D0049573

THE COMPLETE HUMOROUS SKETCHES AND TALES
OF MARK TWAIN

ALSO BY CHARLES NEIDER

Fiction

NAKED EYE
THE AUTHENTIC DEATH OF HENDRY JONES
THE WHITE CITADEL

Biography

SUSY: A CHILDHOOD

Criticism

MARK TWAIN
THE FROZEN SEA, A STUDY OF FRANZ KAFKA

EDITED BY CHARLES NEIDER

THE AUTOBIOGRAPHY OF MARK TWAIN
THE COMPLETE SHORT STORIES OF MARK TWAIN
THE COMPLETE ESSAYS OF MARK TWAIN
THE COMPLETE NOVELS OF MARK TWAIN
THE COMPLETE TRAVEL BOOKS OF MARK TWAIN
MARK TWAIN: THE ADVENTURES OF COLONEL SELLERS
MARK TWAIN: LIFE AS I FIND IT
THE COMPLETE SHORT STORIES OF ROBERT LOUIS STEVENSON
OUR SAMOAN ADVENTURE, BY FANNY AND ROBERT LOUIS STEVENSON
SHORT NOVELS OF THE MASTERS
GREAT SHORT STORIES FROM THE WORLD'S LITERATURE
THE STATURE OF THOMAS MANN
THE GREAT WEST
MAN AGAINST NATURE

The Complete
Humorous Sketches and Tales
of
Mark Twain

NOW COLLECTED FOR THE FIRST TIME

Edited and with an introduction by

Charles Neider

Drawings by Mark Twain

DOUBLEDAY & COMPANY, INC., GARDEN CITY, NEW YORK

ISBN: 0-385-01094-X
Library of Congress Catalog Card Number 61-6503

EDITOR'S NOTE

The present volume contains all of Mark Twain's humorous sketches which the author saw fit to issue in book form, also a number published in such form by his literary executor, A. B. Paine. Mark Twain changed his mind about the worth of certain of these sketches and did not include them in later editions of his books. For this reason, the reader will here encounter sketches not to be found in the collected works. It can be argued that I ought not to have resurrected sketches which the author himself judged ought to be left in the relative obscurity of first editions. My desire to be as complete as possible within the scope of a single volume has overridden this argument, despite the fact that I am aware of a certain cogency which it possesses. The current volume is not only the first substantial collection of Mark Twain's humorous sketches ever to be made; it is also the most complete such collection which can be made, short of exhuming certain materials which the author never cared to dignify with book appearance. I refer to those numberless and fugitive items which he wrote for newspapers and magazines, some of the files of which, unfortunately, have been badly scattered or even lost.

The present volume contains 136 sketches, thirty of them gathered from the five books of travel. The contents are arranged chronologically according to the years of first publication, and alphabetically within a given year whenever more than one item was published in that year. I have indicated the source of the sketches taken from the books of travel, and in such cases have given as the date of publication the date of the first edition of the particular book of travel.

C. N.

CONTENTS

Mark Twain and No Hogwash

By Charles Neider

I am writing this introduction in October of 1960, five or six weeks prior to the 125th anniversary of Mark Twain's birth. (He was born in Florida, Missouri, on November 30, 1835. He died April 21, 1910, just a little more than half a century ago.) This has been an unusual Mark Twain year, with many celebrations of his life and work on both the popular and the esoteric fronts. There have been television shows, spreads of text and photographs in national magazines, and the issuance of various books and articles.

Even the Russians, late last year, had a hand in heightening the great humorist's popularity. In the spirit of shoring up the other fellow's virtue they attacked the most recent edition of his *Autobiography* and then proceeded, without precedent, to allow the American editor of the *Autobiography* an opportunity to state his case and to attack them in turn in their own chief literary journal. They even went so far as to send the editor a check for $49 for his trouble, drawn on the Morgan Guaranty Trust Company of New York. If the editor was only surprised to be allowed to defend his views before an audience of Russian readers, he was dumbfounded to be the recipient of Moscow gold, knowing how rare an event it is that witnesses the movement of dollars from the Soviet Union to the United States for merely literary reasons.

Mark Twain's popularity has not always been as intense in his own country as it has been the past couple of years, and particularly during the present one. As recently as four years ago, when writing the introduction to his *Complete Short Stories*, I had occasion to complain, "Here is a man, a very great man, a national monument, you might say, who has been dead these forty-odd years without having had his stories collected, when lesser men, just recently dead, or still living, have had that mark of honor offered them by the publishing world and the public."

It was not merely that an edition of his collected stories had been overlooked, which was the case. It was also that certain editors in high places believed his vogue had waned to the extent that such an edition would amount to an expensive hobby. The success of the collected stories has made it possible to issue this volume of sketches as a companion volume.

A friend of mine, a novelist who was born and raised in Missouri and who has long been a student of Mark Twain, recently wrote me that he had been reading some current deep analyses of Mark Twain's works. As a result of his reading, which left him alternately astonished and numbed, he decided, "I have pretty well given up writing any book about Mr. Clemens. I am a charter member of the Mark Twain and No Hogwash Society [he used a more pithy and less polite term], and the perfessers have sifted the old man's ashes back and forth until there's nothing left but some sour-smelling talc. All the time the perfessers are trying to figure out what Mark Twain meant by this or that. Hell, he wrote about as clearly as anyone could write and I see no reason to doubt that he meant what he said. There's a perfesser wrote a book in which Huck's trip on the raft symbolized Sam's journey west in the stage coach, and the purpose of the journey was search for a father. Keee-rist! Another perfesser wrote a book for which he did an astonishing amount of research. Of course a lot of the research adds up to nothing important but, being a scholar, he had to put it all in."

Some of the deep analyses are removed from the reality by a distance of not less than several light-years. Mark Twain was not that remote from reality, nor did he have all those anemic theories flowing in his veins. He knew the reality as well as any writing man of his time and better than most. His works, when observed without coyness and without a succession of mirrors, show it.

The Russians are not to be found trailing the field, in this or any other area. They have made substantial contributions to the literature on Mark Twain and hogwash. They insist that America has an official line on Mark Twain, that the nation tries to suppress or forget him, and that his editors have followed the line carefully. Their line in general consists of this: Mark Twain is of primary significance as a social and political observer; his objects of attack are chiefly aspects of the American scene; and the United States officially and unofficially suppresses or distorts his attacks against itself. This notion of America's being a monolithic structure, with control stemming from the top, naturally strikes most Americans as a curious one.

Even more curious, perhaps, is the way in which Soviet literary spokesmen view us as if we were a mirror image of themselves, and this despite their protestation that we are so different from them. *They* live under an official line and under censorship; *they* are primarily social and political critics; and it follows that we closely resemble them. One wonders what the mass of Soviet readers think. Can they digest the official line? And are they as humorless as their literary spokesmen often give the impression of being? I like to believe that they are not, and that Mark Twain's great popularity among them is an indication not so much that the official line has been getting through as that Mark Twain has. That he is very popular among them is indicated by some recent statistics published in the Moscow *Literary Gazette*. There have been 250 printings of Mark Twain's works in 25 languages of the Soviet Union, with a distribution of some 11,000,000 copies. A twelve-volume edition of his collected works is now being prepared.

Mark Twain is of course primarily a humorist. If he had never possessed his humorous gift, if he had only written his social criticisms, he would not now be read by millions of Russian readers and it would be useless for Soviet literary spokesmen to point to him as the great critic of democratic morals. He is also of course primarily a writer of fiction. It was through these two great gifts that he made the reputation which is so well sustained fifty years after his death. His American readers on the whole have no difficulty in comprehending this simple fact, and I like to think that most Russian readers have the same common sense, that they read him basically not for the lessons he teaches of the inherent "evils" of the nation across the Iron Curtain but because he enlarges their lives imaginatively through a flow of pleasure. Great humor, after all, being so rare, is a very exportable commodity. When blended with wisdom and humanitarianism it is irresistible.

If one were exposed only to the official Soviet view one might think that Mark Twain spent most of his time in attacking aspects of his own country. If he did not write much concerning his love of his country it was not only because professed patriotism embarrassed him, it was also and chiefly because love of his country was implicit in all he wrote. He was, after all, *the* American writer close to the native soil; and *the* American writer who in *The Innocents Abroad* forever put out of fashion the literary habit of fawning on Europe while finding no worth back home. In both of these respects, by the way, he resembles Dostoyevsky, just as his opposite number, Henry James, resembles Turgenev the Francophile. Among the great American writers of his period he was the most representative, at a time when it was already fashionable to expatriate oneself in Europe.

From the way official Soviet critics sometimes speak of him, one might imagine that if he were alive today he would be delighted to take up permanent residence in Moscow. If he were unpredictable enough to do such a thing he would soon complain of the quality of the borsht there. It is not the sort of borsht they served up in Missouri or Nevada or California in his day—or even in Connecticut and New York. And he would be instructed forcefully that criticizing Moscow borsht is strictly forbidden in the Soviet Union—a lesson which Boris Pasternak recently learned to his sorrow.

Mark Twain is useful to the Soviet spokesmen—and to most Americans as well—as a critic of certain aspects of American life. What the spokesmen fail to acknowledge is that his criticism of America was a department of a larger criticism, his criticism of man, and that under that heading he would now be criticizing the Russian form of government as well as various lapses in the American way of life. The fact is of course that Americans are better prepared to admire and value self-criticism than the spokesmen of a nation which still remains an autocracy. Democracy for all its shortcomings prizes self-criticism as it cannot be prized in an autocracy, inasmuch as democracy flourishes under self-criticism, whereas an autocracy dies by it.

Mark Twain's sketches never won for themselves the illustrious reputation won by his other kinds of writing, but no one interested in American humor can long remain indifferent to them. They comprised a substantial share of his literary apprenticeship and developed so thoroughly into a flair of genius that they made their way into his important books long after he had decided he had broken their spell. As with the short story he was long on hodgepodge in form and short on French neatness. It is often not easy to say which is a story and which a sketch, and sometimes it is not possible. In the long run it makes little difference, for fortunately his minor works carry the impress of his literary features so strongly that they possess an intrinsic value quite apart from any which they might have gathered to themselves by being more akin to the usual genres.

Some of Clemens's well-wishers were embarrassed by his sketches and were ready to consign them to oblivion. His official biographer, Albert Bigelow Paine, for example, in discussing a collection of items entitled *Sketches New and Old*, published in 1875, said, "Many of them are amusing, some of them delightful, but most of them seem ephemeral. If we except 'The Jumping Frog,' and possibly 'A True Story' (and the latter was altogether out of place in the collection), there is no reason to suppose that any of its contents will escape oblivion." Its contents included such tales as "My Watch," "Political Economy," and "The Experience of the McWilliamses with Membranous Croup," all published in the volume of collected stories. The remainder are included in the present volume. So much for Paine's clouded crystal ball. William Dean Howells praised the book in the *Atlantic* on its publication, however. The sketches are a minor side of Mark Twain, but it ought to be noted that they are a particularly brilliant and representative side.

He began writing them at an early age, before he left Hannibal, and the newspapers of the day made their publication possible. The blights of bigness and sameness had not yet come to the papers. There were no press associations and no syndicates. Each paper had an intimate, personal, local tone rare today and reflected the personality of its editor, also of the town or area in which it was read. Today a reader's only, slim hope of a hearing is in the Letters to the Editor section of the editorial pages. In those earlier times the papers welcomed contributions from its readers, particularly pithy paragraphs from clever men. If you were clever enough you could work your way up to whole sketches. The reward was a haven from anonymity.

It was not only a question of appearing in your local paper. Because papers did not jealously guard their copyright status, if you were good other papers would pick up your items and reprint them along with your name, and your fame might spread over a whole region, as it did in the case of Mark Twain. Those paragraphs of comment, news, observation, hoax, skit, and sketch were the apprenticeship of Samuel Clemens on the American literary scene, although it is altogether doubtful that he ever regarded them in so portentous a manner. He used what was available to him in outlet and in matter, and the result is that his beginnings and his career were so different from those of the masters of the predominant New England school and from those of the emerging Henry James. If anyone strayed into literature (the phrase is Thomas Mann's as applied to himself) it was Samuel Clemens.

But anonymity was only the first part of the reward. Later there was payment in greenbacks and in gold. Thus did Clemens write sketches for the Hannibal *Journal,* the New Orleans *True Delta,* the *Territorial Enterprise* of Virginia City, Nevada, the San Francisco *Morning Call* and *Alta California,* for the *Californian* and the *Golden Era* and the Buffalo *Express* and the *Galaxy.* Beginning in the fifties, he continued writing these sketches into the seventies. He traveled a familiar road to fame, the road of Artemus Ward, Josh Billings, and Petroleum Vesuvius Nasby, all humorists, all commentators—and all lecturers and showmen. For once one's fame was established in the paragraphic way the lecture circuit beckoned with its gold as it competed with other forms of entertainment—with the minstrel show, the music hall, the variety show, the circus.

The humorous lecturer in those days was invariably a showman and invariably "quaint" in matter and style. He availed himself of the appurtenances of showmanship: pseudonyms, advance agents, puff advertisements, colored lithographs, and quaint posters. The poster announcing Mark Twain's first lecture, held in San Francisco in 1866, contained the following information:

Maguire's Academy of Music/Pine Street, near Montogomery/The Sandwich Islands/Mark Twain/(Honolulu Correspondent of the Sacramento Union)/Will Deliver A/Lecture on the Sandwich Islands/at the Academy of Music/On Tuesday Evening, Oct. 2d/(1866)/In which passing mention will be made of Harris, Bishop/Staley, the American missionaries, etc., and the absurd/customs and characteristics of the natives duly discussed/and described. The great volcano of Kilauea will also/receive proper attention./A Splendid Orchestra/is in town, but *has not* been engaged/Also/A Den of Ferocious Wild Beasts/will be on exhibition in the next block/Magnificent Fireworks/were in contemplation for this occa-/sion, but the idea has been abandoned/A Grand Torchlight Procession/may be expected; in fact, the public are/ privileged to expect whatever they please./Dress Circle, $1.00 Family Circle, 50¢./Doors open at 7 o'clock. The Trouble to begin at 8 o'clock.

Lectures had a wide audience, for they were written up in the newspapers and often quoted at length. Just as Mark Twain the lecturer was aggrandized by Mark Twain the writer of sketches, so the writer of sketches benefited from the lecturer, by the creation of a greater market for his wares. And just as the lectures were influenced by the competing forms of entertainment, so they in turn influenced them. The sketches in particular established Mark Twain's fame as "the wild humorist of the Pacific slope" and "the moralist of the Main." In the sketches we find more than mere echoes of the variety shows he no doubt enjoyed during his years of piloting on the great river (he did not pilot showboats, but they flourished on the river in his time) and of the Negro minstrel shows he so loved. The "nigger show," as it was known, with its formalized dialogue between the middleman (who was the straight man) and the end men Tambo (for tambourine) (also Banjo for banjo) and Bones (for castanets) made itself felt in Clemens's early writings, and even in his later ones. "When the Buffalo Climbed a Tree" from *Roughing It* is an example of what I have in mind; it is included in these pages.

Long after the minstrel show gave way in popularity to the variety show, Samuel Clemens, now an old man, wrote nostalgically: "Where now is Billy Rice? He was a joy to me and so were the other stars of the nigger show—Billy Birch, David Wambold, Backus and a delightful dozen of their brethren who made life a pleasure to me forty years ago and later. Birch, Wambold and Backus are gone years ago; and with them departed to return no more forever, I suppose, the real nigger show—the genuine nigger show, the extravagant nigger show—the show which to me had no peer and whose peer has not yet arrived, in my experience. We have the grand opera; and I have witnessed and greatly enjoyed the first act of everything which Wagner created, but the effect on me has always been so powerful that one act was quite sufficient; whenever I have witnessed two acts I have gone away physically exhausted; and whenever I have ventured an entire opera the result has been the next thing to suicide. But if I could have the nigger show back again in its pristine purity and perfection I should have but little further use for opera. It seems to me that to the elevated mind and the sensitive spirit the hand organ and the nigger show are a standard and a summit to whose rarefied altitude the other forms of musical art may not hope to reach." And he continued in the same vein, recreating the color and the technique of the minstrel show.

It is all right to scout around for devious influences on Mark Twain's work, but it is downright foolish to neglect obvious native sources of his humor.

Mark Twain's first book was *The Celebrated Jumping Frog*, a collection of sketches. He referred to the title story as a sketch in a letter to Bret Harte written in May 1867, the month of publication of the book. "The book is out, and is handsome. It is full of damnable errors of grammar and deadly inconsistencies of spelling in the Frog sketch because I was away and did not read the proofs; but be a friend and say nothing about these things. When my hurry is over, I will send you an autograph copy to pisen the children with." He mentioned the book in a letter to his mother: "As for the Frog book, I don't believe that will ever pay anything worth a cent. I published it simply to advertise myself—not with the hope of making anything out of it." The book contained twenty-six sketches in addition to the title story.

His next book is *The Innocents Abroad*, published in 1869, which included four sketches. "Mark Twain's Burlesque Autobiography and First Romance" appeared in 1871, a pamphlet-sized little book. *Roughing It*, in 1872, included nine sketches. In 1874 a thin volume of sketches appeared under the title *Number One*. It was presumably the first in a series but the other numbers failed to materialize. *Sketches New and Old* was published in July of the following year. (The title was *Sketches Old and New* on the cover and *Sketches New and Old* on the title page.) A few of the pieces were new, but most were reprinted from the magazines and newspapers for which Clemens had been writing the past several years. "Answers from Correspondents" was in part from the *Californian*, "To Raise Poultry" was from the Buffalo *Express*, "My First Literary Venture" was from the *Galaxy*, "Information Wanted" was from the New York *Tribune*, "The Siamese Twins" was from *Packard's Monthly*, "Concerning Chambermaids" was from the New York *Weekly Review*, "Honored as a Curiosity" was from the Sacramento *Union*, "Curing a Cold" was from the *Golden Era*, and so on.

According to Paine, Clemens gave up the writing of sketches in 1871, when he relinquished his humor column in the monthly *Galaxy*. Around this time he also sold his one-third interest in the Buffalo *Express*. He was pressed for time now and wanted to devote himself more thoroughly to the writing of books. His old sketches kept appearing in his books, however—in *Punch, Brothers, Punch!* (1878), *The Stolen White Elephant* (1882), *The £ 1,000,000 Bank-Note* (1893), and several others. At the same time new sketches were written for the travel books—thirteen for *A Tramp Abroad* (1880), two for *Life on the Mississippi* (1883) (but one of these was lifted from a novel in progress), and two for *Following the Equator* (1897).

Mark Twain's sketches contain his brand of humor in what is perhaps its purest form. Here more than elsewhere he indulged in fun for its own sake. It is true that in his *Autobiography* he denied that he had ever been a humorist of the "mere" sort, but his practice belied him. In a discussion of a pirated edition of *Mark Twain's Library of Humor*, he said, "This book is a very interesting curiosity, in one way. It reveals the surprising fact that within the compass of these forty years wherein I have been playing professional humorist before the public, I have had for company seventy-eight other American humorists. Each and every one of the seventy-eight rose in my time, became conspicuous and popular, and by and by vanished. A number of these names were as familiar in their day as are the names of George Ade and Dooley today—yet they have all so completely passed from sight now that there is probably not a youth of fifteen years of age in the country whose eye would light with recognition at the mention of any one of the seventy-eight names. . . . In this mortuary volume I find Nasby, Artemus Ward, Yawcob Strauss, Derby, Burdette, Eli Perkins, the 'Danbury News Man,' Orpheus C. Kerr, Smith O'Brien, Josh Billings and a score of others, maybe two score, whose writings and sayings were once in everybody's mouth but are now heard of no more and are no longer mentioned. . . . Why have they perished? Because they were merely humorists. Humorists of the 'mere' sort cannot survive. Humor is only a fragrance, a decoration. Often it is merely an odd trick of speech and of spelling, as in the case of Ward and Billings and Nasby and the 'Disbanded Volunteer,' and presently the fashion passes and the fame along with it. There are those who say a novel should be a work of art solely and you must not preach in it, you must not teach in it. That may be true as regards novels but it is not true as regards humor. Humor must not professedly teach and it must not professedly preach, but it must do both if it would live forever. By forever, I mean thirty years. . . . I have always preached. That is the reason that I have lasted thirty years. If the humor came of its own accord and uninvited I have allowed it a place in my sermon but I was not writing the sermon for the sake of the humor. I should have written the sermon just the same, whether any humor applied for admission or not."

The reader need only read the present sketches to see that Mark Twain, fortunately, did not always consider it necessary to "preach." Nor did he always consider humor only a fragrance. Is laughter indeed only a fragrance, and is frowning the substance of life? Some of Mark Twain's "merely" humorous things *have* survived "forever"—because of their play of fancy, their wit, their fresh and always idiomatic prose. The vogue of coy illiteracy practiced by Ward and Billings was bound to die, if only because it represented not a way of seeing life but a way of exploiting tricks of style and manner. Clemens *saw* life as a strange and comic affair, and that is why his humor needs no surface help. Also, his statement notwithstanding, he was graced by the power to enjoy the comic aspect of things for its own sake, and to enjoy laughter as few have enjoyed it, with invective when he was aroused, but for the most part with a kindliness which makes the use of his great gift seem little short of epic.

Even with a giant like Mark Twain—perhaps always with the giants —it is wise to use a grain of salt when examining his statements regarding himself.

THE COMPLETE HUMOROUS SKETCHES AND TALES
OF MARK TWAIN

Curing a Cold

It is a good thing, perhaps, to write for the amusement of the public, but it is a far higher and nobler thing to write for their instruction, their profit, their actual and tangible benefit. The latter is the sole object of this article. If it prove the means of restoring to health one solitary sufferer among my race, of lighting up once more the fire of hope and joy in his faded eyes, or bringing back to his dead heart again the quick, generous impulses of other days, I shall be amply rewarded for my labor; my soul will be permeated with the sacred delight a Christian feels when he has done a good, unselfish deed.

Having led a pure and blameless life, I am justified in believing that no man who knows me will reject the suggestions I am about to make, out of fear that I am trying to deceive him. Let the public do itself the honor to read my experience in doctoring a cold, as herein set forth, and then follow in my footsteps.

When the White House was burned in Virginia City, I lost my home, my happiness, my constitution, and my trunk. The loss of the two first-named articles was a matter of no great consequence, since a home without a mother, or a sister, or a distant young female relative in it, to remind you, by putting your soiled linen out of sight and taking your boots down off the mantelpiece, that there are those who think about you and care for you, is easily obtained. And I cared nothing for the loss of my happiness, because, not being a poet, it could not be possible that melancholy would abide with me long. But to lose a good constitution and a better trunk were serious misfortunes. On the day of the fire my constitution succumbed to a severe cold, caused by undue exertion in getting ready to do something. I suffered to no purpose, too, because the plan I was figuring at for the extinguishing of the fire was so elaborate that I never got it completed until the middle of the following week.

The first time I began to sneeze, a friend told me to go and bathe my feet in hot water and go to bed. I did so. Shortly afterward, another

friend advised me to get up and take a cold shower-bath. I did that
also. Within the hour, another friend assured me that it was policy to
"feed a cold and starve a fever." I had both. So I thought it best to fill
myself up for the cold, and then keep dark and let the fever starve
awhile.

In a case of this kind, I seldom do things by halves; I ate pretty
heartily; I conferred my custom upon a stranger who had just opened
his restaurant that morning; he waited near me in respectful silence
until I had finished feeding my cold, when he inquired if the people
about Virginia City were much afflicted with colds? I told him I
thought they were. He then went out and took in his sign.

I started down toward the office, and on the way encountered another bosom friend, who told me that a quart of salt-water, taken
warm, would come as near curing a cold as anything in the world. I
hardly thought I had room for it, but I tried it anyhow. The result was
surprising. I believed I had thrown up my immortal soul.

Now, as I am giving my experience only for the benefit of those who
are troubled with the distemper I am writing about, I feel that they
will see the propriety of my cautioning them against following such
portions of it as proved inefficient with me, and acting upon this conviction, I warn them against warm salt-water. It may be a good enough
remedy, but I think it is too severe. If I had another cold in the head,
and there were no course left me but to take either an earthquake or a
quart of warm salt-water, I would take my chances on the earthquake.

After the storm which had been raging in my stomach had subsided,
and no more good Samaritans happening along, I went on borrowing
handkerchiefs again and blowing them to atoms, as had been my custom in the early stages of my cold, until I came across a lady who had
just arrived from over the plains, and who said she had lived in a part
of the country where doctors were scarce, and had from necessity
acquired considerable skill in the treatment of simple "family complaints." I knew she must have had much experience, for she appeared to be a hundred and fifty years old.

She mixed a decoction composed of molasses, aquafortis, turpen-
tine, and various other drugs, and instructed me to take a wine-glass
full of it every fifteen minutes. I never took but one dose; that was
enough, it robbed me of all moral principle, and awoke every unworthy impulse of my nature. Under its malign influence my brain
conceived miracles of meanness, but my hands were too feeble to
execute them; at that time, had it not been that my strength had
surrendered to a succession of assaults from infallible remedies for my

cold, I am satisfied that I would have tried to rob the graveyard. Like most other people, I often feel mean, and act accordingly; but until I took that medicine I had never reveled in such supernatural depravity, and felt proud of it. At the end of two days I was ready to go to doctoring again. I took a few more unfailing remedies, and finally drove my cold from my head to my lungs.

I got to coughing incessantly, and my voice fell below zero; I conversed in a thundering bass, two octaves below my natural tone; I could only compass my regular nightly repose by coughing myself down to a state of utter exhaustion, and then the moment I began to talk in my sleep, my discordant voice woke me up again.

My case grew more and more serious every day. Plain gin was recommended; I took it. Then gin and molasses; I took that also. Then gin and onions; I added the onions, and took all three. I detected no particular result, however, except that I had acquired a breath like a buzzard's.

I found I had to travel for my health. I went to Lake Bigler with my reportorial comrade, Wilson. It is gratifying to me to reflect that we traveled in considerable style; we went in the Pioneer coach, and my friend took all his baggage with him, consisting of two excellent silk handkerchiefs and a daguerreotype of his grandmother. We sailed and hunted and fished and danced all day, and I doctored my cough all night. By managing in this way, I made out to improve every hour in the twenty-four. But my disease continued to grow worse.

A sheet-bath was recommended. I had never refused a remedy yet, and it seemed poor policy to commence then; therefore I determined to take a sheet-bath, notwithstanding I had no idea what sort of arrangement it was. It was administered at midnight, and the weather was very frosty. My breast and back were bared, and a sheet (there appeared to be a thousand yards of it) soaked in ice-water, was wound around me until I resembled a swab for a Columbiad.

It is a cruel expedient. When the chilly rag touches one's warm flesh, it makes him start with sudden violence, and gasp for breath just as men do in the death-agony. It froze the marrow in my bones and stopped the beating of my heart. I thought my time had come.

Young Wilson said the circumstance reminded him of an anecdote about a negro who was being baptized, and who slipped from the parson's grasp, and came near being drowned. He floundered around, though, and finally rose up out of the water considerably strangled and furiously angry, and started ashore at once, spouting water like a whale, and remarking, with great asperity, that "one o' dese days some gen'l'man's nigger gwyne to get killed wid jis' such damn foolishness as dis!"

Never take a sheet-bath—never. Next to meeting a lady acquaintance who, for reasons best known to herself, don't see you when she looks at you, and don't know you when she does see you, it is the most uncomfortable thing in the world.

But, as I was saying, when the sheet-bath failed to cure my cough, a lady friend recommended the application of a mustard plaster to my breast. I believe that would have cured me effectually, if it had not been for young Wilson. When I went to bed, I put my mustard plaster—which was a very gorgeous one, eighteen inches square—where I could reach it when I was ready for it. But young Wilson got hungry in the night, and—here is food for the imagination.

After sojourning a week at Lake Bigler, I went to Steamboat Springs, and, besides the steam-baths, I took a lot of the vilest medicines that were ever concocted. They would have cured me, but I had to go back to Virginia City, where, notwithstanding the variety of new remedies I absorbed every day, I managed to aggravate my disease by carelessness and undue exposure.

I finally concluded to visit San Francisco, and the first day I got there a lady at the hotel told me to drink a quart of whisky every twenty-four hours, and a friend up-town recommended precisely the same course. Each advised me to take a quart; that made half a gallon. I did it, and still live.

Now, with the kindest motives in the world, I offer for the consideration of consumptive patients the variegated course of treatment I have lately gone through. Let them try it; if it don't cure, it can't more than kill them.

1863

Aurelia's Unfortunate Young Man

The facts in the following case came to me by letter from a young lady who lives in the beautiful city of San José; she is perfectly unknown to me, and simply signs herself "Aurelia Maria," which may possibly be a fictitious name. But no matter, the poor girl is almost heartbroken by the misfortunes she has undergone, and so confused by the conflicting counsels of misguided friends and insidious enemies that she does not know what course to pursue in order to extricate herself from the web of difficulties in which she seems almost hopelessly involved. In this dilemma she turns to me for help, and supplicates for my guidance and instruction with a moving eloquence that would touch the heart of a statue. Hear her sad story:

She says that when she was sixteen years old she met and loved, with all the devotion of a passionate nature, a young man from New Jersey, named Williamson Breckinridge Caruthers, who was some six years her senior. They were engaged, with the free consent of their friends and relatives, and for a time it seemed as if their career was destined to be characterized by an immunity from sorrow beyond the usual lot of humanity. But at last the tide of fortune turned; young Caruthers became infected with smallpox of the most virulent type, and when he recovered from his illness his face was pitted like a waffle-mold, and his comeliness gone forever. Aurelia thought to break off the engagement at first, but pity for her unfortunate lover caused her to postpone the marriage-day for a season, and give him another trial.

The very day before the wedding was to have taken place, Breckinridge, while absorbed in watching the flight of a balloon, walked into a well and fractured one of his legs, and it had to be taken off above the knee. Again Aurelia was moved to break the engagement, but again love triumphed, and she set the day forward and gave him another chance to reform.

And again misfortune overtook the unhappy youth. He lost one arm by the premature discharge of a Fourth of July cannon, and within three months he got the other pulled out by a carding-machine. Aurelia's heart was almost crushed by these latter calamities. She could not but be deeply grieved to see her lover passing from her by piecemeal, feeling, as she did, that he could not last forever under this disastrous process of reduction, yet knowing of no way to stop its dreadful career, and in her tearful despair she almost regretted, like brokers who hold on and lose, that she had not taken him at first, before he had suffered such an alarming depreciation. Still, her brave soul bore her up, and she resolved to bear with her friend's unnatural disposition yet a little longer.

Again the wedding-day approached, and again disappointment overshadowed it; Caruthers fell ill with the erysipelas, and lost the use of one of his eyes entirely. The friends and relatives of the bride, considering that she had already put up with more than could reasonably be expected of her, now came forward and insisted that the match should be broken off; but after wavering awhile, Aurelia, with a generous spirit which did her credit, said she had reflected calmly upon the matter, and could not discover that Breckinridge was to blame.

So she extended the time once more, and he broke his other leg.

It was a sad day for the poor girl when she saw the surgeons reverently bearing away the sack whose uses she had learned by previous experience, and her heart told her the bitter truth that some more of her lover was gone. She felt that the field of her affections was growing more and more circumscribed every day, but once more she frowned down her relatives and renewed her betrothal.

Shortly before the time set for the nuptials another disaster occurred. There was but one man scalped by the Owens River Indians last year. That man was Williamson Breckinridge Caruthers of New Jersey. He was hurrying home with happiness in his heart, when he lost his hair forever, and in that hour of bitterness he almost cursed the mistaken mercy that had spared his head.

At last Aurelia is in serious perplexity as to what she ought to do. She still loves her Breckinridge, she writes, with truly womanly feeling—she still loves what is left of him—but her parents are bitterly opposed to the match, because he has no property and is disabled from working, and she has not sufficient means to support both comfortably. "Now, what should she do?" she asked with painful and anxious solicitude.

It is a delicate question; it is one which involves the lifelong happiness of a woman, and that of nearly two-thirds of a man, and I feel that it would be assuming too great a responsibility to do more than make a mere suggestion in the case. How would it do to build to him? If Aurelia can afford the expense, let her furnish her mutilated lover with wooden arms and wooden legs, and a glass eye and a wig, and give him another show; give him ninety days, without grace, and if he does not break his neck in the mean time, marry him and take the chances. It does not seem to me that there is much risk, anyway, Aurelia, because if he sticks to his singular propensity for damaging himself every time he sees a good opportunity, his next experiment is bound to finish him, and then you are safe, married or single. If married, the wooden legs and such other valuables as he may possess revert to the widow, and you see you sustain no actual loss save the cherished fragment of a noble but most unfortunate husband, who honestly strove to do right, but whose extraordinary instincts were against him. Try it, Maria. I have thought the matter over carefully and well, and it is the only chance I see for you. It would have been a happy conceit on the part of Caruthers if he had started with his neck and broken that first; but since he has seen fit to choose a different policy and string himself out as long as possible, I do not think we ought to upbraid him for it if he has enjoyed it. We must do the best we can under the circumstances, and try not to feel exasperated at him.

1864

Information for the Million

A young man anxious for information writes to a friend residing in Virginia City, Nevada, as follows:

"*Springfield, Mo., April 12*

"DEAR SIR: My object in writing to you is to have you give me a full history of Nevada. What is the character of its climate? What are the productions of the earth? Is it healthy? What diseases do they die of mostly? Do you think it would be advisable for a man who can make a living in Missouri to emigrate to that part of the country? There are several of us who would emigrate there in the spring if we could ascertain to a certainty that it is a much better country than this. I suppose you know Joel H. Smith? He used to live here; he lives in Nevada now; they say he owns considerable in a mine there. Hoping to hear from you soon, etc., I remain yours, truly,

WILLIAM—"

The letter was handed in to a newspaper office for reply. For the benefit of all who contemplate moving to Nevada, it is perhaps best to publish the correspondence in its entirety:

DEAREST WILLIAM: Pardon my familiarity—but that name touchingly reminds me of the loved and lost, whose name was similar. I have taken the contract to answer your letter, and although we are now strangers, I feel we shall cease to be so if we ever become acquainted with each other. The thought is worthy of attention, William. I will now respond to your several propositions in the order in which you have fulminated them.

Your object in writing is to have me give you a full history of Nevada. The flattering confidence you repose in me, William, is only equaled by the modesty of your request. I could detail the history of Nevada in five hundred pages octavo; but as you have never done me any harm, I will spare you, though it will be apparent to every body that I would be justified in taking advantage of you if I were a mind to. However, I will condense. Nevada was discovered many years ago by the Mormons, and was called Carson county. It only became Nevada in 1861, by act of Congress. There is a popular tradition that the Almighty created it; but when you come to see it, William, you will think differently. Do not let that discourage you, though. The country looks something like a singed cat, owing to the scarcity of shrubbery, and also resembles that animal in the respect that is has more merits than its personal appearance would seem to indicate. The Grosch brothers found the first silver lead here in 1857. They also founded Silver City, I believe. Signify to your friends, however, that all the mines here do not pay dividends as yet; you may make this statement with the utmost unyielding inflexibility—it will not be contradicted from this quarter. The population of this Territory is about 35,000, one half of which number reside in the united cities of Virginia and Gold Hill. However, I will discontinue this history for the present, lest I get you too deeply interested in this distant land, and cause you to neglect your family or your religion. But I will address you again upon the subject next year. In the mean time, allow me to answer your inquiry as to the character of our climate.

It has no character to speak of, William, and alas! in this respect it resembles many, ah! too many chambermaids in this wretched, wretched world. Sometimes we have the seasons in their regular order, and then again we have winter all the summer, and summer all winter. Consequently, we have never yet come across an almanac that would just exactly fit this latitude. It is mighty regular about not raining, though, William. It will start in here in November and rain about four, and sometimes as much as seven days on a stretch; after that you may loan out your umbrella for twelve months, with the serene confidence which a Christian feels in four aces. Sometimes the winter begins in November and winds up in June; and sometimes there is a bare suspicion of winter in March and April, and summer all the balance of the year. But as a general thing, William, the climate is good, what there is of it.

What are the productions of the earth? You mean in Nevada, of course. On our ranches here any thing can be raised that can be produced on the fertile fields of Missouri. But ranches are very scattering —as scattering, perhaps, as lawyers in heaven. Nevada, for the most part, is a barren waste of sand, embellished with melancholy sagebrush, and fenced in with snow-clad mountains. But these ghastly features were the salvation of the land, William; for no rightly constituted American would have ever come here if the place had been easy of access, and none of our pioneers would have staid after they got here, if they had not felt satisfied that they could not find a smaller chance for making a living anywhere else. Such is man, William, as he crops out in America.

"Is it healthy?" Yes, I think it is as healthy here as it is in any part of the West. But never permit a question of that kind to vegetate in your brain, William; because as long as Providence has an eye on you, you will not be likely to die until your time comes.

"What diseases do they die of mostly?" Well, they used to die of conical balls and cold steel, mostly, but here lately erysipelas and the intoxicating bowl have got the bulge on those things, as was very justly remarked by Mr. Rising last Sunday. I will observe, for your information, William, that Mr. Rising is our Episcopal minister, and has done as much as any man among us to redeem this community from its pristine state of semi-barbarism. We are afflicted with all the diseases incident to the same latitude in the States, I believe, with one or two added and half a dozen subtracted on account of our superior altitude. However, the doctors are about as successful here, both in killing and curing, as they are anywhere.

Now, as to whether it would be advisable for a man who can make a living in Missouri to emigrate to Nevada, I confess I am somewhat mixed. If you are not content in your present condition, it naturally follows that you would be entirely satisfied if you could make either more or less than a living. You would exult in the cheerful exhilaration always produced by a change. Will, you can find your opportunity here, where, if you retain your health, and are sober and industrious, you will inevitably make more than a living, and if you don't, you won't. You can rely upon this statement, William. It contemplates any line of business except the selling of tracts. You can not sell tracts here, William; the people take no interest in tracts; the very best efforts in the tract line—even with pictures on them—have met with no encouragement. Besides, the newspapers have been interfering; a man gets his regular text or so from the Scriptures in his paper, along with the stock sales and the war news, every day now. If you are in the tract business, William, take no chances on Washoe; but you can succeed at any thing else here.

"I suppose you know Joel H. Smith?" Well—the fact is—I believe I don't. Now isn't that singular? Isn't it very singular? And he owns "considerable" in a mine here too. Happy man! Actually owns in a mine here in Nevada Territory, and I never even heard of him. Strange—strange—do you know, William, it is the strangest thing that ever happened to me? And then he not only owns in a mine, but owns "considerable;" that is the strangest part about it—how a man could own considerable in a mine in Washoe, and I not know any thing about it. He is a lucky dog, though. But I strongly suspect that you have made a mistake in the name; I am confident you have; you mean John Smith—I know you do; I know it from the fact that he owns considerable in a mine here, because I sold him the property at a ruinous sacrifice on the very day he arrived here from over the plains. That man will be rich one of these days. I am just as well satisfied of it as I am of any precisely similar instance of the kind that has come under my notice. I said as much to him yesterday, and he said he was satisfied of it also. But he did not say it with that air of of triumphant exultation which a heart like mine so delights to behold in one to whom I have endeavored to be a benefactor in a small way. He looked pensive awhile, but, finally, says he, "Do you know, I think I'd a been a rich man long ago if they'd ever found the d—d ledge?" That was my idea about it. I always throught, and I still think, that if they ever do find that ledge, his chances will be better than they are now. I guess Smith will be all right one of these centuries, if he keeps up his assessments—he is a young man yet. Now, William, I have taken a liking to you, and I would like to sell you "considerable" in a mine in Washoe. Let me hear from you on the subject. Greenbacks at par is as good a thing as I want. But seriously, William, don't you ever invest in a mining stock which you don't know any thing about; beware of John Smith's experience!

You hope to hear from me soon? Very good. I shall also hope to hear from you soon, about that little matter above referred to. Now, William, ponder this epistle well; never mind the sarcasm here and there, and the nonsense, but reflect upon the plain facts set forth, because they *are* facts, and are meant to be so understood and believed.

Remember me affectionately to your friends and relations, and especially to your venerable grandmother, with whom I have not the pleasure to be acquainted—but that is of no consequence, you know. I have been in your town many a time, and all the towns of the neighboring counties—the hotel-keepers will recollect me vividly. Remember me to them—I bear them no animosity.

Yours affectionately.

1864

The Killing of Julius Caesar "Localized"

*Being the only true and reliable account ever published;
taken from the Roman "Daily Evening Fasces,"
of the date of that tremendous occurrence.*

Nothing in the world affords a newspaper reporter so much satisfaction as gathering up the details of a bloody and mysterious murder and writing them up with aggravating circumstantiality. He takes a living delight in this labor of love—for such it is to him, especially if he knows that all the other papers have gone to press, and his will be the only one that will contain the dreadful intelligence. A feeling of regret has often come over me that I was not reporting in Rome when Caesar was killed—reporting on an evening paper, and the only one in the city, and getting at least twelve hours ahead of the morning-paper boys with this most magnificent "item" that ever fell to the lot of the craft. Other events have happened as startling as this, but none that possessed so peculiarly all the characteristics of the favorite "item" of the present day, magnified into grandeur and sublimity by the high rank, fame, and social and political standing of the actors in it.

However, as I was not permitted to report Caesar's assassination in the regular way, it has at least afforded me rare satisfaction to translate the following able account of it from the original Latin of the Roman *Daily Evening Fasces* of that date—second edition:

Our usually quiet city of Rome was thrown into a state of wild excitement yesterday by the occurrence of one of those bloody affrays which sicken the heart and fill the soul with fear, while they inspire all thinking men with fore-bodings for the future of a city where human life is held so cheaply and the gravest laws are so openly set at defiance. As the result of that affray, it is our painful duty, as public journalists, to record the death of one of our most esteemed citizens—a man whose name is known wherever this paper cir-culates, and whose fame it has been our pleasure and our privilege to extend, and also to protect from the tongue of slander and falsehood, to the best of our poor ability. We refer to Mr. J. Caesar, the Emperor-elect.

The facts of the case, as nearly as our reporter could determine them from the conflicting statements of eye-witnesses, were about as follows:—The affair was an election row, of course. Nine-tenths of the ghastly butcheries that disgrace the city nowadays grow out of the bickerings and jealousies and animosities engendered by these accursed elections. Rome would be the gainer by it if her very constables were elected to serve a century; for in our experience we have never even been able to choose a dog-pelter without celebrating the event with a dozen knockdowns and a general cramming of the station-house with drunken vagabonds overnight. It is said that when the immense majority for Caesar at the polls in the market was declared the other day, and the crown was offered to that gentleman, even his amazing unself-ishness in refusing it three times was not sufficient to save him from the whispered insults of such men as Casca, of the Tenth Ward, and other hire-lings of the disappointed candidate, hailing mostly from the Eleventh and Thirteenth and other outside districts, who were overheard speaking ironically and contemptuously of Mr. Caesar's conduct upon that occasion.

We are further informed that there are many among us who think they are justified in believing that the assassination of Julius Caesar was a put-up thing—a cut-and-dried arrangement, hatched by Marcus Brutus and a lot of his hired roughs, and carried out only too faithfully according to the program. Whether there be good grounds for this suspicion or not, we leave to the people to judge for themselves, only asking that they will read the following account of the sad occurrence carefully and dispassionately before they render that judgment.

The Senate was already in session, and Caesar was coming down the street toward the capitol, conversing with some personal friends, and followed, as usual, by a large number of citizens. Just as he was passing in front of Demosthenes and Thucydides' drug store, he was observing casually to a gentleman, who, our informant thinks, is a fortune-teller, that the Ides of March were come. The reply was, "Yes, they are come, but not gone yet." At this moment Artemidorus stepped up and passed the time of day, and asked Caesar to read a schedule or a tract or something of the kind, which he had brought for his perusal. Mr. Decius Brutus also said something about an "humble suit" which *he* wanted read. Artemidorus begged that attention might be paid to his first, because it was of personal consequence to Caesar. The latter replied that what concerned himself should be read last, or words to that effect. Artemidorus begged and beseeched him to read the paper instantly.[1] However, Caesar shook him off, and refused to read any petition in the street. He then entered the capitol, and the crowd followed him.

About this time the following conversation was overheard, and we consider that, taken in connection with the events which succeeded it, it bears an appalling significance: Mr. Papilius Lena remarked to George W. Cassius (commonly known as the "Nobby Boy of the Third Ward"), a bruiser in the pay of the Opposition, that he hoped his enterprise to-day might thrive; and when Cassius asked "What enterprise?" he only closed his left eye temporarily and said with simulated indifference, "Fare you well," and sauntered toward Caesar. Marcus Brutus, who is suspected of being the ringleader of the band that killed Caesar, asked what it was that Lena had said. Cassius told him, and added in a low tone, "*I fear our purpose is discovered.*"

Brutus told his wretched accomplice to keep an eye on Lena, and a moment after Cassius urged that lean and hungry vagrant, Casca, whose reputation here is none of the best, to be sudden, for *he feared prevention.* He then turned to Brutus, apparently much excited, and asked what should be done, and swore that either he or Caesar *should never turn back*—he would kill himself first. At this time Caesar was talking to some of the back-country members about the approaching fall elections, and paying little attention to what was going on around him. Billy Trebonius got into conversation with the people's friend and Caesar's—Mark Antony—and under some pretense or other got him away, and Brutus, Decius, Casca, Cinna, Metellus Cimber, and others of the gang of infamous desperadoes that infest Rome at present, closed around the doomed Caesar. Then Metellus Cimber knelt down and begged that his brother might be recalled from banishment, but Caesar rebuked him for his fawning conduct, and refused to grant his petition. Immediately, at Cimber's request, first Brutus and then Cassius begged for the return of the banished Publius; but Caesar still refused. He said he could not be moved; that he was as fixed as the North Star, and proceeded to speak in the most complimentary terms of the firmness of that star and its steady character. Then he said he was like it, and he believed he was the only man in the country that was; therefore, since he was "constant" that Cimber should be banished, he was also "constant" that he should stay banished, and he'd be hanged if he didn't keep him so!

Instantly seizing upon this shallow pretext for a fight, Casca sprang at Caesar and struck him with a dirk, Caesar grabbing him by the arm with his right hand, and launching a blow straight from the shoulder with his left, that sent the reptile bleeding to the earth. He then backed up against

[1] Mark that: It is hinted by William Shakespeare, who saw the beginning and the end of the unfortunate affray, that this "schedule" was simply a note discovering to Caesar that a plot was brewing to take his life.

Pompey's statue, and squared himself to receive his assailants. Cassius and Cimber and Cinna rushed upon him with their daggers drawn, and the former succeeded in inflicting a wound upon his body; but before he could strike again, and before either of the others could strike at all, Caesar stretched the three miscreants at his feet with as many blows of his powerful fist. By this time the Senate was in an indescribable uproar; the throng of citizens in the lobbies had blockaded the doors in their frantic efforts to escape from the building, the sergeant-at-arms and his assistants were struggling with the assassins, venerable senators had cast aside their encumbering robes, and were leaping over benches and flying down the aisles in wild confusion toward the shelter of the committee-rooms, and a thousand voices were shouting "Po-lice! Po-lice!" in discordant tones that rose above the frightful din like shrieking winds above the roaring of a tempest. And amid it all great Caesar stood with his back against the statue, like a lion at bay, and fought his assailants weaponless and hand to hand, with the defiant bearing and the unwavering courage which he had shown before on many a bloody field. Billy Trebonius and Caius Legarius struck him with their daggers and fell, as their brother-conspirators before them had fallen. But at last, when Caesar saw his old friend Brutus step forward armed with a murderous knife, it is said he seemed utterly overpowered with grief and amazement, and, dropping his invincible left arm by his side, he hid his face in the folds of his mantle and received the treacherous blow without an effort to stay the hand that gave it. He only said, "*Et tu, Brute?*" and fell lifeless on the marble pavement.

We learn that the coat deceased had on when he was killed was the same one he wore in his tent on the afternoon of the day he overcame the Nervii, and that when it was removed from the corpse it was found to be cut and gashed in no less than seven different places. There was nothing in the pockets. It will be exhibited at the coroner's inquest, and will be damning proof of the fact of the killing. These latter facts may be relied on, as we get them from Mark Antony, whose position enables him to learn every item of news connected with the one subject of absorbing interest of-to-day.

LATER.—While the coroner was summoning a jury, Mark Antony and other friends of the late Caesar got hold of the body and lugged it off to the Forum, and at last accounts Antony and Brutus were making speeches over it and raising such a row among the people that, as we go to press, the chief of police is satisfied there is going to be a riot, and is taking measures accordingly.

1864

Lucretia Smith's Soldier

I am an ardent admirer of those nice, sickly war stories which have lately been so popular, and for the last three months I have been at work upon one of that character, which is now completed. It can be relied upon as true in every particular, inasmuch as the facts it contains were compiled from the official records in the War Department at Washington. It is but just, also, that I should confess that I have drawn largely on *Jomini's Art of War*, the *Message of the President and Accompanying Documents*, and sundry maps and military works, so necessary for reference in building a novel like this. To the accommodating Directors of the Overland Telegraph Company I take pleasure in returning my thanks for tendering me the use of their wires at the customary rates. And finally, to all those kind friends who have, by good deeds or encouraging words, assisted me in my labors upon this story of "Lucretia Smith's Soldier," during the past three months, and whose names are too numerous for special mention, I take this method of tendering my sincerest gratitude.

CHAPTER I

On a balmy May morning in 1861, the little village of Bluemass, in Massachusetts, lay wrapped in the splendor of the newly-risen sun. Reginald de Whittaker, confidential and only clerk in the house of Bushrod & Ferguson, general drygoods and grocery dealers and keepers of the post-office, rose from his bunk under the counter, and shook himself. After yawning and stretching comfortably, he sprinkled the floor and proceeded to sweep it. He had only half finished his task, however, when he sat down on a keg of nails and fell into a reverie. "This is my last day in this shanty," said he. "How it will surprise Lucretia when she hears I am going for a soldier! How proud she will be, the little darling!" He pictured himself in all manner of warlike situations; the hero of a thousand extraordinary adventures; the man of rising fame; the pet of Fortune at last; and beheld himself, finally, returning to his own home, a bronzed and scarred brigadier-general, to cast his honors and his matured and perfect love at the feet of his Lucretia Borgia Smith.

At this point a thrill of joy and pride suffused his system; but he looked down and saw his broom, and blushed. He came toppling down from the clouds he had been soaring among, and was an obscure clerk again, on a salary of two dollars and a half a week.

CHAPTER II

At eight o'clock that evening, with a heart palpitating with the proud news he had brought for his beloved, Reginald sat in Mr. Smith's parlor awaiting Lucretia's appearance. The moment she entered, he sprang to meet her, his face lighted by the torch of love that was blazing in his head somewhere and shining through, and ejaculated, "Mine own!" as he opened his arms to receive her.

"Sir!" said she, and drew herself up like an offended queen.

Poor Reginald was stricken dumb with astonishment. This chilling demeanor, this angry rebuff, where he had expected the old, tender welcome, banished the gladness from his heart as the cheerful brightness is swept from the landscape when a dark cloud drifts athwart the face of the sun. He stood bewildered a moment, with a sense of goneness on him like one who finds himself suddenly overboard upon a midnight sea, and beholds the ship pass into shrouding gloom, while the dreadful conviction falls upon his soul that he has not been missed. He tried to speak, but his pallid lips refused their office. At last he murmured:

"O Lucretia! what have I done; what is the matter; why this cruel coldness? Don't you love your Reginald any more?"

Her lips curled in bitter scorn, and she replied, in mocking tones:

"Don't I love my Reginald any more? No, I *don't* love my Reginald any more! Go back to your pitiful junk-shop and grab your pitiful yard-stick, and stuff cotton in your ears, so that you can't hear your country shout to you to fall in and shoulder arms. Go!" And then, unheeding the new light that flashed from his eyes, she fled from the room and slammed the door behind her.

Only a moment more! Only a single moment more, he thought, and he could have told her how he had already answered the summons and signed his name to the muster-roll, and all would have been well; his lost bride would have come back to his arms with words of praise and thanksgiving upon her lips. He made a step forward, once, to recall her, but he remembered that he was no longer an effeminate drygoods student, and his warrior soul scorned to sue for quarter. He strode from the place with martial firmness, and never looked behind him.

CHAPTER III

When Lucretia awoke next morning, the faint music of fife and the roll of a distant drum came floating upon the soft spring breeze, and as she listened the sounds grew more subdued, and finally passed out of hearing. She lay absorbed in thought for many minutes, and then she sighed and said: "Oh! if he were only with that band of fellows, how I could love him!"

In the course of the day a neighbor dropped in, and when the conversation turned upon the soldiers, the visitor said:

"Reginald de Whittaker looked rather down-hearted, and didn't shout when he marched along with the other boys this morning. I expect it's owing to you, Miss Loo, though when I met him coming here yesterday evening to tell you he'd enlisted, he thought you'd like it and be proud of— Mercy! what in the nation's the matter with the girl?"

Nothing, only a sudden misery had fallen like a blight upon her heart, and a deadly pallor telegraphed it to her countenance. She rose up without a word and walked with a firm step out of the room; but once within the sacred seclusion of her own chamber, her strong will gave way and she burst into a flood of passionate tears. Bitterly she upbraided herself for her foolish haste of the night before, and her harsh treatment of her lover at the very moment that he had come to anticipate the proudest wish of her heart, and to tell her that he had enrolled himself under the battle-flag, and was going forth to fight as *her* soldier. Alas! other maidens would have soldiers in those glorious fields, and be entitled to the sweet pain of feeling a tender solicitude for them, but she would be unrepresented. No soldier in all the vast armies would breathe her name as he breasted the crimson tide of war! She wept again—or, rather, she went on weeping where she left off a moment before. In her bitterness of spirit she almost cursed the precipitancy that had brought all this sorrow upon her young life. "Drat it!" The words were in her bosom, but she locked them there, and closed her lips against their utterance.

For weeks she nursed her grief in silence, while the roses faded from her cheeks. And through it all she clung to the hope that some day the old love would bloom again in Reginald's heart, and he would write to her; but the long summer days dragged wearily along, and still no letter came. The newspapers teemed with stories of battle and carnage, and eagerly she read them, but always with the same result: the tears welled up and blurred the closing lines—the name she sought was looked for in vain, and the dull aching returned to her sinking heart. Letters to the other girls sometimes contained brief mention of him, and presented always the same picture of him—a morose, unsmiling, desperate man, always in the thickest of the fight, begrimed with powder, and moving calm and unscathed through tempests of shot and shell, as if he bore a charmed life.

But at last, in a long list of maimed and killed, poor Lucretia read these terrible words, and fell fainting to the floor: "*R. D. Whittaker, private soldier, desperately wounded!*"

CHAPTER IV

On a couch in one of the wards of a hospital at Washington lay a wounded soldier; his head was so profusely bandaged that his features were not visible; but there was no mistaking the happy face of the young girl who sat beside him—it was Lucretia Borgia Smith's. She had hunted him out several weeks before, and since that time she had patiently watched by him and nursed him, coming in the morning as soon as the surgeon had finished dressing his wounds, and never leaving him until relieved at nightfall. A ball had shattered his lower jaw, and he could not utter a syllable; through all her weary vigils she had never once been blessed with a grateful word from his dear lips; yet she stood to her post bravely and without a murmur, feeling that when he did get well again she would hear that which would more than reward her for all her devotion.

At the hour we have chosen for the opening of this chapter, Lucretia was in a tumult of happy excitement; for the surgeon had told her that at last her Whittaker had recovered sufficiently to admit of the removal of the bandages from his head, and she was now waiting with feverish impatience for the doctor to come and disclose the loved features to her view. At last he came, and Lucretia, with beaming eyes and fluttering heart, bent over the couch with anxious expectancy. One bandage was removed, then another and another, and lo! the poor wounded face was revealed to the light of day.

"O my own dar——"

What have we here! What is the matter! Alas! it was the face of a stranger!

Poor Lucretia! With one hand covering her upturned eyes, she staggered back with a moan of anguish. Then a spasm of fury distorted her countenance as she brought her fist down with a crash that made the medicine bottles on the table dance again, and exclaimed:

"Oh! confound my cats, if I haven't gone and fooled away three mortal weeks here, snuffling and slobbering over the wrong soldier!"

It was a sad, sad truth. The wretched but innocent and unwitting impostor was R. D., or Richard Dilworthy Whittaker, of Wisconsin, the soldier of dear little Eugenie Le Mulligan, of that State, and utterly unknown to our unhappy Lucretia B. Smith.

Such is life, and the tail of the serpent is over us all. Let us draw the curtain over this melancholy history—for melancholy it must still remain, during a season at least, for the real Reginald de Whittaker has not turned up yet.

1864

A Touching Story of
George Washington's Boyhood

If it please your neighbor to break the sacred calm of night with the snorting of an unholy trombone, it is your duty to put up with his wretched music and your privilege to pity him for the unhappy instinct that moves him to delight in such discordant sounds. I did not always think thus: this consideration for musical amateurs was born of certain disagreeable personal experiences that once followed the development of a like instinct in myself. Now this infidel over the way, who is learning to play on the trombone, and the slowness of whose progress is almost miraculous, goes on with his harrowing work every night, uncursed by me, but tenderly pitied. Ten years ago, for the same offense, I would have set fire to his house. At that time I was a prey to an amateur violinist for two or three weeks, and the sufferings I endured at his hands are inconceivable. He played "Old Dan Tucker," and he never played any thing else; but he performed that so badly that he could throw me into fits with it if I were awake,

or into a nightmare if I were asleep. As long as he confined himself
to "Dan Tucker," though, I bore with him and abstained from violence;
but when he projected a fresh outrage, and tried to do "Sweet Home,"
I went over and burnt him out. My next assailant was a wretch who
felt a call to play the clarionet. He only played the scale, however, with
his distressing instrument, and I let him run the length of his tether,
also; but finally, when he branched out into a ghastly tune, I felt my
reason deserting me under the exquisite torture, and I sallied forth
and burnt him out likewise. During the next two years I burned out an
amateur cornet player, a bugler, a bassoon-sophomore, and a barbarian whose talents ran in the base-drum line.

I would certainly have scorched this trombone man if he had
moved into my neighborhood in those days. But as I said before, I
leave him to his own destruction now, because I have had experience
as an amateur myself, and I feel nothing but compassion for that kind
of people. Besides, I have learned that there lies dormant in the souls
of all men a penchant for some particular musical instrument, and
an unsuspected yearning to learn to play on it, that are bound to
wake up and demand attention some day. Therefore, you who rail
at such as disturb your slumbers with unsuccessful and demoralizing
attempts to subjugate a fiddle, beware! for sooner or later your own
time will come. It is customary and popular to curse these amateurs
when they wrench you out of a pleasant dream at night with a peculiarly diabolical note; but seeing that we are all made alike, and
must all develop a distorted talent for music in the fullness of time,
it is not right. I am charitable to my trombone maniac; in a moment
of inspiration he fetches a snort, sometimes, that brings me to a sitting
posture in bed, broad awake and weltering in a cold perspiration.
Perhaps my first thought is, that there has been an earthquake; perhaps I hear the trombone, and my next thought is, that suicide and
the silence of the grave would be a happy release from this nightly
agony; perhaps the old instinct comes strong upon me to go after my
matches; but my first cool, collected thought is, that the trombone
man's destiny is upon him, and he is working it out in suffering and
tribulation; and I banish from me the unworthy instinct that would
prompt me to burn him out.

After a long immunity from the dreadful insanity that moves a man
to become a musician in defiance of the will of God that he should
confine himself to sawing wood, I finally fell a victim to the instrument
they call the accordeon. At this day I hate that contrivance as fervently
as any man can, but at the time I speak of I suddenly acquired a

disgusting and idolatrous affection for it. I got one of powerful capacity, and learned to play "Auld Lang Syne" on it. It seems to me, now,
that I must have been gifted with a sort of inspiration to be enabled,
in the state of ignorance in which I then was, to select out of the
whole range of musical composition the one solitary tune that sounds
vilest and most distressing on the accordeon. I do not suppose there is
another tune in the world with which I could have inflicted so much
anguish upon my race as I did with that one during my short musical
career.

After I had been playing "Lang Syne" about a week, I had the
vanity to think I could improve the original melody, and I set about
adding some little flourishes and variations to it, but with rather
indifferent success, I suppose, as it brought my landlady into my
presence with an expression about her of being opposed to such
desperate enterprises. Said she, "Do you know any other tune but
that, Mr. Twain?" I told her, meekly, that I did not. "Well, then," said
she, "stick to it just as it is; don't put any variations to it, because it's
rough enough on the boarders the way it is now."

The fact is, it was something more than simply "rough enough" on
them; it was altogether too rough; half of them left, and the other half
would have followed, but Mrs. Jones saved them by discharging me
from the premises.

I only staid one night at my next lodginghouse. Mrs. Smith was
after me early in the morning. She said, "You can go, sir; I don't want
you here; I have had one of your kind before—a poor lunatic, that
played the banjo and danced breakdowns, and jarred the glass all
out of the windows. You kept me awake all night, and if you was to do
it again, I'd take and mash that thing over your head!" I could see that
this woman took no delight in music, and I moved to Mrs. Brown's.

For three nights in succession I gave my new neighbors "Auld Lang
Syne," plain and unadulterated, save by a few discords that rather
improved the general effect than otherwise. But the very first time
I tried the variations the boarders mutinied. I never did find any
body that would stand those variations. I was very well satisfied with
my efforts in that house, however, and I left it without any regrets;
I drove one boarder as mad as a March hare, and another one tried
to scalp his mother. I reflected, though, that if I could only have been
allowed to give this latter just one more touch of the variations, he
would have finished the old woman.

I went to board at Mrs. Murphy's, an Italian lady of many excellent qualities. The very first time I struck up the variations, a haggard, care-worn, cadaverous old man walked into my room and stood beaming upon me a smile of ineffable happiness. Then he placed his hand upon my head, and looking devoutly aloft, he said with feeling unction, and in a voice trembling with emotion, "God bless you, young man! God bless you! for you have done that for me which is beyond all praise. For years I have suffered from an incurable disease, and knowing my doom was sealed and that I must die, I have striven with all my power to resign myself to my fate, but in vain—the love of life was too strong within me. But Heaven bless you, my benefactor! for since I heard you play that tune and those variations, I do not want to live any longer—I am entirely resigned—I am willing to die— in fact, I am anxious to die." And then the old man fell upon my neck and wept a flood of happy tears. I was surprised at these things; but I could not help feeling a little proud at what I had done, nor could I help giving the old gentleman a parting blast in the way of some peculiarly lacerating variations as he went out at the door. They doubled him up like a jack-knife, and the next time he left his bed of pain and suffering he was all right, in a metallic coffin.

My passion for the accordeon finally spent itself and died out, and I was glad when I found myself free from its unwholesome influence. While the fever was upon me, I was a living, breathing calamity wherever I went, and desolation and disaster followed in my wake. I bred discord in families, I crushed the spirits of the light-hearted, I drove the melancholy to despair, I hurried invalids to premature dissolution, and I fear me I disturbed the very dead in their graves. I did incalculable harm, and inflicted untold suffering upon my race with my execrable music; and yet to atone for it all, I did but one single blessed act, in making that weary old man willing to go to his long home.

Still, I derived some little benefit from that accordeon; for while I continued to practice on it, I never had to pay any board—landlords were always willing to compromise, on my leaving before the month was up.

Now, I had two objects in view in writing the foregoing, one of which was to try and reconcile people to those poor unfortunates who feel that they have a genius for music, and who drive their neighbors crazy every night in trying to develop and cultivate it; and the other was to introduce an admirable story about Little George Washington, who could Not Lie, and the Cherry-Tree—or the Apple-

Tree—I have forgotten now which, although it was told me only yesterday. And writing such a long and elaborate introductory has caused me to forget the story itself; but it was very touching.

1864

Advice to Little Girls

Good little girls ought not to make mouths at their teachers for every trifling offense. This retaliation should only be resorted to under peculiarly aggravated circumstances.

If you have nothing but a rag-doll stuffed with sawdust, while one of your more fortunate little playmates has a costly China one, you should treat her with a show of kindness nevertheless. And you ought not to attempt to make a forcible swap with her unless your conscience would justify you in it, and you know you are able to do it.

You ought never to take your little brother's "chewing-gum" away from him by main force; it is better to rope him in with the promise of the first two dollars and a half you find floating down the river on a grindstone. In the artless simplicity natural to his time of life, he will regard it as a perfectly fair transaction. In all ages of the world this eminently plausible fiction has lured the obtuse infant to financial ruin and disaster.

If at any time you find it necessary to correct your brother, do not correct him with mud—never, on any account, throw mud at him, because it will spoil his clothes. It is better to scald him a little, for then you obtain desirable results. You secure his immediate attention to the lessons you are inculcating, and at the same time your hot water will have a tendency to move impurities from his person, and possibly the skin, in spots.

If your mother tells you to do a thing, it is wrong to reply that you won't. It is better and more becoming to intimate that you will do as she bids you, and then afterward act quietly in the matter according to the dictates of your best judgment.

You should ever bear in mind that it is to your kind parents that you are indebted for your food, and your nice bed, and for your beautiful clothes, and for the privilege of staying home from school when you let on that you are sick. Therefore you ought to respect their little prejudices, and humor their little whims, and put up with their little foibles until they get to crowding you too much.

Good little girls always show marked deference for the aged. You ought never to "sass" old people unless they "sass" you first.

1865

"After" Jenkins

A grand affair of a ball—the Pioneers'—came off at the Occidental some time ago. The following notes of the costumes worn by the belles of the occasion may not be uninteresting to the general reader, and Jenkins may get an idea therefrom:

Mrs. W. M. was attired in an elegant *pâté de foie gras*, made expressly for her, and was greatly admired. Miss S. had her hair done up. She was the center of attraction for the gentlemen and the envy of all the ladies. Mrs. G. W. was tastefully dressed in a *tout ensemble*, and was greeted with deafening applause wherever she went. Mrs. C. N. was superbly arrayed in white kid gloves. Her modest and engaging manner accorded well with the unpretending simplicity of her costume and caused her to be regarded with absorbing interest by every one.

The charming Miss M. M. B. appeared in a thrilling waterfall, whose exceeding grace and volume compelled the homage of pioneers and emigrants alike. How beautiful she was!

The queenly Mrs. L. R. was attractively attired in her new and beautiful false teeth, and the *bon jour* effect they naturally produced was heightened by her enchanting and well-sustained smile.

Miss R. P., with that repugnance to ostentation in dress which is so peculiar to her, was attired in a simple white lace collar, fastened with a neat pearlbutton solitaire. The fine contrast between the sparkling vivacity of her natural optic, and the steadfast attentiveness of her placid glass eye, was the subject of general and enthusiastic remark.

Miss C. L. B. had her fine nose elegantly enameled, and the

easy grace with which she blew it from time to time marked her as a cultivated and accomplished woman of the world; its exquisitely modulated tone excited the admiration of all who had the happiness to hear it.

1865

Answers to Correspondents

"MORAL STATISTICIAN."—I don't want any of your statistics; I took your whole batch and lit my pipe with it. I hate your kind of people. You are always ciphering out how much a man's health is injured, and how much his intellect is impaired, and how many pitiful dollars and cents he wastes in the course of ninety-two years' indulgence in the fatal practice of smoking; and in the equally fatal practice of drinking coffee; and in playing billiards occasionally; and in taking a glass of wine at dinner, etc., etc., etc. And you are always figuring out how many women have been burned to death because of the dangerous fashion of wearing expansive hoops, etc., etc., etc. You never see more than one side of the question. You are blind to the fact that most old men in America smoke and drink coffee, although, according to your theory, they ought to have died young; and that hearty old Englishmen drink wine and survive it, and portly old Dutchmen both drink and smoke freely, and yet grow older and fatter all the time. And you never try to find out how much solid comfort, relaxation, and enjoyment a man derives from smoking in the course of a lifetime (which is worth ten times the money he would save by letting it alone), nor the appalling aggregate of happiness lost in a lifetime by your kind of people from *not* smoking. Of course you can save money by denying yourself all those little vicious enjoy-ments for fifty years; but then what can you do with it? What use can you put it to? Money can't save your infinitesimal soul. All the use that money can be put to is to purchase comfort and enjoyment in this life; therefore, as you are an enemy to comfort and enjoyment, where is the use of accumulating cash? It won't do for you to say that you can use it to better purpose in furnishing a good table, and in charities, and in supporting tract societies, because you know yourself that you people who have no petty vices are never known to give away a cent, and that you stint yourselves so in the matter of food that you are always feeble and hungry. And you never dare to laugh in the daytime for fear some poor wretch, seeing you in a good humor, will try to borrow a dollar of you; and in church you are always down on your knees, with your eyes buried in the cushion, when the contribution-box comes around; and you never give the revenue officers a full statement of your income. Now you know all these things yourself, don't you? Very well, then, what is the use of your stringing out your miserable lives to a lean and withered old age? What is the use of your saving money that is so utterly worthless to you? In a word, why don't you go off somewhere and die, and not be always trying to seduce people into becoming as "ornery" and unlovable as you are yourselves, by your villainous "moral statistics"? Now I don't approve of dissipation, and I don't indulge in it, either; but I haven't a particle of confidence in a man who has no redeeming petty vices, and so I don't want to hear from you any more. I think you are the very same man who read me a long lecture last week about the degrading vice of smoking cigars, and then came back, in my absence, with your reprehensible fire-proof gloves on, and carried off my beautiful parlor stove.

"YOUNG AUTHOR."—Yes, Agassiz *does* recommend authors to eat fish, because the phophorus in it makes brain. So far you are correct. But I cannot help you to a decision about the amount you need to eat —at least, not with certainty. If the specimen composition you send is about your fair usual average, I should judge that perhaps a couple of whales would be all you would want for the present. Not the largest kind, but simply good, middling-sized whales.

"SIMON WHEELER," *Sonora.*—The following simple and touching remarks and accompanying poem have just come to hand from the rich gold-mining region of Sonora:

To Mr. Mark Twain: The within parson, which I have set to poetry under the name and style of "He Done His Level Best," was one among the whitest men I ever see, and it ain't every man that knowed him that can find it in his heart to say he's glad the poor cuss is busted and gone home to the States. He was here in an early day, and he was the handyest man about takin' holt of anything that come along you most ever see, I judge. He was a cheerful, stirrin' cretur, always doin' somethin ', and no man can say he ever see him do

anything by halvers. Preachin' was his nateral gait, but he warn't a man
to lay back and twidle his thumbs because there didn't happen to be nothin'
doin' in his own especial line—no, sir, he was a man who would meander forth
and stir up something for hisself. His last acts was to go his pile on "Kings-
and" (calklatin' to fill, but which he didn't fill), when there was a "flush"
out agin him, and naterally, you see, he went under. And so he was cleaned
out, as you may say, and he struck the home-trail, cheerful but flat broke. I
knowed this talonted man in Arkansaw, and if you would print this humbly
tribute to his gorgis abilities, you would greatly obleege his onhappy friend.

HE DONE HIS LEVEL BEST

Was he a mining on the flat—
   He done it with a zest;
Was he a leading of the choir—
   He done his level best.

If he'd a reg'lar task to do,
   He never took no rest;
Or if 'twas off-and-on—the same—
   He done his level best.

If he was preachin' on his beat,
   He'd tramp from east to west,
And north to south—in cold and heat
   He done his level best.

He'd yank a sinner outen (Hades),[1]
   And land him with the blest;
Then snatch a prayer'n waltz in again,
   And do his level best.

He'd cuss and sing and howl and pray,
   And dance and drink and jest,
And lie and steal—all one to him—
   He done his level best.

Whate'er this man was sot to do,
   He done it with a zest;
No matter *what* his contract was,
   HE'D DO HIS LEVEL BEST.

Verily, this man *was* gifted with "gorgis abilities," and it is a happiness to me to embalm the memory of their luster in these columns.
If it were not that the poet crop is unusually large and rank in

[1] Here I have taken a slight liberty with the original MS. "Hades" does not make
such good meter as the other word of one syllable, but it sounds better.

California this year, I would encourage you to continue writing Simon
Wheeler; but, as it is, perhaps it might be too risky in you to enter
against so much opposition.

"PROFESSIONAL BEGGAR."—No; you are not obliged to take greenbacks
at par.

"MELTON MOWBRAY,"[1] *Dutch Flat*.—This correspondent sends a
lot of doggerel, and says it has been regarded as very good in Dutch
Flat. I give a specimen verse:

> The Assyrian came down like a wolf on the fold,
> And his cohorts were gleaming with purple and gold;
> And the sheen of his spears was like stars on the sea,
> When the blue wave rolls nightly on deep Galilee.

There, that will do. That may be very good Dutch Flat poetry, but
it won't do in the metropolis. It is too smooth and blubbery; it reads
like buttermilk gurgling from a jug. What the people ought to have
is something spirited—something like "Johnny Comes Marching Home."
However, keep on practising, and you may succeed yet. There is genius
in you, but too much blubber.

"ST. CLAIR HIGGINS." *Los Angeles*.—"My life is a failure; I have adored,
wildly, madly, and she whom I love has turned coldly from me and shed her
affections upon another. What would you advise me to do?"

You should set your affections on another also—or on several, if there
are enough to go round. Also, do everything you can to make your
former flame unhappy. There is an absurd idea disseminated in novels,
that the happier a girl is with another man, the happier it makes the
old lover she has blighted. Don't allow yourself to believe any such
nonsense as that. The more cause that girl finds to regret that she did
not marry you, the more comfortable you will feel over it. It isn't
poetical, but it is mighty sound doctrine.

"ARITHMETICUS." *Virginia, Nevada*.—"If it would take a cannon-ball $3\text{-}\frac{1}{3}$
seconds to travel four miles, and $3\text{-}\frac{3}{8}$ seconds to travel the next four, and $3\text{-}\frac{5}{8}$
to travel the next four, and if its rate of progress continued to diminish in the
same ratio, how long would it take it to go fifteen hundred million miles?"

[1] This piece of pleasantry, published in a San Francisco paper, was mistaken
by the country journals for seriousness, and many and loud were the denunciations
of the ignorance of author and editor, in not knowing that the lines in question
were "written by Byron."

I don't know.

"AMBITIOUS LEARNER," *Oakland.*—Yes; you are right—America was not discovered by Alexander Selkirk.

"DISCARDED LOVER."—"I loved, and still love, the beautiful Edwitha Howard, and intended to marry her. Yet, during my temporary absence at Benicia, last week, alas! she married Jones. Is my happiness to be thus blasted for life? Have I no redress?"

Of course you have. All the law, written and unwritten, is on your side. The *intention* and not the *act* constitutes crime—in other words, constitutes the *deed*. If you call your bosom friend a fool, and *intend* it for an insult, it *is* an insult; but if you do it playfully, and meaning no insult, it is *not* an insult. If you discharge a pistol *accidentally*, and kill a man, you can go free, for you have done no murder; but if you try to kill a man, and manifestly *intend* to kill him, but fail utterly to do it, the law still holds that the *intention* constituted the crime, and you are guilty of murder. Ergo, if you had married Edwitha *accidentally*, and without really *intending* to do it, you would not actually be married to her at all, because the *act* of marriage could not be complete without the *intention*. And ergo, in the strict spirit of the law, since you deliberately *intended* to marry Edwitha, and didn't do it, you are married to her all the same—because, as I said before, the *intention* constitutes the crime. It is as clear as day that Edwitha is your wife, and your redress lies in taking a club and mutilating Jones with it as much as you can. Any man has a right to protect his own wife from the advances of other men. But you have another alternative—you were married to Edwitha *first*, because of your deliberate intention, and now you can prosecute her for bigamy, in subsequently marrying Jones. But there is another phase in this complicated case: You *intended* to marry Edwitha, and consequently, according to law, she is your wife—there is no getting around that; but she didn't marry you, and if she *never intended* to marry you, *you are not her husband*, of course. Ergo, in marrying Jones, she was guilty of bigamy, because she was the wife of another man at the time; which is all very well as far as it goes—but then, don't you see, she had no other *husband* when she married Jones, and consequently she was *not* guilty of bigamy. Now, according to this view of the case, Jones married a *spinster*, who was a *widow* at the same time and another man's *wife* at the same time, and yet who had no *husband* and *never had one*, and never had any *intention* of getting married, and therefore, of course, *never had* been married; and by the same reasoning you are a *bachelor*, because you have never been any one's *husband;* and a *married man*, because you have a wife living; and to all intents and purposes a *widower*, because you have been deprived of that wife; and a consummate *ass* for going off to Benicia in the first place, while things were so mixed. And by this time I have got myself so tangled up in the intricacies of this extraordinary case that I shall have to give up any further attempt to advise you—I might get confused and fail to make myself understood. I think I could take up the argument where I left off, and by following it closely awhile, perhaps I could prove to your satisfaction, either that you never existed at all, or that you are dead now, and consequently don't need the faithless Edwitha— I think I could do that, if it would afford you any comfort.

"Arthur Augustus."—No; you are wrong; that is the proper way to throw a brickbat or a tomahawk; but it doesn't answer so well for a bouquet; you will hurt somebody if you keep it up. Turn your nosegay upside down, take it by the stems, and toss it with an upward sweep. Did you ever pitch quoits? that is the idea. The practice of recklessly heaving immense solid bouquets, of the general size and weight of prize cabbages, from the dizzy altitude of the galleries, is dangerous and very reprehensible. Now, night before last, at the Academy of Music, just after Signorina —— had finished that exquisite melody, "The Last Rose of Summer," one of these floral pile-drivers came cleaving down through the atmosphere of applause, and if she hadn't deployed suddenly to the right, it would have driven her into the floor like a shinglenail. Of course that bouquet was well meant; but how would you like to have been the target? A sincere compliment is always grateful to a lady, so long as you don't try to knock her down with it.

"Young Mother."—And so you think a baby is a thing of beauty and a joy forever? Well, the idea is pleasing, but not original; every cow thinks the same of its own calf. Perhaps the cow may not think it so elegantly, but still she thinks it nevertheless. I honor the cow for it. We all honor this touching maternal instinct wherever we find it, be it in the home of luxury or in the humble cow-shed. But really, madam, when I come to examine the matter in all its bearings, I find that the correctness of your assertion does not assert itself in all cases. A soiled baby, with a neglected nose, cannot be conscientiously regarded as a thing of beauty; and inasmuch as babyhood spans but three short years, no baby is competent to be a joy "forever." It pains me thus to demolish two-thirds of your pretty sentiment in a single sentence; but the position I hold in this chair requires that I shall not permit you to deceive and mislead the public with your plausible figures of speech. I know a female baby, aged eighteen months, in this city, which cannot hold out as a "joy" twenty-four hours on a stretch, let alone "forever." And it possesses some of the most remarkable eccentricities of character and appetite that have ever fallen under my notice. I will set down here a statement of this infant's operations (conceived, planned, and carried out by itself, and without suggestion or assistance from its mother or any one else), during a single day; and what I shall say can be substantiated by the sworn testimony of witnesses.

It commenced by eating one dozen large blue-mass pills, box and all; then it fell down a flight of stairs, and arose with a blue and purple knot on its forehead, after which it proceeded in quest of further refreshment and amusement. It found a glass trinket ornamented with brass-work—smashed up and ate the glass, and then swallowed the brass. Then it drank about twenty drops of laudanum, and more than a dozen tablespoonfuls of strong spirits of camphor. The reason why it took no more laudanum was because there was no more to take. After this it lay down on its back, and shoved five or six inches of a silver-headed whalebone cane down its throat; got it fast there, and it was all its mother could do to pull the cane out again, without pulling out some of the child with it. Then, being hungry for glass again, it broke up several wineglasses, and fell to eating and swallowing the fragments, not minding a cut or two. Then it ate a quantity of butter, pepper, salt, and California matches, actually taking a spoonful of butter, a spoonful of salt, a spoonful of pepper, and three or four lucifer matches at each mouthful. (I will remark here that this thing of beauty likes painted German lucifers, and eats all she can get of them; but she prefers California matches, which I regard as a compliment to our home manufactures of more than ordinary value, coming, as it does, from one who is too young to flatter.) Then she washed her head with soap and water, and afterward ate what soap was left, and drank as much of the suds as she had room for; after which she sallied forth and took the cow familiarly by the tail, and got kicked heels over head. At odd times during the day, when this joy forever happened to have nothing particular on hand, she put in the time by climbing up on places, and falling down off them, uniformly damaging herself in the operation. As young as she is, she speaks many words tolerably distinctly; and being plain-spoken in other respects, blunt and to the point, she opens conversation with all strangers, male or female, with the same formula, "How do, Jim?" Not being familiar with the ways of children, it is possible that I have been magnifying into matter of surprise things which may not strike any one who is familiar with infancy as being at all astonishing. However, I cannot believe that such is the case, and so I repeat that my report of this baby's performances is strictly true; and if any one doubts it, I can produce the child. I will further engage that she will devour anything that is given her (reserving to myself only the right to exclude anvils), and fall down from any place to which she may be elevated (merely stipulating that her preference for alighting on her head shall be respected, and, therefore, that the elevation chosen shall be high enough to enable her to accomplish this to her satisfaction). But I find I have wandered from my subject; so, without further argument, I will reiterate my conviction that not *all* babies are things of beauty and joys forever.

"ARITHMETICUS." *Virginia, Nevada.*—"I am an enthusiastic student of mathematics, and it is so vexatious to me to find my progress constantly impeded by these mysterious arithmetical technicalities. Now do tell me what the difference is between geometry and conchology?"

Here *you* come again with your arithmetical conundrums, when I am suffering death with a cold in the head. If you could have seen the expression of scorn that darkened my countenance a moment ago, and was instantly split from the center in every direction like a fractured looking-glass by my last sneeze, you never would have written that disgraceful question. Conchology is a science which has nothing to do with mathematics; it relates only to shells. At the same time, however, a man who opens oysters for a hotel, or shells a fortified town, or sucks eggs, is not, strickly speaking, a conchologist—a fine stroke of sarcasm that, but it will be lost on such an unintellectual clam as you. Now compare conchology and geometry together, and you will see what the difference is, and your question will be answered. But don't torture me with any more arithmetical horrors until you know I am rid of my cold. I feel the bitterest animosity toward you at this moment—bothering me in this way, when I can do nothing but sneeze and rage and snort pocket-handkerchiefs to atoms. If I had you in range of my nose now I would blow your brains out.

1865

Mr. Bloke's Item

Our esteemed friend, Mr. John William Bloke, of Virginia City, walked into the office where we are sub-editor at a late hour last night, with an expression of profound and heartfelt suffering upon his countenance, and, sighing heavily, laid the following item reverently upon the desk, and walked slowly out again. He paused a moment at the door, and seemed struggling to command his feelings sufficiently to enable him to speak, and then, nodding his head toward his manuscript, ejaculated in a broken voice, "Friend of mine—oh! how sad!" and burst into tears. We were so moved at his distress that we did not think to call him back and endeavor to comfort him until he was gone, and it was too late. The paper had already gone to press, but knowing that our friend would consider the publication of this item important, and cherishing the hope that to print it would afford a melancholy satisfaction to his sorrowing heart, we stopped the press at once and inserted it in our columns:

DISTRESSING ACCIDENT.—Last evening, about six o'clock, as Mr. William Schuyler, an old and respectable citizen of South Park, was leaving his residence to go down-town, as has been his usual custom for many years with the exception only of a short interval in the spring of 1850, during which he was confined to his bed by injuries received in attempting to stop a runaway horse by thoughtlessly placing himself directly in its wake and throwing up his hands and shouting, which if he had done so even a single moment sooner, must inevitably have frightened the animal still more instead of checking its speed, although disastrous enough to himself as it was, and rendered more melancholy and distressing by reason of the presence of his wife's mother, who was there and saw the sad occurrence notwithstanding it is at least likely, though not necessarily so, that she should be reconnoitering in another direction when incidents occur, not being vivacious and on the lookout, as a general thing, but even the reverse, as her own mother is said to have stated, who is no more, but died in the full hope of a glorious resurrection, upwards of three years ago, aged eighty-six, being a Christian woman and without guile, as it were, or property, in consequence of the fire of 1849, which destroyed every single thing she had in the world. But such is life. Let us all take warning by this solemn occurrence, and let us endeavor so to conduct ourselves that when we come to die we can do it. Let us place our hands upon our heart, and say with earnestness and sincerity that from this day forth we will beware of the intoxicating bowl.—*First Edition of the Californian.*

The head editor has been in here raising the mischief, and tearing his hair and kicking the furniture about, and abusing me like a pick-pocket. He says that every time he leaves me in charge of the paper for half an hour I get imposed upon by the first infant or the first idiot that comes along. And he says that that distressing item of Mr. Bloke's is nothing but a lot of distressing bosh, and has no point to it, and no sense in it, and no information in it, and that there was no sort of necessity for stopping the press to publish it.

Now all this comes of being good-hearted. If I had been as unaccommodating and unsympathetic as some people, I would have told Mr. Bloke that I wouldn't receive his communication at such a late hour; but no, his snuffling distress touched my heart, and I jumped at the chance of doing something to modify his misery. I never read his item to see whether there was anything wrong about it, but hastily wrote the few lines which preceded it, and sent it to the printers. And what has my kindness done for me? It has done nothing but bring down upon me a storm of abuse and ornamental blasphemy.

Now I will read that item myself, and see if there is any foundation for all this fuss. And if there is, the author of it shall hear from me.

I have read it, and I am bound to admit that it seems a little mixed at a first glance. However, I will peruse it once more.

I have read it again, and it does really seem a good deal more mixed than ever.

I have read it over five times, but if I can get at the meaning of it I wish I may get my just deserts. It won't bear analysis. There are things about it which I cannot understand at all. It don't say whatever became of William Schuyler. It just says enough about him to get one interested in his career, and then drops him. Who is William Schuyler, anyhow, and what part of South Park did he live in, and if he started down-town at six o'clock, did he ever get there, and if he did, did anything happen to him? Is *he* the individual that met with the "distressing accident"? Considering the elaborate circumstantiality of detail observable in the item, it seems to me that it ought to contain more information than it does. On the contrary, it is obscure—and not only obscure, but utterly incomprehensible. Was the breaking of Mr. Schuyler's leg, fifteen years ago, the "distressing accident" that plunged Mr. Bloke into unspeakable grief, and caused him to come up here at dead of night and stop our press to acquaint the world with the circumstance? Or did the "distressing accident" consist in the destruction of Schuyler's mother-in-law's property in early times? Or did it consist in the death of that person herself three years ago (albeit it does not appear that she died by accident)? In a word, what *did* that "distressing accident" consist in? What did that driveling ass of a Schuyler stand *in the wake* of a runaway horse for, with his shouting and gesticulating, if he wanted to stop him? And how the mischief could he get run over by a horse that had already passed beyond him? And what are we to take "warning" by? And how is this extraordinary chapter of incomprehensibilities going to be a "lesson" to us? And, above all, what has the intoxicating "bowl" got to do with it, anyhow? It is not stated that Schuyler drank, or that his wife drank, or that his mother-in-law drank, or that the horse drank—wherefore, then, the reference to the intoxicating bowl? It does seem to me that if Mr. Bloke had let the intoxicating bowl alone himself, he never would have got into so much trouble about this exasperating imaginary accident. I have read this absurd item over and over again, with all its insinuating plausibility, until my head swims; but I can make neither head nor tail of it. There certainly seems to have been an accident of some kind or other, but it is impossible to determine what the nature of it was, or who was the sufferer by it. I do not like to do it, but I feel compelled to request that the next time anything happens to one of Mr. Bloke's friends, he will append such explanatory notes to his account of it as will enable me to find out what sort of an accident it was and whom it happened to. I had rather all his friends should die than that I should be driven to the verge of lunacy again in trying to cipher out the meaning of another such production as the above.

1865

A Page from a Californian Almanac

At the instance of several friends who feel a boding anxiety to know beforehand what sort of phenomena we may expect the elements to exhibit during the next month or two, and who have lost all con-

fidence in the various patent medicine almanacs, because of the unaccountable reticence of those works concerning the extraordinary
event of the 8th inst., I have compiled the following almanac expressly
for the latitude of San Francisco:

Oct. 17.—Weather hazy; atmosphere murky and dense. An expression of profound melancholy will be observable upon most countenances.

Oct. 18.—Slight earthquake. Countenances grow more melancholy.

Oct. 19.—Look out for rain. It would be absurd to look in for it.
The general depression of spirits increased.

Oct. 20.—More weather.

Oct. 21.—Same.

Oct. 22.—Light winds, perhaps. If they blow, it will be from the
"east'ard, or the nor'ard, or the west'ard, or the suth'ard," or from
some general direction approximating more or less to these points of
the compass or otherwise. Winds are uncertain—more especially when
they blow from whence they cometh and whither they listeth. N. B.
—Such is the nature of winds.

Oct. 23.—Mild, balmy earthquakes.

Oct. 24.—Shaky.

Oct. 25.—Occasional shakes, followed by light showers of bricks and
plastering. N. B.—Stand from under!

Oct. 26.—Considerable phenomenal atmospheric foolishness. About
this time expect more earthquakes; but do not look for them, on account of the bricks.

Oct. 27.—Universal despondency, indicative of approaching disaster.
Abstain from smiling, or indulgence in humorous conversation, or
exasperating jokes.

Oct. 28.—Misery, dismal forebodings, and despair. Beware of all
light discourse—a joke uttered at this time would produce a popular
outbreak.

Oct. 29.—Beware!

Oct. 30.—Keep dark!

Oct. 31.—Go slow!

Nov. 1.—Terrific earthquake. This is the great earthquake month.
More stars fall and more worlds are slathered around carelessly and
destroyed in November than in any other month of the twelve.

Nov. 2.—Spasmodic but exhilarating earthquakes, accompanied by
occasional showers of rain and churches and things.

Nov. 3.—Make your will.

Nov. 4.—Sell out.

Nov. 5.—Select your "last words." Those of John Quincy Adams will do, with the addition of a syllable, thus: "This is the last of earthquakes."

Nov. 6.—Prepare to shed this mortal coil.

Nov. 7.—Shed!

Nov. 8.—The sun will rise as usual, perhaps; but if he does, he will doubtless be staggered some to find nothing but a large round hole eight thousand miles in diameter in the place where he saw this world serenely spinning the day before.

1865

The Scriptural Panoramist

"There was a fellow traveling around in that country," said Mr. Nickerson, "with a moral-religious show—a sort of scriptural panorama —and he hired a wooden-headed old slab to play the piano for him. After the first night's performance the showman says:

"'My friend, you seem to know pretty much all the tunes there are, and you worry along first rate. But then, didn't you notice that some- times last night the piece you happened to be playing was a little rough on the proprieties, so to speak—didn't seem to jibe with the general gait of the picture that was passing at the time, as it were— was a little foreign to the subject, you know—as if you didn't either trump or follow suit, you understand?'

"'Well, no,' the fellow said; 'he hadn't noticed, but it might be; he had played along just as it came handy.'

"So they put it up that the simple old dummy was to keep his eye on the panorama after that, and as soon as a stunning picture was reeled out he was to fit it to a dot with a piece of music that would help the audience to get the idea of the subject, and warm them up like a camp-meeting revival. That sort of thing would corral their sympathies, the showman said.

"There was a big audience that night—mostly middle-aged and old people who belong to the church, and took a strong interest in Bible matters, and the balance were pretty much young bucks and heifers—

they always come out strong on panoramas, you know, because it gives them a chance to taste one another's complexions in the dark.

"Well, the showman began to swell himself up for his lecture, and the old mud-dobber tackled the piano and ran his fingers up and down once or twice to see that she was all right, and the fellows behind the curtain commenced to grind out the panorama. The showman balanced his weight on his right foot, and propped his hands over his hips, and flung his eyes over his shoulder at the scenery, and said:

"'Ladies and gentlemen, the painting now before you illustrates the beautiful and touching parable of the Prodigal Son. Observe the happy expression just breaking over the features of the poor, suffering youth —so worn and weary with his long march; note also the ecstasy beaming from the uplifted countenance of the aged father, and the joy that sparkles in the eyes of the excited group of youths and maidens, and seems ready to burst into the welcoming chorus from their lips. The lesson, my friends, is as solemn and instructive as the story is tender and beautiful.'

"The mud-dobber was all ready, and when the second speech was finished, struck up:

> "Oh, we'll all get blind drunk
> When Johnny comes marching home!

"Some of the people giggled, and some groaned a little. The showman couldn't say a word; he looked at the pianist sharp, but he was all lovely and serene—*he* didn't know there was anything out of gear.

"The panorama moved on, and the showman drummed up his grit and started in fresh.

"'Ladies and gentlemen, the fine picture now unfolding itself to your gaze exhibits one of the most notable events in Bible history— our Saviour and His disciples upon the Sea of Galilee. How grand, how awe-inspiring are the reflections which the subject invokes! What sublimity of faith is revealed to us in this lesson from the sacred writings! The Saviour rebukes the angry waves, and walks securely upon the bosom of the deep!'

"All around the house they were whispering, 'Oh, how lovely, how beautiful!' and the orchestra let himself out again:

> "A life on the ocean wave,
> And a home on the rolling deep!

"There was a good deal of honest snickering turned on this time, and considerable groaning, and one or two old deacons got up and went out. The showman grated his teeth, and cursed the piano man to himself; but the fellow sat there like a knot on a log, and seemed to think he was doing first-rate.

"After things got quiet the showman thought he would make one more stagger at it, anyway, though his confidence was beginning to get mighty shaky. The supes started the panorama grinding along again, and he says:

"'Ladies and gentlemen, this exquisite painting represents the raising of Lazarus from the dead by our Saviour. The subject has been handled with marvelous skill by the artist, and such touching sweetness and tenderness of expression has he thrown into it that I have known peculiarly sensitive persons to be even affected to tears by looking at it. Observe the half-confused, half-inquiring look upon the countenance of the awakened Lazarus. Observe, also, the attitude and expression of the Saviour, who takes him gently by the sleeve of his shroud with one hand, while He points with the other toward the distant city.'

"Before anybody could get off an opinion in the case the innocent old ass at the piano struck up:

"Come rise up, William Ri-i-ley,
And go along with me!

"Whe-ew! All the solemn old flats got up in a huff to go, and everybody else laughed till the windows rattled.

"The showman went down and grabbed the orchestra and shook him up and says:

"'That lets you out, you know, you chowder-headed old clam. Go to the doorkeeper and get your money, and cut your stick—vamose the ranch! Ladies and gentlemen, circumstances over which I have no control compel me prematurely to dismiss the house.'"

1865

Among the Spirits

There was a *séance* in town a few nights since. As I was making for it, in company with the reporter of an evening paper, he said he had seen a gambler named Gus Graham shot down in a town in Illinois years ago by a mob, and as he was probably the only person in San Francisco who knew of the circumstance, he thought he would "give the spirits Graham to chaw on awhile." [N. B.—This young creature is a Democrat, and speaks with the native strength and inelegance of his tribe.] In the course of the show he wrote his old pal's name on a slip of paper, and folded it up tightly and put it in a hat which was passed around, and which already had about five hundred similar documents in it. The pile was dumped on the table, and the medium began to take them up one by one and lay them aside, asking, "Is this spirit present? or this? or this?" About one in fifty would rap, and the person who sent up the name would rise in his place and question the defunct. At last a spirit seized the medium's hand and wrote "Gus Graham" backward. Then the medium went skirmishing through the papers for the corresponding name. And that old sport knew his card by the back! When the medium came to it, after picking up fifty others, he rapped! A committeeman unfolded the paper, and it was the right one. I sent for it and got it. It was all right. However, I suppose all Democrats are on sociable terms with the devil. The young man got up and asked:

"Did you die in '51? '52? '53? '54?——"

Ghost—"Rap, rap, rap."

"Did you die of cholera? diarrhea? dysentery? dog-bite? small-pox? violent death?——"

"Rap, rap, rap."

"Were you hanged? drowned? stabbed? shot?——"

"Rap, rap, rap."

"Did you die in Mississippi? Kentucky? New-York? Sandwich Islands? Texas? Illinois?——"

"Rap, rap, rap."

"In Adams county? Madison? Randolph?——"

"Rap, rap, rap."

It was no use trying to catch the departed gambler. He knew his hand, and played it like a major.

About this time a couple of Germans stepped forward, an elderly man and a spry young fellow, cocked and primed for a sensation. They wrote some names. Then young Ollendorff said something which sounded like—

"Ist ein geist hieraus?" [Bursts of laughter from the audience.]

Three raps—signifying that there *was* a geist hieraus.

"Vollen sie schriehen?" [More laughter.]

Three raps.

"Finzig stollen, linsowfterowlickterhairowfterfrowleineruhackfolde-rol?"

Incredible as it may seem, the spirit cheerfully answered Yes to that astonishing proposition.

The audience grew more and more boisterously mirthful with every fresh question, and they were informed that the performance could not go on in the midst of so much levity. They became quiet.

The German ghost didn't appear to know any thing at all—couldn't answer the simplest questions. Young Ollendorff finally stated some numbers, and tried to get at the time of the spirit's death; it appeared to be considerably mixed as to whether it died in 1811 or 1812, which was reasonable enough, as it had been so long ago. At last it wrote "12."

Tableau! Young Ollendorff sprang to his feet in a state of consuming excitement. He exclaimed:

"Laties und shentlemen! I write de name fon a man vot lifs! Speerit-rabbing dells me he ties in yahr eighteen hoondred und dwelf, but he yoos as live und helty as——"

The Medium—"Sit down, sir!"

Ollendorff—"But I vant to——"

Medium—"You are not here to make speeches, sir—sit down!" [Mr. O. had squared himself for an oration.]

Mr. O. "But de speerit cheat!—dere is no such speerit——" [All this time applause and laughter by turns from the audience.]

Medium—"Take your seat, sir, and I will explain this matter."

And she explained. And in that explanation she let off a blast which was so terrific that I half expected to see young Ollendorff shot up through the roof. She said he had come up there with fraud and deceit and cheating in his heart, and a kindred spirit had come from the land of shadows to commune with him! She was terribly bitter. She said in substance, though not in words, that perdition was full of just such fellows as Ollendorff, and they were ready on the slightest pretext to rush in and assume any body's name, and rap and write and lie and swindle with a perfect looseness whenever they could rope in a living affinity like poor Ollendorff to communicate with! [Great applause and laughter.]

Ollendorff stood his ground with good pluck, and was going to open his batteries again, when a storm of cries arose all over the house, "Get down! Go on! Clear out! Speak on—we'll hear you! Climb down from that platform! Stay where you are! Vamose! Stick to your post—say your say!"

The medium rose up and said if Ollendorff remained, she would not. She recognized no one's right to come there and insult her by practicing a deception upon her, and attempting to bring ridicule upon so solemn a thing as her religious belief. The audience then became quiet, and the subjugated Ollendorff retired from the platform.

The other German raised a spirit, questioned it at some length in his own language, and said the answers were correct. The medium claimed to be entirely unacquainted with the German language.

Just then a gentleman called me to the edge of the platform and asked me if I were a Spiritualist. I said I was not. He asked me if I were prejudiced. I said not more than any other unbeliever; but I could not believe in a thing which I could not understand, and I had not seen any thing yet that I could by any possibility cipher out. He said, then, that he didn't think I was the cause of the diffidence shown by the spirits, but he knew there was an antagonistic influence around that table somewhere; he had noticed it from the first; there was a painful negative current passing to his sensitive organization from that direction constantly. I told him I guessed it was that other fellow; and I said, Blame a man who was all the time shedding these infernal negative currents! This appeared to satisfy the mind of the inquiring fanatic, and he sat down.

I had a very dear friend, who, I had heard, had gone to the spirit-land, or perdition, or some of those places, and I desired to know something concerning him. There was something so awful, though, about talking with living, sinful lips to the ghostly dead, that I could hardly bring myself to rise and speak. But at last I got tremblingly up and said with a low and trembling voice:

"Is the spirit of John Smith present?"

(You never can depend on these Smiths; you call for one, and the whole tribe will come clattering out of hell to answer you.)

"Whack! whack! whack! whack!"

Bless me! I believe all the dead and damned John Smiths between San Francisco and perdition boarded that poor little table at once! I was considerably set back—stunned, I may say. The audience urged me to go on, however, and I said:

"What did you die of?"

The Smiths answered to every disease and casualty that men can die of.

"Where did you die?"

They answered Yes to every locality I could name while my geography held out.

"Are you happy where you are?"

There was a vigorous and unanimous "No!" from the late Smiths.

"Is it warm there?"

An educated Smith seized the medium's hand and wrote:

"It's no name for it."

"Did you leave any Smiths in that place when you came away!"

"Dead loads of them!"

I fancied I heard the shadowy Smiths chuckle at this feeble joke— the rare joke that there could be live loads of Smiths where all are dead.

"How many Smiths are present?"

"Eighteen millions—the procession now reaches from here to the other side of China."

"Then there are many Smiths in the kingdom of the lost?"

"The Prince Apollyon calls all new comers Smith on general principles; and continues to do so until he is corrected, if he chances to be mistaken."

"What do lost spirits call their dread abode?"

"They call it the Smithsonian Institute."

I got hold of the right Smith at last—the particular Smith I was after—my dear, lost, lamented friend—and learned that he died a violent death. I feared as much. He said his wife talked him to death. Poor wretch!

By and by up started another Smith. A gentleman in the audience said that this was his Smith. So he questioned him, and this Smith said he too died by violence. He had been a good deal tangled in his religious belief, and was a sort of a cross between a Universalist and a Unitarian; has got straightened out and changed his opinions since he left here; said he was perfectly happy. We proceeded to question this talkative and frolicsome old parson. Among spirits I judge he is the gayest of the gay. He said he had no tangible body; a bullet could pass through him and never make a hole; rain could pass through him as through vapor, and not discommode him in the least, (so I suppose he don't know enough to come in when it rains—or don't care enough;) says heaven and hell are simply mental conditions; spirits in the former have happy and contented minds, and those in the latter are torn by remorse of conscience; says as far as he is concerned, he is all right—he is happy; would not say whether he was a very good or a very bad man on earth, (the shrewd old water-proof non-entity! I asked the question so that I might average my own chances for his luck in the other world, but he saw my drift;) says he has an occupation there—puts in his time teaching and being taught; says there are spheres—grades of perfection—he is making very good progress—has been promoted a sphere or so since his matriculation; (I said mentally, "Go slow, old man, go slow, you have got all eternity before you," and he replied not;) he don't know how many spheres there are, (but I suppose there must be millions, because if a man goes galloping through them at the rate this old Universalist is doing, he will get through an infinitude of them by the time he has been there as long as old Sesostris and those ancient mummies; and there is no estimating how high he will get in even the infancy of eternity—I am afraid the old man is scouring along rather too fast for the style of his surroundings, and the length of time he has got on his hands;) says spirits can not feel heat or cold, (which militates somewhat against all my notions of orthodox damnation—fire and brimstone;) says spirits commune with each other by thought—they have no language; says the distinctions of sex are preserved there—and so forth and so on.

The old parson wrote and talked for an hour, and showed by his quick, shrewd, intelligent replies, that he had not been sitting up nights in the other world for nothing; he had been prying into every thing worth knowing, and finding out every thing he possibly could—as he said himself—when he did not understand a thing he hunted up a spirit who could explain it, consequently he is pretty thoroughly posted. And for his accommodating conduct and his uniform courtesy to me, I sincerely hope he will continue to progress at his present velocity until he lands on the very roof of the highest sphere of all, and thus achieves perfection.

1866

Brief Biographical Sketch
of George Washington

This day, many years ago precisely, George Washington was born. How full of significance the thought! Especially to those among us who have had a similar experience, though subsequently; and still more especially to the young, who should take him for a model, and faithfully try to be like him, undeterred by the frequency with which the same thing has been attempted by American youths before them and not satisfactorily accomplished. George Washington was the youngest of nine children, eight of whom were the offspring of his uncle and his aunt. As a boy, he gave no promise of the greatness he was one day to achieve. He was ignorant of the commonest accomplishments of youth. He could not even lie. But then he never had any of those precious advantages which are within the reach of the humblest of the boys of the present day. Any boy can lie now. I could lie before I could stand—yet this sort of sprightliness was so common in our family that little notice was taken of it. Young George appears to have had no sagacity whatever. It is related of him that he once chopped down his father's favorite cherry-tree, and then didn't know enough to keep dark about it. He came near going to sea once, as a midshipman; but when his mother represented to him that he must necessarily be absent when he was away from home, and that this must continue to be the case until he got back, the sad truth struck him so forcibly that he ordered his trunk ashore, and quietly but firmly refused to serve in the navy and fight the battles of his king so long as the effect of it would be to discommode his mother. The great rule of his life was, that procrastination was the thief of time, and that we should always do unto others somehow. This is the golden rule. Therefore, he would never discommode his mother.

Young George Washington was actuated in all things by the highest and purest principles of morality, justice, and right. He was a model in every way worthy of the emulation of youth. Young George was always prompt and faithful in the discharge of every duty. It has been said of him, by the historian, that he was always on hand, like a thousand of brick. And well deserved was this compliment. The aggregate of the building material specified might have been largely increased—might have been doubled, even—without doing full justice to these high qualities in the subject of this sketch. Indeed, it would hardly be possible to express in bricks the exceeding promptness and fidelity of young George Washington. His was a soul whose manifold excellencies were beyond the ken and computation of mathematics, and bricks are, at the least, but an inadequate vehicle for the conveyance of a comprehension of the moral sublimity of a nature so pure as his.

Young George W. was a surveyor in early life—a surveyor of an inland port—a sort of county surveyor; and under a commission from Governor Dinwiddie, he set out to survey his way four hundred miles through trackless forests, infested with Indians, to procure the liberation of some English prisoners. The historian says the Indians were the most depraved of their species, and did nothing but lay for white men, whom they killed for the sake of robbing them. Considering that white men only traveled through the country at the rate of one a year, they were probably unable to do what might be termed a land-office business in their line. They did not rob young G. W.; one savage made the attempt, but failed; he fired at the subject of this sketch from behind a tree, but the subject of this sketch immediately snaked him out from behind the tree and took him prisoner.

The long journey failed of success; the French would not give up the prisoners, and Wash went sadly back home again. A regiment was raised to go and make a rescue, and he took command of it. He caught the French out in the rain and tackled them with great intrepidity. He defeated them in ten minutes, and their commander handed in his checks. This was the battle of Great Meadows.

After this, a good while, George Washington became Commander-in-Chief of the American armies, and had an exceedingly dusty time of it all through the Revolution. But every now and then he turned a Jack from the bottom and surprised the enemy. He kept up his lick for seven long years, and hazed the British from Harrisburg to Halifax—and America was free! He served two terms as President, and would have been President yet if he had lived—even so did the people honor the Father of his Country. Let the youth of America take his incomparable character for a model, and try it one jolt, any how. Success is possible—let them remember that—success is possible, though there are chances against it.

I could continue this biography with profit to the rising generation, but I shall have to drop the subject at present, because of other matters which must be attended to.

1866

A Complaint about Correspondents

What do you take us for, on this side or the continent? I am addressing myself personally, and with asperity, to every man, woman, and child east of the Rocky Mountains. How do you suppose our minds are constituted, that you will write us such execrable letters—such poor, bald, uninteresting trash? You complain that by the time a man has been on the Pacific coast six months, he seems to lose all concern about matters and things and people in the distant East, and ceases to answer the letters of his friends and even his relatives. It is your own fault. You need a lecture on the subject—a lecture which ought to read about as follows:

There is only one brief, solitary law for letter-writing, and yet you either do not know that law, or else you are so stupid that you never think of it. It is very easy and simple: Write only about things and people your correspondent takes a living interest in.

Can not you remember that law, hereafter, and abide by it? If you are an old friend of the person you are writing to, you know a number of his acquaintances, and you can rest satisfied that even the most trivial things you can write about them will be read with avidity out here on the edge of sunset.

Yet how *do* you write?—how do the most of you write? Why, you drivel and drivel and drivel along in your wooden-headed way about people one never heard of before, and things which one knows nothing at all about and cares less. There is no sense in that. Let me show up your style with a specimen or so. Here is a paragraph from my Aunt Nancy's last letter—received four years ago, and not answered immediately—not at all, I may say:

"*St. Louis, 1862*

"DEAR MARK: We spent the evening very pleasantly at home yesterday. The Rev. Dr. Macklin and wife, from Peoria, were here. He is an humble laborer in the vineyard, and takes his coffee strong. He is also subject to neuralgia—neuralgia in the head—and is so unassuming and prayerful. There are few such men. We had soup for dinner likewise. Although I am not fond of it. O Mark! why *don't* you try to lead a better life? Read II. Kings, from chap. 2 to chap. 24 inclusive. It would be so gratifying to me if you would experience a change of heart. Poor Mrs. Gabrick is dead. You did not know her. She had fits, poor soul. On the 14th the entire army took up the line of march from——"

I always stopped there, because I knew what was coming—the war news, in minute and dry detail—for I could never drive it into those numskulls that the overland telegraph enabled me to know here in San Francisco every day all that transpired in the United States the day before, and that the pony express brought me exhaustive details of all matters pertaining to the war at least two weeks before their letters could possibly reach me. So I naturally skipped their stale war reports, even at the cost of also skipping the inevitable suggestions to read this, that, and the other batch of chapters in the Scriptures, with which they were interlarded at intervals, like snares wherewith to trap the unwary sinner.

Now what was the Rev. Macklin to me? Of what consequence was it to me that he was "an humble laborer in the vineyard," and "took his coffee strong"?—and was "unassuming," and "neuralgic," and "prayerful"? Such a strange conglomeration of virtues could only excite my admiration—nothing more. It could awake no living interest. That there are few such men, and that we had soup for dinner, is simply gratifying—that is all. "Read twenty-two chapters of II. Kings" is a nice shell to fall in the camp of a man who is not studying for the ministry. The intelligence that "poor Mrs. Gabrick" was dead, aroused no enthusiasm—mostly because of the circumstance that I had never heard of her before, I presume. But I was glad she had fits—although a stranger.

Don't you begin to understand, now? Don't you see that there is not a sentence in that letter of any interest in the world to me? I had the war news in advance of it; I could get a much better sermon at church when I needed it; I didn't care any thing about poor Gabrick, not knowing deceased; nor yet the Rev. Macklin, not knowing him either. I said to myself, "Here's not a word about Mary Anne Smith—

I wish there was; nor about Georgiana Brown, or Zeb Leavenworth, or Sam Bowen, or Strother Wiley—or about any body else I care a straw for." And so, as this letter was just of a pattern with all that went before it, it was not answered, and one useless correspondence ceased.

My venerable mother is a tolerably good correspondent—she is above the average, at any rate. She puts on her spectacles and takes her scissors and wades into a pile of newspapers, and slashes out column after column—editorials, hotel arrivals, poetry, telegraph news, advertisements, novelettes, old jokes, recipes for making pies, cures for "biles"—any thing that comes handy; it don't matter to her; she is entirely impartial; she slashes out a column, and runs her eye down it over her spectacles—(she looks over them because she can't see through them, but she prefers them to her more serviceable ones because they have got gold rims to them)—runs her eye down the column, and says, "Well, it's from a St. Louis paper, any way," and jams it into the envelope along with her letter. She writes about every body I ever knew or ever heard of; but unhappily, she forgets that when she tells me that "J. B. is dead," and that "W. L. is going to marry T. D." and that "B. K. and R. M. and L. P. J. have all gone to New-Orleans to live," it is more than likely that years of absence may have so dulled my recollection of once familiar names, that their unexplained initials will be as unintelligible as Hebrew unto me. She never writes a name in full, and so I never know whom she is talking about. Therefore I have to guess—and this was how it came that I mourned the death of Bill Kribben when I should have rejoiced over the dissolution of Ben Kenfuron. I failed to cipher the initials out correctly.

The most useful and interesting letters we get here from home are from children seven or eight years old. This is petrified truth. Happily they have got nothing to talk about but home, and neighbors, and family—things their betters think unworthy of transmission thousands of miles. They write simply and naturally, and without straining for effect. They tell all they know, and then stop. They seldom deal in abstractions or moral homilies. Consequently their epistles are brief; but, treating as they do of familiar scenes and persons, always entertaining. Now, therefore, if you would learn the art of letter-writing, let a little child teach you. I have preserved a letter from a small girl eight years of age—preserved it as a curiosity, because it was the only letter I ever got from the States that had any information in it. It runs thus:

St. Louis, 1865

"Uncle Mark, if you was here, I could tell you about Moses in the Bul-
rushers again, I know it better now. Mr. Sowerby has got his leg broke off a
horse. He was riding it on Sunday. Margaret, that's the maid, Margaret has
took all the spittoons, and slop-buckets, and old jugs out of your room,
because she says she don't think you're ever coming back any more, you
been gone so long. Sissy McElroy's mother has got another little baby. She
has them all the time. It has got little blue eyes, like Mr. Swimley that
boards there, and looks just like him. I have got a new doll, but Johnny
Anderson pulled one of its legs out. Miss Doosenberry was here to-day;
I give her your picture, but she said she didn't want it. My cat has got more
kittens—oh! you can't think—twice as many as Lottie Belden's. And there's
one, such a sweet little buff one with a short tail, and I named it for you. All
of them's got names now—General Grant, and Halleck, and Moses, and
Margaret, and Deuteronomy, and Captain Semmes, and Exodus, and Le-
viticus, and Horace Greeley—all named but one, and I am saving it because
the one that I named for You's been sick all the time since, and I reckon it'll
die. [It appears to have been mighty rough on the short-tailed kitten, naming
it for me—I wonder how the reserved victim will stand it.] Uncle Mark, I
do believe Hattie Caldwell likes you, and I know she thinks you are pretty,
because I heard her say nothing couldn't hurt your good looks—nothing at
all—she said, even if you was to have the small-pox ever so bad, you would
be just as good-looking as you was before. And my ma says she's ever so
smart. [Very.] So no more this time, because General Grant and Moses is
fighting.

ANNIE"

This child treads on my toes, in every other sentence, with a perfect
looseness, but in the simplicity of her time of life she doesn't know it.

I consider that a model letter—an eminently readable and entertaining letter, and, as I said before, it contains more matter of interest and
more real information than any letter I ever received from the East.
I had rather hear about the cats at home and their truly remarkable
names, than listen to a lot of stuff about people I am not acquainted
with, or read "The Evil Effects of the Intoxicating Bowl," illustrated
on the back with a picture of a ragged scalliwag pelting away right
and left, in the midst of his family circle, with a junk bottle.

1866

Concerning Chambermaids

Against all chambermaids, of whatsoever age or nationality, I launch the curse of bachelordom! Because:

They always put the pillows at the opposite end of the bed from the gas-burner, so that while you read and smoke before sleeping (as is the ancient and honored custom of bachelors), you have to hold your book aloft, in an uncomfortable position, to keep the light from dazzling your eyes.

When they find the pillows removed to the other end of the bed in the morning, they receive not the suggestion in a friendly spirit; but, glorying in their absolute sovereignty, and unpitying your helplessness, they make the bed just as it was originally, and gloat in secret over the pang their tyranny will cause you.

Always after that, when they find you have transposed the pillows, they undo your work, and thus defy and seek to embitter the life that God has given you.

If they cannot get the light in an inconvenient position any other way, they move the bed.

If you pull your trunk out six inches from the wall, so that the lid will stay up when you open it, they always shove that trunk back again. They do it on purpose.

If you want the spittoon in a certain spot, where it will be handy, they don't, and so they move it.

They always put your other boots into inaccessible places. They chiefly enjoy depositing them as far under the bed as the wall will permit. It is because this compels you to get down in an undignified attitude and make wild sweeps for them in the dark with the bootjack, and swear.

They always put the matchbox in some other place. They hunt up a new place for it every day, and put up a bottle, or other perishable glass thing, where the box stood before. This is to cause you to break that glass thing, groping in the dark, and get yourself into trouble.

They are for ever and ever moving the furniture. When you come in in the night you can calculate on finding the bureau where the wardrobe was in the morning. And when you go out in the morning, if you leave the slop-bucket by the door and rocking-chair by the window, when you come in at midnight or thereabout, you will fall over that rocking-chair, and you will proceed toward the window and sit down in that slop-tub. This will disgust you. They like that.

No matter where you put anything, they are not going to let it stay there. They will take it and move it the first chance they get. It is their nature. And, besides, it gives them pleasure to be mean and contrary this way. They would die if they couldn't be villains.

They always save up all the old scraps of printed rubbish you throw on the floor, and stack them up carefully on the table, and start the fire with your valuable manuscripts. If there is any one particular old scrap that you are more down on than any other, and which you are gradually wearing your life out trying to get rid of, you may take all the pains you possibly can in that direction, but it won't be of any use, because they will always fetch that old scrap back and put it in the same old place again every time. It does them good.

And they use up more hair-oil than any six men. If charged with purloining the same, they lie about it. What do they care about a hereafter? Absolutely nothing.

If you leave the key in the door for convenience' sake, they will carry it down to the office and give it to the clerk. They do this under the vile pretense of trying to protect your property from thieves; but actually they do it because they want to make you tramp back downstairs after it when you come home tired, or put you to the trouble of sending a waiter for it, which waiter will expect you to pay him something. In which case I suppose the degraded creatures divide.

They keep always trying to make your bed before you get up, thus destroying your rest and inflicting agony upon you; but after you get up, they don't come any more till next day.

They do all the mean things they can think of, and they do them just out of pure cussedness, and nothing else.

Chambermaids are dead to every human instinct.

If I can get a bill through the legislature abolishing chambermaids, I mean to do it.

1866

Honored as a Curiosity

If you get into conversation with a stranger in Honolulu, and experience that natural desire to know what sort of ground you are treading on by finding out what manner of man your stranger is, strike out boldly and address him as "Captain." Watch him narrowly, and if you see by his countenance that you are on the wrong track, ask him where he preaches. It is a safe bet that he is either a missionary or captain of a whaler. I became personally acquainted with seventy-two captains and ninety-six missionaries. The captains and ministers form one-half of the population; the third fourth is composed of common Kanakas and mercantile foreigners and their families; and the final fourth is made up of high officers of the Hawaiian Government. And there are just about cats enough for three apiece all around.

A solemn stranger met me in the suburbs one day, and said:

"Good morning, your reverence. Preach in the stone church yonder, no doubt!"

"No, I don't. I'm not a preacher."

"Really, I beg your pardon, captain. I trust you had a good season. How much oil—"

"Oil! Why, what do you take me for? I'm not a whaler."

"Oh! I beg a thousand pardons, your Excellency. Major-General in the household troops, no doubt? Minister of the Interior, likely? Secretary of War? First Gentleman of the Bedchamber? Commissioner of the Royal—"

"Stuff, man! I'm not connected in any way with the government."

"Bless my life! Then who the mischief are you? what the mischief are you? and how the mischief did you get here? and where in thunder did you come from?"

"I'm only a private personage—an unassuming stranger—lately arrived from America."

"No! Not a missionary! not a whaler! not a member of his Majesty's government! not even a Secretary of the Navy! Ah! Heaven! it is too blissful to be true, alas! I do but dream. And yet that noble, honest countenance—those oblique, ingenuous eyes—that massive head, incapable of—of anything; your hand; give me your hand, bright waif.

Excuse these tears. For sixteen weary years I have yearned for a moment like this, and—"

Here his feelings were too much for him, and he swooned away. I pitied this poor creature from the bottom of my heart. I was deeply moved. I shed a few tears on him, and kissed him for his mother. I then took what small change he had, and "shoved."

1866

An Inquiry about Insurances

Coming down from Sacramento the other night, I found on a centertable in the saloon of the steamboat, a pamphlet advertisement of an Accident Insurance Company. It interested me a good deal, with its General Accidents, and its Hazardous Tables, and Extra-Hazardous furniture of the same description, and I would like to know something more about it. It is a new thing to me. I want to invest if I come to like it. I want to ask merely a few questions of the man who carries on this Accident shop. For I am an orphan.

He publishes this list as accidents he is willing to insure people against.

General accidents include the Traveling Risk, and also all forms of Dislocations, Broken Bones, Ruptures, Tendons, Sprains, Concussions, Crushings, Bruising, Cuts, Stabs, Gunshot Wounds, Poisoned Wounds, Burns and Scalds, Freezing, Bites, Unprovoked Assaults by Burglars, Robbers, or Murderers, the action of Lightning or Sunstroke, the effects of Explosions, Chemicals, Floods, and Earthquakes, Suffocation by Drowning or Choking—where such accidental injury totally disables the person insured from following his usual avocation, or causes death within three months from the time of the happening of the injury.

I want to address this party as follows:

Now, Smith—I suppose likely your name is Smith—you don't know me and I don't know you, but I am willing to be friendly. I am acquainted with a good many of your family—I know John as well as I know any man—and I think we can come to an understanding about your little game without any hard feelings. For instance:

Do you allow the same money on a dog-bite that you do on an earthquake? Do you take special risks for specific accidents?—that is to say, could I, by getting a policy for dog-bites alone, get it cheaper than if I took a chance in your whole lottery? And if so, and supposing I got insured against earthquakes, would you charge any more for San Francisco earthquakes than for those that prevail in places that are better anchored down? And if I had a policy on earthquakes alone, I couldn't collect on a dog-bite, may be, could I?

If a man had such a policy, and an earthquake shook him up and loosened his joints a good deal, but not enough to incapacitate him from engaging in pursuits which did not require him to be tight, wouldn't you pay him some of his pension? I notice you do not mention Biles. How about Biles? Why do you discriminate between Provoked and Unprovoked Assaults by Burglars? If a burglar entered my house at dead of night, and I, in the excitement natural to such an occasion, should forget myself and say something that provoked him, and he should cripple me, wouldn't I get any thing? But if I provoked him by pure accident, I would have you there, I judge; because you would have to pay for the Accident part of it any how, seeing that insuring against accidents is just your strong suit, you know. Now, that item about protecting a man against freezing is good. It will procure you all the custom you want in this country. Because, you understand, the people hereabouts have suffered a good deal from just such climatic drawbacks as that. Why, three years ago, if a man—being a small fish in the matter of money—went over to Washoe, and bought into a good silver mine, they would let that man go on and pay assessments till his purse got down to about thirty-two Fahrenheit, and then the big fish would close in on him and freeze him out. And from that day forth you might consider that man in the light of a bankrupt community; and you would have him down to a spot, too. But if you are ready to insure against that sort of thing, and can stand it, you can give Washoe a fair start. You might send me an agency. Business? Why, Smith, I could get you more business than you could attend to. With such an understanding as that, the boys would all take a chance.

You don't appear to make any particular mention of taking risks on blighted affections. But if you should conclude to do a little business in that line, you might put me down for six or seven chances. I wouldn't mind expense—you might enter it on the extra hazardous. I suppose I would get ahead of you in the long run any how, likely. I have been blighted a good deal in my time.

But now as to those "Effects of Lightning." Suppose the lightning were to strike out at one of your men and miss him, and fetch another party—could that other party come on you for damages? Or could the relatives of the party thus suddenly snaked out of the bright world in the bloom of his youth come on you in case he was crowded for time? as of course he would be, you know, under such circumstances.

You say you have "issued over sixty thousand policies, forty-five of which have proved fatal and been paid for." Now, do you know, Smith, that that looks just a little shaky to me, in a measure? You appear to have it pretty much all your own way, you see. It is all very well for the lucky forty-five that have died "and been paid for," but how about the other fifty-nine thousand nine hundred and fifty-five? You have got their money, haven't you? but somehow the lightning don't seem to strike them and they don't get any chance at you. Won't their families get fatigued waiting for their dividends? Don't your customers drop off rather slow, so to speak?

You will ruin yourself publishing such damaging statements as that, Smith. I tell you as a friend. If you had said that the fifty-nine thousand nine hundred and fifty-five died, and that forty-five lived, you would have issued about four tons of policies the next week. But people are not going to get insured, when you take so much pains to prove that there is such precious little use in it. Good-by Smith!

1866

Literature in the Dry Diggings

Although a resident of San Francisco, I never heard much about the "Art Union Association" of that city until I got hold of some old newspapers during my three months' stay in the Big Tree region of Calaveras county. Up there, you know, they read *every thing*, because in most of those little camps they have no libraries, and no books to speak of, except now and then a patent office report or a prayer-book, or literature of that kind, in a general way, that will hang on and last a good while when people are careful with it, like miners; but as for novels, they pass them around and wear them out in a

week or two. Now there was Coon, a nice, bald-headed man at the
hotel in Angels' Camp, I asked him to lend me a book, one rainy day;
he was silent a moment, and a shade of melancholy flitted across his
fine face, and then he said: "Well, I've got a mighty responsible old
Webster Unabridged, what there is left of it, but they started her
sloshing around and sloshing around and sloshing around the camp
before ever I got a chance to read her myself; and next she went
to Murphy's, and from there she went to Jackass Gulch, and now she's
gone to San Andreas, and I don't expect I'll ever see that book again.
But what makes me mad is, that for all they're so handy about
keeping her sashshaying around from shanty to shanty and from camp
to camp, none of 'em's ever got a good word for her. Now Coddington
had her a week, and she was too many for *him*—he couldn't spell
the words; he tackled some of them regular busters, tow'rd the middle,
you know, and they throwed him; next, Dyer, *he* tried her a jolt, but he
couldn't *pronounce* 'em—Dyer can hunt quail or play seven-up as
well as any man, understand, but he can't *pronounce* worth a cuss;
he used to worry along well enough, though, till he'd flush one of
them rattlers with a clatter of syllables as long as a string of sluice-
boxes, and then he'd lose his grip and throw up his hand; and so, finally,
Dick Stoker harnessed her, up there at his cabin, and sweated over
her and cussed over her and rastled with her for as much as three
weeks, night and day, till he got as far as R, and then passed her over
to 'Lige Pickerell, and said she was the all-firedest dryest reading
that ever *he* struck. Well, well, if she's come back from San Andreas,
you can get her, and prospect her, but I don't reckon there's a good
deal left of her by this time, though time was when she was as likely
a book as any in the State, and as hefty, and had an amount of
general information in her that was astonishing, if any of these cattle
had known enough to get it out of her." And ex-corporal Coon proceeded cheerlessly to scout with his brush after the straggling hairs on
the rear of his head and drum them to the front for inspection and
roll-call, as was his usual custom before turning in for his regular
afternoon nap.

1867

Origin of Illustrious Men

John Smith was the son of his father. He formerly lived in New-York and other places, but he has removed to San Francisco now.

William Smith was the son of his mother. This party's grandmother is deceased. She was a brick.

John Brown was the son of old Brown. The body of the latter lies mouldering in the grave.

Edward Brown was the son of old Brown by a particular friend.

Henry Jones was the son of a sea-cook.

Ed Jones was a son of a gun.

John Jones was a son of temperance.

In early life Gabriel Jones was actually a shoemaker. He is a shoemaker yet.

Previous to the age of eighty-five, Caleb Jones had never given evidence of extraordinary ability. He has never given any since.

Patrick Murphy is said to have been of Irish extraction.

James Peterson was the son of a common weaver, who was so miraculously poor that his friends were encouraged to believe that in case the Scriptures were carried out he would "inherit the earth." He never got his property.

John Davis's father was the son of a soap-boiler, and not a very good soap-boiler at that. John never arrived at maturity—died in childbirth—he and his mother.

John Johnson was a blacksmith. He died. It was published in the papers, with a head over it, "Deaths." It was, therefore, thought he died to gain notoriety. He has got an aunt living somewhere.

Up to the age of thirty-four Hosea Wilkerson never had any home but Home Sweet Home, and even then he had it to sing himself. At one time it was believed that he would have been famous if he became celebrated. He died. He was greatly esteemed for his many virtues. There was not a dry eye in the crowd when they planted him.

1867

The Facts Concerning
the Recent Resignation

Washington, December 2, 1867

I have resigned. The government appears to go on much the same, but there is a spoke out of its wheel, nevertheless. I was clerk of the Senate Committee on Conchology, and I have thrown up the position. I could see the plainest disposition on the part of the other members of the government to debar me from having any voice in the counsels of the nation, and so I could no longer hold office and retain my self-respect. If I were to detail all the outrages that were heaped upon me during the six days that I was connected with the government in an official capacity, the narrative would fill a volume. They appointed me clerk of that Committee on Conchology, and then allowed me no amanuensis to play billiards with. I would have borne that, lonesome as it was, if I had met with that courtesy from the other members of the Cabinet which was my due. But I did not. Whenever I observed that the head of a department was pursuing a wrong course, I laid down everything and went and tried to set him right, as it was my duty to do; and I never was thanked for it in a single instance. I went, with the best intentions in the world, to the Secretary of the Navy, and said:

"Sir, I cannot see that Admiral Farragut is doing anything but skirmishing around there in Europe, having a sort of picnic. Now, that may be all very well, but it does not exhibit itself to me in that light. If there is no fighting for him to do, let him come home. There is no use in a man having a whole fleet for a pleasure excursion. It is too expensive. Mind, I do not object to pleasure excursions for the naval officers—pleasure excursions that are in reason—pleasure excursions that are economical. Now, they might go down the Mississippi on a raft—"

You ought to have heard him storm! One would have supposed I had committed a crime of some kind. But I didn't mind. I said it was cheap, and full of republican simplicity, and perfectly safe. I said that, for a tranquil pleasure excursion, there was nothing equal to a raft.

Then the Secretary of the Navy asked me who I was; and when I told him I was connected with the government, he wanted to know in what capacity. I said that, without remarking upon the singularity of such a question, coming, as it did, from a member of that same government, I would inform him that I was clerk of the Senate Committee on Conchology. Then there was a fine storm! He finished by ordering me to leave the premises, and give my attention strictly to my own business in future. My first impulse was to get him removed. However, that would harm others besides himself, and do me no real good, and so I let him stay.

I went next to the Secretary of War, who was not inclined to see me at all until he learned that I was connected with the government. If I had not been on important business, I suppose I could not have got in. I asked him for a light (he was smoking at the time), and then I told him I had no fault to find with his defending the parole stipulations of General Lee and his comrades in arms, but that I could not approve of his method of fighting the Indians on the Plains. I said he fought too scattering. He ought to get the Indians more together—get them together in some convenient place, where he could have provisions enough for both parties, and then have a general massacre. I said there was nothing so convincing to an Indian as a general massacre. If he could not approve of the massacre, I said the next surest thing for an Indian was soap and education. Soap and education are not as sudden as a massacre, but they are more deadly in the long run; because a half-massacred Indian may recover, but if you educate him and wash him, it is found to finish him some time or other. It undermines his constitution; it strikes at the foundation of his being. "Sir," I said, "the time has come when blood-curdling cruelty has become necessary. Inflict soap and a spelling-book on every Indian that ravages the Plains, and let them die!"

The Secretary of War asked me if I was a member of the Cabinet, and I said I was. He inquired what position I held, and I said I was clerk of the Senate Committee on Conchology. I was then ordered under arrest for contempt of court, and restrained of my liberty for the best part of the day.

I almost resolved to be silent thenceforward, and let the Government get along the best way it could. But duty called, and I obeyed. I called on the Secretary of the Treasury. He said:

"What will *you* have?"

The question threw me off my guard. I said, "Rum punch."

He said: "If you have got any business here, sir, state it—and in as few words as possible."

I then said that I was sorry he had seen fit to change the subject so abruptly, because such conduct was very offensive to me; but under the circumstances I would overlook the matter and come to the point. I now went into an earnest expostulation with him upon the extravagant length of his report. I said it was expensive, unnecessary, and awkwardly constructed; there were no descriptive passages in it, no poetry, no sentiment—no heroes, no plot, no pictures—not even woodcuts. Nobody would read it, that was a clear case. I urged him not to ruin his reputation by getting out a thing like that. If he ever hoped to succeed in literature he must throw more variety into his writings. He must beware of dry detail. I said that the main popularity of the almanac was derived from its poetry and conundrums, and that a few conundrums distributed around through his Treasury report would help the sale of it more than all the internal revenue he could put into it. I said these things in the kindest spirit, and yet the Secretary of the Treasury fell into a violent passion. He even said I was an ass. He abused me in the most vindictive manner, and said that if I came there again meddling with his business he would throw me out of the window. I said I would take my hat and go, if I could not be treated with the respect due to my office, and I did go. It was just like a new author. They always think they know more than anybody else when they are getting out their first book. Nobody can tell *them* anything.

During the whole time that I was connected with the government it seemed as if I could not do anything in an official capacity without getting myself into trouble. And yet I did nothing, attempted nothing, but what I conceived to be for the good of my country. The sting of my wrongs may have driven me to unjust and harmful conclusions, but it surely seemed to me that the Secretary of State, the Secretary of War, the Secretary of the Treasury, and others of my *confrères* had conspired from the very beginning to drive me from the Administration. I never attended but one Cabinet meeting while I was connected with the government. That was sufficient for me. The servant at the White House door did not seem disposed to make way for me until I asked if the other members of the Cabinet had arrived. He said they had, and I entered. They were all there; but nobody offered me a seat. They stared at me as if I had been an intruder. The President said:

"Well, sir, who are *you?*"

I handed him my card, and he read: "The HON. MARK TWAIN, Clerk of the Senate Committee on Conchology." Then he looked at me from head to foot, as if he had never heard of me before. The Secretary of the Treasury said:

"This is the meddlesome ass that came to recommend me to put poetry and conundrums in my report, as if it were an almanac."

The Secretary of War said: "It is the same visionary that came to me yesterday with a scheme to educate a portion of the Indians to death, and massacre the balance."

The Secretary of the Navy said: "I recognize this youth as the person who has been interfering with my business time and again during the week. He is distressed about Admiral Farragut's using a whole fleet for a pleasure excursion, as he terms it. His proposition about some insane pleasure excursion on a raft is too absurd to repeat."

I said: "Gentlemen, I perceive here a disposition to throw discredit upon every act of my official career; I perceive, also, a disposition to debar me from all voice in the counsels of the nation. No notice whatever was sent to me to-day. It was only by the merest chance that I learned that there was going to be a Cabinet meeting. But let these things pass. All I wish to know is, is this a Cabinet meeting or is it not?"

The President said it was.

"Then," I said, "let us proceed to business at once, and not fritter away valuable time in unbecoming fault-findings with each other's official conduct."

The Secretary of State now spoke up, in his benignant way, and said, "Young man, you are laboring under a mistake. The clerks of the Congressional committees are not members of the Cabinet. Neither are the doorkeepers of the Capitol, strange as it may seem. Therefore, much as we could desire your more than human wisdom in our deliberations, we cannot lawfully avail ourselves of it. The counsels of the nation must proceed without you; if disaster follows, as follow full well it may, be it balm to your sorrowing spirit that by deed and voice you did what in you lay to avert it. You have my blessing. Farewell."

These gentle words soothed my troubled breast, and I went away. But the servants of a nation can know no peace. I had hardly reached my den in the Capitol, and disposed my feet on the table like a representative, when one of the Senators on the Conchological Committee came in in a passion and said:

"Where have you been all day?"

I observed that, if that was anybody's affair but my own, I had been to a Cabinet meeting.

"To a Cabinet meeting? I would like to know what business you had at a Cabinet meeting?"

I said I went there to consult—allowing for the sake of argument that he was in any wise concerned in the matter. He grew insolent then, and ended by saying he had wanted me for three days past to copy a report on bomb-shells, egg-shells, clam-shells, and I don't know what all, connected with conchology, and nobody had been able to find me.

This was too much. This was the feather that broke the clerical camel's back. I said, "Sir, do you suppose that I am going to *work* for six dollars a day? If that is the idea, let me recommend the Senate Committee on Conchology to hire somebody else. I am the slave of *no* faction! Take back your degrading commission. Give me liberty, or give me death!"

From that hour I was no longer connected with the government. Snubbed by the department, snubbed by the Cabinet, snubbed at last by the chairman of a committee I was endeavoring to adorn, I yielded to persecution, cast far from me the perils and seductions of my great office, and forsook my bleeding country in the hour of her peril.

But I had done the state some service, and I sent in my bill:

The United States of America in account with
     the Hon. Clerk of the Senate Committee on Conchology, Dr.

To consultation with Secretary of War	$50
To consultation with Secretary of Navy	50
To consultation with Secretary of the Treasury	50
Cabinet consultation . . . . No charge.	
To mileage to and from Jerusalem,[1] *via* Egypt, Algiers,	
Gibraltar, and Cadiz, 14,000 miles, at 20c. a mile	2,800
To salary as Clerk of Senate Committee on Conchology,	
six days, at $6 per day	36
Total	$2,986

Not an item of this bill has been paid, except that trifle of thirty-six dollars for clerkship salary. The Secretary of the Treasury, pursuing me to the last, drew his pen through all the other items, and simply

---

[1] Territorial delegates charge mileage both ways, although they never go back when they get here once. Why my mileage is denied me is more than I can understand.

marked in the margin "Not allowed." So, the dread alternative is embraced at last. Repudiation had begun! The nation is lost.

I am done with official life for the present. Let those clerks who are
willing to be imposed on remain. I know numbers of them in the
departments who are never informed when there is to be a Cabinet
meeting, whose advice is never asked about war, or finance, or commerce, by the heads of the nation, any more than if they were not
connected with the government, and who actually stay in their offices
day after day and work! They know their importance to the nation,
and they unconsciously show it in their bearing, and the way
they order their sustenance at the restaurant—but they work. I
know one who has to paste all sorts of little scraps from the newspapers into a scrapbook—sometimes as many as eight or ten scraps a
day. He doesn't do it well, but he does it as well as he can. It is very
fatiguing. It is exhausting to the intellect. Yet he only gets eighteen
hundred dollars a year. With a brain like his, that young man could
amass thousands and thousands of dollars in some other pursuit, if he
chose to do it. But no—his heart is with his country, and he will serve
her as long as she has got a scrapbook left. And I know clerks that
don't know how to write very well, but such knowledge as they possess
they nobly lay at the feet of their country, and toil on and suffer for
twenty-five hundred dollars a year. What they write has to be written
over again by other clerks sometimes; but when a man has done his
best for his country, should his country complain? Then there are
clerks that have no clerkships, and are waiting, and waiting, and
waiting for a vacancy—waiting patiently for a chance to help their
country out—and while they are waiting, they only get barely two
thousand dollars a year for it. It is sad—it is very, very sad. When a
member of Congress has a friend who is gifted, but has no employment
wherein his great powers may be brought to bear, he confers
him upon his country, and gives him a clerkship in a department. And
there that man has to slave his life out, fighting documents for the
benefit of a nation that never thinks of him, never sympathizes with
him—and all for two thousand or three thousand dollars a year. When
I shall have completed my list of all the clerks in the several departments, with my statement of what they have to do, and what they
get for it, you will see that there are not half enough clerks, and that
what there are do not get half enough pay.

1868

General Washington's
Negro Body-Servant

The stirring part of this celebrated colored man's life properly began with his death—that is to say, the notable features of his biography begin with the first time he died. He had been little heard of up to that time, but since then we have never ceased to hear of him; we have never ceased to hear of him at stated, unfailing intervals. His was a most remarkable career, and I have thought that its history would make a valuable addition to our biographical literature. Therefore, I have carefully collated the materials for such a work, from authentic sources, and here present them to the public. I have rigidly excluded from these pages everything of a doubtful character, with the object in view of introducing my work into the schools for the instruction of the youth of my country.

The name of the famous body-servant of General Washington was George. After serving his illustrious master faithfully for half a century, and enjoying throughout this long term his high regard and confidence, it became his sorrowful duty at last to lay that beloved master to rest in his peaceful grave by the Potomac. Ten years afterward— in 1809—full of years and honors, he died himself, mourned by all who knew him. The Boston *Gazette* of that date thus refers to the event:

George, the favorite body-servant of the lamented Washington, died in Richmond, Va., last Tuesday, at the ripe age of 95 years. His intellect was unimpaired, and his memory tenacious, up to within a few minutes of his decease. He was present at the second installation of Washington as President, and also at his funeral, and distinctly remembered all the prominent incidents connected with those noted events.

From this period we hear no more of the favorite body-servant of General Washington until May, 1825, at which time he died again. A Philadelphia paper thus speaks of the sad occurrence:

At Macon, Ga., last week, a colored man named George, who was the favorite body-servant of General Washington, died at the advanced age of 95 years. Up to within a few hours of his dissolution he was in full

possession of all his faculties, and could distinctly recollect the second installation of Washington, his death and burial, the surrender of Cornwallis, the
battle of Trenton, the griefs and hardships of Valley Forge, etc. Deceased was
followed to the grave by the entire population of Macon.

On the Fourth of July, 1830, and also of 1834 and 1836, the subject
of this sketch was exhibited in great state upon the rostrum of the
orator of the day, and in November of 1840 he died again. The St. Louis
Republican of the 25th of that month spoke as follows:

ANOTHER RELIC OF THE REVOLUTION GONE

"George, once the favorite body-servant of General Washington, died
yesterday at the house of Mr. John Leavenworth in this city, at the venerable
age of 95 years. He was in the full possession of his faculties up to the hour
of his death, and distinctly recollected the first and second installations and
death of President Washington, the surrender of Cornwallis, the battles
of Trenton and Monmouth, the sufferings of the patriot army at Valley
Forge, the proclamation of the Declaration of Independence, the speech
of Patrick Henry in the Virginia House of Delegates, and many other old-
time reminiscenses of stirring interest. Few white men die lamented as was
this aged negro. The funeral was very largely attended."

During the next ten or eleven years the subject of this sketch
appeared at intervals at Fourth-of-July celebrations in various parts
of the country, and was exhibited upon the rostrum with flattering
success. But in the fall of 1855 he died again. The California papers
thus speak of the event:

ANOTHER OLD HERO GONE

Died, at Dutch Flat, on the 7th of March, George (once the confidential
body-servant of General Washington), at the great age of 95 years. His
memory, which did not fail him till the last, was a wonderful storehouse
of interesting reminiscences. He could distinctly recollect the first and second
installations and death of President Washington, the surrender of Cornwallis,
the battles of Trenton and Monmouth, and Bunker Hill, the proclamation
of the Declaration of Independence, and Braddock's defeat. George was
greatly respected in Dutch Flat, and it is estimated that there were 10,000
people present at his funeral.

The last time the subject of this sketch died was in June, 1864; and
until we learn the contrary, it is just to presume that he died permanently this time. The Michigan papers thus refer to the sorrowful
event:

ANOTHER CHERISHED REMNANT OF THE REVOLUTION GONE

George, a colored man, and once the favorite body-servant of General Washington, died in Detroit last week, at the patriarchal age of 95 years. To the moment of his death his intellect was unclouded, and he could distinctly remember the first and second installations and death of Washington, the surrender of Cornwallis, the battles of Trenton and Monmouth, and Bunker Hill, the proclamation of the Declaration of Independence, Braddock's defeat, the throwing over of the tea in Boston harbor, and the landing of the Pilgrims. He died greatly respected, and was followed to the grave by a vast concourse of people.

The faithful old servant is gone! We shall never see him more until he turns up again. He has closed his long and splendid career of dissolution, for the present, and sleeps peacefully, as only they sleep who have earned their rest. He was in all respects a remarkable man. He held his age better than any celebrity that has figured in history; and the longer he lived the stronger and longer his memory grew. If he lives to die again, he will distinctly recollect the discovery of America.

The above résumé of his biography I believe to be substantially correct, although it is possible that he may have died once or twice in obscure places where the event failed of newspaper notoriety. One fault I find in all notices of his death which I have quoted, and this ought to be correct. In them he uniformly and impartially died at the age of 95. This could not have been. He might have done that once, or maybe twice, but he could not have continued it indefinitely. Allowing that when he first died, he died at the age of 95, he was 151 years old when he died last, in 1864. But his age did not keep pace with his recollections. When he died the last time, he distinctly remembered the landing of the Pilgrims, which took place in 1620. He must have been about twenty years old when he witnessed that event, wherefore it is safe to assert that the body-servant of General Washington was in the neighborhood of two hundred and sixty or seventy years old when he departed this life finally.

Having waited a proper length of time, to see if the subject of this sketch had gone from us reliably and irrevocably, I now publish his biography with confidence, and respectfully offer it to a mourning nation.

P. S.—I see by the papers that this infamous old fraud has just died again, in Arkansas. This makes six times that he is known to have died, and always in a new place. The death of Washington's body-servant has ceased to be a novelty; its charm is gone; the people are tired of it; let it cease. This well-meaning but misguided negro has now put six different communities to the expense of burying him in state, and has swindled tens of thousands of people into following him to the grave under the delusion that a select and peculiar distinction was being conferred upon them. Let him stay buried for good now; and let that newspaper suffer the severest censure that shall ever, in all future time, publish to the world that General Washington's favorite colored body-servant has died again.

1868

Information Wanted

"Washington, December 10, 1867
"Could you give me any information respecting such islands, if any, as the government is going to purchase?"

It is an uncle of mine that wants to know. He is an industrious man and well disposed, and wants to make a living in an honest, humble way, but more especially he wants to be quiet. He wishes to settle down, and be quiet and unostentatious. He has been to the new island St. Thomas, but he says he thinks things are unsettled there. He went there early with an *attaché* of the State Department, who was sent down with money to pay for the island. My uncle had his money in the same box, and so when they went ashore, getting a receipt, the sailors broke open the box and took all the money, not making any distinction between government money, which was legitimate money to be stolen, and my uncle's, which was his own private property, and should have been respected. But he came home and got some more and went back. And then he took the fever. There are seven kinds of fever down there, you know; and, as his blood was out of order by reason of loss of sleep and general wear and tear of mind, he failed to cure the first fever, and then somehow he got the other six. He is not a kind of man that enjoys fevers, though he is well meaning and always does what he thinks is right, and so he was a good deal annoyed when it appeared he was going to die.

But he worried through, and got well and started a farm. He fenced it in, and the next day that great storm came on and washed the most of it over to Gibraltar, or around there somewhere. He only said, in his patient way, that it was gone, and he wouldn't bother about trying to find out where it went to, though it was his opinion it went to Gibraltar.

Then he invested in a mountain, and started a farm up there, so as to be out of the way when the sea came ashore again. It was a good mountain, and a good farm, but it wasn't any use; an earthquake came the next night and shook it all down. It was all fragments, you know, and so mixed up with another man's property that he could not tell which were his fragments without going to law; and he would not do that, because his main object in going to St. Thomas was to be quiet. All that he wanted was to settle down and be quiet.

He thought it all over, and finally he concluded to try the low ground again, especially as he wanted to start a brickyard this time. He bought a flat, and put out a hundred thousand bricks to dry pre- paratory to baking them. But luck appeared to be against him. A volcano shoved itself through there that night, and elevated his brick- yard about two thousand feet in the air. It irritated him a good deal. He has been up there, and he says the bricks are all baked right enough, but he can't get them down. At first, he thought maybe the government would get the bricks down for him, because since govern- ment bought the island, it ought to protect the property where a man has invested in good faith; but all he wants is quiet, and so he is not going to apply for the subsidy he was thinking about.

He went back there last week in a couple of ships of war, to prospect around the coast for a safe place for a farm where he could be quiet; but a great "tidal wave" came, and hoisted both of the ships out into one of the interior counties, and he came near losing his life. So he has given up prospecting in a ship, and is discouraged.

Well, now he don't know what to do. He has tried Alaska; but the bears kept after him so much, and kept him so much on the jump, as it were, that he had to leave the country. He could not be quiet there with those bears prancing after him all the time. That is how he came to go to the new island we have bought—St. Thomas. But he is getting to think St. Thomas is not quiet enough for a man of his turn of mind, and that is why he wishes me to find out if government is likely to buy some more islands shortly. He has heard that government is thinking about buying Porto Rico. If that is true, he wishes to try Porto Rico, if it is a quiet place. How is Porto Rico for his style of man? Do you think the government will buy it?

1868

My Late Senatorial
Secretaryship

I am not a private secretary to a senator any more now. I held the berth two months in security and in great cheerfulness of spirit, but my bread began to return from over the waters then—that is to say, my works came back and revealed themselves. I judged it best to resign. The way of it was this. My employer sent for me one morning tolerably early, and, as soon as I had finished inserting some conundrums clandestinely into his last great speech upon finance, I entered the presence. There was something portentous in his appearance. His cravat was untied, his hair was in a state of disorder, and his countenance bore about it the signs of a suppressed storm. He held a package of letters in his tense grasp, and I knew that the dreaded Pacific mail was in. He said:

"I thought you were worthy of confidence."

I said, "Yes, sir."

He said, "I gave you a letter from certain of my constituents in the State of Nevada, asking the establishment of a post-office at Baldwin's Ranch, and told you to answer it, as ingeniously as you could, with arguments which should persuade them that there was no real necessity for an office at that place."

I felt easier. "Oh, if that is all, sir, I *did* do that."

"Yes, you *did*. I will read your answer for your own humiliation:

"*Washington, Nov. 24*

"'*Messrs. Smith, Jones, and others.*

"'GENTLEMEN: What the mischief do you suppose you want with a post-office at Baldwin's Ranch? It would not do you any good. If any letters came there, you couldn't read them, you know; and, besides, such letters as ought to pass through, with money in them, for other localities, would not be likely to *get* through, you must perceive at once; and that would make trouble for us all. No, don't bother about a post-office in your camp. I have your best interests at heart, and feel that it would only be an ornamental folly. What you want is a nice jail, you know—a nice, substantial jail and a free school.

These will be a lasting benefit to you. These will make you really contented and happy. I will move in the matter at once.

> " 'Very truly, etc.,
> " 'MARK TWAIN,
> "For James W. N——, U. S. Senator.'

"That is the way you answered that letter. Those people say they will hang me, if I ever enter that district again; and I am perfectly satisfied they *will*, too."

"Well, sir, I did not know I was doing any harm. I only wanted to convince them."

"Ah. Well, you *did* convince them, I make no manner of doubt. Now, here is another specimen. I gave you a petition from certain gentlemen of Nevada, praying that I would get a bill through Congress incorporating the Methodist Episcopal Church of the State of Nevada. I told you to say, in reply, that the creation of such a law came more properly within the province of the state legislature; and to endeavor to show them that, in the present feebleness of the religious element in that new commonwealth, the expediency of incorporating the church was questionable. What did you write?

> " 'Washington, Nov. 24

" 'Rev. John Halifax and others.

" 'GENTLEMEN: You will have to go to the state legislature about the speculation of yours—Congress don't know anything about religion. But don't you hurry to go there, either; because this thing you propose to do out in that new country isn't expedient—in fact, it is ridiculous. Your religious people there are too feeble, in intellect, in morality, in piety—in everything, pretty much. You had better drop this—you can't make it work. You can't issue stock on an incorporation like that—or if you could, it would only keep you in trouble all the time. The other denominations would abuse it, and "bear" it, and "sell it short," and break it down. They would do with it just as they would with one of your silver-mines out there—they would try to make all the world believe it was "wildcat." You ought not to do anything that is calculated to bring a sacred thing into disrepute. You ought to be ashamed of yourselves—that is what *I* think about it. You close your petition with the words: "And we will ever pray." I think you had better—you need to do it.

> " 'Very truly, etc.,
> " 'MARK TWAIN,
> " 'For James W. N——, U. S. Senator.'

"*That* luminous epistle finishes me with the religious element among my constituents. But that my political murder might be made sure, some evil instinct prompted me to hand you this memorial from the grave company of elders composing the board of aldermen of the city of San Francisco, to try your hand upon—a memorial praying that the city's right to the water-lots upon the city front might be established by law of Congress. I told you this was a dangerous matter to move in. I told you to write a non-committal letter to the aldermen —an ambiguous letter—a letter that should avoid, as far as possible, all real consideration and discussion of the water-lot question. If there is any feeling left in you—any shame—surely this letter you wrote, in obedience to that order, ought to evoke it, when its words fall upon your ears:

" 'Washington, Nov. 27

" 'The Honorable Board of Aldermen, etc.

    " 'GENTLEMEN: George Washington, the revered Father of his Country, is dead. His long and brilliant career is closed, alas! forever. He was greatly respected in this section of the country, and his untimely decease cast a gloom over the whole community. He died on the 14th day of December, 1799. He passed peacefully away from the scene of his honors and his great achievements, the most lamented hero and the best beloved that ever earth hath yielded unto Death. At such a time as this, *you* speak of water-lots!— what a lot was his!

    " 'What is fame! Fame is an accident. Sir Isaac Newton discovered an apple falling to the ground—a trivial discovery, truly, and one which a million men had made before him—but his parents were influential, and so they tortured that small circumstance into something wonderful, and, lo! the simple world took up the shout and, in almost the twinkling of an eye, that man was famous. Treasure these thoughts.

    " 'Poesy, sweet poesy, who shall estimate what the world owes to thee!
"Mary had a little lamb, its fleece was white as snow—
And everywhere that Mary went, the lamb was sure to go."

> "Jack and Gill went up the hill
> To draw a pail of water;
> Jack fell down and broke his crown,
> And Gill came tumbling after."

    " 'For simplicity, elegance of diction, and freedom from immoral tendencies, I regard those two poems in the light of gems. They are suited to all grades of intelligence, to every sphere of life—to the field, to the nursery, to the guild. Especially should no Board of Aldermen be without them.

    " 'Venerable fossils! write again. Nothing improves one so much as friendly correspondence. Write again—and if there is anything in this memorial of yours that refers to anything in particular, do not be backward about explaining it. We shall always be happy to hear you chirp.

" 'Very truly, etc.,
" 'MARK TWAIN,
" 'For James W. N——, U. S. Senator.'

"That is an atrocious, a ruinous epistle! Distraction!"

"Well, sir, I am really sorry if there is anything wrong about it—but—but it appears to me to dodge the water-lot question."

"Dodge the mischief! Oh!—but never mind. As long as destruction must come now, let it be complete. Let it be complete—let this last of your performances, which I am about to read, make a finality of it. I am a ruined man. I *had* my misgivings when I gave you the letter from Humboldt, asking that the post route from Indian Gulch to Shakespeare Gap and intermediate points be changed partly to the old Mormon trail. But I told you it was a delicate question, and warned you to deal with it deftly—to answer it dubiously, and leave them a little in the dark. And your fatal imbecility impelled you to make *this* disastrous reply. I should think you would stop your ears, if you are not dead to all shame:

"'*Washington, Nov. 30*

"'*Messrs. Perkins, Wagner, et al.*

"'GENTLEMEN: It is a delicate question about this Indian trail, but, handled with proper deftness and dubiousness, I doubt not we shall succeed in some measure or otherwise, because the place where the route leaves the Lassen Meadows, over beyond where those two Shawnee chiefs, Dilapidated-Vengeance and Biter-of-the-Clouds, were scalped last winter, this being the favorite direction to some, but others preferring something else in consequence of things, the Mormon trail leaving Mosby's at three in the morning, and passing through Jawbone Flat to Blucher, and then down by Jug-Handle, the road passing to the right of it, and naturally leaving it on the right, too, and Dawson's on the left of the trail where it passes to the left of said Dawson's and onward thence to Tomahawk, thus making the route cheaper, easier of access to all who can get at it, and compassing all the desirable objects so considered by others, and, therefore, conferring the most good upon the greatest number, and, consequently, I am encouraged to hope we shall. However, I shall be ready, and happy, to afford you still further information upon the subject, from time to time, as you may desire it and the Post-office Department be enabled to furnish it to me.

"'Very truly, etc.,

"'MARK TWAIN,

"'For James W. N——, U. S. Senator.'

"There—now *what* do you think of that?"

"Well, I don't know, sir. It—well, it appears to me—to be dubious enough."

"Du—leave the house! I am a ruined man. Those Humboldt savages never will forgive me for tangling their brains up with this inhuman letter. I have lost the respect of the Methodist Church, the board of aldermen—"

"Well, I haven't anything to say about that, because I may have missed it a little in their cases, but I *was* too many for the Baldwin's Ranch people, General!"

"Leave the house! Leave it forever and forever, too."

I regarded that as a sort of covert intimation that my service could be dispensed with, and so I resigned. I never will be a private secretary to a senator again. You can't please that kind of people. They don't know anything. They can't appreciate a party's efforts.

1868

An Ancient Playbill

For me was reserved the high honor of discovering among the rubbish of the ruined Coliseum the only playbill of that establishment now extant. There was a suggestive smell of mint-drops about it still, a corner of it had evidently been chewed, and on the margin, in choice Latin, these words were written in a delicate female hand:

Meet me on the Tarpeian Rock to-morrow evening, dear, at sharp seven. Mother will be absent on a visit to her friends in the Sabine Hills.

CLAUDIA

Ah, where is that lucky youth to-day, and where the little hand that wrote those dainty lines? Dust and ashes these seventeen hundred years!

Thus reads the bill:

ROMAN COLISEUM

UNPARALLELED ATTRACTION!

NEW PROPERTIES! NEW LIONS! NEW GLADIATORS!

Engagement of the renowned

MARCUS MARCELLUS VALERIAN!

FOR SIX NIGHTS ONLY!

The management beg leave to offer to the public an entertainment surpassing in magnificence anything that has heretofore been attempted on any stage. No expense has been spared to make the opening season one which shall be worthy the generous patronage which the management feel sure will crown their efforts. The management beg leave to state that they have succeeded in securing the services of a

GALAXY OF TALENT!

such as has not been beheld in Rome before.

The performance will commence this evening with a

GRAND BROADSWORD COMBAT!

between two young and promising amateurs and a celebrated Parthian gladiator who has just arrived a prisoner from the Camp of Verus.

This will be followed by a grand moral

BATTLE-AX ENGAGEMENT!

between the renowned Valerian (with one hand tied behind him) and two gigantic savages from Britain.

After which the renowned Valerian (if he survive) will fight with the broadsword,

LEFT HANDED!

against six Sophomores and a Freshman from the Gladiatorial College!

A long series of brilliant engagements will follow, in which the finest talent of the Empire will take part.

After which the celebrated Infant Prodigy known as

"THE YOUNG ACHILLES,"

will engage four tiger whelps in combat, armed with no other weapon than his little spear!

The whole to conclude with a chaste and elegant

GENERAL SLAUGHTER!

In which thirteen African Lions and twenty-two Barbarian Prisoners will war with each other until all are exterminated.

BOX OFFICE NOW OPEN

Dress Circle One Dollar; Children and servants half price.

An efficient police force will be on hand to preserve order and keep the wild beasts from leaping the railings and discommoding the audience.

Doors open at 7; performance begins at 8.

POSITIVELY NO FREE LIST

Diodorus Job Press.

It was as singular as it was gratifying that I was also so fortunate as to find among the rubbish of the arena a stained and mutilated copy of the *Roman Daily Battle-Ax*, containing a critique upon this very performance. It comes to hand too late by many centuries to rank as news, and therefore I translate and publish it simply to show how very little the general style and phraseology of dramatic criticism has altered in the ages that have dragged their slow length along since the carriers laid this one damp and fresh before their Roman patrons:

THE OPENING SEASON.—COLISEUM.—Notwithstanding the inclemency of the weather, quite a respectable number of the rank and fashion of the city assembled last night to witness the debut upon metropolitan boards of the young tragedian who has of late been winning such golden opinions in the amphitheaters of the provinces. Some sixty thousand persons were present, and but for the fact that the streets were almost impassable, it is fair to presume that the house would have been full. His august Majesty, the Emperor Aurelius, occupied the imperial box, and was the cynosure of all eyes. Many illustrious nobles and generals of the Empire graced the occasion with their presence, and not the least among them was the young patrician lieutenant whose laurels, won in the ranks of the "Thundering Legion," are still so green upon his brow. The cheer which greeted his entrance was heard beyond the Tiber!

The late repairs and decorations add both to the comeliness and the comfort of the Coliseum. The new cushions are a great improvement upon the hard marble seats we have been so long accustomed to. The present management deserve well of the public. They have restored to the Coliseum the gilding, the rich upholstery, and the uniform magnificence which old Coliseum frequenters tell us Rome was so proud of fifty years ago.

The opening scene last night—the broadsword combat between two young amateurs and a famous Parthian gladiator who was sent here a prisoner—was very fine. The elder of the two young gentlemen handled his weapon with a grace that marked the possession of extraordinary talent. His feint of thrusting, followed instantly by a happily delivered blow which unhelmeted the Parthian, was received with hearty applause. He was not thoroughly up in the backhanded stroke, but it was very gratifying to his numerous friends to know that in time, practice would have overcome this defect. However, he was killed. His sisters, who were present, expressed considerable regret. His mother left the Coliseum. The other youth maintained the contest with such spirit as to call forth enthusiastic bursts of applause. When at last he fell a corpse, his aged mother ran screaming, with hair disheveled and tears streaming from her eyes, and swooned away just as her hands were clutching at the railings of the arena. She was promptly removed by the police. Under the circumstances the woman's conduct was pardonable, perhaps, but we suggest that such exhibitions interfere with the decorum which should be preserved during the performances, and are highly improper in the presence of the Emperor. The Parthian prisoner fought bravely and well; and well he might, for he was fighting for both life and liberty. His wife and children were there to nerve his arm with their love, and to remind him of the old home he should see again if he conquered. When his second assailant fell, the woman clasped her children to her breast and wept for joy. But it was only a transient happiness. The captive staggered toward her and she saw that the liberty he had earned was earned too late. He was wounded unto death. Thus the first act closed in a manner which was entirely satisfactory. The manager was called before the curtain and returned his thanks for the honor done him, in a speech which was replete with wit and humor, and closed by hoping that his humble efforts to afford cheerful and instructive entertainment would continue to meet with the approbation of the Roman public.

The star now appeared, and was received with vociferous applause and the simultaneous waving of sixty thousand handkerchiefs. Marcus Marcellus Velerian (stage-name—his real name is Smith) is a splendid specimen of physical development, and an artist of rare merit. His management of the battle-ax is wonderful. His gaiety and his playfulness are irresistible, in his comic parts, and yet they are inferior to his sublime conceptions in the grave realm of tragedy. When his ax was describing fiery circles about the heads of the bewildered barbarians, in exact time with his springing body and his prancing legs, the audience gave way to uncontrollable bursts of laughter; but when the back of his weapon broke the skull of one and almost in the same instant its edge clove the other's body in twain, the howl of enthusiastic applause that shook the building was the acknowledgment of a critical assemblage that he was a master of the noblest department of his profession. If he has a fault (and we are sorry to even intimate that he has), it is that of glancing at the audience, in the midst of the most exciting moments of the performance, as if seeking admiration. The pausing in a fight to bow when bouquets are thrown to him is also in bad taste. In the great left-handed combat he appeared to be looking at the audience half the time, instead of carving his adversaries; and when he had slain all the sophomores and was dallying with the freshman, he stooped and snatched a bouquet as it fell, and offered it to his adversary at a time when a blow was descending which promised favorably to be his death-warrant. Such levity is proper enough in the provinces, we make no doubt, but it ill suits the dignity of the metropolis. We trust our young friend will take these remarks in good part, for we mean them solely for his benefit. All who know us are aware that although we are at times justly severe upon tigers and martyrs, we never intentionally offend gladiators.

The Infant Prodigy performed wonders. He overcame his four tiger whelps with ease, and with no other hurt than the loss of a portion of his scalp. The General Slaughter was rendered with a faithfulness to details which reflects the highest credit upon the late participants in it.

Upon the whole, last night's performances shed honor not only upon the management but upon the city that encourages and sustains such wholesome and instructive entertainments. We would simply suggest that the practice of vulgar young boys in the gallery of shying peanuts and paper pellets at the tigers, and saying "Hi-yi!" and manifesting approbation or dissatisfaction by such observations as "Bully for the lion!" "Go it, Gladdy!" "Boots!" "Speech!" "Take a walk round the block!" and so on, are extremely reprehensible, when the Emperor is present, and ought to be stopped by the police. Several times last night when the supernumeraries entered the arena to drag out the bodies, the young ruffians in the gallery shouted, "Supe! supe!" and also, "Oh, what a coat!" and "Why don't you pad them shanks?" and made use of various other remarks expressive of derision. These things are very annoying to the audience.

A matinée for the little folks is promised for this afternoon, on which occasion several martyrs will be eaten by the tigers. The regular performance will continue every night till further notice. Material change of program every evening. Benefit of Valerian, Tuesday, 29, if he lives.

I have been a dramatic critic myself, in my time, and I was often surprised to notice how much more I knew about Hamlet than Forrest did; and it gratifies me to observe, now, how much better my brethren of ancient times knew how a broadsword battle ought to be fought than the gladiators.

From THE INNOCENTS ABROAD, 1869

Back from "Yurrup"

Have you ever seen a family of geese just back from Europe—or Yurrup, as they pronounce it? They never talk *to* you, of course, being strangers, but they talk to each other and *at* you till you are pretty nearly distracted with their clatter; till you are sick of their ocean experiences; their mispronounced foreign names; their dukes and emperors; their trivial adventures; their pointless reminiscences; till you are sick of their imbecile faces and their relentless clack, and wish it had pleased Providence to leave the clapper out of their empty skulls.

I travelled with such a family one eternal day, from New York to Boston, last week. They had spent just a year in "Yurrup," and were returning home to Boston. Papa said little, and looked bored—he had simply been down to New York to receive and cart home his cargo of travelled imbecility. Sister Angeline, aged 23, sister Augusta, aged 25, and brother Charles, aged 33, did the conversational drivel, and mamma purred and admired, and threw in some help when occasion offered, in the way of remembering some French barber's—I should say some French Count's—name, when they pretended to have forgotten it. They occupied the choice seats in the parlour of the drawing-room car, and for twelve hours I sat opposite to them—was their *vis-à-vis*, they would have said, in their charming French way.

AUGUSTA "Plague that nahsty (nasty) steamer! I've the headache yet, she rolled so the fifth day out."

ANGELINE "And well you may. *I* never saw such a nahsty old tub. I never want to go in the *Ville de Paris* again. Why *didn't* we go over to London and come in the *Scotia?*"

AUG. "Because we were fools!"

[I endorsed that sentiment.]

ANGIE. "Gustie, what made Count Nixkumarouse drive off looking so blue, that last Thursday in Pairy? (Paris, she meant.) Ah, own up, now!" (tapping her arm *so* roguishly with her ivory fan.)

AUG. "Now, Angie, how you talk! I *told* the nahsty creature I would not receive his attentions any longer. And the old duke, his father, kept boring me about him and his two million francs a year till I sent *him* off with a flea in his ear."

CHORUS "Ke-he-he! Ha-ha-ha!"

CHARLES [Pulling a small silken cloak to pieces.] "Angie, where'd you get this cheap thing?"

ANGIE. "You, Cholly, let that alone! Cheap! Well, how could I help it? There we were, tied up in Switzerland—just down from Mon Blong (Mont Blanc, doubtless)—couldn't buy anything in those nahsty shops so far away from Pairy. I had to put up with that slimpsy forty-dollar rag—but bless you, I couldn't go naked!"

CHORUS "Ke-he-he!"

AUG. "Guess who I was thinking of? Those ignorant persons we saw first in Rome and afterwards in Venice—those——"

ANGIE. "Oh, ha-ha-ha! He-he-he! It *was* so funny! Papa, one of them called the Santa della Spiggiola the Santa della Spizziola! Ha-ha-ha! And she thought it was Canova that did Michael Angelo's Moses! Only *think* of it!—Canova, a sculptor, and the Moses a picture! I thought I should die! I guess I let them see by the way I laughed, that they'd made fools of themselves, because they blushed and sneaked off."

[Papa laughed faintly, but not with the easy grace of a man who was certain he knew what he was laughing about.]

AUG. "Why, Cholly! Where did you get those nahsty Beaumarchais gloves? Well, I *wouldn't*, if I were you!"

MAMMA [With uplifted hands] "Beaumarchais, my son!"

ANGIE. "Beaumarchais! Why how can you! Nobody in Pairy wears those nahsty things but the commonest people."

CHARLES "They *are* a rum lot, but then Tom Blennerhasset gave 'em to me—he wanted to do something or other to curry favour, I s'pose."

ANGIE. "Tom Blennerhasset!"

AUG. "Tom Blennerhasset!"

MAMMA "Tom Blennerhasset! And have you been associating with *him!*"

PAPPA [suddenly interested] "Heavens, what has the son of an honoured and honourable old friend been doing?"

CHORUS "Doing! Why his father has endorsed himself bankrupt for friends—that's what's the matter!"

ANGIE. "Oh, mon Dieu, j'ai faim! Avezvous quelque chose de bon, en votre poche, mon cher frere? Excuse me for speaking French, for, to tell the truth, I haven't spoken English for so long that it comes dreadful awkward. Wish we were back in Yurrup—c'est votre desire aussi, n'est-ce pas, mes cheres?"

And from that moment they lapsed into barbarous French and kept it up for an hour—hesitating, gasping for words, stumbling head over heels through adverbs and participles, floundering among adjectives, working miracles of villainous pronunciation—and neither one of them by any chance ever understanding what another was driving at.

By that time some newcomers had entered the car, and so they lapsed into English again, and fell to holding everything American up to scorn and contumely in order that they might thus let those newcomers know they were just home from "Yurrup." To use their pet and best beloved phrase, they were a "nahsty" family of American snobs, and there ought to be a law against allowing such to go to Europe and misrepresent the nation. It will take these insects five years, without doubt, to get done turning up their noses at everything American and making damaging comparisons between their own country and "Yurrup." Let us pity their waiting friends in Boston in their affliction.

1869

The Benton House

Alexandria was too much like a European city to be novel, and we soon tired of it. We took the cars and came up here to ancient Cairo, which *is* an Oriental city and of the completest pattern. There is little about it to disabuse one's mind of the error if he should take it into his head that he was in the heart of Arabia. Stately camels and dromedaries, swarthy Egyptians, and likewise Turks and black Ethiopians, turbaned, sashed, and blazing in a rich variety of Oriental costumes of all shades of flashy colors, are what one sees on every hand crowding the narrow streets and the honeycombed bazars. We are stopping at Shepherd's Hotel, which is the worst on earth except the one I stopped at once in a small town in the United States. It is pleasant to read this sketch in my note-book, now, and know that I can stand

Shepherd's Hotel, sure, because I have been in one just like it in
America and survived:

I stopped at the Benton House. It used to be a good hotel, but that
proves nothing—I used to be a good boy, for that matter. Both of us
have lost character of late years. The Benton is not a good hotel.
The Benton lacks a very great deal of being a good hotel. Perdition
is full of better hotels than the Benton.

It was late at night when I got there, and I told the clerk I would
like plenty of lights, because I wanted to read an hour or two. When
I reached No. 15 with the porter (we came along a dim hall that was
clad in ancient carpeting, faded, worn out in many places, and patched
with old scraps of oilcloth—a hall that sank under one's feet, and
creaked dismally to every footstep) he struck a light—two inches of
sallow, sorrowful, consumptive tallow candle, that burned blue, and
sputtered, and got discouraged and went out. The porter lit it again,
and I asked if that was all the light the clerk sent. He said, "Oh no, I've
got another one here," and he produced another couple of inches of
tallow candle. I said, "Light them both—I'll have to have one to see the
other by." He did it, but the result was drearier than darkness itself.
He was a cheery, accommodating rascal. He said he would go "some-
wheres" and steal a lamp. I abetted and encouraged him in his
criminal design. I heard the landlord get after him in the hall ten
minutes afterward.

"Where are you going with that lamp?"

"Fifteen wants it, sir."

"Fifteen! why he's got a double lot of candles—does the man want to
illuminate the house?—does he want to get up a torch-light procession?—what *is* he up to, anyhow?"

"He don't like them candles—says he wants a lamp."

"Why, what in the nation does—why I never heard of such a thing?
What on earth can he want with that lamp?"

"Well, he only wants to read—that's what he says."

"Wants to read, does he?—ain't satisfied with a thousand candles,
but has to have a lamp!—I do wonder what the devil that fellow wants
that lamp for? Take him another candle, and then if—"

"But he wants the lamp—says he'll burn the d—d old house down if
he don't get a lamp!" [A remark which I never made.]

"I'd like to see him at it once. Well, you take it along—but I swear it
beats *my* time, though—see if you can't find out what in the very
nation he *wants* with that lamp."

And he went off growling to himself and still wondering and wondering over the unaccountable conduct of No. 15. The lamp was a good one, but it revealed some disagreeable things—a bed in the suburbs of a desert of room—a bed that had hills and valleys in it, and you'd have to accommodate your body to the impression left in it by the man that slept there last, before you could lie comfortably; a carpet that had seen better days; a melancholy washstand in a remote corner, and a dejected pitcher on it sorrowing over a broken nose; a looking-glass split across the center, which chopped your head off at the chin and made you look like some dreadful unfinished monster or other; the paper peeling in shreds from the walls.

I sighed and said: "This is charming; and now don't you think you could get me something to read?"

The porter said, "Oh, certainly; the old man's got dead loads of books"; and he was gone before I could tell him what sort of literature I would rather have. And yet his countenance expressed the utmost confidence in his ability to execute the commission with credit to himself. The old man made a descent on him.

"What are you going to do with that pile of books?"

"Fifteen wants 'em, sir."

"Fifteen, is it? He'll want a warming-pan, next—he'll want a nurse! Take him everything there is in the house—take him the barkeeper—take him the baggage-wagon—take him the chambermaid! Confound me, I never saw anything like it. What did he say he wants with those books?"

"Wants to read 'em, like enough; it ain't likely he wants to eat 'em, I don't reckon."

"Wants to read 'em—wants to read 'em this time of night, the infernal lunatic! Well he can't have them."

"But he says he's mor'ly bound to have 'em: he says he'll just go a-rairin' and a-chargin' through this house and raise more—well, there's no tellin' what he won't do if he don't get 'em; because he's drunk and crazy and desperate, and nothing'll soothe him down but them cussed books." [I had not made any threats and was not in the condition ascribed to me by the porter.]

"Well, go on; but I will be around when he goes to rairing and charging, and the first rair he makes I'll make him rair out of the window." And then the old gentleman went off growling as before.

The genius of that porter was something wonderful. He put an armful of books on the bed and said "Good night" as confidently as if he knew perfectly well that those books were exactly my style of

reading-matter. And well he might. His selection covered the whole
range of legitimate literature. It comprised *The Great Consummation,*
by Rev. Dr. Cummings—theology; *Revised Statutes of the State of
Missouri*—law; *The Complete Horse-Doctor*—medicine; *The Toilers
of the Sea,* by Victor Hugo—romance; the works of William Shakespeare—poetry. I shall never cease to admire the tact and the intelligence of that gifted porter.

From THE INNOCENTS ABROAD, 1869

A Fine Old Man

John Wagner, the oldest man in Buffalo—one hundred and four
years old—recently walked a mile and a half in two weeks.

He is as cheerful and bright as any of these other old men that
charge around so persistently and tiresomely in the newspapers, and
in every way as remarkable.

Last November he walked five blocks in a rainstorm, without any
shelter but an umbrella, and cast his vote for Grant, remarking that
he had voted for forty-seven presidents—which was a lie.

His "second crop" of rich brown hair arrived from New York
yesterday, and he has a new set of teeth coming—from Philadelphia.

He is to be married next week to a girl one hundred and two years
old, who still takes in washing.

They have been engaged eighty years, but their parents persistently
refused their consent until three days ago.

John Wagner is two years older than the Rhode Island veteran, and
yet has never tasted a drop of liquor in his life—unless—unless you
count whisky.

1869

Guying the Guides

I used to worship the mighty genius of Michael Angelo—that man who was great in poetry, painting, sculpture, architecture—great in everything he undertook. But I do not want Michael Angelo for breakfast—for luncheon—for dinner—for tea—for supper—for between meals. I like a change, occasionally. In Genoa, he designed everything; in Milan he or his pupils designed everything; he designed the Lake of Como; in Padua, Verona, Venice, Bologna, who did we ever hear of, from guides, but Michael Angelo? In Florence, he painted everything, designed everything, nearly, and what he did not design he used to sit on a favorite stone and look at, and they showed us the stone. In Pisa he designed everything but the old shot-tower, and they would have attributed that to him if it had not been so awfully out of the perpendicular. He designed the piers of Leghorn and the custom-house regulations of Civita Vecchia. But, here—here it is frightful. He designed St. Peter's; he designed the Pope; he designed the Pantheon, the uniform of the Pope's soldiers, the Tiber, the Vatican, the Coliseum, the Capitol, the Tarpeian Rock, the Barberini Palace, St. John Lateran, the Campagna, the Appian Way, the Seven Hills, the Baths of Caracalla, the Claudian Aqueduct, the Cloaca Maxima—the eternal bore designed the Eternal City, and unless all men and books do lie, he painted everything in it! Dan said the other day to the guide, "Enough, enough, enough! Say no more! Lump the whole thing! Say that the Creator made Italy from designs by Michael Angelo!"

I never felt so fervently thankful, so soothed, so tranquil, so filled with a blessed peace, as I did yesterday when I learned that Michael Angelo was dead.

But we have taken it out of this guide. He has marched us through miles of pictures and sculpture in the vast corridors of the Vatican; and through miles of pictures and sculpture in twenty other palaces; he has shown us the great picture in the Sistine Chapel, and frescoes enough to fresco the heavens—pretty much all done by Michael Angelo. So with him we have played that game which has vanquished so many guides for us—imbecility and idiotic questions. These creatures never suspect—they have no idea of a sarcasm.

He shows us a figure and says: "Statoo brunzo." (Bronze statue.)

We look at it indifferently and the doctor asks: "By Michael Angelo?"

"No—not know who."

Then he shows us the ancient Roman Forum. The doctor asks: "Michael Angelo?"

A stare from the guide. "No—a thousan' year before he is born."

Then an Egyptian obelisk. Again: "Michael Angelo?"

"Oh, *mon dieu*, genteelmen! Zis is *two* thousan' year before he is born!"

He grows so tired of that unceasing question sometimes, that he dreads to show us anything at all. The wretch has tried all the ways he can think of to make us comprehend that Michael Angelo is only responsible for the creation of a *part* of the world, but somehow he has not succeeded yet. Relief for overtasked eyes and brain from study and sight-seeing is necessary, or we shall become idiotic sure enough. Therefore this guide must continue to suffer. If he does not enjoy it, so much the worse for him. We do.

In this place I may as well jot down a chapter concerning those necessary nuisances, European guides. Many a man has wished in his heart he could do without his guide; but knowing he could not, has wished he could get some amusement out of him as a remuneration for the affliction of his society. We accomplished this latter matter, and if our experience can be made useful to others they are welcome to it.

Guides know about enough English to tangle everything up so that a man can make neither head nor tail of it. They know their story by heart—the history of every statue, painting, cathedral, or other wonder they show you. They know it and tell it as a parrot would—and if you interrupt, and throw them off the track, they have to go back and begin over again. All their lives long, they are employed in showing strange things to foreigners and listening to their bursts of admiration. It is human nature to take delight in exciting admiration. It is what prompts children to say "smart" things, and do absurd ones, and in other ways "show off" when company is present. It is what makes gossips turn out in rain and storm to go and be the first to tell a startling bit of news. Think, then, what a passion it becomes with a guide, whose privilege it is, every day, to show to strangers wonders that throw them into perfect ecstasies of admiration! He gets so that he could not by any possibility live in a soberer atmosphere. After we discovered this, we *never* went into ecstasies any more—we never admired anything—we never showed any but impassible faces and stupid indifference in the presence of the sublimest wonders a guide had to display. We had found their weak point. We have made good use of it ever since. We have made some of those people savage, at times, but we have never lost our own serenity.

The doctor asks the questions, generally, because he can keep his countenance, and look more like an inspired idiot, and throw more imbecility into the tone of his voice than any man that lives. It comes natural to him.

The guides in Genoa are delighted to secure an American party, because Americans so much wonder, and deal so much in sentiment and emotion before any relic of Columbus. Our guide there fidgeted about as if he had swallowed a spring mattress. He was full of animation—full of impatience. He said:

"Come wis me, genteelmen!—come! I show you ze letter-writing by Christopher Colombo!—write it himself!—write it wis his own hand! —come!"

He took us to the municipal palace. After much impressive fumbling of keys and opening of locks, the stained and aged document was spread before us. The guide's eyes sparkled. He danced about us and tapped the parchment with his finger:

"What I tell you, genteelmen! Is it not so? See! handwriting Christopher Colombo!—write it himself!"

We looked indifferent—unconcerned. The doctor examined the document very deliberately, during a painful pause. Then he said, without any show of interest:

"Ah—Ferguson—what—what did you say was the name of the party who wrote this?"

"Christopher Colombo! ze great Christopher Colombo!"

Another deliberate examination.

"Ah—did he write it himself, or—or how?"

"He write it himself!—Christopher Colombo! he's own handwriting, write by himself!"

Then the doctor laid the document down and said:

"Why, I have seen boys in America only fourteen years old that could write better than that."

"But zis is ze great Christo—"

"I don't care who it is! It's the worst writing I ever saw. Now you musn't think you can impose on us because we are strangers. We are

not fools, by a good deal. If you have got any specimens of penmanship of real merit, trot them out!—and if you haven't, drive on!"

We drove on. The guide was considerably shaken up, but he made
one more venture. He had something which he thought would overcome us. He said:

"Ah, genteelmen, you come wis me! I show you beautiful, oh, magnificent bust Christopher Colombo!—splendid, grand, magnificent!"

He brought us before the beautiful bust—for it *was* beautiful—and
sprang back and struck an attitude:

"Ah, look, genteelmen!—beautiful, grand,—bust Christopher Colombo!—beautiful bust, beautiful pedestal!"

The doctor put up his eyeglass—procured for such occasions:

"Ah—what did you say this gentleman's name was?"

"Christopher Colombo!—ze great Christopher Colombo!"

"Christopher Colombo—the great Christopher Colombo. Well, what
did *he* do?"

"Discover America!—discover America, oh, ze devil!"

"Discover America. No—that statement will hardly wash. We are
just from America ourselves. We heard nothing about it. Christopher
Colombo—pleasant name—is—is he dead?"

"Oh, *corpo di Baccho!*—three hundred year!"

"What did he die of?"

"I do not know!—I cannot tell."

"Smallpox, think?"

"I do not know, genteelmen!—I do not know *what* he die of!"

"Measles, likely?"

"Maybe—maybe—I do *not* know—I think he die of somethings."

"Parents living?"

"Im-posseeble!"

"Ah—which is the bust and which is the pedestal?"

"Santa Maria!—*zis* ze bust!—*zis* ze pedestal!"

"Ah, I see, I see—happy combination—very happy combination, indeed. Is—is this the first time this gentleman was ever on a bust?"

That joke was lost on the foreigner—guides cannot master the sub-
tleties of the American joke.

We have made it interesting for this Roman guide. Yesterday we
spent three or four hours in the Vatican again, that wonderful world
of curiosities. We came very near expressing interest, sometimes—
even admiration—it was very hard to keep from it. We succeeded
though. Nobody else ever did, in the Vatican museums. The guide

was bewildered—nonplussed. He walked his legs off, nearly, hunting up extraordinary things, and exhausted all his ingenuity on us, but it was a failure; we never showed any interest in anything. He had reserved what he considered to be his greatest wonder till the last—a royal Egyptian mummy, the best-preserved in the world, perhaps. He took us there. He felt so sure, this time, that some of his old enthusiasm came back to him:

"See, genteelmen!—Mummy! Mummy!"

The eyeglass came up as calmly, as deliberately as ever.

"Ah,—Ferguson—what did I understand you to say the gentleman's name was?"

"Name?—he got no name!—Mummy!—'Gyptian mummy!"

"Yes, yes. Born here?"

"No! 'Gyptian mummy!"

"Ah, just so. Frenchman, I presume?"

"No!—not Frenchman, not Roman!—born in Egypta!"

"Born in Egypta. Never heard of Egypta before. Foreign locality, likely. Mummy—mummy. How calm he is—how self-possessed. Is, ah—is he dead?"

"Oh, sacré bleu, been dead three thousan' year!"

The doctor turned on him savagely:

"Here, now, what do you mean by such conduct as this! Playing us for Chinamen because we are strangers and trying to learn! Trying to impose your vile second-hand carcasses on us!—thunder and lightning, I've a notion to—to—if you've got a nice fresh corpse, fetch him out!—or, by George, we'll brain you!"

We make it exceedingly interesting for this Frenchman. However, he has paid us back, partly, without knowing it. He came to the hotel this morning to ask if we were up, and he endeavored as well as he could to describe us, so that the landlord would know which persons he meant. He finished with the casual remark that we were lunatics. The observation was so innocent and so honest that it amounted to a very good thing for a guide to say.

There is one remark (already mentioned) which never yet has failed to disgust these guides. We use it always, when we can think of nothing else to say. After they have exhausted their enthusiasm pointing out to us and praising the beauties of some ancient bronze image or broken-legged statue, we look at it stupidly and in silence for five, ten, fifteen minutes—as long as we can hold out, in fact—and then ask:

"Is—is he dead?"

That conquers the serenest of them. It is not what they are looking for—especially a new guide. Our Roman Ferguson is the most patient, unsuspecting, long-suffering subject we have had yet. We shall be sorry to part with him. We have enjoyed his society very much. We trust he has enjoyed ours, but we are harassed with doubts.

From THE INNOCENTS ABROAD, 1869

Mental Photographs

I have received from the publishers, New York, a neatly printed page of questions, with blanks for answers, and am requested to fill those blanks. These questions are so arranged as to ferret out the most secret points of a man's nature without his ever noticing what the idea is until it is all done and his "character" gone for ever. A number of these sheets are bound together and called a Mental Photograph Album. Nothing could induce me to fill those blanks but the asseveration of my pastor that it will benefit my race by enabling young people to see what I am and giving them an opportunity to become like somebody else. This overcomes my scruples. I have but little character, but what I have I am willing to part with for the public good. I do not boast of this character, further than that I built it up by myself, at odd hours, during the last thirty years, and without other educational aid than I was able to pick up in the ordinary schools and colleges. I have filled the blanks as follows:

WHAT IS YOUR FAVOURITE

Colour?—Any thing but dun.
Flower?—The night-blooming Sirius.*
Tree?—Any that bears forbidden fruit.
Object in Nature?—A dumb belle.
Hour in the Day?—The leisure hour.
Perfume?—Cent. per cent.

* I grant you this is a little obscure—but in explaining to the unfortunate that Sirius is the dog-star and blooms only at night, I am afforded an opportunity to air my erudition. [It is only lately acquired.]

Gem?—The Jack of Diamonds, when it is trump.

Style of Beauty?—The Subscriber's.

Names, Male and Female?—*M'aimez* (Maimie) for a female, and Tacus and Marius, for males.

Painters?—Sign-painters.

Piece of Sculpture?—The Greek Slave, with his hod.

Poet?—Robert Browning, when he has a lucid interval.

Poetess?—Timothy Titcomb.

Prose Author?—Noah Webster, LL.D.

Characters in Romance?—The Napoleon Family.

In History?—King Herod.

Book to take up for an hour?—Rothschild's pocket-book.

What book (not religious) would you part with last?—The one I might happen to be reading on a railroad during the disaster season.

What epoch would you choose to have lived in?—Before the present Erie—it was safer.

Where would you like to live?—In the moon, because there is no water there.

Favourite Amusement?—Hunting the "tiger," or some kindred game.

Favourite Occupation?—"Like dew on the gowan—lying."

What trait of Character do you most admire in man?—The noblest form of cannibalism—love for his fellow-man.

In Woman?—Love for *her* fellow-man.

What trait do you most detest in each?—That "trait" which you put "or" to to describe its possessor.*

If not yourself, who would you rather be?—The Wandering Jew, with a nice annuity.

What is your idea of Happiness?—Finding the buttons all on.

Your idea of Misery?—Breaking an egg in your pocket.

What is your *bête noir?*—[What is my which?]

What is your Dream?—Nightmare, as a general thing.

What do you most dread?—Exposure.

What do you believe to be your Distinguishing Characteristic?—Hunger.

What is the Sublimest Passion of which human nature is capable?—Loving your sweetheart's enemies.

What are the Saddest?—"Dust unto dust."

What are the Sweetest Words in the world?—"Not Guilty."

---

* I have to explain it every single time—"TRAIT-OR." I should think a fine, cultivated intellect might guess that without any help.

What is your Aim in Life?—To endeavour to be absent when my time comes.

What is your Motto?—Be virtuous and you will be eccentric.

1869

Rev. Henry Ward Beecher's Farm

Mr. B.'s farm consists of thirty-six acres, and is carried on on strict scientific principles. He never puts in any part of a crop without consulting his book. He ploughs and reaps and digs and sows according to the best authorities, and the authorities cost more than the other farming implements do. As soon as the library is complete, the farm will begin to be a profitable investment. But book farming has its drawbacks. Upon one occasion, when it seemed morally certain that the hay ought to be cut, the hay book could not be found, and before it was found it was too late, and the hay was all spoiled. Mr. Beecher raises some of the finest crops of wheat in the country, but the unfavourable difference between the cost of producing it and its market value after it is produced has interfered considerably with its success as a commercial enterprise. His special weakness is hogs, however. He considers hogs the best game a farm produces. He buys the original pig for a dollar and a half, and feeds him forty dollars' worth of corn, and then sells him for about nine dollars. This is the only crop he ever makes any money on. He loses on the corn, but he makes seven dollars and a half on the hog. He does not mind this, because he never expects to make anything on corn, anyway. And any way it turns out, he has the excitement of raising the hog any how, whether he gets the worth of him or not. His strawberries would be a comfortable success if the robins would eat turnips, but they won't, and hence the difficulty.

One of Mr. Beecher's most harassing difficulties in his farming operations comes of the close resemblance of different sorts of seeds and plants to each other. Two years ago his farsightedness warned him that there was going to be a great scarcity of water melons, and therefore he put in a crop of seven acres of that fruit. But when they came up they turned out to be pumpkins, and a dead loss was the consequence. Sometimes a portion of his crop goes into the ground the most promising sweet potatoes, and comes up the most execrable carrots. When he bought his farm he found one egg in every hen's nest on the place. He said that here was just the reason why so many farmers failed—they scattered their forces too much—concentration was the idea. So he gathered those eggs together, and put them all under one experienced hen. That hen roosted over the contract night and day for many weeks, under Mr. Beecher's personal supervision, but she could not "phase" those eggs. Why? Because they were those shameful porcelain things which are used by modern farmers as "nest eggs."

Mr. Beecher's farm is not a triumph. It would be easier if he worked it on shares with some one; but he cannot find any body who is willing to stand half the expense, and not many that are able. Still, persistence in any cause is bound to succeed. He was a very inferior farmer when he first began, but a prolonged and unflinching assault upon his agricultural difficulties has had its effect at last, and he is now fast rising from affluence to poverty.

1869

The Turkish Bath

When I think how I have been swindled by books of Oriental travel, I want a tourist for breakfast. For years and years I have dreamed of the wonders of the Turkish bath; for years and years I have promised myself that I would yet enjoy one. Many and many a time, in fancy, I have lain in the marble bath, and breathed the slumbrous fragrance of Eastern spices that filled the air; then passed through a weird and complicated system of pulling and hauling and drenching and scrubbing, by a gang of naked savages who loomed vast and vaguely through the steaming mists, like demons; then rested for a while on a divan fit for a king; then passed through another complex ordeal, and one more fearful than the first; and, finally, swathed in soft fabrics, been conveyed to a princely saloon and laid on a bed of eiderdown, where eunuchs, gorgeous of costume, fanned me while I drowsed and dreamed, or contentedly gazed at the rich hangings of the apartment, the soft carpets, the sumptuous furniture, the pictures, and drank delicious coffee, smoked the soothing narghili, and dropped, at the last, into tranquil repose, lulled by sensuous odors from unseen censers, by the gentle influence of the narghili's Persian tobacco, and by the music of fountains that counterfeited the pattering of summer rain.

That was the picture, just as I got it from incendiary books of travel. It was a poor, miserable imposture. The reality is no more like it than the Five Points are like the Garden of Eden. They received me in a great court, paved with marble slabs; around it were broad galleries, one above another, carpeted with seedy matting, railed with unpainted balustrades, and furnished with huge rickety chairs, cushioned with rusty old mattresses, indented with impressions left by the forms of nine successive generations of men who had reposed upon them. The place was vast, naked, dreary; its court a barn, its galleries stalls for human horses. The cadaverous, half-nude varlets that served in the establishment had nothing of poetry in their appearance, nothing of romance, nothing of Oriental splendor. They shed no entrancing odors—just the contrary. Their hungry eyes and their lank forms continually suggested one glaring, unsentimental fact—they wanted what they term in California "a square meal."

I went into one of the racks and undressed. An unclean starveling wrapped a gaudy table-cloth about his loins, and hung a white rag over my shoulders. If I had had a tub then, it would have come natural to me to take in washing. I was then conducted down-stairs into the wet, slippery court, and the first things that attracted my attention were my heels. My fall excited no comment. They expected it, no doubt. It belonged in the list of softening, sensuous influences peculiar to this home of Eastern luxury. It was softening enough, certainly, but its application was not happy. They now gave me a pair of wooden clogs—benches in miniature, with leather straps over them to confine my feet (which they would have done, only I do not wear No. 13's). These things dangled uncomfortably by the straps when I lifted up my feet, and came down in awkward and unexpected places when I put them on the floor again, and sometimes turned sideways and wrenched my ankles out of joint. However, it was all Oriental luxury, and I did what I could to enjoy it.

They put me in another part of the barn and laid me on a stuffy sort of pallet, which was not made of cloth of gold, or Persian shawls, but was merely the unpretending sort of thing I have seen in the negro quarters of Arkansas. There was nothing whatever in this dim marble prison but five more of these biers. It was a very solemn place. I expected that the spiced odors of Araby were going to steal over my senses, now, but they did not. A copper-colored skeleton, with a rag around him, brought me a glass decanter of water, with a lighted tobacco pipe in the top of it, and a pliant stem a yard long, with a brass mouthpiece to it.

It was the famous "narghili" of the East—the thing the Grand Turk smokes in the pictures. This began to look like luxury. I took one blast at it, and it was sufficient; the smoke went in a great volume down into my stomach, my lungs, even into the uttermost parts of my frame. I exploded one mighty cough, and it was as if Vesuvius had let go. For the next five minutes I smoked at every pore, like a frame house that is on fire on the inside. Not any more narghili for me. The smoke had a vile taste, and the taste of a thousand infidel tongues that remained on that brass mouthpiece was viler still. I was getting discouraged. Whenever, hereafter, I see the cross-legged Grand Turk smoking his narghili, in pretended bliss, on the outside of a paper of Connecticut tobacco, I shall know him for the shameless humbug he is.

This prison was filled with hot air. When I had got warmed up sufficiently to prepare me for a still warmer temperature, they took me where it was—into a marble room, wet, slippery, and steamy, and laid me out on a raised platform in the center. It was very warm. Presently my man sat me down by a tank of hot water, drenched me well, gloved his hand with a coarse mitten, and began to polish me all over with it. I began to smell disagreeably. The more he polished the worse I smelt. It was alarming. I said to him:

"I perceive that I am pretty far gone. It is plain that I ought to be buried without any unnecessary delay. Perhaps you had better go after my friends at once, because the weather is warm, and I cannot 'keep' long."

He went on scrubbing, and paid no attention. I soon saw that he was reducing my size. He bore hard on his mitten, and from under it rolled little cylinders, like macaroni. It could not be dirt, for it was too white. He pared me down in this way for a long time. Finally I said:

"It is a tedious process. It will take hours to trim me to the size you want me; I will wait; go and borrow a jack-plane."

He paid no attention at all.

After a while he brought a basin, some soap, and something that seemed to be the tail of a horse. He made up a prodigious quantity of soap-suds, deluged me with them from head to foot, without warning me to shut my eyes, and then swabbed me viciously with the horse-tail. Then he left me there, a snowy statue of lather, and went away. When I got tired of waiting I went and hunted him up. He was propped against the wall, in another room, asleep. I woke him. He was not disconcerted. He took me back and flooded me with hot water, then turbaned my head, swathed me with dry table-cloths, and conducted me to a latticed chicken-coop in one of the galleries, and pointed to one of those Arkansas beds. I mounted it, and vaguely expected the odors of Araby again. They did not come.

The blank, unornamented coop had nothing about it of that oriental voluptuousness one reads of so much. It was more suggestive of the county hospital than anything else. The skinny servitor brought a narghili, and I got him to take it out again without wasting any time about it. Then he brought the world-renowned Turkish coffee that poets have sung so rapturously for many generations, and I seized upon it as the last hope that was left of my old dreams of Eastern luxury. It was another fraud. Of all the unchristian beverages that ever passed my lips, Turkish coffee is the worst. The cup is small, it is smeared with grounds; the coffee is black, thick, unsavory of smell, and execrable in taste. The bottom of the cup has a muddy sediment in it half an inch deep. This goes down your throat, and portions of it lodge by the way, and produce a tickling aggravation that keeps you barking and coughing for an hour.

Here endeth my experience of the celebrated Turkish bath, and here also endeth my dream of the bliss the mortal revels in who passes through it. It is a malignant swindle. The man who enjoys it is qualified to enjoy anything that is repulsive to sight or sense, and he that can invest it with a charm of poetry is able to do the same with anything else in the world that is tedious, and wretched, and dismal, and nasty.

From THE INNOCENTS ABROAD, 1869

The Case of George Fisher

This is history. It is not a wild extravaganza, like "John Wilson Mackenzie's Great Beef Contract," but is a plain statement of facts and circumstances with which the Congress of the United States has interested itself from time to time during the long period of half a century.

I will not call this matter of George Fisher's a great deathless and unrelenting swindle upon the government and people of the United States—for it has never been so decided, and I hold that it is a grave and solemn wrong for a writer to cast slurs or call names when such is the case—but will simply present the evidence and let the reader deduce his own verdict. Then we shall do nobody injustice, and our consciences shall be clear.

On or about the 1st day of September, 1813, the Creek war being then in progress in Florida, the crops, herds, and houses of Mr. George Fisher, a citizen, were destroyed, either by the Indians or by the United States troops in pursuit of them. By the terms of the law, if the *Indians* destroyed the property, there was no relief for Fisher; but if the *troops* destroyed it, the Government of the United States was debtor to Fisher for the amount involved.

George Fisher must have considered that the *Indians* destroyed the property, because, although he lived several years afterward, he does not appear to have ever made any claim upon the government.

In the course of time Fisher died, and his widow married again. And by and by, nearly twenty years after that dimly remembered raid upon Fisher's corn-fields, *the widow Fisher's new husband* petitioned Congress for pay for the property, and backed up the petition with many depositions and affidavits which purported to prove that the troops, and not the Indians, destroyed the property; that the troops, for some inscrutable reason, deliberately burned down "houses" (or cabins) valued at $600, the same belonging to a peaceable private citizen, and also destroyed various other property belonging to the same citizen. But Congress declined to believe that the troops were such idiots (after overtaking and scattering a band of Indians proved to have been found destroying Fisher's property) as to calmly

continue the work of destruction themselves, and make a complete
job of what the Indians had only commenced. So Congress denied the
petition of the heirs of George Fisher in 1832, and did not pay them
a cent.

We hear no more from them officially until 1848, sixteen years after
their first attempt on the Treasury, and a full generation after the
death of the man whose fields were destroyed. The new generation
of Fisher heirs then came forward and put in a bill for damages.
The Second Auditor awarded them $8,873, being half the damage
sustained by Fisher. The Auditor said the testimony showed that at
least half the destruction was done by the Indians *"before the troops
started in pursuit,"* and of course the government was not responsible
for that half.

2. That was in April, 1848. In December, 1848, the heirs of George
Fisher, deceased, came forward and pleaded for a "revision" of their
bill of damages. The revision was made, but nothing new could be
found in their favor except an error of $100 in the former calculation.
However, in order to keep up the spirits of the Fisher family, the
Auditor concluded to go back and allow *interest* from the date of the
first petition (1832) to the date when the bill of damages was awarded.
This sent the Fishers home happy with sixteen years' interest on
$8,873—the same amounting to $8,997.94. Total, $17,870.94.

3. For an entire year the suffering Fisher family remained quiet—
even satisfied, after a fashion. Then they swooped down upon the
government with their wrongs once more. That old patriot, Attorney-
General Toucey, burrowed through the musty papers of the Fishers
and discovered one more chance for the desolate orphans—interest on
that original award of $8,873 from date of destruction of the property
(1813) up to 1832! Result, $10,004.89 for the indigent Fishers. So
now we have: First, $8,873 damages; second, interest on it from 1832
to 1848, $8,997.94: third, interest on it dated back to 1813, $10,004.89.
Total, $27,875.83! What better investment for a great-grandchild than
to get the Indians to burn a corn-field for him sixty or seventy years
before his birth, and plausibly lay it on lunatic United States troops?

4. Strange as it may seem, the Fishers let Congress alone for five
years—or, what is perhaps more likely, failed to make themselves
heard by Congress for that length of time. But at last, in 1854, they
got a hearing. They persuaded Congress to pass an act requiring the
Auditor to re-examine their case. But this time they stumbled upon
the misfortune of an honest Secretary of the Treasury (Mr. James
Guthrie), and he spoiled everything. He said in very plain language

that the Fishers were not only not entitled to another cent, but that those children of many sorrows and acquainted with grief *had been paid too much already*.

5. Therefore another interval of rest and silence ensued—an interval which lasted four years—*viz.*, till 1858. The "right man in the right place" was then Secretary of War—John B. Floyd, of peculiar renown! Here was a master intellect; here was the very man to succor the suffering heirs of dead and forgotten Fisher. They came up from Florida with a rush—a great tidal wave of Fishers freighted with the same old musty documents about the same immortal corn-fields of their ancestor. They straightway got an act passed transferring the Fisher matter from the dull Auditor to the ingenious Floyd. What did Floyd do? He said, "IT WAS PROVED *that the Indians destroyed everything they could before the troops entered in pursuit.*" He considered, therefore, that what they destroyed must have consisted of "*the houses with all their contents, and the liquor*" (the most trifling part of the destruction, and set down at only $3,200 all told), and that the government troops then drove them off and calmly proceeded to destroy—

Two hundred and twenty acres of corn in the field, thirty-five acres of wheat, and nine hundred and eighty-six head of live stock! [What a singularly intelligent army we had in those days, according to Mr. Floyd—though not according to the Congress of 1832.]

So Mr. Floyd decided that the Government was not responsible for that $3,200 worth of rubbish which the Indians destroyed, but was responsible for the property destroyed by the troops—which property consisted of (I quote from the printed United States Senate document):

	DOLLARS
Corn at Bassett's Creek,	3,000
Cattle,	5,000
Stock Hogs,	1,050
Drove hogs,	1,204
Wheat,	350
Hides,	4,000
Corn on the Alabama River,	3,500
Total,	18,104

That sum, in his report, Mr. Floyd calls the "*full value* of the property destroyed by the troops." He allows that sum to the starving Fishers, TOGETHER WITH INTEREST FROM 1813. From this new sum total the amounts already paid to the Fishers were deducted, and then the cheerful remainder (a fraction under *forty thousand dollars*) was handed to them, and again they retired to Florida in a condition of temporary tranquillity. Their ancestor's farm had now yielded them altogether nearly *sixty-seven thousand dollars* in cash.

6. Does the reader suppose that that was the end of it? Does he suppose those diffident Fishers were satisfied? Let the evidence show. The Fishers were quiet just two years. Then they came swarming up out of the fertile swamps of Florida with their same old documents, and besieged Congress once more. Congress capitulated on the 1st of June, 1860, and instructed Mr. Floyd to overhaul those papers again and pay that bill. A Treasury clerk was ordered to go through those papers and report to Mr. Floyd what amount was still due the emaciated Fishers. This clerk (I can produce him whenever he is wanted) discovered what was apparently a glaring and recent forgery in the papers, whereby a witness's testimony as to the price of corn in Florida in 1813 was made to name double the amount which that witness had originally specified as the price! The clerk not only called his superior's attention to this thing, but in making up his brief of the case called particular attention to it in writing. That part of the brief *never got before Congress*, nor has Congress ever yet had a hint of a forgery existing among the Fisher papers. Nevertheless, on the basis of the double prices (and totally ignoring the clerk's assertion that the figures were manifestly and unquestionably a recent forgery), Mr. Floyd remarks in his new report that "the testimony, *particularly in regard to the corn crops,* DEMANDS A MUCH HIGHER ALLOWANCE than any *heretofore* made by the Auditor or myself." So he estimates the crop at *sixty bushels* to the acre (double what Florida acres produce), and then virtuously allows pay for only half the crop, *but* allows *two dollars and a half* a bushel for that half, when there are rusty old books and documents in the Congressional library to show just what the Fisher testimony showed before the forgery—*viz.*, that in the fall of 1813 corn was only worth from $1.25 to $1.50 a bushel. Having accomplished this, what does Mr. Floyd do next? Mr. Floyd ("with an earnest desire to execute truly the legislative will," as he piously remarks) goes to work and makes out an entirely new bill of Fisher damages, and in this new bill he placidly *ignores the Indians* altogether—puts no particle of the destruction of the Fisher property upon them, but, even repenting him of charging them with burning the cabins and drinking the whisky and breaking the crockery, lays the *entire* damage at the door of the imbecile United States

troops down to the very last item! And not only that, but uses the
forgery to double the loss of corn at "Bassett's Creek," and uses it
again to absolutely *treble* the loss of corn on the "Alabama River."
This new and ably conceived and executed bill of Mr. Floyd's figures
up as follows (I copy again from the printed United States Senate
document):

*The United States in account with the legal representatives of
George Fisher, deceased.*

		DOL. C.
1813.—To 550 head of cattle, at 10 dollars,	. . . . . .	5,500.00
To 86 head of drove hogs,	. . . .	1,204.00
To 350 head of stock hogs,	. . . .	1,750.00
To 100 ACRES OF CORN ON BASSETT'S CREEK,	. . .	6,000.00
To 8 barrels of whisky,	. . . .	350.00
To 2 barrels of brandy,	. . . .	280.00
To 1 barrel of rum,	. . . .	70.00
To dry-goods and merchandise in store,	. . . . .	1,100.00
To 35 acres of wheat,	. . . .	350.00
To 2,000 hides,	. . . .	4,000.00
To furs and hats in store,	. . . .	600.00
To crockery ware in store,	. . . .	100.00
To smith's and carpenter's tools,	. . . . . .	250.00
To houses burned and destroyed,	. . . . . .	600.00
To 4 dozen bottles of wine,	. . . .	48.00
1814.—To 120 acres of corn on Alabama River,	. . . . .	9,500.00
To crops of peas, fodder, etc.,	. . . .	3,250.00
Total,	. . . .	34,952.00
To interest on $22,202, from July 1813 to		
November 1860, 47 years and 4 months,	. . . .	63,053.68
To interest on $12,750, from September		
1814 to November 1860, 46 years and 2		
months,	. . . .	35,317.50
Total,	. . . .	133,323.18

He puts everything in this time. He does not even allow that the
Indians destroyed the crockery or drank the four dozen bottles of
(currant) wine. When it came to supernatural comprehensiveness in
"gobbling," John B. Floyd was without his equal, in his own or any
other generation. Subtracting from the above total the $67,000 already
paid to George Fisher's implacable heirs, Mr. Floyd announced that
the government was still indebted to them in the sum of *sixty-six
thousand five hundred and nineteen dollars and eighty-five cents,*
"which," Mr. Floyd complacently remarks, "will be paid, accordingly,

to the administrator of the estate of George Fisher, deceased, or to his attorney in fact."

But, sadly enough for the destitute orphans, a new President came in just at this time, Buchanan and Floyd went out, and they never got their money. The first thing Congress did in 1861 was to rescind the resolution of June 1, 1860, under which Mr. Floyd had been ciphering. Then Floyd (and doubtless the heirs of George Fisher likewise) had to give up financial business for a while, and go into the Confederate army and serve their country.

Were the heirs of George Fisher killed? No. They are back now at this very time (July, 1870), beseeching Congress through that blushing and diffident creature, Garrett Davis, to commence making payments again on their interminable and insatiable bill of damages for corn and whisky destroyed by a gang of irresponsible Indians, so long ago that even government red-tape has failed to keep consistent and intelligent track of it.

Now the above are facts. They are history. Any one who doubts it can send to the Senate Document Department of the Capitol for H. R. Ex. Doc. No. 21, 36th Congress, 2d Session, and for S. Ex. Doc. No. 106, 41st Congress, 2d Session, and satisfy himself. The whole case is set forth in the first volume of the Court of Claims Reports.

It is my belief that as long as the continent of America holds together, the heirs of George Fisher, deceased, will still make pilgrimages to Washington from the swamps of Florida, to plead for just a little more cash on their bill of damages (even when they received the last of that sixty-seven thousand dollars, they said it was only *one-fourth* what the government owed them on that fruitful corn-field), and as long as they choose to come they will find Garrett Davises to drag their vampire schemes before Congress. This is not the only hereditary fraud (if fraud it is—which I have before repeatedly remarked is not proven) that is being quietly handed down from generation to generation of fathers and sons, through the persecuted Treasury of the United States.

1870

An Entertaining Article

I take the following paragraph from an article in the Boston *Advertiser*:

AN ENGLISH CRITIC ON MARK TWAIN

Perhaps the most successful flights of the humor of Mark Twain have been descriptions of the persons who did not appreciate his humor at all. We have become familiar with the Californians who were thrilled with terror by his burlesque of a newspaper reporter's way of telling a story, and we have heard of the Pennsylvania clergyman who sadly returned his *Innocents Abroad* to the book-agent with the remark that "the man who could shed tears over the tomb of Adam must be an idiot." But Mark Twain may now add a much more glorious instance to his string of trophies. The *Saturday Review,* in its number of October 8th, reviews his book of travels, which has been republished in England, and reviews it seriously. We can imagine the delight of the humorist in reading this tribute to his power; and indeed it is so amusing in itself that he can hardly do better than reproduce the article in full in his next monthly Memoranda.

(Publishing the above paragraph thus, gives me a sort of authority for reproducing the *Saturday Review's* article in full in these pages. I dearly wanted to do it, for I cannot write anything half so delicious myself. If I had a cast-iron dog that could read this English criticism and preserve his austerity, I would drive him off the door-step.)

(From the London "Saturday Review.")

REVIEWS OF NEW BOOKS

THE INNOCENTS ABROAD. A Book of Travels. By Mark Twain.
London: Hotten, publisher. 1870.

Lord Macaulay died too soon. We never felt this so deeply as when we finished the last chapter of the above-named extravagant work. Macaulay died too soon—for none but he could mete out complete and comprehensive justice to the insolence, the impertinence, the presumption, the mendacity, and, above all, the majestic ignorance of this author.

To say that the *Innocents Abroad* is as curious book, would be to use the faintest language—would be to speak of the Matterhorn as a neat elevation or of Niagara as being "nice" or "pretty." "Curious" is too tame a word wherewith to describe the imposing insanity of this work. There is no word that is large enough or long enough. Let us, therefore, photograph a passing glimpse of book and author, and trust the rest to the reader. Let the cultivated English student of human nature picture to himself this Mark Twain as a person capable of doing the following-described things—and not only doing them, but with incredible innocence *printing them* calmly and tranquilly in a book. For instance:

He states that he entered a hair-dresser's in Paris to get shaved, and the first *"rake"* the barber gave with his razor it *loosened his "hide"* and *lifted him out of the chair.*

This is unquestionably exaggerated. In Florence he was so annoyed by beggars that he pretends to have seized and eaten one in a frantic spirit of revenge. There is, of course, no truth in this. He gives at full length a theatrical program seventeen or eighteen hundred years old, which he professes to have found in the ruins of the Coliseum, among the dirt and mold and rubbish. It is a sufficient comment upon this statement to remark that even a cast-iron program would not have lasted so long under such circumstances. In Greece he plainly betrays both fright and flight upon one occasion, but with frozen effrontery puts the latter in this falsely tamed form: "We *sidled* toward the Piraeus." "Sidled," indeed! He does not hesitate to intimate that at Ephesus, when his mule strayed from the proper course, he got down, took him under his arm, carried him to the road again, pointed him right, remounted, and went to sleep contentedly till it was time to restore the beast to the path once more. He states that a growing youth among his ship's passengers was in the constant habit of appeasing his hunger with soap and oakum between meals. In Palestine he tells of ants that came eleven miles to spend the summer in the desert and brought their provisions with them; yet he shows by his description of the country that the feat was an impossibility. He mentions, as if it were the most commonplace of matters, that he cut a Moslem in two in broad daylight in Jerusalem, with Godfrey de Bouillon's sword, and would have shed more blood *if he had had a graveyard of his own.* These statements are unworthy a moment's attention. Mr. Twain or any other foreigner who did such a thing in Jerusalem would be mobbed, and would infallibly lose his life. But why go on? Why repeat more of his audacious and exasperating falsehoods? Let us close fittingly with this one: he affirms that "in the mosque of St. Sophia at Constantinople I got my feet so stuck up with a complication of gums, slime, and general impurity, that I wore out more than two thousand pair of bootjacks getting my boots off that night, and even then some Christian hide peeled off with them." It is monstrous. Such statements are simply lies—there is no other name for them. Will the reader longer marvel at the brutal ignorance that pervades the American nation when we tell him that we are informed upon perfectly good authority that this extravagant compilation of falsehoods, this exhaustless mine of stupendous lies, this *Innocents Abroad*, has actually been adopted by the schools and colleges of several of the states as a text-book!

But if his falsehoods are distressing, his innocence and his ignorance are enough to make one burn the book and despise the author. In one place he was so appalled at the sudden spectacle of a murdered man, unveiled by the moonlight, that he jumped out of the window, going through sash and all, and then remarks with the most childlike simplicity that he "was not scared, but was considerably agitated." It puts us out of patience to note that the simpleton is densely unconscious that Lucrezia Borgia ever existed off the stage. He is vulgarly ignorant of all foreign languages, but is frank enough to criticize, the Italians' use of their own tongue. He says they spell the name of their great painter "Vinci, but pronounce it Vinchy"—and then adds with a naïveté possible only to helpless ignorance, "foreigners always spell better than they pronounce." In another place he commits the bald absurdity of putting the phrase "tare an ouns" into an Italian's mouth. In Rome he unhesitatingly believes the legend that St. Philip Neri's heart was so inflamed with divine love that it burst his ribs—believes it wholly because an author with a learned list of university degrees strung after his name indorses it—"otherwise," says this gentle idiot,"I should have felt a curiosity to know what Philip had for dinner." Our author makes a long, fatiguing journey to the Grotto del Cane on purpose to test its poisoning powers on a dog—got elaborately ready for the experiment, and then discovered that he had no dog. A wiser person would have kept such a thing discreetly to himself, but with this harmless creature everything comes out. He hurts his foot in a rut two thousand years old in exhumed Pompeii, and presently, when staring at one of the cinder-like corpses unearthed in the next square, conceives the idea that maybe it is the remains of the ancient Street Commissioner, and straightway his horror softens down to a sort of chirpy contentment with the condition of things. In Damascus he visits the well of Ananias, three thousand years old, and is as surprised and delighted as a child to find that the water is "as pure and fresh as if the well had been dug yesterday." In the Holy Land he gags desperately at the hard Arabic and Hebrew Biblical names, and finally concludes to call them Baldwinsville, Williamsburgh, and so on, "for convenience of spelling."

We have thus spoken freely of this man's stupefying simplicity and innocence, but we cannot deal similarly with this colossal ignorance. We do not know where to begin. And if we knew where to begin, we certainly would not know where to leave off. We will give one specimen, and one only. He did not know, until he got to Rome, that Michael Angelo was dead! And then, instead of crawling away and hiding his shameful ignorance somewhere, he proceeds to express a pious, grateful sort of satisfaction that he is gone and out of his troubles!

No, the reader may seek out the author's exhibition of his uncultivation for himself. The book is absolutely dangerous, considering the magnitude and variety of its misstatements, and the convincing confidence with which they are made. And yet it is a text-book in the schools of America.

The poor blunderer mouses among the sublime creations of the Old Masters, trying to acquire the elegant proficiency in art-knowledge, which he has a groping sort of comprehension is a proper thing for the traveled man to be able to display. But what is the manner of his study? And what is the progress he achieves? To what extent does he familiarize himself with the great pictures of Italy, and what degree of appreciation does he arrive at? Read:

"When we see a monk going about with a lion and looking up into heaven, we know that that is St. Mark. When we see a monk with a book and a pen, looking tranquilly up to heaven, trying to think of a word, we know that that is St. Matthew. When we see a monk sitting on a rock, looking tranquilly up to heaven, with a human skull beside him, and without other baggage, we know that that is St. Jerome. Because we know that he always went flying light in the matter of baggage. When we see other monks looking tranquilly up to heaven, but having no trade-mark, we always ask who those parties are. We do this because we humbly wish to learn."

He then enumerates the thousands and thousands of copies of these several pictures which he has seen, and adds with accustomed simplicity that he feels encouraged to believe that when he has seen "Some More" of each, and had a larger experience, he will eventually "begin to take an absorbing interest in them"—the vulgar boor.

That we have shown this to be a remarkable book, we think no one will deny. That it is a pernicious book to place in the hands of the confiding and uninformed, we think we have also shown. That the book is a deliberate and wicked creation of a diseased mind, is apparent upon every page. Having placed our judgment thus upon record, let us close with what charity we can, by remarking that even in this volume there is some good to be found; for whenever the author talks of his own country and lets Europe alone, he never fails to make himself interesting, and not only interesting, but instructive. No one can read without benefit his occasional chapters and paragraphs, about life in the gold and silver mines of California and Nevada; about the Indians of the plains and deserts of the West, and their cannibalism; about the raising of vegetables in kegs of gunpowder by the aid of two or three teaspoonfuls of guano; about the moving of small farms from place to place at night in wheelbarrows to avoid taxes; and about a sort of cows and mules in the Humboldt mines, that climb down chimneys and disturb the people at night. These matters are not only new, but are well worth knowing. It is a pity the author did not put in more of the same kind. His book is well written and is exceedingly entertaining, and so it just barely escaped being quite valuable also.

(One month later)

Latterly I have received several letters, and see a number of newspaper paragraphs, all upon a certain subject, and all of about the same tenor. I here give honest specimens. One is from a New York paper, one is from a letter from an old friend, and one is from a letter from a New York publisher who is a stranger to me. I humbly endeavor to make these bits toothsome with the remark that the article they are praising (which appeared in the December *Galaxy*, and *pretended* to be a criticism from the London *Saturday Review* on my *Innocents Abroad*) *was written by myself, every line of it:*

The *Herald* says the richest thing out is the "serious critique" in the London *Saturday Review*, on Mark Twain's *Innocents Abroad*. We thought before we read it that it must be "serious," as everybody said so, and were even ready to shed a few tears; but since perusing it, we are bound to confess that next to Mark Twain's "Jumping Frog" it's the finest bit of humor and sarcasm that we've come across in many a day.

(I do not get a compliment like that every day.)

I used to think that your writings were pretty good, but after reading the criticism in *The Galaxy* from the *London Review*, have discovered what an ass I must have been. If suggestions are in order, mine is, that you put that article in your next edition of the *Innocents*, as an extra chapter, if you are not afraid to put you own humor in competition with it. It is as rich a thing as I ever read.

(Which is strong commendation from a book publisher.)

The London Reviewer, my friend, is not the stupid, "serious" creature he pretends to be, *I* think; but, on the contrary, has a keen appreciation and enjoyment of your book. As I read his article in *The Galaxy*, I could imagine him giving vent to many a hearty laugh. But he is writing for Catholics and Established Church people, and high-toned, antiquated, conservative gentility, whom it is a delight to him to help you shock, while he pretends to shake his head with owlish density. He is a magnificent humorist himself.

(Now that is graceful and handsome. I take off my hat to my life-long friend and comrade, and with my feet together and my fingers spread over my heart, I say, in the language of Alabama, "You do me proud.")

I stand guilty of the authorship of the article, but I did not mean any harm. I saw by an item in the Boston *Advertiser* that a solemn, serious critique on the English edition of my book had appeared in the London *Saturday Review*, and the idea of *such* a literary breakfast by a stolid, ponderous British ogre of the quill was too much for a naturally weak virtue, and I went home and burlesqued it—reveled in it, I may say. I never saw a copy of the real *Saturday Review* criticism until after my burlesque was written and mailed to the printer. But when I did get hold of a copy, I found it to be vulgar, awkwardly written, ill-natured, and entirely serious and in earnest. The gentleman who wrote the newspaper paragraph above quoted had not been misled as to its character.

If any man doubts my word now, I will kill him. No, I will not kill him; I will win his money. I will bet him twenty to one, and let any New York publisher hold the stakes, that the statements I have above made as to the authorship of the article in question are entirely true. Perhaps I may get wealthy at this, for I am willing to take all the bets that offer; and if a man wants larger odds, I will give him all he requires. But he ought to find out whether I am betting on what is termed "a sure thing" or not before he ventures his money, and he can do that by going to a public library and examining the London *Saturday Review* of October 8th, which contains the real critique.

Bless me, some people thought that *I* was the "sold" person!

P. S.—I cannot resist the temptation to toss in this most savory thing of all—this easy, graceful, philosophical disquisition, with its happy, chirping confidence. It is from the Cincinnati *Enquirer:*

Nothing is more uncertain than the value of a fine cigar. Nine smokers out of ten would prefer an ordinary domestic article, three for a quarter, to a fifty-cent Partaga, if kept in ignorance of the cost of the latter. The flavor of the Partaga is too delicate for palates that have been accustomed to Connecticut seed leaf. So it is with humor. The finer it is in quality, the more danger of its not being recognized at all. Even Mark Twain has been taken in by an English review of his *Innocents Abroad*. Mark Twain is by no means a coarse humorist, but the Englishman's humor is so much finer than his, that he mistakes it for solid earnest, and "larfs most consumedly."

A man who cannot learn stands in his own light. Hereafter, when I write an article which I know to be good, but which I may have reason to fear will not, in some quarters, be considered to amount to much, coming from an American, I will aver that an Englishman wrote it and that it is copied from a London journal. And then I will occupy a back seat and enjoy the cordial applause.

(*Still later*)

Mark Twain at last sees that the *Saturday Review's* criticism of his *Innocents Abroad* was not serious, and he is intensely mortified at the thought of having been so badly sold. He takes the only course left him, and in the last *Galaxy* claims that *he* wrote the criticism himself, and published it in *The Galaxy* to sell the public. This is ingenious, but unfortunately it is not true.

If any of our readers will take the trouble to call at this office we will show them the original article in the *Saturday Review* of October 8th, which, on comparison, will be found to be identical with the one published in *The Galaxy*. The best thing for Mark to do will be to admit that he was sold, and say no more about it.

The above is from the Cincinnati *Enquirer*, and is a falsehood. Come to the proof. If the *Enquirer* people, through any agent, will produce at *The Galaxy* office a London *Saturday Review* of October 8th, containing an "article which, on comparison, will be found to be identical with the one published in *The Galaxy*, I will pay to that agent five hundred dollars cash. Moreover, if at any specified time I fail to produce at the same place a copy of the London *Saturday Review* of October 8th, containing a lengthy criticism upon the *Innocents Abroad*, entirely different, in every paragraph and sentence, from the one I published in *The Galaxy*, I will pay to the *Enquirer* agent another five hundred dollars cash. I offer Sheldon & Co., publishers, 500 Broadway, New York, as my "backers." Any one in New York, authorized by the *Enquirer*, will receive prompt attention. It is an easy and profitable way for the *Enquirer* people to prove that they have not uttered a pitiful, deliberate falsehood in the above paragraphs. Will they swallow that falsehood ignominiously, or will they send an agent to *The Galaxy* office. I think the Cincinnati *Enquirer* must be edited by children.

1870

History Repeats Itself

The following I find in a Sandwich Island paper which some friend has sent me from that tranquil far-off retreat. The coincidence between my own experience and that here set down by the late Mr. Benton is so remarkable that I cannot forbear publishing and commenting upon the paragraph. The Sandwich Island paper says:

How touching is this tribute of the late Hon. T. H. Benton to his mother's influence:—"My mother asked me never to use tobacco; I have never touched it from that time to the present day. She asked me not to gamble, and I have never gambled. I cannot tell who is losing in games that are being played. She admonished me, too, against liquor-drinking, and whatever capacity for endurance I have at present, and whatever usefulness I may have attained through life, I attribute to having complied with her pious and correct wishes. When I was seven years of age she asked me not to drink, and then I made a resolution of total abstinence; and that I have adhered to it through all time I owe to my mother."

I never saw anything so curious. It is almost an exact epitome of my own moral career—after simply substituting a grandmother for a mother. How well I remember my grandmother's asking me not to use tobacco, good old soul! She said, "You're at it again, are you, you whelp? Now don't ever let me catch you chewing tobacco before breakfast again, or I lay I'll blacksnake you within an inch of your life!" I have never touched it at that hour of the morning from that time to the present day.

She asked me not to gamble. She whispered and said, "Put up those wicked cards this minute!—two pair and a jack, you numskull, and the other fellow's got a flush!"

I never have gambled from that day to this—never once—without a "cold deck" in my pocket. I cannot even tell who is going to lose in games that are being played unless I deal myself.

When I was two years of age she asked me not to drink, and then I made a resolution of total abstinence. That I have adhered to it and enjoyed the beneficent effects of it through all time, I owe to my grandmother. I have never drunk a drop from that day to this of any kind of water.

1870

John Chinaman in New York

As I passed along by one of those monster American tea stores in New York, I found a Chinaman sitting before it acting in the capacity of a sign. Everybody that passed by gave him a steady stare as long as their heads would twist over their shoulders without dislocating their necks, and a group had stopped to stare deliberately.

Is it not a shame that we, who prate so much about civilization and humanity, are content to degrade a fellow-being to such an office as this? Is it not time for reflection when we find ourselves willing to see in such a being matter for frivolous curiosity instead of regret and grave reflection? Here was a poor creature whom hard fortune had exiled from his natural home beyond the seas, and whose troubles ought to have touched these idle strangers that thronged about him; but did it? Apparently not. Men calling themselves the superior race, the race of culture and of gentle blood, scanned his quaint Chinese hat, with peaked roof and ball on top, and his long queue dangling down his back; his short silken blouse, curiously frogged and figured (and, like the rest of his raiment, rusty, dilapidated, and awkwardly put on); his blue cotton, tight-legged pants, tied close around the ankles; and his clumsy blunt-toed shoes with thick cork soles; and having so scanned him from head to foot, cracked some unseemly joke about his outlandish attire or his melancholy face, and passed on. In my heart I pitied the friendless Mongol. I wondered what was passing behind his sad face, and what distant scene his vacant eye was dreaming of. Were his thoughts with his heart, ten thousand miles away, beyond the billowy wastes of the Pacific? among the rice-fields and the plumy palms of China? under the shadows of remembered mountain peaks, or in groves of bloomy shrubs and strange forest trees unknown to climes like ours? And now and then, rippling among his visions and his dreams, did he hear familiar laughter and half-forgotten voices, and did he catch fitful glimpses of the friendly faces of a bygone time? A cruel fate it is, I said, that is befallen this bronzed wanderer. In order that the group of idlers might be touched at least by the words of the poor fellow, since the appeal of his pauper dress and his dreary exile was lost upon them, I touched him on the shoulder and said:

"Cheer up—don't be downhearted. It is not America that treats you in this way, it is merely one citizen, whose greed of gain has eaten the humanity out of his heart. America has a broader hospitality for the exiled and oppressed. America and Americans are always ready to help the unfortunate. Money shall be raised—you shall go back to China—you shall see your friends again. What wages do they pay you here?"

"Divil a cint but four dollars a week and find meself; but it's aisy, barrin' the troublesome furrin clothes that's so expinsive."

The exile remains at his post. The New York tea merchants who need picturesque signs are not likely to run out of Chinamen.

1870

The Judge's "Spirited Woman"

"I was sitting here," said the judge, "in this old pulpit, holding court, and we were trying a big, wicked-looking Spanish desperado for killing the husband of a bright, pretty Mexican woman. It was a lazy summer day, and an awfully long one, and the witnesses were tedious. None of us took any interest in the trial except that nervous, uneasy devil of a Mexican woman—because you know how they love and how they hate, and this one had loved her husband with all her might, and now she had boiled it all down into hate, and stood here spitting it at that Spaniard with her eyes; and I tell you she would stir *me* up, too, with a little of her summer lightning, occasionally. Well, I had my coat off and my heels up, lolling and sweating, and smoking one of those cabbage cigars the San Francisco people used to think were good enough for us in those times; and the lawyers they all had their coats off, and were smoking and whittling, and the witnesses the same, and so was the prisoner. Well, the fact is, there warn't any interest in a murder trial then, because the fellow was always brought in 'not guilty,' the jury expecting him to do as much for them some time; and, although the evidence was straight and square against this Spaniard, we knew we could not convict him without seeming to be rather high-handed and sort of reflecting on every gentleman in the community; for there warn't any carriages and liveries then, and so the only 'style' there was, was to keep your private graveyard. But that woman seemed to have her heart set on hanging that Spaniard; and you'd ought to have seen how she would glare on him a minute, and then look up at me in her pleading way, and then turn and for the next five minutes search the jury's faces, and by and by drop her face in her hands for just a little while as if she was most ready to give up; but out she'd come again directly, and be as live and anxious as ever. But when the jury announced the verdict—Not Guilty—and I told the prisoner he was acquitted and free to go, that woman rose up till she appeared to be as tall and grand as a seventy-four-gun ship, and says she:

"'Judge, do I understand you to say that this man is not guilty that murdered my husband without any cause before my own eyes

and my little children's, and that all has been done to him that ever
justice and the law can do?'

"'The same,' says I.

"And then what do you reckon she did? Why, she turned on that
smirking Spanish fool like a wildcat, and out with a 'navy' and shot
him dead in open court!"

"That *was* spirited, I am willing to admit."

"Wasn't it, though?" said the judge admiringly. "I wouldn't have
missed it for anything. I adjourned court right on the spot, and we
put on our coats and went out and took up a collection for her and
her cubs, and sent them over the mountains to their friends. Ah, she
was a spirited wench!"

1870

The Late Benjamin Franklin

["Never put off till to-morrow what you can do day after to-morrow just
as well."—B. F.]

This party was one of those persons whom they call Philosophers.
He was twins, being born simultaneously in two different houses in
the city of Boston. These houses remain unto this day, and have signs
upon them worded in accordance with the facts. The signs are considered well enough to have, though not necessary, because the inhabitants point out the two birthplaces to the stranger anyhow, and
sometimes as often as several times in the same day. The subject of
this memoir was of a vicious disposition, and early prostituted his
talents to the invention of maxims and aphorisms calculated to inflict
suffering upon the rising generation of all subsequent ages. His simplest acts, also, were contrived with a view to their being held up
for the emulation of boys forever—boys who might otherwise have
been happy. It was in this spirit that he became the son of a soap-
boiler, and probably for no other reason than that the efforts of all
future boys who tried to be anything might be looked upon with
suspicion unless they were the sons of soap-boilers. With a malevolence

which is without parallel in history, he would work all day, and then sit up nights, and let on to be studying algebra by the light of a smoldering fire, so that all other boys might have to do that also, or else have Benjamin Franklin thrown up to them. Not satisfied with these proceedings, he had a fashion of living wholly on bread and water, and studying astronomy at meal-time—a thing which has brought affliction to millions of boys since, whose fathers had read Franklin's pernicious biography.

His maxims were full of animosity toward boys. Nowadays a boy cannot follow out a single natural instinct without tumbling over some of those everlasting aphorisms and hearing from Franklin on the spot. If he buys two cents' worth of peanuts, his father says, "Remember what Franklin has said, my son—'A groat a day's a penny a year'"; and the comfort is all gone out of those peanuts. If he wants to spin his top when he has done work, his father quotes, "Procrastination is the thief of time." If he does a virtuous action, he never gets anything for it, because "Virtue is its own reward." And that boy is hounded to death and robbed of his natural rest, because Franklin said once, in one of his inspired flights of malignity:

> Early to bed and early to rise
> Makes a man healthy and wealthy and wise.

As if it were any object to a boy to be healthy and wealthy and wise on such terms. The sorrow that that maxim has cost me, through my parents, experimenting on me with it, tongue cannot tell. The legitimate result is my present state of general debility, indigence, and mental aberration. My parents used to have me up before nine o'clock in the morning sometimes when I was a boy. If they had let me take my natural rest where would I have been now? Keeping store, no doubt, and respected by all.

And what an adroit old adventurer the subject of this memoir was! In order to get a chance to fly his kite on Sunday he used to hang a key on the string and let on to be fishing for lightning. And a guileless public would go home chirping about the "wisdom" and the "genius" of the hoary Sabbath-breaker. If anybody caught him playing "mumble-peg" by himself, after the age of sixty, he would immediately appear to be ciphering out how the grass grew—as if it was any of his business. My grandfather knew him well, and he says Franklin was always fixed—always ready. If a body, during his old age, happened on him unexpectedly when he was catching flies, or making mud-pies, or sliding on a cellar door, he would immediately look wise, and rip out a maxim, and walk off with his nose in the air and his cap turned wrong side before, trying to appear absent-minded and eccentric. He was a hard lot.

He invented a stove that would smoke your head off in four hours by the clock. One can see the almost devilish satisfaction he took in it by his giving it his name.

He was always proud of telling how he entered Philadelphia for the first time, with nothing in the world but two shillings in his pocket and four rolls of bread under his arm. But really, when you come to examine it critically, it was nothing. Anybody could have done it.

To the subject of this memoir belongs the honor of recommending the army to go back to bows and arrows in place of bayonets and muskets. He observed, with his customary force, that the bayonet was very well under some circumstances, but that he doubted whether it could be used with accuracy at a long range.

Benjamin Franklin did a great many notable things for his country, and made her young name to be honored in many lands as the mother of such a son. It is not the idea of this memoir to ignore that or cover it up. No; the simple idea of it is to snub those pretentious maxims of his, which he worked up with a great show of originality out of truisms that had become wearisome platitudes as early as the dispersion from Babel; and also to snub his stove, and his military inspirations, his unseemly endeavor to make himself conspicuous when he entered Philadelphia, and his flying his kite and fooling away his time in all sorts of such ways when he ought to have been foraging for soap-fat, or constructing candles. I merely desired to do away with somewhat of the prevalent calamitous idea among heads of families that Franklin *acquired* his great genius by working for nothing, studying by moonlight, and getting up in the night instead of waiting till morning like a Christian; and that this program, rigidly inflicted, will make a Franklin of every father's fool. It is time these gentlemen were finding out that these execrable eccentricities of instinct and conduct are only the *evidences* of genius, not the *creators* of it. I wish I had been the father of my parents long enough to make them comprehend this truth, and thus prepare them to let their son have an easier time of it. When I was a child I had to boil soap, notwithstanding my father was wealthy, and I had to get up early and study geometry at breakfast, and peddle my own poetry, and do everything just as Franklin did, in the solemn hope that I would be a Franklin some day. And here I am.

1870

Map of Paris

The accompanying map explains itself.

The idea of this map is not original with me, but is borrowed from the great metropolitan journals.

I claim no other merit for this production (if I may so call it) than that it is accurate. The main blemish of the city paper maps, of which it is an imitation, is that in them more attention seems paid to artistic picturesqueness than geographical reliability.

Inasmuch as this is the first time I ever tried to draft and engrave a map, or attempted anything in any line of art, the commendations the work has received and the admiration it has excited among the people have been very grateful to my feelings. And it is touching to reflect that by far the most enthusiastic of these praises have come from people who knew nothing at all about art.

By an unimportant oversight I have engraved the map so that it reads wrong end first, except to left-handed people. I forgot that in order to make it right in print, it should be drawn and engraved upside down. However, let the student who desires to contemplate the map stand on his head or hold it before a looking-glass. That will bring it right.

The reader will comprehend at a glance that that piece of river with the "High Bridge" over it got left out to one side by reason of a slip of the graving-tool, which rendered it necessary to change the entire course of the River Rhine, or else spoil the map. After having spent two days in digging and gouging at the map, I would have changed the course of the Atlantic Ocean before I would lose so much work.

I never had so much trouble with anything in my life as I had with this map. I had heaps of little fortifications scattered all around Paris at first, but every now and then my instruments would slip and fetch away whole miles of batteries, and leave the vicinity as clean as if the Prussians had been there.

The reader will find it well to frame this map for future reference, so that it may aid in extending popular intelligence and in dispelling the wide-spread ignorance of the day.   MARK TWAIN

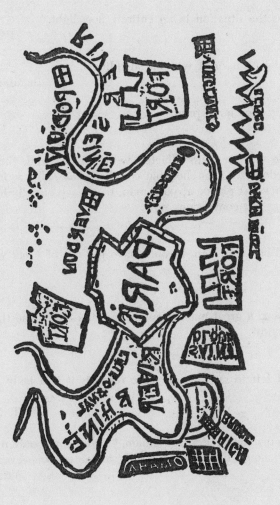

OFFICIAL COMMENDATIONS

It is the only map of the kind I ever saw.

U. S. GRANT

It places the situation in an entirely new light.

BISMARCK

I cannot look upon it without shedding tears.

BRIGHAM YOUNG

It is very nice large print.

NAPOLEON

My wife was for years afflicted with freckles, and, though everything was done for her relief that could be done, all was in vain. But, sir, since her first glance at your map, they have entirely left her. She has nothing but convulsions now.

J. SMITH

If I had had this map, I could have got out of Metz without any trouble.

BAZAINE

I have seen a great many maps in my time, but none that this one reminds me of.

TROCHU

It is but fair to say that in some respects it is a truly remarkable map.

W. T. SHERMAN

I said to my son Frederick William, "If you could only make a map like that, I should be perfectly willing to see you die—even anxious."

WILLIAM III

1870

My Bloody Massacre*

The other burlesque I have referred to was my fine satire upon the financial expedients of "cooking dividends," a thing which became shamefully frequent on the Pacific coast for a while. Once more, in my self-complacent simplicity I felt that the time had arrived for me to rise up and be a reformer. I put this reformatory satire in the shape of a fearful "Massacre at Empire City." The San Francisco papers were making a great outcry about the iniquity of the Daney Silver-Mining Company, whose directors had declared a "cooked" or false divident, for the purpose of increasing the value of their stock, so that they could sell out at a comfortable figure, and then scramble from under the tumbling concern. And while abusing the Daney, those papers did not forget to urge the public to get rid of all their silver stocks and invest in sound and safe San Francisco stocks, such as the Spring Valley Water Company, etc. But right at this unfortunate juncture, behold the Spring Valley cooked a dividend too! And so, under the insidious mask of an invented "bloody massacre," I stole upon the public unawares with my scathing satire upon the dividend-cooking system. In about half a column of imaginary human carnage I told how a citizen had murdered his wife and nine children, and then committed suicide. And I said slyly, at the bottom, that the sudden madness of which this melancholy massacre was the result had been brought about by his having allowed himself to be persuaded by the California papers to sell his sound and lucrative Nevada silver stocks, and buy into Spring Valley just in time to get cooked along with that company's fancy dividend, and sink every cent he had in the world.

Ah, it was a deep, deep satire, and most ingeniously contrived. But I made the horrible details so carefully and conscientiously interesting that the public devoured *them* greedily, and wholly overlooked the following distinctly stated facts, to wit: The murderer was perfectly well known to every creature in the land as a *bachelor*, and consequently he could not murder his wife and nine children; he murdered them "in his splendid dressed-stone mansion just in the edge of the

* See appendix for original hoax.—C.N.

great pine forest between Empire City and Dutch Nick's," when even the very pickled oysters that came on our tables knew that there was not a "dressed-stone mansion" in all Nevada Territory; also that, so far from there being a "great pine forest between Empire City and Dutch Nick's," there wasn't a solitary tree within fifteen miles of either place; and, finally, it was patent and notorious that Empire City and Dutch Nick's were one and the same place, and contained only six houses anyhow, and consequently there could be no forest *between* them; and on top of all these absurdities I stated that this diabolical murderer, after inflicting a wound upon himself that the reader ought to have seen would kill an elephant in the twinkling of an eye, jumped on his horse and rode *four miles,* waving his wife's reeking scalp in the air, and thus performing entered Carson City with tremendous *éclat,* and dropped dead in front of the chief saloon, the envy and admiration of all beholders.

Well, in all my life I never saw anything like the sensation that little satire created. It was the talk of the town, it was the talk of the territory. Most of the citizens dropped gently into it at breakfast, and they never finished their meal. There was something about those minutely faithful details that was a sufficing substitute for food. Few people that were able to read took food that morning. Dan and I (Dan was my reportorial associate) took our seats on either side of our customary table in the "Eagle Restaurant," and, as I unfolded the shred they used to call a napkin in that establishment, I saw at the next table two stalwart innocents with that sort of vegetable dandruff sprinkled about their clothing which was the sign and evidence that they were in from the Truckee with a load of hay. The one facing me had the morning paper folded to a long, narrow strip, and I knew, without any telling, that that strip represented the column that contained my pleasant financial satire. From the way he was excitedly mumbling, I saw that the heedless son of a hay-mow was skipping with all his might, in order to get to the bloody details as quickly as possible; and so he was missing the guide-boards I had set up to warn him that the whole thing was a fraud. Presently his eyes spread wide open, just as his jaws swung asunder to take in a potato approaching it on a fork; the potato halted, the face lit up redly, and the whole man was on fire with excitement. Then he broke into a disjointed checking off of the particulars—his potato cooling in mid-air meantime, and his mouth making a reach for it occasionally, but always bringing up suddenly against a new and still more direful performance of my hero. At last he looked his stunned and rigid comrade impressively in the face, and said, with an expression of concentrated awe:

"Jim, he b'iled his baby, and he took the old 'oman's skelp. Cuss'd if *I* want any breakfast!"

And he laid his lingering potato reverently down, and he and his friend departed from the restaurant empty but satisfied.

He *never got down* to where the satire part of it began. Nobody ever did. They found the thrilling particulars sufficient. To drop in with a poor little moral at the fag-end of such a gorgeous massacre was like following the expiring sun with a candle and hope to attract the world's attention to it.

The idea that anybody could ever take my massacre for a genuine occurrence never once suggested itself to me, hedged about as it was by all those telltale absurdities and impossibilities concerning the "great pine forest," the "dressed-stone mansion," etc. But I found out then, and never have forgotten since, that we never *read* the dull explanatory surroundings of marvelously exciting things when we have no occasion to suppose that some irresponsible scribler is trying to defraud us; we skip all that, and hasten to revel in the blood-curdling particulars and be happy.

1870

A Mysterious Visit

The first notice that was taken of me when I "settled down" recently was by a gentleman who said he was an assessor, and connected with the U. S. Internal Revenue Department. I said I had never heard of his branch of business before, but I was very glad to see him all the same. Would he sit down? He sat down. I did not know anything particular to say, and yet I felt that people who have arrived at the dignity of keeping house must be conversational, must be easy and sociable in company. So, in default of anything else to say, I asked him if he was opening his shop in our neighborhood.

He said he was. [I did not wish to appear ignorant, but I *had* hoped he would mention what he had for sale.]

I ventured to ask him "How was trade?" And he said "So-so."

I then said we would drop in, and if we liked his house as well as any other, we would give him our custom.

He said he thought we would like his establishment well enough to confine ourselves to it—said he never saw anybody who would go off and hunt up another man in his line after trading with him once.

That sounded pretty complacent, but barring that natural expression of villainy which we all have, the man looked honest enough.

I do not know how it came about exactly, but gradually we appeared to melt down and run together, conversationally speaking, and then everything went along as comfortably as clockwork.

We talked, and talked, and talked—at least I did; and we laughed, and laughed, and laughed—at least he did. But all the time I had my presence of mind about me—I had my native shrewdness turned on "full head," as the engineers say. I was determined to find out all about his business in spite of his obscure answers—and I was determined I would have it out of him without his suspecting what I was at. I meant to trap him with a deep, deep ruse. I would tell him all about my own business, and he would naturally so warm to me during this seductive burst of confidence that he would forget himself, and tell me all about *his* affairs before he suspected what I was about. I thought to myself, My son, you little know what an old fox you are dealing with. I said:

"Now you never would guess what I made lecturing this winter and last spring?"

"No—don't believe I could, to save me. Let me see—let me see. About two thousand dollars, maybe? But no; no, sir, I know you couldn't have made that much. Say seventeen hundred, maybe?"

"Ha! ha! I knew you couldn't. My lecturing receipts for last spring and this winter were fourteen thousand seven hundred and fifty dollars. What do you think of that?"

"Why, it is amazing—perfectly amazing. I will make a note of it. And you say even this wasn't all?"

"All! Why bless you, there was my income from the *Daily Warwhoop* for four months—about—about—well, what should you say to about eight thousand dollars, for instance?"

"Say! Why, I should say I should like to see myself rolling in just such another ocean of affluence. Eight thousand! I'll make a note of it. Why man!—and on top of all this am I to understand that you had still more income?"

"Ha! ha! ha! Why, you're only in the suburbs of it, so to speak.

There's my book, *The Innocents Abroad*—price $3.50 to $5, according to the binding. Listen to me. Look me in the eye. During the last four months and a half, saying nothing of sales before that, but just simply during the four months and a half, we've sold ninety-five thousand copies of that book. Ninety-five thousand! Think of it. Average four dollars a copy, say. It's nearly four hundred thousand dollars, my son. I get half."

"The suffering Moses! I'll set *that* down. Fourteen-seven-fifty—eight—two hundred. Total, say—well, upon my word, the grand total is about two hundred and thirteen or fourteen thousand dollars! *Is* that possible?"

"Possible! If there's any mistake it's the other way. Two hundred and fourteen thousand, cash, is my income for this year if *I* know how to cipher."

Then the gentleman got up to go. It came over me most uncomfortably that maybe I had made my revelations for nothing, besides being flattered into stretching them considerably by the stranger's astonished exclamations. But no; at the last moment the gentleman handed me a large envelope, and said it contained his advertisement; and that I would find out all about his business in it; and that he would be happy to have my custom—would, in fact, be *proud* to have the custom of a man of such prodigious income; and that he used to think there were several wealthy men in the city, but when they came to trade with him he discovered that they barely had enough to live on; and that, in truth, it had been such a weary, weary age since he had seen a rich man face to face, and talked to him, and touched him with his hands, that he could hardly refrain from embracing me—in fact, would esteem it a great favor if I would *let* him embrace me.

This so pleased me that I did not try to resist, but allowed this simple-hearted stranger to throw his arms about me and weep a few tranquilizing tears down the back of my neck. Then he went his way.

As soon as he was gone I opened his advertisement. I studied it attentively for four minutes. I then called up the cook, and said:

"Hold me while I faint! Let Marie turn the griddle-cakes."

By and by, when I came to, I sent down to the rum-mill on the corner and hired an artist by the week to sit up nights and curse that stranger, and give me a lift occasionally in the daytime when I came to a hard place.

Ah, what a miscreant he was! His "advertisement" was nothing in the world but a wicked tax-return—a string of impertinent questions about

my private affairs, occupying the best part of four foolscap pages of
fine print—questions, I may remark, gotten up with such marvelous
ingenuity that the oldest man in the world couldn't understand what
the most of them were driving at—questions, too, that were calculated
to make a man report about four times his actual income to keep from
swearing to a falsehood. I looked for a loophole, but there did not
appear to be any. Inquiry No. 1 covered my case as generously and
as amply as an umbrella could cover an ant-hill:

What were your profits, during the past year, from any trade, business,
or vocation, wherever carried on?

And that inquiry was backed up by thirteen others of an equally
searching nature, the most modest of which required information as
to whether I had committed any burglary or highway robbery, or by
any arson or other secret source of emolument had acquired property
which was not enumerated in my statement of income as set opposite
to inquiry No. 1.

It was plain that that stranger had enabled me to make a goose of
myself. It was very, very plain; and so I went out and hired another
artist. By working on my vanity, the stranger had seduced me into
declaring an income of two hundred and fourteen thousand dollars.
By law, one thousand dollars of this was exempt from income tax—
the only relief I could see, and it was only a drop in the ocean. At the
legal five per cent., I must pay to the government the sum of ten
thousand six hundred and fifty dollars, income tax!

[I may remark, in this place, that I did not do it.]

I am acquainted with a very opulent man, whose house is a palace,
whose table is regal, whose outlays are enormous, yet a man who has
no income, as I have often noticed by the revenue returns; and to
him I went for advice in my distress. He took my dreadful exhibition of
receipts, he put on his glasses, he took his pen, and presto!—I was a
pauper! It was the neatest thing that ever was. He did it simply
by deftly manipulating the bill of "DEDUCTIONS." He set down my
"State, national, and municipal taxes" at so much; my "losses by shipwreck, fire, etc.," at so much; my "losses on sales of real estate"—on
"live stock sold"—on "payments for rent of homestead"—on "repairs,
improvements, interest"—on "previously taxed salary an as officer of the
United States army, navy, revenue service," and other things. He got
astonishing "deductions" out of each and every one of these matters
—each and every one of them. And when he was done he handed me
the paper, and I saw at a glance that during the year my income, in

the way of profits, had been *one thousand two hundred and fifty dollars and forty cents*.

"Now," said he, "the thousand dollars is exempt by law. What you want to do is to go and swear this document in and pay tax on the two hundred and fifty dollars."

[While he was making this speech his little boy Willie lifted a two-dollar greenback out of his vest pocket and vanished with it, and I would wager anything that if my stranger were to call on that little boy to-morrow he would make a false return of his income.]

"Do you," said I, "do you always work up the 'deductions' after this fashion in your own case, sir?"

Well, I should say so! If it weren't for those eleven saving clauses under the head of 'Deductions' I should be beggared every year to support this hateful and wicked, this extortionate and tyrannical government."

This gentleman stands away up among the very best of the solid men of the city—the men of moral weight, of commercial integrity, of unimpeachable social spotlessness—and so I bowed to his example. I went down to the revenue office, and under the accusing eyes of my old visitor I stood up and swore to lie after lie, fraud after fraud, villainy after villainy, till my soul was coated inches and inches thick with perjury, and my self-respect gone for ever and ever.

But what of it? It is nothing more than thousands of the richest and proudest, and most respected, honored, and courted men in America do every year. And so I don't care. I am not ashamed. I shall simply, for the present, talk little and eschew fire-proof gloves, lest I fall into certain dreadful habits irrevocably.

1870

Note on "The Petrified Man"*

Now, to show how really hard it is to foist a moral or a truth upon an unsuspecting public through a burlesque without entirely and absurdly missing one's mark, I will here set down two experiences of

* See appendix for the original hoax.—C.N.

my own in this thing. In the fall of 1862, in Nevada and California, the people got to running wild about extraordinary petrifactions and other natural marvels. One could scarcely pick up a paper without finding in it one or two glorified discoveries of this kind. The mania was becoming a little ridiculous. I was a brand-new local editor in Virginia City, and I felt called upon to destroy this growing evil; we all have our benignant, fatherly moods at one time or another, I suppose. I chose to kill the petrifaction mania with a delicate, a very delicate satire. But maybe it was altogether too delicate, for nobody ever preceived the satire part of it at all. I put my scheme in the shape of the discovery of a remarkably petrified man.

I had had a temporary falling out with Mr. ——, the new coroner and justice of the peace of Humboldt, and thought I might as well touch him up a little at the same time and make him ridiculous, and thus combine pleasure with business. So I told, in patient, belief-compelling detail, all about the finding of a petrified man at Gravelly Ford (exactly a hundred and twenty miles, over a breakneck mountain trail from where —— lived); how all the savants of the immediate neighborhood had been to examine it (it was notorious that there was not a living creature within fifty miles of there, except a few starving Indians, some crippled grasshoppers, and four or five buzzards out of meat and too feeble to get away); how those savants all pronounced the petrified man to have been in a state of complete petrifaction for over ten generations; and then, with a seriousness that I ought to have been ashamed to assume, I stated that as soon as Mr. —— heard the news he summoned a jury, mounted his mule, and posted off, with noble reverence for official duty, on that awful five days' journey, through alkali, sagebrush, peril of body, and imminent starvation, to *hold an inquest* on this man that had been dead and turned to everlasting stone for more than three hundred years! And then, my hand being "in," so to speak, I went on, with the same unflinching gravity, to state that the jury returned a verdict that deceased came to his death from *protracted exposure*. This only moved me to higher flights of imagination, and I said that the jury, with that charity so characteristic of pioneers, then dug a grave, and were about to give the petrified man Christian burial, when they found that for ages a limestone sediment had been trickling down the face of the stone against which he was sitting, and this stuff had run under him and cemented him fast to the "bed-rock"; that the jury (they were all silver-miners) canvassed the difficulty a moment, and then got out their powder and fuse, and proceeded to drill a hole under him, in order to *blast*

him from his position, when Mr. ——, "with that delicacy so characteristic of him, forbade them, observing that it would be little less
than sacrilege to do such a thing."

From beginning to end the "Petrified Man" squib was a string of
roaring absurdities, albeit they were told with an unfair pretense of
truth that even imposed upon me to some extent, and I was in some
danger of believing in my own fraud. But I really had no desire to
deceive anybody, and no expectation of doing it. I depended on the
way the petrified man was *sitting* to explain to the public that he was
a swindle. Yet I purposely mixed that up with other things, hoping to
make it obscure—and I did. I would describe the position of one foot,
and then say his right thumb was against the side of his nose; then talk
about his other foot, and presently come back and say the fingers of
his right hand were spread apart; then talk about the back of his
head a little, and return and say the left thumb was hooked into the
right little finger; then ramble off about something else, and by and by
drift back again and remark that the fingers of the left hand were
spread like those of the right. But I was too ingenious. I mixed it up
rather too much; and so all that description of the attitude, as a key to
the humbuggery of the article, was entirely lost, for nobody but me
ever discovered and comprehended the peculiar and suggestive position
of the petrified man's hands.

As a *satire* on the petrifaction mania, or anything else, my Petrified
Man was a disheartening failure; for everybody received him in innocent good faith, and I was stunned to see the creature I had begotten to pull down the wonder-business with, and bring derision upon it,
calmly exalted to the grand chief place in the list of the genuine marvels our Nevada had produced. I was so disappointed at the curious
miscarriage of my scheme, that at first I was angry, and did not like
to think about it; but by and by, when the exchanges began to come in
with the Petrified Man copied and guilelessly glorified, I began to
feel a soothing secret satisfaction; and as my gentleman's field of
travels broadened, and by the exchanges I saw that he steadily and
implacably penetrated territory after territory, state after state, and
land after land, till he swept the great globe and culminated in sublime and unimpeached legitimacy in the august London *Lancet,* my
cup was full, and I said I was glad I had done it. I think that for about
eleven months, as nearly as I can remember, Mr. ——'s daily mail-bag
continued to be swollen by the addition of half a bushel of newspapers hailing from many climes with the Petrified Man in them,
marked around with a prominent belt of ink. I sent them to him. I did

it for spite, not for fun. He used to shovel them into his back yard and curse. And every day during all those months the miners, his constituents (for miners never quit joking a person when they get started), would call on him and ask if he could tell them where they could get hold of a paper with the Petrified Man in it. He could have accommodated a continent with them. I hated —— in those days, and these things pacified me and pleased me. I could not have gotten more real comfort out of him without killing him.

1870

Post-Mortem Poetry

In Philadelphia they have a custom which it would be pleasant to see adopted throughout the land. It is that of appending to published death-notices a little verse or two of comforting poetry. Any one who is in the habit of reading the daily Philadelphia *Ledger* must frequently be touched by these plaintive tributes to extinguished worth. In Philadelphia, the departure of a child is a circumstance which is not more surely followed by a burial than by the accustomed solacing poesy in the *Public Ledger*. In that city death loses half its terror because the knowledge of its presence comes thus disguised in the sweet drapery of verse. For instance, in a late *Ledger* I find the following (I change the surname):

DIED

HAWKS.—On the 17th inst., Clara, the daughter of Ephraim and Laura Hawks, aged 21 months and 2 days.

> That merry shout no more I hear,
>   No laughing child I see,
> No little arms are round my neck,
>   No feet upon my knee;
>
> No kisses drop upon my cheek,
>   These lips are sealed to me.
> Dear Lord, how could I give Clara up
>   To any but to Thee?

A child thus mourned could not die wholly discontented. From the *Ledger* of the same date I make the following extract, merely changing the surname, as before:

BECKET.—On Sunday morning, 19th inst., John P., infant son of George and Julia Becket, aged 1 year, 6 months, and 15 days.

> That merry shout no more I hear,
>   No laughing child I see,
> No little arms are round my neck,
>   No feet upon my knee;
>
> No kisses drop upon my cheek,
>   These lips are sealed to me.
> Dear Lord, how could I give Johnnie up
>   To any but to Thee?

The similarity of the emotions as produced in the mourners in these two instances is remarkably evidenced by the singular similarity of thought which they experienced, and the surprising coincidence of language used by them to give it expression.

In the same journal, of the same date, I find the following (surname suppressed, as before):

WAGNER.—On the 10th inst., Ferguson G., the son of William L. and Martha Theresa Wagner, aged 4 weeks and 1 day.

> That merry shout no more I hear,
>   No laughing child I see,
> No little arms are round my neck,
>   No feet upon my knee;
>
> No kisses drop upon my cheek,
>   These lips are sealed to me.
> Dear Lord, how could I give Ferguson up
>   To any but to Thee?

It is strange what power the reiteration of an essentially poetical thought has upon one's feelings. When we take up the *Ledger* and read the poetry about little Clara, we feel an unaccountable depression of the spirits. When we drift further down the column and read the poetry about little Johnnie, the depression of spirits acquires an added emphasis, and we experience tangible suffering. When we saunter along down the column further still and read the poetry about little Ferguson, the word torture but vaguely suggests the anguish that rends us.

In the *Ledger* (same copy referred to above) I find the following (I alter surname, as usual):

WELCH.—On the 5th inst., Mary C. Welch, wife of William B. Welch, and daughter of Catharine and George W. Markland, in the 29th year of her age.

> A mother dear, a mother kind,
> Has gone and left us all behind.
> Cease to weep, for tears are vain,
> Mother dear is out of pain.
>
> Farewell, husband, children dear,
> Serve thy God with filial fear,
> And meet me in the land above,
> Where all is peace, and joy, and love.

What could be sweeter than that? No collection of salient facts (without reduction to tabular form) could be more succinctly stated than is done in the first stanza by the surviving relatives, and no more concise and comprehensive program of farewells, post-mortuary general orders, etc., could be framed in any form than is done in verse by deceased in the last stanza. These things insensibly make us wiser and tenderer, and better. Another extract:

BALL.—On the morning of the 15th inst., Mary E., daughter of John and Sarah F. Ball.

> 'Tis sweet to rest in lively hope
> That when my change shall come
> Angels will hover round my bed,
> To waft my spirit home.

The following is apparently the customary form for heads of families:

BURNS.—On the 20th inst., Michael Burns, aged 40 years.

> Dearest father, thou hast left us,
> Here thy loss we deeply feel;
> But 'tis God that has bereft us,
> He can all our sorrows heal.

Funeral at 2 o'clock sharp.

There is something very simple and pleasant about the following, which, in Philadelphia, seems to be the usual form for consumptives of long standing. (It deplores four distinct cases in the single copy of the *Ledger* which lies on the Memoranda editorial table):

BROMLEY.—On the 29th inst., of consumption, Philip Bromley, in the 50th year of his age.

> Affliction sore long time he bore,
>   Physicians were in vain—
> Till God at last did hear him mourn,
>   And eased him of his pain.
>
> The friend whom death from us has torn,
>   We did not think so soon to part;
> An anxious care now sinks the thorn
>   Still deeper in our bleeding heart.

This beautiful creation loses nothing by repetition. On the contrary, the oftener one sees it in the *Ledger*, the more grand and awe-inspiring it seems.

With one more extract I will close:

DOBLE.—On the 4th inst., Samuel Peveril Worthington Doble, aged 4 days.

> Our little Sammy's gone,
>   His tiny spirit's fled;
> Our little boy we loved so dear
>   Lies sleeping with the dead,
>
> A tear within a father's eye,
>   A mother's aching heart,
> Can only tell the agony
>   How hard it is to part.

Could anything be more plaintive than that, without requiring further concessions of grammar? Could anything be likely to do more toward reconciling deceased to circumstances, and making him willing to go? Perhaps not. The power of song can hardly be estimated. There is an element about some poetry which is able to make even physical suffering and death cheerful things to contemplate and consummations to be desired. This element is present in the mortuary poetry of Philadelphia degree of development.

The custom I have been treating of is one that should be adopted in all the cities of the land.

It is said that once a man of small consequence died, and the Rev. T. K. Beecher was asked to preach the funeral sermon—a man who abhors the lauding of people, either dead or alive, except in dignified and simple language, and then only for merits which they actually possessed or possess, not merits which they merely ought to have possessed. The friends of the deceased got up a stately funeral. They must have had misgivings that the corpse might not be praised strongly enough, for they prepared some manuscript headings and notes in which nothing was left unsaid on that subject that a fervid imagination and an unabridged dictionary could compile, and these they handed to the minister as he entered the pulpit. They were merely intended as suggestions, and so the friends were filled with consternation when the minister stood up in the pulpit and proceeded to read off the curious odds and ends in ghastly detail and in a loud voice! And their consternation solidified to petrification when he paused at the end, contemplated the multitude reflectively, and then said, impressively:

"The man would be a fool who tried to add anything to that. Let us pray!"

And with the some strict adhesion to truth it can be said that the man would be a fool who tried to add anything to the following transcendent obituary poem. There is something so innocent, so guileless, so complacent, so unearthly serene and self-satisfied about this peerless "hog-wash," that the man must be made of stone who can read it without a dulcet ecstasy creeping along his backbone and quivering in his marrow. There is no need to say that this poem is genuine and in earnest, for its proofs are written all over its face. An ingenious scribbler might imitate it after a fashion, but Shakespeare himself could not counterfeit it. It is noticeable that the country editor who published it did not know that it was a treasure and the most perfect thing of its kind that the storehouses and museums of literature could show. He did not dare to say no to the dread poet—for such a poet must have been something of an apparition—but he just shoveled it into his paper anywhere that came handy, and felt ashamed, and put that disgusted "Published by Request" over it, and hoped that his subscribers would overlook it or not feel an impulse to read it:

(*Published by request*)

LINES

Composed on the death of Samuel and Catharine Belknap's children

BY M. A. GLAZE

> Friends and neighbors all draw near,
>   And listen to what I have to say;
> And never leave your children dear
>   When they are small, and go away.

But always think of that sad fate,
   That happened in year of '63;
Four children with a house did burn,
   Think of their awful agony.

Their mother she had gone away,
   And left them there alone to stay;
The house took fire and down did burn,
   Before their mother did return.

Their piteous cry the neighbors heard,
   And then the cry of fire was given;
But, ah! before they could them reach,
   Their little spirits had flown to heaven.

Their father he to war had gone,
   And on the battle-field was slain;
But little did he think when he went away,
   But what on earth they would meet again.

The neighbors often told his wife
   Not to leave his children there,
Unless she got someone to stay,
   And of the little ones take care.

The oldest he was years not six,
   And the youngest only eleven months old,
But often she had left them there alone,
   As, by the neighbors, I have been told.

How can she bear to see the place.
   Where she so oft has left them there,
Without a single one to look to them,
   Or of the little ones to take good care.

Oh, can she look upon the spot,
   Whereunder their little burnt bones lay,
But what she thinks she hears them say,
   'Twas God had pity, and took us on high.'

And there may she kneel down and pray,
   And ask God her to forgive;
And she may lead a different life
   While she on earth remains to live.

Her husband and her children too,
   God has took from pain and woe.
May she reform and mend her ways,
   That she may also to them go.

And when it is God's holy will,
    O, may she be prepared
To meet her God and friends in peace,
    And leave this world of care.

1870

Riley — Newspaper Correspondent

One of the best men in Washington—or elsewhere—is RILEY, correspondent of one of the great San Francisco dailies.

Riley is full of humor, and has an unfailing vein of irony, which
makes his conversation to the last degree entertaining (as long as
the remarks are about somebody else). But notwithstanding the
possession of these qualities, which should enable a man to write a
happy and an appetizing letter, Riley's newspaper letters often display a more than earthly solemnity, and likewise an unimaginative
devotion to petrified facts, which surprise and distress all men who
know him in his unofficial character. He explains this curious thing by
saying that his employers sent him to Washington to write facts,
not fancy, and that several times he has come near losing his situation
by inserting humorous remarks which, not being looked for at headquarters, and consequently not understood, were thought to be dark
and bloody speeches intended to convey signals and warnings to
murderous secret societies, or something of that kind, and so were
scratched out with a shiver and a prayer and cast into the stove.
Riley says that sometimes he is so afflicted with a yearning to
write a sparkling and absorbingly readable letter that he simply cannot
resist it, and so he goes to his den and revels in the delight of un-
trammeled scribbling; and then, with suffering such as only a mother
can know, he destroys the pretty children of his fancy and reduces
his letter to the required dismal accuracy. Having seen Riley do this
very thing more than once, I know whereof I speak. Often I have
laughed with him over a happy passage, and grieved to see him plow
his pen through it. He would say, "I had to write that or die; and I've
got to scratch it out or starve. *They* wouldn't stand it, you know."

I think Riley is about the most entertaining company I ever saw. We lodged together in many places in Washington during the winter of '67-8, moving comfortably from place to place, and attracting attention by paying our board—a course which cannot fail to make a person conspicuous in Washington. Riley would tell all about his trip to California in the early days, by way of the Isthmus and the San Juan River; and about his baking bread in San Francisco to gain a living, and setting up tenpins, and practising law, and opening oysters, and delivering lectures, and teaching French, and tending bar, and reporting for the newspapers, and keeping dancing-schools, and interpreting Chinese in the courts—which latter was lucrative, and Riley was doing handsomely and laying up a little money when people began to find fault because his translations were too "free," a thing for which Riley considered he ought not to be held responsible, since he did not know a word of the Chinese tongue, and only adopted interpreting as a means of gaining an honest livelihood. Through the machinations of enemies he was removed from the position of official interpreter, and a man put in his place who was familiar with the Chinese language, but did not know any English. And Riley used to tell about publishing a newspaper up in what is Alaska now, but was only an iceberg then, with a population composed of bears, walruses, Indians, and other animals; and how the iceberg got adrift at last, and left all his paying subscribers behind, and as soon as the commonwealth floated out of the jurisdiction of Russia the people rose and threw off their allegiance and ran up the English flag, calculating to hook on and become an English colony as they drifted along down the British Possessions; but a land breeze and a crooked current carried them by, and they ran up the Stars and Stripes and steered for California, missed the connection again and swore allegiance to Mexico, but it wasn't any use; the anchors came home every time, and away they went with the northeast trades drifting off sideways toward the Sandwich Islands, whereupon they ran up the Cannibal flag and had a grand human barbecue in honor of it, in which it was noticed that the better a man liked a friend the better he enjoyed him; and as soon as they got fairly within the tropics the weather got so fearfully hot that the iceberg began to melt, and it got so sloppy under foot that it was almost impossible for ladies to get about at all; and at last, just as they came in sight of the islands, the melancholy remnant of the once majestic iceberg canted first to one side and then to the other, and then plunged under forever, carrying the national archives along with it—and not only the archives and the populace, but some eligible town lots which had increased in value

as fast as they diminished in size in the tropics, and which Riley
could have sold at thirty cents a pound and made himself rich if he
could have kept the province afloat ten hours longer and got her into
port.

Riley is very methodical, untiringly accommodating, never forgets
anything that is to be attended to, is a good son, a stanch friend, and
a permanent reliable enemy. He will put himself to any amount of
trouble to oblige a body, and therefore always has his hands full of
things to be done for the helpless and the shiftless. And he knows how
to do nearly everything, too. He is a man whose native benevolence is
a well-spring that never goes dry. He stands always ready to help whoever needs help, as far as he is able—and not simply with his money,
for that is a cheap and common charity, but with hand and brain,
and fatigue of limb and sacrifice of time. This sort of man is rare.

Riley has a ready wit, a quickness and aptness at selecting and
applying quotations, and a countenance that is as solemn and as blank
as the back side of a tombstone when he is delivering a particularly
exasperating joke. One night a negro woman was burned to death in
a house next door to us, and Riley said that our landlady would be
oppressively emotional at breakfast, because she generally made use
of such opportunities as offered, being of a morbidly sentimental turn,
and so we should find it best to let her talk along and say nothing
back—it was the only way to keep her tears out of the gravy. Riley
said there never was a funeral in the neighborhood but that the
gravy was watery for a week.

And, sure enough, at breakfast the landlady was down in the very
sloughs of woe—entirely brokenhearted. Everything she looked at
reminded her of that poor old negro woman, and so the buckwheat
cakes made her sob, the coffee forced a groan, and when the beefsteak
came on she fetched a wail that made our hair rise. Then she got to
talking about deceased, and kept up a steady drizzle till both of us
were soaked through and through. Presently she took a fresh breath
and said, with a world of sobs:

"Ah, to think of it, only to think of it!—the poor old faithful creature.
For she was *so* faithful. Would you believe it, she had been a
servant in that selfsame house and that selfsame family for twenty-
seven years come Christmas, and never a cross word and never a lick!
And, oh, to think she should meet such a death at last!—a-sitting over
the red-hot stove at three o'clock in the morning and went to sleep
and fell on it and was actually *roasted!* Not just frizzled up a bit,
but literally roasted to a crisp! Poor faithful creature, how she *was*

cooked! I am but a poor woman, but even if I have to scrimp to do it, I will put up a tombstone over that lone sufferer's grave—and Mr. Riley if you would have the goodness to think up a little epitaph to put on it which would sort of describe the awful way in which she met her—"

"Put it, 'Well done, good and faithful servant,'" said Riley, and never smiled.

1870

Running for Governor

A few months ago I was nominated for Governor of the great state of New York, to run against Mr. John T. Smith and Mr. Blank J. Blank on an independent ticket. I somehow felt that I had one prominent advantage over these gentlemen, and that was—good character. It was easy to see by the newspapers that if ever they had known what it was to bear a good name, that time had gone by. It was plain that in these latter years they had become familiar with all manner of shameful crimes. But at the very moment that I was exalting my advantage and joying in it in secret, there was a muddy undercurrent of discomfort "riling" the deeps of my happiness, and that was—the having to hear my name bandied about in familiar connection with those of such people. I grew more and more disturbed. Finally I wrote my grandmother about it. Her answer came quick and sharp. She said:

You have never done one single thing in all your life to be ashamed of—not one. Look at the newspapers—look at them and comprehend what sort of characters Messrs. Smith and Blank are, and then see if you are willing to lower yourself to their level and enter a public canvass with them.

It was my very thought! I did not sleep a single moment that night. But, after all, I could not recede. I was fully committed, and must go on with the fight. As I was looking listlessly over the papers at breakfast I came across this paragraph, and I may truly say I never was so confounded before.

PERJURY.—Perhaps, now that Mr. Mark Twain is before the people as a candidate for Governor, he will condescend to explain how he came to be convicted of perjury by thirty-four witnesses in Wakawak, Cochin China, in 1863, the intent of which perjury being to rob a poor native widow and her helpless family of a meager plantain-patch, their only stay and support in their bereavement and desolation. Mr. Twain owes it to himself, as well as to the great people whose suffrages he asks, to clear this matter up. Will he do it?

I thought I should burst with amazement! Such a cruel, heartless charge! I never had *seen* Cochin China! I never had *heard* of Wakawak! I didn't know a plantain-patch from a kangaroo! I did not know what to do. I was crazed and helpless. I let the day slip away without doing anything at all. The next morning the same paper had this—nothing more:

SIGNIFICANT.—Mr. Twain, it will be observed, is suggestively silent about the Cochin China perjury.

[*Mem.*—During the rest of the campaign this paper never referred to me in any other way than as "the infamous perjurer Twain."]

Next came the *Gazette*, with this:

WANTED TO KNOW.—Will the new candidate for Governor deign to explain to certain of his fellow-citizens (who are suffering to vote for him!) the little circumstance of his cabin-mates in Montana losing small valuables from time to time, until at last, these things having been invariably found on Mr. Twain's person or in his "Trunk" (newspaper he rolled his traps in), they felt compelled to give him a friendly admonition for his own good, and so tarred and feathered him, and rode him on a rail, and then advised him to leave a permanent vacuum in the place he usually occupied in the camp. Will he do this?

Could anything be more deliberately malicious than that? For I never was in Montana in my life.

[After this, this journal customarily spoke of me as "Twain, the Montana Thief."]

I got to picking up papers apprehensively—much as one would lift a desired blanket which he had some idea might have a rattlesnake under it. One day this met my eye:

THE LIE NAILED.—By the sworn affidavits of Michael O'Flanagan, Esq., of the Five Points, and Mr. Snub Rafferty and Mr. Catty Mulligan, of Water Street, it is established that Mr. Mark Twain's vile statement that the lamented grandfather of our noble standard-bearer, Blank J. Blank, was hanged for highway robbery, is a brutal and gratuitous LIE, without a shadow of foundation in fact. It is disheartening to virtuous men to see such shameful means resorted to to achieve political success as the attacking of the dead in their graves, and defiling their honored names with slander. When we think of the anguish this miserable falsehood must cause the innocent relatives and friends of the deceased, we are almost driven to incite an outraged and insulated public to summary and unlawful vengeance upon the traducer. But no! let us leave him to the agony of a lacerated conscience (though if passion should get the better of the public, and in its blind fury they should do the traducer bodily injury, it is but too obvious that no jury could convict and no court punish the perpetrators of the deed).

The ingenious closing sentence had the effect of moving me out of bed with despatch that night, and out at the back door also, while the "outraged and insulted public" surged in the front way, breaking furniture and windows in their righteous indignation as they came, and taking off such property as they could carry when they went. And yet I can lay my hand upon the Book and say that I never slandered Mr. Blank's grandfather. More: I had never even heard of him or mentioned him up to that day and date.

[I will state, in passing, that the journal above quoted from always referred to me afterward as "Twain, the Body-Snatcher."]

The next newspaper article that attracted my attention was the following:

A SWEET CANDIDATE.—Mr. Mark Twain, who was to make such a blighting speech at the mass-meeting of the Independents last night, didn't come to time! A telegram from his physician stated that he had been knocked down by a runaway team, and his leg broken in two places—sufferer lying in great agony, and so forth, and so forth, and a lot more bosh of the same sort. And the Independents tried hard to swallow the wretched subterfuge, and pretend that they did not know what was the *real* reason of the absence of the abandoned creature whom they denominate their standard-bearer. A *certain man was seen to reel into Mr. Twain's hotel last night in a state of beastly intoxication.* It is the imperative duty of the Independents to prove that this besotted brute was not Mark Twain himself. We have them at last! This is a case that admits of no shirking. The voice of the people demands in thunder tones, "WHO WAS THAT MAN?"

It was incredible, absolutely incredible, for a moment, that it was really my name that was coupled with this disgraceful suspicion. Three long years had passed over my head since I had tasted ale, beer, wine, or liquor of any kind.

[It shows what effect the times were having on me when I say that I saw myself confidently dubbed "Mr. Delirium Tremens Twain" in the next issure of that journal without a pang—notwithstanding I knew that with monotonous fidelity the paper would go on calling me so to the very end.]

By this time anonymous letters were getting to be an important part of my mail matter. This form was common:

> How about that old woman you kiked of your premises which was beging.
> POL. PRY.

And this:

> There is things which you have done which is unbeknowens to anybody but me. You better trot out a few dols, to yours truly, or you'll hear through the papers from
> HANDY ANDY.

This is about the idea. I could continue them till the reader was surfeited, if desirable.

Shortly the principal Republican journal "convicted" me of whole-sale bribery, and the leading Democratic paper "nailed" an aggravated case of blackmailing to me.

[In this way I acquired two additional names: "Twain the Filthy Corruptionist" and "Twain the Loathsome Embracer."]

By this time there had grown to be such a clamor for an "answer" to all the dreadful charges that were laid to me that the editors and leaders of my party said it would be political ruin for me to remain silent any longer. As if to make their appeal the more imperative, the following appeared in one of the papers the very next day:

> BEHOLD THE . MAN!—The independent candidate still maintains silence. Because he dare not speak. Every accusation against him has been amply proved, and they have been indorsed and reindorsed by his own eloquent silence, till at this day he stands forever convicted. Look upon your candidate, Independents! Look upon the Infamous Perjurer! the Montana Thief! the Body-Snatcher! Contemplate your incarnate Delirium Tremens! your Filthy Corruptionist! your Loathsome Embracer! Gaze upon him—ponder him well —and then say if you can give your honest votes to a creature who has earned this dismal array of titles by his hideous crimes, and dares not open his mouth in denial of any one of them!

There was no possible way of getting out of it, and so, in deep humiliation, I set about preparing to "answer" a mass of baseless charges and mean and wicked falsehoods. But I never finished the task, for the very next morning a paper came out with a new horror, a fresh malignity, and seriously charged me with burning a lunatic asylum with all its inmates, because it obstructed the view from my house. This threw me into a sort of panic. Then came the charge of poisoning my uncle to get his property, with an imperative demand that the grave should be opened. This drove me to the verge of distraction. On top of this I was accused of employing toothless and incompetent old relatives to prepare the food for the foundling hospital when I was warden. I was wavering—wavering. And at last, as a due and fitting climax to the shameless persecution that party rancor had inflicted upon me, nine little toddling children, of all shades of color and degrees of raggedness, were taught to rush onto the platform at a public meeting, and clasp me around the legs and call me Pa!

I gave it up. I hauled down my colors and surrendered. I was not equal to the requirements of a Gubernatorial campaign in the state of New York, and so I sent in my withdrawal from the candidacy, and in bitterness of spirit signed it, "Truly yours, *once* a decent man, but now

MARK TWAIN, I.P., M.T., B.S., D.T., F.C., and L.E."

1870

To Raise Poultry*

Seriously, from early youth I have taken an especial interest in the subject of poultry-raising, and so this membership touches a ready sympathy in my breast. Even as a school-boy, poultry-raising was a study with me, and I may say without egotism that as early as the age of seventeen I was acquainted with all the best and speediest methods of raising chickens, from raising them off a roost by burning lucifer matches under their noses, down to lifting them off a fence on a frosty night by insinuating the end of a warm board under their heels. By the time I was twenty years old, I really suppose I had raised more poultry than any one individual in all the section round about there. The very chickens came to know my talent by and by. The youth of both sexes ceased to paw the earth for worms, and

* Being a letter written to a Poultry Society that had conferred a complimentary membership upon the author.

old roosters that came to crow, "remained to pray," when I passed by.

I have had so much experience in the raising of fowls that I cannot but think that a few hints from me might be useful to the society. The two methods I have already touched upon are very simple, and are only used in the raising of the commonest class of fowls; one is for summer, the other for winter. In the one case you start out with a friend along about eleven o'clock on a summer's night (not later, because in some states—especially in California and Oregon—chickens always rouse up just at midnight and crow from ten to thirty minutes, according to the ease or difficulty they experience in getting the public waked up), and your friend carries with him a sack. Arrived at the henroost (your neighbor's, not your own), you light a match and hold it under first one and then another pullet's nose until they are willing to go into that bag without making any trouble about it. You then return home, either taking the bag with you or leaving it behind, according as circumstances shall dictate. *N.B.*—I *have* seen the time when it was eligible and appropriate to leave the sack behind and walk off with considerable velocity, without ever leaving any word where to send it.

In the case of the other method mentioned for raising poultry, your friend takes along a covered vessel with a charcoal fire in it, and you carry a long slender plank. This is a frosty night, understand. Arrived at the tree, or fence, or other henroost (your own if you are an idiot), you warm the end of your plank in your friend's fire vessel, and then raise it aloft and ease it up gently against a slumbering chicken's foot. If the subject of your attentions is a true bird, he will infallibly return thanks with a sleepy cluck or two, and step out and take up quarters on the plank, thus becoming so conspicuously accessory before the fact to his own murder as to make it a grave question in our minds, as it once was in the mind of Blackstone, whether he is not really and deliberately committing suicide in the second degree. [But you enter into a contemplation of these legal refinements subsequently—not then.]

When you wish to raise a fine, large, donkey-voiced Shanghai rooster, you do it with a lasso, just as you would a bull. It is because he must be choked, and choked effectually, too. It is the only good, certain way, for whenever he mentions a matter which he is cordially interested in, the chances are ninety-nine in a hundred that he secures somebody else's immediate attention to it too, whether it be day or night.

The Black Spanish is an exceedingly fine bird and a costly one. Thirty-five dollars is the usual figure, and fifty a not uncommon price for a specimen. Even its eggs are worth from a dollar to a dollar and a half apiece, and yet are so unwholesome that the city physician seldom or never orders them for the workhouse. Still I have once or twice procured as high as a dozen at a time for nothing, in the dark of the moon. The best way to raise the Black Spanish fowl is to go late in the evening and raise coop and all. The reason I recommend this method is that, the birds being so valuable, the owners do not permit them to roost around promiscuously, but put them in a coop as strong as a fireproof safe, and keep it in the kitchen at night. The method I speak of is not always a bright and satisfying success, and yet there are so many little articles of *vertu* about a kitchen, that if you fail on the coop you can generally bring away something else. I brought away a nice steel trap one night, worth ninety cents.

But what is the use in my pouring out my whole intellect on this subject? I have shown the Western New York Poultry Society that they have taken to their bosom a party who is not a spring chicken by any means, but a man who knows all about poultry, and is just as high up in the most efficient methods of raising it as the president of the institution himself. I thank these gentlemen for the honorary membership they have conferred upon me, and shall stand at all times ready and willing to testify my good feeling and my official zeal by deeds as well as by this hastily penned advice and information. Whenever they are ready to go to raising poultry, let them call for me any evening after eleven o'clock, and I shall be on hand promptly.

1870

The Undertaker's Chat

"Now that corpse," said the undertaker, patting the folded hands of deceased approvingly, "was a brick—every way you took him he was a brick. He was so real accommodating, and so modest-like and simple in his last moments. Friends wanted metallic burial-case—

nothing else would do. *I* couldn't get it. There warn't going to be time
—anybody could see that.

"Corpse said never mind, shake him up some kind of a box he
could stretch out in comfortable, *he* warn't particular 'bout the general
style of it. Said he went more on room than style, anyway in a last
final container.

"Friends wanted a silver door-plate on the coffin, signifying who he
was and wher' he was from. Now *you* know a fellow couldn't roust
out such a gaily thing as that in a little country-town like this. What
did corpse say?

"Corpse said, whitewash his old canoe and dob his address and
general destination onto it with a blacking-brush and a stencil-plate,
'long with a verse from some likely hymn or other, and p'int him for
the tomb, and mark him C. O. D., and just let him flicker. *He* warn't
distressed any more than you be—on the contrary, just as ca'm and
collected as a hearse-horse; said he judged that wher' he was going
to a body would find it considerable better to attract attention by a
picturesque moral character than a natty burial-case with a swell
door-plate on it.

"Splendid man, he was. I'd druther do for a corpse like that 'n any
I've tackled in seven year. There's some satisfaction in buryin' a man
like that. You feel that what you're doing is appreciated. Lord bless
you, so's he got planted before he sp'iled, he was perfectly satisfied;
said his relations meant well, *per*fectly well, but all them preparations
was bound to delay the thing more or less, and he didn't wish to be
kept layin' around. You never see such a clear head as what he had—
and so ca'm and so cool. Jist a hunk of brains—that is what *he* was.
Perfectly awful. It was a ripping distance from one end of that man's
head to t'other. Often and over again he's had brain-fever a-raging in
one place, and the rest of the pile didn't know anything about it—
didn't affect it any more than an Injun insurrection in Arizona affects
the Atlantic States.

"Well, the relations they wanted a big funeral, but corpse said he
was down on flummery—didn't want any procession—fill the hearse
full of mourners, and get out a stern line and tow *him* behind. He *was*
the most down on style of any remains I ever struck. A beautiful,
simple-minded creature—it was what he was, you can depend on
that. He was just set on having things the way he wanted them, and
he took a solid comfort in laying his little plans. He had me measure
him and take a whole raft of directions; then he had the minister
stand up behind a long box with a table-cloth over it, to represent

the coffin, and read his funeral sermon, saying 'Angcore, angcore!' at the good places, and making him scratch out every bit of brag about him, and all the hifalutin; and then he made them trot out the choir, so's he could help them pick out the tunes for the occasion, and he got them to sing 'Pop Goes the Weasel,' because he'd always liked that tune when he was downhearted, and solemn music made him sad; and when they sung that with tears in their eyes (because they all loved him), and his relations grieving around, he just laid there as happy as a bug, and trying to beat time and showing all over how much he enjoyed it; and presently he got worked up and excited, and tried to join in, for, mind you, he was pretty proud of his abilities in the singing line; but the first time he opened his mouth and was just going to spread himself his breath took a walk.

"I never see a man snuffed out so sudden. Ah, it was a great loss—a powerful loss to this poor little one-horse town. Well, well, well, I hain't got time to be palavering along here—got to nail on the lid and mosey along with him; and if you'll just give me a lift we'll skeet him into the hearse and meander along. Relations bound to have it so— don't pay no attention to dying injunctions, minute a corpse's gone; but, if I had *my* way, if I didn't respect his last wishes and tow him behind the hearse I'll be cuss'd. I consider that whatever a corpse wants done for his comfort is little enough matter, and a man hain't got no right to deceive him or take advantage of him; and whatever a corpse trusts me to do I'm a-going to *do*, you know, even if it's to stuff him and paint him yaller and keep him for a keepsake—you hear *me!*"

He cracked his whip and went lumbering away with his ancient ruin of a hearse, and I continued my walk with a valuable lesson learned—that a healthy and wholesome cheerfulness is not necessarily impossible to *any* occupation. The lesson is likely to be lasting, for it will take many months to obliterate the memory of the remarks and circumstances that impressed it.

1870

The Widow's Protest

One of the saddest things that ever came under my notice (said the banker's clerk) was there in Corning during the war. Dan Murphy enlisted as a private, and fought very bravely. The boys all liked him, and when a wound by and by weakened him down till carrying a musket was too heavy work for him, they clubbed together and fixed him up as a sutler. He made money then, and sent it always to his wife to bank for him. She was a washer and ironer, and knew enough by hard experience to keep money when she got it. She didn't waste a penny. On the contrary, she began to get miserly as her bank-account grew. She grieved to part with a cent, poor creature, for twice in her hard-working life she had known what it was to be hungry, cold, friendless, sick, and without a dollar in the world, and she had a haunting dread of suffering so again. Well, at last Dan died; and the boys, in testimony of their esteem and respect for him, telegraphed to Mrs. Murphy to know if she would like to have him embalmed and sent home; when you know the usual custom was to dump a poor devil like him into a shallow hole, and *then* inform his friends what had become of him. Mrs. Murphy jumped to the conclusion that it would only cost two or three dollars to embalm her dead husband, and so she telegraphed "Yes." It was at the "wake" that the bill for embalming arrived and was presented to the widow.

She uttered a wild, sad wail that pierced every heart, and said, "Sivinty-foive dollars for stooffin' Dan, blister their sowls! Did thim divils suppose I was goin' to start a Museim, that I'd be dalin' in such expinsive curiassities!"

The banker's clerk said there was not a dry eye in the house.

1870

Wit Inspirations of the
"Two-Year-Olds"

All infants appear to have an impertinent and disagreeable fashion nowadays of saying "smart" things on most occasions that offer, and especially on occasions when they ought not to be saying anything at all. Judging by the average published specimens of smart sayings, the rising generation of children are little better than idiots. And the parents must surely be but little better than the children, for in most cases they are the publishers of the sunbursts of infantile imbecility which dazzle us from the pages of our periodicals. I may seem to speak with some heat, not to say a suspicion of personal spite; and I do admit that it nettles me to hear about so many gifted infants in these days, and remember that I seldom said anything smart when I was a child. I tried it once or twice, but it was not popular. The family were not expecting brilliant remarks from me, and so they snubbed me sometimes and spanked me the rest. But it makes my flesh creep and my blood run cold to think what might have happened to me if I had dared to utter some of the smart things of this generation's "four-year-olds" where my father could hear me. To have simply skinned me alive and considered his duty at an end would have seemed to him criminal leniency toward one so sinning. He was a stern, unsmiling man, and hated all forms of precocity. If I had said some of the things I have referred to, and said them in his hearing, he would have destroyed me. He would, indeed. He would, provided the opportunity remained with him. But it would not, for I would have had judgment enough to take some strychnine first, and say my smart thing afterward. The fair record of my life has been tarnished by just one pun. My father overheard that, and he hunted me over four or five townships seeking to take my life. If I had been full-grown, of course he would have been right; but, child as I was, I could not know how wicked a thing I had done.

I made one of those remarks ordinarily called "smart things" before that, but it was not a pun. Still, it came near causing a serious rupture between my father and myself. My father and mother, my uncle

Ephraim and his wife, and one or two others were present, and the conversation turned on a name for me. I was lying there trying some India-rubber rings of various patterns, and endeavoring to make a selection, for I was tired of trying to cut my teeth on people's fingers, and wanted to get hold of something that would enable me to hurry the thing through and get something else. Did you ever notice what a nuisance it was cutting your teeth on your nurse's finger, or how back-breaking and tiresome it was trying to cut them on your big toe? And did you never get out of patience and wish your teeth were in Jericho long before you got them half cut? To me it seems as if these things happened yesterday. And they did, to some children. But I digress. I was lying there trying the India-rubber rings. I remember looking at the clock and noticing that in an hour and twenty-five minutes I would be two weeks old, and thinking how little I had done to merit the blessings that were so unsparingly lavished upon me. My father said:

"Abraham is a good name. My grandfather was named Abraham."

My mother said:

"Abraham is a good name. Very well. Let us have Abraham for one of his names."

I said:

"Abraham suits the subscriber."

My father frowned, my mother looked pleased; my aunt said:

"What a little darling it is!"

My father said:

"Isaac is a good name, and Jacob is a good name."

My mother assented, and said:

"No names are better. Let us add Isaac and Jacob to his names."

I said:

"All right. Isaac and Jacob are good enough for yours truly. Pass me that rattle, if you please. I can't chew India-rubber rings all day."

Not a soul made a memorandum of these sayings of mine, for publication. I saw that, and did it myself, else they would have been utterly lost. So far from meeting with a generous encouragement like other children when developing intellectually, I was now furiously scowled upon by my father; my mother looked grieved and anxious, and even my aunt had about her an expression of seeming to think that maybe I had gone too far. I took a vicious bite out of an India-rubber ring, and covertly broke the rattle over the kitten's head, but said nothing. Presently my father said:

"Samuel is a very excellent name."

I saw that trouble was coming. Nothing could prevent it. I laid down my rattle; over the side of the cradle I dropped my uncle's silver watch, the clothes-brush, the toy dog, my tin soldier, the nutmeg-grater, and other matters which I was accustomed to examine, and meditate upon and make pleasant noises with, and bang and batter and break when I needed wholesome entertainment. Then I put on my little frock and my little bonnet, and took my pygmy shoes in one hand and my licorice in the other, and climbed out on the floor. I said to myself, Now, if the worst comes to worst, I am ready. Then I said aloud, in a firm voice:

"Father, I cannot, cannot wear the name of Samuel."

"My son!"

"Father, I mean it. I cannot."

"Why?"

"Father, I have an invincible antipathy to that name."

"My son, this is unreasonable. Many great and good men have been named Samuel."

"Sir, I have yet to hear of the first instance."

"What! There was Samuel the prophet. Was not he great and good?"

"No so very."

"My son! With His own voice the Lord called him."

"Yes, sir, and had to call him a couple of times before he would come!"

And then I sallied forth, and that stern old man sallied forth after me. He overtook me at noon the following day, and when the interview was over I had acquired the name of Samuel, and a thrashing, and other useful information; and by means of this compromise my father's wrath was appeased and a misunderstanding bridged over which might have become a permanent rupture if I had chosen to be unreasonable. But just judging by this episode, what would my father have done to me if I had ever uttered in his hearing one of the flat, sickly things these "two-year-olds" say in print nowadays? In my opinion there would have been a case of infanticide in our family.

1870

About Barbers

All things change except barbers, the ways of barbers, and the surroundings of barbers. These never change. What one experiences in a barber's shop the first time he enters one is what he always experiences in barbers' shops afterward till the end of his days. I got shaved this morning as usual. A man approached the door from Jones Street as I approached it from Main—a thing that always happens. I hurried up, but it was of no use; he entered the door one little step ahead of me, and I followed in on his heels and saw him take the only vacant chair, the one presided over by the best barber. It always happens so. I sat down, hoping that I might fall heir to the chair belonging to the better of the remaining two barbers, for he had already begun combing his man's hair, while his comrade was not yet quite done rubbing up and oiling his customer's locks. I watched the probabilities with strong interest. When I saw that No. 2 was gaining on No. 1 my interest grew to solicitude. When No. 1 stopped a moment to make change on a bath ticket for a new-comer, and lost ground in the race, my solicitude rose to anxiety. When No. 1 caught up again, and both he and his comrade were pulling the towels away and brushing the powder from their customers' cheeks, and it was about an even thing which one would say "Next!" first, my very breath stood still with the suspense. But when at the culminating moment No. 1 stopped to pass a comb a couple of times through his customer's eyebrows, I saw that he had lost the race by a single instant, and I rose indignant and quitted the shop, to keep from falling into the hands of No. 2; for I have none of that enviable firmness that enables a man to look calmly into the eyes of a waiting barber and tell him he will wait for his fellow-barber's chair.

I stayed out fifteen minutes, and then went back, hoping for better luck. Of course all the chairs were occupied now, and four men sat waiting, silent, unsociable, distraught, and looking bored, as men always do who are waiting their turn in a barber's shop. I sat down in one of the iron-armed compartments of an old sofa, and put in the time for a while reading the framed advertisements of all sorts of quack nostrums for dyeing and coloring the hair. Then I read the greasy names on the private bay-rum bottles; read the names and noted the numbers on the private shaving-cups in the pigeonholes; studied the stained and damaged cheap prints on the walls, of battles, early Presidents, and voluptuous recumbent sultanas, and the tiresome and everlasting young girl putting her grandfather's spectacles on; execrated in my heart the cheerful canary and the distracting parrot that few barbers' shops are without. Finally, I searched out the least dilapidated of last year's illustrated papers that littered the foul center-table, and conned their unjustifiable misrepresentations of old forgotten events.

At last my turn came. A voice said "Next!" and I surrendered to— No. 2, of course. It always happens so. I said meekly that I was in a hurry, and it affected him as strongly as if he had never heard it. He shoved up my head, and put a napkin under it. He plowed his fingers into my collar and fixed a towel there. He explored my hair with his claws and suggested that it needed trimming. I said I did not want it trimmed. He explored again and said it was pretty long for the present style—better have a little taken off; it needed it behind especially. I said I had had it cut only a week before. He yearned over it reflectively a moment, and then asked with a disparaging manner, who cut it? I came back at him promptly with a "You did!" I had him there. Then he fell to stirring up his lather and regarding himself in the glass, stopping now and then to get close and examine his chin critically or inspect a pimple. Then he lathered one side of my face thoroughly, and was about to lather the other, when a dog-fight attracted his attention, and he ran to the window and stayed and saw it out, losing two shillings on the result in bets with the other barbers, a thing which gave me great satisfaction. He finished lathering, and then began to rub in the suds with his hand.

He now began to sharpen his razor on an old suspender, and was delayed a good deal on account of a controversy about a cheap masquerade ball he had figured at the night before, in red cambric and bogus ermine, as some kind of a king. He was so gratified with being chaffed about some damsel whom he had smitten with his charms that he used every means to continue the controversy by pretending to be annoyed at the chaffings of his fellows. This matter begot more surveyings of himself in the glass, and he put down his razor and brushed his hair with elaborate care, plastering an inverted arch of it down on his forehead, accomplishing an accurate "part" behind, and brushing the two wings forward over his ears with nice exactness. In the mean time the lather was drying on my face, and apparently eating into my vitals.

Now he began to shave, digging his fingers into my countenance to stretch the skin and bundling and tumbling my head this way and that as convenience in shaving demanded. As long as he was on the tough sides of my face I did not suffer; but when he began to rake, and rip, and tug at my chin, the tears came. He now made a handle of my nose, to assist him shaving the corners of my upper lip, and it was by this bit of circumstantial evidence that I discovered that a part of his duties in the shop was to clean the kerosense-lamps. I had often wondered in an indolent way whether the barbers did that, or whether it was the boss.

About this time I was amusing myself trying to guess where he would be most likely to cut me this time, but he got ahead of me, and sliced me on the end of the chin before I had got my mind made up. He immediately sharpened his razor—he might have done it before. I do not like a close shave, and would not let him go over me a second time. I tried to get him to put up his razor, dreading that he would make for the side of my chin, my pet tender spot, a place which a razor cannot touch twice without making trouble; but he said he only wanted to just smooth off one little roughness, and in the same moment he slipped his razor along the forbidden ground, and the dreaded pimple-signs of a close shave rose up smarting and answered to the call. Now he soaked his towel in bay rum, and slapped it all over my face nastily; slapped it over as if a human being ever yet washed his face in that way. Then he dried it by slapping with the dry part of the towel, as if a human being ever dried his face in such a fashion; but a barber seldom rubs you like a Christian. Next he poked bay rum into the cut place with his towel, then choked the wound with powdered starch, then soaked it with bay rum again, and would have gone on soaking and powdering it forevermore, no doubt, if I had not rebelled and begged off. He powdered my whole face now, straightened me up, and began to plow my hair thoughtfully with his hands. Then he suggested a shampoo, and said my hair needed it badly, very badly. I observed that I shampooed it myself very thoroughly in the bath yesterday. I "had him" again. He next recommended some of "Smith's Hair Glorifier," and offered to sell me a bottle. I declined. He praised the new perfume, "Jones's Delight of the Toilet," and proposed to sell me some of that. I declined again. He tendered me a tooth-wash atrocity of his own invention, and when I declined offered to trade knives with me.

He returned to business after the miscarriage of this last enterprise, sprinkled me all over, legs and all, greased my hair in defiance of my protest against it, rubbed and scrubbed a good deal of it out by the roots, and combed and brushed the rest, parting it behind, and plastering the eternal inverted arch of hair down on my forehead, and then, while combing my scant eyebrows and defiling them with pomade, strung out an account of the achievements of a six-ounce black-and-tan terrier of his till I heard the whistles blow for noon, and knew I was five minutes too late for the train. Then he snatched away the towel, brushed it lightly about my face, passed his comb through my eyebrows once more, and gaily sang out "Next!"

This barber fell down and died of apoplexy two hours later. I am waiting over a day for my revenge—I am going to attend his funeral.

1871

A Burlesque Biography

Two or three persons having at different times intimated that if I would write an autobiography they would read it when they got leisure, I yield at last to this frenzied public demand and herewith tender my history.

Ours is a noble old house, and stretches a long way back into antiquity. The earliest ancestor the Twains have any record of was a friend of the family by the name of Higgins. This was in the eleventh century, when our people were living in Aberdeen, county of Cork, England. Why it is that our long line has ever since borne the maternal name (except when one of them now and then took a playful refuge in an alias to avert foolishness), instead of Higgins, is a mystery which none of us has ever felt much desire to stir. It is a kind of vague, pretty romance, and we leave it alone. All the old families do that way.

Arthour Twain was a man of considerable note—a solicitor on the highway in William Rufus's time. At about the age of thirty he went to one of those fine old English places of resort called Newgate, to see about something, and never returned again. While there he died suddenly.

Augustus Twain seems to have made something of a stir about the year 1160. He was as full of fun as he could be, and used to take his old saber and sharpen it up, and get in a convenient place on a dark night, and stick it through people as they went by, to see them jump. He was a born humorist. But he got to going too far with it; and the first time he was found stripping one of these parties, the authorities removed one end of him, and put it up on a nice high place on Temple Bar, where it could contemplate the people and have a good time. He never liked any situation so much or stuck to it so long.

Then for the next two hundred years the family tree shows a succession of soldiers—noble, high-spirited fellows, who always went into battle singing, right behind the army, and always went out a-whooping, right ahead of it.

This is a scathing rebuke to old dead Froissart's poor witticism that our family tree never had but one limb to it, and that that one stuck out at right angles, and bore fruit winter and summer.

Early in the fifteenth century we have Beau Twain, called "the Scholar." He wrote a beautiful, beautiful hand. And he could imitate anybody's hand so closely that it was enough to make a person laugh his head off to see it. He had infinite sport with his talent. But by and by he took a contract to break stone for a road, and the roughness of the work spoiled his hand. Still, he enjoyed life all the time he was in the stone business, which, with inconsiderable intervals, was some forty-two years. In fact, he died in harness. During all those long years he gave such satisfaction that he never was through with one contract a week till the government gave him another. He was a perfect pet. And he was always a favorite with his fellow-artists, and was a conspicuous member of their benevolent secret society, called the Chain Gang. He always wore his hair short, had a preference for striped clothes, and died lamented by the government. He was a sore loss to his country. For he was so regular.

Some years later we have the illustrious John Morgan Twain. He came over to this country with Columbus in 1492 as a passenger. He appears to have been of a crusty, uncomfortable disposition. He complained of the food all the way over, and was always threatening to go ashore unless there was a change. He wanted fresh shad. Hardly a day passed over his head that he did not go idling about the ship with his nose in the air, sneering about the commander, and saying he did not believe Columbus knew where he was going to or had ever been there before. The memorable cry of "Land ho!" thrilled every heart in the ship but his. He gazed awhile through a piece of smoked glass at the penciled line lying on the distant water, and then said: "Land be hanged—it's a raft!"

When this questionable passenger came on board the ship, he brought nothing with him but an old newspaper containing a handkerchief marked "B. G.," one cotton sock marked "L. W. C.," one woollen one marked "D. F.," and a night-shirt marked "O. M. R." And yet during the voyage he worried more about his "trunk," and gave himself more airs about it, than all the rest of the passengers put together. If the ship was "down by the head," and would not steer, he would go and move his "trunk" farther aft, and then watch the effect. If the ship was "by the stern," he would suggest to Columbus to detail some men to "shift that baggage." In storms he had to be gagged, because his wailings about his "trunk" made it impossible for the men to hear the orders. The man does not appear to have been openly charged with any gravely unbecoming thing, but it is noted in the ship's log as a "curious circumstance" that albeit he brought his baggage on board the ship in a newspaper, he took it ashore in four trunks, a queensware crate, and a couple of champagne baskets. But when he came back insinuating, in an insolent, swaggering way, that some of his things were missing, and was going to search the other passengers' baggage, it was too much, and they threw him overboard. They watched long and wonderingly for him to come up, but not even a bubble rose on the quietly ebbing tide. But while every one was most absorbed in gazing over the side, and the interest was momentarily increasing, it was observed with consternation that the vessel was adrift and the anchor-cable hanging limp from the bow. Then in the ship's dimmed and ancient log we find this quaint note:

"In time it was discouvered yt ye troblesome passenger hadde gonne downe and got ye anchor, and toke ye same and solde it to ye dam sauvages from ye interior, saying yt he hadde founde it, ye sonne of a ghun!"

Yet this ancestor had good and noble instincts, and it is with pride that we call to mind the fact that he was the first white person who ever interested himself in the work of elevating and civilizing our Indians. He built a commodious jail and put up a gallows, and to his dying day he claimed with satisfaction that he had had a more restraining and elevating influence on the Indians than any other reformer that ever labored among them. At this point the chronicle becomes less frank and chatty, and closes abruptly by saying that the old voyager went to see his gallows perform on the first white man ever hanged in America, and while there received injuries which terminated in his death.

The great-grandson of the "Reformer" flourished in sixteen hundred and something, and was known in our annals as "the old Admiral," though in history he had other titles. He was long in command of fleets of swift vessels, well armed and manned, and did great service in hurrying up merchantmen. Vessels which he followed and kept his eagle eye on, always made good fair time across the ocean. But if a ship still loitered in spite of all he could do, his indignation would grow till he could contain himself no longer—and then he would take that ship home where he lived and keep it there carefully, expecting the owners to come for it, but they never did. And he would try to get the idleness and sloth out of the sailors of that ship by compelling them to take invigorating exercise and a bath. He called it "walking a plank." All the pupils liked it. At any rate, they never found any fault with it after trying it. When the owners were late coming for their ships, the Admiral always burned them, so that the insurance money should not be lost. At last this fine old tar was cut down in the fullness of his years and honors. And to her dying day, his poor heartbroken widow believed that if he had been cut down fifteen minutes sooner he might have been resuscitated.

Charles Henry Twain lived during the latter part of the seventeenth century, and was a zealous and distinguished missionary. He converted sixteen thousand South Sea islanders, and taught them that a dog-tooth necklace and a pair of spectacles was not enough clothing to come to divine service in. His poor flock loved him very, very dearly; and when his funeral was over, they got up in a body (and came out of the restaurant) with tears in their eyes, and saying, one to another, that he was a good tender missionary, and they wished they had some more of him.

Pah-go-to-wah-wah-pukketekeewis (Mighty-Hunter-with-a-Hog-Eye-Twain) adorned the middle of the eighteenth century, and aided General Braddock with all his heart to resist the oppressor Washington. It was this ancestor who fired seventeen times at our Washington from behind a tree. So far the beautiful romantic narrative in the moral story-books is correct; but when that narrative goes on to say that at the seventeenth round the awe-stricken savage said solemnly that that man was being reserved by the Great Spirit for some mighty mission, and he dared not lift his sacrilegious rifle against him again, the narrative seriously impairs the integrity of history. What he did say was:

"It ain't no (hic) no use. 'At man's so drunk he can't stan' still long enough for a man to hit him. I (hic) I can't 'ford to fool away any more am'nition on him."

That was why he stopped at the seventeenth round, and it was a good, plain, matter-of-fact reason, too, and one that easily commends itself to us by the eloquent, persuasive flavor of probability there is about it.

I always enjoyed the story-book narrative, but I felt a marring misgiving that every Indian at Braddock's Defeat who fired at a soldier a couple of times (two easily grows to seventeen in a century), and missed him, jumped to the conclusion that the Great Spirit was reserving that soldier for some grand mission; and so I somehow feared that the only reason why Washington's case is remembered and the others forgotten is, that in his the prophecy came true, and in that of the others it didn't. There are not books enough on earth to contain the record of the prophecies Indians and other unauthorized parties have made; but one may carry in his overcoat pockets the record of all the prophecies that have been fulfilled.

I will remark here, in passing, that certain ancestors of mine are so thoroughly well-known in history by their aliases, that I have not felt it to be worth while to dwell upon them, or even mention them in the order of their birth. Among these may be mentioned Richard Brinsley Twain, alias Guy Fawkes; John Wentworth Twain, alias Sixteen-String Jack; William Hogarth Twain, alias Jack Sheppard; Ananias Twain, alias Baron Munchausen; John George Twain, alias Captain Kydd; and then there are George Francis Train, Tom Pepper, Nebuchadnezzar, and Baalam's Ass—they all belong to our family, but to a branch of it somewhat distinctly removed from the honorable direct line—in fact, a collateral branch, whose members chiefly differ from the ancient stock in that, in order to acquire the notoriety we have always yearned and hungered for, they have got into a low way of going to jail instead of getting hanged.

It is not well, when writing an autobiography, to follow your ancestry down too close to your own time—it is safest to speak only vaguely of your great-grandfather, and then skip from there to yourself, which I now do.

I was born without teeth—and there Richard III had the advantage of me; but I was born without a humpback, likewise, and there I had the advantage of him. My parents were neither very poor nor conspicuously honest.

But now a thought occurs to me. My own history would really seem so tame contrasted with that of my ancestors, that it is simply wisdom to leave it unwritten until I am hanged. If some other biographies I have read had stopped with the ancestry until a like event occurred, it would have been a felicitous thing for the reading public. How does it strike you?

1871

The Danger of Lying in Bed

The man in the ticket-office said:

"Have an accident insurance ticket, also?"

"No," I said, after studying the matter over a little. "No, I believe not; I am going to be traveling by rail all day to-day. However, to-morrow I don't travel. Give me one for to-morrow."

The man looked puzzled. He said:

"But it is for accident insurance, and if you are going to travel by rail—"

"If I am going to travel by rail I sha'n't need it. Lying at home in bed is the thing I am afraid of."

I had been looking into this matter. Last year I traveled twenty thousand miles, almost entirely by rail; the year before, I traveled over twenty-five thousand miles, half by sea and half by rail; and the year before that I traveled in the neighborhood of ten thousand miles, exclusively by rail. I suppose if I put in all the little odd journeys here and there, I may say I have traveled sixty thousand miles during the three years I have mentioned. *And never an accident.*

For a good while I said to myself every morning: "Now I have escaped thus far, and so the chances are just that much increased that I shall catch it this time. I will be shrewd, and buy an accident ticket." And to a dead moral certainty I drew a blank, and went to bed that night without a joint started or a bone splintered. I got tired of that sort of daily bother, and fell to buying accident tickets that were good for a month. I said to myself, "A man *can't* buy thirty blanks in one bundle."

But I was mistaken. There was never a prize in the lot. I could read of railway accidents every day—the newspaper atmosphere was foggy with them; but somehow they never came my way. I found I had spent a good deal of money in the accident business, and had nothing to show for it. My suspicions were aroused, and I began to hunt around for somebody that had won in this lottery. I found plenty of people who had invested, but not an individual that had ever had an accident or made a cent. I stopped buying accident tickets and went to ciphering. The result was astounding. THE PERIL LAY NOT IN TRAVELING, BUT IN STAYING AT HOME.

I hunted up statistics, and was amazed to find that after all the glaring newspaper headings concerning railroad disasters, less than *three hundred* people had really lost their lives by those disasters in the preceding twelve months. The Erie road was set down as the most murderous in the list. It had killed forty-six—or twenty-six, I do not exactly remember which, but I know the number was double that of any other road. But the fact straightway suggested itself that the Erie was an immensely long road, and did more business than any other line in the country; so the double number of killed ceased to be matter for surprise.

By further figuring, it appeared that between New York and Rochester the Erie ran eight passenger-trains each way every day—16 altogether; and carried a daily average of 6,000 persons. That is about a million in six months—the population of New York City. Well, the Erie kills from 13 to 23 persons out of *its* million in six months; and in the same time 13,000 of New York's million die in their beds! My flesh crept, my hair stood on end. "This is appalling!" I said. "The danger isn't in traveling by rail, but in trusting to those deadly beds. I will never sleep in a bed again."

I had figured on considerably less than one-half the length of the Erie road. It was plain that the entire road must transport at least eleven or twelve thousand people every day. There are many short roads running out of Boston that do fully half as much; a great many such roads. There are many roads scattered about the Union that do a prodigious passenger business. Therefore it was fair to presume that an average of 2,500 passengers a day for each road in the country would be about correct. There are 846 railway lines in our country, and 846 times 2,500 are 2,115,000. So the railways of America move more than two millions of people every day; six hundred and fifty millions of people a year, without counting the Sundays. They do that, too— there is no question about it; though where they get the raw material is clear beyond the jurisdiction of my arithmetic; for I have hunted the census through and through, and I find that there are not that many people in the United States, by a matter of six hundred and ten millions at the very least. They must use some of the same people over again, likely.

San Francisco is one-eighth as populous as New York; there are 60 deaths a week in the former and 500 a week in the latter—if they have luck. That is 3,120 deaths a year in San Francisco, and eight times as many in New York—say about 25,000 or 26,000. The health of the two places is the same. So we will let it stand as a fair presumption that this will hold good all over the country, and that consequently 25,000 out of every million of people we have must die every year. That amounts to one-fortieth of our total population. One million of us, then, die annually. Out of this million ten or twelve thousand are stabbed, shot, drowned, hanged, poisoned, or meet a similarly violent death in some other popular way, such as perishing by kerosene-lamp and hoop-skirt conflagrations, getting buried in coal-mines, falling off house-tops, breaking through church or lecture-room floors, taking patent medicines, or committing suicide in other forms. The Erie railroad kills from 23 to 46; the other 845 railroads kill an average of one-third of a man each; and the rest of that million, amounting in the aggregate to the appalling figure of 987,631 corpses, die naturally in their beds!

You will excuse me from taking any more chances on those beds. The railroads are good enough for me.

And my advice to all people is, Don't stay at home any more than you can help; but when you have *got* to stay at home a while, buy a package of those insurance tickets and sit up nights. You cannot be too cautious.

[One can see now why I answered that ticket-agent in the manner recorded at the top of this sketch.]

The moral of this composition is, that thoughtless people grumble more than is fair about railroad management in the United States.

When we consider that every day and night of the year full fourteen thousand railway-trains of various kinds, freighted with life and armed with death, go thundering over the land, the marvel is, *not* that they kill three hundred human beings in a twelvemonth, but that they do not kill three hundred times three hundred!

1871

A Fashion Item

At General G——'s reception the other night, the most fashionably dressed lady was Mrs. G. C. She wore a pink satin dress, plain in front but with a good deal of rake to it—to the train, I mean; it was said to be two or three yards long. One could see it creeping along the floor some little time after the woman was gone. Mrs. C. wore also a white bodice, cut bias, with Pompadour sleeves, flounced with ruches; low neck, with the inside handkerchief not visible, with white kid gloves. She had on a pearl necklace, which glinted lonely, high up the midst of that barren waste of neck and shoulders. Her hair was frizzled into a tangled chaparral, forward of her ears, aft it was drawn together, and compactly bound and plaited into a stump like a pony's tail, and furthermore was canted upward at a sharp angle, and ingeniously supported by a red velvet crupper, whose forward extremity was made fast with a half-hitch around a hairpin on the top of her head. Her whole top hamper was neat and becoming. She had a beautiful complexion when she first came, but it faded out by degrees in an unaccountable way. However, it is not lost for good. I found the most of it on my shoulder afterward. (I stood near the door when she squeezed out with the throng.) There were other ladies present, but I only took notes of one as a specimen. I would gladly enlarge upon the subject were I able to do it justice.

1871

First Interview with Artemus Ward

I had never seen him before. He brought letters of introduction from mutual friends in San Francisco, and by invitation I breakfasted with him. It was almost religion, there in the silver-mines, to precede such a meal with whisky cocktails. Artemus, with the true cosmopolitan instinct, always deferred to the customs of the country he was in, and so he ordered three of those abominations. Hingston was present. I said I would rather not drink a whisky cocktail. I said it would go right to my head, and confuse me so that I would be in a helpless tangle in ten minutes. I did not want to act like a lunatic before strangers. But Artemus gently insisted, and I drank the treasonable mixture under protest, and felt all the time that I was doing a thing I might be sorry for. In a minute or two I began to imagine that my ideas were clouded. I waited in great anxiety for the conversation to open, with a sort of vague hope that my understanding would prove clear, after all, and my misgivings groundless.

Artemus dropped an unimportant remark or two, and then assumed a look of superhuman earnestness, and made the following astounding speech. He said:

"Now there is one thing I ought to ask you about before I forget it. You have been here in Silverland—here in Nevada—two or three years, and, of course, your position on the daily press has made it necessary for you to go down in the mines and examine them carefully in detail, and therefore you know all about the silver-mining business. Now what I want to get at is—is, well, the way the deposits of ore are made, you know. For instance. Now, as I understand it, the vein which contains the silver is sandwiched in between casings of granite, and runs along the ground, and sticks up like a curbstone. Well, take a vein forty feet thick, for example, or eighty, for that matter, or even a hundred—say you go down on it with a shaft, straight down, you know, or with what you call 'incline'—maybe you go down five hundred feet, or maybe you don't go down but two hundred—anyway, you go down, and all the time this vein grows narrower, when the casings come nearer or approach each other, you may say—that is, when they do approach, which, of course, they do not always do, particularly in cases where the nature of the formation is such that they stand apart wider than they otherwise would, and which geology has failed to account for, although everything in that science goes to prove that, all things being equal, it would if it did not, or would not certainly if it did, and then, of course, they are. Do not you think it is?"

I said to myself:

"Now I just knew how it would be—that whisky cocktail has done the business for me; I don't understand any more than a clam."

And then I said aloud:

"I—I—that is—if you don't mind, would you—would you say that over again? I ought—"

"Oh, certainly, certainly! You see I am very unfamiliar with the subject, and perhaps I don't present my case clearly, but I—"

"No, no—no, no—you state it plain enough, but that cocktail has muddled me a little. But I will—no, I do understand for that matter; but I would get the hang of it all the better if you went over it again—and I'll pay better attention this time."

He said, "Why, what I was after was this."

[Here he became even more fearfully impressive than ever, and emphasized each particular point by checking it off on his finger-ends.]

"This vein, or lode, or ledge, or whatever you call it, runs along between two layers of granite, just the same as if it were a sandwich. Very well. Now suppose you go down on that, say a thousand feet, or maybe twelve hundred (it don't really matter) before you drift, and then you start your drifts, some of them across the ledge, and others along the length of it, where the sulphurets—I believe they call them sulphurets, though why they should, considering that, so far as I can see, the main dependence of a miner does not so lie, as some suppose, but in which it cannot be successfully maintained, wherein the same should not continue, while part and parcel of the same ore not committed to either in the sense referred to, whereas, under different circumstances, the most inexperienced among us could not detect it if it were, or might overlook it if it did, or scorn the very idea of such a thing, even though it were palpably demonstrated as such. Am I not right?"

I said, sorrowfully: "I feel ashamed of myself, Mr. Ward. I know I ought to understand you perfectly well, but you see that treacherous whisky cocktail has got into my head, and now I cannot understand even the simplest proposition. I told you how it would be."

"Oh, don't mind it, don't mind it; the fault was my own, no doubt—though I did think it clear enough for—"

"Don't say a word. Clear! Why, you stated it as clear as the sun to anybody but an abject idiot; but it's that confounded cocktail that has played the mischief."

"No; now don't say that. I'll begin it all over again, and—"

"Don't now—for goodness' sake, don't do anything of the kind, because I tell you my head is in such a condition that I don't believe I could understand the most trifling question a man could ask me."

"Now don't you be afraid. I'll put it so plain this time that you can't help but get the hang of it. We will begin at the very beginning." [Leaning far across the table, with determined impressiveness wrought upon his every feature, and fingers prepared to keep tally of each point enumerated; and I, leaning forward with painful interest, resolved to comprehend or perish.] "You know the vein, the ledge, the thing that contains the metal, whereby it constitutes the medium between all other forces, whether of present or remote agencies, so brought to bear in favor of the former against the latter, or the latter against the former or all, or both, or compromising the relative differences existing within the radius whence culminate the several degrees of similarity to which—"

I said: "Oh, hang my wooden head, it ain't any use!—it ain't any use to try—I can't understand anything. The plainer you get it the more I can't get the hang of it."

I heard a suspicious noise behind me, and turned in time to see Hingston dodging behind a newspaper, and quaking with a gentle ecstasy of laughter. I looked at Ward again, and he had thrown off his dread solemnity and was laughing also. Then I saw that I had been sold—that I had been made a victim of a swindle in the way of a string of plausibly worded sentences that didn't mean anything under the sun. Artemus Ward was one of the best fellows in the world, and one of the most companionable. It has been said that he was not fluent in conversation, but, with the above experience in my mind, I differ.

1871

My First Literary Venture

I was a very smart child at the age of thirteen—an unusually smart child, I thought at the time. It was then that I did my first newspaper scribbling, and most unexpectedly to me it stirred up a fine sensation in the community. It did, indeed, and I was very proud of it, too. I was a printer's "devil," and a progressive and aspiring one. My uncle had me on his paper (the *Weekly Hannibal Journal*, two dollars a year in advance—five hundred subscribers, and they paid in cordwood, cabbages, and unmarketable turnips), and on a lucky summer's day he left town to be gone a week, and asked me if I thought I could edit one issue of the paper judiciously. Ah! didn't I want to try! Higgins was the editor on the rival paper. He had lately been jilted, and one night a friend found an open note on the poor fellow's bed, in which he stated that he could not longer endure life and had drowned himself in Bear Creek. The friend ran down there and discovered Higgins wading back to shore. He had concluded he wouldn't. The village was full of it for several days, but Higgins did not suspect it. I thought this was a fine opportunity. I wrote an elaborately wretched account of the whole matter, and then illustrated it with villainous cuts engraved on the bottoms of wooden type with a jackknife—one of them a picture of Higgins wading out into the creek in his shirt, with a lantern, sounding the depth of the water with a walking-stick. I thought it was desperately funny, and was densely unconscious that there was any moral obliquity about such a publication. Being satisfied with this effort I looked around for other worlds to conquer, and it struck me that it would make good, interesting matter to charge the editor of a neighboring country paper with a piece of gratuitous rascality and "see him squirm."

I did it, putting the article into the form of a parody on the "Burial of Sir John Moore"—and a pretty crude parody it was, too.

Then I lampooned two prominent citizens outrageously—not because they had done anything to deserve, but merely because I thought it was my duty to make the paper lively.

Next I gently touched up the newest stranger—the lion of the day, the gorgeous journeyman tailor from Quincy. He was a simpering coxcomb of the first water, and the "loudest" dressed man in the state. He was an inveterate woman-killer. Every week he wrote lushy "poetry" for the *Journal*, about his newest conquest. His rhymes for my week were headed, "To MARY IN H——L," meaning to Mary in Hannibal, of course. But while setting up the piece I was suddenly riven from head to heel by what I regarded as a perfect thunderbolt of humor, and I compressed it into a snappy footnote at the bottom —thus: "We will let this thing pass, just this once; but we wish Mr. J. Gordon Runnels to understand distinctly that we have a character to sustain, and from this time forth when he wants to commune with his friends in h——l, he must select some other medium than the columns of this journal!"

The paper came out, and I never knew any little thing attract so much attention as those playful trifles of mine.

For once the *Hannibal Journal* was in demand—a novelty it had not experienced before. The whole town was stirred. Higgins dropped in with a double-barreled shotgun early in the forenoon. When he found that it was an infant (as he called me) that had done him the damage, he simply pulled my ears and went away; but he threw up his situation that night and left town for good. The tailor came with his goose and a pair of shears; but he despised me, too, and departed for the South that night. The two lampooned citizens came with threats of libel, and went away incensed at my insignificance. The country editor pranced in with a war-whoop next day, suffering for blood to drink; but he ended by forgiving me cordially and inviting me down to the drug store to wash away all animosity in a friendly bumper of "Fahnestock's Vermifuge." It was his little joke. My uncle was very angry when he got back—unreasonably so, I thought, considering what an impetus I had given the paper, and considering also that gratitude for his preservation ought to have been uppermost in his mind, inasmuch as by his delay he had so wonderfully escaped dissection, tomahawking, libel, and getting his head shot off. But he softened when he looked at the accounts and saw that I had actually booked the unparalleled number of thirty-three new subscribers, and had the vegetables to show for it, cordwood, cabbage, beans, and unsalable turnips enough to run the family for two years!

1871

A New Beecher Church

If the Rev. Mr. Smith, or the Rev. Mr. Jones, or the Rev. Mr. Brown, were about to build a new church edifice, it would be projected on the same old pattern, and be like pretty much all the other churches in the country, and so I would naturally mention it as a new Presbyterian church, or a new Methodist, or a new Baptist church, and never think of calling it by the pastor's name; but when a Beecher projects a church, that edifice is necessarily going to be something entirely fresh and original; it is not going to be like any other church in the world; it is going to be as variegated, eccentric, and marked with as peculiar and striking an individuality as a Beecher himself; it is going to have a deal more Beecher in it than any one narrow creed can fit into without rattling, or any one arbitrary order of architecture can symmetrically enclose and cover. Consequently to call it simply a Congregational church would not give half an idea of the thing. There is only one word broad enough, and wide enough, and deep enough to take in the whole affair, and express it cleanly, luminously, and concisely—and that is *Beecher*. The projected edifice I am about to speak of is, therefore, properly named in my caption as a new *"Beecher* Church."

The projector is the Rev. Thomas K. Beecher—brother of the other one, of course—I never knew but one Beecher that wasn't, and *he* was a nephew. The new church is to be built in Elmira, N.Y., where Mr. B. has been preaching to one and the same congregation for the last sixteen years, and is thoroughly esteemed and beloved by his people. I have had opportunity to hear all about the new church, for I have lately been visiting in Elmira.

Now, when one has that disease which gives its possessor the title of "humorist," he must make oath to his statements, else the public will not believe him. Therefore I make solemn oath that what I am going to tell about the new church is the strict truth.

The main building—for there are to be three, massed together in a large grassy square, ornamented with quite a forest of shade trees—will be the church proper. It will be lofty, in order to secure good air and ventilation. The auditorium will be *circular*—an amphitheatre, after the ordinary pattern of an opera-house, *without galleries*. It is to seat a thousand persons. On one side (or one end, if you choose) will be an ample, raised platform for the minister, the rear half of which will be occupied by the organ and the choir. Before the minister will be the circling amphitheatre of pews, the first thirty or forty on the level floor, and the next rising in graduated tiers to the walls. The seats on the level floor will be occupied by the aged and infirm, who can enter the church through a hall under the speaker's platform, without climbing any stairs. The people occupying the raised tiers will enter by a dozen doors opening into the church from a lobby like an opera-house lobby, and descend the various aisles to their places. In case of fire or earth-quakes, these numerous exits will be convenient and useful.

No space is to be wasted. Under the raised tiers of pews are to be stalls for horses and carriages, so that these may be sheltered from sun and rain. There will be twenty-four of these stalls, each stall to be en-tered by an arch of ornamental masonry—no doors to open or shut. Consequently, the outside base of the church will have a formidable port-holed look, like a man-of-war. The stalls are to be so mailed with "deadeners," and so thoroughly plastered, that neither sound nor smell can ascend to the church and offend the worshippers. The horses will be in attendance at church but an hour or two at a time, of course, and can defile the stalls but little; an immediate cleansing after they leave is to set that all right again.

There is to be no steeple on the church—merely because no practical use can be made of it.

There is to be no bell, because all men know what time church serv-ice begins without that exasperating nuisance. In explanation of this remark, I will state that at home I suffer in the vicinity and under the distracting clangour of thirteen church bells, all of whom (is that right?) clamour at once, and no two in accord. A large part of my time is taken up in devising cruel and unusual sufferings and in fancy inflicting them on those bell-ringers and having a good time.

The second building is to be less lofty than the church; is to be built right against the rear of it, and communicate with it by a door. It is to have two stories. On the first floor will be three distinct Sunday school rooms; all large, but one considerably larger than the other two. The Sunday school connected with Mr. Beecher's church has always been a "graded" one, and each department singularly thorough in its grade of instruction; the pupil wins his advancement to the higher grades by hard-won proficiency, not by mere added years. The largest of the three compartments will be used as the main Sunday school room, and for the week-day evening lecture.

The whole upper story of this large building will be well lighted and ventilated, and occupied wholly as a play-room for the children of the church, and it will stand open and welcome to them through all the week-days. They can fill it with their playthings if they choose, and besides it will be furnished with dumb-bells, swings, rocking-horses, and all such matters as children delight in. The idea is to make a child look upon a church as only another *home,* and a sunny one, rather than as a dismal exile or a prison.

The third building will be less lofty than the second; it will adjoin the rear of the second, and communicate with it by a door or doors. It will consist of three stories. Like the other two buildings, it will cover considerable ground. On the first floor will be the "church parlours" where the usual social gatherings of modern congregations are held. On the same floor, and opening into the parlours, will be a reception-room, and also a circulating library—a *free* library—not simply free to the church membership, but to everybody, just as is the present library of Mr. Beecher's church (and few libraries are more extensively and more diligently and gratefully used than this one). Also on this first floor, and communicating with the parlours, will be—tell it not in Gath, publish it not in Askalon!—six *bath-rooms!*—hot and cold water—free tickets issued to any applicant among the unclean of the congregation! The idea is sound and sensible, for this reason. Many members of all congregations have no good bathing facilities, and are not able to pay for them at the barber-shops without feeling the expense; and yet a luxurious bath is a thing that all civilized beings greatly enjoy and derive healthful benefit from. The church buildings are to be heated by steam, and consequently the waste steam can be very judiciously utilised in the proposed bath-rooms. In speaking of this bath-room project, I have revealed a state secret—but I never could keep one of any kind, state or otherwise. Even the congregation were not to know of this matter, the building committee were to leave it unmentioned in their report; but I got hold of it—and from a member of that committee, too—and I had rather part with one of my hind legs than keep still about it. The bath-rooms are unquestionably to be built, and so why not tell it?

In the second story of this third building will be the permanent residence of the "church missionary," a lady who constantly looks after the poor and sick of the church; also a set of lodging and living rooms for the janitors (or janitresses?—for they will be women, Mr. Beecher holding that women are tidier and more efficient in such a position than men, and that they ought to dwell upon the premises and give them their undivided care); also on this second floor are to be six rooms to do duty as a church infirmary for the sick poor of the congregation, this church having always supported and taken care of its own unfortunates instead of leaving them to the public charity. In the infirmary will be kept one or two water-beds (for invalids whose pains will not allow them to lie on a less yielding substance), and half-a-dozen reclining invalid-chairs on wheels. The water-beds and invalid-chairs at present belonging to the church are always in demand and never out of service. Part of the appurtenances of the new church will be a horse and an easy vehicle, to be kept and driven by a janitor, and used wholly for giving the church's indigent invalids air and exercise. It is found that such an establishment is daily needed—so much so, indeed, as to almost amount to a church necessity.

The third story of this third building is to be occupied as the church *kitchen*, and it is sensibly placed aloft, so that the ascending noises and boarding-house smells shall go up and aggravate the birds instead of the saints—except such of the latter as are above the clouds, and they can easily keep out of the way of it, no doubt. Dumb-waiters will carry the food *down* to the church parlours, instead of up. Why is it that nobody has thought of the simple wisdom of this arrangement before? Is it for a church to step forward and tell us how to get rid of kitchen smells and noises? If it be asked why the new church will need a kitchen, I remind the reader of the infirmary occupants, etc. They must eat; and, besides, social gatherings of members of this congregation meet at the church parlours as often as three and four evenings a week, and sew, drink tea, and g——. G——. It commences with g, I think, but somehow I cannnot think of the word. The new church parlours will be large, and it is intended that these social gatherings shall be promoted and encouraged, and that they shall take an added phase, viz.: when several families want to indulge in a little reunion, and have not room in their small houses at home, they can have it in the church parlours. You will notice in every feature of this new church one predominant idea and purpose always discernible—the banding together of the congregation as a *family*, and the making of the church a *home*. You see it in the play-room, the library, the parlours, the baths, the infirmary—it is everywhere. It is the great central, ruling idea. To entirely consummate such a thing would be impossible with nearly any other congregation in the Union; but after sixteen years of moulding and teaching, Mr. Beecher has made it wholly possible and practicable with this one. It is not stretching metaphor too far to say that he is the father of his people, and his church their mother.

If the new church project is a curiosity, it is still but an inferior curiosity compared to the plan of raising the money for it. One could have told, with his eyes shut and one hand tied behind him, that it originated with a Beecher—I was going to say with a lunatic, but the success of the plan robs me of the opportunity.

When it was decided to build a new church edifice at a cost of not less than 40,000 dollars nor more than 50,000 dollars (for the membership is not three hundred and fifty strong, and there are not six men in it who can strictly be called rich), Mr. Beecher gave to each member a printed circular worded as follows—each circular enclosed in an envelope prepaid and addressed to himself, to be returned through the post-office:

[CONFIDENTIAL.]

It is proposed to build a meeting-house and other rooms for the use of the church. To do this work honestly and well, it is proposed to spend *one year* in raising a part of the money *in advance,* and in getting plans and making contracts.

1 year–plans and contracts . . .	Ap. 1, 1871, to 1872
" " build and cover in . . .	" 1872, " 1873
" " plaster, finish, and furnish,	" 1873, " 1874
" " pay for in full and dedicate,	" 1874, " 1875

It is proposed to expend not less than twenty thousand dollars nor more than fifty thousand—according to the ability shown by the returns of these cards of *confidential* subscription. Any member of the Church and congregation, or any friend of the Church, is allowed and invited to subscribe, but no one is urged.

                                              T. K. BEECHER, Pastor.

To help build our meeting-house, I think that I shall be able to give not less than $, and not more than $, each year for four years, beginning April 1, 1871.

Or I can make in one payment $.

Trusting in the Lord to help me, I hereby subscribe the same as noted above.

                                              Name,   •
                                              Residence,   •

The subscriptions were to be wholly *voluntary* and strictly *confidential;* no one was to know the amount of a man's subscription except himself and the minister; nobody was *urged* to give anything at all; all were simply invited to give whatever sum they felt was right and just, from ten cents upward, and no questions asked, no criticisms made, no revealments uttered. There was no possible chance for glory, for even though a man gave his whole fortune nobody would ever know it. I do not know when anything has struck me as being so utopian, so absurdly romantic, so ignorant, on its face, of human nature. And so anybody would have thought. Parties said Mr. Beecher had "educated" his people, and that each would give as he privately felt able, and not bother about the glory. I believed human nature to be a more potent educator than any minister, and that the result would show it. But I was wrong. At the end of a month or two, some two-thirds of the circulars had wended back, one by one, to the pastor, silently and secretly, through the post-office, and then, without mentioning the name of any giver or the amount of his gift, Mr. Beecher announced from the pulpit that all the money needed was pledged—the *certain* amount being over 45,000 dollars, and the possible amount over 53,000 dollars! When the remainder of the circulars have come in, it is confidently expected and believed that they will add to these amounts a sum of not less than 10,000 dollars. A great many subscriptions from children and working men consisted of cash enclosures ranging from a ten cent. currency stamp up to five, ten, and fifteen dollars. As I said before, the plan of levying the building tax, and the success of the plan, are much more curious and surprising than the exceedingly curious edifice the money is to create.

The reason the moneys are to be paid in four annual instalments—for that is the plan—is, partly to make the payments easy, but chiefly because the church is to be substantially built, and its several parts allowed time to settle and season, each in its turn. For instance, the substructures will be allowed a good part of the first year to settle and compact themselves, after completion; the walls the second year, and so forth and so on. There is to be no work done by contract, and no unseasoned wood used. The materials are to be sound and good; and honest, competent, conscientious workmen (Beecher says there are such, the opinion of the world to the contrary notwithstanding) hired at full wages, by the day, to put them together.

The above statements are all true and genuine, according to the oath I have already made thereto, and which I am now about to repeat before a notary, in legal form, with my hand upon the Book. Consequently we are going to have at least one sensible, but very, very curious church in America.

I am aware that I had no business to tell all these matters, but the reporter instinct was strong upon me and I could not help it. And besides they were in everybody's mouth in Elmira, anyway.

1871

Portrait of King William III

I never can look at those periodical portraits in *The Galaxy* magazine without feeling a wild, tempestuous ambition to be an artist. I have
seen thousands and thousands of pictures in my time—acres of them
here and leagues of them in the galleries of Europe—but never any that
moved me as these portraits do.

There is the portrait of Monsignore Capel in the November number,
now *could* anything be sweeter than that? And there was Bismarck's, in
the October number; who can look at that without being purer and
stronger and nobler for it? And Thurlow Weed's picture in the September number; I would not have died without seeing that, no, not for
anything this world can give. But look back still further and recall my
own likeness as printed in the August number; if I had been in my
grave a thousand years when that appeared, I would have got up and
visited the artist.

I sleep with all these portraits under my pillow every night, so that
I can go on studying them as soon as the day dawns in the morning. I
know them all as thoroughly as if I had made them myself; I know
every line and mark about them. Sometimes when company are present I shuffle the portraits all up together, and then pick them out one
by one and call their names, without referring to the printing at the bottom. I seldom make a mistake—never, when I am calm.

I have had the portraits framed for a long time, waiting till my
aunt gets everything ready for hanging them up in the parlor. But first
one thing and then another interferes, and so the thing is delayed. Once
she said they would have more of the peculiar kind of light they
needed in the attic. The old simpleton! it is as dark as a tomb up there.
But she does not know anything about art, and so she has no reverence for it. When I showed her my "Map of the Fortifications of Paris,"
she said it was rubbish.

Well, from nursing those portraits so long, I have come at last to
have a perfect infatuation for art. I have a teacher now, and my
enthusiasm continually and tumultuously grows, as I learn to use
with more and more facility the pencil, brush, and graver. I am
studying under De Mellville, the house and portrait painter. [His

name was Smith when he lived West.] He does any kind of artist
work a body wants, having a genius that is universal, like Michael
Angelo. Resembles that great artist, in fact. The back of his head
is like his, and he wears his hat-brim tilted down on his nose to expose
it.

I have been studying under De Mellville several months now. The
first month I painted fences, and gave general satisfaction. The next
month I whitewashed a barn. The third, I was doing tin roofs; the
fourth, common signs; the fifth, statuary to stand before cigar shops.
This present month is only the sixth, and I am already in portraits!

The humble offering which accompanies these remarks—the portrait
of his Majesty William III, King of Prussia—is my fifth attempt in portraits, and my greatest success. It has received unbounded praise from
all classes of the community, but that which gratifies me most is the frequent and cordial verdict that it resembles the *Galaxy* portraits. Those
were my first love, my earliest admiration, the original source and in-
centive of my art-ambition. Whatever I am in Art to-day, I owe to
these portraits. I ask no credit for myself—I deserve none. And I never
take any, either. Many a stranger has come to my exhibition (for I have
had my portrait of King William on exhibition at one dollar a ticket),
and would have gone away blessing *me*, if I had let him, but I never
did. I always stated where I got the idea.

King William wears large bushy side-whiskers, and some critics
have thought that this portrait would be more complete if they were
added. But it was not possible. There was not room for side-whiskers
and epaulettes both, and so I let the whiskers go, and put in the epaulettes, for the sake of style. That thing on his hat is an eagle. The Prus-
sian eagle—it is a national emblem. When I say hat I mean helmet; but
it seems impossible to make a picture of a helmet that a body can have
confidence in.

I wish kind friends everywhere would aid me in my endeavor to attract a little attention to the *Galaxy* portraits. I feel persuaded it can be
accomplished, if the course to be pursued be chosen with judgment. I
write for that magazine all the time, and so do many abler men, and if
I can get these portraits into universal favor, it is all I ask; the reading-
matter will take care of itself.

WILLIAM III.,
King of Prussia.

COMMENDATIONS OF THE PORTRAIT

There is nothing like it in the Vatican.   Pius IX

It has none of that vagueness, that dreamy spirituality about it, which many of the first critics of Arkansas have objected to in the Murillo school of Art.   Ruskin

The expression is very interesting.   J. W. Titian

        (*Keeps a macaroni store in Venice, at the old family stand.*)

It is the neatest thing in still life I have seen for years.   Rosa Bonheur

The smile may be almost called unique.   Bismarck

I never saw such character portrayed in a pictured face before.
                                                                            De Mellville

There is a benignant simplicity about the execution of this work which warms the heart toward it as much, full as much, as it fascinates the eye.
                                                                              Landseer

One cannot see it without longing to contemplate the artist.
                                                                  Frederick William

Send me the entire edition—together with the plate and the original portrait—and name your own price. And—would you like to come over and stay awhile with Napoleon at Wilhelmshöe? It shall not cost you a cent.
                                                                            William iii

1871

"Blanketing" the Admiral

After a three months' absence, I found myself in San Francisco again, without a cent. When my credit was about exhausted (for I had become too mean and lazy, now, to work on a morning paper, and there were no vacancies on the evening journals), I was created San Francisco correspondent of the *Enterprise,* and at the end of five months I was out of debt, but my interest in my work was gone; for, my correspondence being a daily one, without rest or respite, I got unspeakably tired of it. I wanted another change. The vagabond instinct was strong upon me. Fortune favored, and I got a new berth and a delightful one. It was to go down to the Sandwich Islands and write some letters for the Sacramento *Union,* an excellent journal and liberal with employees.

We sailed in the propeller *Ajax,* in the middle of winter. The almanac called it winter, distinctly enough, but the weather was a compromise between spring and summer. Six days out of port, it became summer altogether. We had some thirty passengers; among them a cheerful soul by the name of Williams, and three sea-worn old whale-ship captains going down to join their vessels. These latter played euchre in the smoking-room day and night, drank astonishing quantities of raw whisky without being in the least affected by it, and were the happiest people I think I ever saw. And then there was "the old Admiral"—a retired whaleman. He was a roaring, terrific combination of wind and lightning and thunder, and earnest, whole-souled profanity. But nevertheless he was tender-hearted as a girl. He was a raving, deafening, devastating typhoon, laying waste the cowering seas, but with an unvexed refuge in the center where all comers were safe and at rest. Nobody could know the "Admiral" without liking him; and in a sudden and dire emergency I think no friend of his would know which to choose—to be cursed by him or prayed for by a less efficient person.

His title of "Admiral" was more strictly "official" than any ever worn by a naval officer before or since, perhaps—for it was the voluntary offering of a whole nation, and came direct from the *people* themselves without any intermediate red tape—the people of the Sandwich Islands. It was a title that came to him freighted with affection, and honor, and appreciation of his unpretending merit. And in testimony of the genuineness of the title it was publicly ordained that an exclusive flag should be devised for him and used solely to welcome his coming and wave him god-speed in his going. From that time forth, whenever his ship was signaled in the offing, or he catted his anchor and stood out to sea, that ensign streamed from the royal halliards on the parliament house, and the nation lifted their hats to it with spontaneous accord.

Yet he had never fired a gun or fought a battle in his life. When I knew him on board the *Ajax,* he was seventy-two years old and had plowed the salt-water sixty-one of them. For sixteen years he had gone in and out of the harbor of Honolulu in command of a whale-ship, and for sixteen more had been captain of a San Francisco and Sandwich Island passenger-packet and had never had an accident or lost a vessel. The simple natives knew him for a friend who never failed them, and regarded him as children regard a father. It was a dangerous thing to oppress them when the roaring Admiral was around.

Two years before I knew the Admiral, he had retired from the sea on a competence, and had sworn a colossal nine-jointed oath that he would "never go within *smelling* distance of the salt-water again as long as he lived." And he had conscientiously kept it. That is to say, *he* considered he had kept it, and it would have been more than dangerous to suggest to him, even in the gentlest way, that making eleven long sea-voyages, as a passenger, during the two years that had transpired since he "retired," was only keeping the general spirit of it and not the strict letter.

The Admiral knew only one narrow line of conduct to pursue in any and all cases where there was a fight, and that was to shoulder his way straight in without an inquiry as to the rights or the merits of it, and take the part of the weaker side. And this was the reason why he was always sure to be present at the trial of any universally execrated criminal to oppress and intimidate the jury with a vindictive pantomime of what he would do to them if he ever caught them out of the box. And this was why harried cats and outlawed dogs that knew him confidently took sanctuary under his chair in time of trouble. In the beginning he was the most frantic and bloodthirsty Union man that drew breath in the shadow of the flag; but the instant the Southerners began to go down before the sweep of the Northern armies, he ran up the Confederate colors, and from that time till the end was a rampant and inexorable secessionist.

He hated intemperance with a more uncompromising animosity than any individual I have ever met, of either sex; and he was never tired of storming against it and beseeching friends and strangers alike to be wary and drink with moderation. And yet if any creature had been guileless enough to intimate that his absorbing nine gallons of "straight" whisky during our voyage was any fraction short of rigid or inflexible abstemiousness, in that self-same moment the old man would have spun him to the uttermost parts of the earth in the whirlwind of his wrath. Mind, I am not saying his whisky ever affected his head or his legs, for it did not, in even the slightest degree. He was a capacious container, but he did not hold enough for that. He took a level tumblerful of whisky every morning before he put his clothes on—"to sweeten his bilgewater," he said. He took another after he got the most of his clothes on, "to settle his mind and give him his bearings." He then shaved, and put on a clean shirt; after which he recited the Lord's Prayer in a fervent, thundering bass that shook the ship to her kelson and suspended all conversation in the main cabin. Then, at this stage, being invariably "by the head," or "by the stern," or "listed to port or starboard," he took one more to "put him on an even keel so that he would mind his hellum and not miss stays and go about, every time he came up in the wind." And now, his stateroom door swung open and the sun of his benignant face beamed redly out upon men and women and children, and he roared his "Shipmets ahoy!" in a way that was calculated to wake the dead and precipitate the final resurrection; and forth he strode, a picture to look at and a presence to enforce attention. Stalwart and portly; not a gray hair; broad-brimmed slouch hat; semi-sailor toggery of blue navy flannel—roomy and ample; a stately expanse of shirt-front and a liberal amount of black-silk neck-cloth tied with a sailor-knot; large chain and imposing seals impending from his fob; awe-inspiring feet, and "a hand like the hand of Providence," as his whaling brethren expressed it; wristbands and sleeves pushed back half-way to the elbow, out of respect for the warm weather, and exposing hairy arms, gaudy with red and blue anchors, ships, and goddesses of liberty tattooed in India ink. But these details were only secondary matters—his face was the lodestone that chained the eye. It was a sultry disk, glowing determinedly out through a weather-beaten mask of mahogany, and studded with warts, seamed with scars, "blazed" all over with unfailing fresh slips of the razor; and with cheery eyes, under shaggy brows, contemplating the world from over the back of a gnarled crag of a nose that loomed vast and lonely out of the undulating immensity that spread away from its foundations. At his heels frisked the darling of his bachelor estate, his terrier "Fan," a creature no larger than a squirrel. The main part of his daily life was occupied in looking after "Fan," in a motherly way, and doctoring her for a hundred ailments which existed only in his imagination.

The Admiral seldom read newspapers; and when he did he never believed anything they said. He read nothing, and believed in nothing, but *The Old Guard*, a secession periodical published in New York. He carried a dozen copies of it with him, always, and referred to them for all required information. If it was not there, he supplied it himself, out of a bountiful fancy, inventing history, names, dates, and everything else necessary to make his point good in an argument. Consequently, he was a formidable antagonist in a dispute. Whenever he swung clear of the record and began to create history, the enemy was helpless and had to surrender. Indeed, the enemy could not keep from betraying some little spark of indignation at his manufactured history—and when it came to indignation, that was the Admiral's very "best hold." He was always ready for a political argument, and if nobody started one he would do it himself. With his third retort his temper would begin to rise, and within five minutes he would be blowing a gale, and within fifteen minutes his smoking-room audience would be utterly stormed away and the old man left solitary and alone, banging the table with his fist, kicking the chairs, and roaring a hurricane of profanity. It got so, after a while, that whenever the Admiral approached, with politics in his eye, the passengers would drop out with quiet accord, afraid to meet him; and he would camp on a deserted field.

But he found his match at last, and before a full company. At one time or another, everybody had entered the lists against him and been routed, except the quiet passenger Williams. He had never been able to get an expression of opinion out of him on politics. But now, just as the Admiral drew near the door and the company were about to slip out, Williams said:

"Admiral, are you *certain* about that circumstance concerning the clergyman you mentioned the other day?"—referring to a piece of the Admiral's manufactured history.

Every one was amazed at the man's rashness. The idea of deliberately inviting annihilation was a thing incomprehensible. The retreat came to a halt; then everybody sat down again wondering, to await the upshot of it. The Admiral himself was as surprised as any one. He paused in the door, with his red handkerchief half raised to his sweating face, and contemplated the daring reptile in the corner.

"*Certain* of it? Am I *certain* of it? Do you think I've been lying about it? What do you take me for? Anybody that don't know that circumstance, don't know anything; a child ought to know it. Read up your history! Read it up —— —— —— ——, and don't come asking a man if he's *certain* about a bit of A B C stuff that the very Southern niggers know all about."

Here the Admiral's fires began to wax hot, the atmosphere thickened, the coming earthquake rumbled, he began to thunder and lighten. Within three minutes his volcano was in full irruption and he was discharging flames and ashes of indignation, belching black volumes of foul history aloft, and vomiting red-hot torrents of profanity from his crater. Meantime Williams sat silent, and apparently deeply and earnestly interested in what the old man was saying. By and by, when the lull came, he said in the most deferential way, and with the gratified air of a man who has had a mystery cleared up which had been puzzling him uncomfortably:

"*Now*, I understand it. I always thought I knew that piece of history well enough, but was still afraid to trust it, because there was not that convincing particularity about it that one likes to have in history; but when you mentioned every name, the other day, and every date, and every little circumstance, in their just order and sequence, I said to myself, *this* sounds something like—*this* is history—*this* is putting it in a shape that gives a man confidence; and I said to myself afterward, I will just ask the Admiral if he is perfectly certain about the details, and if he is I will come out and thank him for clearing this matter up for me. And that is what I want to do now—for until you set that matter right it was nothing but just a confusion in my mind, without head or tail to it."

Nobody ever saw the Admiral look so mollified before, and so pleased. Nobody had ever received his bogus history as gospel before; its genuineness had always been called in question either by words or looks; but here was a man that not only swallowed it all down, but was grateful for the dose. He was taken aback; he hardly knew what to say; even his profanity failed him. Now, Williams continued, modestly and earnestly:

"But, Admiral, in saying that this was the first stone thrown, and that this precipitated the war, you have overlooked a circumstance which you are perfectly familiar with, but which has escaped your memory. Now I grant you that what you have stated is correct in every detail— to wit: that on the 16th of October, 1860, two Massachusetts clergymen, named Waite and Granger, went in disguise to the house of John Moody, in Rockport, at dead of night, and dragged forth two Southern women and their two little children, and after tarring and feathering them conveyed them to Boston and burned them alive in the State House square; and I also grant your proposition that this deed is what led to the secession of South Carolina on the 20th of December following. Very well." [Here the company were pleasantly surprised to hear Williams proceed to come back at the Admiral with his own invincible weapon—clean, pure, *manufactured history*, without a word of truth in it.] "Very well, I say. But, Admiral, why overlook the Willis and Morgan case in South Carolina? You are too well informed a man not to know all about that circumstance. Your arguments and your conversations have shown you to be intimately conversant with every detail of this national quarrel. You develop matters of history every day that show plainly that you are no smatterer in it, content to nibble about the surface, but a man who has searched the depths and possessed yourself of everything that has a bearing upon the great question. Therefore, let me just recall to your mind that Willis and Morgan case —though I see by your face that the whole thing is already passing through your memory at this moment. On the 12th of August, 1860, *two months* before the Waite and Granger affair, two South Carolina clergymen, named John H. Morgan and Winthrop L. Willis, one a Methodist and the other an Old School Baptist, disguised themselves, and went at midnight to the house of a planter named Thompson—Archibald F. Thompson, vice-president under Thomas Jefferson—and took thence, at midnight, his widowed aunt (a Northern woman), and her adopted child, an orphan named Mortimer Highie, afflicted with epilepsy and suffering at the time from white swelling on one of his legs, and compelled to walk on crutches in consequence; and the two ministers, in spite of the pleadings of the victims, dragged them to the bush, tarred and feathered them, and afterward burned them at the stake in the city of Charleston. You remember perfectly well what a stir it made; you remember perfectly well that even the Charleston *Courier* stigmatized the act as being unpleasant, of questionable propriety, and scarcely justifiable, and likewise that it would not be matter of surprise if retaliation ensued. And you remember also, that this thing was the *cause* of the Massachusetts outrage. Who, indeed, were the two Massachusetts ministers? and who were the two Southern women they burned? I do not need to remind *you*, Admiral, with your intimate knowledge of history, that Waite was the nephew of the woman burned in Charleston; that Granger was her cousin in the second degree, and that the women they burned in Boston were the wife of John H. Morgan, and the still loved but divorced wife of Winthrop L. Willis. Now, Admiral, it is only fair that you should acknowledge that the first provocation came from the Southern preachers and that the Northern ones were justified in retaliating. In your arguments you never yet have shown the least disposition to withhold a just verdict or be in anywise unfair, when authoritative history condemned your position, and therefore I have no hesitation in asking you to take the original blame from the Massachusetts ministers, in this matter, and transfer it to the South Carolina clergymen where it justly belongs."

The Admiral was conquered. This sweet-spoken creature who swallowed his fraudulent history as if it were the bread of life; basked in his furious blasphemy as if it were generous sunshine; found only calm, even-handed justice in his rampant partisanship; and flooded him with invented history so sugar-coated with flattery and deference that there was no rejecting it, was "too many" for him. He stammered some awkward, profane sentences about the —— —— —— — Willis and Morgan business having escaped his memory, but that he "remembered it now," and then, under pretense of giving Fan some medicine for an imaginary cough, drew out of the battle and went away, a vanquished man. Then cheers and laughter went up, and Williams, the ship's benefactor, was a hero. The news went about the vessel, champagne was ordered, an enthusiastic reception instituted in the smoking-room, and everybody flocked thither to shake hands with the conqueror. The wheelsman said afterward, that the Admiral stood up behind the pilothouse and "ripped and cursed all to himself" till he loosened the smoke-stack guys and becalmed the mainsail.

The Admiral's power was broken. After that, if he began an argument, somebody would bring Williams, and the old man would grow weak and begin to quiet down at once. And as soon as he was done, Williams in his dulcet, insinuating way, would invent some history (referring for proof, to the old man's own excellent memory and to copies of *The Old Guard* known not to be in his possession) that would turn the tables completely and leave the Admiral all abroad and helpless. By and by he came to so dread Williams and his gilded tongue that he would stop talking when he saw him approach, and finally ceased to mention politics altogether, and from that time forward there was entire peace and serenity in the ship.

From ROUGHING IT, 1872

A Deception

You may remember that I lectured lately for the young gentlemen of the Clayonian Society? During the afternoon of that day I was talking with one of the young gentlemen referred to, and he said he had an uncle who, from some cause or other, seemed to have grown permanently bereft of all emotion. And with tears in his eyes this young man said:

"Oh, if I could only see him laugh once more! Oh, if I could only see him weep!"

I was touched. I could never withstand distress. I said:

"Bring him to my lecture. I'll start him for you."

"Oh, if you could but do it! If you could but do it, all our family would bless you for evermore; for he is very dear to us. Oh, my benefactor, can you make him laugh? Can you bring soothing tears to those parched orbs?"

I was profoundly moved. I said:

"My son, bring the old party round. I have got some jokes in my lecture that will make him laugh, if there is any laugh in him; and, if they miss fire, I have got some others that'll make him cry or kill him, one or the other."

Then the young man wept on my neck, and presently spread both hands on my head and looked up towards heaven, mumbling something reverently; and then he went after his uncle. He placed him in full view, in the second row of benches, that night, and I began on him. I tried him with mild jokes—then with severe ones; I dosed him with bad jokes, and riddled him with good ones; I fired old, stale jokes on him, and peppered him fore and aft with red-hot new ones. I warmed up to my work, and assaulted him on the right and left, in front and behind; I fumed, and charged, and ranted, till I was hoarse and sick, and frantic and furious; but I never moved him once—I never started a smile or a tear! Never a ghost of a smile, and never a suspicion of moisture! I was astounded. I closed the lecture at last with one despairing shriek—with one wild burst of humor—and hurled a joke of supernatural atrocity full at him. It never phased him! Then I sat down bewildered and exhausted.

The president of the society came up and bathed my head with cold water, and said:

"What made you carry on so towards the last?"

I said, "I was trying to make that confounded old idiot laugh in the second row."

And he said, "Well, you were wasting your time; because he is deaf and dumb, and as blind as a badger."

Now was that any way for that old man's nephew to impose on a stranger and an orphan like me?

1872

A Genuine Mexican Plug

I resolved to have a horse to ride. I had never seen such wild, free, magnificent horsemanship outside of a circus at these picturesquely clad Mexicans, Californians, and Mexicanized Americans displayed in Carson streets every day. How they rode! Leaning just gently forward out of the perpendicular, easy and nonchalant, with broad slouch-hat brim blown square up in front, and long *riata* swinging above the head, they swept through the town like the wind! The next minute they were only a sailing puff of dust on the far desert. If they trotted, they sat up gallantly and gracefully, and seemed part of the horse; did not go jiggering up and down after the silly Miss-Nancy fashion of the riding-schools. I had quickly learned to tell a horse from a cow, and was full of anxiety to learn more. I resolved to buy a horse.

While the thought was rankling in my mind, the auctioneer came scurrying through the plaza on a black beast that had as many humps and corners on him as a dromedary, and was necessarily uncomely; but he was "going, going, at twenty-two!—horse, saddle and bridle at twenty-two dollars, gentlemen!" and I could hardly resist.

A man whom I did not know (he turned out to be the auctioneer's brother) noticed the wistful look in my eye, and observed that that was a very remarkable horse to be going at such a price; and added that the saddle alone was worth the money. It was a Spanish saddle, with ponderous *tapidaros*, and furnished with the ungainly sole-leather covering with the unspellable name. I said I had half a notion to bid. Then this keen-eyed person appeared to me to be "taking my measure"; but I dismissed the suspicion when he spoke, for his manner was full of guileless candor and truthfulness. Said he:

"I know that horse—know him well. You are a stranger, I take it, and so you might think he was an American horse, maybe, but I assure you he is not. He is nothing of the kind; but—excuse my speaking in a low voice, other people being near—he is, without the shadow of a doubt, a Genuine Mexican Plug!"

I did not know what a Genuine Mexican Plug was, but there was something about this man's way of saying it, that made me swear inwardly that I would own a Genuine Mexican Plug, or die.

"Has he any other—er—advantages?" I inquired, suppressing what eagerness I could.

He hooked his forefinger in the pocket of my army shirt, led me to one side, and breathed in my ear impressively these words:

"He can out-buck anything in America!"

"Going, going, going—at *twent-ty*-four dollars and a half, gen—"

"Twenty-seven!" I shouted, in a frenzy.

"And sold!" said the auctioneer, and passed over the Genuine Mexican Plug to me.

I could scarcely contain my exultation. I paid the money, and put the animal in a neighboring livery stable to dine and rest himself.

In the afternoon I brought the creature into the plaza, and certain citizens held him by the head, and others by the tail, while I mounted him. As soon as they let go, he placed all his feet in a bunch together, lowered his back, and then suddenly arched it upward, and shot me straight into the air a matter of three or four feet! I came as straight down again, lit in the saddle, went instantly up again, came down almost on the high pommel, shot up again, and came down on the horse's neck—all in the space of three or four seconds. Then he rose and stood almost straight up on his hind feet, and I, clasping his lean neck desperately, slid back into the saddle, and held on. He came down, and immediately hoisted his heels into the air, delivering a vicious kick at the sky, and stood on his fore feet. And then down he came once more, and began the original exercise of shooting me straight up again.

The third time I went up I heard a stranger say: "Oh *don't* he buck, though!"

While I was up, somebody struck the horse a sounding thwack with a leathern strap, and when I arrived again the Genuine Mexican Plug was not there. A Californian youth chased him up and caught him, and asked if he might have a ride. I granted him that luxury. He mounted the Genuine, got lifted into the air once, but sent his spurs home as he descended, and the horse darted away like a telegram. He soared over three fences like a bird, and disappeared down the road toward the Washoe Valley.

I sat down on a stone with a sigh, and by a natural impulse one of my hands sought my forehead, and the other the base of my stomach. I believe I never appreciated, till then, the poverty of the human machinery—for I still needed a hand or two to place elsewhere. Pen cannot describe how I was jolted up. Imagination cannot conceive how disjointed I was—how internally, externally, and universally I was unsettled, mixed up, and ruptured. There was a sympathetic crowd around me, though.

One elderly-looking comforter said:

"Stranger, you've been taken in. Everybody in this camp knows that horse. Any child, any Injun, could have told you that he'd buck; he is the very worst devil to buck on the continent of America. You hear *me*. I'm Curry. *Old* Curry. Old *Abe* Curry. And moreover, he is a simon-pure, out-and-out, genuine d—d Mexican plug, and an uncommon mean one at that, too. Why, you turnip, if you had laid low and kept dark, there's chances to buy an *American* horse for mighty little more than you paid for that bloody old foreign relic."

I gave no sign; but I made up my mind that if the auctioneer's brother's funeral took place while I was in the territory I would postpone all other recreations and attend it.

After a gallop of sixteen miles the Californian youth and the Genuine Mexican Plug came tearing into town again, shedding foam-flakes like the spume-spray that drives before a typhoon, and, with one final skip over a wheelbarrow and a Chinaman, cast anchor in front of the "ranch."

Such panting and blowing! Such spreading and contracting of the red equine nostrils, and glaring of the wild equine eye! But was the imperial beast subjugated? Indeed, he was not. His lordship the Speaker of the House thought he was, and mounted him to go down to the Capitol; but the first dash the creature made was over a pile of telegraph-poles half as high as a church; and his time to the Capitol—one mile and three-quarters—remains unbeaten to this day. But then he took an advantage—he left out the mile, and only did the three-quarters. That is to say, he made a straight cut across lots, preferring fences and ditches to a crooked road; and when the Speaker got to the Capitol he said he had been in the air so much he felt as if he had made the trip on a comet.

In the evening the Speaker came home afoot for exercise, and got the Genuine towed back behind a quartz-wagon. The next day I loaned the animal to the Clerk of the House to go down to the Dana silver-mine, six miles, and *he* walked back for exercise, and go the horse towed. Everybody I loaned him to always walked back; they never could get enough exercise any other way. Still, I continued to loan him to anybody who was willing to borrow him, my idea being to get him crippled, and throw him on the borrower's hands, or killed, and make the borrower pay for him. But somehow nothing ever happened to him. He took chances that no other horse ever took and survived, but he always came out safe. It was his daily habit to try experiments that had always before been considered impossible, but he always got through. Sometimes he miscalculated a little, and did not get his rider through intact, but *he* always got through himself. Of course I had tried to sell him; but that was a stretch of simplicity which met with little sympathy. The auctioneer stormed up and down the streets on him for four days, dispersing the populace, interrupting business, and destroying children, and never got a bid—at least never any but the eighteen-dollar one he hired a notoriously substanceless bummer to make. The people only smiled pleasantly, and restrained their desire to buy, if they had any. Then the auctioneer brought in his bill, and I withdrew the horse from the market. We tried to trade him off at private vendue next, offering him at a sacrifice for second-hand tombstones, old iron, temperance tracts—any kind of property. But holders were stiff, and we retired from the market again. I never tried to ride the horse any more. Walking was good enough exercise for a man like me, that had nothing the matter with him except ruptures, internal injuries, and such things. Finally I tried to *give* him away. But it was a failure. Parties said earthquakes were handy enough on the Pacific coast—they did not wish to own one. As a last resort I offered him to the Governor for the use of the "Brigade." His face lit up eagerly at first, but toned down again, and he said the thing would be too palpable.

Just then the livery-stable man brought in his bill for six weeks' keeping—stall-room for the horse, fifteen dollars; hay for the horse, two hundred and fifty! The Genuine Mexican Plug had eaten a ton of the article, and the man said he would have eaten a hundred if he had let him.

I will remark here, in all seriousness, that the regular price of hay during that year and a part of the next was really two hundred and fifty dollars a ton. During a part of the previous year it had sold at five hundred a ton, in gold, and during the winter before that there was such scarcity of the article that in several instances small quanities had brought eight hundred dollars a ton in coin! The consequence might be guessed without my telling it: people turned their stock loose to starve, and before the spring arrived Carson and Eagle Valleys were almost literally carpeted with their carcasses! Any old settler there will verify these statements.

I managed to pay the livery bill, and that same day I gave the Genuine Mexican Plug to a passing Arkansas emigrant whom fortune delivered into my hand. If this ever meets his eye, he will doubtless remember the donation.

Now whoever has had the luck to ride a real Mexican plug will recognize the animal depicted in this chapter, and hardly consider him exaggerated—but the uninitiated will feel justified in regarding his portrait as a fancy sketch, perhaps.

From ROUGHING IT, 1872

The Great Landslide Case

The mountains are very high and steep about Carson, Eagle, and Washoe Valleys—very high and very steep, and so when the snow gets to melting off fast in the spring and the warm surface-earth begins to moisten and soften, the disastrous landslides commence. The reader cannot know what a landslide is, unless he has lived in that country and seen the whole side of a mountain taken off some fine morning and deposited down in the valley, leaving a vast, treeless, unsightly scar upon the mountain's front to keep the circumstance fresh in his memory all the years that he may go on living within seventy miles of that place.

General Buncombe was shipped out to Nevada in the invoice of territorial officers, to be United States Attorney. He considered himself a lawyer of parts, and he very much wanted an opportunity to manifest it—partly for the pure gratification of it and partly because his salary was territorially meager (which is a strong expression). Now the older citizens of a new territory look down upon the rest of the world with a calm, benevolent compassion, as long as it keeps out of the way—when it gets in the way they snub it. Sometimes this latter takes the shape of a practical joke.

One morning Dick Hyde rode furiously up to General Buncombe's door in Carson City and rushed into his presence without stopping to tie his horse. He seemed much excited. He told the General that he wanted him to conduct a suit for him and would pay him five hundred dollars if he achieved a victory. And then, with violent gestures and a world of profanity, he poured out his griefs. He said it was pretty well known that for some years he had been farming (or ranching, as the more customary term is) in Washoe District, and making a successful thing of it, and furthermore it was known that his ranch was situated just in the edge of the valley, and that Tom Morgan owned a ranch immediately above it on the mountainside. And now the trouble was, that one of those hated and dreaded landslides had come and slid Morgan's ranch, fences, cabins, cattle, barns, and everything down on top of *his* ranch and exactly covered up every single vestige of his property, to a depth of about thirty-eight feet. Morgan was in possession and refused to vacate the premises—said he was occupying his own cabin and not interfering with anybody else's—and said the cabin was standing on the same dirt and same ranch it had always stood on, and he would like to see anybody make him vacate.

"And when I reminded him," said Hyde, weeping, "that it was on top of my ranch and that he was trespassing, he had the infernal meanness to ask me why didn't I *stay* on my ranch and hold possession when I see him a-coming! Why didn't I *stay* on it, the blathering lunatic—by George, when I heard that racket and looked up that hill it was just like the whole world was a-ripping and a-tearing down that mountainside —splinters and cord-wood, thunder and lightning, hail and snow, odds and ends of haystacks, and awful clouds of dust!—trees going end over end in the air, rocks as big as a house jumping 'bout a thousand feet high and busting into ten million pieces, cattle turned inside out and a-coming head on with their tails hanging out between their teeth!— and in the midst of all that wrack and destruction sot that cussed Morgan on his gatepost, a-wondering why I didn't *stay and hold possession!* Laws bless me, I just took one glimpse, General, and lit out'n the county in three jumps exactly.

"But what grinds me is that that Morgan hangs on there and won't move off'n that ranch—says it's his'n and he's going to keep it—likes it better'n he did when it was higher up the hill. Mad! Well, I've been so mad for two days I couldn't find my way to town—been wandering around in the brush in a starving condition—got anything here to drink, General? But I'm here *now,* and I'm a-going to law. You hear *me!*"

Never in all the world, perhaps, were a man's feelings so outraged as were the General's. He said he had never heard of such high-handed conduct in all his life as this Morgan's. And he said there was no use in going to law—Morgan had no shadow of right to remain where he was —nobody in the wide world would uphold him in it, and no lawyer would take his case and no judge listen to it. Hyde said that right there was where he was mistaken—everybody in town sustained Morgan; Hal Brayton, a very smart lawyer, had taken his case; the courts being in vacation, it was to be tried before a referee, and ex-Governor Roop had already been appointed to that office, and would open his court in a large public hall near the hotel at two that afternoon.

The General was amazed. He said he had suspected before that the people of that territory were fools, and now he knew it. But he said rest easy, rest easy and collect the witnesses, for the victory was just as certain as if the conflict were already over. Hyde wiped away his tears and left.

At two in the afternoon referee Roop's Court opened, and Roop appeared throned among his sheriffs, the witnesses, and spectators, and wearing upon his face a solemnity so awe-inspiring that some of his fellow-conspirators had misgivings that maybe he had not comprehended, after all, that this was merely a joke. An unearthly stillness prevailed, for at the slightest noise the judge uttered sternly the command:

"Order in the Court!"

And the sheriffs promptly echoed it. Presently the General elbowed his way through the crowd of spectators, with his arms full of law-books, and on his ears fell an order from the judge which was the first respectful recognition of his high official dignity that had ever saluted them, and it trickled pleasantly through his whole system:

"Way for the United States Attorney!"

The witnesses were called—legislators, high government officers, ranchmen, miners, Indians, Chinamen, negroes. Three-fourths of them were called by the defendant Morgan, but no matter, their testimony invariably went in favor of the plaintiff Hyde. Each new witness only added new testimony to the absurdity of a man's claiming to own another man's property because his farm had slid down on top of it. Then the Morgan lawyers made their speeches, and seemed to make singularly weak ones—they did really nothing to help the Morgan cause. And now the General, with exultation in his face, got up and made an impassioned effort; he pounded the table, he banged the law-books, he shouted, and roared, and howled, he quoted from everything and everybody, poetry, sarcasm, statistics, history, pathos, bathos, blasphemy, and wound up with a grand war-whoop for free speech, freedom of the press, free schools, the Glorious Bird of America and the principles of eternal justice! [Applause.]

When the General sat down, he did it with the conviction that if there was anything in good strong testimony, a great speech and believing and admiring countenances all around, Mr. Morgan's case was killed. Ex-Governor Roop leaned his head upon his hand for some minutes, thinking, and the still audience waited for his decision. And then he got up and stood erect, with bended head, and thought again. Then he walked the floor with long, deliberate strides, his chin in his hand, and still the audience waited. At last he returned to his throne, seated himself, and began, impressively:

"Gentlemen, I feel the great responsibility that rests upon me this day. This is no ordinary case. On the contrary, it is plain that it is the most solemn and awful that ever man was called upon to decide. Gentlemen, I have listened attentively to the evidence, and have perceived that the weight of it, the overwhelming weight of it, is in favor of the plaintiff Hyde. I have listened also to the remark of counsel, with high interest—and especially will I commend the masterly and irrefutable logic of the distinguished gentleman who represents the plaintiff. But, gentlemen, let us beware how we allow mere human testimony, human ingenuity in argument and human ideas of equity, to influence us at a moment so solemn as this. Gentlemen, it ill becomes us, worms as we are, to meddle with the decrees of Heaven. It is plain to me that Heaven, in its inscrutable wisdom, has seen fit to move this defendant's ranch for a purpose. We are but creatures, and we must submit. If Heaven has chosen to favor the defendant Morgan in this marked and wonderful manner; and if Heaven, dissatisfied with the position of the Morgan ranch upon the mountainside, has chosen to remove it to a position more eligible and more advantageous for its owner, it ill becomes us, insects as we are, to question the legality of the act or inquire into the reasons that prompted it. No—Heaven created the ranches, and it is Heaven's prerogative to rearrange them, to experiment with them, to shift them around at its pleasure. It is for us to submit, without repining. I warn you that this thing which has happened is a thing with which the sacrilegious hands and brains and tongues of men must not meddle. Gentlemen, it is the verdict of this court that the plaintiff, Richard Hyde, has been deprived of his ranch by the visitation of God! And from this decision there is no appeal."

Buncombe seized his cargo of law-books and plunged out of the court-room frantic with indignation. He pronounced Roop to be a miraculous fool, an inspired idiot. In all good faith he returned at night and remonstrated with Roop upon his extravagant decision, and implored him to walk the floor and think for half an hour, and see if he could not figure out some sort of modification of the verdict. Roop yielded at last and got up to walk. He walked two hours and a half, and at last his face lit up happily and he told Buncombe it had occurred to him that the ranch underneath the new Morgan ranch still belonged to Hyde, that his title to the ground was just as good as it had ever been, and therefore he was of opinion that Hyde had a right to dig it out from under there and—

The General never waited to hear the end of it. He was always an impatient and irascible man, that way. At the end of two months the fact that he had been played upon with a joke had managed to bore itself, like another Hoosac Tunnel, through the solid adamant of his understanding.

From ROUGHING IT, 1872

How the Author Was Sold in Newark

It is seldom pleasant to tell on oneself, but sometimes it is a sort of relief to a man to make a confession. I wish to unburden my mind now, and yet I almost believe that I am moved to do it more because I long to bring censure upon another man than because I desire to pour balm upon my wounded heart. (I don't know what balm is, but I believe it is the correct expression to use in this connection—never having seen any balm.) You may remember that I lectured in Newark lately for the young gentlemen of the —— Society? I did at any rate. During the afternoon of that day I was talking with one of the young gentlemen just referred to, and he said he had an uncle who, from some cause or other, seemed to have grown permanently bereft of all emotion. And with tears in his eyes, this young man said, "Oh, if I could only see him laugh once more! Oh, if I could only see him weep!" I was touched. I could never withstand distress.

I said: "Bring him to my lecture. I'll start him for you."

"Oh, if you could but do it! If you could but do it, all our family would bless you for evermore—for he is so very dear to us. Oh, my benefactor, can you make him laugh? can you bring soothing tears to those parched orbs?"

I was profoundly moved. I said: "My son, bring the old party round. I have got some jokes in that lecture that will make him laugh if there is any laugh in him; and if they miss fire, I have got some others that will make him cry or kill him, one or the other." Then the young man blessed me, and wept on my neck, and went after his uncle. He placed

him in full view, in the second row of benches, that night, and I began
on him. I tried him with mild jokes, then with severe ones; I dosed
him with bad jokes and riddled him with good ones; I fired old stale
jokes into him, and peppered him fore and aft with red-hot new ones;
I warmed up to my work, and assaulted him on the right and left, in
front and behind; I fumed and sweated and charged and ranted till I
was hoarse and sick and frantic and furious; but I never moved him
once—I never started a smile or a tear! Never a ghost of a smile, and
never a suspicion of moisture! I was astounded. I closed the lecture at
last with one despairing shriek—with one wild burst of humor, and
hurled a joke of supernatural atrocity full at him!

Then I sat down bewildered and exhausted.

The president of the society came up and bathed my head with
cold water, and said: "What made you carry on so toward the last?"

I said: "I was trying to make that confounded old fool laugh, in the
second row."

And he said: "Well, you were wasting your time, because he is deaf
and dumb, and as blind as a badger!"

Now, was that any way for that old man's nephew to impose on a
stranger and orphan like me? I ask you as a man and brother, if that
was any way for him to do?

1872

A Hundred and Ten Tin Whistles

It is a luscious country for thrilling evening stories about assassinations of intractable Gentiles. I cannot easily conceive of anything more
cozy than the night in Salt Lake which we spent in a Gentile den,
smoking pipes and listening to tales of how Burton galloped in among
the pleading and defenseless "Morisites" and shot them down, men
and women, like so many dogs. And how Bill Hickman, a Destroying
Angel, shot Drown and Arnold dead for bringing suit against him for a
debt. And how Porter Rockwell did this and that dreadful thing. And
how heedless people often come to Utah and make remarks about
Brigham, or polygamy, or some other sacred matter, and the very next

morning at daylight such parties are sure to be found lying up some back alley, contentedly waiting for the hearse. And the next most interesting thing is to sit and listen to these Gentiles talk about polygamy; and how some portly old frog of an elder, or a bishop, marries a girl—likes her, marries her sister—likes her, marries another sister—likes her, takes another—likes her, marries her mother—likes her, marries her father, grandfather, great grandfather, and then comes back hungry and asks for more. And how the pert young thing of eleven will chance to be the favorite wife, and her own venerable grandmother have to rank away down toward D 4 in their mutual husband's esteem, and have to sleep in the kitchen, as like as not. And how this dreadful sort of thing, this hiving together in one foul nest of mother and daughters, and the making a young daughter superior to her own mother in rank and authority, are things which Mormon women submit to because their religion teaches them that the more wives a man has on earth, and the more children he rears, the higher the place they will all have in the world to come—and the warmer, maybe, though they do not seem to say anything about that.

According to these Gentile friends of ours, Brigham Young's harem contains twenty or thirty wives. They said that some of them had grown old and gone out of active service, but were comfortably housed and cared for in the hennery—or the Lion House, as it is strangely named. Along with each wife were her children—fifty altogether. The house was perfectly quiet and orderly, when the children were still. They all took their meals in one room, and a happy and homelike sight it was pronounced to be. None of our party got an opportunity to take dinner with Mr. Young, but a Gentile by the name of Johnson professed to have enjoyed a sociable breakfast in the Lion House. He gave a preposterous account of the "calling of the roll," and other preliminaries, and the carnage that ensued when the buckwheat-cakes came in. But he embellished rather too much. He said that Mr. Young told him several smart sayings of certain of his "two-year-olds," observing with some pride that for many years he had been the heaviest contributor in that line to one of the Eastern magazines; and then he wanted to show Mr. Johnson one of the pets that had said the last good thing, but he could not find the child. He searched the faces of the children in detail, but could not decide which one it was. Finally, he give it up with a sigh and said: "I thought I would know the little cub again, but I don't." Mr. Johnson said further, that Mr. Young observed that life was a sad, sad thing—"because the joy of every new marriage a man contracted was so apt to be blighted by the inopportune funeral of a less recent bride." And Mr. Johnson said that while he and Mr. Young were pleasantly conversing in private, one of the Mrs. Youngs came in and demanded a breastpin, remarking that she had found out that he had been giving a breastpin to No. 6, and *she*, for one, did not propose to let this partiality go on without making a satisfactory amount of trouble about it. Mr. Young reminded her that there was a stranger present. Mrs. Young said that if the state of things inside the house was not agreeable to the stranger, he could find room outside. Mr. Young promised the breastpin, and she went away. But in a minute or two another Mrs. Young came in and demanded a breastpin. Mr. Young began a remonstrance, but Mrs. Young cut him short. She said No. 6 had got one, and No. 11 was promised one, and it was "no use for him to try to impose on her—she hoped she knew her rights." He gave his promise, and she went. And presently three Mrs. Youngs entered in a body and opened on their husband a tempest of tears, abuse, and entreaty. They had heard all about No. 6, No. 11, and No. 14. Three more breastpins were promised. They were hardly gone when nine more Mrs. Youngs filed into the presence, and a new tempest burst forth and raged round about the prophet and his guest. Nine breastpins were promised, and the weird sisters filed out again. And in came eleven more, weeping and wailing and gnashing their teeth. Eleven promised breastpins purchased peace once more.

"That is a specimen," said Mr. Young. "You see how it is. You see what a life I lead. A man *can't* be wise all the time. In a heedless moment I gave my darling No. 6—excuse my calling her thus, as her other name has escaped me for the moment—a breastpin. It was only worth twenty-five dollars—that is, *apparently* that was its whole cost—but its ultimate cost was inevitably bound to be a good deal more. You yourself have seen it climb up to six hundred and fifty dollars—and alas, even that is not the end! For I have wives all over this territory of Utah. I have dozens of wives whose *numbers*, even, I do not know without looking in the family Bible. They are scattered far and wide among the mountains and valleys of my realm. And, mark you, every solitary one of them will hear of this wretched breastpin, and every last one of them will have one or die. No. 6's breastpin will cost me twenty-five hundred dollars before I see the end of it. And these creatures will compare these pins together, and if one is a shade finer than the rest, they will all be thrown on my hands, and I will have to order a new lot to keep peace in the family. Sir, you probably did not know it, but all the time you were present with my children your every

movement was watched by vigilant servitors of mine. If you had offered to give a child a dime, or a stick of candy, or any trifle of the
kind, you would have been snatched out of the house instantly, provided it could be done before your gift left your hand. Otherwise it
would be absolutely necessary for you to make an exactly similar gift
to all my children—and knowing by experience the importance of the
thing, I would have stood by and seen to it myself that you did it, and
did it thoroughly. Once a gentleman gave one of my children a tin
whistle—a veritable invention of Satan, sir, and one which I have an
unspeakable horror of, and so would you if you had eighty or ninety
children in your house. But the deed was done—the man escaped. I
knew what the result was going to be, and I thirsted for vengeance. I
ordered out a flock of Destroying Angels, and they hunted the man
far into the fastnesses of the Nevada mountains. But they never caught
him. I am not cruel, sir—I am not vindictive except when sorely outraged—but if I had caught him, sir, so help me Joseph Smith, I would
have locked him into the nursery till the brats whistled him to death.
By the slaughtered body of St. Parley Pratt (whom God assoil!) there
was never anything on this earth like it! I knew who gave the whistle
to the child, but I could not make those jealous mothers believe me.
They believed I did it, and the result was just what any man of reflection could have foreseen: I had to order a hundred and ten whistles—
I think we had a hundred and ten children in the house then, but some
of them are off at college now—I had to order a hundred and ten of
those shrieking things, and I wish I may never speak another word if
we didn't have to talk on our fingers entirely, from that time forth
until the children got tired of the whistles. And if ever another man
gives a whistle to a child of mine and I get my hands on him, I will
hang him higher than Haman! That is the word with the bark on it!
Shade of Nephi! You don't know anything about married life. I am
rich, and everybody knows it. I am benevolent, and everybody takes
advantage of it. I have a strong fatherly instinct, and all the foundlings
are foisted on me. Every time a woman wants to do well by her darling, she puzzles her brain to cipher out some scheme for getting it
into my hands. Why, sir, a woman came here once with a child of a
curious lifeless sort of complexion (and so had the woman), and
swore that the child was mine and she my wife—that I had married her at such-and-such a time in such-and-such a place, but she had
forgotten her number, and of course I could not remember her name.
Well, sir, she called my attention to the fact that the child looked like

me, and really it did seem to resemble me—a common thing in the territory—and, to cut the story short, I put it in my nursery, and she left. And, by the ghost of Orson Hyde, when they came to wash the paint off that child it was an Injun! Bless my soul, you don't know anything about married life. It is a perfect dog's life, sir—a perfect dog's life. You can't economize. It isn't possible. I have tried keeping one set of bridal attire for all occasions. But it is of no use. First you'll marry a combination of calico and consumption that's as thin as a rail, and next you'll get a creature that's nothing more than the dropsy in disguise, and then you've got to eke out that bridal dress with an old balloon. That is the way it goes. And think of the wash-bill—(excuse these tears)—nine hundred and eighty-four pieces a week! No, sir, there is no such a thing as economy in a family like mine. Why, just the one item of cradles—think of it! And vermifuge! Soothing-syrup! Teething-rings! And 'papa's watches' for the babies to play with! And things to scratch the furniture with! And lucifer matches for them to eat, and pieces of glass to cut themselves with! The item of glass alone would support *your* family, I venture to say, sir. Let me scrimp and squeeze all I can, I still can't get ahead as fast as I feel I ought to, with my opportunities. Bless you, sir, at a time when I had seventy-two wives in this house, I groaned under the pressure of keeping thousands of dollars tied up in seventy-two bedsteads when the money ought to have been out at interest; and I just sold out the whole stock, sir, at a sacrifice, and built a bedstead seven feet long and ninety-six feet wide. But it was a failure, sir. I could *not* sleep. It appeared to me that the whole seventy-two women snored at once. The roar was deafening. And then the danger of it! That was what I was looking at. They would all draw in their breath at once, and you could actually see the walls of the house suck in—and then they would all exhale their breath at once, and you could see the walls swell out, and strain, and hear the rafters crack, and the shingles grind together. My friend, take an old man's advice and *don't* encumber yourself with a large family—mind, I tell you, don't do it. In a small family, and in a small family only, you will find that comfort and that peace of mind which are the best at last of the blessings this world is able to afford us, and for the lack of which no accumulation of wealth, and no acquisition of fame, power, and greatness can ever compensate us. Take my word for it, ten or eleven wives is all you need—never go over it."

Some instinct or other made me set this Johnson down as being unreliable. And yet he was a very entertaining person, and I doubt if some of the information he gave us could have been acquired from any other source. He was a pleasant contrast to those reticent Mormons.

From ROUGHING IT, 1872

Lionizing Murderers

I had heard so much about the celebrated fortune-teller Madame ——, that I went to see her yesterday. She has a dark complexion naturally, and this effect is heightened by artificial aids which cost her nothing. She wears curls—very black ones, and I had an impression that she gave their native attractiveness a lift with rancid butter. She wears a reddish check handkerchief, cast loosely around her neck, and it was plain that her other one is slow getting back from the wash. I presume she takes snuff. At any rate, something resembling it had lodged among the hairs sprouting from her upper lip. I know she likes garlic—I knew that as soon as she sighed. She looked at me searchingly for nearly a minute, with her black eyes, and then said:

"It is enough. Come!"

She started down a very dark and dismal corridor—I stepping close after her. Presently she stopped, and said that, as the way was so crooked and dark, perhaps she had better get a light. But it seemed ungallant to allow a woman to put herself to so much trouble for me, and so I said:

"It is not worth while, madam. If you will heave another sigh, I think I can follow it."

So we got along all right. Arrived at her official and mysterious den, she asked me to tell her the date of my birth, the exact hour of that occurrence, and the color of my grandmother's hair. I answered as accurately as I could. Then she said:

"Young man, summon your fortitude—do not tremble. I am about to reveal the past."

"Information concerning the *future* would be, in a general way, more—"

"Silence! You have had much trouble, some joy, some good fortune, some bad. Your great grandfather was hanged."

"That is a l—"

"Silence! Hanged sir. But it was not his fault. He could not help it."

"I am glad you do him justice."

"Ah—grieve, rather, that the jury did. He was hanged. His star crosses yours in the fourth division, fifth sphere. Consequently you will be hanged also."

"In view of this cheerful—"

"I *must* have silence. Yours was not, in the beginning, a criminal nature, but circumstances changed it. At the age of nine you stole sugar. At the age of fifteen you stole money. At twenty you stole horses. At twenty-five you committed arson. At thirty, hardened in crime, you became an editor. You are now a public lecturer. Worse things are in store for you. You will be sent to Congress. Next, to the penitentiary. Finally, happiness will come again—all will be well—you will be hanged."

I was now in tears. It seemed hard enough to go to Congress; but to be hanged—this was too sad, too dreadful. The woman seemed surprised at my grief. I told her the thoughts that were in my mind. Then she comforted me.

"Why, man,"[1] she said, "hold up your head—*you* have nothing to

[1] In this paragraph the fortune-teller details the exact history of the Pike-Brown assassination case in New Hampshire, from the succoring and saving of the stranger Pike by the Browns, to the subsequent hanging and coffining of that treacherous miscreant. She adds nothing, invents nothing, exaggerates nothing (see any New England paper for November, 1869). This Pike-Brown case is selected merely as a type, to illustrate a custom that prevails, not in New Hampshire alone, but in every state in the Union—I mean the sentimental custom of visiting, petting, glorifying, and snuffling over murderers like this Pike, from the day they enter the jail under sentence of death until they swing from the gallows. The following extract from the *Temple Bar* (1866) reveals the fact that this custom is not confined to the United States:—"On December 31, 1841, a man named John Johnes, a shoemaker, murdered his sweetheart, Mary Hallam, the daughter of a respectable laborer, at Mansfield, in the county of Nottingham. He was executed on March 23, 1842. He was a man of unsteady habits, and gave way to violent fits of passion. The girl declined his addresses, and he said if he did not have her no one else should. After he had inflicted the first wound, which was not immediately fatal, she begged for her life, but seeing him resolved, asked for time to pray. He said that he would pray for both, and completed the crime. The wounds were inflicted by a shoemaker's knife, and her throat was cut barbarously. After this he dropped on his knees some time, and prayed God to have mercy on two unfortunate lovers. He made no attempt to escape, and confessed the crime. After his imprisonment he behaved in a most decorous manner; he won upon the good opinion of the jail chaplain, and he was visited by the Bishop of Lincoln. It does not appear that he expressed any contrition for the crime, but seemed to pass away with triumphant certainty that he was going to rejoin his victim in heaven. *He was*

grieve about. Listen. You will live in New Hampshire. In your sharp need and distress the Brown family will succor you—such of them as Pike the assassin left alive. They will be benefactors to you. When you shall have grown fat upon their bounty, and are grateful and happy, you will desire to make some modest return for these things, and so you will go to the house some night and brain the whole family with an ax. You will rob the dead bodies of your benefactors, and disburse your gains in riotous living among the rowdies and courtesans of Boston. Then you will be arrested, tried, condemned to be hanged, thrown into prison. Now is your happy day. You will be converted—you will be converted just as soon as every effort to compass pardon, commutation, or reprieve has failed—and then! Why, then, every morning and every afternoon, the best and purest young ladies of the village will assemble in your cell and sing hymns. This will show that assassination is respectable. Then you will write a touching letter, in which you will forgive all those recent Browns. This will excite the public admiration. No public can withstand magnanimity. Next, they will take you to the scaffold, with great *éclat*, at the head of an imposing procession composed of clergymen, officials, citizens generally, and young ladies walking pensively two and two, and bearing bouquets and immortelles. You will mount the scaffold, and while the great concourse stand uncovered in your presence, you will read your sappy little speech which the minister has written for you. And then, in the midst of a grand and impressive silence, they will swing you into per—Paradise, my son. There will not be a dry eye on the ground. You will be a hero! Not a rough there but will envy you. Not a rough there but will resolve to emulate you. And next, a great procession will follow you to the tomb —will weep over your remains—the young ladies will sing again the hymns made dear by sweet associations connected with the jail, and, as a last tribute of affection, respect, and appreciation of your many sterling qualities, they will walk two and two around your bier, and strew wreaths of flowers on it. And lo! you are canonized. Think of it, son—ingrate, assassin, robber of the dead, drunken brawler among thieves and harlots in the slums of Boston one month, and the pet of the pure and innocent daughters of the land the next! A bloody and hateful devil—a bewept, bewailed, and sainted martyr—all in a month! Fool!—so noble a fortune, and yet you sit here grieving!"

"No, madam," I said, "you do me wrong, you do, indeed. I am per-

---

visited by some pious and benevolent ladies of Nottingham, some of whom declared he was a child of God, if ever there was one. One of the ladies sent him a white camellia to wear at his execution."

fectly satisfied. I did not know before that my great-grandfather was hanged, but it is of no consequence. He has probably ceased to bother about it by this time—and I have not commenced yet. I confess, madam, that I do something in the way of editing and lecturing, but the other crimes you mention have escaped my memory. Yet I must have committed them—you would not deceive a stranger. But let the past be as it was, and let the future be as it may—these are nothing. I have only cared for one thing. I have always felt that I should be hanged some day, and somehow the thought has annoyed me considerably; but if you can only assure me that I shall be hanged in New Hampshire—"

"Not a shadow of a doubt!"

"Bless you, my benefactress!—excuse this embrace—you have removed a great load from my breast. To be hanged in New Hampshire is happiness—it leaves an honored name behind a man, and introduces him at once into the best New Hampshire society in the other world."

I then took leave of the fortune-teller. But, seriously, is it well to glorify a murderous villain on the scaffold, as Pike was glorified in New Hampshire? Is it well to turn the penalty for a bloody crime into a reward? Is it just to do it? Is it safe?

1872

Markiss, King of Liars

I stumbled upon one curious character in the island of Maui. He became a sore annoyance to me in the course of time. My first glimpse of him was in a sort of public room in the town of Lahaina. He occupied a chair at the opposite side of the apartment, and sat eying our party with interest for some minutes, and listening as critically to what we were saying as if he fancied we were talking to him and expecting him to reply. I thought it very sociable in a stranger. Presently, in the course of conversation, I made a statement bearing upon the subject under discussion—and I made it with due modesty, for there was nothing extraordinary about it, and it was only put forth in illustration of a point at issue. I had barely finished when this person spoke out with rapid utterance and feverish anxiety:

"Oh, that was certainly remarkable, after a fashion, but you ought to have seen *my* chimney—you ought to have seen *my* chimney, sir! Smoke! I wish I may hang if—Mr. Jones, *you* remember that chimney—you *must* remember that chimney! No, no—I recollect, now, you warn't living on this side of the island then. But I am telling you nothing but the truth, and I wish I may never draw another breath if that chimney didn't smoke so that the smoke actually got *caked* in it and I had to dig it out with a pickax! You may smile, gentlemen, but the high sheriff's got a hunk of it which I dug out before his eyes, and so it's perfectly easy for you to go and examine for yourselves."

The interruption broke up the conversation, which had already begun to lag, and we presently hired some natives and an outrigger canoe or two, and went out to overlook a grand surf-bathing contest.

Two weeks after this, while talking in a company, I looked up and detected this same man boring through and through me with his intense eye, and noted again his twitching muscles and his feverish anxiety to speak. The moment I paused, he said:

"*Beg* your pardon, sir, beg your pardon, but it can only be considered remarkable when brought into strong outline by isolation. Sir, contrasted with a circumstance which occurred in my own experience, it instantly becomes commonplace. No, not that—for I will not speak so discourteously of any experience in the career of a stranger and a gentleman—but I am *obliged* to say that you could not, and you *would* not ever again refer to this tree as a *large* one, if you could behold, as I have, the great Yakmatack tree, in the island of Ounaska, sea of Kamtchatka—a tree, sir, not one inch less than four hundred and fifteen feet in solid diameter!—and I wish I may die in a minute if it isn't so! Oh, you needn't look so questioning, gentlemen; here's old Cap Saltmarsh can say whether I know what I'm talking about or not. I showed him the tree."

CAPTAIN SALTMARSH: "Come, now, cat your anchor, lad—you're heaving too taut. You *promised* to show me that stunner, and I walked more than eleven mile with you through the cussedest jungle *I* ever see, a-hunting for it; but the tree you showed me finally warn't as big around as a beer-cask, and *you* know that your own self, Markiss."

"Hear the man talk! Of *course* the tree was reduced that way, but didn't I *explain* it? Answer me, didn't I? Didn't I say I wished you could have seen it when *I* first saw it? When you got up on your ear and called me names, and said I had brought you eleven miles to look at a sapling, didn't I *explain* to you that all the whale-ships in the North Seas had been wooding off of it for more than twenty-seven years? And did you s'pose the tree could last for*ever*, con*found* it? I don't see why you want to keep back things that way, and try to injure a person that's never done *you* any harm."

Somehow this man's presence made me uncomfortable, and I was glad when a native arrived at that moment to say that Muckawow, the most companionable and luxurious among the rude war-chiefs of the Islands, desired us to come over and help him enjoy a missionary whom he had found trespassing on his grounds.

I think it was about ten days afterward that, as I finished a statement I was making for the instruction of a group of friends and acquaintances, and which made no pretense of being extraordinary, a familiar voice chimed instantly in on the heels of my last word, and said:

"But, my dear sir, there was *nothing* remarkable about that horse, or the circumstance either—nothing in the world! I mean no sort of offense when I say it, sir, but you really do not know anything whatever about speed. Bless your heart, if you could only have seen my mare Margaretta; *there* was a beast!—*there* was lightning for you! Trot! Trot is no name for it—she flew! How she *could* whirl a buggy along! I started her out once, sir—Colonel Bilgewater, *you* recollect that animal perfectly well—I started her out about thirty or thirty-five yards ahead of the awfulest storm I ever saw in my life, and it chased us upward of eighteen miles! It did, by the everlasting hills! And I'm telling you nothing but the unvarnished truth when I say that not one single drop of rain fell on me—not a single *drop* sir! And I swear to it! But my dog was a-swimming behind the wagon all the way!"

For a week or two I stayed mostly within doors, for I seemed to meet this person everywhere, and he had become utterly hateful to me. But one evening I dropped in on Captain Perkins and his friends, and we had a sociable time. About ten o'clock I chanced to be talking about a merchant friend of mine, and without really intending it, the remark slipped out that he was a little mean and parsimonious about paying his workmen. Instantly, through the steam of a hot whisky punch on the opposite side of the room, a remembered voice shot— and for a moment I trembled on the imminent verge of profanity:

"Oh, my dear sir, really you expose yourself when you parade *that* as a surprising circumstance. Bless your heart and hide, you are ignorant of the very A B C of meanness! ignorant as the unborn babe! ignorant as unborn *twins!* You don't know *anything* about it! It is pitiable to see you, sir, a well-spoken and prepossessing stranger, making such an enormous pow-wow here about a subject concerning which your ignorance is perfectly humiliating! Look me in the eye, if you please; look me in the eye. John James Godfrey was the son of poor but honest parents in the state of Mississippi—boyhood friend of mine—bosom comrade in later years. Heaven rest his noble spirit, he is gone from us now. John James Godfrey was hired by the Hayblossom Mining Company in California to do some blasting for them—the 'Incorporated Company of Mean Men,' the boys used to call it. Well, one day he drilled a hole about four feet deep and put in an awful blast of powder, and was standing over it ramming it down with an iron crowbar about nine foot long, when the cussed thing struck a spark and fired the powder, and scat! away John Godfrey whizzed like a sky-rocket, him and his crowbar! Well, sir, he kept on going up in the air higher and higher, till he didn't look any bigger than a boy— and he kept going on up higher and higher, till he didn't look any bigger than a doll—and he kept on going up higher and higher, till he didn't look any bigger than a little small bee—and then he went out of sight! Presently he came in sight again, looking like a little small bee— and he came along down further and further, till he looked as big as a doll again—and down further and further, till he was as big as a boy again—and further and further, till he was a full-sized man once more; and then him and his crowbar came a-whizzing down and lit right exactly in the same old tracks and went to r-ramming down, and r-ramming down, and r-ramming down again, just the same as if nothing had happened! Now, do you know, that poor cuss warn't gone only sixteen minutes, and yet that incorporated company of mean men DOCKED HIM FOR THE LOST TIME!"

I said I had the headache, and so excused myself and went home. And on my diary I entered "another night spoiled" by this offensive loafer. And a fervent curse was sent down with it to keep the item company. And the very next day I packed up, out of all patience, and left the island.

Almost from the very beginning, I regarded that man as a liar.

. . . .

The line of points represents an interval of years. At the end of which time the opinion hazarded in that last sentence came to be gratifyingly and remarkably indorsed, and by wholly disinterested persons. The man Markiss was found one morning hanging to a beam of his own bedroom (the doors and windows securely fastened on the inside), dead; and on his breast was pinned a paper in his own handwriting begging his friends to suspect no innocent person of having anything to do with his death, for that it was the work of his own hands entirely. Yet the jury brought in the astounding verdict that deceased came to his death "by the hands of some person or persons unknown"! They explained that the perfectly undeviating consistency of Markiss's character for thirty years towered aloft as colossal and indestructible testimony, that whatever statement he chose to make was entitled to instant and unquestioning acceptance as a *lie*. And they furthermore stated their belief that he was not dead, and instanced the strong circumstantial evidence of his own word that he *was* dead—and beseeched the coroner to delay the funeral as long as possible, which was done. And so in the tropical climate of Lahaina the coffin stood open for seven days, and then even the loyal jury gave him up. But they sat on him again, and changed their verdict to "suicide induced by mental aberration"—because, said they, with penetration, "he said he was dead, and he *was* dead; and would he have told the truth if he had been in his right mind? *No*, sir."

From ROUGHING IT, 1872

Mr. Arkansas

There were two men in the company who caused me particular discomfort. One was a little Swede, about twenty-five years old, who knew only one song, and he was forever singing it. By day we were all crowded into one small, stifling barroom, and so there was no escaping this person's music. Through all the profanity, whisky-guzzling, "old sledge," and quarreling, his monotonous song meandered with never a variation in its tiresome sameness, and it seemed to me, at last, that I would be content to die, in order to be rid of the torture. The other man was a stalwart ruffian called "Arkansas," who carried two revolvers in his belt and a bowie-knife projecting from his boot, and who was always drunk and always suffering for a fight. But he was so feared, that nobody would accommodate him. He would try all manner of little wary ruses to entrap somebody into an offensive remark, and his face would light up now and then when he fancied he was fairly on the scent of a fight, but invariably his victim would elude his toils and then he would show a disappointment that was almost pathetic. The landlord, Johnson, was a meek, well-meaning fellow, and Arkansas fastened on him early, as a promising subject, and gave him no rest day or night, for a while. On the fourth morning, Arkansas got drunk and sat himself down to wait for an opportunity. Presently Johnson came in, just comfortably sociable with whisky, and said:

"I reckon the Pennsylvania 'lection—"

Arkansas raised his finger impressively and Johnson stopped. Arkansas rose unsteadily and confronted him. Said he:

"Wha-what do you know a-about Pennsylvania? Answer me that. Wha-what do you know 'bout Pennsylvania?"

"I was only goin' to say—"

"You was only goin' to *say*. *You* was! You was only goin' to say— *what* was you goin' to say? That's it! That's what *I* want to know. *I* want to know wha-what you (*'ic*) what you know about Pennsylvania, since you're makin' yourself so d—d free. Answer me that!"

"Mr. Arkansas, if you'd only let me—"

"Who's a-henderin' you? Don't you insinuate nothing agin me!— don't you do it. Don't you come in bullyin' around, and cussin' and goin' on like a lunatic—don't you do it. 'Coz I won't *stand* it. If fight's what you want, out with it! I'm your man! Out with it!"

Said Johnson, backing into a corner, Arkansas following, menacingly:

"Why, I never said nothing, Mr. Arkansas. You don't give a man no chance. I was only goin' to say that Pennsylvania was goin' to have an election next week—that was all—that was everything I was goin' to say—I wish I may never stir if it wasn't."

"Well then why d'n't you say it? What did you come swellin' around that way for, and tryin' to raise trouble?"

"Why, I didn't come swellin' around, Mr. Arkansas—I just—"

"I'm a liar am I! Ger-reat Caesar's ghost—"

"Oh, please, Mr. Arkansas, I never meant such a thing as that, I wish I may die if I did. All the boys will tell you that I've always spoke well of you, and respected you more'n any man in the house. Ask Smith. Ain't it so, Smith? Didn't I say, no longer ago than last night, that for a man that was a gentleman *all* the time and every way you took him, give me Arkansas? I'll leave it to any gentleman here if them warn't the very words I used. Come, now, Mr. Arkansas, le's take a drink—le's shake hands and take a drink. Come up—everybody! It's my treat. Come up, Bill, Tom, Bob, Scotty—come up. I want you all to

take a drink with me and Arkansas—*old* Arkansas, I call him—bully
old Arkansas. Gimme your hand ag'in. Look at him, boys—just take a
look at him. Thar stands the whitest man in America!—and the man
that denies it has got to fight *me*, that's all. Gimme that old flipper
ag'in!"

They embraced, with drunken affection on the landlords part and
unresponsive toleration on the part of Arkansas, who, bribed by a
drink, was disappointed of his prey once more. But the foolish landlord was so happy to have escaped butchery, that he went on talking
when he ought to have marched himself out of danger. The consequence was that Arkansas shortly began to glower upon him danger-
ously, and presently said:

"Lan'lord, will you p-please make that remark over ag'in if you
please?"

"I was a-sayin' to Scotty that my father was up'ards of eighty year
old when he died."

"Was that *all* that you said?"

"Yes, that was all."

"Didn't say nothing but that?"

"No—nothing."

Then an uncomfortable silence.

Arkansas played with his glass a moment, lolling on his elbows on
the counter. Then he meditatively scratched his left shin with his right
boot, while the awkward silence continued. But presently he loafed
away toward the stove, looking dissatisfied; roughly shouldered two or
three men out of comfortable position; occupied it himself, gave a
sleeping dog a kick that sent him howling under a bench, then spread
his long legs and his blanket-coat tails apart and proceeded to warm
his back. In a little while he fell to grumbling to himself, and soon he
slouched back to the bar and said:

"Lan'lord, what's your idea for rakin' up old personalities and
blowin' about your father? Ain't this company agreeable to you? Ain't
it? If this company ain't agreeable to you, p'r'aps we'd better leave. Is
that your idea? Is that what you're coming at?"

"Why, bless your soul, Arkansas, I warn't thinking of such a thing.
My father and my mother—"

"Lan'lord, *don't* crowd a man! Don't do it. If nothing'll do you but a
disturbance, out with it like a man (*'ic*)—but *don't* rake up old bygones
and fling 'em in the teeth of a passel of people that wants to be
peaceable if they could git a chance. What's the matter with you this
mornin', anyway? I never see a man carry on so."

"Arkansas, I reely didn't mean no harm, and I won't go on with it if it's onpleasant to you. I reckon my licker's got into my head, and what with the flood, and havin' so many to feed and look out for—"

"So *that's* what's a-ranklin' in your heart, is it? You want us to leave, do you? There's too many on us. You want us to pack up and swim. Is that it? Come!"

"Please be reasonable, Arkansas. Now *you* know that I ain't the man to—"

"Are you a-threatenin' me? Are you? By George, the man don't live that can skeer me! Don't you try to come that game, my chicken—'cuz I can stand a good deal, but I won't stand that. Come out from behind that bar till I clean you! You want to drive us out, do you, you sneakin' underhanded hound! Come out from behind that bar! *I'll* learn you to bully and badger and browbeat a gentleman that's forever trying to befriend you and keep you out of trouble!"

"Please, Arkansas, please don't shoot! If there's got to be blood-shed—"

"Do you hear that, gentlemen? Do you hear him talk about blood-shed? So it's blood you want, is it, you ravin' desperado! You'd made up your mind to murder somebody this mornin'—I knowed it perfectly well. I'm the man, am I? It's me you're goin' to murder, is it? But you can't do it 'thout I get one chance first, you thievin' black-hearted, white-livered son of a nigger! Draw your weepon!"

With that, Arkansas began to shoot, and the landlord to clamber over benches, men, and every sort of obstacle in a frantic desire to escape. In the midst of the wild hubbub the landlord crashed through a glass door, and as Arkansas charged after him the landlord's wife suddenly appeared in the doorway and confronted the desperado with a pair of scissors! Her fury was magnificent. With head erect and flashing eye she stood a moment and then advanced, with her weapon raised. The astonished ruffian hesitated, and then fell back a step. She followed. She backed him step by step into the middle of the barroom, and then, while the wondering crowd closed up and gazed, she gave him such another tongue-lashing as never a cowed and shame-faced braggart got before, perhaps! As she finished and retired victorious, a roar of applause shook the house, and every man ordered "drinks for the crowd" in one and the same breath.

The lesson was entirely sufficient. The reign of terror was over, and the Arkansas domination broken for good. During the rest of the sea-son of island captivity, there was one man who sat apart in a state of

permanent humiliation, never mixing in any quarrel or uttering a
boast, and never resenting the insults the once cringing crew now
constantly leveled at him, and that man was Arkansas.

From ROUGHING IT, 1872

Nevada Nabobs

In Nevada there used to be current the story of an adventure of two
of her nabobs, which may or may not have occurred. I give it for what
it is worth.

Col. Jim had seen somewhat of the world, and knew more or less of
its ways; but Col. Jack was from the back settlements of the States,
had led a life of arduous toil, and had never seen a city. These two,
blessed with sudden wealth, projected a visit to New York—Col. Jack
to see the sights, and Col. Jim to guard his unsophistication from misfortune. They reached San Francisco in the night, and sailed in the
morning. Arrived in New York, Col. Jack said:

"I've heard tell of carriages all my life, and now I mean to have a
ride in one; I don't care what it costs. Come along."

They stepped out on the sidewalk, and Col. Jim called a stylish
barouche. But Col. Jack said:

"*No,* sir! None of your cheap-John turnouts for me. I'm here to have
a good time, and money ain't any object. I mean to have the nobbiest
rig that's going. Now here comes the very trick. Stop that yaller one
with the pictures on it—don't you fret—I'll stand all the expenses myself."

So Col. Jim stopped an empty omnibus, and they got in. Said Col.
Jack:

"Ain't it gay, though? Oh, no, I reckon not! Cushions, and windows,
and pictures, till you can't rest. What would the boys say if they could
see us cutting a swell like this in New York? By George, I wish they
could see us."

Then he put his head out of the window, and shouted to the driver:

"Say, Johnny, this suits *me!*—suits yours truly, you bet you! I want
this shebang all day. I'm *on* it, old man! Let 'em out! Make 'em go!
We'll make it all right with *you,* sonny!"

The driver passed his hand through the straphold, and tapped for his fare—it was before the gongs came into common use. Col. Jack took the hand, and shook it cordially. He said:

"You twig me, old pard! All right between gents. Smell of *that,* and see how you like it!"

And he put a twenty-dollar gold piece in the driver's hand. After a moment the driver said he could not make change.

"Bother the change! Ride it out. Put it in your pocket."

Then to Col. Jim, with a sounding slap on his thigh:

"*Ain't* it style, though? Hanged if I don't hire this thing every day for a week."

The omnibus stopped, and a young lady got in. Col. Jack stared a moment, then nudged Col. Jim with his elbow:

"Don't say a word," he whispered. "Let her ride, if she wants to. Gracious, there's room enough."

The young lady got out her porte-monnaie, and handed her fare to Col. Jack.

"What's this for?" said he.

"Give it to the driver, please."

"Take back your money, madam. We can't allow it. You're welcome to ride here as long as you please, but this shebang's chartered, and can't let you pay a cent."

The girl shrunk into a corner, bewildered. An old lady with a basket climbed in, and proffered her fare.

"Excuse me," said Col. Jack. "You're perfectly welcome here, madam, but we can't allow you to pay. Set right down there, mum, and don't you be the least uneasy. Make yourself just as free as if you was in your own turnout."

Within two minutes, three gentlemen, two fat women, and a couple of children, entered.

"Come right along, friends," said Col. Jack; "don't mind *us.* This is a free blowout." Then he whispered to Col. Jim, "New York ain't no sociable place, I don't reckon—it ain't no *name* for it!"

He resisted every effort to pass fares to the driver, and made everybody cordially welcome. The situation dawned on the people, and they pocketed their money, and delivered themselves up to covert enjoyment of the episode. Half a dozen more passengers entered.

"Oh, there's *plenty* of room," said Col. Jack. "Walk right in, and make yourselves at home. A blowout ain't worth anything *as* a blowout, unless a body has company." Then in a whisper to Col. Jim: "But *ain't* these New-Yorkers friendly? And ain't they cool about it, too?

Icebergs ain't anywhere. I reckon they'd tackle a hearse, if it was
going their way."

More passengers got in; more yet, and still more. Both seats were
filled, and a file of men were standing up, holding on to the cleats
overhead. Parties with baskets and bundles were climbing up on the
roof. Half-suppressed laughter rippled up from all sides.

"Well, for clean, cool, out-and-out cheek, if this don't bang anything
that ever I saw, I'm an Injun!" whispered Col. Jack.

A Chinaman crowded his way in.

"I weaken!" said Col. Jack. "Hold on, driver! Keep your seats, ladies
and gents. Just make yourselves free—everything's paid for. Driver, rustle these folks around as long as they're a mind to go—friends of ours,
you know. Take them everywheres—and if you want more money,
come to the St. Nicholas, and we'll make it all right. Pleasant journey
to you, ladies and gents—go it just as long as you please—it sha'n't cost
you a cent!"

The two comrades got out, and Col. Jack said:

"Jimmy, it's the sociablest place *I* ever saw. The Chinaman
waltzed in as comfortable as anybody. If we'd stayed awhile, I reckon
we'd had some niggers. B'George, we'll have to barricade our doors
to-night, or some of these ducks will be trying to sleep with us."

From ROUGHING IT, 1872

What Hank Said to Horace Greeley

On the western verge of the desert we halted a moment at Ragtown. It consisted of one log house and is not set down on the map.

This reminds me of a circumstance. Just after we left Julesburg, on the Platte, I was sitting with the driver, and he said:

"I can tell you a most laughable thing indeed, if you would like to listen to it. Horace Greeley went over this road once. When he was leaving Carson City he told the driver, Hank Monk, that he had an engagement to lecture at Placerville and was very anxious to go through quick. Hank Monk cracked his whip and started off at an awful pace. The coach bounced up and down in such a terrific way that it jolted the buttons all off of Horace's coat, and finally shot his head clean through the roof of the stage, and then he yelled at Hank Monk and begged him to go easier—said he warn't in as much of a hurry as he was awhile ago. But Hank Monk said, 'Keep your seat, Horace, and I'll get you there on time'—and you bet you he did, too, what was left of him!"

A day or two after that we picked up a Denver man at the crossroads, and he told us a good deal about the country and the Gregory Diggings. He seemed a very entertaining person and a man well posted in the affairs of Colorado. By and by he remarked:

"I can tell you a most laughable thing indeed, if you would like to listen to it. Horace Greeley went over this road once. When he was leaving Carson City he told the driver, Hank Monk, that he had an engagement to lecture at Placerville and was very anxious to go through quick. Hank Monk cracked his whip and started off at an awful pace. The coach bounced up and down in such a terrific way that it jolted the buttons all off of Horace's coat, and finally shot his head clean through the roof of the stage, and then he yelled at Hank Monk and begged him to go easier—said he warn't in as much of a hurry as he was awhile ago. But Hank Monk said, 'Keep your seat, Horace, and I'll get you there on time'—and you bet you he did, too, what was left of him!"

At Fort Bridger, some days after this, we took on board a cavalry sergeant, a very proper and soldierly person indeed. From no other

man during the whole journey did we gather such a store of concise
and well-arranged military information. It was surprising to find in the
desolate wilds of our country a man so thoroughly acquainted with
everything useful to know in his line of life, and yet of such inferior
rank and unpretentious bearing. For as much as three hours we listened to him with unabated interest. Finally he got upon the subject
of transcontinental travel, and presently said:

"I can tell you a very laughable thing indeed, if you would like to
listen to it. Horace Greeley went over this road once. When he was
leaving Carson City he told the driver, Hank Monk, that he had an
engagement to lecture at Placerville and was very anxious to go
through quick. Hank Monk cracked his whip and started off at an
awful pace. The coach bounced up and down in such a terrific way
that it jolted the buttons all off of Horace's coat, and finally shot his
head clean through the roof of the stage, and then he yelled at Hank
Monk and begged him to go easier—said he warn't in as much of a
hurry as he was awhile ago. But Hank Monk said, 'Keep your seat,
Horace, and I'll get you there on time'—and you bet you he did, too,
what was left of him!"

When we were eight hours out from Salt Lake City a Mormon
preacher got in with us at a way-station—a gentle, soft-spoken, kindly
man, and one whom any stranger would warm to at first sight. I can
never forget the pathos that was in his voice as he told, in simple
language, the story of his people's wanderings and unpitied sufferings.
No pulpit eloquence was ever so moving and so beautiful as this outcast's picture of the first Mormon pilgrimage across the plains, struggling sorrowfully onward to the land of its banishment and marking
its desolate way with graves and watering it with tears. His words so
wrought upon us that it was a relief to us all when the conversation
drifted into a more cheerful channel and the natural features of the
curious country we were in came under treatment. One matter after
another was pleasantly discussed, and at length the stranger said:

"I can tell you a most laughable thing indeed, if you would like to
listen to it. Horace Greeley went over this road once. When he was
leaving Carson City he told the driver, Hank Monk, that he had an
engagement to lecture in Placerville, and was very anxious to go
through quick. Hank Monk cracked his whip and started off at an
awful pace. The coach bounced up and down in such a terrific way
that it jolted the buttons all off of Horace's coat, and finally shot his
head clean through the roof of the stage, and then he yelled at Hank
Monk and begged him to go easier—said he warn't in as much of a

hurry as he was awhile ago. But Hank Monk said, 'Keep your seat, Horace, and I'll get you there on time'—and you bet you he did, too, what was left of him!"

Ten miles out of Ragtown we found a poor wanderer who had lain down to die. He had walked as long as he could, but his limbs had failed him at last. Hunger and fatigue had conquered him. It would have been inhuman to leave him there. We paid his fare to Carson and lifted him into the coach. It was some little time before he showed any very decided signs of life; but by dint of chafing him and pouring brandy between his lips we finally brought him to a languid consciousness. Then we fed him a little, and by and by he seemed to comprehend the situation and a grateful light softened his eye. We made his mail-sack bed as comfortable as possible, and constructed a pillow for him with our coats. He seemed very thankful. Then he looked up in our faces, and said in a feeble voice that had a tremble of honest emotion in it:

"Gentlemen, I know not who you are, but you have saved my life; and although I can never be able to repay you for it, I feel that I can at least make one hour of your long journey lighter. I take it you are strangers to this great thoroughfare, but I am entirely familiar with it. In this connection I can tell you a most laughable thing indeed, if you would like to listen to it. Horace Greeley—"

I said, impressively:

"Suffering stranger, proceed at your peril. You see in me the melancholy wreck of a once stalwart and magnificent manhood. What has brought me to this? That thing which you are about to tell. Gradually, but surely, that tiresome old anecdote has sapped my strength, undermined my constitution, withered my life. Pity my helplessness. Spare me only just this once, and tell me about young George Washington and his little hatchet for a change."

We were saved. But not so the invalid. In trying to retain the anecdote in his system he strained himself and died in our arms.

I am aware, now, that I ought not to have asked of the sturdiest citizen of all that region, what I asked of that mere shadow of a man; for, after seven years' residence on the Pacific coast, I know that no passenger or driver on the Overland ever corked that anecdote in, when a stranger was by, and survived. Within a period of six years I crossed and recrossed the Sierras between Nevada and California thirteen times by stage and listened to that deathless incident four hundred and eighty-one or eighty-two times. I have the list somewhere. Drivers always told it, conductors told it, landlords told it, chance passengers

told it, the very Chinamen and vagrant Indians recounted it. I have
had the same driver tell it to me two or three times in the same afternoon. It has come to me in all the multitude of tongues that Babel bequeathed to earth, and flavored with whisky, brandy, beer, cologne,
sozodont, tobacco, garlic, onions, grasshoppers—everything that has a
fragrance to it through all the long list of things that are gorged or guz-
zled by the sons of men. I never have smelt any anecdote as often as I
have smelt that one; never have smelt any anecdote that smelt so variegated as that one. And you never could learn to know it by its smell,
because every time you thought you had learned the smell of it, it
would turn up with a different smell. Bayard Taylor has written about
this hoary anecdote, Richardson has published it; so have Jones, Smith,
Johnson, Ross Browne, and every other correspondence-inditing being
that ever set his foot upon the great overland road anywhere between
Julesburg and San Francisco; and I have heard that it is in the Talmud.
I have seen it in print in nine different foreign languages; I have been
told that it is employed in the inquisition in Rome; and I now learn
with regret that it is going to be set to music. I do not think that such
things are right.

Stage-coaching on the Overland is no more, and stage-drivers are a
race defunct. I wonder if they bequeathed that bald-headed anecdote
to their successors, the railroad brakemen and conductors, and if these
latter still persecute the helpless passenger with it until he concludes, as
did many a tourist of other days, that the real grandeurs of the Pacific
coast are not Yo Semite and the Big Trees, but Hank Monk and his adventure with Horace Greeley.[1]

[1] And what makes that worn anecdote the more aggravating, is, that the
adventure it celebrates *never occurred*. If it were a good anecdote, that seeming
demerit would be its chiefest virtue, for creative power belongs to greatness; but
what ought to be done to a man who would wantonly contrive so flat a one as this?
If *I* were to suggest what ought to be done to him, I should be called extravagant—
but what does the sixteenth chapter of Daniel say? Aha!

From ROUGHING IT, 1872

When the Buffalo Climbed a Tree

It did seem strange enough to see a town again after what appeared to us such a long acquaintance with deep, still, almost lifeless and houseless solitude! We tumbled out into the busy street feeling like meteoric people crumbled off the corner of some other world, and wakened up suddenly in this. For an hour we took as much interest in Overland City as if we had never seen a town before. The reason we had an hour to spare was because we had to change our stage (for a less sumptuous affair, called a "mud-wagon") and transfer our freight of mails.

Presently we got under way again. We came to the shallow, yellow, muddy South Platte, with its low banks and its scattering flat sand-bars and pygmy islands—a melancholy stream straggling through the center of the enormous flat plain, and only saved from being impossible to find with the naked eye by its sentinel rank of scattering trees standing on either bank. The Platte was "up," they said—which made me wish I could see it when it was down, if it could look any sicker and sorrier. They said it was a dangerous stream to cross, now, because its quicksands were liable to swallow up horses, coach, and passengers if an attempt was made to ford it. But the mails had to go, and we made the attempt. Once or twice in midstream the wheels sunk into the yielding sands so threateningly that we half believed we had dreaded and avoided the sea all our lives to be shipwrecked in a "mud-wagon" in the middle of a desert at last. But we dragged through and sped away toward the setting sun.

Next morning just before dawn, when about five hundred and fifty miles from St. Joseph, our mud-wagon broke down. We were to be delayed five or six hours, and therefore we took horses, by invitation, and joined a party who were just starting on a buffalo-hunt. It was noble sport galloping over the plain in the dewy freshness of the morning, but our part of the hunt ended in disaster and disgrace, for a wounded buffalo bull chased the passenger Bemis nearly two miles, and then he forsook his horse and took to a lone tree. He was very sullen about the matter for some twenty-four hours, but at last he began to soften little by little, and finally he said:

"Well, it was not funny, and there was no sense in those gawks making themselves so facetious over it. I tell you I was angry in earnest for a while. I should have shot that long gangly lubber they called Hank, if I could have done it without crippling six or seven other people—but of course I couldn't, the old 'Allen' 's so confounded comprehensive. I wish those loafers had been up in the tree; they wouldn't have wanted to laugh so. If I had had a horse worth a cent—but no, the minute he saw that buffalo bull wheel on him and give a bellow, he raised straight up in the air and stood on his heels. The saddle began to slip, and I took him round the neck and laid close to him, and began to pray. Then he came down and stood up on the other end awhile, and the bull actually stopped pawing sand and bellowing to contemplate the inhuman spectacle. Then the bull made a pass at him and uttered a bellow that sounded perfectly frightful, it was so close to me, and that seemed to literally prostrate my horse's reason, and make a raving distracted maniac of him, and I wish I may die if he didn't stand on his head for a quarter of a minute and shed tears. He was absolutely out of his mind—he was, as sure as truth itself, and he really didn't know what he was doing. Then the bull came charging at us, and my horse dropped down on all fours and took a fresh start —and then for the next ten minutes he would actually throw one handspring after another so fast that the bull began to get unsettled, too, and didn't know where to start in—and so he stood there sneezing, and shoveling dust over his back, and bellowing every now and then, and thinking he had got a fifteen-hundred-dollar circus horse for breakfast, certain. Well, I was first out on his neck—the horse's, not the bull's—and then underneath, and next on his rump, and sometimes head up, and sometimes heels—but I tell you it seemed solemn and awful to be ripping and tearing and carrying on so in the presence of death, as you might say. Pretty soon the bull made a snatch for us and brought away some of my horse's tail (I suppose, but do not know, being pretty busy at the time), but *something* made him hungry for solitude and suggested to him to get up and hunt for it. And then you ought to have seen that spider-legged old skeleton go! and you ought to have seen the bull cut out after him, too—head down, tongue out, tail up, bellowing like everything, and actually mowing down the weeds, and tearing up the earth, and boosting up the sand like a whirlwind! By George, it was a hot race! I and the saddle were back on the rump, and I had the bridle in my teeth and holding on to the pommel with both hands. First we left the dogs behind; then we passed a jackass-rabbit; then we overtook a coyote, and were gain-

ing on an antelope when the rotten girths let go and threw me about
thirty yards off to the left, and as the saddle went down over the horse's
rump he gave it a lift with his heels that sent it more than four hundred
yards up in the air, I wish I may die in a minute if he didn't. I fell at
the foot of the only solitary tree there was in nine counties adjacent (as
any creature could see with the naked eye), and the next second I had
hold of the bark with four sets of nails and my teeth, and the next second after that I was astraddle of the main limb and blaspheming my
luck in a way that made my breath smell of brimstone. I *had* the bull,
now, if he did not think of *one* thing. But that one thing I dreaded. I
dreaded it very seriously. There was a possibility that the bull might
not think of it, but there were greater chances that he would. I made
up my mind what I would do in case he did. It was a little over forty
feet to the ground from where I sat. I cautiously unwound the lariat
from the pommel of my saddle—"

"Your *saddle?* Did you take your saddle up in the tree with you?"

"Take it up in the tree with me? Why, how you talk! Of course I
didn't. No man could do that. It *fell* in the tree when it came down."

"Oh—exactly."

"Certainly. I unwound the lariat, and fastened one end of it to the
limb. It was the very best green rawhide, and capable of sustaining
tons. I made a slip-noose in the other end, and then hung it down to see
the length. It reached down twenty-two feet—half-way to the ground.
I then loaded every barrel of the Allen with a double charge. I felt satisfied. I said to myself, if he never thinks of that one thing that I dread,
all right—but if he does, all right anyhow—I am fixed for him. But don't
you know that the very thing a man dreads is the thing that always
happens? Indeed it is so. I watched the bull, now, with anxiety—anxiety which no one can conceive of who has not been in such a situation
and felt that at any moment death might come. Presently a thought
came into the bull's eye. I knew it! said I—if my nerve fails now, I am
lost. Sure enough, it was just as I had dreaded, he started in to climb
the tree—"

"What, the bull?"

"Of course—who else?"

"But a bull can't climb a tree."

"He can't, can't he? Since you know so much about it, did you ever
see a bull try?"

"No! I never dreamt of such a thing."

"Well, then, what is the use of your talking that way, then? Because you never saw a thing done, is that any reason why it can't be done?"

"Well, all right—go on. What did you do?"

"The bull started up, and got along well for about ten feet, then slipped and slid back. I breathed easier. He tried it again—got up a little higher—slipped again. But he came at it once more, and this time he was careful. He got gradually higher and higher, and my spirits went down more and more. Up he came—an inch at a time—with his eyes hot, and his tongue hanging out. Higher and higher—hitched his foot over the stump of a limb, and looked up, as much as to say, 'You are my meat, friend.' Up again—higher and higher, and getting more excited the closer he got. He was within ten feet of me! I took a long breath— and then said I, 'It is now or never.' I had the coil of the lariat all ready; I paid it out slowly, till it hung right over his head; all of a sudden I let go of the slack and the slip-noose fell fairly round his neck! Quicker than lightning I out with the Allen and let him have it in the face. It was an awful roar, and must have scared the bull out of his senses. When the smoke cleared away, there he was, dangling in the air, twenty foot from the ground, and going out of one convulsion into another faster than you could count! I didn't stop to count, anyhow —I shinned down the tree and shot for home."

"Bemis, is all that true, just as you have stated it?"

"I wish I may rot in my tracks and die the death of a dog if it isn't."

"Well, we can't refuse to believe it, and we don't. But if there were some proofs—"

"Proofs! Did I bring back my lariat?"

"No."

"Did I bring back my horse?"

"No."

"Did you ever see the bull again?"

"No."

"Well, then, what more do you want? I never saw anybody as particular as you are about a little thing like that."

I made up my mind that if this man was not a liar he only missed it by the skin of his teeth.

From ROUGHING IT, 1872

A Curious Pleasure Excursion*

[We have received the following advertisement, but, inasmuch as it concerns a matter of deep and general interest, we feel fully justified in inserting it in our reading-columns. We are confident that our conduct in this regard needs only explanation, not apology.—Ed., *N. Y. Herald.*]

ADVERTISEMENT

This is to inform the public that in connection with Mr. Barnum I have leased the comet for a term of years; and I desire also to solicit the public patronage in favor of a beneficial enterprise which we have in view.

We propose to fit up comfortable, and even luxurious, accommodations in the comet for as many persons as will honor us with their patronage, and make an extended excursion among the heavenly bodies. We shall prepare 1,000,000 state-rooms in the tail of the comet (with hot and cold water, gas, looking-glass, parachute, umbrella, etc., in each), and shall construct more if we meet with a sufficiently generous encouragement. We shall have billiard-rooms, card-rooms, music-rooms, bowling-alleys and many spacious theaters and free libraries; and on the main deck we propose to have a driving-park, with upward of 100,000 miles of roadway in it. We shall publish daily newspapers also.

DEPARTURE OF THE COMET.

The comet will leave New York at 10 P.M. on the 20th inst., and therefore it will be desirable that the passengers be on board by eight at the latest, to avoid confusion in getting under way. It is not known whether passports will be necessary or not, but it is deemed best that passengers provide them, and so guard against all contingencies. No dogs will be allowed on board. This rule has been made in deference to the existing state of feeling regarding these animals, and will be strictly adhered to. The safety of the passengers will in all ways be jealously looked to. A substantial iron railing will be put up all around the comet, and no one

* Published at the time of the "Comet Scare" in the summer of 1874.

will be allowed to go to the edge and look over unless accompanied by either my partner or myself.

THE POSTAL SERVICE

will be of the completest character. Of course the telegraph, and the telegraph only, will be employed; consequently friends occupying state-rooms 20,000,000 and even 30,000,000 miles apart will be able to send a message and receive a reply inside of eleven days. Night messages will be half-rate. The whole of this vast postal system will be under the personal superintendence of Mr. Hale of Maine. Meals served at all hours. Meals served in staterooms charged extra.

Hostility is not apprehended from any great planet, but we have thought it best to err on the safe side, and therefore have provided a proper number of mortars, siege-guns, and boarding-pikes. History shows that small, isolated communities, such as the people of remote islands, are prone to be hostile to strangers, and so the same may be the case with

THE INHABITANTS OF STARS

of the tenth or twentieth magnitude. We shall in no case wantonly offend the people of any star, but shall treat all alike with urbanity and kindliness, never conducting ourselves toward an asteroid after a fashion which we could not venture to assume toward Jupiter or Saturn. I repeat that we shall not wantonly offend any star; but at the same time we shall promptly resent any injury that may be done us, or any insolence offered us, by parties or governments residing in any star in the firmament. Although averse to the shedding of blood, we shall still hold this course rigidly and fearlessly, not only toward single stars, but toward constellations. We shall hope to leave a good impression of America behind us in every nation we visit, from Venus to Uranus. And, at all events, if we cannot inspire love we shall at least compel respect for our country wherever we go. We shall take with us, free of charge,

A GREAT FORCE OF MISSIONARIES,

and shed the true light upon all the celestial orbs which, physically aglow, are yet morally in darkness. Sunday-schools will be established wherever practicable. Compulsory education will also be introduced.

The comet will visit Mars first, and proceed to Mercury, Jupiter, Venus, and Saturn. Parties connected with the government of the District of Columbia and with the former city government of New York, who may desire to inspect the rings, will be allowed time and every facility. Every star of prominent magnitude will be visited, and time allowed for excursions to points of interest inland.

THE DOG STAR

has been stricken from the program. Much time will be spent in the Great Bear, and, indeed, in every constellation of importance. So, also, with the Sun and Moon and the Milky Way, otherwise the Gulf Stream of the skies. Clothing suitable for wear in the sun should be provided. Our program has been so arranged that we shall seldom go more than 100,000,000 of miles at a time without stopping at some star. This will necessarily make the stoppages frequent and preserve the interest of the tourist. Baggage checked through to any point on the route. Parties desiring to make only a part of the proposed tour, and thus save expense, may stop over at any star they choose and wait for the return voyage.

After visiting all the most celebrated stars and constellations in our system and personally inspecting the remotest sparks that even the most powerful telescope can now detect in the firmament, we shall proceed with good heart upon

A STUPENDOUS VOYAGE

of discovery among the countless whirling worlds that make turmoil in the mighty wastes of space that stretch their solemn solitudes, their unimaginable vastness billions upon billions of miles away beyond the farthest verge of telescopic vision, till by comparison the little sparkling vault we used to gaze at on Earth shall seem like a remembered phosphorescent flash of spangles which some tropical voyager's prow stirred into life for a single instant, and which ten thousand miles of phosphorescent seas and tedious lapse of time had since diminished to an incident utterly trivial in his recollection. Children occupying seats at the first table will be charged full fare.

FIRST-CLASS FARE

from the Earth to Uranus, including visits to the Sun and Moon and all the principal planets on the route, will be charged at the low rate of $2 for every 50,000,000 miles of actual travel. A great reduction will be made where parties wish to make the round trip. This comet is new and in thorough repair and is now on her first voyage. She is confessedly the fastest on the line. She makes 20,000,000 miles a day, with her present facilities; but, with a picked American crew and good weather, we are confident we can get 40,000,000 out of her. Still, we shall never push her to a dangerous speed, and we shall rigidly prohibit racing with other comets. Passengers desiring to diverge at any point or return will be transferred to other comets. We make close connections at all principal points with all reliable lines. Safety can be depended upon. It is not to be denied that the heavens are infested with

OLD RAMSHACKLE COMETS

that have not been inspected or overhauled in 10,000 years, and which ought long ago to have been destroyed or turned into hail-barges, but with these we have no connection whatever. Steerage passengers not allowed abaft the main hatch.

Complimentary round-trip tickets have been tendered to General Butler, Mr. Shepherd, Mr. Richardson, and other eminent gentlemen, whose public services have entitled them to the rest and relaxation of a voyage of this kind. Parties desiring to make the round trip will have extra accommodation. The entire voyage will be completed, and the passengers landed in New York again, on the 14th of December, 1991. This is, at least, forty years quicker than any other comet can do it in. Nearly all the back-pay members contemplate making the round trip with us in case their constituents will allow them a holiday. Every harmless amusement will be allowed on board, but no pools permitted on the run of the comet—no gambling of any kind. All fixed stars will be respected by us, but such stars as seem to need fixing we shall fix. If it makes trouble, we shall be sorry, but firm.

Mr. Coggia having leased his comet to us, she will no longer be called by his name, but by my partner's. N. B.—Passengers by paying double fare will be entitled to a share in all the new stars, suns moons, comets, meteors, and magazines of thunder and lightning we may discover. Patent-medicine people will take notice that

WE CARRY BULLETIN-BOARDS

and a paint-brush along for use in the constellations, and are open to terms. Cremationists are reminded that we are going straight to—some hot places—and are open to terms. To other parties our enterprise is a pleasure excursion, but individually we mean business. We shall fly our comet for all it is worth.

FOR FURTHER PARTICULARS,

or for freight or passage, apply on board, or to my partner, but not to me, since I do not take charge of the comet until she is under way. It is necessary, at a time like this, that my mind should not be burdened with small business details.

MARK TWAIN

1874

Rogers

This man Rogers happened upon me and introduced himself at the town of——, in the South of England, where I stayed awhile. His stepfather had married a distant relative of mine who was afterward hanged, and so he seemed to think a blood relationship existed between us. He came in every day and sat down and talked. Of all the bland, serene human curiosities I ever saw, I think he was the chiefest. He desired to look at my new chimney-pot hat. I was very willing, for I thought he would notice the name of the great Oxford Street hatter in it, and respect me accordingly. But he turned it about with a sort of grave compassion, pointed out two or three blemishes, and said that I, being so recently arrived, could not be expected to know where to supply myself. Said he would send me the address of *his* hatter. Then he said, "Pardon me," and proceeded to cut a neat circle of red tissue-paper; daintily notched the edges of it; took the mucilage and pasted it in my hat so as to cover the manufacturer's name. He said, "No one will know now where you got it. I will send you a hot-tip of my hatter, and you can paste it over this tissue circle." It was the calmest, coolest thing—I never admired a man so much in my life. Mind, he did this while his own hat sat offensively near our noses, on the table—an ancient extinguisher of the "slouch" pattern, limp and shapeless with age, discolored by vicissitudes of the weather, and banded by an equator of bear's grease that had stewed through.

Another time he examined my coat. I had no terrors, for over my tailor's door was the legend, "By Special Appointment Tailor to H. R. H. the Prince of Wales," etc. I did not know at the time that the most of the tailor shops had the same sign out, and that whereas it takes nine tailors to make an ordinary man, it takes a hundred and fifty to make a prince. He was full of compassion for my coat. Wrote down the address of his tailor for me. Did not tell me to mention my *nom de plume* and the tailor would put his best work on my garment, as complimentary people sometimes do, but said his tailor would hardly trouble himself for an unknown person (unknown person, when I thought I was so celebrated in England!—that was the cruelest cut), but cautioned me to mention *his* name, and it would be all right. Thinking to be facetious, I said:

"But he might sit up all night and injure his health."

"Well, *let* him," said Rogers; "I've done enough for him, for him to show some appreciation of it."

I might as well have tried to disconcert a mummy with my facetiousness. Said Rogers: "I get all my coats there—they're the only coats fit to be seen in."

I made one more attempt. I said, "I wish you had brought one with you—I would like to look at it."

"Bless your heart, haven't I got one on?—*this* article is Morgan's make."

I examined it. The coat had been bought ready-made, of a Chatham Street Jew, without any question—about 1848. It probably cost four dollars when it was new. It was ripped, it was frayed, it was napless and greasy. I could not resist showing him where it was ripped. It so affected him that I was almost sorry I had done it. First he seemed plunged into a bottomless abyss of grief. Then he roused himself, made a feint with his hands as if waving off the pity of a nation, and said— with what seemed to me a manufactured emotion—"No matter; no matter; don't mind me; do not bother about it. I can get another."

When he was thoroughly restored, so that he could examine the rip and command his feelings, he said, ah, *now* he understood it—his servant must have done it while dressing him that morning.

His servant! There was something awe-inspiring in effrontery like this.

Nearly every day he interested himself in some article of my clothing. One would hardly have expected this sort of infatuation in a man who always wore the same suit, and it a suit that seemed coeval with the Conquest.

It was an unworthy ambition, perhaps, but I *did* wish I could make this man admire *something* about me or something I did—you would have felt the same way. I saw my opportunity: I was about to return to London, and had "listed" my soiled linen for the wash. It made quite an imposing mountain in the corner of the room—fifty-four pieces. I hoped he would fancy it was the accumulation of a single week. I took up the wash-list, as if to see that it was all right, and then tossed it on the table, with pretended forgetfulness. Sure enough, he took it up and ran his eye along down to the grand total. Then he said, "You get off easy," and laid it down again.

His gloves were the saddest ruin, but he told me where I could get some like them. His shoes would hardly hold walnuts without leaking, but he liked to put his feet up on the mantelpiece and contemplate them. He wore a dim glass breastpin, which he called a "morphylitic diamond"—whatever that may mean—and said only two of them had ever been found—the Emperor of China had the other one.

Afterward, in London, it was a pleasure to me to see this fantastic vagabond come marching into the lobby of the hotel in his grand-ducal way, for he always had some new imaginary grandeur to develop—there was nothing stale about him but his clothes. If he addressed me when strangers were about, he always raised his voice a little and called me "Sir Richard," or "General," or "Your Lordship"—and when people began to stare and look deferential, he would fall to inquiring in a casual way why I disappointed the Duke of Argyll the night before; and then remind me of our engagement at the Duke of Westminster's for the following day. I think that for the time being these things were realities to him. He once came and invited me to go with him and spend the evening with the Earl of Warwick at his town house. I said I had received no formal invitation. He said that that was of no consequence, the Earl had no formalities for him or his friends. I asked if I could go just as I was. He said no, that would hardly do; evening dress was requisite at night in any gentleman's house. He said he would wait while I dressed, and then we would go to his apartments and I could take a bottle of champagne and a cigar while he dressed. I was very willing to see how this enterprise would turn out, so I dressed, and we started to his lodgings. He said if I didn't mind we would walk. So we tramped some four miles through the mud and fog, and finally found his "apartments"; they consisted of a single room over a barber's shop in a back street. Two chairs, a small table, an ancient valise, a

wash-basin and pitcher (both on the floor in a corner), an unmade
bed, a fragment of a looking-glass, and a flower-pot, with a perishing
little rose geranium in it, which he called a century plant, and said it
had not bloomed now for upward of two centuries—given to him by the
late Lord Palmerston—(been offered a prodigious sum for it)—these
were the contents of the room. Also a brass candlestick and a part of a
candle. Rogers lit the candle, and told me to sit down and make myself
at home. He said he hoped I was thirsty, because he would surprise my
palate with an article of champagne that seldom got into a commoner's
system; or would I prefer sherry, or port? Said he had port in bottles
that were swathed in stratified cobwebs, every stratum representing a
generation. And as for his cigars—well, I should judge of them myself.
Then he put his head out at the door and called:

"Sackville!" No answer.

"Hi—Sackville!" No answer.

"Now what the devil can have become of that butler? I *never* allow
a servant to—Oh, confound that idiot, he's got the *keys*. Can't get into
the other rooms without the keys."

(I was just wondering at his intrepidity in still keeping up the delusion of the champagne, and trying to imagine how he was going to
get out of the difficulty.)

Now he stopped calling Sackville and began to call "Anglesy." But
Anglesy didn't come. He said, "This is the *second* time that that equerry
has been absent without leave. To-morrow I'll discharge him."

Now he began to whoop for "Thomas," but Thomas didn't answer.
Then for "Theodore," but no Theodore replied.

"Well, I give it up," said Rogers. "The servants never expect me
this hour, and so they're all off on a lark. Might get along without the
equerry and the page, but can't have any wine or cigars without the
butler, and can't dress without my valet."

I offered to help him dress, but he would not hear of it; and besides,
he said he would not feel comfortable unless dressed by a practised
hand. However, he finally concluded that he was such old friends with
the Earl that it would not make any difference how he was dressed. So
we took a cab, he gave the driver some directions, and we started. By
and by we stopped before a large house and got out. I never had seen
this man with a collar on. He now stepped under a lamp and got a venerable paper collar out of his coat pocket, along with a hoary cravat,
and put them on. He ascended the stoop, and entered. Presently he re-
appeared, descended rapidly, and said:

"Come—quick!"

We hurried away, and turned the corner.

"Now we're safe," he said, and took off his collar and cravat and returned them to his pocket.

"Made a mighty narrow escape," said he.

"How?" said I.

"B' George, the Countess was there!"

"Well, what of that?—don't she know you?"

"Know me? Absolutely worships me. I just did happen to catch a glimpse of her before she saw me—and out I shot. Haven't seen her for two months—to rush in on her without any warning might have been fatal. She could *not* have stood it. I didn't know *she* was in town—thought she was at the castle. Let me lean on you—just a moment—there; now I am better—thank you; thank you ever so much. Lord bless me, what an escape!"

So I never got to call on the Earl, after all. But I marked the house for future reference. It proved to be an ordinary family hotel, with about a thousand plebeians roosting in it.

In most things Rogers was by no means a fool. In some things it was plain enough that he was a fool, but he certainly did not know it. He was in the "deadest" earnest in these matters. He died at sea, last summer, as the "Earl of Ramsgate."

1874

After-Dinner Speech

[At a Fourth of July Gathering, in London, of Americans]

MR. CHAIRMAN AND LADIES AND GENTLEMEN: I thank you for the compliment which has just been tendered me, and to show my appreciation of it I will not afflict you with many words. It is pleasant to celebrate in this peaceful way, upon this old mother soil, the anniversary of an experiment which was born of war with this same land so long ago, and wrought out to a successful issue by the devotion of our ancestors. It has taken nearly a hundred years to bring the English and Americans into kindly and mutually appreciative relations, but I believe it has been accomplished at last. It was a great step when the two last misunderstandings were settled by arbitration instead of cannon. It is another great step when England adopts our sewing-machines without claiming the invention—as usual. It was another when they imported one of our sleeping-cars the other day. And it warmed my heart more than I can tell, yesterday, when I witnessed the spectacle of an Englishman ordering an American sherry cobbler of his own free will and accord—and not only that but with a great brain and a level head reminding the barkeeper not to forget the strawberries. With a common origin, a common language, a common literature, a common religion and—common drinks, what is longer needful to the cementing of the two nations together in a permanent bond of brotherhood?

This is an age of progress, and ours is a progressive land. A great and glorious land, too—a land which has developed a Washington, a Franklin, a William M. Tweed, a Longfellow, a Motley, a Jay Gould, a Samuel C. Pomeroy, a recent Congress which has never had its equal (in some respects), and a United States Army which conquered sixty Indians in eight months by tiring them out—which is much better than uncivilized slaughter, God knows. We have a criminal jury system which is superior to any in the world; and its efficiency is only marred by the difficulty of finding twelve men every day who don't know anything and can't read. And I may observe that we have an insanity plea that would have saved Cain. I think I can say, and say with pride, that we have some legislatures that bring higher prices than any in the world.

I refer with effusion to our railway system, which consents to let us live, though it might do the opposite, being our owners. It only destroyed three thousand and seventy lives last year by collisions, and twenty-seven thousand two hundred and sixty by running over heedless and unnecessary people at crossings. The companies seriously regretted the killing of these thirty thousand people, and went so far as to pay for some of them—voluntarily, of course, for the meanest of us would not claim that we possess a court treacherous enough to enforce a law against a railway company. But, thank Heaven, the railway companies are generally disposed to do the right and kindly thing without compulsion. I know of an instance which greatly touched me at the time. After an accident the company sent home the remains of a dear distant old relative of mine in a basket, with the remark, "Please state what figure you hold him at—and return the basket." Now there couldn't be anything friendlier than that.

But I must not stand here and brag all night. However, you won't mind a body bragging a little about his country on the fourth of July. It is a fair and legitimate time to fly the eagle. I will say only one more word of brag—and a hopeful one. It is this. We have a form of government which gives each man a fair chance and no favor. With us no individual is born with a right to look down upon his neighbor and hold him in contempt. Let such of us as are not dukes find our consolation in that. And we may find hope for the future in the fact that as unhappy as is the condition of our political morality to-day, England has risen up out of a far fouler since the days when Charles I. ennobled courtesans and all political place was a matter of bargain and sale. There is hope for us yet.[1]

1875

A Couple of Poems by Twain and Moore

THOSE EVENING BELLS

BY THOMAS MOORE

Those evening bells! those evening bells!
How many a tale their music tells
Of youth, and home, and that sweet time
When last I heard their soothing chime.

[1] At least the above is the speech which I was going to make, but our minister, General Schenck, presided, and after the blessing, got up and made a great long inconceivably dull harangue, and wound up by saying that inasmuch as speech-making did not seem to exhilarate the guests much, all further oratory would be dispensed with during the evening, and we could just sit and talk privately to our elbow-neighbors and have a good sociable time. It is known that in consequence of that remark forty-four perfected speeches died in the womb. The depression, the gloom, the solemnity that reigned over the banquet from that time forth will be a lasting memory with many that were there. By that one thoughtless remark General Schenck lost forty-four of the best friends he had in England. More than one said that night, "And this is the sort of person that is sent to represent us in a great sister empire!"

Those joyous hours are passed away;
And many a heart that then was gay,
Within the tomb now darkly dwells,
And hears no more those evening bells.

And so 'twill be when I am gone—
That tuneful peal will still ring on;
While other bards shall walk these dells,
And sing your praise, sweet evening bells.

THOSE ANNUAL BILLS

BY MARK TWAIN

These annual bills! these annual bills!
How many a song their discord trills
Of "truck" consumed, enjoyed, forgot,
Since I was skinned by last year's lot!

Those joyous beans are passed away;
Those onions blithe, O where are they?
Once loved, lost, mourned—*now* vexing ILLS
Your shades troop back in annual bills!

And so 'twill be when I'm aground—
These yearly duns will still go round,
While other bards, with frantic quills,
Shall damn and *damn* these annual bills!

1875

An Encounter with an Interviewer

The nervous, dapper, "peart" young man took the chair I offered him,
and said he was connected with the *Daily Thunderstorm*, and added:
"Hoping it's no harm, I've come to interview you."

"Come to what?"

"*Interview* you."

"Ah! I see. Yes—yes. Um! Yes—yes."

I was not feeling bright that morning. Indeed, my powers seemed a bit under a cloud. However, I went to the bookcase, and when I had been looking six or seven minutes I found I was obliged to refer to the young man. I said:

"How do you spell it?"

"Spell what?"

"Interview."

"Oh, my goodness! what do you want to spell it for?"

"I don't want to spell it; I want to see what it means."

"Well, this is astonishing, I must say. *I* can tell you what it means, if you—if you—"

"Oh, all right! That will answer, and much obliged to you, too."

"In, *in*, ter, *ter*, *inter*—"

"Then you spell it with an *I?*"

"Why, certainly!"

"Oh, that is what took me so long."

"Why, my *dear* sir, what did *you* propose to spell it with?"

"Well, I—I—hardly know. I had the Unabridged, and I was ciphering around in the back end, hoping I might tree her among the pictures. But it's a very old edition."

"Why, my friend, they wouldn't have a *picture* of it in even the latest e— My dear sir, I beg your pardon, I mean no harm in the world, but you do not look as—as—intelligent as I had expected you would. No harm—I mean no harm at all."

"Oh, don't mention it! It has often been said, and by people who would not flatter and who could have no inducement to flatter, that I am quite remarkable in that way. Yes—yes; they always speak of it with rapture."

"I can easily imagine it. But about this interview. You know it is the custom, now, to interview any man who has become notorious."

"Indeed, I had not heard of it before. It must be very interesting. What do you do it with?"

"Ah, well—well—well—this is disheartening. It *ought* to be done with a club in some cases; but customarily it consists in the interviewer asking questions and the interviewed answering them. It is all the rage now. Will you let me ask you certain questions calculated to bring out the salient points of your public and private history?"

"Oh, with pleasure—with pleasure. I have a very bad memory, but I

hope you will not mind that. That is to say, it is an irregular memory
—singularly irregular. Sometimes it goes in a gallop, and then again it
will be as much as a fortnight passing a given point. This is a great
grief to me."

"Oh, it is no matter, so you will try to do the best you can."

"I will. I will put my whole mind on it."

"Thanks. Are you ready to begin?"

"Ready."

Q. How old are you?

A. Nineteen, in June.

Q. Indeed. I would have taken you to be thirty-five or six. Where
were you born?

A. In Missouri.

Q. When did you begin to write?

A. In 1836.

Q. Why, how could that be, if you are only nineteen now?

A. I don't know. It does seem curious, somehow.

Q. It does, indeed. Whom do you consider the most remarkable
man you ever met?

A. Aaron Burr.

Q. But you never could have met Aaron Burr, if you are only nineteen years—

A. Now, if you know more about me than I do, what do you ask me
for?

Q. Well, it was only a suggestion; nothing more. How did you happen to meet Burr?

A. Well, I happened to be at his funeral one day, and he asked me to
make less noise, and—

Q. But, good heavens! if you were at his funeral, he must have been
dead, and if he was dead how could he care whether you made a noise
or not?

A. I don't know. He was always a particular kind of a man that way.

Q. Still, I don't understand it at all. You say he spoke to you, and
that he was dead.

A. I didn't say he was dead.

Q. But wasn't he dead?

A. Well, some said he was, some said he wasn't.

Q. What did you think?

A. Oh, it was none of my business! It wasn't any of my funeral.

Q. Did you— However, we can never get this matter straight. Let
me ask about something else. What was the date of your birth?

A. Monday, October 31, 1693.

Q. What! Impossible! That would make you a hundred and eighty years old. How do you account for that?

A. I don't account for it at all.

Q. But you said at first you were only nineteen, and now you make yourself out to be one hundred and eighty. It is an awful discrepancy.

A. Why, have you noticed that? (Shaking hands.) Many a time it has seemed to me like a discrepancy, but somehow I couldn't make up my mind. How quick you notice a thing!

Q. Thank you for the compliment, as far as it goes. Had you, or have you, any brothers or sisters?

A. Eh! I—I—I think so—yes—but I don't remember.

Q. Well, that is the most extraordinary statement I ever heard!

A. Why, what makes you think that?

Q. How could I think otherwise? Why, look here! Who is this a picture of on the wall? Isn't that a brother of yours?

A. Oh, yes, yes, yes! Now you remind me of it; that *was* a brother of mine. That's William—*Bill* we called him. Poor old Bill!

Q. Why? Is he dead, then?

A. Ah! Well, I suppose so. We never could tell. There was a great mystery about it.

Q. That is sad, very sad. He disappeared, then?

A. Well, yes, in a sort of general way. We buried him.

Q. *Buried* him! *Buried* him, without knowing whether he was dead or not?

A. Oh, no! Not that. He was dead enough.

Q. Well, I confess that I can't understand this. If you buried him, and you knew he was dead—

A. No! no! We only thought he was.

Q. Oh, I see! He came to life again?

A. I bet he didn't.

Q. Well, I never heard anything like this. *Somebody* was dead. *Somebody* was buried. Now, where was the mystery?

A. Ah! that's just it! That's it exactly. You see, we were twins—defunct and I—and we got mixed in the bathtub when we were only two weeks old, and one of us was drowned. But we didn't know which. Some think it was Bill. Some think it was me.

Q. Well, that *is* remarkable. What do *you* think?

A. Goodness knows! I would give whole worlds to know. This solemn, this awful mystery has cast a gloom over my whole life. But I

will tell you a secret now, which I never have revealed to any creature
before. One of us had a peculiar mark—a large mole on the back of his
left hand; that was *me*. *That child was the one that was drowned!*

Q. Very well, then, I don't see that there is any mystery about it, after
all.

A. You don't? Well, *I* do. Anyway, I don't see how they could ever
have been such a blundering lot as to go and bury the wrong child. But,
'sh!—don't mention it where the family can hear of it. Heaven knows
they have heartbreaking troubles enough without adding this.

Q. Well, I believe I have got material enough for the present, and I
am very much obliged to you for the pains you have taken. But I was a
good deal interested in that account of Aaron Burr's funeral. Would you
mind telling me what particular circumstance it was that made you
think Burr was such a remarkable man?

A. Oh! it was a mere trifle! Not one man in fifty would have noticed
it at all. When the sermon was over, and the procession all ready to
start for the cemetery, and the body all arranged nice in the hearse, he
said he wanted to take a last look at the scenery, and so he *got up and
rode with the driver*.

Then the young man reverently withdrew. He was very pleasant
company, and I was sorry to see him go.

1875

Johnny Greer

"The church was densely crowded that lovely summer Sabbath," said
the Sunday-school superintendent, "and all, as their eyes rested upon
the small coffin, seemed impressed by the poor black boy's fate. Above
the stillness the pastor's voice rose, and chained the interest of every
ear as he told, with many an envied compliment, how that the brave,
noble, daring little Johnny Greer, when he saw the drowned body
sweeping down toward the deep part of the river whence the agonized
parents never could have recovered it in this world, gallantly sprang
into the stream, and, at the risk of his life, towed the corpse to shore,
and held it fast till help came and secured it. Johnny Greer was sitting

just in front of me. A ragged street-boy, with eager eye, turned upon
him instantly, and said in a hoarse whisper:

" 'No; but did you, though?'

" 'Yes.'

" 'Towed the carkiss ashore and saved it yo'self?'

" 'Yes.'

" 'Cracky! What did they give you?'

" 'Nothing.'

" 'W-h-a-t [with intense disgust]! D'you know what I'd 'a' done? I'd
'a' anchored him out in the stream, and said, *Five dollars, gents, or you
carn't have yo' nigger.*' "

1875

The Jumping Frog

*In English. Then in French. Then clawed back
into a civilized language once more
by patient, unremunerated toil.* .

Even a criminal is entitled to fair play; and certainly when a man
who has done no harm has been unjustly treated, he is privileged to do
his best to right himself. My attention has just been called to an article
some three years old in a French Magazine entitled, *Revue des Deux
Mondes* (Review of Some Two Worlds), wherein the writer treats of
"Les Humoristes Americaines" (These Humorists Americans). I am
one of these humorists Americans dissected by him, and hence the
complaint I am making.

This gentleman's article is an able one (as articles go, in the French,
where they always tangle up everything to that degree that when you
start into a sentence you never know whether you are going to come out
alive or not). It is a very good article, and the writer says all manner of
kind and complimentary things about me—for which I am sure I thank
him with all my heart; but then why should he go and spoil all his
praise by one unlucky experiment? What I refer to is this: he says my
Jumping Frog is a funny story, but still he can't see why it should
ever really convulse any one with laughter—and straightway proceeds

to translate it into French in order to prove to his nation that there is
nothing so very extravagantly funny about it. Just there is where my
complaint originates. He has not translated it at all; he has simply
mixed it all up; it is no more like the Jumping Frog when he gets
through with it than I am like a meridian of longitude. But my mere
assertion is not proof; wherefore I print the French version, that all
may see that I do not speak falsely; furthermore, in order that even the
unlettered may know my injury and give me their compassion, I have
been at infinite pains and trouble to retranslate this French version back
into English; and to tell the truth I have well-nigh worn myself out
at it, having scarcely rested from my work during five days and nights.
I cannot speak the French language, but I can translate very well,
though not fast, I being self-educated. I ask the reader to run his eye
over the original English version of the Jumping Frog, and then read
the French or my retranslation, and kindly take notice how the Frenchman has riddled the grammar. I think it is the worst I ever saw; and yet
the French are called a polished nation. If I had a boy that put sentences together as they do, I would polish him to some purpose. Without further introduction, the Jumping Frog, as I originally wrote it, was
as follows [after it will be found the French version, and after the latter
my retranslation from the French]:

THE NOTORIOUS JUMPING FROG OF
CALAVERAS[1] COUNTY

In compliance with the request of a friend of mine, who wrote me
from the East, I called on good-natured, garrulous old Simon Wheeler,
and inquired after my friend's friend, Leonidas W. Smiley, as requested to do, and I hereunto append the result. I have a lurking suspicion that *Leonidas W.* Smiley is a myth; that my friend never knew
such a personage; and that he only conjectured that if I asked old
Wheeler about him, it would remind him of his infamous *Jim* Smiley,
and he would go to work and bore me to death with some exasperating
reminiscence of him as long and as tedious as it should be useless to
me. If that was the design, it succeeded.

I found Simon Wheeler dozing comfortably by the bar-room stove of
the dilapidated tavern in the decayed mining camp of Angel's, and I
noticed that he was fat and bald-headed, and had an expression of winning gentleness and simplicity upon his tranquil countenance. He
roused up, and gave me good day. I told him that a friend of mine

[1] Pronounced Cal-e-*va*-ras.

had commissioned me to make some inquiries about a cherished companion of his boyhood named *Leonidas W.* Smiley—*Rev. Leonidas W.* Smiley, a young minister of the Gospel, who he had heard was at one time a resident of Angel's Camp. I added that if Mr. Wheeler could tell me anything about this Rev. Leonidas W. Smiley, I would feel under many obligations to him.

Simon Wheeler backed me into a corner and blockaded me there with his chair, and then sat down and reeled off the monotonous narrative which follows this paragraph. He never smiled, he never frowned, he never changed his voice from the gentle-flowing key to which he tuned his initial sentence, he never betrayed the slightest suspicion of enthusiasm; but all through the interminable narrative there ran a vein of impressive earnestness and sincerity, which showed me plainly that, so far from his imagining that there was anything ridiculous or funny about his story, he regarded it as a really important matter, and admired its two heroes as men of transcendent genius in *finesse.* I let him go on in his own way, and never interrupted him once.

"Rev. Leonidas W. H'm, Reverend Le—well, there was a feller here once by the name of *Jim* Smiley, in the winter of '49—or maybe it was the spring of '50—I don't recollect exactly, somehow though what makes me think it was one or the other is because I remember the big flume warn't finished when he first come to the camp; but anyway, he was the curiousest man about always betting on anything that turned up you ever see, if he could get anybody to bet on the other side; and if he couldn't he'd change sides. Any way that suited the other man would suit *him*—any way just so's he got a bet, *he* was satisfied. But still he was lucky, uncommon lucky; he most always come out winner. He was always ready and laying for a chance; there couldn't be no solit'ry thing mentioned but that feller'd offer to bet on it, and take ary side you please, as I was just telling you. If there was a horse-race, you'd find him flush or you'd find him busted at the end of it; if there was a dog-fight, he'd bet on it; if there was a cat-fight, he'd bet on it; if there was a chicken-fight, he'd bet on it; why, if there was two birds setting on a fence, he would bet you which one would fly first; or if there was a camp-meeting, he would be there reg'lar to bet on Parson Walker, which he judged to be the best exhorter about here, and so he was too, and a good man. If he even see a straddle-bug start to go anywheres, he would bet you how long it would take him to get to—to wherever he was going to, and if you took him up, he would foller that straddle-bug to Mexico but what he would find out where he was bound for and how long he was on the road. Lots of the boys here has seen that Smiley, and

can tell you about him. Why, it never made no difference to *him*—he'd
bet on *any* thing—the dangdest feller. Parson Walker's wife laid very
sick once, for a good while, and it seemed as if they warn't going to
save her; but one morning he come in, and Smiley up and asked him
how she was, and he said she was considerable better—thank the Lord
for his inf'nite mercy—and coming on so smart that with the blessing of
Prov'dence she'd get well yet; and Smiley, before he thought, says,
'Well, I'll resk two-and-a-half she don't anyway.'

"Thish-yer Smiley had a mare—the boys called her the fifteen-minute
nag, but that was only in fun, you know, because of course she was
faster than that—and he used to win money on that horse, for all she
was so slow and always had the asthma, or the distemper, or the consumption, or something of that kind. They used to give her two or three
hundred yards' start, and then pass her under way; but always at the
fag end of the race she'd get excited and desperate like, and come ca-
vorting and straddling up, and scattering her legs around limber, sometimes in the air, and sometimes out to one side among the fences, and
kicking up m-o-r-e dust and raising m-o-r-e racket with her coughing
and sneezing and blowing her nose—and *always* fetch up at the stand
just about a neck ahead, as near as you could cipher it down.

"And he had a little small bull-pup, that to look at him you'd think he
warn't worth a cent but to set around and look ornery and lay for a
chance to steal something. But as soon as money was up on him he
was a different dog; his under-jaw'd begin to stick out like the fo'castle
of a steamboat, and his teeth would uncover and shine like the furnaces.
And a dog might tackle him and bully-rag him, and bite him, and
throw him over his shoulder two or three times, and Andrew Jackson
—which was the name of the pup—Andrew Jackson would never let on
but what *he* was satisfied, and hadn't expected nothing else—and the
bets being doubled and doubled on the other side all the time, till the
money was all up; and then all of a sudden he would grab that other
dog jest by the j'int of his hind leg and freeze to it—not chaw, you understand, but only just grip and hang on till they throwed up the
sponge, if it was a year. Smiley always come out winner on that pup,
til he harnessed a dog once that didn't have no hind legs, because
they'd been sawed off in a circular saw, and when the thing had gone
along far enough, and the money was all up, and he come to make a
snatch for his pet holt, he see in a minute how he'd been imposed on
and how the other dog had him in the door, so to speak, and he 'peared
surprised, and then he looked sorter discouraged-like, and didn't try no
more to win the fight, and so he got shucked out bad. He give Smiley

a look, as much as to say his heart was broke, and it was *his* fault, for putting up a dog that hadn't no hind legs for him to take holt of, which was his main dependence in a fight, and then he limped off a piece and laid down and died. It was a good pup, was that Andrew Jackson, and would have made a name for hisself if he'd lived, for the stuff was in him and he had genius—I know it, because he hadn't no opportunities to speak of, and it don't stand to reason that a dog could make such a fight as he could under them circumstances if he hadn't no talent. It always makes me feel sorry when I think of that last fight of his'n, and the way it turned out.

"Well, thish-yer Smiley had rat-tarriers, and chicken cocks, and tomcats and all them kind of things, till you couldn't rest, and you couldn't fetch nothing for him to bet on but he'd match you. He ketched a frog one day, and took him home, and said he cal'lated to educate him; and so he never done nothing for three months but set in his back yard and learn that frog to jump. And you bet you he *did* learn him, too. He'd give him a little punch behind, and the next minute you'd see that frog whirling in the air like a doughnut—see him turn one summerset, or maybe a couple, if he got a good start, and come down flat-footed and all right, like a cat. He got him up so in the matter of ketching flies, and kep' him in practice so constant, that he'd nail a fly every time as fur as he could see him. Smiley said all a frog wanted was education, and he could do 'most anything—and I believe him. Why, I've seen him set Dan'l Webster down here on this floor—Dan'l Webster was the name of the frog—and sing out, 'Flies, Dan'l, flies!' and quicker'n you could wink he'd spring straight up and snake a fly off'n the counter there, and flop down on the floor ag'in as solid as a gob of mud, and fall to scratching the side of his head with his hind foot as indifferent as if he hadn't no idea he'd been doin' any more'n any frog might do. You never see a frog so modest and straightfor'ard as he was, for all he was so gifted. And when it come to fair and square jumping on a dead level, he could get over more ground at one straddle than any animal of his breed you ever see. Jumping on a dead level was his strong suit, you understand; and when it come to that, Smiley would ante up money on him as long as he had a red. Smiley was monstrous proud of his frog, and well he might be, for fellers that had traveled and been everywheres all said he laid over any frog that ever *they* see.

"Well, Smiley kep' the beast in a little lattice box, and he used to fetch him down-town sometimes and lay for a bet. One day a feller—a stranger in the camp, he was—come acrost him with his box, and says:

"'What might it be that you've got in the box?'"

"And Smiley says, sorter indifferent-like, 'It might be a parrot, or it might be a canary, maybe, but it ain't—it's only just a frog.'

"And the feller took it, and looked at it careful, and turned it round this way and that, and says, 'H'm—so 'tis. Well, what's *he* good for?'

"'Well,' Smiley says, easy and careless, 'he's good enough for *one* thing, I should judge—he can outjump any frog in Calaveras County.'

"The feller took the box again, and took another long, particular look, and give it back to Smiley, and says, very deliberate, 'Well,' he says, 'I don't see no p'ints about that frog that's any better'n any other frog.'

"'Maybe you don't,' Smiley says. 'Maybe you understand frogs and maybe you don't understand 'em; maybe you've had experience, and maybe you ain't only a amature, as it were. Anyways, I've got *my* opinion, and I'll resk forty dollars that he can outjump any frog in Calaveras County.'

"And the feller studied a minute, and then says, kinder sadlike, 'Well, I'm only a stranger here, and I ain't got no frog; but if I had a frog, I'd bet you.'

"And then Smiley says, 'That's all right—that's all right—if you'll hold my box a minute, I'll go and get you a frog.' And so the feller took the box, and put up his forty dollars along with Smiley's, and set down to wait.

"So he set there a good while thinking and thinking to himself, and then he got the frog out and prized his mouth open and took a teaspoon and filled him full of quail-shot—filled him pretty near up to his chin—and set him on the floor. Smiley he went to the swamp and slopped around in the mud for a long time, and finally he ketched a frog, and fetched him in, and give him to this feller, and says:

"'Now, if you're ready, set him alongside of Dan'l, with his fore paws just even with Dan'l's, and I'll give the word.' Then he says, 'One—two—three—*git!*' and him and the feller touched up the frogs from behind, and the new frog hopped off lively, but Dan'l give a heave, and hysted up his shoulders—so—like a Frenchman, but it warn't no use—he couldn't budge; he was planted as solid as a church, and he couldn't no more stir than if he was anchored out. Smiley was a good deal surprised, and he was disgusted too, but he didn't have no idea what the matter was, of course.

"The feller took the money and started away; and when he was going out at the door, he sorter jerked his thumb over his shoulder—so—at Dan'l, and says again, very deliberate, 'Well,' he says, '*I* don't see no p'ints about that frog that's any better'n any other frog.'

"Smiley he stood scratching his head and looking down at Dan'l a long time, and at last he says, 'I do wonder what in the nation that frog throw'd off for—I wonder if there ain't something the matter with him —he 'pears to look mighty baggy, somehow.' And he ketched Dan'l by the nap of the neck, and hefted him, and says, 'Why blame my cats if he don't weigh five pound!' and turned him upside down and he belched out a double handful of shot. And then he see how it was, and he was the maddest man—he set the frog down and took out after that feller, but he never ketched him. And—"

[Here Simon Wheeler heard his name called from the front yard, and got up to see what was wanted.] And turning to me as he moved away, he said: "Just set where you are, stranger, and rest easy —I ain't going to be gone a second."

But, by your leave, I did not think that a continuation of the history of the enterprising vagabond *Jim* Smiley would be likely to afford me much information concerning the Rev. *Leonidas W.* Smiley, and so I started away.

At the door I met the sociable Wheeler returning, and he button-holed me and recommenced:

"Well, thish-yer Smiley had a yaller one-eyed cow that didn't have no tail, only just a short stump like a bannanner, and—"

However, lacking both time and inclination, I did not wait to hear about the afflicted cow, but took my leave.

Now let the learned look upon this picture and say if iconoclasm can further go:

[From the *Revue des Duex Mondes*, of July 15th, 1872.]

LA GRENOUILLE SAUTEUSE DU COMTE DE CALAVERAS

"—Il y avait une fois ici un individu connu sous le nom de Jim Smiley: c'était dans l'hiver de 49, peut-être bien au printemps de 50, je ne me rappelle pas exactement. Cequi me fait croire que c'était l'un ou l'autre, c'est que je me souviens que le grand bief n'était pas achevé lorsqu'il arriva au camp pour la premiére fois, mais de toutes façons il était l'homme le plus friand de paris qui se pût voir, pariant sur tout ce qui se présentait, quand il pouvait trouver un adversaire, et, quand il n'en trouvait pas il passait du côté opposé. Tout ce qui convenait à l'autre lue convenait; pourvu qu'il eût un pari, Smiley était satisfait. Et il avati une chance! une chance inouie: presque toujours il gagnait. Il faut dire qu'il était toujours prêt à s'exposer, qu'on ne pouvait men-

tionner la moindre chose sans que ce gaillard offrît de parier là-
dessus n'importe quoi et de prendre le côté que l'on voudrait, comme
je vous le disais tout à l'heure. S'il y avait des courses, vous le trouviez
riche ou ruiné à la fin; s'il y avait un combat de chiens, il apportait
son enjeu; il l'apportait pour un combat de chats, pour un combat de
coqs;—parbleu! si vous aviez vu deux oiseaux sur une haie, il vous
aurait offert de parier lequel s'envolerait le premier, et, s'il y avait
meeting au camp, il venait parier régulièrement pour le curé Walker,
qu'il jugeait être le meilleur prédicateur des environs, et qui l'était en
effet, et un brave homme. Il aurait rencontré une punaise de bois en
chemin, qu'il aurait parié sur le temps qu'il lui faudrait pour aller où
elle voudrait aller, et si vous l'aviez pris au mot, il aurait suivi la
punaise jusqu'au Mexique, sans se soucier d'aller si loin, ni du temps
qu'il y perdrait. Une fois la femme du curé Walker fut très malade
pendant longtemps, il semblait qu'on ne la sauverait pas; mais un
matin le curé arrive, et Smiley lui demande comment ella va, et il dit
qu'elle est bien mieux, grâce à l'infinie miséricorde, tellement mieux
qu'avec la bénédiction de la Providence elle s'en tirerait, et voilá que,
sans y penser, Smiley répond:—Eh bien! ye gage deux et demi qu'elle
mourra tout de même.

"Ce Smiley avait une jument que les gars appelaient le bidet du
quart d'heure, mais seulement pour plaisanter, vous comprenez, parce
que, bien entendu, elle était plus *vite* que ça! Et il avait coutume de
gagner de l'argent avec cette bête, quoiqu'elle fût poussive, cornarde,
toujours prise d'asthme, de coliques ou de consomption, ou de quelque
chose d'approchant. On lui donnait 2 ou 300 *yards* au départ, puis on la
dépassait sans peine; mais jamais à la fin elle ne manquait de s'échauffer, de s'exaspérer, et elle arrivait, s'écartant, se dèfendant, ses jambs
grêles en l'air devant les obstacles, quelquefois les évitant et faisant
avec cela plus de poussière qu'aucun cheval, plus de bruit surtout
avec ses éternumens et reniflemens.—crac! elle arrivait donc toujours
première d'une tête, aussi juste qu'on peut le mesurer. Et il avait un
petit bouledogue qui, à le voir, ne valait pas un sou; on aurait cru que
parier contre lui c'était voler, tant il était ordinaire; mais aussitôt les
enjeux faits, il devenait un autre chien. Sa mâchoire inférieure com-
mençait à ressortir comme un gaillard d'avant, ses dents se découvra-
ient brillantes commes des fournaises, et un chien pouvait le taquiner,
l'exciter, le mordre, le jeter deux ou trois fois par-dessus son épaule,
André Jackson, c'était le nom du chien, André Jackson prenait cela
tranquillement, comme s'il ne se fût jamais attendu à autre chose, et
quand les paris étaient doublés et redoublés contre lui, il vous saisissait

l'autre chien juste à l'articulation de la jambe de derrière, et il ne la lâchait plus, non pas qu'il la mâchât, vous concevez, mais il s'y serait tenu pendu jusqu'à ce qu'on jetât l'éponge en l'air, fallût-il attendre un an. Smiley gagnait toujours avec cette bête-là; malheureusement ils ont fini par dresser un chien qui n'avait pas de pattes de derrière, parce qu'on les avait sciées, et quand les choses furent au point qu'il voulait, et qu'il en vint à se jeter sur son morceau favori, le pauvre chien comprit en un instant qu'on s'était moqué de lui, et que l'autre le tenait. Vous n'avez jamais vu personne avoir l'air plus penaud et plus découragé; il ne fit aucun effort pour gagner le combat et fut rudement secoué, de sorte que, regardant Smiley comme pour lui dire:— Mon coeur est brisé, c'est ta faute; pourquoi m'avoir livré à un chien qui n'a pas de pattes de derrière, puisque c'est par là que je les bats? —il s'en alla en clopinant, et se coucha pour mourir. Ah! c'était un bon chien, cet André Jackson, et il se serait fait un nom, s'il avait vécu, car il y avait de l'etoffe en lui, il avait du génie, je la sais, bien que de grandes occasions lui aient manqué; mais il est impossible de supposer qu'un chien capable de se battre comme lui, certaines circonstances étant données, ait manqué de talent. Je me sens triste toutes les fois que je pense à son dernier combat et au dénoûment qu'il a eu. Eh bien! ce Smiley nourrissait des terriers à rats, et des coqs combat, et des chats, et toute sorte de choses, au point qu'il était toujours en mesure de vous tenir tête, et qu'avec sa rage de paris on n'avait plus de repos. Il attrapa un jour une grenouille et l'emporta chez lui, disant qu'il prétendait faire son éducation; vous me croirez si vous voulez, mais pendant trois mois il n'a rien fait que lue apprendre á sauter dans une cour retirée de sa maison. Et je vous réponds qu'il avait réussi. Il lui donnait un petit coup par derrière, et l'instant d'après vous voyiez la grenouille tourner en l'air comme un beignet au-dessus de la poêle, faire une culbute, quelquefois deux, lorsqu'elle était bien partie, et retomber sur ses pattes comme un chat. Il l'avait dressée dans l'art de gober des mouches, er l'y exerçait continuellement, si bien qu'une mouche, du plus loin qu'elle apparaissait, était une mouche perdue. Smiley avait coutume de dire que tout ce qui manquait à une grenouille, c'était l'éducation, qu'avec l'éducation elle pouvait faire presque tout, et je le crois. Tenez, je l'ai vu poser Daniel Webster là sur se plancher,—Daniel Webster était le nom de la grenouille,—et lui chanter:—Des mouches! Daniel, des mouches!—En un clin d'oeil, Daniel avait bondi et saisi une mouche ici sur le comptoir, puis sauté de nouveau par terre, où il restait vraiment à se gratter la tête avec sa patte de derrière, comme s'il n'avait pas eu la moindre idée de sa

supériorité. Jamais vous n'avez grenouille vu de aussi modeste, aussi
naturelle, douée comme elle l'était! Et quand il s'agissait de sauter
purement et simplement sur terrain plat, elle faisait plus de chemin en
un saut qu'aucune bête de son espèce que vous puissiez connaître.
Sauter à plat, c'était son fort! Quand il s'agissait de cela, Smiley en-
tassait les enjeux sur elle tant qu'il lui, restait un rouge liard. Il faut le
reconnaître, Smiley était monstrueusement fier de sa grenouille, et il
en avait le droit, car des gens qui avaient voyagé, qui avaient tout vu,
disaient qu'on lui ferait injure de la comparer à une autre; de façon
que Smiley gardait Daniel dans une petite boîte à claire-voie qu'il
emportait parfois à la ville pour quelque pari.

"Un jour, un individu étranger au camp l'arrête avec sa boîte et lui
dit:—Qu'est-ce que vous avez donc serré là dedans?

"Smiley dit d'un air indifférent:—Cela pourrait être un perroquet ou
un serin, mais ce n'est rien de pareil, ce n'est qu'une grenouille.

"L'individu la prend, la regarde avec soin, la tourne d'un côté et de
l'autre puis il dit.—Tiens! en effet! A quoi estelle bonne?

"—Mon Dieu! répond Smiley, toujours d'un air dégagé, elle est
bonne pour une chose à mon avis, elle peut battre en sautant toute
grenouille du comté de Calaveras.

"L'individu reprend la boîte, l'examine de nouveau longuement, et
la rend à Smiley en disant d'un air délibéré:—Eh bien! je ne vois pas
que cette grenouille ait rien de mieux qu'aucune grenouille.

"—Possible que vous ne le voyiez paz, dit Smiley, possible que vous
vous entendiez en grenouilles, possible que vous ne vous y entendez
point, possible que vous ayez de l'expérience, et possible que vous ne
soyez qu'un amateur. De toute maniére, je parie guarante dollars
qu'elle battra en sautant n'importe quelle grenouille du comté de
Calaveras.

"L'individu réfléchit une seconde et dit comme attristé:—Je ne suis
qu'un étranger ici, je n'ai pas de grenouille; mais, si j'en avais une, je
tiendrais le pari.

"—Fort bien! répond Smiley. Rien de plus facile. Si vous voulez tenir
ma boîte une minute, j'irai vous chercher une grenouille.—Voilà donc
l'individu qui garde la boîte, qui met ses quarante dollars sur ceux de
Smiley et qui attend. Il attend assez longtemps, réflechissant tout
seul, et figurez-vous qu'il prend Daniel, lui ouvre la bouche de force at
avec une cuiller à thé l'emplit de menu plomb de chasse, mais
l'emplit jusqu'au menton, puis il le pose par terre. Smiley pendant ce
temps était à barboter dans une mare. Finalement il attrape une
grenouille, l'apporte à cet individu et dit:—Maintenant, si vous êtes

prêt, mettez-la tout contre Daniel, avec leurs pattes de devant sur la même ligne, et je donnerai le signal;—puis il ajoute:—Un, deux, trois, sautez!

"Lui et l'individu touchent leurs grenouilles par derrière, et la grenouille neuve se met à sautiller, mais Daniel se soulève lourdement, hausse les épaules ainsi, comme un Français; à quoi bon? il ne pouvait bouger, il était planté solide comme une enclume, il n'avançait pas plus que si on l'eût mis à l'ancre. Smiley fut surpris et dégoûté, mais il ne se doutait pas du tour, bien entendu. L'individu empoche l'argent, s'en va, et en s'en allant est-ce qu'il ne donne pas un coup de pouce par-dessus l'épaule, comme ça, au pauvre Daniel, en disant de son air délibéré:—Eh bien! je ne vois pas que cette grenouille ait rien de muiex qu'une autre.

"Smiley se gratta longtemps la tête, les yeux fixés sur Daniel, jusqu'à ce qu'enfin il dit:—Je me demande comment diable il se fait que cette bête ait refusé. . . . Est-ce qu'elle aurait quelque chose? . . . On croirait qu'elle est enflée.

"Il empoigne Daniel par la peau du cou, le soulève et dit:—Le loup me croque, s'il ne pèse pas cinq livres.

"Il le retourne, et le malheureux crache deux poignées de plomb. Quand Smiley reconnut ce qui en était, il fut comme fou. Vous le voyez d'ici poser sa grenouille par terre et courir après cet individu, mais il ne le rattrapa jamais, et. . . .

[Translation of the above back from the French.]

THE FROG JUMPING OF THE COUNTY OF CALAVERAS

It there was one time here an individual known under the name of Jim Smiley; it was in the winter of '49, possibly well at the spring of '50, I no me recollect not exactly. This which me makes to believe that it was the one or the other, it is that I shall remember that the grand flume is not achieved when he arrives at the camp for the first time, but of all sides he was the man the most fond of to bet which one have seen, betting upon all that which is presented, when he could find an adversary; and when he not of it could not, he passed to the side opposed. All that which convenienced to the other, to him convenienced also; seeing that he had a bet, Smiley was satisfied. And he had a chance! a chance even worthless; nearly always he gained. It must to say that he was always near to himself expose, but one no could mention the least thing without that this gaillard offered to bet the bottom,

no matter what, and to take the side that one him would, as I you it
said all at the hour (tout à l'heure). If it there was of races, you him
find rich or ruined at the end; if it there is a combat of dogs, he bring
his bet; he himself laid always for a combat of cats, for a combat of
cocks;—by-blue! If you have see two birds upon a fence, he you should
have offered of to bet which of those birds shall fly the first; and if
there is *meeting* at the camp (*meeting* au camp) he comes to bet
regularly for the curé Walker, which he judged to be the best predi-
cator of the neighborhood (prédicateur des environs) and which he
was in effect, and a brave man. He would encounter a bug of wood in
the road, whom he will bet upon the time which he shall take to go
where she would go—and if you him have take at the word, he will
follow the bug as far as Mexique, without himself caring to go so far;
neither of the time which he there lost. One time the woman of the
curé Walker is very sick during long time, it seemed that one not her
saved not; but one morning the curé arrives, and Smiley him demanded how she goes, and he said that she is well better, grace to the
infinite misery (lui demande comment elle va, et il dit qu'elle est bien
mieux, grâce à l'infinie miséricorde) so much better that with the
benediction of the Providence she herself of it would pull out (elle
s'en tirerait); and behold that without there thinking Smiley responds:
"Well, I gage two-and-half that she will die all of same."

This Smiley had an animal which the boys called the nag of the
quarter of hour, but solely for pleasantry, you comprehend, because,
well understand, she was more fast as that! [Now why that exclamation?—M. T.] And it was custom of to gain of the silver with this beast,
notwithstanding she was poussive, cornarde, always taken of asthma,
of colics or of consumption, or something of approaching. One him
would give two or three hundred yards at the departure, then one him
passed without pain; but never at the last she not fail of herself
échauffer, of herself exasperate, and she arrives herself écartant, se
défendant, her legs grêles in the air before the obstacles, sometimes
them elevating and making with this more of dust than any horse,
more of noise above with his éternumens and reniflemens—crac! she
arrives then always first by one head, as just as one can it measure. An
he had a small bulldog (bouledogue!) who, to him see, no value, not a
cent; one would believe that to bet against him it was to steal, so much
he was ordinary; but as soon as the game made, she becomes another
dog. Her jaw inferior commence to project like a deck of before, his
teeth themselves discover brilliant like some furnaces, and a dog could

him tackle (le taquiner), him excite, him murder (le mordre), him throw two or three times over his shoulder, André Jackson—this was the name of the dog—André Jackson takes that tranquilly, as if he not himself was never expecting other thing, and when the bets were doubled and redoubled against him, he you seize the other dog just at the articulation of the leg of behind, and he not it leave more, not that he it masticate, you conceive, but he himself there shall be holding during until that one throws the sponge in the air, must he wait a year. Smiley gained always with this beast-là; unhappily they have finished by elevating a dog who no had not of feet of behind, because one them had sawed; and when things were at the point that he would, and that he came to himself throw upon his morsel favorite, the poor dog comprehended in an instant that he himself was deceived in him, and that the other dog him had. You no have never seen person having the air more penaud and more discouraged; he not made no effort to gain the combat, and was rudely shucked.

Eh bien! this Smiley nourished some terriers à rats, and some cocks of combat, and some cats, and all sorts of things; and with his rage of betting one no had more of repose. He trapped one day a frog and him imported with him (et l'emporta chez lui) saying that he pretended to make his education. You me believe if you will, but during three months he not has nothing done but to him apprehend to jump (apprendre à sauter) in a court retired of her mansion (de sa maison). And I you respond that he have succeeded. He him gives a small blow by behind, and the instant after you shall see the frog turn in the air like a grease-biscuit, make one summersault, sometimes two, when she was well started, and refall upon his feet like a cat. He him had accomplished in the art of to gobble the flies (gober des mouches), and him there exercised continually—so well that a fly at the most far that she appeared was a fly lost. Smiley had custom to say that all which lacked to a frog it was the education, but with the education she could do nearly all—and I him believe. Tenez, I him have seen pose Daniel Webster there upon this plank—Daniel Webster was the name of the frog—and to him sing, "Some flies, Daniel, some flies!"—in a flash of the eye Daniel had bounded and seized a fly here upon the counter, then jumped anew at the earth, where he rested truly to himself scratch the head with his behind foot, as if he no had not the least idea of his superiority. Never you not have seen frog as modest, as natural, sweet as she was. And when he himself agitated to jump purely and simply upon plain earth, she does more ground in one jump than any beast of his species than you can know. To jump plain—this was his strong. When he himself agitated for that, Smiley multiplied the bets upon her as long as there to him remained a red. It must to know, Smiley was monstrously proud of his frog, and he of it was right, for some men who were traveled, who had all seen, said that they to him would be injurious to him compare to another frog. Smiley guarded Daniel in a little box latticed which he carried by-times to the village for some bet.

One day an individual stranger at the camp him arrested with his box and him said:

"What is this that you have them shut up there within?"

Smiley said, with an air indifferent:

"That could be a paroquet, or a syringe (ou un serin), but this no is nothing of such, it not is but a frog."

The individual it took, it regarded with care, it turned from one side and from the other, then he said:

"Tiens! in effect!—At what is she good?"

"My God!" respond Smiley, always with an air disengaged, "she is good for one thing, to my notice (à mon avis), she can batter in jumping (elle peut battre en sautant) all frogs of the county of Calaveras."

The individual retook the box, it examined of new longly, and it rendered to Smiley in saying with an air deliberate:

"Eh bien! I no saw not that that frog had nothing of better than each frog." (Je ne vois pas que cette grenouille ait rien de mieux qu'aucune grenouille.) [If that isn't grammar gone to seed, then I count myself no judge.—M. T.]

"Possible that you not it saw not," said Smiley, "possible that you—you comprehend frogs; possible that you not you there comprehend nothing; possible that you had of the experience, and possible that you not be but an amateur. Of all manner (De toute manière) I bet forty dollars that she batter in jumping no matter which frog of the county of Calaveras."

The individual reflected a second, and said like sad:

"I not am but a stranger here, I no have not a frog; but if I of it had one, I would embrace the bet."

"Strong well!" respond Smiley; "nothing of more facility. If you will hold my box a minute, I go you to search a frog (j'irai vous chercher)."

Behold, then, the individual, who guards the box, who puts his forty dollars upon those of Smiley, and who attends (et qui attend). He attended enough longtimes, reflecting all solely. And figure you that he takes Daniel, him opens the mouth by force and with a teaspoon him fills with shot of the hunt, even him fills just to the chin, then he him puts by the earth. Smiley during these times was at slopping in a swamp. Finally he trapped (attrape) a frog, him carried to that individual, and said:

"Now if you be ready, put him all against Daniel, with their before feet upon the same line, and I give the signal"—then he added: "One, two, three—advance!"

Him and the individual touched their frogs by behind, and the frog new put to jump smartly, but Daniel himself lifted ponderously, exalted the shoulders thus, like a Frenchman—to what good? he not could budge, he is planted solid like a church, he not advance no more than if one him had put at the anchor.

Smiley was surprised and disgusted, but he not himself doubted not of the turn being intended (mais il ne se doutait pas du tour, bien entendu). The individual empocketed the silver, himself with it went, and of it himself in going is it that he no gives not a jerk of thumb over the shoulder—like that—at the poor Daniel, in saying with his air deliberate—(L'individu empoche l'argent, s'en va et en s'en allant est-ce qu'il ne donne pas un coup de pouce par-dessus l'épaule, comme ça au pauvre Daniel, en disant de son air délibéré):

"Eh bien! *I no see not that that frog has nothing of better than another.*"

Smiley himself scratched longtimes the head, the eyes fixed upon Daniel, until that which at last he said:

"I me demand how the devil it makes itself that this beast has refused. Is it that she had something? One would believe that she is stuffed."

He grasped Daniel by the skin of the neck, him lifted and said:

"The wolf me bite if he no weigh not five pounds."

He him reversed and the unhappy belched two handfuls of shot (et le malheureux, etc.). When Smiley recognized how it was, he was like mad. He deposited his frog by the earth and ran after that individual, but he not him caught never.

Such is the Jumping Frog, to the distorted French eye. I claim that I never put together such an odious mixture of bad grammar and delirium tremens in my life. And what has a poor foreigner like me done, to be abused and misrepresented like this? When I say, "Well, I don't see no p'ints about that frog that's any better'n any other frog," is it kind, is it just, for this Frenchman to try to make it appear that I said,

"Eh bien! I no saw not that that frog had nothing of better than each frog"? I have no heart to write more. I never felt so about anything before.

1875

The Office Bore

He arrives just as regularly as the clock strikes nine in the morning. And so he even beats the editor sometimes, and the porter must leave his work and climb two or three pairs of stairs to unlock the "Sanctum" door and let him in. He lights one of the office pipes—not reflecting, perhaps, that the editor may be one of those "stuck-up" people who would as soon have a stranger defile his tooth-brush as his pipe-stem. Then he begins to loll—for a person who can consent to loaf his useless life away in ignominious indolence has not the energy to sit up straight. He stretches full length on the sofa awhile; then draws up to half length; then gets into a chair, hangs his head back and his arms abroad, and stretches his legs till the rims of his boot-heels rest upon the floor; by and by sits up and leans forward, with one leg or both over the arm of the chair. But it is still observable that with all his changes of position, he never assumes the upright or a fraudful affectation of dignity. From time to time he yawns, and stretches, and scratches himself with a tranquil, mangy enjoyment, and now and then he grunts a kind of stuffy, overfed grunt, which is full of animal contentment. At rare and long intervals, however, he sighs a sigh that is the eloquent expression of a secret confession, to wit: "I am useless and a nuisance, a cumberer of the earth." The bore and his comrades—for there are usually from two to four on hand, day and night—mix into the conversation when men come in to see the editors for a moment on business; they hold noisy talks among themselves about politics in particular, and all other subjects in general—even warming up, after a fashion, sometimes, and seeming to take almost a real interest in what they are discussing. They ruthlessly call an editor from his work with such a remark as: "Did you see this, Smith, in the *Gazette*?" and proceed to read the paragraph while the sufferer reins in his impatient pen and listens; they often loll and sprawl round the office hour after hour, swapping anecdotes and relating personal experiences to each other—hair-breadth escapes, social encounters with distinguished men, election reminiscences, sketches of odd characters, etc. And through all those hours they never seem to comprehend that they are robbing the editors of their time, and the public of journalistic excellence in next day's paper. At other times they drowse, or dreamily pore over exchanges, or droop limp and pensive over the chair-arms for an hour. Even this solemn silence is small respite to the editor, for the next uncomfortable thing to having people look over his shoulders, perhaps, is to have them sit by in silence and listen to the scratching of his pen. If a body desires to talk private business with one of the editors, he must call him outside, for no hint milder than blasting-powder or nitroglycerin would be likely to move the bores out of listening-distance. To have to sit and endure the presence of a bore day after day; to feel your cheerful spirits begin to sink as his footstep sounds on the stair, and utterly vanish away as his tiresome form enters the door; to suffer through his anecdotes and die slowly to his reminiscences; to feel always the fetters of his clogging presence; to long hopelessly for one single day's privacy; to note with a shudder, by and by, that to contemplate his funeral in fancy has ceased to soothe, to imagine him undergoing in strict and fearful detail the tortures of the ancient Inquisition has lost its power to satisfy the heart, and that even to wish him millions and millions and millions of miles in Tophet is able to bring only a fitful gleam of joy; to have to endure all this, day after day, and week after week, and month after month, is an affliction that transcends any other that men suffer. Physical pain is pastime to it, and hanging a pleasure excursion.

1875

"Party Cries" in Ireland

Belfast is a peculiarly religious community. This may be said of the whole of the North of Ireland. About one-half of the people are Protestants and the other half Catholics. Each party does all it can to make its own doctrines popular and draw the affections of the irreligious toward them. One hears constantly of the most touching instances of this zeal. A week ago a vast concourse of Catholics assembled at Armagh to dedicate a new Cathedral; and when they started home again the roadways were lined with groups of meek and lowly Protestants who stoned them till all the region round about was marked with blood. I thought that only Catholics argued in that way, but it seems to be a mistake.

Every man in the community is a missionary and carries a brick to admonish the erring with. The law has tried to break this up, but not with perfect success. It has decreed that irritating "party cries" shall not be indulged in, and that persons uttering them shall be fined forty shillings and costs. And so, in the police court reports every day, one sees these fines recorded. Last week a girl of twelve years old was fined the usual forty shillings and costs for proclaiming in the public streets that she was "a Protestant." The usual cry is, "To hell with the Pope!" or "To hell with the Protestants!" according to the utterer's system of salvation.

One of Belfast's local jokes was very good. It referred to the uniform and inevitable fine of forty shillings and costs for uttering a party cry—and it is no economical fine for a poor man, either, by the way. They say that a policeman found a drunken man lying on the ground, up a dark alley, entertaining himself with shouting, "To *hell* with!" "To *hell* with!" The officer smelt a fine—informers get half.

"What's that you say?"

"To *hell* with!"

"To hell with *who?* To hell with *what?*"

"Ah, bedad, ye can finish it yourself—it's too expinsive for me!"

I think the seditious disposition, restrained by the economical instinct, is finely put in that.

1875

Petition Concerning Copyright

Whereas, The Constitution guarantees equal rights to all, backed by the Declaration of Independence; and

Whereas, Under our laws, the right of property in real estate is perpetual; and

Whereas, Under our laws, the right of property in the literary result of a citizen's intellectual labor is restricted to forty-two years; and

Whereas, Forty-two years seems an exceedingly just and righteous term, and a sufficiently long one for the retention of property;

Therefore, Your petitioner, having the good of his country solely at heart, humbly prays that "equal rights" and fair and equal treatment may be meted out to all citizens, by the restriction of rights in *all* property, real estate included, to the beneficent term of forty-two years. Then shall all men bless your honorable body and be happy. And for this will your petitioner ever pray.

MARK TWAIN

A PARAGRAPH NOT ADDED TO THE PETITION

The charming absurdity of restricting property-rights in books to forty-two years sticks prominently out in the fact that hardly any man's books ever *live* forty-two years, or even the half of it; and so, for the sake of getting a shabby advantage of the heirs of about one Scott or Burns or Milton in a hundred years, the lawmakers of the "Great" Republic are content to leave that poor little pilfering edict upon the statute-books. It is like an emperor lying in wait to rob a phenix's nest, and waiting the necessary century to get the chance.

1875

The Siamese Twins

I do not wish to write of the personal *habits* of these strange creatures solely, but also of certain curious details of various kinds concerning them, which, belonging only to their private life, have never crept into print. Knowing the Twins intimately, I feel that I am peculiarly well qualified for the task I have taken upon myself.

The Siamese Twins are naturally tender and affectionate in disposition, and have clung to each other with singular fidelity throughout a long and eventful life. Even as children they were inseparable companions; and it was noticed that they always seemed to prefer each other's society to that of any other persons. They nearly always played together; and, so accustomed was their mother to this peculiarity, that, whenever both of them chanced to be lost, she usually only hunted for one of them—satisfied that when she found that one she would find his brother somewhere in the immediate neighborhood. And yet these creatures were ignorant and unlettered—barbarians themselves and the offspring of barbarians, who knew not the light of philosophy and science. What a withering rebuke is this to our boasted civilization, with its quarrelings, its wranglings, and its separations of brothers!

As men, the Twins have not always lived in perfect accord; but still there has always been a bond between them which made them unwilling to go away from each other and dwell apart. They have even occupied the same house, as a general thing, and it is believed that they have never failed to even sleep together on any night since they were born. How surely do the habits of a lifetime become second nature to us! The Twins always go to bed at the same time; but Chang usually gets up about an hour before his brother. By an understanding between themselves, Chang does all the indoor work and Eng runs all the errands. This is because Eng likes to go out; Chang's habits are sedentary. However, Chang always goes along. Eng is a Baptist, but Chang is a Roman Catholic; still, to please his brother, Chang consented to be baptized at the same time that Eng was, on condition that it should not "count." During the war they were strong partisans, and both fought gallantly all through the great struggle—Eng on the Union

side and Chang on the Confederate. They took each other prisoners at
Seven Oaks, but the proofs of capture were so evenly balanced in
favor of each, that a general army court had to be assembled to determine which one was properly the captor and which the captive. The
jury was unable to agree for a long time; but the vexed question was
finally decided by agreeing to consider them both prisoners, and then
exchanging them. At one time Chang was convicted of disobedience
of orders, and sentenced to ten days in the guard-house, but Eng, in
spite of all arguments, felt obliged to share his imprisonment, notwithstanding he himself was entirely innocent; and so, to save the blameless brother from suffering, they had to discharge both from custody—
the just reward of faithfulness.

Upon one occasion the brothers fell out about something, and
Chang knocked Eng down, and then tripped and fell on him, whereupon both clinched and began to beat and gouge each other without
mercy. The bystanders interfered, and tried to separate them, but they
could not do it, and so allowed them to fight it out. In the end both
were disabled, and were carried to the hospital on one and the same
shutter.

Their ancient habit of going always together had its drawbacks
when they reached man's estate, and entered upon the luxury of
courting. Both fell in love with the same girl. Each tried to steal
clandestine interviews with her, but at the critical moment the other
would always turn up. By and by Eng saw, with distraction, that
Chang had won the girl's affections; and, from that day forth, he had
to bear with the agony of being a witness to all their dainty billing and
cooing. But with a magnanimity that did him infinite credit, he succumbed to his fate, and gave countenance and encouragement to a
state of things that bade fair to sunder his generous heart-strings. He
sat from seven every evening until two in the morning, listening to the
fond foolishness of the two lovers, and to the concussion of hundreds
of squandered kisses—for the privilege of sharing only one of which he
would have given his right hand. But he sat patiently, and waited,
and gaped, and yawned, and stretched, and longed for two o'clock to
come. And he took long walks with the lovers on moonlight evenings—
sometimes traversing ten miles, notwithstanding he was usually suffering from rheumatism. He is an inveterate smoker; but he could not
smoke on these occasions, because the young lady was painfully sensitive to the smell of tobacco. Eng cordially wanted them married, and
done with it; but although Chang often asked the momentous question, the young lady could not gather sufficient courage to answer it

while Eng was by. However, on one occasion, after having walked some sixteen miles, and sat up till nearly daylight, Eng dropped asleep, from sheer exhaustion, and then the question was asked and answered. The lovers were married. All acquainted with the circumstance applauded the noble brother-in-law. His unwavering faithfulness was the theme of every tongue. He had stayed by them all through their long and arduous courtship; and when at last they were married, he lifted his hands above their heads, and said with impressive unction, "Bless ye, my children, I will never desert ye!" and he kept his word. Fidelity like this is all too rare in this cold world.

By and by Eng fell in love with his sister-in-law's sister, and married her, and since that day they have all lived together, night and day, in an exceeding sociability which is touching and beautiful to behold, and is a scathing rebuke to our boasted civilization.

The sympathy existing between these two brothers is so close and so refined that the feelings, the impulses, the emotions of the one are instantly experienced by the other. When one is sick, the other is sick; when one feels pain, the other feels it; when one is angered, the other's temper takes fire. We have already seen with what happy facility they both fell in love with the same girl. Now Chang is bitterly opposed to all forms of intemperance, on principle; but Eng is the reverse—for, while these men's feelings and emotions are so closely wedded, their reasoning faculties are unfettered; their *thoughts* are free. Chang belongs to the Good Templars, and is a hard-working, enthusiastic supporter of all temperance reforms. But, to his bitter distress, every now and then Eng gets drunk, and, of course, that makes Chang drunk too. This unfortunate thing has been a great sorrow to Chang, for it almost destroys his usefulness in his favorite field of effort. As sure as he is to head a great temperance procession Eng ranges up alongside of him, prompt to the minute, and drunk as a lord; but yet no more dismally and hopelessly drunk than his brother, who has not tasted a drop. And so the two begin to hoot and yell, and throw mud and bricks at the Good Templars; and, of course, they break up the procession. It would be manifestly wrong to punish Chang for what Eng does, and, therefore, the Good Templars accept the untoward situation, and suffer in silence and sorrow. They have officially and deliberately examined into the matter, and find Chang blameless. They have taken the two brothers and filled Chang full of warm water and sugar and Eng full of whisky, and in twenty-five minutes it was not possible to tell which was the drunkest. Both were as drunk as loons—and on hot whisky punches, by the smell of their breath. Yet all the while Chang's moral principles were unsullied, his conscience clear; and so all just men were forced to confess that he was not morally, but only physically, drunk. By every right and by every moral evidence the man was strictly sober; and, therefore, it caused his friends all the more anguish to see him shake hands with the pump and try to wind his watch with his night-key.

There is a moral in these solemn warnings—or, at least, a warning in these solemn morals; one or the other. No matter, it is somehow. Let us heed it; let us profit by it.

I could say more of an instructive nature about these interesting beings, but let what I have written suffice.

Having forgotten to mention it sooner, I will remark in conclusion that the ages of the Siamese Twins are respectively fifty-one and fifty-three years.

1875

Speech at the Scottish
Banquet in London

At the anniversary festival of the Scottish Corporation of London on Monday evening, in response to the toast of "The Ladies," MARK TWAIN replied. The following is his speech as reported in the London *Observer:*

I am proud, indeed, of the distinction of being chosen to respond to this especial toast, to 'The Ladies,' or to women if you please, for that is the preferable term, perhaps; it is certainly the older, and therefore the more entitled to reverence. [Laughter.] I have noticed that the Bible, with that plain, blunt honesty which is such a conspicuous characteristic of the Scriptures, is always particular to never refer to even the illustrious mother of all mankind herself as a 'lady,' but speaks of her as a woman. [Laughter.] It is odd, but you will find it is so. I am peculiarly proud of this honor, because I think that the toast to women is one which, by right and by every rule of gallantry, should take precedence of all others—of the army, of the navy, of even royalty itself—perhaps, though the latter is not necessary in this day and in this land, for the reason that, tacitly, you do drink a broad general health to all good women when you drink the health of the Queen of England and the Princess of Wales. [Loud cheers.] I have in mind a poem just now which is familiar to you all, familiar to everybody. And what an inspiration that was (and how instantly the present toast recalls the verses to all our minds) when the most noble, the most gracious, the purest, and sweetest of all poets says:

"Woman! O woman!—er—
Wom—"

[Laughter.] However, you remember the lines; and you remember how feelingly, how daintily, how almost imperceptibly the verses raise up before you, feature by feature, the ideal of a true and perfect woman; and how, as you contemplate the finished marvel, your homage grows into worship of the intellect that could create so fair a thing out of mere breath, mere words. And you call to mind now, as I speak, how the poet, with stern fidelity to the history of all humanity, delivers this beautiful child of his heart and his brain over to the trials and sorrows that must come to all, sooner or later, that abide in the earth, and how the pathetic story culminates in that apostrophe—so wild, so regretful, so full of mournful retrospection. The lines run thus:

"Alas!—alas!—a—alas!
——Alas!——alas!"

—and so on. [Laughter.] I do not remember the rest; but, taken together, it seems to me that poem is the noblest tribute to woman that human genius has ever brought forth—[laughter]—and I feel that if I were to talk hours I could not do my great theme completer or more graceful justice than I have now done in simply quoting that poet's matchless words. [Renewed laughter.] The phases of the womanly nature are infinite in their variety. Take any type of woman, and you shall find in it something to respect, something to admire, something to love. And you shall find the whole joining you heart and hand. Who was more patriotic than Joan of Arc? Who was braver? Who has given us a grander instance of self-sacrificing devotion? Ah? you remember, you remember well, what a throb of pain, what a great tidal wave of grief swept over us all when Joan of Arc fell at Waterloo. [Much laughter.] Who does not sorrow for the loss of Sappho, the

sweet singer of Israel? [Laughter.] Who among us does not miss the
gentle ministrations, the softening influences, the humble piety of
Lucretia Borgia? [Laughter.] Who can join in the heartless libel that
says woman is extravagant in dress when he can look back and call to
mind our simple and lowly mother Eve arrayed in her modification of
the Highland costume. [Roars of laughter.] Sir, women have been
soldiers, women have been painters, women have been poets. As long
as language lives the name of Cleopatra will live. And, not because
she conquered George III.—[laughter]—but because she wrote those
divine lines:—

"Let dogs delight to bark and bite,
For God hath made them so."

[More laughter.] The story of the world is adorned with the names of
illustrious ones of our own sex—some of them sons of St. Andrew, too—
Scott, Bruce, Burns, the warrior Wallace, Ben Nevis—[laughter]—the
gifted Ben Lomond, and the great new Scotchman, Ben Disraeli.[1]
[Great laughter.] Out of the great plains of history tower whole
mountain ranges of sublime women—the Queen of Sheba, Josephine,
Semiramis, Sairey Gamp; the list is endless—[laughter]—but I will not
call the mighty roll, the names rise up in your own memories at the
mere suggestion, luminous with the glory of deeds that cannot die,
hallowed by the loving worship of the good and the true of all epochs
and all climes. [Cheers.] Suffice it for our pride and our honor that we
in our day have added to it such names as those of Grace Darling and
Florence Nightingale. [Cheers.] Woman is all that she should be—
gentle, patient, long suffering, trustful, unselfish, full of generous impulses. It is her blessed mission to comfort the sorrowing, plead for the
erring, encourage the faint of purpose, succor the distressed, uplift the
fallen, befriend the friendless—in a word, afford the healing of her
sympathies and a home in her heart for all the bruised and persecuted
children of misfortune that knock at its hospitable door. [Cheers.]
And when I say, God bless her, there is none among us who has known
the ennobling affection of a wife, or the steadfast devotion of a mother,
but in his heart will say, Amen! [Loud and prolonged cheering.]

1875

[1] Mr. Benjamin Disraeli, at that time Prime Minister of England, had just been
elected Lord Rector of Glasgow University, and had made a speech which gave
rise to a world of discussion.

Speech on Accident Insurance

Delivered in Hartford, at a Dinner to
Corneluis Walford, of London

Gentlemen: I am glad, indeed, to assist in welcoming the distinguished guest of this occasion to a city whose fame as an insurance center has extended to all lands, and given us the name of being a quadruple band of brothers working sweetly hand in hand—the Colt's Arms Company making the destruction of our race easy and convenient, our life-insurance citizens paying for the victims when they pass away, Mr. Batterson perpetuating their memory with his stately monuments, and our fire-insurance comrades taking care of their hereafter. I am glad to assist in welcoming our guest—first, because he is an Englishman, and I owe a heavy debt of hospitality to certain of his fellow-countrymen; and secondly, because he is in sympathy with insurance and has been the means of making many other men cast their sympathies in the same direction.

Certainly there is no nobler field for human effort than the insurance line of business—especially accident insurance. Ever since I have been a director in an accident-insurance company I have felt that I am a better man. Life has seemed more precious. Accidents have assumed a kindlier aspect. Distressing special providences have lost half their horror. I look upon a cripple now with affectionate interest—as an advertisement. I do not seem to care for poetry any more. I do not care for politics—even agriculture does not excite me. But to me now there is a charm about a railway collision that is unspeakable.

There is nothing more beneficent than accident insurance. I have seen an entire family lifted out of poverty and into affluence by the simple boon of a broken leg. I have had people come to me on crutches, with tears in their eyes, to bless this beneficent institution. In all my experience of life, I have seen nothing so seraphic as the look that comes into a freshly mutilated man's face when he feels in his vest pocket with his remaining hand and finds his accident ticket all right. And I have seen nothing so sad as the look that came into another splintered customer's face when he found he couldn't collect on a wooden leg.

I will remark here, by way of advertisement, that that noble charity which we have named the HARTFORD ACCIDENT INSURANCE COMPANY[1] is an institution which is peculiarly to be depended upon. A man is bound to prosper who gives it his custom. No man can take out a policy in it and not get crippled before the year is out. Now there was one indigent man who had been disappointed so often with other companies that he had grown disheartened, his appetite left him, he ceased to smile—said life was but a weariness. Three weeks ago I got him to insure with us, and now he is the brightest, happiest spirit in this land—has a good steady income and a stylish suit of new bandages every day, and travels around on a shutter.

I will say, in conclusion, that my share of the welcome to our guest is none the less hearty because I talk so much nonsense, and I know that I can say the same for the rest of the speakers.

1875

The Facts Concerning the Recent
Carnival of Crime in Connecticut

I was feeling blithe, almost jocund. I put a match to my cigar, and just then the morning's mail was handed in. The first superscription I glanced at was in a handwriting that sent a thrill of pleasure through and through me. It was Aunt Mary's; and she was the person I loved and honored most in all the world, outside of my own household. She had been my boyhood's idol; maturity, which is fatal to so many enchantments, had not been able to dislodge her from her pedestal; no, it had only justified her right to be there, and placed her dethronement permanently among the impossibilities. To show how strong her influence over me was, I will observe that long after everybody else's "do-stop-smoking" had ceased to affect me in the slightest degree, Aunt Mary could still stir my torpid conscience into faint signs of life when she touched upon the matter. But all things have their limit in this world. A happy day came at last, when even Aunt Mary's words

---

[1] The speaker is a director of the company named.

could no longer move me. I was not merely glad to see that day arrive;
I was more than glad—I was grateful; for when its sun had set, the one
alloy that was able to mar my enjoyment of my aunt's society was
gone. The remainder of her stay with us that winter was in every way
a delight. Of course she pleaded with me just as earnestly as ever,
after that blessed day, to quit my pernicious habit, but to no purpose
whatever; the moment she opened the subject I at once became
calmly, peacefully, contentedly indifferent—absolutely, adamantinely
indifferent. Consequently the closing weeks of that memorable visit
melted away as pleasantly as a dream, they were so freighted for me
with tranquil satisfaction. I could not have enjoyed my pet vice more
if my gentle tormentor had been a smoker herself, and an advocate of
the practice. Well, the sight of her handwriting reminded me that I
was getting very hungry to see her again. I easily guessed what I
should find in her letter. I opened it. Good! just as I expected; she was
coming! Coming this very day, too, and by the morning train; I might
expect her any moment.

I said to myself, "I am thoroughly happy and content now. If my
most pitiless enemy could appear before me at this moment, I would
freely right any wrong I may have done him."

Straightway the door opened, and a shriveled, shabby dwarf entered. He was not more than two feet high. He seemed to be about
forty years old. Every feature and every inch of him was a trifle out of
shape; and so, while one could not put his finger upon any particular
part and say, "This is a conspicuous deformity," the spectator perceived that this little person was a deformity as a whole—a vague,
general, evenly blended, nicely adjusted deformity. There was a fox-
like cunning in the face and the sharp little eyes, and also alertness
and malice. And yet, this vile bit of human rubbish seemed to bear a
sort of remote and ill-defined resemblance to me! It was dully perceptible in the mean form, the countenance, and even the clothes,
gestures, manner, and attitudes of the creature. He was a far-fetched,
dim suggestion of a burlesque upon me, a caricature of me in little.
One thing about him struck me forcibly and most unpleasantly: he
was covered all over with a fuzzy, greenish mold, such as one sometimes sees upon mildewed bread. The sight of it was nauseating.

He stepped along with a chipper air, and flung himself into a doll's
chair in a very free-and-easy way, without waiting to be asked. He
tossed his hat into the waste-basket. He picked up my old chalk pipe
from the floor, gave the stem a wipe or two on his knee, filled the bowl

from the tobacco-box at his side, and said to me in a tone of pert command:

"Gimme a match!"

I blushed to the roots of my hair; partly with indignation, but mainly because it somehow seemed to me that this whole performance was very like an exaggeration of conduct which I myself had sometimes been guilty of in my intercourse with familiar friends—but never, never with strangers, I observed to myself. I wanted to kick the pygmy into the fire, but some incomprehensible sense of being legally and legitimately under his authority forced me to obey his order. He applied the match to the pipe, took a contemplative whiff or two, and remarked, in an irritatingly familiar way:

"Seems to me it's devilish odd weather for this time of year."

I flushed again, and in anger and humiliation as before; for the language was hardly an exaggeration of some that I have uttered in my day, and moreover was delivered in a tone of voice and with an exasperating drawl that had the seeming of a deliberate travesty of my style. Now there is nothing I am quite so sensitive about as a mocking imitation of my drawling infirmity of speech. I spoke up sharply and said:

"Look here, you miserable ash-cat! you will have to give a little more attention to your manners, or I will throw you out of the window!"

The manikin smiled a smile of malicious content and security, puffed a whiff of smoke contemptuously toward me, and said, with a still more elaborate drawl:

"Come—go gently now; don't put on *too* many airs with your betters."

This cool snub rasped me all over, but it seemed to subjugate me, too, for a moment. The pygmy contemplated me awhile with his weasel eyes, and then said, in a peculiarly sneering way:

"You turned a tramp away from your door this morning."

I said crustily:

"Perhaps I did, perhaps I didn't. How do *you* know?"

"Well, I know. It isn't any matter *how* I know."

"Very well. Suppose I *did* turn a tramp away from the door— what of it?"

"Oh, nothing; nothing in particular. Only you lied to him."

"I *didn't!* That is, I—"

"Yes, but you did; you lied to him."

I felt a guilty pang—in truth, I had felt it forty times before that tramp had traveled a block from my door—but still I resolved to make a show of feeling slandered; so I said:

"This is a baseless impertinence. I said to the tramp—"

"There—wait. You were about to lie again. *I* know what you said to him. You said the cook was gone down-town and there was nothing left from breakfast. Two lies. You knew the cook was behind the door, and plenty of provisions behind *her*."

This astonishing accuracy silenced me; and it filled me with wondering speculations, too, as to how this cub could have got his information. Of course he could have culled the conversation from the tramp, but by what sort of magic had he contrived to find out about the concealed cook? Now the dwarf spoke again:

"It was rather pitiful, rather small, in you to refuse to read that poor young woman's manuscript the other day, and give her an opinion as to its literary value; and she had come so far, too, and *so* hopefully. Now *wasn't* it?"

I felt like a cur! And I had felt so every time the thing had recurred to my mind, I may as well confess. I flushed hotly and said:

"Look here, have you nothing better to do than prowl around prying into other people's business? Did that girl tell you that?"

"Never mind whether she did or not. The main thing is, you did that contemptible thing. And you felt ashamed of it afterward. Aha! you feel ashamed of it *now!*"

This was a sort of devilish glee. With fiery earnestness I responded:

"I told that girl, in the kindest, gentlest way, that I could not consent to deliver judgment upon *any* one's manuscript, because an individual's verdict was worthless. It might underrate a work of high merit and lose it to the world, or it might overrate a trashy production and so open the way for its infliction upon the world. I said that the great public was the only tribunal competent to sit in judgment upon a literary effort, and therefore it must be best to lay it before that tribunal in the outset, since in the end it must stand or fall by that mighty court's decision anyway."

"Yes, you said all that. So you did, you juggling, small-souled shuffler! And yet when the happy hopefulness faded out of that poor girl's face, when you saw her furtively slip beneath her shawl the scroll she had so patiently and honestly scribbled at—so ashamed of her darling now, so proud of it before—when you saw the gladness go out of her eyes and the tears come there, when she crept away so humbly who had come so—"

"Oh, peace! peace! peace! Blister your merciless tongue, haven't all these thoughts tortured me enough without *your* coming here to fetch them back again!"

Remorse! remorse! It seemed to me that it would eat the very heart out of me! And yet that small fiend only sat there leering at me with joy and contempt, and placidly chuckling. Presently he began to speak again. Every sentence was an accusation, and every accusation a truth. Every clause was freighted with sarcasm and derision, every slow-dropping word burned like vitriol. The dwarf reminded me of times when I had flown at my children in anger and punished them for faults which a little inquiry would have taught me that others, and not they, had committed. He reminded me of how I had disloyally allowed old friends to be traduced in my hearing, and been too craven to utter a word in their defense. He reminded me of many dishonest things which I had done; of many which I had procured to be done by children and other irresponsible persons; of some which I had planned, thought upon, and longed to do, and been kept from the performance by fear of consequences only. With exquisite cruelty he recalled to my mind, item by item, wrongs and unkindnesses I had inflicted and humiliations I had put upon friends since dead, "who died thinking of those injuries, maybe, and grieving over them," he added, by way of poison to the stab.

"For instance," said he, "take the case of your younger brother, when you two were boys together, many a long year ago. He always lovingly trusted in you with a fidelity that your manifold treacheries were not able to shake. He followed you about like a dog, content to suffer wrong and abuse if he might only be with you; patient under these injuries so long as it was your hand that inflicted them. The latest picture you have of him in health and strength must be such a comfort to you! You pledged your honor that if he would let you blindfold him no harm should come to him; and then, giggling and choking over the rare fun of the joke, you led him to a brook thinly glazed with ice, and pushed him in; and how you did laugh! Man, you will never forget the gentle, reproachful look he gave you as he struggled shivering out, if you live a thousand years! Oho! you see it now, you see it *now!*"

"Beast, I have seen it a million times, and shall see it a million more! and may you rot away piecemeal, and suffer till doomsday what I suffer now, for bringing it back to me again!"

The dwarf chuckled contentedly, and went on with his accusing history of my career. I dropped into a moody, vengeful state, and suffered in silence under the merciless lash. At last this remark of his gave me a sudden rouse:

"Two months ago, on a Tuesday, you woke up, away in the night, and fell to thinking, with shame, about a peculiarly mean and pitiful act of yours toward a poor ignorant Indian in the wilds of the Rocky Mountains in the winter of eighteen hundred and—"

"Stop a moment, devil! Stop! Do you mean to tell me that even my very *thoughts* are not hidden from you?"

"It seems to look like that. Didn't you think the thoughts I have just mentioned?"

"If I didn't, I wish I may never breathe again! Look here, friend—look me in the eye. Who *are* you?"

"Well, who do you think?"

"I think you are Satan himself. I think you are the devil."

"No."

"No? Then who *can* you be?"

"Would you really like to know?"

"*Indeed* I would."

"Well, I am your *Conscience!*"

In an instant I was in a blaze of joy and exultation. I sprang at the creature, roaring:

"Curse you, I have wished a hundred million times that you were tangible, and that I could get my hands on your throat once! Oh, but I will wreak a deadly vengeance on—"

Folly! Lightning does not move more quickly than my Conscience did! He darted aloft so suddenly that in the moment my fingers clutched the empty air he was already perched on the top of the high bookcase, with his thumb at his nose in token of derision. I flung the poker at him, and missed. I fired the bootjack. In a blind rage I flew from place to place, and snatched and hurled any missile that came handy; the storm of books, inkstands, and chunks of coal gloomed the air and beat about the manikin's perch relentlessly, but all to no purpose; the nimble figure dodged every shot; and not only that, but burst into a cackle of sarcastic and triumphant laughter as I sat down exhausted. While I puffed and gasped with fatigue and excitement, my Conscience talked to this effect:

"My good slave, you are curiously witless—no, I mean characteristically so. In truth, you are always consistent, always yourself, always an ass. Otherwise it must have occurred to you that if you attempted this murder with a sad heart and a heavy conscience, I would droop under the burdening influence instantly. Fool, I should have weighed a ton, and could not have budged from the floor; but instead, you are so cheerfully anxious to kill me that your conscience is as light as a feather; hence I am away up here out of your reach. I can almost respect a mere ordinary sort of fool; but *you*—pah!"

I would have given anything, then, to be heavy-hearted, so that I could get this person down from there and take his life, but I could no more be heavy-hearted over such a desire than I could have sorrowed over its accomplishment. So I could only look longingly up at my master, and rave at the ill luck that denied me a heavy conscience the one only time that I had ever wanted such a thing in my life. By and by I got to musing over the hour's strange adventure, and of course my human curiosity began to work. I set myself to framing in my mind some questions for this fiend to answer. Just then one of my boys entered, leaving the door open behind him, and exclaimed:

"My! what *has* been going on here? The bookcase is all one riddle of—"

I sprang up in consternation, and shouted:

"Out of this! Hurry! Jump! Fly! Shut the door! Quick, or my Conscience will get away!"

The door slammed to, and I locked it. I glanced up and was grateful, to the bottom of my heart, to see that my owner was still my prisoner. I said:

"Hang you, I might have lost you! Children are the heedlessest creatures. But look here, friend, the boy did not seem to notice you at all; how is that?"

"For a very good reason. I am invisible to all but you."

I made a mental note of that piece of information with a good deal of satisfaction. I could kill this miscreant now, if I got a chance, and no one would know it. But this very reflection made me so light-hearted that my Conscience could hardly keep his seat, but was like to float aloft toward the ceiling like a toy balloon. I said, presently:

"Come, my Conscience, let us be friendly. Let us fly a flag of truce for a while. I am suffering to ask you some questions."

"Very well. Begin."

"Well, then, in the first place, why were you never visible to me before?"

"Because you never asked to see me before; that is, you never asked in the right spirit and the proper form before. You were just in the right spirit this time, and when you called for your most pitiless enemy I was that person by a very large majority, though you did not suspect it."

"Well, did that remark of mine turn you into flesh and blood?"

"No. It only made me visible to you. I am unsubstantial, just as other spirits are."

This remark prodded me with a sharp misgiving. If he was unsubstantial, how was I going to kill him? But I dissembled, and said persuasively:

"Conscience, it isn't sociable of you to keep at such a distance. Come down and take another smoke."

This was answered with a look that was full of derision, and with this observation added:

"Come where you can get at me and kill me? The invitation is declined with thanks."

"All right," said I to myself; "so it seems a spirit *can* be killed, after all; there will be one spirit lacking in this world, presently, or I lose my guess." Then I said aloud:

"Friend—"

"There; wait a bit. I am not your friend, I am your enemy; I am not your equal, I am your master. Call me 'my lord,' if you please. You are too familiar."

"I don't like such titles. I am willing to call you *sir*. That is as far as—"

"We will have no argument about this. Just obey, that is all. Go on with your chatter."

"Very well, my lord—since nothing but my lord will suit you—I was going to ask you how long you will be visible to me?"

"Always!"

I broke out with strong indignation: "This is simply an outrage. That is what I think of it. You have dogged, and dogged, and *dogged* me, all the days of my life, invisible. That was misery enough; now to have such a looking thing as you tagging after me like another shadow all the rest of my days is an intolerable prospect. You have my opinion, my lord; make the most of it."

"My lad, there was never so pleased a conscience in this world as I was when you made me visible. It gives me an inconceivable advantage. *Now* I can look you straight in the eye, and call you names, and leer at you, jeer at you, sneer at you; and *you* know what eloquence there is in visible gesture and expression, more especially when the effect is heightened by audible speech. I shall always address you henceforth in your o-w-n s-n-i-v-e-l-i-n-g d-r-a-w-l—baby!"

I let fly with the coal-hod. No result. My lord said:

"Come, come! Remember the flag of truce!"

"Ah, I forgot that. I will try to be civil; and *you* try it, too, for a novelty. The idea of a *civil* conscience! It is a good joke; an excellent joke.

All the consciences I have ever heard of were nagging, badgering, fault-finding, execrable savages! Yes; and always in a sweat about some poor little insignificant trifle or other—destruction catch the lot of them, I say! I would trade mine for the smallpox and seven kinds of consumption, and be glad of the chance. Now tell me, why is it that a conscience can't haul a man over the coals once, for an offense, and then let him alone? Why is it that it wants to keep on pegging at him, day and night and night and day, week in and week out, forever and ever, about the same old thing? There is no sense in that, and no reason in it. I think a conscience that will act like that is meaner than the very dirt itself."

"Well, we like it; that suffices."

"Do you do it with the honest intent to improve a man?"

That question produced a sarcastic smile, and this reply:

"No, sir. Excuse me. We do it simply because it is 'business.' It is our trade. The purpose of it is to improve the man, but we are merely disinterested agents. We are appointed by authority, and haven't anything to say in the matter. We obey orders and leave the consequences where they belong. But I am willing to admit this much: we do crowd the orders a trifle when we get a chance, which is most of the time. We enjoy it. We are instructed to remind a man a few times of an error; and I don't mind acknowledging that we try to give pretty good measure. And when we get hold of a man of a peculiarly sensitive nature, oh, but we do haze him! I have consciences to come all the way from China and Russia to see a person of that kind put through his paces, on a special occasion. Why, I knew a man of that sort who had accidentally crippled a mulatto baby; the news went abroad, and I wish you may never commit another sin if the consciences didn't flock from all over the earth to enjoy the fun and help his master exorcise him. That man walked the floor in torture for forty-eight hours, without eating or sleeping, and then blew his brains out. The child was perfectly well again in three weeks."

"Well, you are a precious crew, not to put it too strong. I think I begin to see now why you have always been a trifle inconsistent with me. In your anxiety to get all the juice you can out of a sin, you make a man repent of it in three or four different ways. For instance, you found fault with me for lying to that tramp, and I suffered over that. But it was only yesterday that I told a tramp the square truth, to with, that, it being regarded as bad citizenship to encourage vagrancy, I would give him nothing. What did you do then? Why, you made me say to myself, 'Ah, it would have been so much kinder and more blameless to ease him off with a little white lie, and send him away feeling that if he could not have bread, the gentle treatment was at least something to be grateful for!' Well, I suffered all day about *that*. Three days before I had fed a tramp, and fed him freely, supposing it a virtuous act. Straight off you said, 'Oh, false citizen, to have fed a tramp!' " and I suffered as usual. I gave a tramp work; you objected to it—*after* the contract was made, of course; you never speak up beforehand. Next, I *refused* a tramp work; you objected to *that*. Next, I proposed to kill a tramp; you kept me awake all night, oozing remorse at every pore. Sure I was going to be right *this* time, I sent the next tramp away with my benediction; and I wish you may live as long as I do, if you didn't make me smart all night again because I didn't kill him. Is there *any* way of satisfying that malignant invention which is called a conscience?"

"Ha, ha! this is luxury! Go on!"

"But come, now, answer me that question. *Is* there any way?"

"Well, none that I propose to tell *you*, my son. Ass! I don't care *what* act you may turn your hand to, I can straightway whisper a word in your ear and make you think you have committed a dreadful meanness. It is my *business*—and my joy—to make you repent of *every*thing you do. If I have fooled away any opportunities it was not intentional; I beg to assure you it was not intentional!"

"Don't worry; you haven't missed a trick that *I* know of. I never did a thing in all my life, virtuous or otherwise, that I didn't repent of in twenty-four hours. In church last Sunday I listened to a charity sermon. My first impulse was to give three hundred and fifty dollars; I repented of that and reduced it a hundred; repented of that and reduced it another hundred; repented of that and reduced it another hundred; repented of that and reduced the remaining fifty to twenty-five; repented of that and came down to fifteen; repented of that and dropped to two dollars and a half; when the plate came around at last, I repented once more and contributed ten cents. Well, when I got home, I did wish to goodness I had that ten cents back again! You never *did* let me get through a charity sermon without having something to sweat about."

"Oh, and I never shall, I never shall. You can always depend on me."

"I think so. Many and many's the restless night I've wanted to take you by the neck. If I could only get hold of you now!"

"Yes, no doubt. But I am not an ass; I am only the saddle of an ass. But go on, go on. You entertain me more than I like to confess."

"I am glad of that. (You will not mind my lying a little, to keep in practice.) Look here; not to be too personal, I think you are about the shabbiest and most contemptible little shriveled-up reptile that can be imagined. I am grateful enough that you are invisible to other people, for I should die with shame to be seen with such a mildewed monkey of a conscience as *you* are. Now if you were five or six feet high, and—"

"Oh, come! who is to blame?"

"*I* don't know."

"Why, you are; nobody else."

"Confound you, I wasn't consulted about your personal appearance."

"I don't care, you had a good deal to do with it, nevertheless. When you were eight or nine years old, I was seven feet high, and as pretty as a picture."

"I wish you had died young! So you have grown the wrong way, have you?"

"Some of us grow one way and some the other. You had a large conscience once; if you've a small conscience now I reckon there are reasons for it. However, both of us are to blame, you and I. You see, you used to be conscientious about a great many things; morbidly so, I may say. It was a great many years ago. You probably do not remember it now. Well, I took a great interest in my work, and I so enjoyed the anguish which certain pet sins of yours afflicted you with that I kept pelting at you until I rather overdid the matter. You began to rebel. Of course I began to lose ground, then, and shrivel a little—diminish in stature, get moldy, and grow deformed. The more I weakened, the more stubbornly you fastened on to those particular sins; till at last the places on my person that represent those vices became as callous as shark-skin. Take smoking, for instance. I played that card a little too long, and I lost. When people plead with you at this late day to quit that vice, that old callous place seems to enlarge and cover me all over like a shirt of mail. It exerts a mysterious, smothering effect; and presently I, your faithful hater, your devoted Conscience, go sound asleep! Sound? It is no name for it. I couldn't hear it thunder at such a time. You have some few other vices—perhaps eighty, or maybe ninety—that affect me in much the same way."

"This is flattering; you must be asleep a good part of your time."

"Yes, of late years. I should be asleep *all* the time but for the help I get."

"Who helps you?"

"Other consciences. Whenever a person whose conscience I am acquainted with tries to plead with you about the vices you are callous to, I get my friend to give his client a pang concerning some villainy of his own, and that shuts off his meddling and starts him off to hunt personal consolation. My field of usefulness is about trimmed down to tramps, budding authoresses, and that line of goods now; but don't you worry —I'll harry you on *them* while they last! Just you put your trust in me."

"I think I can. But if you had only been good enough to mention these facts some thirty years ago, I should have turned my particular attention to sin, and I think that by this time I should not only have had you pretty permanently asleep on the entire list of human vices, but reduced to the size of a homeopathic pill, at that. That is about the style of conscience *I* am pining for. If I only had you shrunk down to a homeopathic pill, and could get my hands on you, would I put you in a glass case for a keepsake? No, sir. I would give you to a yellow dog! That is where *you* ought to be—you and all your tribe. You are not fit to be in society, in my opinion. Now another question. Do you know a good many consciences in this section?"

"Plenty of them."

"I would give anything to see some of them! Could you bring them here? And would they be visible to me?"

"Certainly not."

"I suppose I ought to have known that without asking. But no matter, you can describe them. Tell me about my neighbor Thompson's conscience, please."

"Very well. I know him intimately; have known him many years. I knew him when he was eleven feet high and of a faultless figure. But he is very rusty and tough and misshapen now, and hardly ever interests himself about anything. As to his present size—well, he sleeps in a cigar-box."

"Likely enough. There are few smaller, meaner men in this region than Hugh Thompson. Do you know Robinson's conscience?"

"Yes. He is a shade under four and a half feet high; used to be a blond; is a brunette now, but still shapely and comely."

"Well, Robinson is a good fellow. Do you know Tom Smith's conscience?"

"I have known him from childhood. He was thirteen inches high, and rather sluggish, when he was two years old—as nearly all of us are at that age. He is thirty-seven feet high now, and the stateliest figure in America. His legs are still racked with growing-pains, but he has a good time, nevertheless. Never sleeps. He is the most active and energetic member of the New England Conscience Club; is president of it. Night and day you can find him pegging away at Smith, panting with his labor, sleeves rolled up, countenance all alive with enjoyment. He has got his victim splendidly dragooned now. He can make poor Smith imagine that the most innocent little thing he does is an odious sin; and then he sets to work and almost tortures the soul out of him about it."

"Smith is the noblest man in all this section, and the purest; and yet is always breaking his heart because he cannot be good! Only a conscience *could* find pleasure in heaping agony upon a spirit like that. Do you know my aunt Mary's conscience?"

"I have seen her at a distance, but am not acquainted with her. She lives in the open air altogether, because no door is large enough to admit her."

"I can believe that. Let me see. Do you know the conscience of that publisher who once stole some sketches of mine for a 'series' of his, and then left me to pay the law expenses I had to incur in order to choke him off?"

"Yes. He has a wide fame. He was exhibited, a month ago, with some other antiquities, for the benefit of a recent Member of the Cabinet's conscience that was starving in exile. Tickets and fares were high, but I traveled for nothing by pretending to be the conscience of an editor, and got in for half-price by representing myself to be the conscience of a clergyman. However, the publisher's conscience, which was to have been the main feature of the entertainment, was a failure—as an exhibition. He was there, but what of that? The management had provided a microscope with a magnifying power of only thirty thousand diameters, and so nobody got to see him, after all. There was great and general dissatisfaction, of course, but—"

Just here there was an eager footstep on the stair; I opened the door, and my aunt Mary burst into the room. It was a joyful meeting and a cheery bombardment of questions and answers concerning family matters ensued. By and by my aunt said:

"But I am going to abuse you a little now. You promised me, the day I saw you last, that you would look after the needs of the poor family around the corner as faithfully as I had done it myself. Well, I found out by accident that you failed of your promise. *Was* that right?"

In simple truth, I never had thought of that family a second time! And now such a splintering pang of guilt shot through me! I glanced up at my Conscience. Plainly, my heavy heart was affecting him. His body was drooping forward; he seemed about to fall from the bookcase. My aunt continued:

"And think how you have neglected my poor *protégé* at the almshouse, you dear, hard-hearted promise-breaker!" I blushed scarlet, and my tongue was tied. As the sense of my guilty negligence waxed sharper and stronger, my Conscience began to sway heavily back and forth; and when my aunt, after a little pause, said in a grieved tone, "Since you never once went to see her, maybe it will not distress you now to know that that poor child died, months ago, utterly friendless and forsaken!" my Conscience could no longer bear up under the weight of my sufferings, but tumbled headlong from his high perch and struck the floor with a dull, leaden thump. He lay there writhing with pain and quaking with apprehension, but straining every muscle in frantic efforts to get up. In a fever of expectancy I sprang to the door, locked it, placed my back against it, and bent a watchful gaze upon my struggling master. Already my fingers were itching to begin their murderous work.

"Oh, what *can* be the matter!" exclaimed my aunt, shrinking from me, and following with her frightened eyes the direction of mine. My breath was coming in short, quick gasps now, and my excitement was almost uncontrollable. My aunt cried out:

"Oh, do not look so! You appal me! Oh, what can the matter be? What is it you see? Why do you stare so? Why do you work your fingers like that?"

"Peace, woman!" I said, in a hoarse whisper. "Look elsewhere; pay no attention to me; it is nothing—nothing. I am often this way. It will pass in a moment. It comes from smoking too much."

My injured lord was up, wild-eyed with terror, and trying to hobble toward the door. I could hardly breathe, I was so wrought up. My aunt wrung her hands, and said:

"Oh, I knew how it would be; I knew it would come to this at last! Oh, I implore you to crush out that fatal habit while it may yet be time! You must not, you shall not be deaf to my supplications longer!" My struggling Conscience showed sudden signs of weariness! "Oh, promise me you will throw off this hateful slavery of tobacco!" My Conscience began to reel drowsily, and grope with his hands—enchanting spectacle! "I beg you, I beseech you, I implore you! Your reason is deserting you! There is madness in your eye! It flames with frenzy! Oh, hear me, hear me, and be saved! See, I plead with you on my very knees!" As she sank before me my Conscience reeled again, and then drooped languidly to the floor, blinking toward me a last supplication for mercy, with heavy eyes. "Oh, promise, or you are lost! Promise, and be redeemed! Promise! Promise and live!" With a long-drawn sigh my conquered Conscience closed his eyes and fell fast asleep!

With an exultant shout I sprang past my aunt, and in an instant I had my lifelong foe by the throat. After so many years of waiting and longing, he was mine at last. I tore him to shreds and fragments. I rent the fragments to bits. I cast the bleeding rubbish into the fire, and drew into my nostrils the grateful incense of my burnt-offering. At last, and forever, my Conscience was dead!

I was a free man! I turned upon my poor aunt, who was almost petrified with terror, and shouted:

"Out of this with your paupers, your charities, your reforms, your pestilent morals! You behold before you a man whose life-conflict is done, whose soul is at peace; a man whose heart is dead to sorrow, dead to suffering, dead to remorse; a man WITHOUT A CONSCIENCE! In my joy I spare you, though I could throttle you and never feel a pang! Fly!"

She fled. Since that day my life is all bliss. Bliss, unalloyed bliss. Nothing in all the world could persuade me to have a conscience again. I settled all my old outstanding scores, and began the world anew. I killed thirty-eight persons during the first two weeks—all of them on account of ancient grudges. I burned a dwelling that interrupted my view. I swindled a widow and some orphans out of their last cow, which is a very good one, though not thoroughbred, I believe. I have also committed scores of crimes, of various kinds, and have enjoyed my work exceedingly, whereas it would formerly have broken my heart and turned my hair gray, I have no doubt.

In conclusion, I wish to state, by way of advertisement, that medical colleges desiring assorted tramps for scientific purposes, either by the gross, by cord measurement, or per ton, will do well to examine the lot in my cellar before purchasing elsewhere, as these were all selected and prepared by myself, and can be had at a low rate, because I wish to clear out my stock and get ready for the spring trade.

1876

Letter Read at a Dinner

OF THE KNIGHTS OF ST. PATRICK

HARTFORD, CONN., *March 16, 1876*

To the Chairman:

DEAR SIR,—I am very sorry that I cannot be with the Knights of St. Patrick to-morrow evening. In this centennial year we ought to find a peculiar pleasure in doing honor to the memory of a man whose good name has endured through fourteen centuries. We ought to find pleasure in it for the reason that at this time we naturally have a fellow-feeling for such a man. He wrought a great work in his day. He found Ireland a prosperous republic, and looked about him to see if he might find some useful thing to turn his hand to. He observed that the president of that republic was in the habit of sheltering his great officials from deserved punishment, so he lifted up his staff and smote him, and he died. He found that the secretary of war had been so unbecomingly enconomical as to have laid up $12,000 a year out of a salary of $8,000, and he killed him. He found that the secretary of the interior always prayed over every separate and distinct barrel of salt beef that was intended for the unconverted savage, and then kept that beef himself, so he killed him also. He found that the secretary of the navy knew more about handling suspicious claims than he did about handling a ship, and he at once made an end of him. He found that a very foul private secretary had been engineered through a sham trial, so he destroyed him. He discovered that the congress which pretended to prodigious virtue was very anxious to investigate an ambassador who had dishonored the country abroad, but was equally anxious to prevent the appointment of any spotless man to a similar post; that this congress had no God but party; no system of morals but party policy; no vision but a bat's vision; and no reason or excuse for existing anyhow. Therefore he massacred that congress to the last man.

When he had finished his great work, he said, in his figurative way, "Lo, I have destroyed all the reptiles in Ireland."

St. Patrick had no politics; his sympathies lay with the right—that was politics enough. When he came across a reptile, he forgot to inquire

whether he was a democrat or a republican, but simply exalted his
staff and "let him have it." Honored be his name—I wish we had him
here to trim us up for the centennial. But that cannot be. His staff,
which was the symbol of real, not sham reform, is idle. However, we
still have with us the symbol of Truth—George Washington's little
hatchet—for I know where they've buried it.

Yours truly,

MARK TWAIN

1876

Punch, Brothers, Punch

Will the reader please to cast his eye over the following lines, and
see if he can discover anything harmful in them?

> Conductor, when you receive a fare,
> Punch in the presence of the passenjare!
> A blue trip slip for an eight-cent fare,
> A buff trip slip for a six-cent fare,
> A pink trip slip for a three-cent fare,
> Punch in the presence of the passenjare!

CHORUS

> Punch, brothers! punch with care!
> Punch in the presence of the passenjare!

I came across these jingling rhymes in a newspaper, a little while ago,
and read them a couple of times. They took instant and entire possession of me. All through breakfast they went waltzing through my
brain; and when, at last, I rolled up my napkin, I could not tell whether
I had eaten anything or not. I had carefully laid out my day's work the
day before—a thrilling tragedy in the novel which I am writing. I went
to my den to begin my deed of blood. I took up my pen, but all I could
get it to say was, "Punch in the presence of the passenjare." I fought
hard for an hour, but it was useless. My head kept humming, "A blue
trip slip for an eight-cent fare, a buff trip slip for a six-cent fare," and
so on and so on, without peace or respite. The day's work was ruined—

I could see that plainly enough. I gave up and drifted down-town, and presently discovered that my feet were keeping time to that relentless jingle. When I could stand it no longer I altered my step. But it did no good; those rhymes accommodated themselves to the new step and went on harassing me just as before. I returned home, and suffered all the afternoon; suffered all through an unconscious and unrefreshing dinner; suffered, and cried, and jingled all through the evening; went to bed and rolled, tossed, and jingled right along, the same as ever; got up at midnight frantic, and tried to read; but there was nothing visible upon the whirling page except "Punch! punch in the presence of the passenjare." By sunrise I was out of my mind, and everybody marveled and was distressed at the idiotic burden of my ravings—"Punch! oh, punch! punch in the presence of the passenjare!"

Two days later, on Saturday morning, I arose, a tottering wreck, and went forth to fulfil an engagement with a valued friend, the Rev. Mr. ——, to walk to the Talcott Tower, ten miles distant. He stared at me, but asked no questions. We started. Mr. —— talked, talked, talked—as is he wont. I said nothing; I heard nothing. At the end of a mile, Mr. —— said:

"Mark, are you sick? I never saw a man look so haggard and worn and absent-minded. Say something, do!"

Drearily, without enthusiasm, I said: "Punch, brothers, punch with care! Punch in the presence of the passenjare!"

My friend eyed me blankly, looked perplexed, then said:

"I do not think I get your drift, Mark. There does not seem to be any relevancy in what you have said, certainly nothing sad; and yet—maybe it was the way you *said* the words—I never heard anything that sounded so pathetic. What is—"

But I heard no more. I was already far away with my pitiless, heart-breaking "blue trip slip for an eight-cent fare, buff trip slip for a six-cent fare, pink trip slip for a three-cent fare; punch in the presence of the passenjare." I do not know what occurred during the other nine miles. However, all of a sudden Mr. —— laid his hand on my shoulder and shouted:

"Oh, wake up! wake up! wake up! Don't sleep all day! Here we are at the Tower, man! I have talked myself deaf and dumb and blind, and never got a response. Just look at this magnificent autumn landscape! Look at it! look at it! Feast your eyes on it! You have traveled; you have seen boasted landscapes elsewhere. Come, now, deliver an honest opinion. What do you say to this?"

I sighed wearily, and murmured:

"A buff trip slip for a six-cent fare, a pink trip slip for a three-cent fare, punch in the presence of the passenjare."

Rev. Mr. — stood there, very grave, full of concern, apparently, and looked long at me; then he said:

"Mark, there is something about this that I cannot understand. Those are about the same words you said before; there does not seem to be anything in them, and yet they nearly break my heart when you say them. Punch in the—how is it they go?"

I began at the beginning and repeated all the lines.

My friend's face lighted with interest. He said:

"Why, what a captivating jingle it is! It is almost music. It flows along so nicely. I have nearly caught the rhymes myself. Say them over just once more, and then I'll have them, sure."

I said them over. Then Mr. — said them. He made one little mistake, which I corrected. The next time and the next he got them right. Now a great burden seemed to tumble from my shoulders. That torturing jingle departed out of my brain, and a grateful sense of rest and peace descended upon me. I was light-hearted enough to sing; and I did sing for half an hour, straight along, as we went jogging homeward. Then my freed tongue found blessed speech again, and the pent talk of many a weary hour began to gush and flow. It flowed on and on, joyously, jubilantly, until the fountain was empty and dry. As I wrung my friend's hand at parting, I said:

"Haven't we had a royal good time! But now I remember, you haven't said a word for two hours. Come, come, out with something!"

The Rev. Mr. — turned a lack-luster eye upon me, drew a deep sigh, and said, without animation, without apparent consciousness:

"Punch, brothers, punch with care! Punch in the presence of the passenjare!"

A pang shot through me as I said to myself, "Poor fellow, poor fellow! *he* has got it, now."

I did not see Mr. — for two or three days after that. Then, on Tuesday evening, he staggered into my presence and sank dejectedly into a seat. He was pale, worn; he was a wreck. He lifted his faded eyes to my face and said:

"Ah, Mark, it was a ruinous investment that I made in those heartless rhymes. They have ridden me like a nightmare, day and night, hour after hour, to this very moment. Since I saw you I have suffered the torments of the lost. Saturday evening I had a sudden call, by telegraph, and took the night train for Boston. The occasion was the death of a valued old friend who had requested that I should preach his funeral sermon. I took my seat in the cars and set myself to framing the discourse. But I never got beyond the opening paragraph; for then the train started and the car-wheels began their 'clack, clack—clack-clack-clack! clack-clack—clack-clack-clack!' and right away those odious rhymes fitted themselves to that accompaniment. For an hour I sat there and set a syllable of those rhymes to every separate and distinct clack the car-wheels made. Why, I was as fagged out, then, as if I had been chopping wood all day. My skull was splitting with headache. It seemed to me that I must go mad if I sat there any longer; so I undressed and went to bed. I stretched myself out in my berth, and—well, you know what the result was. The thing went right along, just the same. 'Clack-clack-clack, a blue trip slip, clack-clack-clack, for an eight-cent fare; clack-clack-clack, a buff trip slip, clack-clack-clack, for a six cent fare, and so on, and so on, and so on—*punch* in the presence of the passenjare!' Sleep? Not a single wink! I was almost a lunatic when I got to Boston. Don't ask me about the funeral. I did the best I could, but every solemn individual sentence was meshed and tangled and woven in and out with 'Punch, brothers, punch with care, punch in the presence of the passenjare.' And the most distressing thing was that my *delivery* dropped into the undulating rhythm of those pulsing rhymes, and I could actually catch absent-minded people nodding *time* to the swing of it with their stupid heads. And, Mark, you may believe it or not, but before I got through the entire assemblage were placidly bobbing their heads in solemn unison, mourners, undertaker, and all. The moment I had finished, I fled to the anteroom in a state bordering on frenzy. Of course it would be my luck to find a sorrowing and aged maiden aunt of the deceased there, who had arrived from Springfield too late to get into the church. She began to sob, and said:

" 'Oh, oh, he is gone, he is gone, and I didn't see him before he died!'

" 'Yes!' I said, 'he *is* gone, he *is* gone, he *is* gone—oh, *will* this suffering never cease!'

" 'You loved him, then! Oh, you too loved him!'

" 'Loved him! Loved *who?*'

" 'Why, my poor George! my poor nephew!'

" 'Oh—*him!* Yes—oh, yes, yes. Certainly—certainly. Punch—punch—oh, this misery will kill me!'

" 'Bless you! bless you, sir, for these sweet words! *I*, too, suffer in this dear loss. Were you present during his last moments?'

" 'Yes. I—*whose* last moments?'

" '*His*. The dear departed's.'

"'Yes! Oh, yes—yes—*yes!* I suppose so, I think so, *I* don't know! Oh, certainly—I was there—*I* was there!'

"'Oh, what a privilege! what a precious privilege! And his last words —oh, tell me, tell me his last words! What did he say?'

"'He said—he said—oh, my head, my head, my head! He said—he said—he never said *any*thing but Punch, punch, *punch* in the presence of the passenjare! Oh, leave me, madam! In the name of all that is generous, leave me to my madness, my misery, my despair!—a buff trip slip for a six-cent fare, a pink trip slip for a three-cent fare—endu-rance *can* no fur-ther go!—PUNCH in the presence of the passenjare!'"

My friend's hopeless eyes rested upon mine a pregnant minute, and then he said impressively:

"Mark, you do not say anything. You do not offer me any hope. But, ah me, it is just as well—it is just as well. You could not do me any good. The time has long gone by when words could comfort me. Something tells me that my tongue is doomed to wag forever to the jigger of that remorseless jingle. There—there it is coming on me again: a blue trip slip for an eight-cent fare, a buff trip slip for a—"

Thus murmuring faint and fainter, my friend sank into a peaceful trance and forgot his sufferings in a blessed respite.

How did I finally save him from an asylum? I took him to a neighboring university and made him discharge the burden of his persecuting rhymes into the eager ears of the poor, unthinking students. How is it with *them*, now? The result is too sad to tell. Why did I write this article? It was for a worthy, even a noble, purpose. It was to warn you, reader, if you should come across those merciless rhymes, to avoid them—avoid them as you would a pestilence!

1876

Some Rambling Notes of
an Idle Excursion

I

All the journeyings I had ever done had been purely in the way of business. The pleasant May weather suggested a novelty—namely, a trip for pure recreation, the bread-and-butter element left out. The Reverend said he would go, too; a good man, one of the best of men, although a clergyman. By eleven at night we were in New Haven and on board the New York boat. We bought our tickets, and then went wandering around here and there, in the solid comfort of being free and idle, and of putting distance between ourselves and the mails and telegraphs.

After a while I went to my stateroom and undressed, but the night was too enticing for bed. We were moving down the bay now, and it was pleasant to stand at the window and take the cool night breeze and watch the gliding lights on shore. Presently, two elderly men sat down under that window and began a conversation. Their talk was properly no business of mine, yet I was feeling friendly toward the world and willing to be entertained. I soon gathered that they were brothers, that they were from a small Connecticut village, and that the matter in hand concerned the cemetery. Said one:

"Now, John, we talked it all over amongst ourselves, and this is what we've done. You see, everybody was a-movin' from the old buryin'-ground, and our folks was 'most about left to theirselves, as you may say. They was crowded, too, as you know; lot wa'n't big enough in the first place; and last year, when Seth's wife died, we couldn't hardly tuck her in. She sort o' overlaid Deacon Shorb's lot, and he soured on her, so to speak, and on the rest of us, too. So we talked it over, and I was for a lay-out in the new simitery on the hill. They wa'n't unwilling, if it was cheap. Well, the two best and biggest plots was No. 8 and No. 9—both of a size; nice comfortable room for twenty-six—twenty-six full-growns, that is; but you reckon in children and other shorts, and strike an average, and I should say you might lay in thirty, or maybe thirty-two or three, pretty genteel—no crowdin' to signify."

"That's a plenty, William. Which one did you buy?"

"Well, I'm a-comin' to that, John. You see, No. 8 was thirteen dollars, No. 9 fourteen—"

"I see. So's't you took No. 8."

"You wait. I took No. 9. And I'll tell you for why. In the first place, Deacon Shorb wanted it. Well, after the way he'd gone on about Seth's wife overlappin' his prem'ses, I'd 'a' beat him out of that No. 9 if I'd 'a' had to stand two dollars extra, let alone one. That's the way I felt about it. Says, I, what's a dollar, anyway? Life's on'y a pilgrimage, says I; we ain't here for good, and we can't take it with us, says I. So I just dumped it down, knowin' the Lord don't suffer a good deed to go for nothin', and cal'latin' to take it out o' somebody in the course o' trade. Then there was another reason, John. No. 9's a long way the handiest lot in the simitery, and the likeliest for situation. It lays right on top of a knoll in the dead center of the buryin'-ground; and you can see Mill-port from there, and Tracy's, and Hopper Mount, and a raft o' farms, and so on. There ain't no better outlook from a buryin'-plot in the state. Si Higgins says so, and I reckon he ought to know. Well, and that ain't all. 'Course Shorb had to take No. 8; wa'n't no help for 't. Now, No. 8 jines onto No. 9, but it's on the slope of the hill, and every time it rains it'll soak right down onto the Shorbs. Si Higgins says 't when the dea-con's time comes, he better take out fire and marine insurance both on his remains."

Here there was the sound of a low, placid, duplicate chuckle of ap-preciation and satisfaction.

"Now, John, here's a little rough draft of the ground that I've made on a piece of paper. Up here in the left-hand corner we've bunched the departed; took them from the old graveyard and stowed them one alongside o' t'other, on a first-come-first-served plan, no partialities, with Gran'ther Jones for a starter, on'y because it happened so, and windin' up indiscriminate with Seth's twins. A little crowded towards the end of the lay-out, maybe, but we reckoned 'twa'n't best to scatter the twins. Well, next comes the livin'. Here, where it's marked A, we're goin' to put Mariar and her family, when they're called; B, that's for Brother Hosea and hisn; C, Calvin and tribe. What's left is these two lots here—just the gem of the whole patch for general style and out-look; they're for me and my folks, and you and yourn. Which of them would you ruther be buried in?"

"I swan, you've took me mighty unexpected, William! It sort of started the shivers. Fact is, I was thinkin' so busy about makin' things comfortable for the others, I hadn't thought about being buried myself."

"Life's on'y a fleetin' show, John, as the sayin' is. We've all got to go, sooner or later. To go with a clean record's the main thing. Fact is, it's the on'y thing worth strivin' for, John."

"Yes, that's so, William, that's so; there ain't no getting around it. Which of these lots would you recommend?"

"Well, it depends, John. Are you particular about outlook?"

"I don't say I am, William, I don't say I ain't. Reely I don't know. But mainly, I reckon, I'd set store by a south exposure."

"That's easy fixed, John. They're both south exposure. They take the sun, and the Shorbs get the shade."

"How about sile, William?"

"D's a sandy sile, E's mostly loom."

"You may gimme E, then, William; a sandy sile caves in, more or less, and costs for repairs."

"All right, set your name down here, John, under E. Now, if you don't mind payin' me your share of the fourteen dollars, John, while we're on the business, everything's fixed."

After some higgling and sharp bargaining the money was paid, and John bade his brother good night and took his leave. There was silence for some moments; then a soft chuckle welled up from the lonely William, and he muttered: "I declare for 't, if I haven't made a mistake! It's D that's mostly loom, not E. And John's booked for a sandy sile, after all."

There was another soft chuckle, and William departed to his rest also.

The next day, in New York, was a hot one. Still we managed to get more or less entertainment out of it. Toward the middle of the afternoon we arrived on board the stanch steamship *Bermuda*, with bag and baggage, and hunted for a shady place. It was blazing summer weather, until we were half-way down the harbor. Then I buttoned my coat closely; half an hour later I put on a spring overcoat and buttoned that. As we passed the light-ship I added an ulster and tied a handkerchief around the collar to hold it snug to my neck. So rapidly had the summer gone and winter come again!

By nightfall we were far out at sea, with no land in sight. No telegrams could come here, no letters, no news. This was an uplifting thought. It was still more uplifting to reflect that the millions of harrassed people on shore behind us were suffering just as usual.

The next day brought us into the midst of the Atlantic solitudes—out of smoke-colored soundings into fathomless deep blue; no ships visible anywhere over the wide ocean; no company but Mother Carey's chickens wheeling, darting, skimming the waves in the sun. There were some seafaring men among the passengers, and conversation drifted into matters concerning ships and sailors. One said that "true as the needle to the pole" was a bad figure, since the needle seldom pointed to the pole. He said a ship's compass was not faithful to any particular point, but was the most fickle and treacherous of the servants of man. It was forever changing. It changed every day in the year; consequently the amount of the daily variation had to be ciphered out and allowance made for it, else the mariner would go utterly astray. Another said there was a vast fortune waiting for the genius who should invent a compass that would not be affected by the local influences of an iron ship. He said there was only one creature more fickle than a wooden ship's compass, and that was the compass of an iron ship. Then came reference to the well-known fact that an experienced mariner can look at the compass of a new iron vessel, thousands of miles from her birthplace, and tell which way her head was pointing when she was in process of building.

Now an ancient whale-ship master fell to talking about the sort of crews they used to have in his early days. Said he:

"Sometimes we'd have a batch of college students. Queer lot. Ignorant? Why, they didn't know the catheads from the main brace. But if you took them for fools you'd get bit, sure. They'd learn more in a month than another man would in a year. We had one, once, in the *Mary Ann*, that came aboard with gold spectacles on. And besides, he was rigged out from main truck to keelson in the nobbiest clothes that ever saw a fo'castle. He had a chestful, too: cloaks, and broadcloth coats, and velvet vests; everything swell, you know; and didn't the saltwater fix them out for him? I guess not! Well, going to sea, the mate told him to go aloft and help shake out the foreto'gallants'l. Up he shines to the foretop, with his spectacles on, and in a minute down he comes again, looking insulted. Says the mate, 'What did you come down for?' Says the chap, 'P'r'aps you didn't notice that there ain't any ladders above there.' You see we hadn't any shrouds above the foretop. The men bursted out in a laugh such as I guess you never heard the like of. Next night, which was dark and rainy, the mate ordered this chap to go aloft about something, and I'm dummed if he didn't start up with an umbrella and a lantern! But no matter; he made a mighty good sailor before the voyage was done, and we had to hunt up something else to laugh at. Years afterwards, when I had forgot all about him, I comes into Boston, mate of a ship, and was loafing around town with the second mate, and it so happened that we stepped into the Re-

vere House, thinking maybe we would chance the salt-horse in that big
dining-room for a flyer, as the boys say. Some fellows were talking
just at our elbow, and one says, 'Yonder's the new governor of Massachusetts—at that table over there with the ladies.' We took a good look,
my mate and I, for we hadn't either of us ever seen a governor before.
I looked and looked at that face, and then all of a sudden it popped on
me! But I didn't give any sign. Says I, 'Mate, I've a notion to go over
and shake hands with him.' Says he, 'I think I see you doing it, Tom.'
Says I, 'Mate, I'm a-going to do it.' Says he, 'Oh, yes, I guess so! Maybe
you don't want to bet you will, Tom?' Says I, 'I don't mind going a V
on it, mate.' Says he, 'Put it up.' 'Up she goes,' says I, planking the cash.
This surprised him. But he covered it, and says, pretty sarcastic,
'Hadn't you better take your grub with the governor and the ladies,
Tom?' Says I, 'Upon second thoughts, I will.' Says he, 'Well, Tom, you
are a dum fool.' Says I, 'Maybe I am, maybe I ain't; but the main
question is, do you want to risk two and a half that I won't do it?' 'Make
it a V,' says he. 'Done,' says I. I started, him a-giggling and slapping
his hand on his thigh, he felt so good. I went over there and leaned
my knuckles on the table a minute and looked the governor in the face,
and says I, 'Mr. Gardner, don't you know me?' He stared, and I stared,
and he stared. Then all of a sudden he sings out, 'Tom Bowling, by the
holy poker! Ladies, it's old Tom Bowling, that you've heard me talk
about—shipmate of mine in the *Mary Ann.*' He rose up and shook
hands with me ever so hearty—I sort of glanced around and took a re-
alizing sense of my mate's saucer eyes—and then says the governor,
'Plant yourself, Tom, plant yourself; you can't cat your anchor again till
you've had a feed with me and the ladies!' I planted myself alongside
the governor, and canted my eye around toward my mate. Well, sir,
his dead-lights were bugged out like tompions; and his mouth stood
that wide open that you could have laid a ham in it without him noticing it."

There was great applause at the conclusion of the old captain's story;
then, after a moment's silence, a grave, pale young man said:

"Had you ever met the governor before?"

The old captain looked steadily at this inquirer awhile, and then got
up and walked aft without making any reply. One passenger after another stole a furtive glance at the inquirer, but failed to make him out,
and so gave him up. It took some little work to get the talk-machinery
to running smoothly again after this derangement; but at length a conversation sprang up about that important and jealously guarded instru-

ment, a ship's timekeeper, its exceeding delicate accuracy, and the wreck and destruction that have sometimes resulted from its varying a few seemingly trifling moments from the true time; then, in due course, my comrade, the Reverend, got off on a yarn, with a fair wind and everything drawing. It was a true story, too—about Captain Rounceville's shipwreck—true in every detail. It was to this effect:

Captain Rounceville's vessel was lost in mid-Atlantic, and likewise his wife and his two little children. Captain Rounceville and seven seamen escaped with life, but with little else. A small, rudely constructed raft was to be their home for eight days. They had neither provisions nor water. They had scarcely any clothing; no one had a coat but the captain. This coat was changing hands all the time, for the weather was very cold. Whenever a man became exhausted with the cold, they put the coat on him and laid him down between two shipmates until the garment and their bodies had warmed life into him again. Among the sailors was a Portuguese who knew no English. He seemed to have no thought of his own calamity, but was concerned only about the captain's bitter loss of wife and children. By day he would look his dumb compassion in the captain's face; and by night, in the darkness and the driving spray and rain, he would seek out the captain and try to comfort him with caressing pats on the shoulder. One day, when hunger and thirst were making their sure inroads upon the men's strength and spirits, a floating barrel was seen at a distance. It seemed a great find, for doubtless it contained food of some sort. A brave fellow swam to it, and after long and exhausting effort got it to the raft. It was eagerly opened. It was a barrel of magnesia! On the fifth day an onion was spied. A sailor swam off and got it. Although perishing with hunger, he brought it in its integrity and put it into the captain's hand. The history of the sea teaches that among starving, shipwrecked men selfishness is rare, and a wonder-compelling magnanimity the rule. The onion was equally divided into eight parts, and eaten with deep thanksgivings. On the eighth day a distant ship was sighted. Attempts were made to hoist an oar, with Captain Rounceville's coat on it for a signal. There were many failures, for the men were but skeletons now, and strengthless. At last success was achieved, but the signal brought no help. The ship faded out of sight and left despair behind her. By and by another ship appeared, and passed so near that the castaways, every eye eloquent with gratitude, made ready to welcome the boat that would be sent to save them. But this ship also drove on, and left these men staring their unutterable surprise and dismay into each other's ashen faces. Late in the day, still another ship came up out of the distance, but the men noted with a pang that her course was one which would not bring her nearer. Their remnant of life was nearly spent; their lips and tongues were swollen, parched, cracked with eight days' thirst; their bodies starved; and here was their last chance gliding relentlessly from them; they would not be alive when the next sun rose. For a day or two past the men had lost their voices, but now Captain Rounceville whispered, "Let us pray." The Portuguese patted him on the shoulder in sign of deep approval. All knelt at the base of the oar that was waving the signal-coat aloft, and bowed their heads. The sea was tossing; the sun rested, a red, rayless disk, on the sea-line in the west. When the men presently raised their heads they would have roared a hallelujah if they had had a voice—the ship's sails lay wrinkled and flapping against her masts—she was going about! Here was rescue at last, and in the very last instant of time that was left for it. No, not rescue yet—only the imminent prospect of it. The red disk sank under the sea, and darkness blotted out the ship. By and by came a pleasant sound—oars moving in a boat's rowlocks. Nearer it came, and nearer—within thirty steps, but nothing visible. Then a deep voice: "Hol-*lo!*" The castaways could not answer; their swollen tongues refused voice. The boat skirted round and round the raft, started away—the agony of it!—returned, rested the oars, close at hand, listening, no doubt. The deep voice again: "Hol-*lo!* Where are ye, ship-mates?" Captain Rounceville whispered to his men, saying: "Whisper your best, boys! now—all at once!" So they sent out an eightfold whisper in hoarse concert; "Here!" There was life in it if it succeeded; death if it failed. After that supreme moment Captain Rounceville was conscious of nothing until he came to himself on board the saving ship. Said the Reverend, concluding:

"There was one little moment of time in which that raft could be visible from that ship, and only one. If that one little fleeting moment had passed unfruitful, those men's doom was sealed. As close as that does God shave events foreordained from the beginning of the world. When the sun reached the water's edge that day, the captain of that ship was sitting on deck reading his prayer-book. The book fell; he stooped to pick it up, and happened to glance at the sun. In that in-stant that far-off raft appeared for a second against the red disk, its needle-like oar and diminutive signal cut sharp and black against the bright surface, and in the next instant was thrust away into the dusk again. But that ship, that captain, and that pregnant instant had had their work appointed for them in the dawn of time and could not fail of the performance. The chronometer of God never errs!"

There was deep, thoughtful silence for some moments. Then the grave, pale young man said:

"What is the chronometer of God?"

II

At dinner, six o'clock, the same people assembled whom we had talked with on deck and seen at luncheon and breakfast this second day out, and at dinner the evening before. That is to say, three journeying ship-masters, a Boston merchant, and a returning Bermudian who had been absent from his Bermuda thirteen years; these sat on the starboard side. On the port side sat the Reverend in the seat of honor; the pale young man next to him; I next; next to me an aged Bermudian, returning to his sunny islands after an absence of twenty-seven years. Of course, our captain was at the head of the table, the purser at the foot of it. A small company, but small companies are pleasantest.

No racks upon the table; the sky cloudless, the sun brilliant, the blue sea scarcely ruffled; then what had become of the four married couples, the three bachelors, and the active and obliging doctor from the rural districts of Pennsylvania?—for all these were on deck when we sailed down New York harbor. This is the explanation. I quote from my notebook:

Thursday, 3.30 P.M. Under way, passing the Battery. The large party, of four married couples, three bachelors, and a cheery, exhilarating doctor from the wilds of Pennsylvania, are evidently traveling together. All but the doctor grouped in camp-chairs on deck.

Passing principal fort. The doctor is one of those people who has an infallible preventive of seasickness; is flitting from friend to friend administering it and saying, "Don't you be afraid; I *know* this medicine; absolutely infallible; prepared under my own supervision." Takes a dose himself, intrepidly.

4.15 P.M. Two of those ladies have struck their colors, notwithstanding the "infallible." They have gone below. The other two begin to show distress.

5 P.M. Exit one husband and one bachelor. These still and their infallible in cargo when they started, but arrived at the companionway without it.

5.10. Lady No. 3, two bachelors, and one married man have gone below with their own opinion of the infallible.

5.20. Passing Quarantine Hulk. The infallible has done the business for all the party except the Scotchman's wife and the author of that formidable remedy.

Nearing the Light-Ship. Exit the Scotchman's wife, head drooped on stewardess's shoulder.

Entering the open sea. Exit doctor!

The rout seems permanent; hence the smallness of the company at table since the voyage began. Our captain is a grave, handsome Hercules of thirty-five, with a brown hand of such majestic size that one cannot eat for admiring it and wondering if a single kid or calf could furnish material for gloving it.

Conversation not general; drones along between couples. One catches a sentence here and there. Like this, from Bermudian of thirteen years' absence: "It is the nature of women to ask trivial, irrelevant, and pursuing questions—questions that pursue you from a beginning in nothing to a run-to-cover in nowhere." Reply of Bermudian of twenty-seven years' absence: "Yes; and to think they have logical, analytical minds and argumentative ability. You see 'em begin to whet up whenever they smell argument in the air." Plainly these be philosophers.

Twice since we left port our engines have stopped for a couple of minutes at a time. Now they stop again. Says the pale young man, meditatively, "There!—that engineer is sitting down to rest again."

Grave stare from the captain, whose mighty jaws cease to work, and whose harpooned potato stops in midair on its way to his open, paralyzed mouth. Presently he says in measured tones, "Is is it your idea that the engineer of this ship propels her by a crank turned by his own hands?"

The pale young man studies over this a moment, then lifts up his guileless eyes, and says, "Don't he?"

Thus gently falls the death-blow to further conversation, and the dinner drags to its close in a reflective silence, disturbed by no sounds but the murmurous wash of the sea and the subdued clash of teeth.

After a smoke and a promenade on deck, where is no motion to discompose our steps, we think of a game of whist. We ask the brisk and capable stewardess from Ireland if there are any cards in the ship.

"Bless your soul, dear, indeed there is. Not a whole pack, true for ye, but not enough missing to signify."

However, I happened by accident to bethink me of a new pack in a morocco case, in my trunk, which I had placed there by mistake, thinking it to be a flask of something. So a party of us conquered the tedium of the evening with a few games and were ready for bed at six bells, mariner's time, the signal for putting out the lights.

There was much chat in the smoking-cabin on the upper deck after luncheon to-day, mostly whaler yarns from those old sea-captains. Captain Tom Bowling was garrulous. He had that garrulous attention to minor detail which is born of secluded farm life or life at sea on long voyages, where there is little to do and time no object. He would sail along till he was right in the most exciting part of a yarn, and then say, "Well, as I was saying, the rudder was fouled, ship driving before the gale, head-on, straight for the iceberg, all hands holding their breath, turned to stone, top-hamper giving 'way, sails blown to ribbons, first one stick going, then another, boom! smash! crash! duck your head and stand from under! when up comes Johnny Rogers, capstan-bar in hand, eyes a-blazing, hair a-flying . . . no, 'twa'n't Johnny Rogers . . . lemme see . . . seems to me Johnny Rogers wa'n't along that voyage; he was along *one* voyage, I know that mighty well, but somehow it seems to me that he signed the articles for this voyage, but—but—whether he come along or not, or got left, or something happened—"

And so on and so on till the excitement all cooled down and nobody cared whether the ship struck the iceberg or not.

In the course of his talk he rambled into a criticism upon New England degrees of merit in shipbuilding. Said he, "You get a vessel built away down Maine-way; Bath, for instance; what's the result? First thing you do, you want to heave her down for repairs—*that's* the result! Well, sir, she hain't been hove down a week till you can heave a dog through her seams. You send that vessel to sea, and what's the result? She wets her oakum the first trip! Leave it to any man if 'tain't so. Well, you let *our* folks build you a vessel—down New-Bedford-way. What's the result? Well, sir, you might take that ship and heave her down, and keep her hove down six months, and she'll never shed a tear!"

Everybody, landsmen and all, recognized the descriptive neatness of that figure, and applauded, which greatly pleased the old man. A moment later, the meek eyes of the pale young fellow heretofore mentioned came up slowly, rested upon the old man's face a moment, and the meek mouth began to open.

"Shet your head!" shouted the old mariner.

It was a rather startling surprise to everybody, but it was effective in the matter of its purpose. So the conversation flowed on instead of perishing.

There was some talk about the perils of the sea, and a landsman delivered himself of the customary nonsense about the poor mariner wandering in far oceans, tempest-tossed, pursued by dangers, every storm-blast and thunderbolt in the home skies moving the friends by snug firesides to compassion for that poor mariner, and prayers for his succor. Captain Bowling put up with this for a while, and then burst out with a new view of the matter.

"Come, belay there! I have read this kind of rot all my life in poetry and tales and such-like rubbage. Pity for the poor mariner! sympathy for the poor mariner! All right enough, but not in the way the poetry puts it. Pity for the mariner's wife! all right again, but not in the way the poetry puts it. Look-a-here! whose life's the safest in the whole world? The poor mariner's. You look at the statistics, you'll see. So don't you fool away any sympathy on the poor mariner's dangers and privations and sufferings. Leave that to the poetry muffs. Now you look at the other side a minute. Here is Captain Brace, forty years old, been at sea thirty. On his way now to take command of his ship and sail south from Bermuda. Next week he'll be under way; easy times; comfortable quarters; passengers, sociable company; just enough to do to keep his mind healthy and not tire him; king over his ship, boss of everything and everybody; thirty years' safety to learn him that his profession ain't a dangerous one. Now you look back at his home. His wife's a feeble woman; she's a stranger in New York; shut up in blazing hot or freezing cold lodgings, according to the season; don't know anybody hardly; no company but her lonesomeness and her thoughts; husband gone six months at a time. She has borne eight children; five of them she has buried without her husband ever setting eyes on them. She watched them all the long nights till they died—he comfortable on the sea; she followed them to the grave, she heard the clods fall that broke her heart—he comfortable on the sea; she mourned at home, weeks and weeks, missing them every day and every hour— he cheerful at sea, knowing nothing about it. Now look at it a minute— turn it over in your mind and size it: five children born, she among strangers, and him not by to hearten her; buried, and him not by to comfort her; think of that! Sympathy for the poor mariner's perils is rot; give it to his wife's hard lines, where it belongs! Poetry makes out that all the wife worries about is the dangers her husband's running. She's got substantialer things to worry over, I tell you. Poetry's always pitying the poor mariner on account of his perils at sea; better a blamed sight pity him for the nights he can't sleep for thinking of how he had to leave his wife in her very birth-pains, lonesome and friend-less, in the thick of disease and trouble and death. If there's one thing that can make me madder than another, it's this sappy, damned mari-time poetry!"

Captain Brace was a patient, gentle, seldom-speaking man, with a pathetic something in his bronzed face that had been a mystery up to this time, but stood interpreted now since we had heard his story. He had voyaged eighteen times to the Mediterranean, seven times to India, once to the arctic pole in a discovery-ship, and "between times" had visited all the remote seas and ocean corners of the globe. But he said that twelve years ago, on account of his family, he "settled down," and ever since then had ceased to roam. And what do you suppose was this simple-hearted, lifelong wanderer's idea of settling down and ceasing to roam? Why, the making of two five-month voyages a year between Surinam and Boston for sugar and molasses!

Among other talk to-day, it came out that whale-ships carry no doctor. The captain adds the doctorship to his own duties. He not only gives medicines, but sets broken limbs after notions of his own, or saws them off and sears the stump when amputation seems best. The captain is provided with a medicine-chest, with the medicines numbered instead of named. A book of directions goes with this. It describes diseases and symptoms, and says, "Give a teaspoonful of No. 9 once an hour," or "Give ten grains of No. 12 every half-hour," etc. One of our sea-captains came across a skipper in the North Pacific who was in a state of great surprise and perplexity. Said he:

"There's something rotten about this medicine-chest business. One of my men was sick—nothing much the matter. I looked in the book: it said give him a teaspoonful of No. 15. I went to the medicine-chest, and I see I was out of No. 15. I judged I'd got to get up a combination somehow that would fill the bill; so I hove into the fellow half a teaspoonful of No. 8 and half a teaspoonful of No. 7, and I'll be hanged if it didn't kill him in fifteen minutes! There's something about this medicine-chest system that's too many for me!"

There was a good deal of pleasant gossip about old Captain "Hurricane" Jones, of the Pacific Ocean—peace to his ashes! Two or three of us present had known him; I particularly well, for I had made four sea-voyages with him. He was a very remarkable man. He was born in a ship; he picked up what little education he had among his shipmates; he began life in the forecastle, and climbed grade by grade to the captaincy. More than fifty years of his sixty-five were spent at sea. He had sailed all oceans, seen all lands, and borrowed a tint from all climates. When a man has been fifty years at sea he necessarily knows nothing of men, nothing of the world but its surface, nothing of the world's thought, nothing of the world's learning but its A B C, and that blurred and distorted by the unfocused lenses of an untrained mind. Such a man is only a gray and bearded child. That is what old Hur-

ricane Jones was—simply an innocent, lovable old infant. When his
spirit was in repose he was as sweet and gentle as a girl; when his
wrath was up he was a hurricane that made his nickname seem
tamely descriptive. He was formidable in a fight, for he was of powerful build and dauntless courage. He was frescoed from head to heel
with pictures and mottoes tattooed in red and blue India ink. I was
with him one voyage when he got his last vacant space tattooed; this
vacant space was around his left ankle. During three days he stumped
about the ship with his ankle bare and swollen, and this legend gleaming red and angry out from a clouding of India ink: "Virtue is its own
R'd." (There was a lack of room.) He was deeply and sincerely pious,
and swore like a fishwoman. He considered swearing blameless, because sailors would not understand an order unillumined by it. He was
a profound biblical scholar—that is, he thought he was. He believed
everything in the Bible, but he had his own methods of arriving at
his beliefs. He was of the "advanced" school of thinkers, and applied
natural laws to the interpretation of all miracles, somewhat on the
plan of the people who make the six days of creation six geological
epochs, and so forth. Without being aware of it, he was a rather
severe satire on modern scientific religionists. Such a man as I have
been describing is rabidly fond of disquisition and argument; one
knows that without being told it.

One trip the captain had a clergyman on board, but did not know
he was a clergyman, since the passenger-list did not betray the fact.
He took a great liking to this Reverend Mr. Peters, and talked with
him a great deal; told him yarns, gave him toothsome scraps of personal history, and wove a glittering streak of profanity through his
garrulous fabric that was refreshing to a spirit weary of the dull
neutralities of undecorated speech. One day the captain said, "Peters,
do you ever read the Bible?"

"Well—yes."

"I judge it ain't often, by the way you say it. Now, you tackle it in
dead earnest once, and you'll find it'll pay. Don't you get discouraged,
but hang right on. First, you won't understand it; but by and by things
will begin to clear up, and then you wouldn't lay it down to eat."

"Yes, I have heard that said."

"And it's so, too. There ain't a book that begins with it. It lays
over'm all, Peters. There's some pretty tough things in it—there ain't
any getting around that—but you stick to them and think them out,
and when once you get on the inside everything's plain as day."

"The miracles, too, captain?"

"Yes, sir! the miracles, too. Every one of them. Now, there's that business with the prophets of Baal; like enough that stumped you?"

"Well, I don't know but—"

"Own up now; it stumped you. Well, I don't wonder. You hadn't had any experience in raveling such things out, and naturally it was too many for you. Would you like to have me explain that thing to you, and show you how to get at the meat of these matters?"

"Indeed, I would, captain, if you don't mind."

Then the captain proceeded as follows: "I'll do it with pleasure. First, you see, I read and read, and thought and thought, till I got to understand what sort of people they were in the old Bible times, and then after that it was all clear and easy. Now this was the way I put it up, concerning Isaac[1] and the prophets of Baal. There was some mighty sharp men among the public characters of that old ancient day, and Isaac was one of them. Isaac had his failings—plenty of them, too; it ain't for me to apologize for Isaac; he played it on the prophets of Baal, and like enough he was justifiable, considering the odds that was against him. No, all I say is, 'twa'n't any miracle, and that I'll show you so's't you can see it yourself.

"Well, times had been getting rougher and rougher for prophets— that is, prophets of Isaac's denomination. There was four hundred and fifty prophets of Baal in the community, and only one Presbyterian; that is, if Isaac *was* a Presbyterian, which I reckon he was, but it don't say. Naturally, the prophets of Baal took all the trade. Isaac was pretty low-spirited, I reckon, but he was a good deal of a man, and no doubt he went a-prophesying around, letting on to be doing a land-office business, but 'twa'n't any use; he couldn't run any opposition to amount to anything. By and by things got desperate with him; he sets his head to work and thinks it all out, and then what does he do? Why, he begins to throw out hints that the other parties are this and that and t'other—nothing very definite, maybe, but just kind of undermining their reputation in a quiet way. This made talk, of course, and finally got to the king. The king asked Isaac what he meant by his talk. Says Isaac, 'Oh, nothing particular; only, can they pray down fire from heaven on an altar? It ain't much, maybe, your majesty, only can they *do* it? That's the idea.' So the king was a good deal disturbed, and he went to the prophets of Baal, and they said, pretty airy, that if he had an altar ready, *they* were ready; and they intimated he better get it insured, too.

[1] This is the captain's own mistake.

"So next morning all the children of Israel and their parents and the other people gathered themselves together. Well, here was that great crowd of prophets of Baal packed together on one side, and Isaac walking up and down all alone on the other, putting up his job. When time was called, Isaac let on to be comfortable and indifferent; told the other team to take the first innings. So they went at it, the whole four hundred and fifty, praying around the altar, very hopeful, and doing their level best. They prayed an hour—two hours—three hours— and so on, plumb till noon. It wa'n't any use; they hadn't took a trick. Of course they felt kind of ashamed before all those people, and well they might. Now, what would a magnanimous man do? Keep still, wouldn't he? Of course. What did Isaac do? He graveled the prophets of Baal every way he could think of. Says he, 'You don't speak up loud enough; your god's asleep, like enough, or maybe he's taking a walk; you want to holler, you know'—or words to that effect; I don't recollect the exact language. Mind, I don't apologize for Isaac; he had his faults.

"Well, the prophets of Baal prayed along the best they knew how all the afternoon, and never raised a spark. At last, about sundown, they were all tuckered out, and they owned up and quit.

"What does Isaac do now? He steps up and says to some friends of his there, 'Pour four barrels of water on the altar!' Everybody was astonished; for the other side had prayed at it dry, you know, and got whitewashed. They poured it on. Says he, 'Heave on four more barrels.' Then he says, 'Heave on four more.' Twelve barrels, you see, altogether. The water ran all over the altar, and all down the sides, and filled up a trench around it that would hold a couple of hogs- heads—'measures,' it says; I reckon it means about a hogshead. Some of the people were going to put on their things and go, for they allowed he was crazy. They didn't know Isaac. Isaac knelt down and began to pray; he strung along, and strung along, about the heathen in distant lands, and about the sister churches, and about the state and the country at large, and about those that's in authority in the govern- ment, and all the usual program, you know, till everybody had got tired and gone to thinking about something else, and then, all of a sudden, when nobody was noticing, he outs with a match and rakes it on the under side of his leg, and *pff!* up the whole thing blazes like a house afire! Twelve barrels of *water? Petroleum,* sir, PETROLEUM! that's what it was!"

"Petroleum, captain?"

"Yes, sir, the country was full of it. Isaac knew all about that. You read the Bible. Don't you worry about the tough places. They ain't tough when you come to think them out and throw light on them. There ain't a thing in the Bible but what is true; all you want is to go prayerfully to work and cipher out how 'twas done."

At eight o'clock on the third morning out from New York, land was sighted. Away across the sunny waves one saw a faint dark stripe stretched along under the horizon—or pretended to see it, for the credit of his eyesight. Even the Reverend said he saw it, a thing which was manifestly not so. But I never have seen any one who was morally strong enough to confess that he could not see land when others claimed that they could.

By and by the Bermuda Islands were easily visible. The principal one lay upon the water in the distance, a long, dull-colored body, scalloped with slight hills and valleys. We could not go straight at it, but had to travel all the way around it, sixteen miles from shore, because it is fenced with an invisible coral reef. At last we sighted buoys, bobbing here and there, and then we glided into a narrow channel among them, "raised the reef," and came upon shoaling blue water that soon further shoaled into pale green, with a surface scarcely rippled. Now came the resurrection hour; the berths gave up their dead. Who are these pale specters in plug-hats and silken flounces that file up the companionway in melancholy procession and step upon the deck? These are they which took the infallible preventive of seasickness in New York harbor and then disappeared and were forgotten. Also there came two or three faces not seen before until this moment. One's impulse is to ask, "Where did *you* come aboard?"

We followed the narrow channel a long time, with land on both sides—low hills that might have been green and grassy, but had a faded look instead. However, the land-locked water was lovely, at any rate, with its glittering belts of blue and green where moderate soundings were, and its broad splotches of rich brown where the rocks lay near the surface. Everybody was feeling so well that even the grave, pale young man (who, by a sort of kindly common consent, had come latterly to be referred to as "The Ass") received frequent and friendly notice—which was right enough, for there was no harm in him.

At last we steamed between two island points whose rocky jaws allowed only just enough room for the vessel's body, and now before us loomed Hamilton on her clustered hillsides and summits, the whitest mass of terraced architecture that exists in the world, perhaps.

It was Sunday afternoon, and on the pier were gathered one or two hundred Bermudians, half of them black, half of them white, and all of them nobbily dressed, as the poet says.

Several boats came off to the ship, bringing citizens. One of these citizens was a faded, diminutive old gentleman, who approached our most ancient passenger with a childlike joy in his twinkling eyes, halted before him, folded his arms, and said, smiling with all his might and with all the simple delight that was in him, "You don't know me, John! Come, out with it now; you know you don't!"

The ancient passenger scanned him perplexedly, scanned the napless, threadbare costume of venerable fashion that had done Sunday service no man knows how many years, contemplated the marvelous stovepipe hat of still more ancient and venerable pattern, with its poor, pathetic old stiff brim canted up "gallusly" in the wrong places, and said, with a hesitation that indicated strong internal effort to "place" the gentle old apparition, "Why . . . let me see . . . plague on it . . . there's *something* about you that . . . er . . . er . . . but I've been gone from Bermuda for twenty-seven years, and . . . hum, hum . . . I don't seem to get at it, somehow, but there's something about you that is just as familiar to me as—"

"Likely it might be his hat," murmured the Ass, with innocent, sympathetic interest.

III

So the Reverend and I had at last arrived at Hamilton, the principal town in the Bermuda Islands. A wonderfully white town; white as snow itself. White as marble; white as flour. Yet looking like none of these, exactly. Never mind, we said; we shall hit upon a figure by and by that will describe this peculiar white.

It was a town that was compacted together upon the sides and tops of a cluster of small hills. Its outlying borders fringed off and thinned away among the cedar forests, and there was no woody distance of curving coast or leafy islet sleeping upon the dimpled, painted sea, but was flecked with shining white points—half-concealed houses peeping out of the foliage. The architecture of the town was mainly Spanish, inherited from the colonists of two hundred and fifty years ago. Some ragged-topped cocoa-palms, glimpsed here and there, gave the land a tropical aspect.

There was an ample pier of heavy masonry; upon this, under shelter, were some thousands of barrels containing that product which has carried the fame of Bermuda to many lands, the potato. With here and there an onion. That last sentence is facetious; for they grow at least two onions in Bermuda to one potato. The onion is the pride and joy of Bermuda. It is her jewel, her gem of gems. In her conversation, her pulpit, her literature, it is her most frequent and eloquent figure. In Bermuda metaphor it stands for perfection—perfection absolute.

The Bermudian weeping over the departed exhausts praise when he says, "He was an onion!" The Bermudian extolling the living hero bankrupts applause when he says, "He is an onion!" The Bermudian setting his son upon the stage of life to dare and do for himself climaxes all counsel, supplication, admonition, comprehends all ambition, when he says, "Be an onion!"

When parallel with the pier, and ten or fifteen steps outside it, we anchored. It was Sunday, bright and sunny. The groups upon the pier —men, youths, and boys—were whites and blacks in about equal proportion. All were well and neatly dressed, many of them nattily, a few of them very stylishly. One would have to travel far before he would find another town of twelve thousand inhabitants that could represent itself so respectably, in the matter of clothes, on a freight-pier, without premeditation or effort. The women and young girls, black and white, who occasionally passed by, were nicely clad, and many were elegantly and fashionably so. The men did not affect summer clothing much, but the girls and women did, and their white garments were good to look at, after so months of familiarity with somber colors.

Around one isolated potato-barrel stood four young gentlemen, two black, two white, becomingly dressed, each with the head of a slender cane pressed against his teeth, and each with a foot propped up on the barrel. Another young gentleman came up, looked longingly at the barrel, but saw no rest for his foot there, and turned pensively away to seek another barrel. He wandered here and there, but without result. Nobody sat upon a barrel, as is the custom of the idle in other lands, yet all the isolated barrels were humanly occupied. Whosoever had a foot to spare put it on a barrel, if all the places on it were not already taken. The habits of all peoples are determined by their circumstances. The Bermudians lean upon barrels because of the scarcity of lamp-posts.

Many citizens came on board and spoke eagerly to the officers—inquiring about the Turco-Russian war news, I supposed. However, by listening judiciously I found that this was not so. They said, "What is the price of onions?" or, "How's onions?" Naturally enough this was their first interest; but they dropped into the war the moment it was satisfied.

We went ashore and found a novelty of a pleasant nature: there were no hackmen, hacks, or omnibuses on the pier or about it anywhere, and nobody offered his services to us, or molested us in any way. I said it was like being in heaven. The Reverend rebukingly and rather pointedly advised me to make the most of it, then. We knew of a boarding-house, and what we needed now was somebody to pilot us to it. Presently a little barefooted colored boy came along, whose raggedness was conspicuously un-Bermudian. His rear was so marvelously bepatched with colored squares and triangles that one was half persuaded he had got it out of an atlas. When the sun struck him right, he was as good to follow as a lightning-bug. We hired him and dropped into his wake. He piloted us through one picturesque street after another, and in due course deposited us where we belonged. He charged nothing for his map, and but a trifle for his services: so the Reverend doubled it. The little chap received the money with a beaming applause in his eye which plainly said, "This man's an onion!"

We had brought no letters of introduction; our names had been misspelled in the passenger-list; nobody knew whether we were honest folk or otherwise. So we were expecting to have a good private time in case there was nothing in our general aspect to close boarding-house doors against us. We had no trouble. Bermuda has had but little experience of rascals, and is not suspicious. We got large, cool, well-lighted rooms on a second floor, overlooking a bloomy display of flowers and flowering shrubs—calla and annunciation lilies, lantanas, heliotrope, jasmine, roses, pinks, double geraniums, oleanders, pomegranates, blue morning-glories of a great size, and many plants that were unknown to me.

We took a long afternoon walk, and soon found out that that exceedingly white town was built of blocks of white coral. Bermuda is a coral island, with a six-inch crust of soil on top of it, and every man has a quarry on his own premises. Everywhere you go you see square recesses cut into the hillsides, with perpendicular walls unmarred by crack or crevice, and perhaps you fancy that a house grew out of the ground there, and has been removed in a single piece from the mold. If you do, you err. But the material for a house has been quarried there. They cut right down through the coral, to any depth that is convenient—ten to twenty feet—and take it out in great square blocks. This cutting is done with a chisel that has a handle twelve or fifteen feet long, and is used as one uses a crowbar when he is drilling a hole, or a dasher when he is churning. Thus soft is this stone. Then with a common handsaw they saw the great blocks into handsome, huge bricks that are two feet long, a foot wide, and about six inches thick. These stand loosely piled during a month to harden; then the work of building begins.

The house is built of these blocks; it is roofed with broad coral slabs an inch thick, whose edges lap upon each other, so that the roof looks like a succession of shallow steps or terraces; the chimneys are built of the coral blocks, and sawed into graceful and picturesque patterns; the ground-floor veranda is paved with coral blocks; also the walk to the gate; the fence is built of coral blocks—built in massive panels, with broad capstones and heavy gate-posts, and the whole trimmed into easy lines and comely shape with the saw. Then they put a hard coat of whitewash, as thick as your thumb-nail, on the fence and all over the house, roof, chimneys, and all; the sun comes out and shines on this spectacle, and it is time for you to shut your unaccustomed eyes, lest they be put out. It is the whitest white you can conceive of, and the blindingest. A Bermuda house does not look like marble; it is a much intenser white than that; and, besides, there is a dainty, indefinable something else about its look that is not marble-like. We put in a great deal of solid talk and reflection over this matter of trying to find a figure that would describe the unique white of a Bermuda house, and we contrived to hit upon it at last. It is exactly the white of the icing of a cake, and has the same unemphasized and scarcely perceptible polish. The white of marble is modest and retiring compared with it.

After the house is cased in its hard scale of whitewash, not a crack, or sign of a seam, or joining of the blocks is detectable, from base-stone to chimney-top; the building looks as if it had been carved from a single block of stone, and the doors and windows sawed out afterward. A white marble house has a cold, tomb-like, unsociable look, and takes the conversation out of a body and depresses him. Not so with a Bermuda house. There is something exhilarating, even hilarious, about its vivid whiteness when the sun plays upon it. If it be of picturesque shape and graceful contour—and many of the Bermudian dwellings are—it will so fascinate you that you will keep your eyes on it until they ache. One of those clean-cut, fanciful chimneys—too pure and white for this world—with one side glowing in the sun and the other touched with a soft shadow, is an object that will charm one's gaze by the hour. I know of no other country that has chimneys worthy to be gazed at and gloated over. One of those snowy houses, half concealed and half glimpsed through green foliage, is a pretty thing to see; and if it takes one by surprise and suddenly, as he turns a sharp corner of a country road, it will wring an exclamation from him, sure.

Wherever you go, in town or country, you find those snowy houses, and always with masses of bright-colored flowers about them, but with no vines climbing their walls; vines cannot take hold of the smooth, hard whitewash. Wherever you go, in the town or along the country roads, among little potato farms and patches or expensive country-seats, these stainless white dwellings, gleaming out from flowers and foliage, meet you at every turn. The least little bit of a cottage is as white and blemishless as the stateliest mansion. Nowhere is there dirt or stench, puddle or hog-wallow, neglect, disorder, or lack of trimness and neatness. The roads, the streets, the dwellings, the people, the clothes—this neatness extends to everything that falls under the eye. It is the tidiest country in the world. And very much the tidiest, too.

Considering these things, the question came up, Where do the poor live? No answer was arrived at. Therefore, we agreed to leave this conundrum for future statesmen to wrangle over.

What a bright and startling spectacle one of those blazing white country palaces, with its brown-tinted window-caps and ledges, and green shutters, and its wealth of caressing flowers and foliage, would be in black London! And what a gleaming surprise it would be in nearly any American city one could mention, too!

Bermuda roads are made by cutting down a few inches into the solid white coral—or a good many feet, where a hill intrudes itself—and smoothing off the surface of the road-bed. It is a simple and easy process. The grain of the coral is coarse and porous; the road-bed has the look of being made of coarse white sugar. Its excessive cleanness and whiteness are a trouble in one way: the sun is reflected into your eyes with such energy as you walk along that you want to sneeze all the time. Old Captain Tom Bowling found another difficulty. He joined us in our walk, but kept wandering unrestfully to the roadside. Finally he explained. Said he, "Well, I chew, you know, and the road's so plaguy clean."

We walked several miles that afternoon in the bewildering glare of the sun, the white roads, and the white buildings. Our eyes got to paining us a good deal. By and by a soothing, blessed twilight spread its cool balm around. We looked up in pleased surprise and saw that it proceeded from an intensely black negro who was going by. We answered his military salute in the grateful gloom of his near presence, and then passed on into the pitiless white glare again.

The colored women whom we met usually bowed and spoke; so did the children. The colored men commonly gave the military salute. They borrow this fashion from the soldiers, no doubt; England has kept a garrison here for generations. The younger men's custom of carrying small canes is also borrowed from the soldiers, I suppose, who always carry a cane, in Bermuda as everywhere else in Britain's broad dominions.

The country roads curve and wind hither and thither in the delight-fulest way, unfolding pretty surprises at every turn: billowy masses of oleander that seem to float out from behind distant projections like the pink cloud-banks of sunset; sudden plunges among cottages and gardens, life and activity, followed by as sudden plunges into the somber twilight and stillness of the woods; flitting visions of white fortresses and beacon towers pictured against the sky on remote hilltops; glimpses of shining green sea caught for a moment through opening headlands, then lost again; more woods and solitude; and by and by another turn lays bare, without warning, the full sweep of the inland ocean, enriched with its bars of soft color and graced with its wandering sails.

Take any road you please, you may depend upon it you will not stay in it half a mile. Your road is everything that a road ought to be: it is bordered with trees, and with strange plants and flowers; it is shady and pleasant, or sunny and still pleasant; it carries you by the prettiest and peacefulest and most homelike of homes, and through stretches of forest that lie in a deep hush sometimes, and sometimes are alive with the music of birds; it curves always, which is a continual promise, whereas straight roads reveal everything at a glance and kill interest. Your road is all this, and yet you will not stay in it half a mile, for the reason that little seductive, mysterious roads are always branching out from it on either hand, and as these curve sharply also and hide what is beyond, you cannot resist the temptation to desert your own chosen road and explore them. You are usually paid for your trouble; consequently, your walk inland always turns out to be one of the most crooked, involved, purposeless, and interesting experiences a body can imagine. There is enough of variety. Sometimes you are in the level open, with marshes thick grown with flag-lances that are ten feet high on the one hand, and potato and onion orchards on the other; next, you are on a hilltop, with the ocean and the islands spread around you; presently the road winds through a deep cut, shut in by perpendicular walls thirty or forty feet high, marked with the oddest and abruptest stratum lines, suggestive of sudden and eccentric old upheavals, and garnished with here and there a clinging adventurous flower, and here and there a dangling vine; and by and by your way is along the sea edge, and you may look down a fathom or two through the transparent water and watch the diamond-like flash and play of the light upon the rocks and sands on the bottom until you are tired of it—if you are so constituted as to be able to get tired of it.

You may march the country roads in maiden meditation, fancy free, by field and farm, for no dog will plunge out at you from unsuspected gate, with breath-taking surprise of ferocious bark, notwithstanding it is a Christian land and a civilized. We saw upward of a million cats in Bermuda, but the people are very abstemious in the matter of dogs. Two or three nights we prowled the country far and wide, and never once were accosted by a dog. It is a great privilege to visit such a land. The cats were no offense when properly distributed, but when piled they obstructed travel.

As we entered the edge of the town that Sunday afternoon, we stopped at a cottage to get a drink of water. The proprietor, a middle-aged man with a good face, asked us to sit down and rest. His dame brought chairs, and we grouped ourselves in the shade of the trees by the door. Mr. Smith—that was not his name, but it will answer—questioned us about ourselves and our country, and we answered him truthfully, as a general thing, and questioned him in return. It was all very simple and pleasant and sociable. Rural, too; for there was a pig and a small donkey and a hen anchored out, close at hand, by cords to their legs, on a spot that purported to be grassy. Presently, a woman passed along, and although she coldly said nothing she changed the drift of our talk. Said Smith:

"She didn't look this way, you noticed? Well, she is our next neighbor on one side, and there's another family that's our next neighbors on the other side; but there's a general coolness all around now, and we don't speak. Yet these three families, one generation and another, have lived here side by side and been as friendly as weavers for a hundred and fifty years, till about a year ago."

"Why, what calamity could have been powerful enough to break up so old a friendship?"

"Well, it was too bad, but it couldn't be helped. It happened like this: About a year or more ago, the rats got to pestering my place a good deal, and I set up a steel trap in my back yard. Both of these neighbors run considerable to cats, and so I warned them about the trap, because their cats were pretty sociable around here nights, and they might get into trouble without my intending it. Well, they shut up their cats for a while, but you know how it is with people; they got careless, and sure enough one night the trap took Mrs. Jones's principal tomcat into camp and finished him up. In the morning Mrs. Jones comes here with the corpse in her arms, and cries and takes on the same as if it was a child. It was a cat by the name of Yelverton—Hector G. Yelverton—a troublesome old rip, with no more principle than an Injun, though you couldn't make *her* believe it. I said all a man could to comfort her, but no, nothing would do but I must pay for him. Finally, I said I warn't investing in cats now as much as I was, and with that she walked off in a huff, carrying the remains with her. That closed our intercourse with the Joneses. Mrs. Jones joined another church and took her tribe with her. She said she would not hold fellowship with assassins. Well, by and by comes Mrs. Brown's turn—she that went by here a minute ago. She had a disgraceful old yellow cat that she thought as much of as if he was twins, and one night he tried that trap on his neck, and it fitted him so, and was so sort of satisfactory, that he laid down and curled up and stayed with it. Such was the end of Sir John Baldwin."

"Was that the name of the cat?"

"The same. There's cats around here with names that would surprise you. Maria" (to his wife), "what was that cat's name that eat a keg of ratsbane by mistake over at Hooper's, and started home and got struck by lightning and took the blind staggers and fell in the well and was 'most drowned before they could fish him out?"

"That was that colored Deacon Jackson's cat. I only remember the last end of its name, which was Hold-The-Fort-For-I-Am-Coming Jackson."

"Sho! that ain't the one. That's the one that eat up an entire box of Seidlitz powders, and then hadn't any more judgment than to go and take a drink. He was considered to be a great loss, but I never could see it. Well, no matter about the names. Mrs. Brown wanted to be reasonable, but Mrs. Jones wouldn't let her. She put her up to going to law for damages. So to law she went, and had the face to claim seven shillings and sixpence. It made a great stir. All the neighbors went to court. Everybody took sides. It got hotter and hotter, and broke up all the friendships for three hundred yards around—friendships that had lasted for generations and generations.

"Well, I proved by eleven witnesses that the cat was of a low character and very ornery, and warn't worth a canceled postage-stamp, anyway, taking the average of cats here; but I lost the case. What could I expect? The system is all wrong here, and is bound to make revolution and bloodshed some day. You see, they give the magistrate a poor little starvation salary, and then turn him loose on the public to gouge for fees and costs to live on. What is the natural result? Why, he never looks into the justice of a case—never once. All he looks at is which client has got the money. So this one piled the fees and costs and everything on to me. I could pay specie, don't you see? and he knew mighty well that if he put the verdict on to Mrs. Brown, where it belonged, he'd have to take his swag in currency."

"Currency? Why, has Bermuda a currency?"

"Yes—onions. And they were forty per cent. discount, too, then, because the season had been over as much as three months. So I lost my case. I had to pay for that cat. But the general trouble the case made was the worst thing about it. Broke up so much good feeling. The neighbors don't speak to each other now. Mrs. Brown had named a child after me. But she changed its name right away. She is a Baptist. Well, in the course of baptizing it over again it got drowned. I was hoping we might get to be friendly again some time or other, but of course this drowning the child knocked that all out of the question. It would have saved a world of heartbreak and ill blood if she had named it dry."

I knew by the sigh that this was honest. All this trouble and all this destruction of confidence in the purity of the bench on account of a seven-shilling lawsuit about a cat! Somehow, it seemed to "size" the country.

At this point we observed that an English flag had just been placed at half-mast on a building a hundred yards away. I and my friends were busy in an instant trying to imagine whose death, among the island dignitaries, could command such a mark of respect at this. Then a shudder shook them and me at the same moment, and I knew that we had jumped to one and the same conclusion: "The governor has gone to England; it is for the British admiral!"

At this moment Mr. Smith noticed the flag. He said with emotion: "That's on a boarding-house. I judge there's a boarder dead."

A dozen other flags within view went to half-mast.

"It's a boarder, sure," said Smith.

"But would they half-mast the flags here for a boarder, Mr. Smith?"

"Why, certainly they would, if he was *dead*."

That seemed to size the country again.

IV

The early twilight of a Sunday evening in Hamilton, Bermuda, is an alluring time. There is just enough of whispering breeze, fragrance of flowers, and sense of repose to raise one's thoughts heavenward; and just enough amateur piano music to keep him reminded of the other place. There are many venerable pianos in Hamilton, and they all play at twilight. Age enlarges and enriches the powers of some musical instruments—notably those of the violin—but it seems to set a piano's teeth on edge. Most of the music in vogue there is the same that those pianos prattled in their innocent infancy; and there is something very pathetic about it when they go over it now, in their asthmatic second childhood, dropping a note here and there, where a tooth is gone.

We attended evening service at the stately Episcopal church on the hill, where were five or six hundred people, half of them white and the other half black, according to the usual Bermudian proportions; and all well dressed—a thing which is also usual in Bermuda and to be confidently expected. There was good music, which we heard, and doubtless a good sermon, but there was a wonderful deal of coughing, and so only the high parts of the argument carried over it. As we came out, after service, I overheard one young girl say to another:

"Why, you don't mean to say you pay duty on gloves and laces! I only pay postage; have them done up and sent in the Boston *Advertiser*."

There are those that believe that the most difficult thing to create is a woman who can comprehend that it is wrong to smuggle; and that an impossible thing to create is a woman who will not smuggle, whether or no, when she gets a chance. But these may be errors.

We went wandering off toward the country, and were soon far down in the lonely black depths of a road that was roofed over with the dense foliage of a double rank of great cedars. There was no sound of any kind there; it was perfectly still. And it was so dark that one could detect nothing but somber outlines. We strode farther and farther down this tunnel, cheering the way with chat.

Presently the chat took this shape: "How insensibly the character of the people and of a government makes its impress upon a stranger, and gives him a sense of security or of insecurity without his taking deliberate thought upon the matter or asking anybody a question! We have been in this land half a day; we have seen none but honest faces;

we have noted the British flag flying, which means efficient government and good order; so without inquiry we plunge unarmed and with perfect confidence into this dismal place, which in almost any other country would swarm with thugs and garroters—"

'Sh! What was that? Stealthy footsteps! Low voices! We gasp, we close up together, and wait. A vague shape glides out of the dusk and confronts us. A voice speaks—demands money!

"A shilling, gentlemen, if you please, to help build the new Methodist church."

Blessed sound! Holy sound! We contribute with thankful avidity to the new Methodist church, and are happy to think how lucky it was that those little colored Sunday-school scholars did not seize upon everything we had with violence, before we recovered from our momentary helpless condition. By the light of cigars we write down the names of weightier philanthropists than ourselves on the contribution cards, and then pass on into the farther darkness, saying, What sort of a government do they call this, where they allow little black pious children, with contribution cards, to plunge out upon peaceable strangers in the dark and scare them to death?

We prowled on several hours, sometimes by the seaside, sometimes inland, and finally managed to get lost, which is a feat that requires talent in Bermuda. I had on new shoes. They were No. 7's when I started, but were not more than 5's now, and still diminishing. I walked two hours in those shoes after that, before we reached home. Doubtless I could have the reader's sympathy for the asking. Many people have never had the headache or the toothache, and I am one of those myself; but everybody has worn tight shoes for two or three hours, and known the luxury of taking them off in a retired place and seeing his feet swell up and obscure the firmament. Once when I was a callow, bashful cub, I took a plain, unsentimental country girl to a comedy one night. I had known her a day; she seemed divine; I wore my new boots. At the end of the first half-hour she said, "Why do you fidget so with your feet?" I said, "Did I?" Then I put my attention there and kept still. At the end of another half-hour she said, "Why do you say, 'Yes, oh yes!' and 'Ha, ha, oh, certainly! very true!' to everything I say, when half the time those are entirely irrelevant answers?" I blushed, and explained that I had been a little absent-minded. At the end of another half-hour she said, "Please, why do you grin so steadfastly at vacancy, and yet look so sad?" I explained that I always did that when I was reflecting. An hour passed, and then she turned and contemplated me with her earnest eyes and said, "Why do you cry all the time?" I explained that very funny comedies always made me cry. At last human nature surrendered, and I secretly slipped my boots off. This was a mistake. I was not able to get them on any more. It was a rainy night; there were no omnibuses going our way; and as I walked home, burning up with shame, with the girl on one arm and my boots under the other, I was an object worthy of some compassion—especially in those moments of martydom when I had to pass through the glare that fell upon the pavement from streetlamps. Finally, this child of the forest said, "Where are your boots?" and being taken unprepared, I put a fitting finish to the follies of the evening with the stupid remark, "The higher classes do not wear them to the theater."

The Reverend had been an army chaplain during the war, and while we were hunting for a road that would lead to Hamilton he told a story about two dying soldiers which interested me in spite of my feet. He said that in the Potomac hospitals rough pine coffins were furnished by government, but that it was not always possible to keep up with the demand; so, when a man died, if there was no coffin at hand he was buried without one. One night, late, two soldiers lay dying in a ward. A man came in with a coffin on his shoulder, and stood trying to make up his mind which of these two poor fellows would be likely to need it first. Both of them begged for it with their fading eyes—they were past talking. Then one of them protruded a wasted hand from his blankets and made a feeble beckoning sign with the fingers, to signify, "Be a good fellow; put it under my bed, please." The man did it, and left. The lucky soldier painfully turned himself in his bed until he faced the other warrior, raised himself partly on his elbow, and began to work up a mysterious expression of some kind in his face. Gradually, irksomely, but surely and steadily, it developed, and at last it took definite form as a pretty successful *wink*. The sufferer fell back exhausted with his labor, but bathed in glory. Now entered a personal friend of No. 2, the despoiled soldier. No. 2 pleaded with him with eloquent eyes, till presently he understood, and removed the coffin from under No. 1's bed and put it under No. 2's. No. 2 indicated his joy, and made some more signs; the friend understood again, and put his arm under No. 2's shoulders and lifted him partly up. Then the dying hero turned the dim exultation of his eye upon No. 1, and began a slow and labored work with his hands; gradually he lifted one hand up toward his face; it grew weak and dropped back again; once more he made the effort, but failed again. He took a rest; he gathered all the remnant of his strength, and this time he slowly but surely carried his thumb to the side of his nose, spread the gaunt fingers wide in triumph, and dropped back dead. That picture sticks by me yet. The "situation" is unique.

The next morning, at what seemed a very early hour, the little white table-waiter appeared suddenly in my room and shot a single word out of himself: "Breakfast!"

This was a remarkable boy in many ways. He was about eleven years old; he had alert, intent black eyes; he was quick of movement; there was no hesitation, no uncertainty about him anywhere; there was a military decision in his lip, his manner, his speech, that was an astonishing thing to see in a little chap like him; he wasted no words; his answers always came so quick and brief that they seemed to be part of the question that had been asked instead of a reply to it. When he stood at table with his fly-brush, rigid, erect, his face set in a cast-iron gravity, he was a statue till he detected a dawning want in somebody's eye; then he pounced down, supplied it, and was instantly a statue again. When he was sent to the kitchen for anything, he marched upright till he got to the door; he turned hand-springs the rest of the way.

"Breakfast!"

I thought I would make one more effort to get some conversation out of this being.

"Have you called the Reverend, or are—"

"Yes s'r!"

"Is it early, or is—"

"Eight-five."

"Do you have to do all the 'chores,' or is there somebody to give you a—"

"Colored girl."

"Is there only one parish in this island, or are there—"

"Eight!"

"Is the big church on the hill a parish church, or is it—"

"Chapel-of-easel"

"Is taxation here classified into poll, parish, town, and—"

"Don't know!"

Before I could cudgel another question out of my head, he was below, hand-springing across the back yard. He had slid down the balusters, head first. I gave up trying to provoke a discussion with him. The essential element of discussion had been left out of him; his answers were so final and exact that they did not leave a doubt to hang conversation on. I suspect that there is the making of a mighty man or a mighty rascal in this boy—according to circumstances—but they are going to apprentice him to a carpenter. It is the way the world uses its opportunities.

During this day and the next we took carriage drives about the island and over to the town of St. George's, fifteen or twenty miles away. Such hard, excellent roads to drive over are not to be found elsewhere out of Europe. An intelligent young colored man drove us, and acted as guide-book. In the edge of the town we saw five or six mountain-cabbage palms (atrocious name!) standing in a straight row, and equidistant from each other. These were not the largest or the tallest trees I have ever seen, but they were the stateliest, the most majestic. That row of them must be the nearest that nature has ever come to counterfeiting a colonnade. These trees are all the same height, say sixty feet; the trunks as gray as granite, with a very gradual and perfect taper; without sign of branch or knot or flaw; the surface not looking like bark, but like granite that has been dressed and not polished. Thus all the way up the diminishing shaft for fifty feet; then it begins to take the appearance of being closely wrapped, spool-fashion, with gray cord, or of having been turned in a lathe. Above this point there is an outward swell, and thence upward for six feet or more the cylinder is a bright, fresh green, and is formed of wrappings like those of an ear of green Indian corn. Then comes the great, spraying palm plume, also green. Other palm trees always lean out of the perpendicular, or have a curve in them. But the plumb-line could not detect a deflection in any individual of this stately row; they stand as straight as the colonnade of Baalbec; they have its great height, they have its gracefulness, they have its dignity; in moonlight or twilight, and shorn of their plumes, they would duplicate it.

The birds we came across in the country were singularly tame; even that wild creature, the quail, would pick around in the grass at ease while we inspected it and talked about it at leisure. A small bird of the canary species had to be stirred up with the butt-end of the whip before it would move, and then it moved only a couple of feet. It is said that even the suspicious flea is tame and sociable in Bermuda, and will allow himself to be caught and caressed without misgivings. This should be taken with allowance, for doubtless there is more or less brag about it. In San Francisco they used to claim that their native flea could kick a child over, as if it were a merit in a flea to be able to do that; as if the knowledge of it trumpeted abroad ought to entice immigration. Such a thing in nine cases out of ten would be almost sure to deter a thinking man from coming.

We saw no bugs or reptiles to speak of, and so I was thinking of say-

ing in print, in a general way, that there were none at all; but one night
after I had gone to bed, the Reverend came into my room carrying
something, and asked, "Is this your boot?" I said it was, and he said he
had met a spider going off with it. Next morning he stated that just at
dawn the same spider raised his window and was coming in to get a
shirt, but saw him and fled.

I inquired, "Did he get the shirt?"

"No."

"How did you know it was a shirt he was after?"

"I could see it in his eye."

We inquired around, but could hear of no Bermudian spider capable of doing these things. Citizens said that their largest spiders could
not more than spread their legs over an ordinary saucer, and that
they had always been considered honest. Here was testimony of a clergyman against the testimony of mere worldlings—interested ones, too.
On the whole, I judged it best to lock up my things.

Here and there on the country roads we found lemon, papaw,
orange, lime, and fig trees; also several sorts of palms, among them the
cocoa, the date, and the palmetto. We saw some bamboos forty feet
high, with stems as thick as a man's arm. Jungles of the mangrove tree
stood up out of swamps, propped on their interlacing roots as upon a
tangle of stilts. In drier places the noble tamarind sent down its grateful cloud of shade. Here and there the blossomy tamarisk adorned the
roadside. There was a curious gnarled and twisted black tree, without
a single leaf on it. It might have passed itself off for a dead apple tree
but for the fact that it had a star-like, red-hot flower sprinkled sparsely
over its person. It had the scattery red glow that a constellation might
have when glimpsed through smoked glass. It is possible that our constellations have been so constructed as to be invisible through smoked
glass; if this is so it is a great mistake.

We saw a tree that bears grapes, and just as calmly and unostenta-
tiously as a vine would do it. We saw an India-rubber tree, but out of
season, possibly, so there were no shoes on it, nor suspenders, nor
anything that a person would properly expect to find there. This gave
it an impressively fraudulent look. There was exactly one mahogany
tree on the island. I know this to be reliable, because I saw a man who
said he had counted it many a time and could not be mistaken. He was
a man with a harelip and a pure heart, and everybody said he was as
true as steel. Such men are all too few.

One's eye caught near and far the pink cloud of the oleander and
the red blaze of the pomegranate blossom. In one piece of wild wood

the morning-glory vines had wrapped the trees to their very tops, and decorated them all over with couples and clusters of great bluebells—a fine and striking spectacle, at a little distance. But the dull cedar is everywhere, and is the prevailing foliage. One does not appreciate how dull it is until the varnished, bright green attire of the infrequent lemon tree pleasantly intrudes its contrast. In one thing Bermuda is eminently tropical—was in May, at least—the unbrilliant, slightly faded, unrejoicing look of the landscape. For forests arrayed in a blemishless magnificence of glowing green foliage that seems to exult in its own existence and can move the beholder to an enthusiasm that will make him either shout or cry, one must go to countries that have malignant winters.

We saw scores of colored farmers digging their crops of potatoes and onions, their wives and children helping—entirely contented and comfortable, if looks go for anything. We never met a man, or woman, or child anywhere in this sunny island who seemed to be unprosperous, or discontented, or sorry about anything. This sort of monotony became very tiresome presently, and even something worse. The spectacle of an entire nation groveling in contentment is an infuriating thing. We felt the lack of something in this community—a vague, an indefinable, an elusive something, and yet a lack. But after considerable thought we made out what it was—tramps. Let them go there, right now, in a body. It is utterly virgin soil. Passage is cheap. Every true patriot in America will help buy tickets. Whole armies of these excellent beings can be spared from our midst and our polls; they will find a delicious climate and a green, kind-hearted people. There are potatoes and onions for all, and a generous welcome for the first batch that arrives, and elegant graves for the second.

It was the Early Rose potato the people were digging. Later in the year they have another crop, which they call the Garnet. We buy their potatoes (retail) at fifteen dollars a barrel; and those colored farmers buy ours for a song, and live on them. Havana might exchange cigars with Connecticut in the same advantageous way, if she thought of it.

We passed a roadside grocery with a sign up, "Potatoes Wanted." An ignorant stranger, doubtless. He could not have gone thirty steps from his place without finding plenty of them.

In several fields the arrowroot crop was already sprouting. Bermuda used to make a vast annual profit out of this staple before firearms came into such general use.

The island is not large. Somewhere in the interior a man ahead of us had a very slow horse. I suggested that we had better go by him;

but the driver said the man had but a little way to go. I waited to see, wondering how he could know. Presently the man did turn down another road. I asked, "How did you know he would?"

"Because I knew the man, and where he lived."

I asked him, satirically, if he knew everybody in the island; he answered, very simply, that he did. This gives a body's mind a good substantial grip on the dimensions of the place.

At the principal hotel at St. George's, a young girl, with a sweet, serious face, said we could not be furnished with dinner, because we had not been expected, and no preparation had been made. Yet it was still an hour before dinner-time. We argued, she yielded not; we supplicated, she was serene. The hotel had not been expecting an inundation of two people, and so it seemed that we should have to go home dinnerless. I said we were not very hungry; a fish would do. My little maid answered, it was not the market-day for fish. Things began to look serious; but presently the boarder who sustained the hotel came in, and when the case was laid before him he was cheerfully willing to divide. So we had much pleasant chat at table about St. George's chief industry, the repairing of damaged ships; and in between we had a soup that had something in it that seemed to taste like the hereafter, but it proved to be only pepper of a particularly vivacious kind. And we had an iron-clad chicken that was deliciously cooked, but not in the right way. Baking was not the thing to convince this sort. He ought to have been put through a quartz-mill until the "tuck" was taken out of him, and then boiled till we came again. We got a good deal of sport out of him, but not enough sustenance to leave the victory on our side. No matter; we had potatoes and a pie and a sociable good time. Then a ramble through the town, which is a quaint one, with interesting, crooked streets, and narrow, crooked lanes, with here and there a grain of dust. Here, as in Hamilton, the dwellings had Venetian blinds of a very sensible pattern. They were not double shutters, hinged at the sides, but a single broad shutter, hinged at the top; you push it outward, from the bottom, and fasten it at any angle required by the sun or desired by yourself.

All about the island one sees great white scars on the hill-slopes. These are dished spaces where the soil has been scraped off and the coral exposed and glazed with hard whitewash. Some of these are a quarter-acre in size. They catch and carry the rainfall to reservoirs; for the wells are few and poor, and there are no natural springs and no brooks.

They say that the Bermuda climate is mild and equable, with never

any snow or ice, and that one may be very comfortable in spring clothing the year round, there. We had delightful and decided summer
weather in May, with a flaming sun that permitted the thinnest of raiment, and yet there was a constant breeze; consequently we were
never discomforted by heat. At four or five in the afternoon the mercury began to go down, and then it became necessary to change to
thick garments. I went to St. George's in the morning clothed in the
thinnest of linen, and reached home at five in the afternoon with two
overcoats on. The nights are said to be always cool and bracing. We
had mosquito-nets, and the Reverend said the mosquitoes persecuted
him a good deal. I often heard him slapping and banging at these imaginary creatures which as much zeal as if they had been real. There
are no mosquitoes in the Bermudas in May.

The poet Thomas Moore spent several months in Bermuda more
than seventy years ago. He was sent out to be registrar of the admiralty.
I am not quite clear as to the function of a registrar of the admiralty
of Bermuda, but I think it is his duty to keep a record of all the admirals born there. I will inquire into this. There was not much doing in
admirals, and Moore got tired and went away. A reverently preserved
souvenir of him is still one of the treasures of the islands. I gathered
the idea, vaguely, that it was a jug, but was persistently thwarted in
the twenty-two efforts I made to visit it. However, it was no matter,
for I found out afterward that it was only a chair.

There are several "sights" in the Bermudas, of course, but they are
easily avoided. This is a great advantage—one cannot have it in Europe. Bermuda is the right country for a jaded man to "loaf" in. There
are no harassments; the deep peace and quiet of the country sink into
one's body and bones and give his conscience a rest, and chloroform
the legion of invisible small devils that are always trying to whitewash
his hair. A good many Americans go there about the first of March and
remain until the early spring weeks have finished their villainies at
home.

The Bermudians are hoping soon to have telegraphic communication
with the world. But even after they shall have acquired this curse it
will still be a good country to go to for a vacation, for there are charming little islets scattered about the inclosed sea where one could live
secure from interruption. The telegraph-boy would have to come in a
boat, and one could easily kill him while he was making his landing.

We had spent four days in Bermuda—three bright ones out of doors
and one rainy one in the house, we being disappointed about getting

a yacht for a sail; and now our furlough was ended, and we entered into the ship again and sailed homeward.

We made the run home to New York quarantine in three days and five hours, and could have gone right along up to the city if we had had a health permit. But health permits are not granted after seven in the evening, partly because a ship cannot be inspected and overhauled with exhaustive thoroughness except in daylight, and partly because health-officers are liable to catch cold if they expose themselves to the night air. Still, you can *buy* a permit after hours for five dollars extra, and the officer will do the inspecting next week. Our ship and passengers lay under expense and in humiliating captivity all night, under the very nose of the little official reptile who is supposed to protect New York from pestilence by his vigilant "inspections." This imposing rigor gave everybody a solemn and awful idea of the beneficent watchfulness of our government, and there were some who wondered if anything finer could be found in other countries.

In the morning we were all a-tiptoe to witness the intricate ceremony of inspecting the ship. But it was a disappointing thing. The health-officer's tug ranged alongside for a moment, our purser handed the lawful three-dollar permit fee to the health-officer's bootblack, who passed us a folded paper in a forked stick, and away we went. The entire "inspection" did not occupy thirteen seconds.

The health-officer's place is worth a hundred thousand dollars a year to him. His system of inspection is perfect, and therefore cannot be improved on; but it seems to me that his system of collecting his fees might be amended. For a great ship to lie idle all night is a most costly loss of time; for her passengers to have to do the same thing works to them the same damage, with the addition of an amount of exasperation and bitterness of soul that the spectacle of that health-officer's ashes on a shovel could hardly sweeten. Now why would it not be better and simpler to let the ships pass in unmolested, and the fees and permits be exchanged once a year by post?

1877-78

Speech on the Weather

*At the New England Society's Seventy-first
Annual Dinner, New York City*

The next toast was: "The Oldest Inhabitant—The Weather of New England."

> Who can lose it and forget it?
> Who can have it and regret it?
>
> Be interposer 'twixt us Twain.
> *Merchant of Venice*

To this Samuel L. Clemens (Mark Twain) replied as follows:—

I reverently believe that the Maker who made us all makes everything in New England but the weather. I don't know who makes that, but I think it must be raw apprentices in the weather-clerk's factory who experiment and learn how, in New England, for board and clothes, and then are promoted to make weather for countries that require a good article, and will take their custom elsewhere if they don't get it. There is a sumptuous variety about the New England weather that compels the stranger's admiration—and regret. The weather is always doing something there; always attending strictly to business; always getting up new designs and trying them on the people to see how they will go. But it gets through more business in spring than in any other season. In the spring I have counted one hundred and thirty-six different kinds of weather inside of four-and-twenty hours. It was I that made the fame and fortune of that man that had that marvelous collection of weather on exhibition at the Centennial, that so astounded the foreigners. He was going to travel all over the world and get specimens from all the climes. I said, "Don't you do it; you come to New England on a favorable spring day." I told him what we could do in the way of style, variety, and quantity. Well, he came and he made his collection in four days. As to variety, why, he confessed that he got hundreds of kinds of weather that he had never heard of before. And as to quantity—well, after he had picked out and discarded all that was blemished in any way, he not only had weather enough, but weather to spare; weather to hire out; weather to sell; to deposit; weather to invest; weather to give to the poor. The people of New England are by nature patient and forbearing, but there are some things which they will not stand. Every year they kill a lot of poets for writing about "Beautiful Spring." These are generally casual visitors, who bring their notions of spring from somewhere else, and cannot, of course, know how the natives feel about spring. And so the first thing they know the opportunity to inquire how they feel has permanently gone by. Old Probabilities has a mighty reputation for accurate prophecy, and thoroughly well deserves it. You take up the paper and observe how crisply and confidently he checks off what to-day's weather is going to be on the Pacific, down South, in the Middle States, in the Wisconsin region. See him sail along in the joy and pride of his power till he gets to New England, and then see his tail drop. *He* doesn't know what the weather is going to be in New England. Well, he mulls over it, and by and by he gets out something about like this: Probable northeast to southwest winds, varying to the southward and westward and eastward, and points between, high and low barometer swapping around from place to place; probable areas of rain, snow, hail, and drought, succeeded or preceded by earthquakes, with thunder and lightning. Then he jots down this postscript from his wandering mind, to cover accidents: "But it is possible that the program may be wholly changed in the mean time." Yes, one of the brightest gems in the New England weather is the dazzling uncertainty of it. There is only one thing certain about it: you are certain there is going to be plenty of it—a perfect grand review; but you never can tell which end of the procession is going to move first. You fix up for the drought; you leave your umbrella in the house and sally out, and two to one you get drowned. You make up your mind that the earthquake is due; you stand from under, and take hold of something to steady yourself, and the first thing you know you get struck by lightning. These are great disappointments; but they can't be helped. The lightning there is peculiar; it is so convincing, that when it strikes a thing it doesn't leave enough of that thing behind for you to tell whether— Well, you'd think it was something valuable, and a Congressman had been there. And the thunder. When the thunder begins to merely tune up and scrape and saw, and key up the instruments for the performance, strangers say, "Why, what awful thunder you have here!" But when the baton is raised and the real concert begins, you'll find that stranger down in the cellar with his head in the ash-barrel. Now as to the *size* of the weather in New England—lengthways, I mean. It is utterly disproportioned to the size of that little country. Half the time, when it is packed as full as it can stick, you will see that New England weather sticking out beyond the edges and projecting around hundreds and hundreds of miles over the neighboring states. She can't hold a tenth part of her weather. You can see cracks all about where she has strained herself trying to do it. I could speak volumes about the inhuman perversity of the New England weather, but I will give but a single specimen. I like to hear rain on a tin roof. So I covered part of my roof with tin, with an eye to that luxury. Well, sir, do you think it ever rains on that tin? No, sir; skips it every time. Mind, in this speech I have been trying merely to do honor to the New England weather—no language could do it justice. But, after all, there is at least one or two things about that weather (or, if you please, effects produced by it) which we residents would not like to part with. If we hadn't our bewitching autumn foliage, we should still have to credit the weather with one feature which compensates for all its bullying vagaries—the ice-storm: when a leafless tree is clothed with ice from the bottom to the top—ice that is as bright and clear as crystal; when every bough and twig is strung with ice-beads, frozen dewdrops, and the whole tree sparkles cold and white, like the Shah of Persia's diamond plume. Then the wind waves the branches and the sun comes out and turns all those myriads of beads and drops to prisms that glow and burn and flash with all manner of colored fires, which change and change again with inconceivable rapidity from blue to red, from red to green, and green to gold—the tree becomes a spraying fountain, a very explosion of dazzling jewels; and it stands there the acme, the climax, the supremest possibility in art or nature, of bewildering, intoxicating, intolerable magnificence. One cannot make the words too strong.

1877

The Whittier Birthday Speech

MR. CHAIRMAN,—This is an occasion peculiarly meet for the digging up of pleasant reminiscences concerning literary folk, therefore I will drop lightly into history myself. Standing here on the shore of the At-

MARK TWAIN

lantic, and contemplating certain of its largest literary billows, I am reminded of a thing which happened to me thirteen years ago, when I had just succeeded in stirring up a little Nevadian literary puddle myself, whose spume-flakes were beginning to blow thinly California-ward. I started an inspection tramp through the southern mines of California. I was callow and conceited, and I resolved to try the virtue of my *nom de guerre*. I very soon had an opportunity. I knocked at a miner's lonely log cabin in the foothills of the Sierras just at nightfall. It was snowing at the time. A jaded, melancholy man of fifty, bare-footed, opened the door to me. When he heard my *nom de guerre* he looked more dejected than before. He let me in—pretty reluctantly, I thought—and after the customary bacon and beans, black coffee and hot whisky, I took a pipe. This sorrowful man had not said three words up to this time. Now he spoke up and said, in the voice of one who is secretly suffering, "You're the fourth—I'm going to move." "The fourth what?" said I. "The fourth littery man that has been here in twenty-four hours—I'm going to move." "You don't tell me!" said I; "who were the others?" "Mr. Longfellow, Mr. Emerson, and Mr. Oliver Wendell Holmes—consound the lot!"

You can easily believe I was interested. I supplicated—three hot whiskies did the rest—and finally the melancholy miner began. Said he:

"They came here just at dark yesterday evening, and I let them in, of course. Said they were going to the Yosemite. They were a rough lot, but that's nothing; everybody looks rough that travels afoot. Mr. Emerson was a seedy little bit of a chap, red-headed. Mr. Holmes was as fat as a balloon; he weighed as much as three hundred, and had double chins all the way down to his stomach. Mr. Longfellow was built like a prize-fighter. His head was cropped and bristly, like as if he had a wig made of hair-brushes. His nose lay straight down in his face, like a finger with the end joint tilted up. They had been drinking, I could see that. And what queer talk they used! Mr. Holmes inspected this cabin, then he took me by the buttonhole and says he:

"'Through the deep caves of thought
I hear a voice that sings,
"Build thee more stately mansions,
O my soul!"'

"Says I, 'I can't afford it, Mr. Holmes, and moreover I don't want to.' Blamed if I liked it pretty well, either, coming from a stranger that way. However, I started to get out my bacon and beans when Mr. Emerson came and looked on awhile, and then *he* takes me aside by the buttonhole and says:

> " 'Give me agates for my meat;
> Give me cantharids to eat;
> From air and ocean bring me foods,
> From all zones and altitudes.'

"Says I, 'Mr. Emerson, if you'll excuse me, this ain't no hotel.' You see, it sort of riled me—I warn't used to the ways of littery swells. But I went on a-sweating over my work, and next comes Mr. Longfellow and buttonholes me and interrupts me. Says he:

> " 'Honor be to Mudjekeewis!
> You shall hear how Pau-Puk-Keewis—'

"But I broke in, and says I, 'Beg your pardon, Mr. Longfellow, if you'll be so kind as to hold your yawp for about five minutes and let me get this grub ready, you'll do me proud.' Well, sir, after they'd filled up I set out the jug. Mr. Holmes looks at it and then he fires up all of a sudden and yells:

> " 'Flash out a stream of blood-red wine!
> For I would drink to other days.'

"By George, I was getting kind of worked up. I don't deny it, I was getting kind of worked up. I turns to Mr. Holmes and says I, 'Looky here, my fat friend, I'm a-running this shanty, and if the court knows herself you'll take whisky straight or you'll go dry.' Them's the very words I said to him. Now I don't want to sass such famous littery people, but you see they kind of forced me. There ain't nothing onreasonable 'bout me. I don't mind a passel of guests a-treadin' on my tail three or four times, but when it comes to *standing* on it it's different, 'and if the court knows herself,' I says, 'you'll take whisky straight or you'll go dry.' Well, between drinks they'd swell around the cabin and strike attitudes and spout; and pretty soon they got out a greasy old deck and went to playing euchre at ten cents a corner—on trust. I began to notice some pretty suspicious things. Mr. Emerson dealt, looked at his hand, shook his head, says—

> " 'I am the doubter and the doubt—'

and calmly bunched the hands and went to shuffling for a new lay-out. Says he:

> " 'They reckon ill who leave me out;
> They know not well the subtle ways I keep.
> I pass and deal *again!*'

Hang'd if he didn't go ahead and do it, too! Oh, he was a cool one!
Well, in about a minute things were running pretty tight, but all of a
sudden I see by Mr. Emerson's eye he judged he had 'em. He had already corralled two tricks and each of the others one. So now he kind
of lifts a little in his chair and says,

> " 'I tire of globes and aces!—
> Too long the game is played!'

and down he fetched a right bower. Mr. Longfellow smiles as sweet
as pie and says,

> " 'Thanks, thanks to thee, my worthy friend,
> For the lesson thou hast taught,'

and blamed if he didn't down with *another* right bower! Emerson claps
his hand on his bowie, Longfellow claps his on his revolver, and I
went under a bunk. There was going to be trouble; but that monstrous
Holmes rose up, wobbling his double chins, and says he, 'Order, gentlemen; the first man that draws I'll lay down on him and smother him!'
All quiet on the Potomac, you bet!

"They were pretty how-come-you-so by now, and they begun to
blow. Emerson says, 'The noblest thing I ever wrote was "Barbara
Frietchie."' Says Longfellow, 'It don't begin with my "Bigelow Papers."' Says Holmes, 'My "Thanatopsis" lays over 'em both.' They
mighty near ended in a fight. Then they wished they had some more
company, and Mr. Emerson pointed to me and says:

> " 'Is yonder squalid peasant all
> That this proud nursery could breed?'

He was a-whetting his bowie on his boot—so I let it pass. Well, sir, next
they took it into their heads that they would like some music; so
they made me stand up and sing, 'When Johnny Comes Marching
Home' till I dropped—at thirteen minutes past four this morning. That's
what I've been through, my friend. When I woke at seven they were
leaving, thank goodness, and Mr. Longfellow had my only boots on and
his'n under his arm. Says I, 'Hold on there, Evangeline, what are you
going to do with *them?*' He says, 'Going to make tracks with 'em, because—

> " 'Lives of great men all remind us
> We can make our lives sublime;
> And, departing, leave behind us
> Footprints on the sands of time.'

As I said, Mr. Twain, you are the fourth in twenty-four hours—and I'm going to move; I ain't suited to a littery atmosphere."

I said to the miner, "Why, my dear sir, *these* were not the gracious singers to whom we and the world pay loving reverence and homage; these were impostors."

The miner investigated me with a calm eye for a while; then said he, "Ah! imposters, were they? Are you?"

I did not pursue the subject, and since then I have not traveled on my *nom de guerre* enough to hurt. Such was the reminiscence I was moved to contribute, Mr. Chairman. In my enthusiasm I may have exaggerated the details a little, but you will easily forgive me that fault, since I believe it is the first time I have ever deflected from perpendicular fact on an occasion like this.

1877

About Magnanimous-Incident
Literature

All my life, from boyhood up, I have had the habit of reading a certain set of anecdotes, written in the quaint vein of The World's ingenious Fabulist, for the lesson they taught me and the pleasure they gave me. They lay always convenient to my hand, and whenever I thought meanly of my kind I turned to them, and they banished that sentiment; whenever I felt myself to be selfish, sordid, and ignoble I turned to them, and they told me what to do to win back my self-respect. Many times I wished that the charming anecdotes had not stopped with their happy climaxes, but had continued the pleasing history of the several benefactors and beneficiaries. This wish rose in my breast so persistently that at last I determined to satisfy it by seeking out the sequels of those anecdotes myself. So I set about it, and after great labor and tedious research accomplished my task. I will lay the result before you, giving you each anecdote in its turn, and following it with its sequel as I gathered it through my investigations.

THE GRATEFUL POODLE

One day a benevolent physician (who had read the books) having found a stray poodle suffering from a broken leg, conveyed the poor creature to his home, and after setting and bandaging the injured limb gave the little outcast its liberty again, and thought no more about the matter. But how great was his surprise, upon opening his door one morning, some days later, to find the grateful poodle patiently waiting there, and in its company another stray dog, one of whose legs, by some accident, had been broken. The kind physician at once relieved the distressed animal, nor did he forget to admire the inscrutable goodness and mercy of God, who had been willing to use so humble an instrument as the poor outcast poodle for the inculcating of, etc., etc., etc.

SEQUEL

The next morning the benevolent physician found the two dogs, beaming with gratitude, waiting at his door, and with them two other dogs—cripples. The cripples were speedily healed, and the four went their way, leaving the benevolent physician more overcome by pious wonder than ever. The day passed, the morning came. There at the door sat now the four reconstructed dogs, and with them four others requiring reconstruction. This day also passed, and another morning came; and now sixteen dogs, eight of them newly crippled, occupied the sidewalk, and the people were going around. By noon the broken legs were all set, but the pious wonder in the good physician's breast was beginning to get mixed with involuntary profanity. The sun rose once more, and exhibited thirty-two dogs, sixteen of them with broken legs, occupying the sidewalk and half of the street; the human spectators took up the rest of the room. The cries of the wounded, the songs of the healed brutes, and the comments of the onlooking citizens made great and inspiring cheer, but traffic was interrupted in that street. The good physician hired a couple of assistant surgeons and got through his benevolent work before dark, first taking the precaution to cancel his church-membership, so that he might express himself with the latitude which the case required.

But some things have their limits. When once more the morning dawned, and the good physician looked out upon a massed and far-reaching multitude of clamorous and beseeching dogs, he said, "I might

as well acknowledge it, I have been fooled by the books; they only tell
the pretty part of the story, and then stop. Fetch me the shotgun; this
thing has gone along far enough."

He issued forth with his weapon, and chanced to step upon the
tail of the original poodle, who promptly bit him in the leg. Now the
great and good work which this poodle had been engaged in had engendered in him such a mighty and augmenting enthusiasm as to
turn his weak head at last and drive him mad. A month later, when the
benevolent physician lay in the death-throes of hydrophobia, he called
his weeping friends about him, and said:

"Beware of the books. They tell but half of the story. Whenever a
poor wretch asks you for help, and you feel a doubt as to what result
may flow from your benevolence, give yourself the benefit of the
doubt and kill the applicant."

And so saying he turned his face to the wall and gave up the ghost.

THE BENEVOLENT AUTHOR

A poor and young literary beginner had tried in vain to get his manuscripts accepted. At last, when the horrors of starvation were staring
him in the face, he laid his sad case before a celebrated author, beseeching his counsel and assistance. This generous man immediately
put aside his own matters and proceeded to peruse one of the despised
manuscripts. Having completed his kindly task, he shook the poor
young man cordially by the hand, saying, "I perceive merit in this;
come again to me on Monday." At the time specified, the celebrated
author, with a sweet smile, but saying nothing, spread open a magazine
which was damp from the press. What was the poor young man's
astonishment to discover upon the printed page his own article. "How
can I ever," said he, falling upon his knees and bursting into tears, "testify my gratitude for this noble conduct!"

The celebrated author was the renowned Snodgrass; the poor young
beginner thus rescued from obscurity and starvation was the afterward equally renowned Snagsby. Let this pleasing incident admonish
us to turn a charitable ear to all beginners that need help.

SEQUEL

The next week Snagsby was back with five rejected manuscripts.
The celebrated author was a little surprised, because in the books the
young struggler had needed but one lift, apparently. However, he

plowed through these papers, removing unnecessary flowers and digging up some acres of adjective stumps, and then succeeded in getting two of the articles accepted.

A week or so drifted by, and the grateful Snagsby arrived with another cargo. The celebrated author had felt a mighty glow of satisfaction within himself the first time he had successfully befriended the poor young struggler, and had compared himself with the generous people in the books with high gratification; but he was beginning to suspect now that he had struck upon something fresh in the noble-episode line. His enthusiasm took a chill. Still, he could not bear to repulse this struggling young author, who clung to him with such pretty simplicity and trustfulness.

Well, the upshot of it all was that the celebrated author presently found himself permanently freighted with the poor young beginner. All his mild efforts to unload this cargo went for nothing. He had to give daily counsel, daily encouragement; he had to keep on procuring magazine acceptances, and then revamping the manuscripts to make them presentable. When the young aspirant got a start at last, he rode into sudden fame by describing the celebrated author's private life with such a caustic humor and such minuteness of blistering detail that the book sold a prodigious edition, and broke the celebrated author's heart with mortification. With his latest gasp he said, "Alas, the books deceived me; they do not tell the whole story. Beware of the struggling young author, my friends. Whom God sees fit to starve, let not man presumptuously rescue to his own undoing."

THE GRATEFUL HUSBAND

One day a lady was driving through the principal street of a great city with her little boy, when the horses took fright and dashed madly away, hurling the coachman from his box and leaving the occupants of the carriage paralyzed with terror. But a brave youth who was driving a grocery-wagon threw himself before the plunging animals, and succeeded in arresting their flight at the peril of his own.[1] The grateful lady took his number, and upon arriving at her home she related the heroic act to her husband (who had read the books), who listened with streaming eyes to the moving recital, and who, after returning thanks, in conjunction with his restored loved ones, to Him who suffereth not even a sparrow to fall to the ground unnoticed, sent for the brave young person, and, placing a check for five hundred dollars in his hand, said,

[1] This is probably a misprint.—M. T.

"Take this as a reward for your noble act, William Ferguson, and if ever you shall need a friend, remember that Thompson McSpadden has a grateful heart." Let us learn from this that a good deed cannot fail to benefit the doer, however humble he may be.

SEQUEL

William Ferguson called the next week and asked Mr. McSpadden to use his influence to get him a higher employment, he feeling capable of better things than driving a grocer's wagon. Mr. McSpadden got him an underclerkship at a good salary.

Presently William Ferguson's mother fell sick, and William— Well, to cut the story short, Mr. McSpadden consented to take her into his house. Before long she yearned for the society of her younger children; so Mary and Julia were admitted also, and little Jimmy, their brother. Jimmy had a pocketknife, and he wandered into the drawing-room with it one day, alone, and reduced ten thousand dollars' worth of furniture to an indeterminable value in rather less than three-quarters of an hour. A day or two later he fell down-stairs and broke his neck, and seventeen of his family's relatives came to the house to attend the funeral. This made them acquainted, and they kept the kitchen occupied after that, and likewise kept the McSpaddens busy hunting up situations of various sorts for them, and hunting up more when they wore these out. The old woman drank a good deal and swore a good deal; but the grateful McSpaddens knew it was their duty to reform her, considering what her son had done for them, so they clave nobly to their generous task. William came often and got decreasing sums of money, and asked for higher and more lucrative employments—which the grateful McSpadden more or less promptly procured for him. McSpadden consented also, after some demur, to fit William for college; but when the first vacation came and the hero requested to be sent to Europe for his health, the persecuted McSpadden rose against the tyrant and revolted. He plainly and squarely refused. William Ferguson's mother was so astounded that she let her gin-bottle drop, and her profane lips refused to do their office. When she recovered she said in a half-gasp, "Is this your gratitude? Where would your wife and boy be now, but for my son?"

William said, "Is this your gratitude? Did I save your wife's life or not? Tell me that!"

Seven relations swarmed in from the kitchen and each said, "And this is his gratitude!"

William's sisters stared, bewildered, and said, "And this is his grat—" but were interrupted by their mother, who burst into tears and exclaimed, "To think that my sainted little Jimmy threw away his life in the service of such a reptile!"

Then the pluck of the revolutionary McSpadden rose to the occasion, and he replied with fervor, "Out of my house, the whole beggarly tribe of you! I was beguiled by the books, but shall never be beguiled again—once is sufficient for me." And turning to William he shouted, "Yes, you did save my wife's life, and the next man that does it shall die in his tracks!"

Not being a clergyman, I place my text at the end of my sermon instead of at the beginning. Here it is, from Mr. Noah Brooks's Recollections of President Lincoln in *Scribner's Monthly*:

J. H. Hackett, in his part of Falstaff, was an actor who gave Mr. Lincoln great delight. With his usual desire to signify to others his sense of obligation, Mr. Lincoln wrote a genial little note to the actor expressing his pleasure at witnessing his performance. Mr. Hackett, in reply, sent a book of some sort; perhaps it was one of his own authorship. He also wrote several notes to the President. One night, quite late, when the episode had passed out of my mind, I went to the White House in answer to a message. Passing into the President's office, I noticed, to my surprise, Hackett sitting in the anteroom as if waiting for an audience. The President asked me if any one was outside. On being told, he said, half sadly, "Oh, I can't see him, I can't see him; I was in hopes he had gone away." Then he added, "Now this just illustrates the difficulty of having pleasant friends and acquaintances in this place. You know how I liked Hackett as an actor, and how I wrote to tell him so. He sent me that book, and there I thought the matter would end. He is a master of his place in the profession, I suppose, and well fixed in it; but just because we had a little friendly correspondence, such as any two men might have, he wants something. What do you suppose he wants?" I could not guess, and Mr. Lincoln added, "Well, he wants to be consul to London. Oh, dear!"

I will observe, in conclusion, that the William Ferguson incident occurred, and within my personal knowledge—though I have changed the nature of the details, to keep William from recognizing himself in it.

All the readers of this article have in some sweet and gushing hour of their lives played the rôle of Magnanimous-Incident hero. I wish I knew how many there are among them who are willing to talk about that episode and like to be reminded of the consequences that flowed from it.

1878

O'Shah

(*A Series of News Letters Describing a Visit to England by the Shah of Persia*)

I

THE ARRIVAL IN ENGLAND

London, June 18, 1873

"Would you like to go over to Belgium and help bring the Shah to England?"

I said I was willing.

"Very well, then; here is an order from the Admiralty which will admit you on board Her Majesty's ship *Lively*, now lying at Ostend, and you can return in her day after to-morrow."

That was all. That was the end of it. Without stopping to think, I had in a manner taken upon myself to bring the Shah of Persia to England. I could not otherwise regard the conversation I had just held with the London representative of the New York *Herald*. The amount of discomfort I endured for the next two or three hours cannot be set down in words. I could not eat, sleep, talk, smoke with any satisfaction. The more I thought the thing over the more oppressed I felt. What was the Shah to me, that I should go to all this worry and trouble on his account? Where was there the least occasion for taking upon myself such a responsibility? If I got him over all right, well. But if I lost him? if he died on my hands? if he got drowned? It was depressing, any way I looked at it. In the end I said to myself, "If I get this Shah over here safe and sound I never will take charge of another one." And yet, at the same time I kept thinking: "This country has treated me well, stranger as I am, and this foreigner is the country's guest—that is enough, I will help him out; I will fetch him over; I will land him in London, and say to the British people, 'Here is your Shah; give me a receipt.'"

I felt easy in my mind now, and was about to go to bed, but something occurred to me. I took a cab and drove downtown and routed out that *Herald* representative.

"Where is Belgium?" said I.

"Where is Belgium? I never heard such a question!"

"That doesn't make any difference to me. If I have got to fetch this Shah I don't wish to go to the wrong place. Where is Belgium? Is it a shilling fare in a cab?"

He explained that it was in foreign parts—the first place I have heard of lately which a body could not go to in a cab for a shilling.

I said I could not go alone, because I could not speak foreign languages well, could not get up in time for the early train without help, and could not find my way. I said it was enough to have the Shah on my hands; I did not wish to have everything piled on me. Mr. Blank was then ordered to go with me. I do like to have somebody along to talk to when I go abroad.

When I got home I sat down and thought the thing all over. I wanted to go into this enterprise understandingly. What was the main thing? That was the question. A little reflection informed me. For two weeks the London papers had sung just one continual song to just one continual tune, and the idea of it all was "how to impress the Shah." These papers had told all about the St. Petersburg splendors, and had said at the end that splendors would no longer answer; that England could not outdo Russia in that respect; therefore some other way of impressing the Shah must be contrived. And these papers had also told all about the Shahstic reception in Prussia and its attendant military pageantry. England could not improve on that sort of thing—she could not impress the Shah with soldiers; something else must be tried. And so on. Column after column, page after page of agony about how to "impress the Shah." At last they had hit upon a happy idea—a grand naval exhibition. That was it! A man brought up in Oriental seclusion and simplicity, a man who had never seen anything but camels and such things, could not help being surprised and delighted with the strange novelty of ships. The distress was at an end. England heaved a great sigh of relief; she knew at last how to impress the Shah.

My course was very plain, now, after that bit of reflection. All I had to do was to go over to Belgium and impress the Shah. I failed to form any definite plan as to the process, but I made up my mind to manage it somehow. I said to myself, "I will impress this Shah or there shall be a funeral that will be worth contemplating."

I went to bed then, but did not sleep a great deal, for the responsibilities were weighing pretty heavily upon me. At six o'clock in the the morning Mr. Blank came and turned me out. I was surprised at this, and not gratified, for I detest early rising. I never like to say severe things, but I was a good deal tried this time. I said I did not mind getting up moderately early, but I hated to be called day before yesterday. However, as I was acting in a national capacity and for a country that I liked, I stopped grumbling and we set out. A grand naval review is a good thing to impress a Shah with, but if he would try getting up at six o'clock in the morning—but no matter; we started.

We took the Dover train and went whistling along over the housetops at the rate of fifty miles an hour, and just as smoothly and pleasantly, too, as if we were in a sleigh. One never can have anything but a very vague idea of what speed is until he travels over an English railway. Our "lightning" expresses are sleepy and indolent by comparison. We looked into the back windows of the endless ranks of houses abreast and below us, and saw many a homelike little family of early birds sitting at their breakfasts. New views and new aspects of London were about me; the mighty city seemed to spread farther and wider in the clear morning air than it had ever done before. There is something awe-inspiring about the mere look of the figures that express the population of London when one comes to set them down in a good large hand—4,000,000! It takes a body's breath away, almost.

We presently left the city behind. We had started drowsy, but we did not stay so. How could we, with the brilliant sunshine pouring down, the balmy wind blowing through the open windows, and the Garden of Eden spread all abroad? We swept along through rolling expanses of growing grain—not a stone or a stump to mar their comeliness, not an unsightly fence or an ill-kept hedge; through broad meadows covered with fresh green grass as clean swept as if a broom had been at work there—little brooks wandering up and down them, noble trees here and there, cows in the shade, groves in the distance and church spires projecting out of them; and there were the quaintest old-fashioned houses set in the midst of smooth lawns or partly hiding themselves among fine old forest trees; and there was one steep-roofed ancient cottage whose walls all around, and whose roof, and whose chimneys, were clothed in a shining mail of ivy leaves!—so thoroughly, indeed, that only one little patch of roof was visible to prove that the house was not a mere house of leaves, with glass windows in it. Imagine those dainty little homes surrounded by flowering shrubs and bright green grass and all sorts of old trees—and then go on and try to imagine something more bewitching.

By and by we passed Rochester, and, sure enough, right there, on the highest ground in the town and rising imposingly up from among clustering roofs, was the gray old castle—roofless, ruined, ragged, the sky beyond showing clear and blue through the glassless windows, the walls partly clad with ivy—a time-scarred, weather-beaten old pile, but ever so picturesque and ever so majestic, too. There it was, a whole book of English history. I had read of Rochester Castle a thousand times, but I had never really believed there was any such building before.

Presently we reached the sea and came to a stand far out on a pier; and here was Dover and more history. The chalk cliffs of England towered up from the shore and the French coast was visible. On the tallest hill sat Dover Castle, stately and spacious and superb, looking just as it has always looked any time these ten or fifteen thousand years—I do not know its exact age, and it does not matter, anyway.

We stepped aboard the little packet and steamed away. The sea was perfectly smooth, and painfully brilliant in the sunshine. There were no curiosities in the vessel except the passengers and a placard in French setting forth the transportation fares for various kinds of people. The lithographer probably considered that placard a triumph. It was printed in green, blue, red, black, and yellow; no individual line in one color, even the individual letters were separately colored. For instance, the first letter of a word would be blue, the next red, the next green, and so on. The placard looked as if it had the smallpox or something. I inquired the artist's name and place of business, intending to hunt him up and kill him when I had time; but no one could tell me. In the list of prices first-class passengers were set down at fifteen shillings and four pence, and dead bodies at one pound ten shillings and eight pence—just double price! That is Belgian morals, I suppose. I never say a harsh thing unless I am greatly stirred; but in my opinion the man who would take advantage of a dead person would do almost any odious thing. I publish this scandalous discrimination against the most helpless class among us in order that people intending to die abroad may come back by some other line.

We skimmed over to Ostend in four hours and went ashore. The first gentleman we saw happened to be the flag lieutenant of the fleet, and he told me where the *Lively* lay, and said she would sail about six in the morning. Heavens and earth. He said he would give my letter to the proper authority, and so we thanked him and bore away for the hotel. Bore away is good sailor phraseology, and I have been at sea portions of two days now. I easily pick up a foreign language.

Ostend is a curious, comfortable-looking, massively built town, where the people speak both the French and the Flemish with exceeding fluency, and yet I could not understand them in either tongue. But I will write the rest about Ostend in to-morrow's letter.

We idled about this curious Ostend the remainder of the afternoon and far into the long-lived twilight, apparently to amuse ourselves, but secretly I had a deeper motive. I wanted to see if there was anything here that might "impress the Shah." In the end I was reassured and content. If Ostend could impress him, England could amaze the head clear off his shoulders and have marvels left that not even the trunk could be indifferent to.

These citizens of Flanders—Flounders, I think they call them, though I feel sure I have eaten a creature of that name or seen it in an aquarium or a menagerie, or in a picture or somewhere—are a thrifty, industrious race, and are as commercially wise and farsighted as they were in Edward the Third's time, and as enduring and patient under adversity as they were in Charles the Bold's. They are prolific in the matter of children; in some of the narrow streets every house seemed to have had a freshet of children, which had burst through and overflowed into the roadway. One could hardly get along for the pack of juveniles, and they were all soiled and all healthy. They all wore wooden shoes, which clattered noisily on the stone pavements. All the women were hard at work; there were no idlers about the houses. The men were away at labor, no doubt. In nearly every door women sat at needlework or something of that marketable nature—they were knitting principally. Many groups of women sat in the street, in the shade of walls, making point lace. The lace maker holds a sort of pillow on her knees with a strip of cardboard fastened on it, on which the lace pattern has been punctured. She sticks bunches of pins in the punctures and about them weaves her web of threads. The numberless threads diverge from the bunch of pins like the spokes of a wheel, and the spools from which the threads are being unwound form the outer circle of the wheel. The woman throws these spools about her with flying fingers, in and out, over and under one another, and so fast that you can hardly follow the evolutions with your eyes. In the chaos and confusion of skipping spools you wonder how she can possibly pick up the right one every time, and especially how she can go on gossiping with her friends all the time and yet never seem to miss a stitch. The laces these ingenious Flounders were making were very dainty and delicate in texture and very beautiful in design.

Most of the shops in Ostend seemed devoted to the sale of sea shells. All sorts of figures of men and women were made of shells; one sort was composed of grotesque and ingenious combinations of lobster

claws in the human form. And they had other figures made of stuffed
frogs—some fencing, some barbering each other, and some were not to
be described at all without indecent language. It must require a barbarian nature to be able to find humor in such nauseating horrors as
these last. These things were exposed in the public windows where
young girls and little children could see them, and in the shops sat the
usual hairy-lipped young woman waiting to sell them.

There was a contrivance attached to the better class of houses which
I had heard of before, but never seen. It was an arrangement of mirrors
outside the window, so contrived that the people within could see
who was coming either up or down the street—see all that might be
going on, in fact—without opening the window or twisting themselves
into uncomfortable positions in order to look.

A capital thing to watch for unwelcome (or welcome) visitors with,
or to observe pageants in cold or rainy weather. People in second and
third stories had, also, another mirror which showed who was passing
underneath.

The dining room at our hotel was very spacious and rather gorgeous. One end of it was composed almost entirely of a single pane of
plate glass, some two inches thick—for this is the plate-glass manufacturing region, you remember. It was very clear and fine. If one were
to enter the place in such a way as not to catch the sheen of the glass,
he would suppose that the end of the house was wide open to the sun
and the storms. A strange boyhood instinct came strongly upon me,
and I could not really enjoy my dinner, I wanted to break that glass
so badly. I have no doubt that every man feels so, and I know that such
a glass must be simply torture to a boy.

This dining room's walls were almost completely covered with large
oil paintings in frames.

It was an excellent hotel; the utmost care was taken that everything
should go right. I went to bed at ten and was called at eleven to "take
the early train." I said I was not the one, so the servant stirred up the
next door and he was not the one; then the next door and the next—no
success—and so on till the reverberations of the knocking were lost in
the distance down the hall, and I fell asleep again. They called me at
twelve to take another early train, but I said I was not the one again,
and asked as a favor that they would be particular to call the rest next
time, but never mind me. However, they could not understand my
English; they only said something in reply to signify that, and then
went on banging up the boarders, none of whom desired to take the
early train.

When they called me at one, it made my rest seem very broken, and
I said if they would skip me at two I would call myself—not really
intending to do it, but hoping to beguile the porter and deceive him.
He probably suspected that and was afraid to trust me, because when
he made his rounds at that hour he did not take any chances on me,
but routed me out along with the others. I got some more sleep after
that, but when the porter called me at three I felt depressed and
jaded and greatly discouraged. So I gave it up and dressed myself.
The porter got me a cup of coffee and kept me awake while I drank it.
He was a good, well-meaning sort of Flounder, but really a drawback
to the hotel, I should think.

Poor Mr. Blank came in then, looking worn and old. He had been
called for all the different trains, too, just as I had. He said it was a
good enough hotel, but they took too much pains. While we sat there
talking we fell asleep and were called again at four. Then we went
out and dozed about town till six, and then drifted aboard the *Lively*.

She was trim and bright, and clean and smart; she was as handsome as a picture. The sailors were in brand-new man-of-war costume,
and plenty of officers were about the decks in the state uniform of the
service—cocked hats, huge epaulettes, claw-hammer coats lined with
white silk—hats and coats and trousers all splendid with gold lace. I
judged that these were all admirals, and so got afraid and went ashore
again. Our vessel was to carry the Shah's brother, also the Grand Vizier,
several Persian princes, who were uncles to the Shah, and other dignitaries of more or less consequence. A vessel alongside was to carry the
luggage, and a vessel just ahead (the *Vigilant*) was to carry nobody
but just the Shah and certain Ministers of State and servants and the
Queen's special ambassador, Sir Henry Rawlinson, who is a Persian
scholar and talks to the Shah in his own tongue.

I was very glad, for several reasons, to find that I was not to go in the
same ship with the Shah. First, with him not immediately under my
eye I would feel less responsibility for him; and, secondly, as I was
anxious to impress him, I wanted to practice on his brother first.

THE SHAH'S QUARTERS

On the afterdeck of the *Vigilant*—very handsome ship—a temporary
cabin had been constructed for the sole and special use of the Shah,
temporary but charmingly substantial and graceful and pretty. It was
about thirty feet long and twelve wide, beautifully gilded, decorated
and painted within and without. Among its colors was a shade of light

green, which reminds me of an anecdote about the Persian party, which I will speak of in to-morrow's letter.

It was getting along toward the time for the Shah to arrive from Brussels, so I ranged up alongside my own ship. I do not know when I ever felt so ill at ease and undecided. It was a sealed letter which I had brought from the Admiralty, and I could not guess what the purport of it might be. I supposed I was intended to command the ship—that is, I had supposed it at first, but, after seeing all those splendid officers, I had discarded that idea. I cogitated a good deal, but to no purpose. Presently a regiment of Belgian troops arrived and formed in line along the pier. Then a number of people began to spread down carpets for fifty yards along the pier, by the railway track, and other carpets were laid from these to the ships. The gangway leading on board my ship was now carpeted and its railings were draped with bright-colored signal flags. It began to look as if I was expected; so I walked on board. A sailor immediately ran and stopped me, and made another sailor bring a mop for me to wipe my feet on, lest I might soil the deck, which was wonderfully clean and nice. Evidently I was not the person expected, after all. I pointed to the group of officers and asked the sailor what the naval law would do to a man if he were to go and speak to some of those admirals—for there was an awful air of etiquette and punctilio about the premises; but just then one of those officers came forward and said that if his instinct was correct an Admiralty order had been received giving me a passage in the ship; and he also said that he was the first lieutenant, and that I was very welcome and he would take pains to make me feel at home, and furthermore there was champagne and soda waiting down below; and furthermore still, all the London correspondents, to the number of six or seven, would arrive from Brussels with the Shah, and would go in our ship, and if our passage were not a lively one, and a jolly and enjoyable one, it would be a very strange thing indeed. I could have jumped for joy if I had not been afraid of breaking some rule of naval etiquette and getting hanged for it.

Now the train was signaled, and everybody got ready for the great event. The Belgian regiment straightened itself up, and some two hundred Flounders arrived and took conspicuous position on a little mound. I was a little afraid that this would impress the Shah; but I was soon occupied with other interests. The train of thirteen cars came tearing in, and stopped abreast the ships. Music and guns began an uproar. Odd-looking Persian faces and felt hats (brimless stovepipes) appeared at the car windows.

Some gorgeous English officials fled down the carpet from the *Vigilant*. They stopped at a long car with the royal arms upon it, uncovered their heads, and unlocked the car door. Then the Shah stood up in it and gave us a good view. He was a handsome, strong-featured man, with a rather European fairness of complexion; had a mustache, wore spectacles, seemed of a good height and graceful build and carriage, and looked about forty or a shade less. He was very simply dressed—brimless stovepipe and close-buttoned dark-green military suit, without ornament. No, not wholly without ornament, for he had a band two inches wide worn over his shoulder and down across his breast, scarf fashion, which band was one solid glory of fine diamonds.

A Persian official appeared in the Shah's rear and enveloped him in an ample quilt—or cloak, if you please—which was lined with fur. The outside of it was of a whitish color and elaborately needleworked in Persian patterns like an India shawl. The Shah stepped out and the official procession formed about him and marched him down the carpet and on board the *Vigilant* to slow music. Not a Flounder raised a cheer. All the small fry swarmed out of the train now.

The Shah walked back alongside his fine cabin, looking at the assemblage of silent, solemn Flounders; the correspondent of the London *Telegraph* was hurrying along the pier and took off his hat and bowed to the "King of Kings," and the King of Kings gave a polite military salute in return. This was the commencement of the excitement. The success of the breathless *Telegraph* man made all the other London correspondents mad, every man of whom flourished his stovepipe recklessly and cheered lustily, some of the more enthusiastic varying the exercise by lowering their heads and elevating their coat tails. Seeing all this, and feeling that if I was to "impress the Shah" at all, now was my time, I ventured a little squeaky yell, quite distinct from the other shouts, but just as hearty. His Shahship heard and saw and saluted me in a manner that was, I considered, an acknowledgment of my superior importance. I do not know that I ever felt so ostentatious and absurd before. All the correspondents came aboard, and then the Persian baggage came also, and was carried across to the ship alongside of ours. When she could hold no more we took somewhere about a hundred trunks and boxes on board our vessel. Two boxes fell into the water, and several sailors jumped in and saved one, but the other was lost. However, it probably contained nothing but a few hundred pounds of diamonds and things.

At last we got under way and steamed out through a long slip, the piers on either side being crowded with Flounders; but never a cheer.

A battery of three guns on the starboard pier boomed a royal salute, and we swept out to sea, the *Vigilant* in the lead, we right in her wake, and the baggage ship in ours. Within fifteen minutes everybody was well acquainted; a general jollification set in, and I was thoroughly glad I had come over to fetch the Shah.

II

MARK TWAIN EXECUTES HIS CONTRACT AND DELIVERS THE SHAH IN LONDON

London, June 19, 1873

SOME PERSIAN FINERY

Leaving Ostend, we went out to sea under a clear sky and upon smooth water—so smooth, indeed, that its surface was scarcely rippled. I say the sky was clear, and so it was, clear and sunny; but a rich haze lay upon the water in the distance—a soft, mellow mist, through which a scattering sail or two loomed vaguely. One may call such a morning perfect.

The corps of correspondents were well jaded with their railway journey, but after champagne and soda downstairs with the officers, everybody came up refreshed and cheery and exceedingly well acquainted all around. The Persian grandees had meantime taken up a position in a glass house on the afterdeck, and were sipping coffee in a grave, Oriental way. They all had much lighter complexions and a more European cast of features than I was prepared for, and several of them were exceedingly handsome, fine-looking men.

They all sat in a circle on a sofa (the deckhouse being circular), and they made a right gaudy spectacle. Their breasts were completely crusted with gold bullion embroidery of a pattern resembling frayed and interlacing ferns, and they had large jeweled ornaments on their breasts also. The Grand Vizier came out to have a look around. In addition to the sumptuous gold fernery on his breast he wore a jeweled star as large as the palm of my hand, and about his neck hung the Shah's miniature, reposing in a bed of diamonds, that gleamed and flashed in a wonderful way when touched by the sunlight. It was said that to receive the Shah's portrait from the Shah was the highest compliment that could be conferred upon a Persian subject. I did not care so much about the diamonds, but I would have liked to have the portrait very much. The Grand Vizier's sword hilt and the whole back of the sheath from end to end were composed of a neat and simple combination of some twelve or fifteen thousand emeralds and diamonds.

"IMPRESSING" A PERSIAN GENERAL

Several of the Persians talked French and English. One of them, who was said to be a general, came up on the bridge where some of us were standing, pointed to a sailor, and asked me if I could tell him what that sailor was doing?

I said he was communicating with the other ships by means of the optical telegraph—that by using the three sticks the whole alphabet could be expressed. I showed him how A, B and C were made, and so forth. Good! This Persian was "impressed"! He showed it by his eyes, by his gestures, by his manifest surprise and delight. I said to myself, if the Shah were only here now, the grand desire of Great Britain could be accomplished. The general immediately called the other grandees and told them about this telegraphic wonder. Then he said:

"Now does everyone on board acquire this knowledge?"

"No, only the officers."

"And this sailor?"

"He is only the signalman. Two or three sailors on board are detailed for this service, and by order and direction of the officers they communicate with the other ships."

"Very good! very fine! Very great indeed!"

These men were unquestionably impressed. I got the sailor to bring the signal book, and the matter was fully explained, to their high astonishment; also the flag signals, and likewise the lamp signals for night telegraphing. Of course, the idea came into my head, in the first place, to ask one of the officers to conduct this bit of instruction, but I at once dismissed it. I judged that this would all go to the Shah, sooner or later. I had come over on purpose to "impress the Shah," and I was not going to throw away my opportunity. I wished the Queen had been there; I would have been knighted, sure. You see, they knight people here for all sorts of things—knight them, or put them into the peerage and make great personages of them. Now, for instance, a king comes over here on a visit; the Lord Mayor and sheriffs do him becoming honors in the city, and straightway the former is created a baronet and the latter are knighted. When the Prince of Wales recovered from his illness one of his chief physicians was made a baronet and the other

was knighted. Charles II made duchesses of one or two female acquaintances of his for something or other—I have forgotten now what
it was. A London shoemaker's apprentice became a great soldier—
indeed, a Wellington—won prodigious victories in many climes and
covered the British arms with glory all through a long life; and when
he was 187 years old they knighted him and made him Constable of
the Tower. But he died next year and they buried him in Westminster
Abbey. There is no telling what that man might have become if he had
lived. So you see what a chance I had; for I have no doubt in the world
that I have been the humble instrument, under Providence, of "impressing the Shah." And I really believe that if the Queen comes to
hear of it I shall be made a duke.

Friends intending to write will not need to be reminded that a duke
is addressed as "Your Grace"; it is considered a great offense to leave
that off.

A PICTURESQUE NAVAL SPECTACLE

When we were a mile or so out from Ostend conversation ceased,
an expectant look came into all faces, and opera glasses began to stand
out from above all noses. This impressive hush lasted a few minutes,
and then some one said:

"There they are!"

"Where?"

"Away yonder ahead—straight ahead."

Which was true. Three huge shapes smothered in the haze—the
Vanguard, the *Audacious*, and the *Devastation*—all great ironclads.
They were to do escort duty. The officers and correspondents gathered
on the forecastle and waited for the next act. A red spout of fire issued
from the *Vanguard's* side, another flashed from the *Audacious*. Beautiful these red tongues were against the dark haze. Then there was a
long pause—ever so long a pause and not a sound, not the suspicion of
a sound; and now, out of the stillness, came a deep, solemn "boom!
boom!" It had not occurred to me that at so great a distance I would
not hear the report as soon as I saw the flash. The two crimson jets
were very beautiful, but not more so than the rolling volumes of
white smoke that plunged after them, rested a moment over the water,
and then went wreathing and curling up among the webbed rigging
and the tall masts, and left only glimpses of these things visible, high
up in the air, projecting as if from a fog.

Now the flashes came thick and fast from the black sides of both vessels. The muffled thunders of the guns mingled together in one continued roll, the two ships were lost to sight, and in their places two mountains of tumbled smoke rested upon the motionless water, their bases in the hazy twilight and their summits shining in the sun. It was good to be there and see so fine a spectacle as that.

THE NAVAL SALUTE

We closed up fast upon the ironclads. They fell apart to let our flotilla come between, and as the *Vigilant* ranged up the rigging of the ironclads was manned to salute the Shah. And, indeed, that was something to see. The shrouds, from the decks clear to the trucks, away up toward the sky, were black with men. On the lower rounds of these rope ladders they stood five abreast, holding each other's hands, and so the tapering shrouds formed attenuated pyramids of humanity, six pyramids of them towering into the upper air, and clear up on the top of each dizzy mast stood a little creature like a clothes pin—a mere black peg against the sky—and that mite was a sailor waving a flag like a postage stamp. All at once the pyramids of men burst into a cheer, and followed it with two more, given with a will; and if the Shah was not impressed he must be the offspring of a mummy.

And just at this moment, while we all stood there gazing——

However breakfast was announced and I did not wait to see.

THE THIRTY-FOUR-TON GUNS SPEAK

If there is one thing that is pleasanter than another it is to take breakfast in the wardroom with a dozen naval officers. Of course, that awe-inspiring monarch, the captain, is aft, keeping frozen state with the Grand Viziers when there are any on board, and so there is nobody in the wardroom to maintain naval etiquette. As a consequence none is maintained. One officer, in a splendid uniform, snatches a champagne bottle from a steward and opens it himself; another keeps the servants moving; another opens soda; everybody eats, drinks, shouts, laughs in the most unconstrained way, and it does seem a pity that ever the thing should come to an end. No individual present seemed sorry he was not in the ship with the Shah. When the festivities had been going on about an hour, some tremendous booming was heard outside. Now here was a question between duty and broiled chicken.

What might that booming mean? Anguish sat upon the faces of the correspondents. I watched to see what they would do, and the precious moments were flying. Somebody cried down a companionway:

"The *Devastation* is saluting!"

The correspondents tumbled over one another, over chairs, over everything in their frenzy to get on deck, and the last gun reverberated as the last heel disappeared on the stairs. The *Devastation,* the pride of England, the mightiest war vessel afloat, carrying guns that outweigh any metal in any service, it is said (thirty-five tons each), and these boys had missed that spectacle—at least I knew that some of them had. I did not go. Age has taught me wisdom. If a spectacle is going to be particularly imposing I prefer to see it through somebody else's eyes, because that man will always exaggerate. Then I can exaggerate his exaggeration, and my account of the thing will be the most impressive.

But I felt that I had missed my figure this time, because I was not sure which of these gentlemen reached the deck in time for a glimpse and which didn't. And this morning I cannot tell by the London papers. They all have imposing descriptions of that thing, and no one of them resembled another. Mr. X's is perhaps the finest, but he was singing a song about "Spring, Spring, Gentle Spring," all through the bombardment, and was overexcited, I fear.

The next best was Mr. Y's; but he was telling about how he took a Russian battery, along with another man, during the Crimean War, and he was not fairly through the story till the salute was over, though I remember he went up and saw the smoke. I will not frame a description of the *Devastation's* salute, for I have no material that I can feel sure is reliable.

THE GRAND SPECTACULAR CLIMAX

When we first sailed away from Ostend I found myself in a dilemma; I had no notebook. But "any port in a storm," as the sailors say. I found a fair, full pack of ordinary playing cards in my overcoat pocket—one always likes to have something along to amuse children with—and really they proved excellent to take notes on, although bystanders were a bit inclined to poke fun at them and ask facetious questions. But I was content; I made all the notes I needed. The aces and low "spot" cards are very good indeed to write memoranda on, but I will not recommend the Kings and Jacks.

SPEAKING BY THE CARDS

Referring to the seven of hearts, I find that this naval exhibition and journey from Ostend to Dover is going to cost the government £500,000. Got it from a correspondent. It is a round sum.

Referring to the ace of diamonds, I find that along in the afternoon we sighted a fresh fleet of men-of-war coming to meet us. The rest of the diamonds, down to the eight spot (nines and tens are no good for notes) are taken up with details of that spectacle. Most of the clubs and hearts refer to matters immediately following that, but I really can hardly do anything with them because I have forgotten what was trumps.

THE SPECTACLE

But never mind. The sea scene grew little by little, until presently it was very imposing. We drew up into the midst of a waiting host of vessels. Enormous five-masted men-of-war, great turret ships, steam packets, pleasure yachts—every sort of craft, indeed—the sea was thick with them; the yards and riggings of the warships loaded with men, the packets crowded with people, the pleasure ships rainbowed with brilliant flags all over and over—some with flags strung thick on lines stretching from bowsprit to foremast, thence to mainmast, thence to mizzenmast, and thence to stern. All the ships were in motion—gliding hither and thither, in and out, mingling and parting—a bewildering whirl of flash and color. Our leader, the vast, black, ugly, but very formidable *Devastation*, plowed straight through the gay throng, our Shah-ships following, the lines of big men-of-war saluting, the booming of the guns drowning the cheering, stately islands of smoke towering everywhere. And so, in this condition of unspeakable grandeur, we swept into the harbor of Dover, and saw the English princes and the long ranks of red-coated soldiers waiting on the pier, civilian multitudes behind them, the lofty hill front by the castle swarming with spectators, and there was the crash of cannon and a general hurrah all through the air. It was rather a contrast to silent Ostend and the unimpressible Flanders.

THE SHAH "IMPRESSED" AT LAST

The Duke of Edinburgh and Prince Arthur received the Shah in state, and then all of us—princes, Shahs, ambassadors, Grand Viziers and newspaper correspondents—climbed aboard the train and started off to London just like so many brothers.

From Dover to London it was a sight to see. Seventy miles of human beings in a jam—the gaps were not worth mentioning—and every man, woman, and child waving hat or handkerchief and cheering. I wondered—could not tell—could not be sure—could only wonder—would this "impress the Shah"? I would have given anything to know. But—well, it ought—but—still one could not tell.

And by and by we burst into the London Railway station—a very large station it is—and found it wonderfully decorated and all the neighboring streets packed with cheering citizens. Would this impress the Shah? I—I—well, I could not yet feel certain.

The Prince of Wales received the Shah—ah, you should have seen how gorgeously the Shah was dressed now—he was like the sun in a total eclipse of rainbows—yes, the Prince received him, put him in a grand open carriage, got in and made him sit over further and not "crowd," the carriage clattered out of the station, all London fell apart on either side and lifted a perfectly national cheer, and just at that instant the bottom fell out of the sky and forty deluges came pouring down at once!

The great strain was over, the crushing suspense at an end. I said, "Thank God, this will impress the Shah."

Now came the long files of Horse Guards in silver armor. We took the great Persian to Buckingham Palace. I never stirred till I saw the gates open and close upon him with my own eyes and knew he was there. Then I said:

"England, here is your Shah; take him and be happy, but don't ever ask me to fetch over another one."

This contract has been pretty straining on me.

III

THE SHAH AS A SOCIAL STAR

London, June 21, 1873

After delivering the Shah at the gates of that unsightly pile of dreary grandeur known as Buckingham Palace I cast all responsibility for him aside for the time being, and experienced a sense of relief and likewise an honest pride in my success, such as no man can feel who has not had a Shah at nurse (so to speak) for three days.

It is said by those who ought to know that when Buckingham Palace was being fitted up as a home for the Shah one of the chief rooms was adorned with a rich carpet which had been designed and manufactured especially to charm the eye of His Majesty. The story goes on to say that a couple of the Persian suite came here a week ago to see that all things were in readiness and nothing overlooked, and that when they reached that particular room and glanced at the lovely combination of green figures and white ones in that carpet they gathered their robes carefully up about their knees and then went elaborately tiptoeing about the floor with the aspect and anxiety of a couple of cats hunting for dry ground in a wet country, and they stepped only on the white figures and almost fainted whenever they came near touching a green one. It is said that the explanation is that these visiting Persians are all Mohammedans, and green being a color sacred to the descendants of the Prophet, and none of these people being so descended, it would be dreadful profanation for them to defile the holy color with their feet. And the general result of it all was that carpet had to be taken up and is a dead loss.

Man is a singular sort of human being, after all, and his religion does not always adorn him. Now, our religion is the right one, and has fewer odd and striking features than any other; and yet my ancestors used to roast Catholics and witches and warm their hands by the fire; but they would be blanched with horror at the bare thought of breaking the Sabbath, and here is a Persian monarch who never sees any impropriety in chopping a subject's head off for the mere misdemeanor of calling him too early for breakfast, and yet would be consumed with pious remorse if unheeding foot were to chance to step upon anything so green as you or I, my reader.

Oriental peoples say that women have no souls to save and, almost without my memory, many American Protestants said the same of

babies. I thought there was a wide gulf between the Persians and ourselves, but I begin to feel that they are really our brothers after all.

After a day's rest the Shah went to Windsor Castle and called on the
Queen. What that suggests to the reader's mind is this:—That the Shah
took a hand satchel and an umbrella, called a cab and said he wanted
to go to the Paddington station; that when he arrived there the driver
charged him sixpence too much, and he paid it rather than have
trouble; that he tried now to buy a ticket, and was answered by a
ticket seller as surly as a hotel clerk that he was not selling tickets for
that train yet; that he finally got his ticket, and was beguiled of his
satchel by a railway porter at once, who put it into a first-class carriage
and got a sixpence, which the company forbids him to receive; that
presently when the guard (or conductor) of the train came along the
Shah slipped a shilling into his hand and said he wanted to smoke,
and straightway the guard signified that it was all right; that when the
Shah arrived at Windsor Castle he rang the bell, and when the girl
came to the door asked her if the Queen was at home, and she left
him standing in the hall and went to see; that by and by she returned
and said would he please sit down in the front room and Mrs. Guelph
would be down directly; that he hung his hat on the hatrack, stood
his umbrella up in the corner, entered the front room and sat down on
a haircloth chair; that he waited and waited and got tired; that he got
up and examined the old piano, the depressing lithographs on the
walls and the album of photographs of faded country relatives on the
center table, and was just about to fall back on the family Bible when
the Queen entered briskly and begged him to sit down and apologized
for keeping him waiting, but she had just got a new girl and everything
was upside down, and so forth and so on; but how are the family, and
when did he arrive, and how long should he stay and why didn't he
bring his wife. I knew that that was the picture which would spring
up in the American reader's mind when it was said the Shah went to
visit the Queen, because that was the picture which the announcement
suggested to my own mind.

But it was far from the facts, very far. Nothing could be farther. In
truth, these people made as much of a to do over a mere friendly call
as anybody else would over a conflagration. There were special railway trains for the occasion; there was a general muster of princes and
dukes to go along, each one occupying room 40; there were regiments
of cavalry to clear the way; railway stations were turned into flower
gardens, sheltered with flags and all manner of gaudy splendor; there
were multitudes of people to look on over the heads of interminable

ranks of policemen standing shoulder to shoulder and facing front; there was braying of music and booming of cannon. All that fuss, in sober truth, over a mere off-hand friendly call. Imagine what it would have been if he had brought another shirt and was going to stay a month.

AT THE GUILDHALL

Truly, I am like to suffocate with astonishment at the things that are going on around me here. It is all odd, it is all queer enough, I can tell you; but last night's work transcends anything I ever heard of in the way of—well, how shall I express it? how can I word it? I find it awkward to get at it. But to say it in a word—and it is a true one, too, as hundreds and hundreds of people will testify—last night the Corporation of the City of London, with a simplicity and ignorance which almost rise to sublimity, actually gave a ball to a Shah who does not dance. If I would allow myself to laugh at a cruel mistake, this would start me. It is the oddest thing that has happened since I have had charge of the Shah. There is some excuse for it in the fact that the Aldermen of London are simply great and opulent merchants, and cannot be expected to know much about the ways of high life—but then they could have asked some of us who have been with the Shah.

The ball was a marvel in its way. The historical Guildhall was a scene of great magnificence. There was a high dais at one end, on which were three state chairs under a sumptuous canopy; upon the middle one sat the Shah, who was almost a Chicago conflagration of precious stones and gold bullion lace. Among other gems upon his breast were a number of emeralds of marvelous size, and from a loop hung an historical diamond of great size and wonderful beauty. On the right of the Shah sat the Princess of Wales, and on his left the wife of the Crown Prince of Russia. Grouped about the three stood a full jury of minor princes, princesses, and ambassadors hailing from many countries.

THE TWO CORRALS

The immense hall was divided in the middle by a red rope. The Shah's division was sacred to blue blood, and there was breathing room there; but the other corral was but a crush of struggling and perspiring humanity. The place was brilliant with gas and was a rare spectacle in the matter of splendid costumes and rich coloring.

The lofty stained-glass windows, pictured with celebrated episodes in the history of the ancient city, were lighted from the outside, and one may imagine the beauty of the effect. The great giants, Gog and Magog (whose origin and history, curiously enough, are unknown even to tradition), looked down from the lofty gallery, but made no observation. Down the long sides of the hall, with but brief spaces between, were imposing groups of marble statuary; and, contrasted with the masses of life and color about them, they made a picturesque effect. The groups were statues (in various attitudes) of the Duke of Wellington. I do not say this knowingly, but only supposingly; but I never have seen a statue in England yet that represented anybody but the Duke of Wellington, and, as for the streets and terraces and courts and squares that are named after him or after selections from his 797 titles, they are simply beyond the grasp of arithmetic. This reminds me that, having named everything after Wellington that there was left to name, in England (even down to Wellington boots), our British brothers, still unsatisfied, still oppressed with adulation, blandly crossed over and named our Californian big trees Wellington, and put it in Latin at that. They did that, calmly ignoring the fact that we, the discoverers and owners of the trees, had long ago named them after a larger man. However, if the ghost of Wellington enjoys such a proceeding, possibly the ghost of Washington will not greatly trouble itself about the matter. But what really disturbs me is that, while Wellington is justly still in the fashion here, Washington is fading out of the fashion with us. It is not a good sign. The idols we have raised in his stead are not to our honor.

Some little dancing was done in the sacred corral in front of the Shah by grandees belonging mainly to "grace-of-God" families, but he himself never agitated a foot. The several thousand commoner people on the other side of the rope could not dance any more than sardines in a box. Chances to view the Guildhall spectacle were so hungered for that people offered £5 for the privilege of standing three minutes in the musicians' gallery and were refused. I cannot convey to you an idea of the inordinate desire which prevails here to see the Shah better than by remarking that speculators who held four-seat opera boxes at Covent Garden Theater to-night were able to get $250 for them. Had all the seats been sold at auction the opera this evening would have produced not less than one hundred and twenty-five thousand dollars in gold! I am below the figures rather than above them. The greatest house (for money) that America ever saw was gathered together upon the occasion of Jenny Lind's first concert at Castle Garden. The seats were sold at auction and produced something over twenty thousand dollars.

I am by no means trying to describe the Guildhall affair of last night. Such a crush of titled swells; such a bewildering array of jeweled uniforms and brilliant feminine costumes; such solemn and awful reception ceremonies in the library; such grim and stately imposing addresses and Persian replies; such imposing processional pageantry later on; such depressing dancing before the apathetic Shah; such ornate tables and imperial good cheer at the banquet—it makes a body tired to merely think of trying to put all that on paper. Perhaps you, sir, will be good enough to imagine it, and thus save one who respects you and honors you five columns of solid writing.

THE LUNATIC ASYLUM IS BLESSED WITH A GLIMPSE

As regards the momentous occasion of the opera, this evening, I found myself in a grievous predicament, for a republican. The tickets were all sold long ago, so I must either go as a member of the royal family or not at all. After a good deal of reflection it seemed best not to mix up with that class lest a political significance might be put upon it. But a queer arrangement had been devised whereby I might have a glimpse of the show, and I took advantage of that. There is an immense barnlike glass house attached to the rear of the theater, and that was fitted up with seats, carpets, mirrors, gas, columns, flowers, garlands, and a meager row of shrubs strung down the sides on brackets—to create an imposing forest effect, I suppose. The place would seat ten or twelve hundred people. All but a hundred paid a dollar and a quarter a seat—for what? To look at the Shah three quarters of a minute, while he walked through to enter the theater. The remaining hundred paid $11 a seat for the same privilege, with the added luxury of rushing on the stage and glancing at the opera audience for one single minute afterward, while the chorus sung "God Save the Queen!" We are all gone mad, I do believe. Eleven hundred five-shilling lunatics and a hundred two-guinea maniacs. The *Herald* purchased a ticket and created me one of the latter, along with two or three more of the staff.

Our cab was about No. 17,342 in the string that worked its slow way through London and past the theater. The Shah was not to come till nine o'clock, and yet we had to be at the theater by half past six, or we would not get into the glass house at all, they said. We were there on time, and seated in a small gallery which overlooked a very brilliantly

dressed throng of people. Every seat was occupied. We sat there two
hours and a half gazing and melting. The wide, red-carpeted central
aisle below offered good display ground for officials in fine uniforms,
and they made good use of it.

ROYALTY ARRIVES

By and by a band in showy uniform came in and stood opposite the
entrance. At the end of a tedious interval of waiting trumpets sounded
outside, there was some shouting, the band played half of "God Save
the Queen," and then the Duke and Duchess of Cambridge and a
dozen gorgeous Persian officials entered. After a little the young Prince
Arthur came, in a blue uniform, with a whole broadside of gold and
silver medals on his breast—for good behavior, punctuality, accurate
spelling, penmanship, etc., I suppose, but I could not see the inscrip-
tions. The band gave him some bars of "God Save the Queen," too,
while he stood under us talking, with altogether unroyal animation,
with the Persians—the crowd of people staring hungrily at him the
while—country cousins, maybe, who will go home and say, "I was as
close to him as I am to that chair this minute."

Then came the Duke of Teck and the Princess Mary, and the band
God-Save-the-Queen'd them also. Now came the Prince of Wales and
the Russian Tsarina—the royal anthem again, with an extra blast at the
end of it. After them came a young, handsome, mighty giant, in showy
uniform, his breast covered with glittering orders, and a general's
chapeau, with a flowing white plume, in his hand—the heir to all the
throne of all the Russias. The band greeted him with the Russian
national anthem, and played it clear through. And they did right; for
perhaps it is not risking too much to say that this is the only national
air in existence that is really worthy of a great nation.

And at last came the long-expected millennium himself, His Imperial
Majesty the Shah, with the charming Princess of Wales on his arm.
He had all his jewels on, and his diamond shaving brush in his hat
front. He shone like a window with the westering sun on it.

WHAT THE ASYLUM SAW

The small space below us was full now—it could accommodate no
more royalty. The august procession filed down the aisle in double
rank, the Shah and the Princess of Wales in the lead, and cheers broke
forth and a waving of handkerchiefs as the Princess passed—all said

this demonstration was meant for her. As the procession disappeared through the farther door, the hundred eleven-dollar maniacs rushed through a small aperture, then through an anteroom, and gathered in a flock on the stage, the chorus striking up "God Save the Queen" at the same moment.

We stood in a mighty bandbox, or a Roman coliseum, with a sea of faces stretching far away over the ground floor, and above them rose five curving tiers of gaudy humanity, the dizzy upper tier in the far distance rising sharply up against the roof, like a flower garden trying to hold an earthquake down and not succeeding. It was a magnificent spectacle, and what with the roaring of the chorus, the waving of handkerchiefs, the cheering of the people, the blazing gas, and the awful splendor of the long file of royalty, standing breast to breast in the royal box, it was wonderfully exhilarating, not to say exciting.

The chorus sang only three-quarters of a minute—one stanza—and down came the huge curtain and shut out the fairyland. And then all those eleven-dollar people hunted their way out again.

A NATION DEMENTED

We are certainly gone mad. We scarcely look at the young colossus who is to reign over 70,000,000 of people and the mightiest empire in extent which exists to-day. We have no eyes but for this splendid barbarian, who is lord over a few deserts and a modest ten million of ragamuffins—a man who has never done anything to win our gratitude or excite our admiration, except that he managed to starve a million of his subjects to death in twelve months. If he had starved the rest I suppose we would set up a monument to him now.

The London theaters are almost absolutely empty these nights. Nobody goes, hardly. The managers are being ruined. The streets for miles are crammed with people waiting whole long hours for a chance glimpse of the Shah. I never saw any man "draw" like this one.

Is there any truth in the report that your bureaus are trying to get the Shah to go over there and lecture? He could get $100,000 a night here and choose his own subject.

I know a showman who has got a pill that belonged to him, and which for some reason he did not take. That showman will not take any money for that pill. He is going to travel with it. And let me tell you he will get more engagements than he can fill in a year.

IV

MARK TWAIN HOOKS THE PERSIAN OUT OF
THE ENGLISH CHANNEL

London, June 26, 1873

I suppose I am the only member of the Shah's family who is not wholly broken down and worn out; and, to tell the truth, there is not much of me left. If you have ever been limited to four days in Paris or Rome or Jerusalem and been "rushed" by a guide you can form a vague, far-away sort of conception of what the Shah and the rest of us have endured during these late momentous days. If this goes on we may as well get ready for the imperial inquest.

When I was called at five o'clock the other morning to go to Portsmouth, and remembered that the Shah's incessant movements had left me only three hours' sleep that night, nothing but a sense of duty drove me forth. A cab could not be found, nor a carriage in all London. I lost an hour and a half waiting and trying, then started on foot and lost my way; consequently I missed one train by a good while, another one by three minutes, and then had more than half an hour to spare before another would go. Most people had had a similar experience, and there was comfort in that. We started at last, and were more than three hours going seventy-two miles. We stopped at no stations, hardly, but we halted every fifteen minutes out in the woods and fields for no purpose that we could discover. Never was such an opportunity to look at scenery. There were five strangers in our car, or carriage, as the English call it, and by degrees their English reserve thawed out and they passed around their sherry and sandwiches and grew sociable.

One of them had met the Russian General of Police in St. Petersburg, and found him a queer old simple-hearted soldier, proud of his past and devoted to his master, the present Tsar, and to the memory of his predecessor, Nicholas. The English gentleman gave an instance of the old man's simplicity which one would not expect in a chief of police. The general had been visiting London and been greatly impressed by two things there—the admirable police discipline and the museum. It transpired that the museum he referred to was not that mighty collection of marvels known to all the world as the British Museum, but Mme. Toussaud's Waxworks Show; and in this waxwork show he had seen a figure of the Emperor Nicholas. And did it please him? Yes, as to the likeness; for it was a good likeness and a commanding figure; but—"*Mon Dieu!* try to fancy it, m'sieu—dressed in the uniform of a simple colonel of infantry!—the great Nicholas of Russia, my august last master, dressed in a colonel's uniform!"

The old general could not abide that. He went to the proprietor and remonstrated against this wanton indignity. The proprietor was grieved; but it was the only Russian uniform he could get, and——

"Say no more!" said the general. "May I get you one?"

The proprietor would be most happy. The general lost not a moment; he wrote it once to the Emperor Alexander, describing with anguish the degradation which the late great Nicholas was suffering day by day through his infamously clothed waxen representative, and imploring His Majesty to send suitable raiment for the imperial dummy, and also a letter to authenticate the raiment. And out of regard for the old servant and respect for his outraged feelings the Emperor of all the Russias descended from his Alpine altitude to send to the Toussaud waxwork the general's uniform worn last by his father, and to write with his own hand an authenticating letter to go with it. So the simple-hearted police chief was happy once more, and never once thought of charging the "museum" $10,000 for these valuable additions to the show, which he might easily have done, and collected the money, too. How like our own chiefs of police this good old soul is!

Another of these English gentlemen told an anecdote, which, he said, was old, but which I had not heard before. He said that one day St. Peter and the devil chanced to be thrown together, and found it pretty dull trying to pass the time. Finally they got to throwing dice for a lawyer. The devil threw sixes. Then St. Peter threw sixes. The devil threw sixes again. St. Peter threw sixes again. The devil threw sixes once more. Then St. Peter threw sevens, and the devil said, "Oh, come now, Your Honor, cheat fair. None of your playing miracles here!" I thought there was a nice bit of humor in that suggestion to "cheat fair."

A SMALL PRIVATE NAUTICAL RACE

I am getting to Portsmouth about as fast in this letter as I did in that train. The Right Honorable the Mayor of Portsmouth had had a steamer placed at his disposal by the Admiralty, and he had invited the Lord Mayor of London and other guests to go in her. This was the ship I was to sail in, and she was to leave her pier at 9 A.M. sharp. I arrived at that pier at ten minutes to eleven exactly. There was one chance left, however. The ship had stopped for something and was floating at ease about a mile away.

A rusty, decayed, little two-oared skiff, the size of a bathtub, came floating by, with a fisherman and his wife and child in it. I entreated the man to come in and take me to the ship. Presently he consented and started toward me. I stood impatient and all ready to jump the moment he should get within thirty yards of me; he halted at the distance of thirty-five and said it would be a long pull; did I think I could pay him two shillings for it, seeing it was a holiday? All this palaver and I in such a state of mind! I jumped aboard and told him to rush, which he did; at least he threw his whole heart into his little, useless oars, and we moved off at the rate of a mile a week. This was solid misery. When we had gone a hundred and nine feet and were gaining on the tenth a long, trim, graceful man-of-war's boat came flying by, bound for the flagship. Without expecting even the courtesy of a response, I hailed and asked the coxswain to take me to the mayor's vessel. He said, "Certainly, sir!—ease her, boys!" I could not have been more astonished at anything in the world. I quickly gave my man his two shillings, and he started to pull me to the boat. Then there was a movement of discontent among the sailors, and they seemed about to move on. I thought—well, you are not such generous fellows, after all, as I took you to be, or so polite, either; but just then the coxswain hailed and said:

"The boys don't mind the pull, and they're perfectly willing to take you, but they say they ain't willing to take the fisherman's job away from him."

Now that was genuine manliness and right conduct. I shall always remember that honorable act. I told them the fisherman was already paid, and I was in their boat the next moment. Then ensued the real fun of the day, as far as I was personally concerned. The boys glanced over their shoulders to measure the distance, and then at the order to "Give way!" they bent to it and the boat sped through the water like an arrow. We passed all kinds of craft and steadily shortened the distance that lay between us and the ship. Presently the coxswain said:

"No use! Her wheels have begun to turn over. Lively now, lively!"

Then we flew. We watched the ship's movement with a sharp interest and calculated our chances.

"Can you steer?" said the coxswain.

"Can a duck swim?" said I.

"Good—we'll make her yet!"

I took the helm and he the stroke oar, and that one oar did appear
to add a deal to that boat's speed. The ship was turning around to go
out to sea, and she did seem to turn unnecessarily fast, too; but just as
she was pointed right and both her wheels began to go ahead our
boat's bow touched her companionway and I was aboard. It was a
handsome race, and very exciting. If I could have had that dainty
boat and those eight white-shirted, blue-trousered sailors for the day I
would not have gone in any ship, but would have gone about in vast
naval style and experienced the feelings of an admiral.

OLD HISTORICAL MEN-OF-WAR

Our ship sailed out through a narrow way, bordered by piers that
swarmed with people, and likewise by prodigious men-of-war of the
fashion of a hundred years ago. There were, perhaps, a dozen of the
stately veterans, these relics of an historic past; and not looking aged
and seedy, either, but as bright and fresh as if they had been launched
and painted yesterday. They were the noblest creatures to look upon;
hulls of huge proportion and great length; four long tiers of cannon
grinning from their tall sides; vast sterns that towered into the air like
the gable end of a church; graceful bows and figureheads; masts as
trim and lofty as spires—surely no spectacle could be so imposing as a
sea fight in the old times, when such beautiful and such lordly ships
as these ruled the seas. And how it must have stirred the heart of
England when a fleet of them used to come sailing in from victory,
with ruined sides and tattered spars and sails, while bells and cannon
pealed a welcome!

One of the grandest of these veterans was the very one upon whose
deck Nelson himself fell in the moment of triumph. I suppose England
would rather part with ten colonies than with that illustrious old ship.
We passed along within thirty steps of her, and I was just trying to
picture in my mind the tremendus scenes that had transpired upon
her deck upon that day, the proudest in England's naval history, when
the venerable craft, stirred by the boom of saluting cannon, perhaps,
woke up out of her long sleep and began to vomit smoke and thunder
herself, and then she looked her own natural self again, and no doubt
the spirit of Nelson was near. Still it would have been pleasanter to be
on her decks than in front of her guns; for, as the white volumes of
smoke burst in our faces, one could not help feeling that a ball might
by accident have got mixed up with a blank cartridge, and might chip
just enough off the upper end of a man to disfigure him for life; and be-

sides, the powder they use in cannon is in grains as large as billiard chalks, and it does not all explode—suppose a few should enter one's system? The crash and roar of these great guns was as unsettling a sound as I have ever heard at short range. I took off my hat and acknowledged the salute, of course, though it seemed to me that it would have been better manners if they had saluted the Lord Mayor, inasmuch as he was on board.

THE WORLD'S GREATEST NAVY ON VIEW

We went out to the Spithead and sailed up and down there for four hours through four long ranks of stately men-of-war—formidable ironclads they were—the most insignificant of which would make a breakfast of a whole fleet of Nelson's prodigious ships and still be hungry. The show was very fine, for there were forty-nine of the finest ironclads the world can show, and many gunboats besides. Indeed, here in its full strength was the finest navy in the world, and this the only time in history that just such a spectacle has been seen, and none who saw it that day is likely to live long enough to see its like again. The vessels were all dressed out with flags, and all about them frolicked a bewildering host of bannered yachts, steamers, and every imaginable sort of craft. It would be hard to contrive a gayer scene. One of the royal yachts came flying along presently and put the Shah on board one of the ironclads, and then the yards of the whole fleet were manned simultaneously, and such another booming and bellowing of great guns ensued as I cannot possibly describe. Within two minutes the huge fleet was swallowed up in smoke, with angry red tongues of fire darting through it here and there. It was wonderful to look upon. Every time the *Devastation* let off one of her thirty-five-ton guns it seemed as if an entire London fog issued from her side, and the report was so long coming that if she were to shoot a man he would be dead before he heard it, and would probably go around wondering through all eternity what it was that happened to him. I returned to London in a great hurry by a train that was in no way excited by it, but failed in the end and object I had in view after all, which was to go to the grand concert as Albert Hall in honor of the Shah. I had a strong desire to see that building filled with people once. Albert Hall is one of the many monuments erected to the memory of the late Prince Albert. It is a huge and costly edifice, but the architectural design is old, not to say in some sense a plagiarism; for there is but little originality in putting a dome on a gasometer. It is said to seat 13,000 people, and

surely that is a thing worth seeing—at least to a man who was not at
the Boston Jubilee. But no tickets were to be had—every seat was full,
they said. It was no particular matter, but what made me mad was to
come so extremely close and then miss. Indeed, I was madder than I
can express, to think that if the architect had only planned the place to
hold 13,001 I could have got in. But, after all, I was not the only person who had occasion to feel vexed. Colonel X, a noted man in
America, bought a seat some days ago for $10 and a little afterward
met a knowing person who said the Shah would be physically worn
out before that concert night and would not be there, and consequently
nobody else; so the seat was immediately sold for $5. Then came an-
other knowing one, who said the Shah would unquestionably be at the
concert, so the colonel went straight and bought his ticket back again.
The temporary holder of it only charged him $250 for carrying it
around for him during the interval! The colonel was at the concert,
and took the Shah's head clerk for the Shah all the evening. Vexation
could go no further than that.

V

MARK TWAIN GIVES THE ROYAL PERSIAN
A "SEND-OFF"

London, June 30, 1873

For the present we are done with the Shah in London. He is gone to
the country to be further "impressed." After all, it would seem that he
was more moved and more genuinely entertained by the military day
at Windsor than by even the naval show at Portsmouth. It is not to be
wondered at, since he is a good deal of a soldier himself and not much
of a sailor. It has been estimated that there were 300,000 people assembled at Windsor—some say 500,000. That was a show in itself. The
Queen of England was there; so was Windsor Castle; also an imposing
array of cavalry, artillery, and infantry. And the accessories to these
several shows were the matchless rural charms of England—a vast
expanse of green sward, walled in by venerable forest trees, and
beyond them glimpses of hills clothed in Summer vegetation. Upon
such a theater a bloodless battle was fought and an honorable victory
won by trained soldiers who have not always been carpet knights, but
whose banners bear the names of many historic fights.

England is now practically done with the Shah. True, his engagement is not yet completed, for he is still billed to perform at one or

two places; but curiosity is becoming sated, and he will hardly draw as good houses as heretofore. Whenever a star has to go to the provinces it is a bad sign. The poor man is well nigh worn out with hard work. The other day he was to have performed before the Duke of Buccleuch and was obliged to send an excuse. Since then he failed of his engagement at the Bank of England. He does not take rest even when he might. He has a telegraphic apparatus in his apartments in Buckingham Palace, and it is said that he sits up late, talking with his capital of Persia by telegraph. He is so fascinated with the wonderful contrivance that he cannot keep away from it. No doubt it is the only homelike thing the exile finds in the hard, practical West, for it is the next of kin to the enchanted carpets that figure in the romance and traditions of his own land, and which carry the wanderer whither he will about the earth, circumscribing the globe in the twinkling of an eye, propelled by only the force of an unspoken wish.

GOSSIP ABOUT THE SHAH

This must be a dreary, unsatisfactory country to him, where one's desires are thwarted at every turn. Last week he woke up at three in the morning and demanded of the Vizier on watch by his bedside that the ballet dancers be summoned to dance before him. The Vizier prostrated himself upon the floor and said:

"O king of kings, light of the world, source of human peace and contentment, the glory and admiration of the age, turn away thy sublime countenance, let not thy fateful frown wither thy slave; for behold the dancers dwell wide asunder in the desert wastes of London, and not in many hours could they be gathered together."

The Shah could not even speak, he was so astounded with the novelty of giving a command that could not be obeyed. He sat still a moment, suffering, then wrote in his tablets these words:

"MEM.—Upon arrival in Teheran, let the Vizier have the coffin which has just been finished for the late general of the household troops—it will save time."

He then got up and set his boots outside the door to be blacked and went back to bed, calm and comfortable, making no more to-do about giving away that costly coffin than I would about spending a couple of shillings.

THE LESSON OF HIS JOURNEY

If the mountains of money spent by civilized Europe in entertaining the Shah shall win him to adopt some of the mild and merciful ways that prevail in Christian realms it will have been money well and wisely laid out. If he learns that a throne may rest as firmly upon the affections of a people as upon their fears; that charity and justice may go hand in hand without detriment to the authority of the sovereign; that an enlarged liberty granted to the subject need not impair the power of the monarch; if he learns these things Persia will be the gainer by his journey, and the money which Europe has expended in entertaining him will have been profitably invested. That the Shah needs a hint or two in these directions is shown by the language of the following petition, which has just reached him from certain Parsees residing here and in India:

THE PETITION

1. A heavy and oppressive poll tax, called the Juzia, is imposed upon the remnant of the ancient Zoroastrain race now residing in Persia. A hundred years ago, when the Zoroastrian population was 30,000 families, and comparatively well-to-do, the tax was only 250 toomans; now, when there are scarcely six thousand souls altogether, and stricken with poverty, they have to pay 800 toomans. In addition to the crushing effect of this tax, the government officials oppress these poor people in enforcing the tax.

2. A Parsee desirous of buying landed property is obliged to pay twenty per cent. on the value of the property as fee to the Kazee and other authorities.

3. When a Parsee dies any member of his family, no matter however distant, who may have previously been converted to Mohammedanism, claims and obtains the whole property of the deceased, to the exclusion of all the rightful heirs. In enforcing this claim the convert is backed and supported by government functionaries.

4. When a Parsee returns to Persia from a foreign country he is harassed with all sorts of exactions at the various places he has to pass through in Persia.

5. When any dispute arises, whether civil or criminal, between a Mohammedan and a Parsee, the officials invariably side with the former, and the testimony of one Mohammedan—no matter how false on its very face—receives more credit than that of a dozen or any number of Parsee witnesses. If a Mohammedan kills a Parsee he is only fined about eight toomans, or four pounds sterling; but on the contrary, if a Parsee wounds or murders a Mohammedan he is not only cut to pieces himself, but all his family and children

are put to the sword, and sometimes all the Parsees living in the same street are harassed in a variety of ways. The Parsees are prevented from dressing themselves well and from riding a horse or donkey. No matter, even if he were ill and obliged to ride, he is compelled to dismount in the presence of a Mohammedan rider, and is forced to walk to the place of his destination. The Parsees are not allowed to trade in European articles, nor are they allowed to deal in domestic produce, as grocers, dyers, or oilmen, tailors, dairymen, &c., on the ground that their touch would pollute the articles and supplies and make them unfit for the use of Mohammedans.

6. The Parsees are often insulted and abused in every way by the Mohammedans, and their children are stolen or forcibly taken away from them by the Mohammedans. These children are concealed in Mohammedan houses, their names are changed, and they are forced to become Mohammedans, and when they refuse to embrace the Mohammedan faith they are maltreated in various ways. When a man is forcibly converted, his wife and family are also forced to join him as Mohammedans. The Mohammedans desecrate the sacred places of worship of the Zoroastrians and the places for the disposal of their dead.

7. In general the Parsees are heavily taxed in various ways, and are subjected to great oppression. In consequence of such persecution the Parsee population of Persia has, during this century, considerably decreased and is now so small that it consists of a few thousand families only. It is possible that these persecutions are practiced on the Zoroastrian inhabitants of Persia without the knowledge of His Majesty the Shah.

THE INGENIOUS BARON REUTER

It is whispered that the Shah's European trip was not suggested by the Shah himself, but by the noted telegraphic newsman, Baron Reuter. People who pretend to know say that Reuter began life very poor; that he was an energetic spirit and improved such opportunities as fell in his way; that he learned several languages, and finally became a European guide, or courier, and employed himself in conducting all sorts of foreigners through all sorts of countries and wearing them out with the usual frantic system of sight-seeing. That was a good education for him; it also gave him an intimate knowledge of all the routes of travel and taught him how certain long ones might be shortened. By and by he got some carrier pigeons and established a news express, which necessarily prospered, since it furnished journals and commercial people with all matters of importance considerably in advance of the mails. When railways came into vogue he obtained concessions which enlarged his facilities and still enabled him to defy competition. He was ready for the telegraph and seized that, too; and now for years

"REUTER'S TELEGRAMS"

has stood in brackets at the head of the telegraphic column of all European journals. He became rich; he bought telegraph lines and built others, purchased a second-hand German baronetcy, and finally sold out his telegraphic property to his government for $3,000,000 and was out of business for once. But he could not stay out.

After building himself a sort of a palace, he looked around for fresh game, singled out the Shah of Persia and "went for him," as the historian Josephus phrases it. He got an enormous "concession" from him and then conceived the admirable idea of exhibiting a Shah of Persia in the capitals of Europe and thus advertising his concession before needful capitalists. It was a sublimer idea than any that any showman's brain has ever given birth to. No Shah had ever voluntarily traveled in Europe before; but then no Shah had ever fallen into the hands of a European guide before.

THE FAT "CONCESSION"

The baron's "concession" is a financial curiosity. It allows him the sole right to build railways in Persia for the next seventy years; also street railroads; gives all the land necessary, free of charge, for double tracks and fifty or sixty yards on each side; all importations of *material*, etc., free of duty; all the baron's exports free of duty also. The baron may appropriate and work all mines (except those of the precious metals) free of charge, the Shah to have 15 per cent of the profits. Any private mine may be "gobbled" (the Persian word is *akbamarish*) by the baron if it has not been worked during five years previously. The baron has the exclusive privilege of making the most of all government forests, he giving the Shah 15 per cent of the profits from the wood sold. After a forest is removed, the baron is to be preferred before all other purchasers if he wants to buy the land. The baron alone may dig wells and construct canals, and he is to own all the land made productive by such works. The baron is empowered to raise $30,000,000 on the capital stock for working purposes, and the Shah agrees to pay 7 per cent interest on it; and Persia is wholly unencumbered with debt. The Shah hands over to the baron the management of his customs for twenty years, and the baron engages to pay for this privilege $100,-000 a year more than the Shah now receives, so the baron means to wake up that sleepy Persian commerce. After the fifth year the baron is to pay the Shah an additional 60 per cent of the profits, if his head

388   MARK TWAIN

is still a portion of his person then. The baron is to have first preference in the establishment of a bank. The baron has preference in establishing gas, road, telegraph, mill, manufacturing, forge, pavement, and all such enterprises. The Shah is to have 20 per cent of the profits arising from the railways. Finally, the baron may sell out whenever he wants to.

It is a good "concession" in its way. It seems to make the Shah say: "Run Persia at my expense and give me a fifth of the profits."

One's first impulse is to envy the baron; but, after all, I do not know. Some day, if things do not go to suit the Shah, he may say, "There is no head I admire so much as this baron's; bring it to me on a plate."

DEPARTURE OF THE IMPERIAL CIRCUS

We are all sorry to see the Shah leave us, and yet are glad on his account. We have had all the fun and he all the fatigue. He would not have lasted much longer here. I am just here reminded that the only way whereby you may pronounce the Shah's title correctly is by taking a pinch of snuff. The result will be "t-Shah!"

1878

The Great Revolution in Pitcairn

Let me refresh the reader's memory a little. Nearly a hundred years ago the crew of the British ship *Bounty* mutinied, set the captain and his officers adrift upon the open sea, took possession of the ship, and sailed southward. They procured wives for themselves among the natives of Tahiti, then proceeded to a lonely little rock in mid-Pacific, called Pitcairn's Island, wrecked the vessel, stripped her of everything that might be useful to a new colony, and established themselves on shore.

Pitcairn's is so far removed from the track of commerce that it was many years before another vessel touched there. It had always been considered an uninhabited island; so when a ship did at last drop its anchor there, in 1808, the captain was greatly surprised to find the place peopled. Although the mutineers had fought among themselves, and gradually killed each other off until only two or three of the original stock remained, these tragedies had not occurred before a number of children had been born; so in 1808 the island had a population of twenty-seven persons. John Adams, the chief mutineer, still survived, and was to live many years yet, as governor and patriarch of the flock. From being mutineer and homicide, he had turned Christian and teacher, and his nation of twenty-seven persons was now the purest and devoutest in Christendom. Adams had long ago hoisted the British flag and constituted his island an appanage of the British crown.

To-day the population numbers ninety persons—sixteen men, nineteen women, twenty-five boys, and thirty girls—all descendants of the mutineers, all bearing the family names of those mutineers, and all speaking English, and English only. The island stands high up out of the sea, and has precipitous walls. It is about three-quarters of a mile long, and in places is as much as half a mile wide. Such arable land as it affords is held by the several families, according to a division made many years ago. There is some live stock—goats, pigs, chickens, and cats; but no dogs, and no large animals. There is one church-building —used also as a capitol, a schoolhouse, and a public library. The title of the governor has been, for a generation or two, "Magistrate and Chief Ruler, in subordination to her Majesty the Queen of Great Britain." It was his province to *make* the laws, as well as execute them. His office was elective; everybody over seventeen years old had a vote—no matter about the sex.

The sole occupations of the people were farming and fishing; their sole recreation, religious services. There has never been a shop in the island, nor any money. The habits and dress of the people have always been primitive, and their laws simple to puerility. They have lived in a deep Sabbath tranquillity, far from the world and its ambitions and vexations, and neither knowing nor caring what was going on in the mighty empires that lie beyond their limitless ocean solitudes. Once in three or four years a ship touched there, moved them with aged news of bloody battles, devastating epidemics, fallen thrones, and ruined dynasties, then traded them some soap and flannel for some yams and breadfruit, and sailed away, leaving them to retire into their peaceful dreams and pious dissipations once more.

On the 8th of last September, Admiral de Horsey, commander-in-chief of the British fleet in the Pacific, visited Pitcairn's Island, and speaks as follows in his official report to the admiralty:

They have beans, carrots, turnips, cabbages, and a little maize; pineapples, fig trees, custard-apples, and oranges; lemons, and cocoanuts. Clothing is obtained alone from passing ships, in barter for refreshments. There are no springs on the island, but as it rains generally once a month they have plenty of water, although at times in former years they have suffered from drought. No alcoholic liquors, except for medicinal purposes, are used, and a drunkard is unknown. . . .

The necessary articles required by the islanders are best shown by those we furnished in barter for refreshments: namely, flannel, serge, drill, half-boots, combs, tobacco, and soap. They also stand much in need of maps and slates for their school, and tools of any kind are most acceptable. I caused them to be supplied from the public stores with a Union Jack for display on the arrival of ships, and a pit-saw, of which they were greatly in need. This, I trust, will meet the approval of their lordships. If the munificent people of England were only aware of the wants of this most deserving little colony, they would not long go unsupplied. . . .

Divine service is held every Sunday at 10.30 A.M. and at 3 P.M., in the house built and used by John Adams for that purpose until he died in 1829. It is conducted strictly in accordance with the liturgy of the Church of England, by Mr. Simon Young, their selected pastor, who is much respected. A Bible class is held every Wednesday, when all who conveniently can attend. There is also a general meeting for prayer on the first Friday in every month. Family prayers are said in every house the first thing in the morning and the last thing in the evening, and no food is partaken of without asking God's blessing before and afterward. Of these islanders' religious attributes no one can speak without deep respect. A people whose greatest pleasure and privilege is to commune in prayer with their God, and to join in hymns of praise, and who are, moreover, cheerful, diligent, and probably freer from vice than any other community, need no priest among them.

Now I come to a sentence in the admiral's report which he dropped carelessly from his pen, no doubt, and never gave the matter a second thought. He little imagined what a freight of tragic prophecy it bore! This is the sentence:

One stranger, an American, has settled on the island—*a doubtful acquisition.*

A doubtful acquisition, indeed! Captain Ormsby, in the American ship *Hornet*, touched at Pitcairn's nearly four months after the admiral's visit, and from the facts which he gathered there we now know all about that American. Let us put these facts together in historical form. The American's name was Butterworth Stavely. As soon as he had become well acquainted with all the people—and this took but a few days, of course—he began to ingratiate himself with them by all the arts he could command. He became exceedingly popular, and much looked up to; for one of the first things he did was to forsake his worldly way of life, and throw all his energies into religion. He was always reading his Bible, or praying, or singing hymns, or asking blessings. In prayer, no one had such "liberty" as he, no one could pray so long or so well.

At last, when he considered the time to be ripe, he began secretly to sow the seeds of discontent among the people. It was his deliberate purpose, from the beginning, to subvert the government, but of course he kept that to himself for a time. He used different arts with different individuals. He awakened dissatisfaction in one quarter by calling attention to the shortness of the Sunday services; he argued that there should be three three-hour services on Sunday instead of only two. Many had secretly held this opinion before; they now privately banded themselves into a party to work for it. He showed certain of the women that they were not allowed sufficient voice in the prayer-meetings; thus another party was formed. No weapon was beneath his notice; he even descended to the children, and awoke discontent in their breasts because—as *he* discovered for them—they had not enough Sunday-school. This created a third party.

Now, as the chief of these parties, he found himself the strongest power in the community. So he proceeded to his next move—a no less important one than the impeachment of the chief magistrate, James Russell Nickoy; a man of character and ability, and possessed of great wealth, he being the owner of a house with a parlor to it, three acres and a half of yam-land, and the only boat in Pitcairn's, a whaleboat; and, most unfortunately, a pretext for his impeachment offered itself at just the right time.

One of the earliest and most precious laws of the island was the law against trespass. It was held in great reverence, and was regarded as the palladium of the people's liberties. About thirty years ago an important case came before the courts under this law, in this wise: a chicken belonging to Elizabeth Young (aged, at that time, fifty-eight, a daughter of John Mills, one of the mutineers of the *Bounty*) trespassed upon the grounds of Thursday October Christian (aged twenty-nine, a grandson of Fletcher Christian, one of the mutineers). Christian killed the chicken. According to the law, Christian could keep the chicken; or, if he preferred, he could restore its remains to the owner and receive damages in "produce" to an amount equivalent to the waste and injury wrought by the trespasser. The court records set forth that "the said Christian aforesaid did deliver the aforesaid remains to the said Elizabeth Young, and did demand one bushel of yams in satisfaction of the damage done." But Elizabeth Young considered the demand exorbitant; the parties could not agree; therefore Christian brought suit in the courts. He lost his case in the justice's court; at least, he was awarded only a half-peck of yams, which he considered insufficient, and in the nature of a defeat. He appealed. The case lingered several years in an ascending grade of courts, and always resulted in decrees sustaining the original verdict; and finally the thing got into the supreme court, and there it stuck for twenty years. But last summer, even the supreme court managed to arrive at a decision at last. Once more the original verdict was sustained. Christian then said he was satisfied; but Stavely was present, and whispered to him and to his lawyer, suggesting, "as a mere form," that the original law be exhibited, in order to make sure that it still existed. It seemed an odd idea, but an ingenious one. So the demand was made. A messenger was sent to the magistrate's house; he presently returned with the tidings that it had disappeared from among the state archives.

The court now pronounced its late decision void, since it had been made under a law which had no actual existence.

Great excitement ensued immediately. The news swept abroad over the whole island that the palladium of the public liberties was lost—maybe treasonably destroyed. Within thirty minutes almost the entire nation were in the court-room—that is to say, the church. The impeachment of the chief magistrate followed, upon Stavely's motion. The accused met his misfortune with the dignity which became his great office. He did not plead, or even argue; he offered the simple defense that he had not meddled with the missing law; that he had kept the state archives in the same candle-box that had been used as their depository from the beginning; and that he was innocent of the removal or destruction of the lost document.

But nothing could save him; he was found guilty of misprision of treason, and degraded from his office, and all his property was confiscated.

The lamest part of the whole shameful matter was the *reason* suggested by his enemies for his destruction of the law, to wit: that he did it to favor Christian, because Christian was his cousin! Whereas Stavely was the only individual in the entire nation who was *not* his cousin. The reader must remember that all these people are the descendants of half a dozen men; that the first children intermarried together and bore grandchildren to the mutineers; that these grandchildren intermarried; after them, great and great-great-grandchildren intermarried; so that to-day everybody is blood kin to everybody. Moreover, the relation-

ships are wonderfully, even astoundingly, mixed up and complicated. A stranger, for instance, says to an islander:

"You speak of that young woman as your cousin; a while ago you
called her your aunt."

"Well, she *is* my aunt, and my cousin, too. And also my stepsister,
my niece, my fourth cousin, my thirty-third cousin, my forty-second
cousin, my greataunt, my grandmother, my widowed sister-in-law—
and next week she will be my wife."

So the charge of nepotism against the chief magistrate was weak. But
no matter; weak or strong, it suited Stavely. Stavely was immediately
elected to the vacant magistracy, and, oozing reform from every pore,
he went vigorously to work. In no long time religious services raged
everywhere and unceasingly. By command, the second prayer of the
Sunday morning service, which had customarily endured some thirty-
five or forty minutes, and had pleaded for the world, first by continent
and then by national and tribal detail, was extended to an hour and a
half, and made to include supplications in behalf of the possible peoples in the several planets. Everybody was pleased with this; everybody said, "Now *this* is something *like*." By command, the usual three-
hour sermons were doubled in length. The nation came in a body to
testify their gratitude to the new magistrate. The old law forbidding
cooking on the Sabbath was extended to the prohibition of eating, also.
By command, Sunday-school was privileged to spread over into the
week. The joy of all classes was complete. In one short month the new
magistrate had become the people's idol!

The time was ripe for this man's next move. He began, cautiously at
first, to poison the public mind against England. He took the chief citizens aside, one by one, and conversed with them on this topic. Presently he grew bolder, and spoke out. He said the nation owed it to itself, to its honor, to its great traditions, to rise in its might and throw
off "this galling English yoke."

But the simple islanders answered:

"We had not noticed that it galled. How does it gall? England sends
a ship once in three or four years to give us soap and clothing, and
things which we sorely need and gratefully receive; but she never troubles us; she lets us go our own way."

"She lets you go your own way! So slaves have felt and spoken in
all the ages! This speech shows how fallen you are, how base, how brutalized you have become, under this grinding tyranny! What! has all
manly pride forsaken you? Is liberty nothing? Are you content to be a
mere appendage to a foreign and hateful sovereignty, when you might

rise up and take your rightful place in the august family of nations, great, free, enlightened, independent, the minion of no sceptered master, but the arbiter of your own destiny, and a voice and a power in decreeing the destinies of your sister-sovereignties of the world?"

Speeches like this produced an effect by and by. Citizens began to feel the English yoke; they did not know exactly how or whereabouts they felt it, but they were perfectly certain they did feel it. They got to grumbling a good deal, and chafing under their chains, and longing for relief and release. They presently fell to hating the English flag, that sign and symbol of their nation's degradation; they ceased to glance up at it as they passed the capitol, but averted their eyes and grated their teeth; and one morning, when it was found trampled into the mud at the foot of the staff, they left it there, and no man put his hand to it to hoist it again. A certain thing which was sure to happen sooner or later happened now. Some of the chief citizens went to the magistrate by night, and said:

"We can endure this hated tyranny no longer. How can we cast it off?"

"By a *coup d'état*."

"How?"

"A *coup d'état*. It is like this: everything is got ready, and at the appointed moment I, as the official head of the nation, publicly and solemnly proclaim its independence, and absolve it from allegiance to any and all other powers whatsoever."

"That sounds simple and easy. We can do that right away. Then what will be the next thing to do?"

"Seize all the defenses and public properties of all kinds, establish martial law, put the army and navy on a war footing, and proclaim the empire!"

This fine program dazzled these innocents. They said:

"This is grand—this is splendid; but will not England resist?"

"Let her. This rock is a Gibraltar."

"True. But about the empire? Do we *need* an empire and an emperor?"

"What you *need*, my friends, is unification. Look at Germany; look at Italy. They are unified. Unification is the thing. It makes living dear. That constitutes progress. We must have a standing army and a navy. Taxes follow, as a matter of course. All these things summed up make grandeur. With unification and grandeur, what more can you want? Very well—only the empire can confer these boons."

So on the 8th day of December Pitcairn's Island was proclaimed a free and independent nation; and on the same day the solemn coronation of Butterworth I., Emperor of Pitcairn's Island, took place, amid great rejoicings and festivities. The entire nation, with the exception of fourteen persons, mainly little children, marched past the throne in single file, with banners and music, the procession being upward of ninety feet long; and some said it was as much as three-quarters of a minute passing a given point. Nothing like it had ever been seen in the history of the island before. Public enthusiasm was measureless.

Now straightway imperial reforms began. Orders of nobility were instituted. A minister of the navy was appointed, and the whale-boat put in commission. A minister of war was created, and ordered to proceed at once with the formation of a standing army. A first lord of the treasury was named, and commanded to get up a taxation scheme, and also open negotiations for treaties, offensive, defensive, and commercial, with foreign powers. Some generals and admirals were appointed; also some chamberlains, some equerries in waiting, and some lords of the bedchamber.

At this point all the material was used up. The Grand Duke of Galilee, minister of war, complained that all the sixteen grown men in the empire had been given great offices, and consequently would not consent to serve in the ranks; wherefore his standing army was at a standstill. The Marquis of Ararat, minister of the navy, made a similar complaint. He said he was willing to steer the whale-boat himself, but he *must* have somebody to man her.

The emperor did the best he could in the circumstances: he took all the boys above the age of ten years away from their mothers, and pressed them into the army, thus constructing a corps of seventeen privates, officered by one lieutenant-general and two major-generals. This pleased the minister of war, but procured the enmity of all the mothers in the land; for they said their precious ones must now find bloody graves in the fields of war, and he would be answerable for it. Some of the more heartbroken and unappeasable among them lay constantly in wait for the emperor and threw yams at him, unmindful of the body-guard.

On account of the extreme scarcity of material, it was found necessary to require the Duke of Bethany, postmaster-general, to pull stroke-oar in the navy, and thus sit in the rear of a noble of lower degree, namely, Viscount Canaan, lord justice of the common pleas. This turned the Duke of Bethany into a tolerably open malcontent and a secret conspirator—a thing which the emperor foresaw, but could not help.

Things went from bad to worse. The emperor raised Nancy Peters to the peerage on one day, and married her the next, notwithstanding, for reasons of state, the cabinet had strenuously advised him to marry Emmeline, eldest daughter of the Archbishop of Bethlehem. This caused trouble in a powerful quarter—the church. The new empress secured the support and friendship of two-thirds of the thirty-six grown women in the nation by absorbing them into her court as maids of honor; but this made deadly enemies of the remaining twelve. The families of the maids of honor soon began to rebel, because there was nobody at home to keep house. The twelve snubbed women refused to enter the imperial kitchen as servants; so the empress had to require the Countess of Jericho and other great court dames to fetch water, sweep the palace, and perform other menial and equally distasteful services. This made bad blood in that department.

Everybody fell to complaining that the taxes levied for the support of the army, the navy, and the rest of the imperial establishment were intolerably burdensome, and were reducing the nation to beggary. The emperor's reply—"Look at Germany; look at Italy. Are you better than they? and haven't you unification?"—did not satisfy them. They said, "People can't *eat* unification, and we are starving. Agriculture has ceased. Everybody is in the army, everybody is in the navy, everybody is in the public service, standing around in a uniform, with nothing whatever to do, nothing to eat, and nobody to till the fields—"

"Look at Germany; look at Italy. It is the same there. Such is unification, and there's no other way to get it—no other way to keep it after you've got it," said the poor emperor always.

But the grumblers only replied, "We can't *stand* the taxes—we can't *stand* them."

Now right on top of this the cabinet reported a national debt amounting to upward of forty-five dollars—half a dollar to every individual in the nation. And they proposed to fund something. They had heard that this was always done in such emergencies. They proposed duties on exports; also on imports. And they wanted to issue bonds; also paper money, redeemable in yams and cabbages in fifty years. They said the pay of the army and of the navy and of the whole governmental machine was far in arrears, and unless something was done, and done immediately, national bankruptcy must ensue, and possibly insurrection and revolution. The emperor at once resolved upon a high-handed measure, and one of a nature never before heard of in Pitcairn's Island. He went in state to the church on Sunday morning, with the army at his back, and commanded the minister of the treasury to take up a collection.

That was the feather that broke the camel's back. First one citizen, and then another, rose and refused to submit to this unheard-of outrage—and each refusal was followed by the immediate confiscation of the malcontent's property. This vigor soon stopped the refusals, and the collection proceeded amid a sullen and ominous silence. As the emperor withdrew with the troops, he said, "I will teach you who is master here." Several persons shouted, "Down with unification!" They were at once arrested and torn from the arms of their weeping friends by the soldiery.

But in the mean time, as any prophet might have foreseen, a Social Democrat had been developed. As the emperor stepped into the gilded imperial wheelbarrow at the church door, the social democrat stabbed at him fifteen or sixteen times with a harpoon, but fortunately with such a perculiarly social democratic unprecision of aim as to do no damage.

That very night the convulsion came. The nation rose as one man—though forty-nine of the revolutionists were of the other sex. The infantry threw down their pitchforks; the artillery cast aside their cocoanuts; the navy revolted; the emperor was seized, and bound hand and foot in his palace. He was very much depressed. He said:

"I freed you from a grinding tyranny; I lifted you up out of your degradation, and made you a nation among nations; I gave you a strong, compact, centralized government; and, more than all, I gave you the blessing of blessings—unification. I have done all this, and my reward is hatred, insult, and these bonds. Take me; do with me as you will. I here resign my crown and all my dignities, and gladly do I release myself from their too heavy burden. For your sake I took them up; for your sake I lay them down. The imperial jewel is no more; now bruise and defile as ye will the useless setting."

By a unanimous voice the people condemned the ex-emperor and the social democrat to perpetual banishment from church services, or to perpetual labor as galley-slaves in the whale-boat—whichever they might prefer. The next day the nation assembled again, and rehoisted the British flag, reinstated the British tyranny, reduced the nobility to the condition of commoners again, and then straightway turned their diligent attention to the weeding of the ruined and neglected yam patches, and the rehabilitation of the old useful industries and the old healing and solacing pieties. The ex-emperor restored the lost trespass law, and explained that he had stolen it—not to injure any one, but to further his political projects. Therefore the nation gave the late chief magistrate his office again, and also his alienated property.

Upon reflection, the ex-emperor and the social democrat chose perpetual banishment from religious services in preference to perpetual labor as galley-slaves *"with* perpetual religious services," as they phrased it; wherefore the people believed that the poor fellows' troubles had unseated their reason, and so they judged it best to confine them for the present. Which they did.

Such is the history of Pitcairn's "doubtful acquisition."

1879

Speech on the Babies

At the Banquet, in Chicago, Given by the Army of the Tennessee to Their First Commander, General U. S. Grant, November, 1879

The fifteenth regular toast was "The Babies—as they comfort us in our sorrows, let us not forget them in our festivities."

I like that. We have not all had the good fortune to be ladies. We have not all been generals, or poets, or statesmen; but when the toast works down to the babies, we stand on common ground. It is a shame that for a thousand years the world's banquets have utterly ignored the baby, as if he didn't amount to anything. If you will stop and think a minute—if you will go back fifty or one hundred years to your early married life and recontemplate your first baby—you will remember that he amounted to a good deal, and even something over. You soldiers all know that when that little fellow arrived at family headquarters you had to hand in your resignation. He took entire command. You became his lackey, his mere body-servant, and you had to stand around, too. He was not a commander who made allowances for time, distance, weather, or anything else. You had to execute his order whether it was possible or not. And there was only one form of marching in his manual of tactics, and that was the double-quick. He treated you with every sort of insolence and disrespect, and the bravest of you didn't dare to say a word. You could face the death-storm at Donelson and Vicksburg,

and give back blow for blow; but when he clawed your whiskers, and
pulled your hair, and twisted your nose, you had to take it. When the
thunders of war were sounding in your ears you set your faces toward
the batteries, and advanced with steady tread; but when he turned on
the terrors of his war-whoop you advanced in the other direction, and
mighty glad of the chance, too. When he called for soothing-syrup,
did you venture to throw out any side remarks about certain services
being unbecoming an officer and a gentleman? No. You got up and *got*
it. When he ordered his pap-bottle and it was not warm, did you talk
back? Not you. You went to work and *warmed* it. You even descended
so far in your menial office as to take a suck at that warm, insipid stuff
yourself, to see if it was right—three parts water to one of milk, a touch
of sugar to modify the colic, and a drop of peppermint to kill those
hiccoughs. I can taste that stuff yet. And how many things you learned
as you went along! Sentimental young folks still take stock in that beautiful old saying that when the baby smiles in his sleep, it is because the
angels are whispering to him. Very pretty, but too thin—simply wind
on the stomach, my friends. If the baby proposed to take a walk at his
usual hour, two o'clock in the morning, didn't you rise up promptly and
remark, with a mental addition which would not improve a Sunday-
school book *much*, that that was the very thing you were about to propose yourself? Oh! you were under good discipline, and as you went
fluttering up and down the room in your undress uniform, you not only
prattled undignified baby-talk, but even tuned up your martial voices
and tried to *sing!*—"Rock-a-by baby in the treetop," for instance. What
a spectacle for an Army of the Tennessee! And what an affliction for
the neighbors, too; for it is not everybody within a mile around that
likes military music at three in the morning. And when you had been
keeping this sort of thing up two or three hours, and your little velvet-
head intimated that nothing suited him like exercise and noise, what
did you do? ["*Go on!*"] You simply *went* on until you dropped in the
last ditch. The idea that a *baby* doesn't *amount* to anything! Why, *one*
baby is just a house and a front yard full by itself. *One* baby can
furnish more business than you and your whole Interior Department
can attend to. He is enterprising, irrepressible, brimful of lawless activities. Do what you please, you can't make him stay on the reservation.
Sufficient unto the day is one baby. As long as you are in your right
mind don't you ever pray for twins. Twins amount to a permanent riot.
And there ain't any real difference between triplets and an insurrection.

Yes, it was high time for a toast-master to recognize the importance

of the babies. Think what is in store for the present crop! Fifty years
from now we shall all be dead, I trust, and then this flag, if it still survive (and let us hope it may), will be floating over a Republic number-
ing 200,000,000 souls, according to the settled laws of our increase. Our
present schooner of State will have grown into a political leviathan—a
Great Eastern. The cradled babies of to-day will be on deck. Let them
be well trained, for we are going to leave a big contract on their hands.
Among the three or four million cradles now rocking in the land are
some which this nation would preserve for ages as sacred things, if we
could know which ones they are. In one of these cradles the unconscious Farragut of the future is at this moment teething—think of it!
—and putting in a world of dead earnest, unarticulated, but perfectly
justifiable profanity over it, too. In another the future renowned as-
tronomer is blinking at the shining Milky Way with but a languid interest—poor little chap!—and wondering what has become of that other
one they call the wet-nurse. In another the future great historian is lying—and doubtless will continue to lie until his earthly missions
ended. In another the future President is busying himself with no profounder problem of state than what the mischief has become of his hair
so early; and in a mighty array of other cradles there are now some
60,000 future office-seekers, getting ready to furnish him occasion to
grapple with that same old problem a second time. And in still one
more cradle, somewhere under the flag, the future illustrious commander-in-chief of the American armies is so little burdened with his
approaching grandeurs and responsibilities as to be giving his whole
strategic mind at this moment to trying to find out some way to get his
big toe into his mouth—an achievement which, meaning no disrespect,
the illustrious guest of this evening turned *his* entire attention to some
fifty-six years ago; and if the child is but a prophecy of the man, there
are mighty few who will doubt that he *succeeded*.

1879

American in Europe

For some days we were content to enjoy looking at the blue lake Lucerne and at the piled-up masses of snow-mountains that border it all around—an enticing spectacle, this last, for there is a strange and fascinating beauty and charm about a majestic snow-peak with the sun blazing upon it or the moonlight softly enriching it—but finally we concluded to try a bit of excursioning around on a steamboat, and a dash on foot at the Rigi. Very well, we had a delightful trip to Fluelen, on a breezy, sunny day. Everybody sat on the upper deck, on benches, under an awning; everybody talked, laughed, and exclaimed at the wonderful scenery; in truth, a trip on that lake is almost the perfection of pleasuring. The mountains were a never-ceasing marvel. Sometimes they rose straight up out of the lake, and towered aloft and overshadowed our pygmy steamer with their prodigious bulk in the most impressive way. Not snow-clad mountains, these, yet they climbed high enough toward the sky to meet the clouds and veil their foreheads in them. They were not barren and repulsive, but clothed in green, and restful and pleasant to the eye. And they were so almost straight-up-and-down, sometimes, that one could not imagine a man being able to keep his footing upon such a surface, yet there are paths, and the Swiss people go up and down them every day.

Sometimes one of these monster precipices had the slight inclination of the huge ship-houses in dockyards—then high aloft, toward the sky, it took a little stronger inclination, like that of a mansard roof—and perched on this dizzy mansard one's eye detected little things like martin boxes, and presently perceived that these were the dwellings of peasants—an airy place for a home, truly. And suppose a peasant should walk in his sleep, or his child should fall out of the front yard?—the friends would have have a tedious long journey down out of those cloud-heights before they found the remains. And yet those far-away homes looked ever so seductive, they were so remote from the troubled world, they dozed in such an atmosphere of peace and dreams—surely no one who had learned to live up there would ever want to live on a meaner level.

We swept through the prettiest little curving arms of the lake, among these colossal green walls, enjoying new delights, always, as the stately panorama unfolded itself before us and rerolled and hid itself behind us; and now and then we had the thrilling surprise of bursting suddenly upon a tremendous white mass like the distant and dominating Jungfrau, or some kindred giant, looming head and shoulders above a tumbled waste of lesser Alps.

Once, while I was hungrily taking in one of these surprises, and doing my best to get all I possibly could of it while it should last, I was interrupted by a young and care-free voice:

"You're an American, I think—so'm I."

He was about eighteen, or possibly nineteen; slender and of medium height; open, frank, happy face; a restless but independent eye; a snub nose, which had the air of drawing back with a decent reserve from the silky new-born mustache below it until it should be introduced; a loosely hung jaw, calculated to work easily in the sockets. He wore a low-crowned, narrow-brimmed straw hat, with a broad blue ribbon around it which had a white anchor embroidered on it in front; nobby short-tailed coat, pantaloons, vest, all trim and neat and up with the fashion; red-striped stockings, very low-quarter patent-leather shoes, tied with black ribbon; blue ribbon around his neck, wide-open collar; tiny diamond studs; wrinkleless kids; projecting cuffs, fastened with large oxydized silver sleeve-buttons, bearing the device of a dog's face —English pug. He carried a slim cane, surmounted with an English pug's head with red glass eyes. Under his arm he carried a German grammar—Otto's. His hair was short, straight, and smooth, and presently when he turned his head a moment, I saw that it was nicely parted behind. He took a cigarette out of a dainty box, stuck it into a meerschaum holder which he carried in a morocco case, and reached for my cigar. While he was lighting, I said:

"Yes—I am an American."

"I knew it—I can always tell them. What ship did you come over in?"

"*Holsatia.*"

"We came in the *Batavia*—Cunard, you know. What kind of a passage did you have?"

"Tolerably rough."

"So did we. Captain said he'd hardly ever seen it rougher. Where are you from?"

"New England."

"So'm I. I'm from New Bloomfield. Anybody with you?"

"Yes—a friend."

"Our whole family's along. It's awful slow, going around alone—don't you think so?"

"Rather slow."

"Ever been over here before?"

"Yes."

"I haven't. My first trip. But we've been all around—Paris and everywhere. I'm to enter Harvard next year. Studying German all the time, now. Can't enter till I know German. I know considerable French—I get along pretty well in Paris, or anywhere where they speak French. What hotel are you stopping at?"

"Schweitzerhof."

"No! is that so? I never see you in the reception-room. I go to the reception-room a good deal of the time, because there's so many Americans there. I make lots of acquaintances. I know an American as soon as I see him—and so I speak to him and make his acquaintance. I like to be always making acquaintances—don't you?"

"Lord, yes!"

"You see it breaks up a trip like this, first rate. I never get bored on a trip like this, if I can make acquaintances and have somebody to talk to. But I think a trip like this would be an awful bore, if a body couldn't find anybody to get acquainted with and talk to on a trip like this. I'm fond of talking, ain't you?"

"Passionately."

"Have you felt bored, on this trip?"

"Not all the time, part of it."

"That's it!—you see you ought to go around and get acquainted, and talk. That's my way. That's the way I always do—I just go 'round, 'round, 'round, and talk, talk, talk—I never get bored. You been up the Rigi yet?"

"No."

"Going?"

"I think so."

"What hotel you going to stop at?"

"I don't know. Is there more than one?"

"Three. You stop at the Schreiber—you'll find it full of Americans. What ship did you say you came over in?"

"*City of Antwerp.*"

"German, I guess. You going to Geneva?"

"Yes."

"What hotel you going to stop at?"

"Hotel de l'Écu de Génève."

"Don't you do it! No Americans there! You stop at one of those big hotels over the bridge—they're packed full of Americans."

"But I want to practise my Arabic."

"Good gracious, do you speak Arabic?"

"Yes—well enough to get along."

"Why, hang it, you won't get along in Geneva—*they* don't speak Arabic, they speak French. What hotel are you stopping at here?"

"Hotel Pension-Beaurivage."

"Sho, you ought to stop at the Schweitzerhof. Didn't you know the Schweitzerhof was the best hotel in Switzerland?—look at your Baedeker."

"Yes, I know—but I had an idea there warn't any Americans there."

"No Americans! Why, bless your soul, it's just alive with them! I'm in the great reception-room most all the time. I make lots of acquaintances there. Not as many as I did at first, because now only the new ones stop in there—the others go right along through. Where are you from?"

"Arkansaw."

"Is that so? I'm from New England—New Bloomfield's my town when I'm at home. I'm having a mighty good time to-day, ain't you?"

"Divine."

"That's what I call it. I like this knocking around, loose and easy, and making acquaintances and talking. I know an American, soon as I see him; so I go and speak to him and make his acquaintance. I ain't ever bored, on a trip like this, if I can make new acquaintances and talk. I'm awful fond of talking when I can get hold of the right kind of a person, ain't you?"

"I prefer it to any other dissipation."

"That's my notion, too. Now some people like to take a book and sit down and read, and read, and read, or moon around yawping at the lake or these mountains and things, but that ain't my way; no, sir, if they like it, let 'em do it, I don't object; but as for me, talking's what *I* like. You been up the Rigi?"

"Yes."

"What hotel did you stop at?"

"Schreiber."

"That's the place!—I stopped there too. *Full* of Americans, *wasn't* it? It always is—always is. That's what they say. Everybody says that. What ship did you come over in?"

"*Ville de Paris.*"

"French, I reckon. What kind of a passage did . . . excuse me a minute, there's some Americans I haven't seen before."

And away he went. He went uninjured, too—I had the murderous impulse to harpoon him in the back with my alpenstock, but as I raised the weapon the disposition left me; I found I hadn't the heart to kill him, he was such a joyous, innocent, good-natured numbskull.

Half an hour later I was sitting on a bench inspecting, with strong interest, a noble monolith which we were skimming by—a monolith not shaped by man, but by Nature's free great hand—a massy pyramidal rock eighty feet high, devised by Nature ten million years ago against the day when a man worthy of it should need it for his monument. The time came at last, and now this grand remembrancer bears Schiller's name in huge letters upon its face. Curiously enough, this rock was not degraded or defiled in any way. It is said that two years ago a stranger let himself down from the top of it with ropes and pulleys, and painted all over it, in blue letters bigger than those in Schiller's name, these words:

"TRY SOZODONT;"
"BUY SUN STOVE POLISH;"
"HELMBOLD'S BUCHU;"
"TRY BENZALINE FOR THE BLOOD."

He was captured, and it turned out that he was an American. Upon his trial the judge said to him:

"You are from a land where any insolent that wants to is privileged to profane and insult Nature, and, through her, Nature's God, if by so doing he can put a sordid penny in his pocket. But here the case is different. Because you are a foreigner and ignorant, I will make your sentence light; if you were a native I would deal strenuously with you. Hear and obey:—You will immediately remove every trace of your offensive work from the Schiller monument; you pay a fine of ten thousand francs; you will suffer two years' imprisonment at hard labor; you will then be horsewhipped, tarred and feathered, deprived of your ears, ridden on a rail to the confines of the canton, and banished forever. The severest penalties are omitted in your case—not as a grace to you, but to that great republic which had the misfortune to give you birth."

The steamer's benches were ranged back to back across the deck. My back hair was mingling innocently with the back hair of a couple of ladies. Presently they were addressed by some one and I overheard this conversation:

"You are Americans, I think? So'm I."

"Yes—we are Americans."

"I knew it—I can always tell them. What ship did you come over in?"

"*City of Chester.*"

"Oh, yes—Inman line. We came in the *Batavia*—Cunard, you know. What kind of a passage did you have?"

"Pretty fair."

"That was luck. We had it awful rough. Captain said he'd hardly ever seen it rougher. Where are you from?"

"New Jersey."

"So'm I. No—I didn't mean that; I'm from New England. New Bloom-field's my place. These your children?—belong to both of you?"

"Only to one of us; they are mine; my friend is not married."

"Single, I reckon? So'm I. Are you two ladies traveling alone?"

"No—my husband is with us."

"Our whole family's along. It's awful slow, going around alone—don't you think so?"

"I suppose it must be."

"Hi, there's Mount Pilatus coming in sight again. Named after Pontius Pilate, you know, that shot the apple off of William Tell's head. Guide-book tells all about it, they say. I didn't read it—an American told me. I don't read when I'm knocking around like this, having a good time. Did you ever see the chapel where William Tell used to preach?"

"I did not know he ever preached there."

"Oh, yes, he did. That American told me so. He don't ever shut up his guide-book. He knows more about this lake than the fishes in it. Besides, they *call* it 'Tell's Chapel'—you know that yourself. You ever been over here before?"

"Yes."

"I haven't. It's my first trip. But we've been all around—Paris and everywhere. I'm to enter Harvard next year. Studying German all the time now. Can't enter till I know German. This book's Otto's grammar. It's a mighty good book to get the *ich habe gehabt haben's* out of. But I don't really study when I'm knocking around this way. If the notion takes me, I just run over my little old *ich habe gehabt, du hast gehabt, er hat gehabt, wir haben gehabt, ihr haben gehabt, sie haben gehabt*—kind of 'Now-I-lay-me-down-to-sleep' fashion, you know, and after that, maybe I don't buckle to it again for three days. It's awful undermining to the intellect, German is; you want to take it in small doses, or first you know your brains all run together, and you feel them sloshing around in your head same as so much drawn butter. But French is different; *French* ain't anything. I ain't any more afraid of French than a tramp's afraid of pie; I can rattle off my little *j'ai, tu as, il a,* and the rest of it, just as easy as a-b-c. I get along pretty well in Paris, or anywhere where they speak French. What hotel are you stopping at?"

"The Schweitzerhof."

"No! is that so? I never see you in the big reception-room. I go in there a good deal of the time, because there's so many Americans there. I make lots of acquaintances. You been up the Rigi yet?"

"No."

"Going?"

"We think of it."

"What hotel you going to stop at?"

"I don't know."

"Well, then, you stop at the Schreiber—it's full of Americans. What ship did you come over in?"

"*City of Chester.*"

"Oh, yes, I remember I asked you that before. But I always ask everybody what ship they came over in, and so sometimes I forget and ask again. You going to Geneva?"

"Yes."

"What hotel you going to stop at?"

"We expect to stop in a pension."

"I don't hardly believe you'll like that; there's very few Americans in the pensions. What hotel are you stopping at here?"

"The Schweitzerhof."

"Oh, yes, I asked you that before, too. But I always ask everybody what hotel they're stopping at, and so I've got my head all mixed up with hotels. But it makes talk, and I love to talk. It refreshes me up so—don't it you—on a trip like this?"

"Yes—sometimes."

"Well, it does me, too. As long as I'm talking I never feel bored— ain't that the way with you?"

"Yes—generally. But there are exceptions to the rule."

"Oh, of course. *I* don't care to talk to everybody, *myself.* If a person starts in to jabber-jabber-jabber about scenery, and history, and pictures, and all sorts of tiresome things, I get the fan-tods mighty soon. I say 'Well, I must be going now—hope I'll see you again'—and then I take a walk. Where you from?"

"New Jersey."

"Why, bother it all, I asked you *that* before, too. Have you seen the Lion of Lucerne?"

"Not yet."

"Nor I, either. But the man who told me about Mount Pilatus says it's one of the things to see. It's twenty-eight feet long. It don't seem reasonable, but he said so, anyway. He saw it yesterday; said it was dying, then, so I reckon it's dead by this time. But that ain't any matter, of course they'll stuff it. Did you say the children are yours—or *hers?*"

"Mine."

"Oh, so you did. Are you going up the . . . no, I asked you that. What ship . . . no, I asked you that, too. What hotel are you . . . no, you told me that. Let me see . . . um. . . . Oh, what kind of a voy . . . no, we've been over that ground, too. Um . . . um . . . well, I believe that is all. *Bonjour*—I am very glad to have made your acquaintance, ladies. *Guten Tag.*"

From A TRAMP ABROAD, 1880

An American Party

The seven-thirty table d'hôte at the great Schweitzerhof furnished a mighty array and variety of nationalities, but it offered a better opportunity to observe costumes than people, for the multitude sat at immensely long tables, and therefore the faces were mainly seen in perspective; but the breakfasts were served at small round tables, and then if one had the fortune to get a table in the midst of the assemblage he could have as many faces to study as he could desire. We used to try to guess out the nationalities, and generally succeeded tolerably well. Sometimes we tried to guess people's names; but that was a failure; that is a thing which probably requires a good deal of practice. We presently dropped it and gave our efforts to less difficult particulars. One morning I said:

"There is an American party."

Harris said:

"Yes—but name the state."

I named one state, Harris named another. We agreed upon one thing, however—that the young girl with the party was very beautiful, and very tastefully dressed. But we disagreed as to her age. I said she was eighteen, Harris said she was twenty. The dispute between us waxed warm, and I finally said, with a pretense of being in earnest:

"Well, there is one way to settle the matter—I will go and ask her."

Harris said, sarcastically, "Certainly, that is the thing to do. All you need to do is to use the common formula over here: go and say, 'I'm an American!' Of course she will be glad to see you."

Then he hinted that perhaps there was no great danger of my venturing to speak to her.

I said, "I was only talking—I didn't intend to approach her, but I see that you do not know what an intrepid person I am. I am not afraid of any woman that walks. I will go and speak to this young girl."

The thing I had in my mind was not difficult. I meant to address her in the most respectful way and ask her to pardon me if her strong resemblance to a former acquaintance of mine was deceiving me; and when she should reply that the name I mentioned was not the name she bore, I meant to beg pardon again, most respectfully, and retire. There would be no harm done. I walked to her table, bowed to the gentleman, then turned to her and was about to begin my little speech when she exclaimed:

"I *knew* I wasn't mistaken—I told John it was you! John said probably wasn't, but I knew I was right. I said you would recognize me presently and come over; and I'm glad you did, for I shouldn't have felt much flattered if you had gone out of this room without recognizing me. Sit down, sit down—how odd it is—you are the last person I was ever expecting to see again."

This was a stupefying surprise. It took my wits clear away, for an instant. However, we shook hands cordially all around, and I sat down. But truly this was the tightest place I ever was in. I seemed to vaguely remember the girl's face, now, but I had no idea where I had seen it before, or what name belonged with it. I immediately tried to get up a diversion about Swiss scenery, to keep her from launching into topics that might betray that I did not know her, but it was of no use, she went right along upon matters which interested her more:

"Oh dear, what a night that was, when the sea washed the forward boats away—do you remember it?"

"Oh, *don't* I!" said I—but I didn't. I wished the sea had washed the rudder and the smoke-stack and the captain away—then I could have located this questioner.

"And don't you remember how frightened poor Mary was, and how she cried?"

"Indeed I do!" said I. "Dear me, how it all comes back!"

I fervently wished it *would* come back—but my memory was a blank. The wise way would have been to frankly own up; but I could not bring myself to do that, after the young girl had praised me so for recognizing her; so I went on, deeper and deeper into the mire, hoping for a chance clue but never getting one. The Unrecognizable continued, with vivacity:

"Do you know, George married Mary, after all?"

"Why, no! Did he?"

"Indeed he did. He said he did not believe she was half as much to blame as her father was, and I thought he was right. Didn't you?"

"Of course he was. It was a perfectly plain case. I always said so."

"Why, no you didn't!—at least that summer."

"Oh, no, not that summer. No, you are perfectly right about that. It was the following winter that I said it."

"Well, as it turned out, Mary was not in the least to blame—it was all her father's fault—at least his and old Darley's."

It was necessary to say something—so I said:

"I always regarded Darley as a troublesome old thing."

"So he was, but then they always had a great affection for him, although he had so many eccentricities. You remember that when the weather was the least cold, he would try to come into the house."

I was rather afraid to proceed. Evidently Darley was not a man—he must be some other kind of animal—possibly a dog, maybe an elephant. However, tails are common to all animals, so I ventured to say:

"And what a tail he had!"

"*One!* He had a thousand!"

This was bewildering. I did not quite know what to say, so I only said:

"Yes, he *was* rather well fixed in the matter of tails."

"For a negro, and a crazy one at that, I should say he was," said she.

It was getting pretty sultry for me. I said to myself, "Is it possible she is going to stop there, and wait for me to speak? If she does, the conversation is blocked. A negro with a thousand tails is a topic which a person cannot talk upon fluently and instructively without more or less preparation. As to diving rashly into such a vast subject—"

But here, to my gratitude, she interrupted my thoughts by saying:

"Yes, when it came to tales of his crazy woes, there was simply no end to them if anybody would listen. His own quarters were comfortable enough, but when the weather was cold, the family were sure to have his company—nothing could keep him out of the house. But they always bore it kindly because he had saved Tom's life, years before. You remember Tom?"

"Oh, perfectly. Fine fellow he was, too."

"Yes he was. And what a pretty little thing his child was!"

"You may well say that. I never saw a prettier child."

"I used to delight to pet it and dandle it and play with it."

"So did I."

"You named it. What *was* that name? I can't call it to mind."

It appeared to me that the ice was getting pretty thin, here. I would have given something to know what the child's sex was. However, I had the good luck to think of a name that would fit either sex— so I brought it out:

"I named it Frances."

"From a relative, I suppose? But you named the one that died, too —one that I never saw. What did you call that one?"

I was out of neutral names, but as the child was dead and she had never seen it, I thought I might risk a name for it and trust to luck. Therefore I said:

"I called that one Thomas Henry."

She said, musingly:

"That is very singular . . . very singular."

I sat still and let the cold sweat run down. I was in a good deal of trouble, but I believed I could worry through if she wouldn't ask me to name any more children. I wondered where the lightning was going to strike next. She was still ruminating over that last child's title, but presently she said:

"I have always been sorry you were away at the time—I would have had you name my child."

"*Your* child! Are you married?"

"I have been married thirteen years."

"Christened, you mean."

"No, married. The youth by your side is my son."

"It seems incredible—even impossible. I do not mean any harm by it, but would you mind telling me if you are any over eighteen?—that is to say, will you tell me how old you are?"

"I was just nineteen the day of the storm we were talking about. That was my birthday."

That did not help matters, much, as I did not know the date of the storm. I tried to think of some non-committal thing to say, to keep up

my end of the talk, and render my poverty in the matter of reminiscences as little noticeable as possible, but I seemed to be about
out of non-committal things. I was about to say, "You haven't changed
a bit since then"—but that was risky. I thought of saying, "You have
improved ever so much since then"—but that wouldn't answer, of
course. I was about to try a shy at the weather, for a saving change,
when the girl slipped in ahead of me and said:

"How I have enjoyed this talk over those happy old times—haven't
you?"

"I never have spent such a half-hour in all my life before!" said I,
with emotion; and I could have added, with a near approach to truth,
"and I would rather be scalped than spend another one like it." I was
holily grateful to be through with the ordeal, and was about to make
my good-bys and get out, when the girl said:

"But there is one thing that is ever so puzzling to me."

"Why, what is that?"

"That dead child's name. What did you say it was?"

Here was another balmy place to be in: I had forgotten the child's
name; I hadn't imagined it would be needed again. However, I had
to pretend to know, anyway, so I said:

"Joseph William."

The youth at my side corrected me, and said:

"No, Thomas Henry."

I thanked him—in words—and said, with trepidation:

"O yes—I was thinking of another child that I named—I have named
a great many, and I get them confused—this one *was* named Henry
Thompson—"

"Thomas Henry," calmly interposed the boy.

I thanked him again—strictly in words—and stammered out:

"Thomas Henry—yes, Thomas Henry was the poor child's name. I
named him for Thomas—er—Thomas Carlyle, the great author, you
know—and Henry—er—er—Henry the Eighth. The parents were very
grateful to have a child named Thomas Henry."

"That makes it more singular than ever," murmured my beautiful
friend.

"Does it? Why?"

"Because when the parents speak of that child now, they always call
it Susan Amelia."

That spiked my gun. I could not say anything. I was entirely out of
verbal obliquities; to go further would be to lie, and that I would not
do; so I simply sat still and suffered—sat mutely and resignedly there,

and sizzled—for I was being slowly fried to death in my own blushes. Presently the enemy laughed a happy laugh and said:

"I *have* enjoyed this talk over old times, but you have not. I saw very soon that you were only pretending to know me, and so as I had wasted a compliment on you in the beginning, I made up my mind to punish you. And I have succeeded pretty well. I was glad to see that you knew George and Tom and Darley, for I had never heard of them before and therefore could not be sure that you had; and I was glad to learn the names of those imaginary children, too. One can get quite a fund of information out of you if one goes at it cleverly. Mary and the storm, and the sweeping away of the forward boats, were facts— all the rest was fiction. Mary was my sister; her full name was Mary —— *Now* do you remember me?"

"Yes," I said, "I do remember you now; and you are as hard-hearted as you were thirteen years ago in that ship, else you wouldn't have punished me so. You haven't changed your nature nor your person, in any way at all; you look just as young as you did then, you are just as beautiful as you were then, and you have transmitted a deal of your comeliness to this fine boy. There—if that speech moves you any, let's fly the flag of truce, with the understanding that I am conquered and confess it."

All of which was agreed to and accomplished, on the spot. When I went back to Harris, I said:

"Now you see what a person with talent and address can do."

"Excuse me, I see what a person of colossal ignorance and simplicity can do. The idea of your going and intruding on a party of strangers, that way, and talking for half an hour; why I never heard of a man in his right mind doing such a thing before. What did you say to them?"

"I never said any harm. I merely asked the girl what her name was."

"I don't doubt it. Upon my word I don't. I think you were capable of it. It was stupid in me to let you go over there and make such an exhibition of yourself. But you know I couldn't really believe you would do such an inexcusable thing. What will those people think of us? But how did you say it?—I mean the manner of it. I hope you were not abrupt."

"No, I was careful about that. I said 'My friend and I would like to know what your name is, if you don't mind.'"

"No, that was not abrupt. There is a polish about it that does you infinite credit. And I am glad you put me in; that was a delicate attention which I appreciate at its full value. What did she do?"

"She didn't do anything in particular. She told me her name."

"Simply told you her name. Do you mean to say she did not show any surprise?"

"Well, now I come to think, she did show something; maybe it was surprise; I hadn't thought of that—I took it for gratification."

"Oh, undoubtedly you were right; it must have been gratification; it could not be otherwise than gratifying to be assaulted by a stranger with such a question as that. Then what did you do?"

"I offered my hand and the party gave me a shake."

"I saw it! I did not believe my own eyes, at the time. Did the gentleman say anything about cutting your throat?"

"No, they all seemed glad to see me, as far as I could judge."

"And do you know, I believe they were. I think they said to themselves, 'Doubtless this curiosity has got away from his keeper—let us amuse ourselves with him.' There is no other way of accounting for their facile docility. You sat down. Did they *ask* you to sit down?"

"No, they did not ask me, but I suppose they did not think of it."

"You have an unerring instinct. What else did you do? What did you talk about?"

"Well, I asked the girl how old she was."

"*Un*doubtedly. Your delicacy is beyond praise. Go on, go on—don't mind my apparent misery—I always look so when I am steeped in a profound and reverent joy. Go on—she told you her age?"

"Yes, she told me her age, and all about her mother, and her grandmother, and her other relations, and all about herself."

"Did she volunteer these statistics?"

"No, not exactly that. I asked the questions and she answered them."

"This is divine. Go on—it is not possible that you forgot to inquire into her politics?"

"No, I thought of that. She is a democrat, her husband is a republican, and both of them are Baptists."

"Her husband? Is that child married?"

"She is not a child. She is married, and that is her husband who is there with her."

"Has she any children?"

"Yes—seven and a half."

"That is impossible."

"No, she has them. She told me herself."

"Well, but seven and a *half*? How do you make out the half? Where does the half come in?"

"There is a child which she had by another husband—not this one but another one—so it is a stepchild, and they do not count it full measure."

"Another husband? Has she had another husband?"

"Yes, four. This one is number four."

"I don't believe a word of it. It is impossible, upon its face. Is that boy there her brother?"

"No, that is her son. He is her youngest. He is not as old as he looks; he is only eleven and a half."

"These things are all manifestly impossible. This is a wretched business. It is a plain case: they simply took your measure, and concluded to fill you up. They seem to have succeeded. I am glad I am not in the mess; they may at least be charitable enough to think there ain't a pair of us. Are they going to stay here long?"

"No, they leave before noon."

"There is one man who is deeply grateful for that. How did you find out? You asked, I suppose?"

"No, along at first I inquired into their plans, in a general way, and they said they were going to be here a week, and make trips round about; but toward the end of the interview, when I said you and I would tour around with them with pleasure, and offered to bring you over and introduce you, they hesitated a little, and asked if you were from the same establishment that I was. I said you were, and then they said they had changed their mind and considered it necessary to start at once and visit a sick relative in Siberia."

"Ah, me, you struck the summit! You struck the loftiest altitude of stupidity that human effort has ever reached. You shall have a monument of jackasses' skulls as high as the Strasburg spire if you die before I do. They wanted to know if I was from the same 'establishment' that you hailed from, did they? What did they mean by 'establishment'?"

"I don't know; it never occurred to me to ask."

"Well *I* know. They meant an asylum—an *idiot* asylum, do you understand? So they *do* think there's a pair of us, after all. Now what do you think of yourself?"

"Well, I don't know. I didn't know I was doing any harm; I didn't *mean* to do any harm. They were very nice people, and they seemed to like me."

Harris made some rude remarks and left for his bedroom—to break some furniture, he said. He was a singularly irascible man; any little thing would disturb his temper.

I had been well scorched by the young woman, but no matter, I took it out of Harris. One should always "get even" in some way, else the sore place will go on hurting.

From A TRAMP ABROAD, 1880

Ascending the Riffelberg

After I had finished my readings, I was no longer myself; I was tranced, uplifted, intoxicated, by the almost incredible perils and adventures I had been following my authors through, and the triumphs I had been sharing with them. I sat silent some time, then turned to Harris and said:

"My mind is made up."

Something in my tone struck him; and when he glanced at my eye and read what was written there, his face paled perceptibly. He hesitated a moment, then said:

"Speak."

I answered, with perfect calmness:

"I WILL ASCEND THE RIFFELBERG."

If I had shot my poor friend he could not have fallen from his chair more suddenly. If I had been his father he could not have pleaded harder to get me to give up my purpose. But I turned a deaf ear to all he said. When he perceived at last that nothing could alter my determination, he ceased to urge, and for a while the deep silence was broken only by his sobs. I sat in marble resolution, with my eyes fixed upon vacancy, for in spirit I was already wrestling with the perils of the mountains, and my friend sat gazing at me in adoring admiration through his tears. At last he threw himself upon me in a loving embrace and exclaimed in broken tones:

"Your Harris will never desert you. We will die together!"

I cheered the noble fellow with praises, and soon his fears were forgotten and he was eager for the adventure. He wanted to summon the guides at once and leave at two in the morning, as he supposed the custom was; but I explained that nobody was looking at that hour; and that the start in the dark was not usually made from the village but from the first night's resting-place on the mountainside. I said we would leave the village at 3 or 4 P.M. on the morrow; meantime he could notify the guides, and also let the public know of the attempt which we proposed to make.

I went to bed, but not to sleep. No man can sleep when he is about to undertake one of these Alpine exploits. I tossed feverishly all night long, and was glad enough when I heard the clock strike half past eleven and knew it was time to get up for dinner. I rose, jaded and rusty, and went to the noon meal, where I found myself the center of interest and curiosity; for the news was already abroad. It is not easy to eat calmly when you are a lion, but it is very pleasant, nevertheless.

As usual, at Zermatt, when a great ascent is about to be undertaken, everybody, native and foreign, laid aside his own projects and took up a good position to observe the start. The expedition consisted of 198 persons, including the mules; or 205, including the cows. As follows:

CHIEFS OF SERVICE		SUBORDINATES	
	Myself	1	Veterinary Surgeon
	Mr. Harris	1	Butler
17	Guides	12	Waiters
4	Surgeons	1	Footman
1	Geologist	1	Barber
1	Botanist	1	Head Cook
3	Chaplains	9	Assistants
2	Draftsmen	4	Pastry Cooks
15	Barkeepers	1	Confectionery Artist
1	Latinist		

TRANSPORTATION, ETC.

27	Porters	3	Coarse Washers and
44	Mules		Ironers
44	Muleteers	1	Fine ditto
		7	Cows
		2	Milkers

Total, 154 men, 51 animals. Grand Total, 205.

RATIONS, ETC.		APPARATUS	
16	Cases Hams	25	Spring Mattresses
2	Barrels Flour	2	Hair ditto
22	Barrels Whisky		Bedding for same
1	Barrel Sugar	2	Mosquito-nets
1	Keg Lemons	29	Tents
2,000	Cigars		Scientific Instruments
1	Barrel Pies	97	Ice-axes
1	Ton of Pemmican	5	Cases Dynamite
143	Pair Crutches	7	Cans Nitroglycerin
2	Barrels Arnica	22	40-foot Ladders
1	Bale of Lint	2	Miles of Rope
27	Kegs Paregoric	154	Umbrellas

It was full four o'clock in the afternoon before my cavalcade was entirely ready. At that hour it began to move. In point of numbers and spectacular effect, it was the most imposing expedition that had ever marched from Zermatt.

I commanded the chief guide to arrange the men and animals in single file, twelve feet apart, and lash them all together on a strong rope. He objected that the first two miles was a dead level, with plenty of room, and that the rope was never used except in very dangerous places. But I would not listen to that. My reading had taught me that many serious accidents had happened in the Alps simply from not having the people tied up soon enough; I was not going to add one to the list. The guide then obeyed my order.

When the procession stood at ease, roped together, and ready to move, I never saw a finer sight. It was 3,122 feet long—over half a mile; every man but Harris and me was on foot, and had on his green veil and his blue goggles, and his white rag around his hat, and his coil of rope over one shoulder and under the other, and his ice-ax in his belt, and carried his alpenstock in his left hand, his umbrella (closed) in his right, and his crutches slung at his back. The burdens of the pack-mules and the horns of the cows were decked with the Edelweiss and the Alpine rose.

I and my agent were the only persons mounted. We were in the post of danger in the extreme rear, and tied securely to five guides apiece. Our armor-bearers carried our ice-axes, alpenstocks, and other implements for us. We were mounted upon very small donkeys, as a measure of safety; in time of peril we could straighten our legs and stand up, and let the donkey walk from under. Still, I cannot recommend this sort of animal—at least for excursions of mere pleasure—because his ears interrupt the view. I and my agent possessed the regulation mountaineering costumes, but concluded to leave them behind. Out of respect for the great numbers of tourists of both sexes who would be assembled in front of the hotels to see us pass, and also out of respect for the many tourists whom we expected to encounter on our expedition, we decided to make the ascent in evening dress.

At fifteen minutes past four I gave the command to move, and my subordinates passed it along the line. The great crowd in front of the Monte Rosa hotel parted in twain, with a cheer, as the procession approached; and as the head of it was filing by I gave the order—"Unlimber—make ready—HOIST!"—and with one impulse up went my half-mile of umbrellas. It was a beautiful sight, and a total surprise to the spectators. Nothing like that had ever been seen in the Alps before.

The applause it brought forth was deeply gratifying to me, and I rode by with my plug hat in my hand to testify my appreciation of it. It was the only testimony I could offer, for I was too full to speak.

We watered the caravan at the cold stream which rushes down a trough near the end of the village, and soon afterward left the haunts of civilization behind us. About half past five o'clock we arrived at a bridge which spans the Visp, and after throwing over a detachment to see if it was safe, the caravan crossed without accident. The way now led, by a gentle ascent, carpeted with fresh green grass, to the church at Winkelmatten. Without stopping to examine this edifice, I executed a flank movement to the right and crossed the bridge over the Findelenbach, after first testing its strength. Here I deployed to the right again, and presently entered an inviting stretch of meadowland which was unoccupied save by a couple of deserted huts toward its furthest extremity. These meadows offered an excellent camping-place. We pitched our tents, supped, established a proper guard, recorded the events of the day, and then went to bed.

We rose at two in the morning and dressed by candle-light. It was a dismal and chilly business. A few stars were shining, but the general heavens were overcast, and the great shaft of the Matterhorn was draped in a sable pall of clouds. The chief guide advised a delay; he said he feared it was going to rain. We waited until nine o'clock, and then got away in tolerably clear weather.

Our course led up some terrific steeps, densely wooded with larches and cedars, and traversed by paths which the rains had guttered and which were obstructed by loose stones. To add to the danger and inconvenience, we were constantly meeting returning tourists on foot or horseback, and as constantly being crowded and battered by ascending tourists who were in a hurry and wanted to get by.

Our troubles thickened. About the middle of the afternoon the seventeen guides called a halt and held a consultation. After consulting an hour they said their first suspicion remained intact—that is to say, they believed they were lost. I asked if they did not *know* it? No, they said, they *couldn't* absolutely know whether they were lost or not, because none of them had ever been in that part of the country before. They had a strong instinct that they were lost, but they had no proofs —except that they did not know where they were. They had met no tourists for some time, and they considered that a suspicious sign.

Plainly we were in an ugly fix. The guides were naturally unwilling to go alone and seek a way out of the difficulty; so we all went together. For better security we moved slow and cautiously, for the forest was

very dense. We did not move up the mountain, but around it, hoping
to strike across the old trail. Toward nightfall, when we were about
tired out, we came up against a rock as big as a cottage. This barrier
took all the remaining spirit out of the men, and a panic of fear and
despair ensued. They moaned and wept, and said they should never
see their homes and their dear ones again. Then they began to upbraid
me for bringing them upon this fatal expedition. Some even muttered
threats against me.

Clearly it was no time to show weakness. So I made a speech in
which I said that other Alp-climbers had been in as perilous a position
as this, and yet by courage and perseverance had escaped. I promised
to stand by them, I promised to rescue them. I closed by saying we
had plenty of provisions to maintain us for quite a siege—and did they
suppose Zermatt would allow half a mile of men and mules to mysteriously disappear during any considerable time, right above their noses,
and make no inquiries? No, Zermatt would send out searching-expedi-
tions and we should be saved.

This speech had a great effect. The men pitched the tents with some
little show of cheerfulness, and we were snugly under cover when the
night shut down. I now reaped the reward of my wisdom in providing
one article which is not mentioned in any book of Alpine adventure
but this. I refer to the paregoric. But for that beneficent drug, not one
of those men would have slept a moment during that fearful night.
But for that gentle persuader they must have tossed, unsoothed, the
night through; for the whisky was for me. Yes, they would have risen
in the morning unfitted for their heavy task. As it was, everybody slept
but my agent and me—only we two and the barkeepers. I would not
permit myself to sleep at such a time. I considered myself responsible
for all those lives. I meant to be on hand and ready, in case of
avalanches. I am aware, now, that there were no avalanches up there,
but I did not know it then.

We watched the weather all through that awful night, and kept an
eye on the barometer, to be prepared for the least change. There was
not the slightest change recorded by the instrument, during the whole
time. Words cannot describe the comfort that that friendly, hopeful,
steadfast thing was to me in that season of trouble. It was a defective
barometer, and had no hand but the stationary brass pointer, but I
did not know that until afterward. If I should be in such a situation
again, I should not wish for any barometer but that one.

All hands rose at two in the morning and took breakfast, and as soon
as it was light we roped ourselves together and went at that rock. For

some time we tried the hook-rope and other means of scaling it, but without success—that is, without perfect success. The hook caught once, and Harris started up it hand over hand, but the hold broke and if there had not happened to be a chaplain sitting underneath at the time, Harris would certainly have been crippled. As it was, it was the chaplain. He took to his crutches, and I ordered the hook-rope to be laid aside. It was too dangerous an implement where so many people were standing around.

We were puzzled for a while; then somebody thought of the ladders. One of these was leaned against the rock, and the men went up it tied together in couples. Another ladder was sent up for use in descending. At the end of half an hour everybody was over, and that rock was conquered. We gave our first grand shout of triumph. But the joy was short-lived, for somebody asked how we were going to get the animals over.

This was a serious difficulty; in fact, it was an impossibility. The courage of the men began to waver immediately; once more we were threatened with a panic. But when the danger was most imminent, we were saved in a mysterious way. A mule which had attracted attention from the beginning by its disposition to experiment, tried to eat a five-pound can of nitroglycerin. This happened right alongside the rock. The explosion threw us all to the ground, and covered us with dirt and debris; it frightened us extremely, too, for the crash it made was deafening, and the violence of the shock made the ground tremble. However, we were grateful, for the rock was gone. Its place was occupied by a new cellar, about thirty feet across, by fifteen feet deep. The explosion was heard as far as Zermatt; and an hour and a half afterward, many citizens of that town were knocked down and quite seriously injured by descending portions of mule meat, frozen solid. This shows, better than any estimate in figures, how high the experimenter went.

We had nothing to do, now, but bridge the cellar and proceed on our way. With a cheer the men went at their work. I attended to the engineering, myself. I appointed a strong detail to cut down trees with ice-axes and trim them for piers to support the bridge. This was a slow business, for ice-axes are not good to cut wood with. I caused my piers to be firmly set up in ranks in the cellar, and upon them I laid six of my forty-foot ladders, side by side, and laid six more on top of them. Upon this bridge I caused a bed of boughs to be spread, and on top of the boughs a bed of earth six inches deep. I stretched ropes upon either side to serve as railings, and then my bridge was complete. A train of elephants could have crossed it in safety and comfort. By nightfall the caravan was on the other side and the ladders taken up.

Next morning we went on in good spirits for a while, though our way was slow and difficult, by reason of the steep and rocky nature of the ground and the thickness of the forest; but at last a dull despondency crept into the men's faces and it was apparent that not only they, but even the guides, were now convinced that we were lost. The fact that we still met no tourists was a circumstance that was but too significant. Another thing seemed to suggest that we were not only lost, but very badly lost; for there must surely be searching-parties on the road before this time, yet we had seen no sign of them.

Demoralization was spreading; something must be done, and done quickly, too. Fortunately, I am not unfertile in expedients. I contrived one now which commended itself to all, for it promised well. I took three-quarters of a mile of rope and fastened one end of it around the waist of a guide, and told him to go and find the road, while the caravan waited. I instructed him to guide himself back by the rope, in case of failure; in case of success, he was to give the rope a series of violent jerks, whereupon the Expedition would go to him at once. He departed, and in two minutes had disappeared among the trees. I payed out the rope myself, while everybody watched the crawling thing with eager eyes. The rope crept away quite slowly, at times, at other times with some briskness. Twice or thrice we seemed to get the signal, and a shout was just ready to break from the men's lips when they perceived it was a false alarm. But at last, when over half a mile of rope had slidden away, it stopped gliding and stood absolutely still —one minute—two minutes—three—while we held our breath and watched.

Was the guide resting? Was he scanning the country from some high point? Was he inquiring of a chance mountaineer? Stop—had he fainted from excess of fatigue and anxiety?

This thought gave us a shock. I was in the very act of detailing an Expedition to succor him, when the cord was assailed with a series of such frantic jerks that I could hardly keep hold of it. The huzza that went up, then, was good to hear. "Saved! saved!" was the word that rang out, all down the long rank of the caravan.

We rose up and started at once. We found the route to be good enough for a while, but it began to grow difficult, by and by, and this feature steadily increased. When we judged we had gone half a mile, we momently expected to see the guide; but no, he was not visible anywhere; neither was he waiting, for the rope was still moving, consequently he was doing the same. This argued that he had not found the road, yet, but was marching to it with some peasant. There was nothing for us to do but plod along—and this we did. At the end of three hours we were still plodding. This was not only mysterious, but exasperating. And very fatiguing, too; for we had tried hard, along at first, to catch up with the guide, but had only fagged ourselves, in vain; for although he was traveling slowly he was yet able to go faster than the hampered caravan over such ground.

At three in the afternoon we were nearly dead with exhaustion—and still the rope was slowly gliding out. The murmurs against the guide had been growing steadily, and at last they were become loud and savage. A mutiny ensued. The men refused to proceed. They declared that we had been traveling over and over the same ground all day, in a kind of circle. They demanded that our end of the rope be made fast to a tree, so as to halt the guide until we could overtake him and kill him. This was not an unreasonable requirement, so I gave the order.

As soon as the rope was tied, the Expedition moved forward with that alacrity which the thirst for vengeance usually inspires. But after a tiresome march of almost half a mile, we came to a hill covered thick with a crumbly rubbish of stones, and so steep that no man of us all was now in a condition to climb it. Every attempt failed, and ended in crippling somebody. Within twenty minutes I had five men on crutches. Whenever a climber tried to assist himself by the rope, it yielded and let him tumble backward. The frequency of this result suggested an idea to me. I ordered the caravan to 'bout face and form in marching order; I then made the tow-rope fast to the rear mule, and gave the command:

"Mark time—by the right flank—forward—march!"

The procession began to move, to the impressive strains of a battle-chant, and I said to myself, "Now, if the rope don't break I judge *this* will fetch that guide into the camp." I watched the rope gliding down the hill, and presently when I was all fixed for triumph I was confronted by a bitter disappointment; there was no guide tied to the rope, it was only a very indignant old black ram. The fury of the baffled Expedition exceeded all bounds. They even wanted to wreak their unreasoning vengeance on this innocent dumb brute. But I stood between them and their prey, menaced by a bristling wall of ice-axes and alpenstocks, and proclaimed that there was but one road to this murder, and it was directly over my corse. Even as I spoke I saw that my doom was sealed, except a miracle supervened to divert these madmen from their fell purpose. I see that sickening wall of weapons now; I see that advancing host as I saw it then, I see the hate in those cruel eyes; I remember how I drooped my head upon my breast, I feel again the sudden earthquake shock in my rear, administered by the very ram I was sacrificing myself to save; I hear once more the typhoon of laughter that burst from the assaulting column as I clove it from van to rear like a Sepoy shot from a Rodman gun.

I was saved. Yes, I was saved, and by the merciful instinct of ingratitude which nature had planted in the breast of that treacherous beast. The grace which eloquence had failed to work in those men's hearts, had been wrought by a laugh. The ram was set free and my life was spared.

We lived to find out that that guide had deserted us as soon as he had placed a half-mile between himself and us. To avert suspicion, he had judged it best that the line should continue to move; so he caught that ram, and at the time that he was sitting on it making the rope fast to it, we were imagining that he was lying in a swoon, overcome by fatigue and distress. When he allowed the ram to get up it fell to plunging around, trying to rid itself of the rope, and this was the signal which we had risen up with glad shouts to obey. We had followed this ram round and round in a circle all day—a thing which was proven by the discovery that we had watered the Expedition seven times at one and the same spring in seven hours. As expert a woodman as I am, I had somehow failed to notice this until my attention was called to it by a hog. This hog was always wallowing there, and as he was the only hog we saw, his frequent repetition, together with his unvarying similarity to himself, finally caused me to reflect that he must be the same hog, and this led me to the deduction that this must be the same spring, also—which indeed it was.

I made a note of this curious thing, as showing in a striking manner the relative difference between glacial action and the action of the hog. It is now a well-established fact that glaciers move; I consider that my observations go to show, with equal conclusiveness, that a hog in a spring does not move. I shall be glad to receive the opinions of other observers upon this point.

To return, for an explanatory moment, to that guide, and then I shall be done with him. After leaving the ram tied to the rope, he had wandered at large a while, and then happened to run across a cow. Judging that a cow would naturally know more than a guide, he took her by the tail, and the result justified his judgment. She nibbled her leisurely way downhill till it was near milking-time, then she struck for home and towed him into Zermatt.

We went into camp on that wild spot to which that ram had brought us. The men were greatly fatigued. Their conviction that we were lost was forgotten in the cheer of a good supper, and before the reaction had a chance to set in, I loaded them up with paregoric and put them to bed.

Next morning I was considering in my mind our desperate situation and trying to think of a remedy, when Harris came to me with a Baedeker map which showed conclusively that the mountain we were on was still in Switzerland—yes, every part of it was in Switzerland. So we were not lost, after all. This was an immense relief; it lifted the weight of two such mountains from my breast. I immediately had the news disseminated and the map exhibited. The effect was wonderful. As soon as the men saw with their own eyes that they knew where they were, and that it was only the summit that was lost and not themselves, they cheered up instantly and said with one accord, let the summit take care of itself, they were not interested in its troubles.

Our distresses being at an end, I now determined to rest the men in camp and give the scientific department of the Expedition a chance. First, I made a barometric observation, to get our altitude, but I could not perceive that there was any result. I knew, by my scientific reading, that either thermometers or barometers ought to be boiled, to make them accurate; I did not know which it was, so I boiled both. There was still no result; so I examined these instruments and discovered that they possessed radical blemishes: the barometer had no hand but the brass pointer and the ball of the thermometer was stuffed with tin-foil. I might have boiled those things to rags, and never found out anything.

I hunted up another barometer; it was new and perfect. I boiled it half an hour in a pot of bean soup which the cooks were making. The result was unexpected: the instrument was not affected at all, but there was such a strong barometer taste to the soup that the head cook, who was a most conscientious person, changed its name in the bill of fare. The dish was so greatly liked by all, that I ordered the cook to have barometer soup every day. It was believed that the barometer might eventually be injured, but I did not care for that. I had demonstrated to my satisfaction that it could not tell how high a mountain was, therefore I had no real use for it. Changes of the weather I could take care of without it; I did not wish to know when the weather was going to be good, what I wanted to know was when it was going to be bad, and this I could find out from Harris's corns. Harris had had his corns tested and regulated at the government observatory in Heidelberg, and one could depend upon them with confidence. So I transferred the new barometer to the cooking department, to be used for the official mess. It was found that even a pretty fair article of soup could be made with the defective barometer; so I allowed that one to be transferred to the subordinate messes.

I next boiled the thermometer, and got a most excellent result; the mercury went up to about 200° Fahrenheit. In the opinion of the other scientists of the Expedition, this seemed to indicate that we had attained the extraordinary altitude of two hundred thousand feet above sea-level. Science places the line of eternal snow at about ten thousand feet above sea-level. There was no snow where we were, consequently it was proven that the eternal snow-line ceases somewhere above the ten-thousand-foot level and does not begin any more. This was an interesting fact, and one which had not been observed by any observer before. It was as valuable as interesting, too, since it would open up the deserted summits of the highest Alps to population and agriculture. It was a proud thing to be where we were, yet it caused us a pang to reflect that but for that ram we might just as well have been two hundred thousand feet higher.

The success of my last experiment induced me to try an experiment with my photographic apparatus. I got it out, and boiled one of my cameras, but the thing was a failure: it made the wood swell up and burst, and I could not see that the lenses were any better than they were before.

I now concluded to boil a guide. It might improve him, it could not impair his usefulness. But I was not allowed to proceed. Guides have no feeling for science, and this one would not consent to be made uncomfortable in its interest.

In the midst of my scientific work, one of those needless accidents happened which are always occurring among the ignorant and thoughtless. A porter shot at a chamois and missed it and crippled the Latinist. This was not a serious matter to me, for a Latinist's duties are as well performed on crutches as otherwise—but the fact remained that if the Latinist had not happened to be in the way a mule would have got that load. That would have been quite another matter, for when it comes down to a question of value there is a palpable difference between a Latinist and a mule. I could not depend on having a Latinist in the right place every time; so, to make things safe, I ordered that in the future the chamois must not be hunted within limits of the camp with any other weapon than the forefinger.

My nerves had hardly grown quiet after this affair when they got another shake-up—one which utterly unmanned me for a moment: a rumor swept suddenly through the camp that one of the barkeepers had fallen over a precipice!

However, it turned out that it was only a chaplain. I had laid in an extra force of chaplains, purposely to be prepared for emergencies like this, but by some unaccountable oversight had come away rather short-handed in the matter of barkeepers.

On the following morning we moved on, well refreshed and in good spirits. I remember this day with peculiar pleasure, because it saw our road restored to us. Yes, we found our road again, and in quite an extraordinary way. We had plodded along some two hours and a half, when we came up against a solid mass of rock about twenty feet high. I did not need to be instructed by a mule this time. I was already beginning to know more than any mule in the Expedition. I at once put in a blast of dynamite, and lifted that rock out of the way. But to my surprise and mortification, I found that there had been a chalet on top of it.

I picked up such members of the family as fell in my vicinity, and subordinates of my corps collected the rest. None of these poor people were injured, happily, but they were much annoyed. I explained to the head chaleteer just how the thing happened, and that I was only searching for the road, and would certainly have given him timely notice if I had known he was up there. I said I had meant no harm, and hoped I had not lowered myself in his estimation by raising him a few rods in the air. I said many other judicious things, and finally when I offered to rebuild his chalet, and pay for the breakages, and throw in the cellar, he was mollified and satisfied. He hadn't any cellar at all, before; he would not have as good a view, now, as formerly, but what he had lost in view he had gained in cellar, by exact measurement. He said there wasn't another hole like that in the mountains— and he would have been right if the late mule had not tried to eat up the nitroglycerin.

I put a hundred and sixteen men at work, and they rebuilt the chalet from its own debris in fifteen minutes. It was a good deal more picturesque than it was before, too. The man said we were now on the Feli-Stutz, above the Schwegmatt—information which I was glad to get, since it gave us our position to a degree of particularity which we had not been accustomed to for a day or so. We also learned that we were standing at the foot of the Riffelberg proper, and that the initial chapter of our work was completed.

We had a fine view, from here, of the energetic Visp, as it makes its first plunge into the world from under a huge arch of solid ice, worn through the foot-wall of the great Gorner Glacier; and we could also see the Furggenbach, which is the outlet of the Furggen Glacier.

The mule-road to the summit of the Riffelberg passed right in front of the chalet, a circumstance which we almost immediately noticed, because a procession of tourists was filing along it pretty much all the time.[1] The chaleteer's business consisted in furnishing refreshments to tourists. My blast had interrupted this trade for a few minutes, by breaking all the bottles on the place; but I gave the man a lot of whisky to sell for Alpine champagne, and a lot of vinegar which would answer for Rhine wine, consequently trade was soon as brisk as ever.

Leaving the Expedition outside to rest, I quartered myself in the chalet, with Harris, purposing to correct my journals and scientific observations before continuing the ascent. I had hardly begun my work when a tall, slender, vigorous American youth of about twenty-three, who was on his way down the mountain, entered and came toward me with that breezy self-complacency which is the adolescent's idea of the well-bred ease of the man of the world. His hair was short and parted accurately in the middle, and he had all the look of an American person who would be likely to begin his signature with an initial, and spell his middle name out. He introduced himself, smiling a smirky smile borrowed from the courtiers of the stage, extended a fair-skinned talon, and while he gripped my hand in it he bent his body forward three times at the hips, as the stage-courtier does, and said in the airiest and most condescending and patronizing way—I quote his exact language:

"Very glad to make your acquaintance, 'm sure; very glad indeed, assure you. I've read all your little efforts and greatly admired them, and when I heard you were here, I . . ."

I indicated a chair, and he sat down. This grandee was the grandson of an American of considerable note in his day, and not wholly forgotten yet—a man who came so near being a great man that he was quite generally accounted one while he lived.

I slowly paced the floor, pondering scientific problems, and heard this conversation:

GRANDSON.   First visit to Europe?

[1] "Pretty much" may not be elegant English, but it is high time it was. There is no elegant word or phrase which means just what it means.—M.T.

HARRIS. Mine? Yes.

G. S. (With a soft reminiscent sigh suggestive of bygone joys that may be tasted in their freshness but once.) Ah, I know what it is to you. A first visit!—ah, the romance of it! I wish I could feel it again.

H. Yes, I find it exceeds all my dreams. It is enchantment. I go . . .

G. S. (With a dainty gesture of the hand signifying "Spare me your callow enthusiasms, good friend.") Yes, I know, I know; you go to cathedrals, and exclaim; and you drag through league-long picture-galleries and exclaim; and you stand here, and there, and yonder, upon historic ground, and continue to exclaim; and you are permeated with your first crude conceptions of Art, and are proud and happy. Ah, yes, proud and happy—that expresses it. Yes-yes, enjoy it—it is right— it is an innocent revel.

H. And you? Don't you do these things now?

G. S. I! Oh, that is *very* good! My dear sir, when you are as old a traveler as I am, you will not ask such a question as that. *I* visit the regulation gallery, moon around the regulation cathedral, do the worn round of the regulation sights, *yet?*—Excuse me!

H. Well, what *do* you do, then?

G. S. Do? I flit—and flit—for I am ever on the wing—but I avoid the herd. To-day I am in Paris, to-morrow in Berlin, anon in Rome; but you would look for me in vain in the galleries of the Louvre or the common resorts of the gazers in those other capitals. If you would find me, you must look in the unvisited nooks and corners where others never think of going. One day you will find me making myself at home in some obscure peasant's cabin, another day you will find me in some forgotten castle worshiping some little gem of art which the careless eye has overlooked and which the unexperienced would despise; again you will find me a guest in the inner sanctuaries of palaces while the herd is content to get a hurried glimpse of the unused chambers by feeing a servant.

H. You are a *guest* in such places?

G. S. And a welcome one.

H. It is surprising. How does it come?

G. S. My grandfather's name is a passport to all the courts in Europe. I have only to utter that name and every door is open to me. I flit from court to court at my own free will and pleasure, and am always welcome. I am as much at home in the palaces of Europe as you are among your relatives. I know every titled person in Europe, I think. I have my pockets full of invitations all the time. I am under promise now to go to Italy, where I am to be the guest of a succession of the

noblest houses in the land. In Berlin my life is a continued round of
gaiety in the imperial palace. It is the same, wherever I go.

H.   It must be very pleasant. But it must make Boston seem a little
slow when you are at home.

G. S.   Yes, of course it does. But I don't go home much. There's no
life there—little to feed a man's higher nature. Boston's very narrow,
you know. She doesn't know it, and you couldn't convince her of it—
so I say nothing when I'm there: where's the use? Yes, Boston is very
narrow, but she has such a good opinion of herself that she can't see
it. A man who has traveled as much as I have, and seen as much of the
world, sees it plain enough, but he can't cure it, you know, so the
best way is to leave it and seek a sphere which is more in harmony
with his tastes and culture. I run across there, once a year, perhaps,
when I have nothing important on hand, but I'm very soon back again.
I spend my time in Europe.

H.   I see. You map out your plans and . . .

G. S.   No, excuse me. I don't map out any plans. I simply follow the
inclination of the day. I am limited by no ties, no requirements, I am
not bound in any way. I am too old a traveler to hamper myself with
deliberate purposes. I am simply a traveler—an inveterate traveler—a
man of the world, in a word—I can call myself by no other name. I do
not say, "I am going here, or I am going there"—I say nothing at all, I
only act. For instance, next week you may find me the guest of a
grandee of Spain, or you may find me off for Venice, or flitting toward
Dresden. I shall probably go to Egypt presently; friends will say to
friends, "He is at the Nile cataracts"—and at that very moment they
will be surprised to learn that I'm away off yonder in India somewhere.
I am a constant surprise to people. They are always saying, "Yes, he
was in Jerusalem when we heard of him last, but goodness knows
where he is now."

Presently the Grandson rose to leave—discovered he had an appointment with some Emperor, perhaps. He did his graces over again:
gripped me with one talon, at arm's-length, pressed his hat against his
stomach with the other, bent his body in the middle three times, murmuring:

"Pleasure, 'm sure; great pleasure, 'm sure. Wish you much success."

Then he removed his gracious presence. It is a great and solemn
thing to have a grandfather.

I have not purposed to misrepresent this boy in any way, for what
little indignation he excited in me soon passed and left nothing behind
it but compassion. One cannot keep up a grudge against a vacuum. I

have tried to repeat the lad's very words; if I have failed anywhere I have at least not failed to reproduce the marrow and meaning of what he said. He and the innocent chatterbox whom I met on the Swiss lake are the most unique and interesting specimens of Young America I came across during my foreign tramping. I have made honest portraits of them, not caricatures. The Grandson of twenty-three referred to himself five or six times as an "old traveler," and as many as three times (with a serene complacency which was maddening) as a "man of the world." There was something very delicious about his leaving Boston to her "narrowness," unreproved and uninstructed.

I formed the caravan in marching order, presently, and after riding down the line to see that it was properly roped together, gave the command to proceed. In a little while the road carried us to open, grassy land. We were above the troublesome forest, now, and had an uninterrupted view, straight before us, of our summit—the summit of the Riffelberg.

We followed the mule-road, a zigzag course, now to the right, now to the left, but always up, and always crowded and incommoded by going and coming files of reckless tourists who were never, in a single instance, tied together. I was obliged to exert the utmost care and caution, for in many places the road was not two yards wide, and often the lower side of it sloped away in slanting precipices eight and even nine feet deep. I had to encourage the men constantly, to keep them from giving way to their unmanly fears.

We might have made the summit before night, but for a delay caused by the loss of an umbrella. I was for allowing the umbrella to remain lost, but the men murmured, and with reason, for in this exposed region we stood in peculiar need of protection against avalanches; so I went into camp and detached a strong party to go after the missing article.

The difficulties of the next morning were severe, but our courage was high, for our goal was near. At noon we conquered the last impediment—we stood at last upon the summit, and without the loss of a single man except the mule that ate the glycerin. Our great achievement was achieved—the possibility of the impossible was demonstrated, and Harris and I walked proudly into the great dining-room of the Riffelberg Hotel and stood our alpenstocks up in the corner.

Yes, I had made the grand ascent; but it was a mistake to do it in evening dress. The plug hats were battered, the swallow-tails were fluttering rags, mud added no grace, the general effect was unpleasant and even disreputable.

There were about seventy-five tourists at the hotel—mainly ladies and little children—and they gave us an admiring welcome which paid us for all our privations and sufferings. The ascent had been made, and the names and dates now stand recorded on a stone monument there to prove it to all future tourists.

I boiled a thermometer and took an altitude, with a most curious result: *the summit was not as high as the point on the mountainside where I had taken the first altitude.* Suspecting that I had made an important discovery, I prepared to verify it. There happened to be a still higher summit (called the Gorner Grat), above the hotel, and notwithstanding the fact that it overlooks a glacier from a dizzy height, and that the ascent is difficult and dangerous, I resolved to venture up there and boil a thermometer. So I sent a strong party, with some borrowed hoes, in charge of two chiefs of service, to dig a stairway in the soil all the way, and this I ascended, roped to the guides. This breezy height was the summit proper—so I accomplished even more than I had originally purposed to do. This foolhardy exploit is recorded on another stone monument.

I boiled my thermometer, and sure enough, this spot, which purported to be two thousand feet higher than the locality of the hotel, turned out to be nine thousand feet *lower.* Thus the fact was clearly demonstrated, that, *above a certain point, the higher a point seems to be, the lower it actually is.* Our ascent itself was a great achievement, but this contribution to science was an inconceivably greater matter.

Cavilers object that water boils at a lower and lower temperature the higher and higher you go, and hence the apparent anomaly. I answer that I do not base my theory upon what the boiling water does, but upon what a boiled thermometer says. You can't go behind the thermometer.

I had a magnificent view of Monte Rosa, and apparently all the rest of the Alpine world, from that high place. All the circling horizon was piled high with a mighty tumult of snowy crests. One might have imagined he saw before him the tented camps of a beleaguering host of Brobdingnagians.

But lonely, conspicuous, and superb, rose that wonderful upright wedge, the Matterhorn. Its precipitous sides were powdered over with

NOTE.—I had the very unusual luck to catch one little momentary glimpse of the Matterhorn wholly unencumbered by clouds. I leveled my photographic apparatus at it without the loss of an instant, and should have got an elegant picure if my donkey had not interfered. It was my purpose to draw this photograph all by myself for my book, but was obliged to put the mountain part of it into the hands of the professional artist because I found I could not do landscape well.

snow, and the upper half hidden in thick clouds which now and then dissolved to cobweb films and gave brief glimpses of the imposing tower as through a veil. A little later the Matterhorn took to himself the semblance of a volcano; he was stripped naked to his apex—around this circled vast wreaths of white cloud which strung slowly out and streamed away slantwise toward the sun, a twenty-mile stretch of rolling and tumbling vapor, and looking just as if it were pouring out of a crater. Later again, one of the mountain's sides was clean and clear, and another side densely clothed from base to summit in thick smoke-like cloud which feathered off and blew around the shaft's sharp_edge like the smoke around the corners of a burning building. The Matterhorn is always experimenting, and always gets up fine effects, too. In the sunset, when all the lower world is palled in gloom, it points toward heaven out of the pervading blackness like a finger of fire. In the sunrise—well, they say it is very fine in the sunrise.

Authorities agree that there is no such tremendous "layout" of snowy Alpine magnitude, grandeur, and sublimity to be seen from any other accessible point as the tourist may see from the summit of the Riffelberg. Therefore, let the tourist rope himself up and go there; for I have shown that with nerve, caution, and judgment, the thing can be done.

I wish to add one remark, here—in parentheses, so to speak—suggested by the word "snowy," which I have just used. We have all seen hills and mountains and levels with snow on them, and so we think we know all the aspects and effects produced by snow. But indeed we do not until we have seen the Alps. Possibly mass and distance add something—at any rate, something *is* added. Among other noticeable things, there is a dazzling, intense whiteness about the distant Alpine snow, when the sun is on it, which one recognizes as peculiar, and not familiar to the eye. The snow which one is accustomed to has a tint to it—painters usually give it a bluish cast—but there is no perceptible tint to the distant Alpine snow when it is trying to look its whitest. As to the unimaginable splendor of it when the sun is blazing down on it —well, it simply *is* unimaginable.

A guide-book is a queer thing. The reader has just seen what a man who undertakes the great ascent from Zermatt to the Riffelberg Hotel must experience. Yet Baedeker makes these strange statements concerning this matter:

1. Distance—3 hours.
2. The road cannot be mistaken.
3. Guide unnecessary.

4. Distance from Riffelberg Hotel to the Gorner Grat, one hour and a half.

5. Ascent simple and easy. Guide unnecessary.

6. Elevation of Zermatt above sea-level, 5,315 feet.

7. Elevation of Riffelberg Hotel above sea-level, 8,429 feet.

8. Elevation of the Gorner Grat above sea-level, 10,289 feet.

I have pretty effectually throttled these errors by sending him the following demonstrated facts:

1. Distance from Zermatt to Riffelberg Hotel, 7 days.

2. The road *can* be mistaken. If I am the first that did it, I want the credit of it, too.

3. Guides *are* necessary, for none but a native can read those finger-boards.

4. The estimate of the elevation of the several localities above sea-level is pretty correct—for Baedeker. He only misses it about a hundred and eighty or ninety thousand feet.

I found my arnica invaluable. My men were suffering excruciatingly, from the friction of sitting down so much. During two or three days, not one of them was able to do more than lie down or walk about; yet so effective was the arnica, that on the fourth all were able to sit up. I consider that, more than to anything else, I owe the success of our great undertaking to arnica and paregoric.

My men being restored to health and strength, my main perplexity, now, was how to get them down the mountain again. I was not willing to expose the brave fellows to the perils, fatigues, and hardships of that fearful route again if it could be helped. First I thought of balloons; but, of course, I had to give that idea up, for balloons were not procurable. I thought of several other expedients, but upon consideration discarded them, for cause. But at last I hit it. I was aware that the movement of glaciers is an established fact, for I had read it in Baedeker; so I resolved to take passage for Zermatt on the great Gorner Glacier.

Very good. The next thing was, how to get down to the glacier comfortably—for the mule-road to it was long, and winding, and wearisome. I set my mind at work, and soon thought out a plan. One looks straight down upon the vast frozen river called the Gorner Glacier, from the Gorner Grat, a sheer precipice twelve hundred feet high. We had one hundred and fifty-four umbrellas—and what is an umbrella but a parachute?

I mentioned this noble idea to Harris, with enthusiasm, and was about to order the Expedition to form on the Gorner Grat, with their umbrellas, and prepare for flight by platoons, each platoon in command of a guide, when Harris stopped me and urged me not to be too hasty. He asked me if this method of descending the Alps had ever been tried before. I said no, I had not heard of an instance. Then, in his opinion, it was a matter of considerable gravity; in his opinion it would not be well to send the whole command over the cliff at once; a better way would be to send down a single individual, first, and see how he fared.

I saw the wisdom of this idea instantly. I said as much, and thanked my agent cordially, and told him to take his umbrella and try the thing right away, and wave his hat when he got down, if he struck in a soft place, and then I would ship the rest right along.

Harris was greatly touched with this mark of confidence, and said so, in a voice that had a perceptible tremble in it; but at the same time he said he did not feel himself worthy of so conspicuous a favor; that it might cause jealousy in the command, for there were plenty who would not hesitate to say he had used underhanded means to get the appointment, whereas his conscience would bear him witness that he had not sought it at all, nor even, in his secret heart, desired it.

I said these words did him extreme credit, but that he must not throw away the imperishable distinction of being the first man to descend an Alp per parachute, simply to save the feelings of some envious underlings. No, I said, he *must* accept the appointment—it was no longer an invitation, it was a command.

He thanked me with effusion, and said that putting the thing in this form removed every objection. He retired, and soon returned with his umbrella, his eyes flaming with gratitude and his cheeks pallid with joy. Just then the head guide passed along. Harris's expression changed to one of infinite tenderness, and he said:

"That man did me a cruel injury four days ago, and I said in my heart he should live to perceive and confess that the only noble revenge a man can take upon his enemy is to return good for evil. I resign in his favor. Appoint him."

I threw my arms around the generous fellow and said:

"Harris, you are the noblest soul that lives. You shall not regret this sublime act, neither shall the world fail to know of it. You shall have opportunities far transcending this one, too, if I live—remember that."

I called the head guide to me and appointed him on the spot. But the thing aroused no enthusiasm in him. He did not take to the idea at all. He said:

"Tie myself to an umbrella and jump over the Gorner Grat! Excuse me, there are a great many pleasanter roads to the devil than that."

Upon a discussion of the subject with him, it appeared that he considered the project distinctly and decidedly dangerous. I was not convinced, yet I was not willing to try the experiment in any risky way—that is, in a way that might cripple the strength and efficiency of the Expedition. I was about at my wits' end when it occurred to me to try it on the Latinist.

He was called in. But he declined, on the plea of inexperience, diffidence in public, lack of curiosity, and I don't know what all. Another man declined on account of a cold in the head; thought he ought to avoid exposure. Another could not jump well—never *could* jump well—did not believe he could jump so far without long and patient practice. Another was afraid it was going to rain, and his umbrella had a hole in it. Everybody had an excuse. The result was what the reader has by this time guessed: the most magnificent idea that was ever conceived had to be abandoned, from sheer lack of a person with enterprise enough to carry it out. Yes, I actually had to give that thing up—while doubtless I should live to see somebody use it and take all the credit from me.

Well, I had to go overland—there was no other way. I marched the Expedition down the steep and tedious mule-path and took up as good a position as I could upon the middle of the glacier—because Baedeker said the middle part travels the fastest. As a measure of economy, however, I put some of the heavier baggage on the shoreward parts, to go as slow freight.

I waited and waited, but the glacier did not move. Night was coming on, the darkness began to gather—still we did not budge. It occurred to me then, that there might be a time-table in Baedeker; it would be well to find out the hours of starting. I called for the book—it could not be found. Bradshaw would certainly contain a time-table; but no Bradshaw could be found.

Very well, I must make the best of the situation. So I pitched the tents, picketed the animals, milked the cows, had supper, paregoricked the men, established the watch, and went to bed—with orders to call me as soon as we came in sight of Zermatt.

I awoke about half past ten next morning, and looked around. We hadn't budged a peg! At first I could not understand it; then it occurred to me that the old thing must be aground. So I cut down some trees and rigged a spar on the starboard and another on the port side, and fooled away upward of three hours trying to spar her off. But it was no use. She was half a mile wide and fifteen or twenty miles long, and there was no telling just whereabouts she *was* aground. The men began to show uneasiness, too, and presently they came flying to me with ashy faces, saying she had sprung a leak.

Nothing but my cool behavior at this critical time saved us from another panic. I ordered them to show me the place. They led me to a spot where a huge boulder lay in a deep pool of clear and brilliant water. It did look like a pretty bad leak, but I kept that to myself. I made a pump and set the men to work to pump out the glacier. We made a success of it. I perceived, then, that it was not a leak at all. This boulder had descended from a precipice and stopped on the ice in the middle of the glacier, and the sun had warmed it up, every day, and consequently it had melted its way deeper and deeper into the ice, until at last it reposed, as we had found it, in a deep pool of the clearest and coldest water.

Presently Baedeker was found again, and I hunted eagerly for the time-table. There was none. The book simply said the glacier was moving all the time. This was satisfactory, so I shut up the book and chose a good position to view the scenery as we passed along. I stood there some time enjoying the trip, but at last it occurred to me that we did not seem to be gaining any on the scenery. I said to myself, "This confounded old thing's aground again, sure,"—and opened Baedeker to see if I could run across any remedy for these annoying interruptions. I soon found a sentence which threw a dazzling light upon the matter. It said, "The Gorner Glacier travels at an average rate of a little less than an inch a day." I have seldom felt so outraged. I have seldom had my confidence so wantonly betrayed. I made a small calculation: One inch a day, say thirty feet a year; estimated distance to Zermatt, three and one-eighteenth miles. Time required to go by glacier, *a little over five hundred years!* I said to myself, "I can *walk* it quicker—and before I will patronize such a fraud as this, I will do it."

When I revealed to Harris the fact that the passenger part of this glacier—the central part—the lightning-express part, so to speak—was not due in Zermatt till the summer of 2378, and that the baggage, coming along the slow edge, would not arrive until some generations later, he burst out with:

"That is European management, all over! An inch a day—think of that! Five hundred years to go a trifle over three miles! But I am not a bit surprised. It's a Catholic glacier. You can tell by the look of it. And the management."

I said, no, I believed nothing but the extreme end of it was in a Catholic canton.

"Well, then, it's a government glacier," said Harris. "It's all the same. Over here the government runs everything—so everything's slow; slow, and ill-managed. But with us, everything's done by private enterprise— and then there ain't much lolling around, you can depend on it. I wish Tom Scott could get his hands on this torpid old slab once—you'd see it take a different gait from this."

I said I was sure he would increase the speed, if there was trade enough to justify it.

"He'd *make* trade," said Harris. "That's the difference between governments and individuals. Governments don't care, individuals do. Tom Scott would take all the trade; in two years Gorner stock would go to two hundred, and inside of two more you would see all the other glaciers under the hammer for taxes." After a reflective pause, Harris added, "A little less than an inch a day; a little less than an *inch*, mind you. Well, I'm losing my reverence for glaciers."

I was feeling much the same way myself. I have traveled by canal-boat, ox-wagon, raft, and by the Ephesus and Smyrna railway; but when it comes down to good solid honest slow motion, I bet my money on the glacier. As a means of passenger transportation, I consider the glacier a failure; but as a vehicle for slow freight, I think she fills the bill. In the matter of putting the fine shades on that line of business, I judge she could teach the Germans something.

I ordered the men to break camp and prepare for the land journey to Zermatt. At this moment a most interesting find was made; a dark object, bedded in the glacial ice, was cut out with the ice-axes, and it proved to be a piece of the undressed skin of some animal—a hair trunk, perhaps; but a close inspection disabled the hair-trunk theory, and further discussion and examination exploded it entirely—that is, in the opinion of all the scientists except the one who had advanced it. This one clung to his theory with the affectionate fidelity characteristic of originators of scientific theories, and afterward won many of the first scientists of the age to his view, by a very able pamphlet which he wrote, entitled, "Evidences going to show that the hair trunk, in a wild state, belonged to the early glacial period, and roamed the wastes of chaos in company with the cave-bear, primeval man, and the other Oölitics of the Old Silurian family."

Each of our scientists had a theory of his own, and put forward an animal of his own as a candidate for the skin. I sided with the geologist of the Expedition in the belief that this patch of skin had once helped to cover a Siberian elephant, in some old forgotten age—but we divided there, the geologist believing that this discovery proved that Siberia had formerly been located where Switzerland is now, whereas I held the opinion that it merely proved that the primeval Swiss was not the dull savage he is represented to have been, but was a being of high intellectual development, who liked to go to the menagerie.

We arrived that evening, after many hardships and adventures, in some fields close to the great ice-arch where the mad Visp boils and surges out from under the foot of the great Gorner Glacier, and here we camped, our perils over and our magnificent undertaking successfully completed. We marched into Zermatt the next day, and were received with the most lavish honors and applause. A document, signed and sealed by all the authorities, was given to me which established and indorsed the fact that I had made the ascent of the Riffelberg. This I wear around my neck, and it will be buried with me when I am no more.

From A TRAMP ABROAD, 1880

The Awful German Language

A little learning makes the whole world kin.—*Proverbs* xxxii, 7.

I went often to look at the collection of curiosities in Heidelberg Castle, and one day I surprised the keeper of it with my German. I spoke entirely in that language. He was greatly interested; and after I had talked a while he said my German was very rare, possibly a "unique"; and wanted to add it to his museum.

If he had known what it had cost me to acquire my art, he would also have known that it would break any collector to buy it. Harris and I had been hard at work on our German during several weeks at that time, and although we had made good progress, it had been accomplished under great difficulty and annoyance, for three of our teachers had died in the mean time. A person who has not studied German can form no idea of what a perplexing language it is.

Surely there is not another language that is so slipshod and systemless, and so slippery and elusive to the grasp. One is washed about in it, hither and thither, in the most helpless way; and when at last he thinks he has captured a rule which offers firm ground to take a rest on amid the general rage and turmoil of the ten parts of speech, he turns over the page and reads, "Let the pupil make careful note of the following *exceptions.*" He runs his eye down and finds that there are more exceptions to the rule than instances of it. So overboard he goes again, to hunt for another Ararat and find another quicksand. Such has been, and continues to be, my experience. Every time I think I have got one of these four confusing "cases" where I am master of it, a seemingly insignificant preposition intrudes itself into my sentence, clothed with an awful and unsuspected power, and crumbles the ground from under me. For instance, my book inquires after a certain bird—(it is always inquiring after things which are of no sort of consequence to anybody): "Where is the bird?" Now the answer to this question—according to the book—is that the bird is waiting in the blacksmith shop on account of the rain. Of course no bird would do that, but then you must stick to the book. Very well, I begin to cipher out the German for that answer. I begin at the wrong end, necessarily, for that is the German idea. I say to myself, "*Regen* (rain) is masculine —or maybe it is feminine—or possibly neuter—it is too much trouble to look now. Therefore, it is either *der* (the) Regen, or *die* (the) Regen, or *das* (the) Regen, according to which gender it may turn out to be when I look. In the interest of science, I will cipher it out on the hypothesis that it is masculine. Very well—then *the* rain is *der* Regen, if it is simply in the quiescent state of being *mentioned,* without enlargement or discussion—Nominative case; but if this rain is lying around, in a kind of a general way on the ground, it is then definitely located, it is *doing something*—that is, *resting* (which is one of the German grammar's ideas of doing something), and this throws the rain into the Dative case, and makes it *dem* Regen. However, this rain is not resting, but is doing something *actively*—it is falling—to interfere with the bird, likely—and this indicates *movement,* which has the effect of sliding it into the Accusative case and changing *dem* Regen into *den* Regen." Having completed the grammatical horoscope of this matter, I answer up confidently and state in German that the bird is staying in the blacksmith shop "wegen (on account of) *den* Regen." Then the teacher lets me softly down with the remark that whenever the word "wegen" drops into a sentence, it *always* throws that subject into the *Genitive* case, regardless of consequences—and that therefore this bird stayed in the blacksmith shop "wegen *des* Regens."

N.B.—I was informed, later, by a higher authority, that there was an "exception" which permits one to say "wegen *den* Regen" in certain peculiar and complex circumstances, but that this exception is not extended to anything *but* rain.

There are ten parts of speech, and they are all troublesome. An average sentence, in a German newspaper, is a sublime and impressive curiosity; it occupies a quarter of a column; it contains all the ten parts of speech—not in regular order, but mixed; it is built mainly of compound words constructed by the writer on the spot, and not to be found in any dictionary—six or seven words compacted into one, without joint or seam—that is, without hyphens; it treats of fourteen or fifteen different subjects, each inclosed in a parenthesis of its own, with here and there extra parentheses which reinclose three or four of the minor parentheses, making pens within pens: finally, all the parentheses and reparentheses are massed together between a couple of king-parentheses, one of which is placed in the first line of the majestic sentence and the other in the middle of the last line of it—*after which comes the* VERB, and you find out for the first time what the man has been talking about; and after the verb—merely by way of ornament, as far as I can make out—the writer shovels in *"haben sind gewesen gehabt haben geworden sein,"* or words to that effect, and the monument is finished. I suppose that this closing hurrah is in the nature of the flourish to a man's signature—not necessary, but pretty. German books are easy enough to read when you hold them before the looking-glass or stand on your head—so as to reverse the construction—but I think that to learn to read and understand a German newspaper is a thing which must always remain an impossibility to a foreigner.

Yet even the German books are not entirely free from attacks of the Parenthesis distemper—though they are usually so mild as to cover only a few lines, and therefore when you at last get down to the verb it carries some meaning to your mind because you are able to remember a good deal of what has gone before.

Now here is a sentence from a popular and excellent German novel —with a slight parenthesis in it. I will make a perfectly literal translation, and throw in the parenthesis-marks and some hyphens for the assistance of the reader—though in the original there are no parenthesis-marks or hyphens, and the reader is left to flounder through to the remote verb the best way he can:

"But when he, upon the street, the (in-satin-and-silk-covered-

now-very-unconstrainedly-after-the-newest-fashion-dressed)   government counselor's wife *met*," etc., etc.[1]

That is from *The Old Mamselle's Secret,* by Mrs. Marlitt. And that
sentence is constructed upon the most approved German model. You
observe how far that verb is from the reader's base of operations; well,
in a German newspaper they put their verb away over on the next
page; and I have heard that sometimes after stringing along on exciting preliminaries and parentheses for a column or two, they get in a
hurry and have to go to press without getting to the verb at all. Of
course, then, the reader is left in a very exhausted and ignorant state.

We have the Parenthesis disease in our literature, too; and one may
see cases of it every day in our books and newspapers: but with us it is
the mark and sign of an unpractised writer or a cloudy intellect,
whereas with the Germans it is doubtless the mark and sign of a
practised pen and of the presence of that sort of luminous intellectual
fog which stands for clearness among these people. For surely it is
not clearness—it necessarily can't be clearness. Even a jury would have
penetration enough to discover that. A writer's ideas must be a good
deal confused, a good deal out of line and sequence, when he starts
out to say that a man met a counselor's wife in the street, and then
right in the midst of this so simple undertaking halts these approaching
people and makes them stand still until he jots down an inventory
of the woman's dress. That is manifestly absurd. It reminds a person of
those dentists who secure your instant and breathless interest in a tooth
by taking a grip on it with the forceps, and then stand there and
drawl through a tedious anecdote before they give the dreaded jerk.
Parentheses in literature and denistry are in bad taste.

The Germans have another kind of parenthesis, which they make
by splitting a verb in two and putting half of it at the beginning of an
exciting chapter and the *other half* at the end of it. Can any one
conceive of anything more confusing than that? These things are
called "separable verbs." The German grammar is blistered all over
with separable verbs; and the wider the two portions of one of them
are spread apart, the better the author of the crime is pleased with
his performance. A favorite one is *reiste ab*—which means *departed.*
Here is an example which I culled from a novel and reduced to
English:

"The trunks being now ready, he DE-after kissing his mother and
sisters, and once more pressing to his bosom his adored Gretchen,

[1] *Wenn er aber auf der Strasse der in Sammt und Seide gehüllten jetz sehr ungenirt
nach der neusten mode gekleideten Regierungsrathin begegnet.*

who, dressed in simple white muslin, with a single tuberose in the ample folds of her rich brown hair, had tottered feebly down the stairs, still pale from the terror and excitement of the past evening, but longing to lay her poor aching head yet once again upon the breast of him whom she loved more dearly than life itself, PARTED."

However, it is not well to dwell too much on the separable verbs. One is sure to lose his temper early; and if he sticks to the subject, and will not be warned, it will at last either soften his brain or petrify it. Personal pronouns and adjectives are a fruitful nuisance in this language, and should have been left out. For instance, the same sound, *sie*, means *you*, and it means *she*, and it means *her*, and it means *it*, and it means *they*, and it means *them*. Think of the ragged poverty of a language which has to make one word do the work of six—and a poor little weak thing of only three letters at that. But mainly, think of the exasperation of never knowing which of these meanings the speaker is trying to convey. This explains why, whenever a person says *sie* to me, I generally try to kill him, if a stranger.

Now observe the Adjective. Here was a case where simplicity would have been an advantage; therefore, for no other reason, the inventor of this language complicated it all he could. When we wish to speak of our "good friend or friends," in our enlightened tongue, we stick to the one form and have no trouble or hard feeling about it; but with the German tongue it is different. When a German gets his hands on an adjective, he declines it, and keeps on declining it until the common sense is all declined out of it. It is as bad as Latin. He says, for instance:

SINGULAR

Nominative—Mein guter Freund, my good friend.
Genitives—Meines guten Freundes, of my good friend.
Dative—Meinem guten Freund, to my good friend.
Accusative—Meinen guten Freund, my good friend.

PLURAL

N.—Meine guten Freunde, my good friends.
G.—Meiner guten Freunde, of my good friends.
D.—Meinen guten Freunden, to my good friends.
A.—Meine guten Freunde, my good friends.

Now let the candidate for the asylum try to memorize those variations, and see how soon he will be elected. One might better go without friends in Germany than take all this trouble about them. I have
shown what a bother it is to decline a good (male) friend; well this is
only a third of the work, for there is a variety of new distortions of the
adjective to be learned when the object is feminine, and still another
when the object is neuter. Now there are more adjectives in this
language than there are black cats in Switzerland, and they must all
be as elaborately declined as the examples above suggested. Difficult?
—troublesome?—these words cannot describe it. I heard a Californian
student in Heidelberg say, in one of his calmest moods, that he would
rather decline two drinks than one German adjective.

The inventor of the language seems to have taken pleasure in
complicating it in every way he could think of. For instance, if one is
casually referring to a house, *Haus*, or a horse, *Pferd*, or a dog, *Hund*,
he spells these words as I have indicated; but if he is referring to them
in the Dative case, he sticks on a foolish and unnecessary *e* and spells
them *Hause*, *Pferde*, *Hunde*. So, as an added *e* often signifies the
plural, as the *s* does with us, the new student is likely to go on for a
month making twins out of a Dative dog before he discovers his
mistake; and on the other hand, many a new student who could ill
afford loss, has bought and paid for two dogs and only got one of
them, because he ignorantly bought that dog in the Dative singular
when he really supposed he was talking plural—which left the law on
the seller's side, of course, by the strict rules of grammar, and therefore
a suit for recovery could not lie.

In German, all the Nouns begin with a capital letter. Now that is a
good idea; and a good idea, in this language, is necessarily conspicuous
from its lonesomeness. I consider this capitalizing of nouns a good idea,
because by reason of it you are almost always able to tell a noun the
minute you see it. You fall into error occasionally, because you mistake
the name of a person for the name of a thing, and waste a good deal of
time trying to dig a meaning out of it. German names almost always
do mean something, and this helps to deceive the student. I translated
a passage one day, which said that "the infuriated tigress broke loose
and utterly ate up the unfortunate fir forest" (*Tannenwald*). When
I was girding up my loins to doubt this, I found out that Tannenwald
in this instance was a man's name.

Every noun has a gender, and there is no sense or system in the
distribution; so the gender of each must be learned separately and by
heart. There is no other way. To do this one has to have a memory

like a memorandum-book. In German, a young lady has no sex, while a turnip has. Think what overwrought reverence that shows for the turnip, and what callous disrespect for the girl. See how it looks in print—I translate this from a conversation in one of the best of the German Sunday-school books:

"*Gretchen.*—Wilhelm, where is the turnip?

"*Wilhelm.*—She has gone to the kitchen.

"*Gretchen.*—Where is the accomplished and beautiful English maiden?

"*Wilhelm.*—It has gone to the opera."

To continue with the German genders: a tree is male, its buds are female, its leaves are neuter; horses are sexless, dogs are male, cats are female—tomcats included, of course; a person's mouth, neck, bosom, elbows, fingers, nails, feet, and body are of the male sex, and his head is male or neuter according to the word selected to signify it, and *not* according to the sex of the individual who wears it—for in Germany all the women wear either male heads or sexless ones; a person's nose, lips, shoulders, breast, hands, and toes are of the female sex; and his hair, ears, eyes, chin, legs, knees, heart, and conscience haven't any sex at all. The inventor of the language probably got what he knew about a conscience from hearsay.

Now, by the above dissection, the reader will see that in Germany a man may *think* he is a man, but when he comes to look into the matter closely, he is bound to have his doubts; he finds that in sober truth he is a most ridiculous mixture; and if he ends by trying to comfort himself with the thought that he can at least depend on a third of this mess as being manly and masculine, the humiliating second thought will quickly remind him that in this respect he is no better off than any woman or cow in the land.

In the German it is true that by some oversight of the inventor of the language, a Woman is a female; but a Wife (*Weib*) is not—which is unfortunate. A Wife, here, has no sex; she is neuter; so, according to the grammar, a fish is *he,* his scales are *she,* but a fishwife is neither. To describe a wife as sexless may be called under-description; that is bad enough, but over-description is surely worse. A German speaks of an Englishman as the *Engländer;* to change the sex, he adds *inn,* and that stands for Englishwoman—*Engländerinn.* That seems descriptive enough, but still it is not exact enough for a German; so he precedes the word with that article which indicates that the creature to follow is feminine, and writes it down thus: "*die* Engländer*inn,*"—which means "the *she-Englishwoman.*" I consider that that person is over-described.

Well, after the student has learned the sex of a great number of nouns, he is still in a difficulty, because he finds it impossible to persuade his tongue to refer to things as "*he*" and "*she*," and "*him*" and "*her*," which it has been always accustomed to refer to as "*it*." When he even frames a German sentence in his mind, with the hims and hers in the right places, and then works up his courage to the utterance-point, it is no use—the moment he begins to speak his tongue flies the track and all those labored males and females come out as "*its*." And even when he is reading German to himself, he always calls those things "*it*," whereas he ought to read in this way:

TALE OF THE FISHWIFE AND ITS SAD FATE[1]

It is a bleak Day. Hear the Rain, how he pours, and the Hail, how he rattles; and see the Snow, how he drifts along, and oh the Mud, how deep he is! Ah the poor Fishwife, it is stuck fast in the Mire; it has dropped its Basket of Fishes; and its Hands have been cut by the Scales as it seized some of the falling Creatures; and one Scale has even got into its Eye, and it cannot get her out. It opens its Mouth to cry for Help; but if any Sound comes out of him, alas he is drowned by the raging of the Storm. And now a Tomcat has got one of the Fishes and she will surely escape with him. No, she bites off a Fin, she holds her in her Mouth—will she swallow her? No, the Fishwife's brave Mother-dog deserts his Puppies and rescues the Fin—which he eats, himself, as his Reward. O, horror, the Lightning has struck the Fish-basket; he sets him on Fire; see the Flame, how she licks the doomed Utensil with her red and angry Tongue; now she attacks the helpless Fishwife's Foot—she burns him up, all but the big Toe, and even *she* is partly consumed; and still she spreads, still she waves her fiery Tongues; she attacks the Fishwife's Leg and destroys *it*; she attacks its Hand and destroys *her*; she attacks its poor worn Garment and destroys *her* also; she attacks its Body and consumes *him*; she wreathes herself about its Heart and *it* is consumed; next about its Breast, and in a Moment *she* is a Cinder; now she reaches its Neck—*he* goes; now its Chin—*it* goes; now its Nose—*she* goes. In another Moment, except Help come, the Fishwife will be no more. Time presses —is there none to succor and save? Yes! Joy, joy, with flying Feet the she-Englishwoman comes! But alas, the generous she-Female is too late: where now is the fated Fishwife? It has ceased from its Sufferings, it has gone to a better Land; all that is left of it for its loved Ones to

[1] I capitalize the nouns, in the German (and ancient English) fashion.

lament over, is this poor smoldering Ash-heap. Ah, woeful, woeful Ash-heap! Let us take him up tenderly, reverently, upon the lowly Shovel, and bear him to his long Rest, with the Prayer that when he rises again it will be in a Realm where he will have one good square responsible Sex, and have it all to himself, instead of having a mangy lot of assorted Sexes scattered all over him in Spots.

There, now, the reader can see for himself that this pronoun business is a very awkward thing for the unaccustomed tongue.

I suppose that in all languages the similarities of look and sound between words which have no similarity in meaning are a fruitful source of perplexity to the foreigner. It is so in our tongue, and it is notably the case in the German. Now there is that troublesome word *vermählt:* to me it has so close a resemblance—either real or fancied— to three or four other words, that I never know whether it means despised, painted, suspected, or married; until I look in the dictionary, and then I find it means the latter. There are lots of such words and they are a great torment. To increase the difficulty there are words which *seem* to resemble each other, and yet do not; but they make just as much trouble as if they did. For instance, there is the word *vermiethen* (to let, to lease, to hire); and the word *verheirathen* (another way of saying to *marry*). I heard of an Englishman who knocked at a man's door in Heidelberg and proposed, in the best German he could command, to *"verheirathen"* that house. Then there are some words which mean one thing when you emphasize the first syllable, but mean something very different if you throw the emphasis on the last syllable. For instance, there is a word which means a runaway, or the act of glancing through a book, according to the placing of the emphasis; and another word which signifies to *associate* with a man, or to *avoid* him, according to where you put the emphasis —and you can generally depend on putting it in the wrong place and getting into trouble.

There are some exceedingly useful words in this language. *Schlag,* for example; and *Zug*. There are three-quarters of a column of *Schlags* in the dictionary, and a column and a half of *Zugs*. The word *Schlag* means Blow, Stroke, Dash, Hit, Shock, Clap, Slap, Time, Bar, Coin, Stamp, Kind, Sort, Manner, Way, Apoplexy, Wood-cutting, Inclosure, Field, Forest-clearing. This is its simple and *exact* meaning—that is to say, its restricted, its fettered meaning; but there are ways by which you can set it free, so that it can soar away, as on the wings of the morning, and never be at rest. You can hang any word you please to its

tail, and make it mean anything you want to. You can begin with
Schlag-ader, which means artery, and you can hang on the whole
dictionary, word by word, clear through the alphabet to *Schlag-wasser,*
which means bilge-water—and including *Schlag-mutter,* which means
mother-in-law.

Just the same with *Zug.* Strictly speaking, *Zug* means Pull, Tug,
Draught, Procession, March, Progress, Flight, Direction, Expedition,
Train, Caravan, Passage, Stroke, Touch, Line, Flourish, Trait of Character, Feature, Lineament, Chess-move, Organ-stop, Team, Whiff,
Bias, Drawer, Propensity, Inhalation, Disposition: but that thing which
it does *not* mean—when all its legitimate pennants have been hung on,
has not been discovered yet.

One cannot overestimate the usefulness of *Schlag* and *Zug.* Armed
just with these two, and the word *Also,* what cannot the foreigner on
German soil accomplish? The German word *Also* is the equivalent of
the English phrase "You know," and does not mean anything at all—in
talk, though it sometimes does in print. Every time a German opens
his mouth an *Also* falls out; and every time he shuts it he bites one
in two that was trying to *get* out.

Now, the foreigner, equipped with these three noble words, is master
of the situation. Let him talk right along, fearlessly; let him pour his
indifferent German forth, and when he lacks for a word, let him heave
a *Schlag* into the vacuum; all the chances are that it fits it like a plug,
but if it doesn't let him promptly heave a *Zug* after it; the two together
can hardly fail to bung the hole; but if, by a miracle, they *should* fail,
let him simply say *Also!* and this will give him a moment's chance to
think of the needful word. In Germany, when you load your conversational gun it is always best to throw in a *Schlag* or two and a *Zug*
or two, because it doesn't make any difference how much the rest of
the charge may scatter, you are bound to bag something with *them.*
Then you blandly say *Also,* and load up again. Nothing gives such
an air of grace and elegance and unconstraint to a German or an
English conversation as to scatter it full of "Also's" or "You-knows."

In my note-book I find this entry:

July 1.—In the hospital yesterday, a word of thirteen syllables was
successfully removed from a patient—a North German from near Ham-
burg; but as most unfortunately the surgeons had opened him in the
wrong place, under the impression that he contained a panorama, he
died. The sad event has cast a gloom over the whole community.

That paragraph furnishes a text for a few remarks about one of the
most curious and notable features of my subject—the length of

German words. Some German words are so long that they have a perspective. Observe these examples:

Freundschaftsbezeigungen.

Dilettantenaufdringlichkeiten.

Stadtverordnetenversammlungen.

These things are not words, they are alphabetical processions. And they are not rare; one can open a German newspaper any time and see them marching majestically across the page—and if he has any imagination he can see the banners and hear the music, too. They impart a martial thrill to the meekest subject. I take a great interest in these curiosities. Whenever I come across a good one, I stuff it and put it in my museum. In this way I have made quite a valuable collection. When I get duplicates, I exchange with other collectors, and thus increase the variety of my stock. Here are some specimens which I lately bought at an auction sale of the effects of a bankrupt bric-à-brac hunter:

GENERALSTAATSVERORDNETENVERSAMMLUNGEN.

ALTERTHUMSWISSENSCHAFTEN.

KINDERBEWAHRUNGSANSTALTEN.

UNABHAENGIGKEITSERKLAERUNGEN.

WIEDERERSTELLUNGSBESTREBUNGEN.

WAFFENSTILLSTANDSUNTERHANDLUNGEN.

Of course when one of these grand mountain ranges goes stretching across the printed page, it adorns and ennobles that literary landscape —but at the same time it is a great distress to the new student, for it blocks up his way; he cannot crawl under it, or climb over it, or tunnel through it. So he resorts to the dictionary for help, but there is no help there. The dictionary must draw the line somewhere—so it leaves this sort of words out. And it is right, because these long things are hardly legitimate words, but are rather combinations of words, and the inventor of them ought to have been killed. They are compound words with the hyphens left out. The various words used in building them are in the dictionary, but in a very scattered condition; so you can hunt the materials out, one by one, and get at the meaning at last, but it is a tedious and harassing business. I have tried this process upon some of the above examples. *"Freundschaftsbezeigungen"* seems to be "Friendship demonstrations," which is only a foolish and clumsy way of saying "demonstrations of friendship." *"Unabhaengigkeitserklaerungen"* seems to be "Independencedeclarations," which is no improvement upon "Declarations of Independence," so far as I can see. *"Generalstaatsverordnetenversammlungen"* seems to be "Generalstatesrepresentativesmeetings," as nearly as I can get at it—a mere rhythmical, gushy euphuism for "meetings of the legislature," I judge. We used to have a good deal of this sort of crime in our literature, but it has gone out now. We used to speak of a thing as a "never-to-be-forgotten" circumstance, instead of cramping it into the simple and sufficient word "memorable" and then going calmly about our business as if nothing had happened. In those days we were not content to embalm the thing and bury it decently, we wanted to build a monument over it.

But in our newspapers the compounding-disease lingers a little to the present day, but with the hyphens left out, in the German fashion. This is the shape it takes: instead of saying "Mr. Simmons, clerk of the county and district courts, was in town yesterday," the new form puts it thus: "Clerk of the County and District Courts Simmons was in town yesterday." This saves neither time nor ink, and has an awkward sound besides. One often sees a remark like this in our papers: "*Mrs.* Assistant District Attorney Johnson returned to her city residence yesterday for the season." That is a case of really unjustifiable compounding; because it not only saves no time or trouble, but confers a title on Mrs. Johnson which she has no right to. But these little instances are trifles indeed, contrasted with the ponderous and dismal German system of piling jumbled compounds together. I wish to submit the following local item, from a Mannheim journal, by way of illustration:

"In the daybeforeyesterdayshortlyaftereleveno'clock Night, the inthistownstandingtavern called 'The Wagoner' was downburnt. When the fire to the onthedownburninghouseresting Stork's Nest reached, flew the parent Storks away. But when the bytheraging, firesurrounded Nest *itself* caught Fire, straightway plunged the quickreturning Motherstork into the Flames and died, her Wings over her young ones outspread."

Even the cumbersome German construction is not able to take the pathos out of that picture—indeed, it somehow seems to strengthen it. This item is dated away back yonder months ago. I could have used it sooner, but I was waiting to hear from the Father-stork. I am still waiting.

"*Also!*" If I have not shown that the German is a difficult language, I have at least intended to do it. I have heard of an American student who was asked how he was getting along with his German, and who answered promptly: "I am not getting along at all. I have worked at it hard for three level months, and all I have got to show for it is one solitary German phrase—'*Zwei glas*'" (two glasses of beer). He paused a moment, reflectively; then added with feeling: "But I've got that *solid!*"

And if I have not also shown that German is a harassing and infuriating study, my execution has been at fault, and not my intent. I heard lately of a worn and sorely tried American student who used to fly to a certain German word for relief when he could bear up under his aggravations no longer—the only word in the whole language whose sound was sweet and precious to his ear and healing to his lacerated spirit. This was the word *Damit.* It was only the *sound* that helped him, not the meaning;[1] and so, at last, when he learned that the emphasis was not on the first syllable, his only stay and support was gone, and he faded away and died.

I think that a description of any loud, stirring, tumultuous episode must be tamer in German than in English. Our descriptive words of this character have such a deep, strong, resonant sound, while their German equivalents do seem so thin and mild and energyless. Boom, burst, crash, roar, storm, bellow, blow, thunder, explosion; howl, cry, shout, yell, groan; battle, hell. These are magnificent words; they have a force and magnitude of sound befitting the things which they describe. But their German equivalents would be ever so nice to sing the children to sleep with, or else my awe-inspiring ears were made for display and not for superior usefulness in analyzing sounds. Would any man want to die in a battle which was called by so tame a term as a *Schlacht?* Or would not a consumptive feel too much bundled up, who was about to go out, in a shirt-collar and a seal-ring, into a storm which the bird-song word *Gewitter* was employed to describe? And observe the strongest of the several German equivalents for explosion —*Ausbruch.* Our word Toothbrush is more powerful than that. It seems to me that the Germans could do worse than import it into their language to describe particularly tremendous explosions with. The German word for hell—Hölle—sounds more like *helly* than anything else; therefore, how necessarily chipper, frivolous, and unimpressive it is. If a man were told in German to go there, could he really rise to the dignity of feeling insulted?

Having pointed out, in detail, the several vices of this language, I now come to the brief and pleasant task of pointing out its virtues. The capitalizing of the nouns I have already mentioned. But far before this virtue stands another—that of spelling a word according to the sound of it. After one short lesson in the alphabet, the student can tell how any German word is pronounced without having to ask; whereas in

[1] It merely means, in its general sense, *"herewith."*

our language if a student should inquire of us, "What does B, O, W, spell?" we should be obliged to reply, "Nobody can tell what it spells when you set it off by itself; you can only tell by referring to the context and finding out what it signifies—whether it is a thing to shoot arrows with, or a nod of one's head, or the forward end of a boat."

There are some German words which are singularly and powerfully effective. For instance, those which describe lowly, peaceful, and affectionate home life; those which deal with love, in any and all forms, from mere kindly feeling and honest good will toward the passing stranger, clear up to courtship; those which deal with outdoor Nature, in its softest and loveliest aspects—with meadows and forests, and birds and flowers, the fragrance and sunshine of summer, and the moonlight of peaceful winter nights; in a word, those which deal with any and all forms of rest, respose, and peace; those also which deal with the creatures and marvels of fairyland; and lastly and chiefly, in those words which express pathos, is the language surpassingly rich and effective. There are German songs which can make a stranger to the language cry. That shows that the *sound* of the words is correct —it interprets the meanings with truth and with exactness; and so the ear is informed, and through the ear, the heart.

The Germans do not seem to be afraid to repeat a word when it is the right one. They repeat it several times, if they choose. That is wise. But in English, when we have used a word a couple of times in a paragraph, we imagine we are growing tautological, and so we are weak enough to exchange it for some other word which only approximates exactness, to escape what we wrongly fancy is a greater blemish. Repetition may be bad, but surely inexactness is worse.

There are people in the world who will take a great deal of trouble to point out the faults in a religion or a language, and then go blandly about their business without suggesting any remedy. I am not that kind of a person. I have shown that the German language needs reforming. Very well, I am ready to reform it. At least I am ready to make the proper suggestions. Such a course as this might be immodest in another; but I have devoted upward of nine full weeks, first and last, to a careful and critical study of this tongue, and thus have acquired a confidence in my ability to reform it which no mere superficial culture could have conferred upon me.

In the first place, I would leave out the Dative case. It confuses the plurals; and, besides, nobody ever knows when he is in the Dative case, except he discover it by accident—and then he does not know when or where it was that he got into it, or how long he has been in it, or how he is ever going to get out of it again. The Dative case is but an ornamental folly—it is better to discard it.

In the next place, I would move the Verb further up to the front. You may load up with ever so good a Verb, but I notice that you never really bring down a subject with it at the present German range—you only cripple it. So I insist that this important part of speech should be brought forward to a position where it may be easily seen with the naked eye.

Thirdly, I would import some strong words from the English tongue —to swear with, and also to use in describing all sorts of vigorous things in a vigorous way.[1]

Fourthly, I would reorganize the sexes, and distribute them according to the will of the Creator. This as a tribute of respect, if nothing else.

Fifthly, I would do away with those great long compounded words; or require the speaker to deliver them in sections, with intermissions for refreshments. To wholly do away with them would be best, for ideas are more easily received and digested when they come one at a time than when they come in bulk. Intellectual food is like any other; it is pleasanter and more beneficial to take it with a spoon than with a shovel.

Sixthly, I would require a speaker to stop when he is done, and not hang a string of those useless *"haben sind gewesen gehabt haben geworden seins"* to the end of his oration. This sort of gewgaws undignify a speech, instead of adding a grace. They are, therefore, an offense, and should be discarded.

Seventhly, I would discard the Parenthesis. Also the reparenthesis, the re-reparenthesis, and the re-re-re-re-re-reparentheses, and likewise the final wide-reaching all-inclosing king-parenthesis. I would require every individual, be he high or low, to unfold a plain straightforward

[1] *"Verdammt,"* and its variations and enlargements, are words which have plenty of meaning, but the *sounds* are so mild and ineffectual that German ladies can use them without sin. German ladies who could not be induced to commit a sin by any persuasion or compulsion, promptly rip out one of these harmless little words when they tear their dresses or don't like the soup. It sounds about as wicked as our "My gracious." German ladies are constantly saying, *"Ach! Gott!" "Mein Gott!" "Gott in Himmel!" "Herr Gott!" "Der Herr Jesus!"* etc. They think our ladies have the same custom, perhaps; for I once heard a gentle and lovely old German lady say to a sweet young American girl: "The two languages are so alike—how pleasant that is; we say 'Ach! Gott!' you say 'Goddam.' "

tale, or else coil it and sit on it and hold his peace. Infractions of this law should be punishable with death.

And eighthly, and last, I would retain *Zug* and *Schlag,* with their pendants, and discard the rest of the vocabulary. This would simplify the language.

I have now named what I regard as the most necessary and important changes. These are perhaps all I could be expected to name for nothing; but there are other suggestions which I can and will make in case my proposed application shall result in my being formally employed by the government in the work of reforming the language.

My philological studies have satisfied me that a gifted person ought to learn English (barring spelling and pronouncing) in thirty hours, French in thirty days, and German in thirty years. It seems manifest, then, that the latter tongue ought to be trimmed down and repaired. If it is to remain as it is, it ought to be gently and reverently set aside among the dead languages, for only the dead have time to learn it.

A FOURTH OF JULY ORATION IN THE GERMAN TONGUE, DELIVERED
AT A BANQUET OF THE ANGLO-AMERICAN CLUB OF STUDENTS
BY THE AUTHOR OF THIS BOOK

GENTLEMEN: Since I arrived, a month ago, in this old wonderland, this vast garden of Germany, my English tongue has so often proved a useless piece of baggage to me, and so troublesome to carry around, in a country where they haven't the checking system for luggage, that I finally set to work, last week, and learned the German language. Also! Es freut mich dass dies so ist, denn es muss, in ein hauptsächlich degree, höflich sein, dass man auf ein occasion like this, sein Rede in die Sprache des Landes worin he boards, aussprechen soll. Dafür habe ich, aus reinische Verlegenheit—no, Vergangenheit—no, I mean Höflichkeit—aus reinische Höflichkeit habe ich resolved to tackle this business in the German language, um Gottes willen! Also! Sie müssen so freundlich sein, und verzeih mich die interlarding von ein oder zwei Englischer Worte, hie und da, denn ich finde dass die deutsche is not a very copious language, and so when you've really got anything to say, you've got to draw on a language that can stand the strain.

Wenn aber man kann nicht meinem Rede verstehen, so werde ich ihm später dasselbe übersetz, wenn er solche Dienst verlangen wollen haben werden sollen sein hätte. (I don't know what wollen haben werden sollen sein hätte means, but I notice they always put it at the

end of a German sentence—merely for general literary gorgeousness,
I suppose.)

This is a great and justly honored day—a day which is worthy of
the veneration in which it is held by the true patriots of all climes
and nationalities—a day which offers a fruitful theme for thought
and speech; und meinem Freunde—no, meinen Freunden—meines
Freundes—well, take your choice, they're all the same price; I don't
know which one is right—also! ich habe gehabt haben worden gewesen
sein, as Goethe says in his Paradise Lost—ich—ich—that is to say—ich—
but let us change cars.

Also! Die Anblick so viele Grossbrittanischer und Amerikanischer
hier zusammengetroffen in Bruderliche concord, ist zwar a welcome and inspiriting spectacle. And what has moved you to it?
Can the terse German tongue rise to the expression of this impulse? Is it Freundschaftsbezeigungenstadtverordnetenversammlungen-
familieneigenthümlichkeiten? Nein, o nein! This is a crisp and noble
word, but it fails to pierce the marrow of the impulse which has
gathered this friendly meeting and produced diese Anblick—eine
Anblick welche ist gut zu sehen—gut für die Augen in a foreign land
and a far country—eine Anblick solche als in die gewöhnliche Heidel-
berger phrase nennt man ein "schönes Aussicht!" Ja, freilich natürlich
wahrscheinlich ebensowohl! Also! Die Aussicht auf dem Königsstuhl
mehr grösserer ist, aber geistlische sprechend nicht so schön, lob' Gott!
Because sie sind hier zusammengetroffen, in Bruderlichem concord,
ein grossen Tag zu feiern, whose high benefits were not for one land
and one locality only, but have conferred a measure of good upon all
lands that know liberty to-day, and love it. Hundert Jahre vorüber,
waren die Engländer und die Amerikaner Feinde; aber heute sind
sie herzlichen Freunde, Gott sei Dank! May this good-fellowship endure; may these banners here blended in amity so remain; may they
never any more wave over opposing hosts, or be stained with blood
which was kindred, is kindred, and always will be kindred, until a line
drawn upon a map shall be able to say: "*This* bars the ancestral blood
from flowing in the veins of the descendant!"

From A TRAMP ABROAD, 1880

The Great French Duel

Much as the modern French duel is ridiculed by certain smart people, it is in reality one of the most dangerous institutions of our day. Since it is always fought in the open air, the combatants are nearly sure to catch cold. M. Paul de Cassagnac, the most inveterate of the French duelists, had suffered so often in this way that he is at last a confirmed invalid; and the best physician in Paris has expressed the opinion that if he goes on dueling for fifteen or twenty years more —unless he forms the habit of fighting in a comfortable room where damps and draughts cannot intrude—he will eventually endanger his life. This ought to moderate the talk of those people who are so stubborn in maintaining that the French duel is the most health-giving of recreations because of the open-air exercise it affords. And it ought also to moderate that foolish talk about French duelists and socialist-hated monarchs being the only people who are immortal.

But it is time to get at my subject. As soon as I heard of the late fiery outbreak between M. Gambetta and M. Fourtou in the French Assembly, I knew that trouble must follow. I knew it because a long personal friendship with M. Gambetta had revealed to me the desperate and implacable nature of the man. Vast as are his physical proportions, I knew that the thirst for revenge would penetrate to the remotest frontiers of his person.

I did not wait for him to call on me, but went at once to him. As I had expected, I found the brave fellow steeped in a profound French calm. I say French calm, because French calmness and English calmness have points of difference. He was moving swiftly back and forth among the debris of his furniture, now and then staving chance fragments of it across the room with his foot; grinding a constant grist of curses through his set teeth; and halting every little while to deposit another handful of his hair on the pile which he had been building of it on the table.

He threw his arms around my neck, bent me over his stomach to his breast, kissed me on both cheeks, hugged me four or five times, and then placed me in his own arm-chair. As soon as I had got well again, we began business at once.

I said I supposed he would wish me to act as his second, and he said, "Of course." I said I must be allowed to act under a French name, so that I might be shielded from obloquy in my country, in case of fatal results. He winced here, probably at the suggestion that dueling was not regarded with respect in America. However, he agreed to my requirement. This accounts for the fact that in all the newspaper reports M. Gambetta's second was apparently a Frenchman.

First, we drew up my principal's will. I insisted upon this, and stuck to my point. I said I had never heard of a man in his right mind going out to fight a duel without first making his will. He said he had never heard of a man in his right mind doing anything of the kind. When he had finished the will, he wished to proceed to a choice of his "last words." He wanted to know how the following words, as a dying exclamation, struck me:

"I die for my God, for my country, for freedom of speech, for progress, and the universal brotherhood of man!"

I objected that this would require too lingering a death; it was a good speech for a consumptive, but not suited to the exigencies of the field of honor. We wrangled over a good many ante-mortem outbursts, but I finally got him to cut his obituary down to this, which he copied into his memorandum-book, purposing to get it by heart:

"I DIE THAT FRANCE MAY LIVE."

I said that this remark seemed to lack relevancy; but he said relevancy was a matter of no consequence in last words, what you wanted was thrill.

The next thing in order was the choice of weapons. My principal said he was not feeling well, and would leave that and the other details of the proposed meeting to me. Therefore I wrote the following note and carried it to M. Fourtou's friend:

SIR: M. Gambetta accepts M. Fourtou's challenge, and authorizes me to propose Plessis-Piquet as the place of meeting; to-morrow morning at daybreak as the time; and axes as the weapons. I am, sir, with great respect,

MARK TWAIN.

M. Fourtou's friend read this note, and shuddered. Then he turned to me, and said, with a suggestion of severity in his tone:

"Have you considered, sir, what would be the inevitable result of such a meeting as this?"

MARK TWAIN

"Well, for instance, what *would* it be?"

"Bloodshed!"

"That's about the size of it," I said. "Now, if it is a fair question, what was your side proposing to shed?"

I had him there. He saw he had made a blunder, so he hastened to explain it away. He said he had spoken jestingly. Then he added that he and his principal would enjoy axes, and indeed prefer them, but such weapons were barred by the French code, and so I must change my proposal.

I walked the floor, turning the thing over in my mind, and finally it occurred to me that Gatling-guns at fifteen paces would be a likely way to get a verdict on the field of honor. So I framed this idea into a proposition.

But it was not accepted. The code was in the way again. I proposed rifles; then double-barreled shotguns; then Colt's navy revolvers. These being all rejected, I reflected awhile, and sarcastically suggested brickbats at three-quarters of a mile. I always hate to fool away a humorous thing on a person who has no perception of humor; and it filled me with bitterness when this man went soberly away to submit the last proposition to his principal.

He came back presently and said his principal was charmed with the idea of brickbats at three-quarters of a mile, but must decline on account of the danger to disinterested parties passing between. Then I said:

"Well, I am at the end of my string, now. Perhaps *you* would be good enough to suggest a weapon? Perhaps you have even had one in your mind all the time?"

His countenance brightened, and he said with alacrity:

"Oh, without doubt, monsieur!"

So he fell to hunting in his pockets—pocket after pocket, and he had plenty of them—muttering all the while, "Now, what could I have done with them?"

At last he was successful. He fished out of his vest pocket a couple of little things which I carried to the light and ascertained to be pistols. They were single-barreled and silver-mounted, and very dainty and pretty. I was not able to speak for emotion. I silently hung one of them on my watch-chain, and returned the other. My companion in crime now unrolled a postage-stamp containing several cartridges, and gave me one of them. I asked if he meant to signify by this that our men were to be allowed but one shot apiece. He replied that the French code permitted no more. I then begged him to go on and suggest a distance, for my mind was growing weak and confused under the strain which had been put upon it. He named sixty-five yards. I nearly lost my patience. I said:

"Sixty-five yards, with these instruments? Squirt-guns would be deadlier at fifty. Consider, my friend, you and I are banded together to destroy life, not make it eternal."

But with all my persuasions, all my arguments, I was only able to get him to reduce the distance to thirty-five yards; and even this concession he made with reluctance, and said with a sigh, "I wash my hands of this slaughter; on your head be it."

There was nothing for me but to go home to my old lion-heart and tell my humiliating story. When I entered, M. Gambetta was laying his last lock of hair upon the altar. He sprang toward me, exclaiming:

"You have made the fatal arrangements—I see it in your eye!"

"I have."

His face paled a trifle, and he leaned upon the table for support. He breathed thick and heavily for a moment or two, so tumultuous were his feelings; then he hoarsely whispered:

"The weapon, the weapon! Quick! what is the weapon?"

"This!" and I displayed that silver-mounted thing. He cast but one glance at it, then swooned ponderously to the floor.

When he came to, he said mournfully:

"The unnatural calm to which I have subjected myself has told upon my nerves. But away with weakness! I will confront my fate like a man and a Frenchman."

He rose to his feet, and assumed an attitude which for sublimity has never been approached by man, and has seldom been surpassed by statues. Then he said, in his deep bass tones:

"Behold, I am calm, I am ready; reveal to me the distance."

"Thirty-five yards." . . .

I could not lift him up, of course; but I rolled him over, and poured water down his back. He presently came to, and said:

"Thirty-five yards—without a rest? But why ask? Since murder was that man's intention, why should he palter with small details? But mark you one thing: in my fall the world shall see how the chivalry of France meets death."

After a long silence he asked:

"Was nothing said about that man's family standing up with him, as an offset to my bulk? But no matter; I would not stoop to make such a suggestion; if he is not noble enough to suggest it himself, he is welcome to this advantage, which no honorable man would take."

He now sank into a sort of stupor of reflection, which lasted some minutes; after which he broke silence with:

"The hour—what is the hour fixed for the collision?"

"Dawn, to-morrow."

He seemed greatly surprised, and immediately said:

"Insanity! I never heard of such a thing. Nobody is abroad at such an hour."

"That is the reason I named it. Do you mean to say you want an audience?"

"It is no time to bandy words. I am astonished that M. Fourtou should ever have agreed to so strange an innovation. Go at once and require a later hour."

I ran down-stairs, threw open the front door, and almost plunged into the arms of M. Fourtou's second. He said:

"I have the honor to say that my principal strenuously objects to the hour chosen, and begs you will consent to change it to half past nine."

"Any courtesy, sir, which it is in our power to extend is at the service of your excellent principal. We agree to the proposed change of time."

"I beg you to accept the thanks of my client." Then he turned to a person behind him, and said, "You hear, M. Noir, the hour is altered to half past nine." Whereupon M. Noir bowed, expressed his thanks, and went away. My accomplice continued:

"If agreeable to you, your chief surgeons and ours shall proceed to the field in the same carriage, as is customary."

"It is entirely agreeable to me, and I am obliged to you for mentioning the surgeons, for I am afraid I should not have thought of them. How many shall I want? I suppose two or three will be enough?"

"Two is the customary number for each party. I refer to 'chief' surgeons; but considering the exalted positions occupied by our clients, it will be well and decorous that each of us appoint several consulting surgeons, from among the highest in the profession. These will come in their own private carriages. Have you engaged a hearse?"

"Bless my stupidity, I never thought of it! I will attend to it right away. I must seem very ignorant to you; but you must try to overlook that, because I have never had any experience of such a swell duel as this before. I have had a good deal to do with duels on the Pacific coast, but I see now that they were crude affairs. A hearse—sho! we used to leave the elected lying around loose, and let anybody cord

them up and cart them off that wanted to. Have you anything further
to suggest?"

"Nothing, except that the head undertakers shall ride together, as is
usual. The subordinates and mutes will go on foot, as is also usual. I
will see you at eight o'clock in the morning, and we will then arrange
the order of the procession. I have the honor to bid you a good day."

I returned to my client, who said, "Very well; at what hour is the
engagement to begin?"

"Half past nine."

"Very good indeed. Have you sent the fact to the newspapers?"

"*Sir!* If after our long and intimate friendship you can for a moment
deem me capable of so base a treachery—"

"Tut, tut! What words are these, my dear friend? Have I wounded
you? Ah, forgive me; I am overloading you with labor. Therefore go on
with the other details, and drop this one from your list. The bloody-
minded Fourtou will be sure to attend to it. Or I myself—yes, to make
certain, I will drop a note to my journalistic friend, M. Noir—"

"Oh, come to think of it, you may save yourself the trouble; that
other second has informed M. Noir."

"H'm! I might have known it. It is just like that Fourtou, who always
wants to make a display."

At half past nine in the morning, the procession approached the field
of Plessis-Piquet in the following order: first came our carriage—nobody in it but M. Gambetta and myself; then a carriage containing
M. Fourtou and his second; then a carriage containing two poet-orators
who did not believe in God, and these had MS. funeral orations
projecting from their breast pockets; then a carriage containing the
head surgeons and their cases of instruments; then eight private carriages containing consulting surgeons; then a hack containing a coroner;
then the two hearses; then a carriage containing the head undertakers;
then a train of assistants and mutes on foot; and after these came
plodding through the fog a long procession of camp followers, police,
and citizens generally. It was a noble turnout, and would have made a
fine display if we had had thinner weather.

There was no conversation. I spoke several times to my principal,
but I judge he was not aware of it, for he always referred to his note-
book and muttered absently, "I die that France may live."

Arrived on the field, my fellow-second and I paced off the thirty-
five yards, and then drew lots for choice of position. This latter was
but an ornamental ceremony, for all the choices were alike in such
weather. These preliminaries being ended, I went to my principal and

asked him if he was ready. He spread himself out to his full width, and said in a stern voice, "Ready! Let the batteries be charged."

The loading was done in the presence of duly constituted witnesses. We considered it best to perform this delicate service with the assistance of a lantern, on account of the state of the weather. We now placed our men.

At this point the police noticed that the public had massed themselves together on the right and left of the field; they therefore begged a delay, while they should put these poor people in a place of safety. The request was granted.

The police having ordered the two multitudes to take positions behind the duelists, we were once more ready. The weather growing still more opaque, it was agreed between myself and the other second that before giving the fatal signal we should each deliver a loud whoop to enable the combatants to ascertain each other's whereabouts.

I now returned to my principal, and was distressed to observe that he had lost a good deal of his spirit. I tried my best to hearten him. I said, "Indeed, sir, things are not as bad as they seem. Considering the character of the weapons, the limited number of shots allowed, the generous distance, the impenetrable solidity of the fog, and the added fact that one of the combatants is one-eyed and the other cross-eyed and near-sighted, it seems to me that this conflict need not necessarily be fatal. There are chances that both of you may survive. Therefore, cheer up; do not be downhearted."

This speech had so good an effect that my principal immediately stretched forth his hand and said, "I am myself again; give me the weapon."

I laid it, all lonely and forlorn, in the center of the vast solitude of his palm. He gazed at it and shuddered. And still mournfully contemplating it, he murmured, in a broken voice:

"Alas, it is not death I dread, but mutilation."

I heartened him once more, and with such success that he presently said, "Let the tragedy begin. Stand at my back; do not desert me in this solemn hour, my friend."

I gave him my promise. I now assisted him to point his pistol toward the spot where I judged his adversary to be standing, and cautioned him to listen well and further guide himself by my fellow-second's whoop. Then I propped myself against M. Gambetta's back, and raised a rousing "Whoop-ee!" This was answered from out the far distances of the fog, and I immediately shouted:

"One—two—three—*fire!*"

Two little sounds like *spit! spit!* broke upon my ear, and in the same instant I was crushed to the earth under a mountain of flesh. Bruised as I was, I was still able to catch a faint accent from above, to this effect:

"I die for . . . for . . . perdition take it, what *is* it I die for? . . . oh, yes—FRANCE! I die that France may live!"

The surgeons swarmed around with their probes in their hands, and applied their microscopes to the whole area of M. Gambetta's person, with the happy result of finding nothing in the nature of a wound. Then a scene ensued which was in every way gratifying and inspiriting.

The two gladiators fell upon each other's neck, with floods of proud and happy tears; that other second embraced me; the surgeons, the orators, the undertakers, the police, everybody embraced, everybody congratulated, everybody cried, and the whole atmosphere was filled with praise and with joy unspeakable.

It seemed to me then that I would rather be a hero of a French duel than a crowned and sceptered monarch.

When the commotion had somewhat subsided, the body of surgeons held a consultation, and after a good deal of debate decided that with proper care and nursing there was reason to believe that I would survive my injuries. My internal hurts were deemed the most serious, since it was apparent that a broken rib had penetrated my left lung, and that many of my organs had been pressed out so far to one side or the other of where they belonged, that it was doubtful if they would ever learn to perform their functions in such remote and unaccustomed localities. They then set my left arm in two places, pulled my right hip into its socket again, and reelevated my nose. I was an object of great interest, and even admiration; and many sincere and warm-hearted persons had themselves introduced to me, and said they were proud to know the only man who had been hurt in a French duel in forty years.

I was placed in an ambulance at the very head of the procession; and thus with gratifying *éclat* I was marched into Paris, the most conspicuous figure in that great spectacle, and deposited at the hospital.

The cross of the Legion of Honor has been conferred upon me. However, few escape that distinction.

Such is the true version of the most memorable private conflict of the age.

I have no complaints to make against any one. I acted for myself, and I can stand the consequences.

Without boasting, I think I may say I am not afraid to stand before a modern French duelist, but as long as I keep in my right mind I will never consent to stand behind one again.

From A TRAMP ABROAD, 1880

The King's Encore

I am told that in a German concert or opera, they hardly ever encore a song; that though they may be dying to hear it again, their good breeding usually preserves them against requiring the repetition.

Kings may encore; that is quite another matter; it delights everybody to see that the King is pleased; and as to the actor encored, his pride and gratification are simply boundless. Still, there are circumstances in which even a royal encore—

But it is better to illustrate. The King of Bavaria is a poet, and has a poet's eccentricities—with the advantage over all other poets of being able to gratify them, no matter what form they may take. He is fond of the opera, but not fond of sitting in the presence of an audience; therefore, it has sometimes occurred, in Munich, that when an opera has been concluded and the players were getting off their paint and finery, a command has come to them to get their paint and finery on again. Presently the King would arrive, solitary and alone, and the players would begin at the beginning and do the entire opera over again with only that one individual in the vast solemn theater for audience. Once he took an odd freak into his head. High up and out of sight, over the prodigious stage of the court theater is a maze of interlacing water-pipes, so pierced that in case of fire, innumerable little threadlike streams of water can be caused to descend; and in case of need, this discharge can be augmented to a pouring flood. American managers might make a note of that. The King was sole audience. The opera proceeded, it was a piece with a storm in it; the mimic thunder began to mutter, the mimic wind began to wail and sough, and the mimic rain to patter. The King's interest rose higher and higher; it developed into enthusiasm. He cried out:

"It is good, very good, indeed! But I will have real rain! Turn on the water!"

The manager pleaded for a reversal of the command; said it would ruin the costly scenery and the splendid costumes, but the King cried:

"No matter, no matter, I will have real rain! Turn on the water!"

So the real rain was turned on and began to descend in gossamer lances to the mimic flower-beds and gravel walks of the stage. The richly dressed actresses and actors tripped about singing bravely and pretending not to mind it. The King was delighted—his enthusiasm grew higher. He cried out:

"Bravo, bravo! More thunder! more lightning! turn on more rain!"

The thunder boomed, the lightning glared, the storm-winds raged, the deluge poured down. The mimic royalty on the stage, with their soaked satins clinging to their bodies, slopped around ankle-deep in water, warbling their sweetest and best, the fiddlers under the eaves of the stage sawed away for dear life, with the cold overflow spouting down the backs of their necks, and the dry and happy King sat in his lofty box and wore his gloves to ribbons applauding.

"More yet!" cried the King; "more yet—let loose all the thunder, turn on all the water! I will hang the man that raises an umbrella!"

When this most tremendous and effective storm that had ever been produced in any theater was at last over, the King's approbation was measureless. He cried:

"Magnificent, magnificent! *Encore!* Do it again!"

But the manager succeeded in persuading him to recall the encore, and said the company would feel sufficiently rewarded and complimented in the mere fact that the encore was desired by his Majesty, without fatiguing him with a repetition to gratify their own vanity.

During the remainder of the act the lucky performers were those whose parts required changes of dress; the others were a soaked, bedraggled, and uncomfortable lot, but in the last degree picturesque. The stage scenery was ruined, trap-doors were so swollen that they wouldn't work for a week afterward, the fine costumes were spoiled, and no end of minor damages were done by that remarkable storm.

It was a royal idea—that storm—and royally carried out. But observe the moderation of the King; he did not insist upon his encore. If he had been a gladsome, unreflecting American opera-audience, he probably would have had his storm repeated and repeated until he drowned all those people.

From A TRAMP ABROAD, 1880

The Laborious Ant

We followed the carriage-road, and had our usual luck; we traveled under a beating sun, and always saw the shade leave the shady places before we could get to them. In all our wanderings we seldom managed to strike a piece of road at its time for being shady. We had a particularly hot time of it on that particular afternoon, and with no comfort but what we could get out of the fact that the peasants at work away up on the steep mountainsides above our heads were even worse off than we were. By and by it became impossible to endure the intolerable glare and heat any longer; so we struck across the ravine and entered the deep cool twilight of the forest, to hunt for what the guide-book called the "old road."

We found an old road, and it proved eventually to be the right one, though we followed it at the time with the conviction that it was the wrong one. If it was the wrong one there could be no use in hurrying, therefore we did not hurry, but sat down frequently on the soft moss and enjoyed the restful quiet and shade of the forest solitudes. There had been distractions in the carriage-road—school-children, peasants, wagons, troops of pedestrianizing students from all over Germany—but we had the old road to ourselves.

Now and then, while we rested, we watched the laborious ant at his work. I found nothing new in him—certainly nothing to change my opinion of him. It seems to me that in the matter of intellect the ant must be a strangely overrated bird. During many summers, now, I have watched him, when I ought to have been in better business, and I have not yet come across a living ant that seemed to have any more sense than a dead one. I refer to the ordinary ant, of course; I have had no experience of those wonderful Swiss and African ones which vote, keep drilled armies, hold slaves, and dispute about religion. Those particular ants may be all that the naturalist paints them, but I am persuaded that the average ant is a sham. I admit his industry, of course; he is the hardest-working creature in the world—when anybody is looking—but his leatherheadedness is the point I make against him. He goes out foraging, he makes a capture, and then what does he do? Go home? No—he goes anywhere but home. He doesn't know where home is. His home may be only three feet away—no matter, he can't find it. He makes his capture, as I have said; it is generally something which can be of no sort of use to himself or anybody else; it is usually seven times bigger than it ought to be; he hunts out the awkwardest place to take hold of it; he lifts it bodily up in the air by main force, and starts; not toward home, but in the opposite direction; not calmly and wisely, but with a frantic haste which is wasteful of his strength; he fetches up against a pebble, and instead of going around it, he climbs over it backward dragging his booty after him, tumbles down on the other side, jumps up in a passion, kicks the dust off his clothes, moistens his hands, grabs his property viciously, yanks it this way, then that, shoves it ahead of him a moment, turns tail and lugs it after him another moment, gets madder and madder, then presently hoists it into the air and goes tearing away in an entirely new direction; comes to a weed; it never occurs to him to go around it; no, he must climb it; and he does climb it, dragging his worthless property to the top—which is as bright a thing to do as it would be for me to carry a sack of flour from Heidelberg to Paris by way of Strasburg steeple; when he gets up there he finds that that is not the place; takes a cursory glance at the scenery and either climbs down again or tumbles down, and starts off once more—as usual, in a new direction. At the end of half an hour, he fetches up within six inches of the place he started from and lays his burden down; meantime he has been over all the ground for two yards around, and climbed all the weeds and pebbles he came across. Now he wipes the sweat from his brow, strokes his limbs, and then marches aimlessly off, in as violent a hurry as ever. He traverses a good deal of zigzag country, and by and by stumbles on his same booty again. He does not remember to have ever seen it before; he looks around to see which is not the way home, grabs his bundle and starts; he goes through the same adventures he had before; finally stops to rest, and a friend comes along. Evidently the friend remarks that a last year's grasshopper leg is a very noble acquisition, and inquires where he got it. Evidently the proprietor does not remember exactly where he did get it, but thinks he got it "around here somewhere." Evidently the friend contracts to help him freight it home. Then, with a judgment peculiarly antic (pun not intentional), they take hold of opposite ends of that grasshopper leg and begin to tug with all their might in opposite directions. Presently they take a rest and confer together. They decide that something is wrong, they can't make out what. Then they go at it again, just as before. Same result. Mutual recriminations follow. Evidently each

accuses the other of being an obstructionist. They warm up, and the
dispute ends in a fight. They lock themselves together and chew each
other's jaws for a while; then they roll and tumble on the ground till
one loses a horn or a leg and has to haul off for repairs. They make up
and go to work again in the same old insane way, but the crippled
ant is at a disadvantage; tug as he may, the other one drags off the
booty and him at the end of it. Instead of giving up, he hangs on, and
gets his shins bruised against every obstruction that comes in the way.
By and by, when that grasshopper leg has been dragged all over the
same old ground once more, it is finally dumped at about the spot
where it originally lay, the two perspiring ants inspect it thoughtfully
and decide that dried grasshopper legs are a poor sort of property
after all, and then each starts off in a different direction to see if he
can't find an old nail or something else that is heavy enough to afford
entertainment and at the same time valueless enough to make an ant
want to own it.

There in the Black Forest, on the mountainside, I saw an ant go
through with such a performance as this with a dead spider of fully
ten times his own weight. The spider was not quite dead, but too far
gone to resist. He had a round body the size of a pea. The little ant—
observing that I was noticing—turned him on his back, sunk his fangs
into his throat, lifted him into the air and started vigorously off with
him, stumbling over little pebbles, stepping on the spider's legs and
tripping himself up, dragging him backward, shoving him bodily ahead,
dragging him up stones six inches high instead of going around them,
climbing weeds twenty times his own height and jumping from their
summits—and finally leaving him in the middle of the road to be
confiscated by any other fool of an ant that wanted him. I measured
the ground which this ass traversed, and arrived at the conclusion that
what he had accomplished inside of twenty minutes would constitute
some such job as this—relatively speaking—for a man; to wit: to strap
two eight-hundred-pound horses together, carry them eighteen hundred feet, mainly over (not around) boulders averaging six feet high,
and in the course of the journey climb up and jump from the top of
one precipice like Niagara, and three steeples, each a hundred and
twenty feet high; and then put the horses down, in an exposed place,
without anybody to watch them, and go off to indulge in some other
idiotic miracle for vanity's sake.

Science has recently discovered that the ant does not lay up anything
for winter use. This will knock him out of literature, to some extent. He
does not work, except when people are looking, and only then when

the observer has a green, naturalistic look, and seems to be taking notes. This amounts to deception, and will injure him for the Sunday-schools. He has not judgment enough to know what is good to eat from what isn't. This amounts to ignorance, and will impair the world's respect for him. He cannot stroll around a stump and find his way home again. This amounts to idiocy, and once the damaging fact is established, thoughtful people will cease to look up to him, the sentimental will cease to fondle him. His vaunted industry is but a vanity and of no effect, since he never gets home with anything he starts with. This disposes of the last remnant of his reputation and wholly destroys his main usefulness as a moral agent, since it will make the sluggard hesitate to go to him any more. It is strange, beyond comprehension, that so manifest a humbug as the ant has been able to fool so many nations and keep it up so many ages without being found out.

From A TRAMP ABROAD, 1880

My Long Crawl in the Dark

When we got back to the hotel I wound and set the pedometer and put it in my pocket, for I was to carry it next day and keep record of the miles we made. The work which we had given the instrument to do during the day which had just closed had not fatigued it perceptibly.

We were in bed by ten, for we wanted to be up and away on our tramp homeward with the dawn. I hung fire, but Harris went to sleep at once. I hate a man who goes to sleep at once; there is a sort of indefinable something about it which is not exactly an insult, and yet is an insolence; and one which is hard to bear, too. I lay there fretting over this injury, and trying to go to sleep; but the harder I tried, the wider awake I grew. I got to feeling very lonely in the dark, with no company but an undigested dinner. My mind got a start by and by, and began to consider the beginning of every subject which has ever been thought of; but it never went further than the beginning; it was touch and go; it fled from topic to topic with a frantic speed. At the end of an hour my head was in a perfect whirl and I was dead tired, fagged out.

The fatigue was so great that it presently began to make some head against the nervous excitement; while imagining myself wide awake, I would really doze into momentary unconsciousness, and come suddenly out of it with a physical jerk which nearly wrenched my joints apart—the delusion of the instant being that I was tumbling backward over a precipice. After I had fallen over eight or nine precipices and thus found out that one half of my brain had been asleep eight or nine times without the wide-awake, hard-working other half suspecting it, the periodical unconsciousnesses began to extend their spell gradually over more of my brain-territory, and at last I sank into a drowse which grew deeper and deeper and was doubtless just on the very point of becoming a solid, blessed dreamless stupor, when—what was that?

My dulled faculties dragged themselves partly back to life and took a receptive attitude. Now out of an immense, a limitless distance, came a something which grew and grew, and approached, and presently was recognizable as a sound—it had rather seemed to be a feeling, before. This sound was a mile away, now—perhaps it was the murmur of a storm; and now it was nearer—not a quarter of a mile away; was it the muffled rasping and grinding of distant machinery? No, it came still nearer; was it the measured tramp of a marching troop? But it came nearer still, and still nearer—and at last it was right in the room: it was merely a mouse gnawing the woodwork. So I had held my breath all that time for such a trifle.

Well, what was done could not be helped; I would go to sleep at once and make up the lost time. That was a thoughtless thought. Without intending it—hardly knowing it—I fell to listening intently to that sound, and even unconsciously counting the strokes of the mouse's nutmeg-grater. Presently I was deriving exquisite suffering from this employment, yet maybe I could have endured it if the mouse had attended steadily to his work; but he did not do that; he stopped every now and then, and I suffered more while waiting and listening for him to begin again than I did while he was gnawing. Along at first I was mentally offering a reward of five—six—seven—ten—dollars for that mouse; but toward the last I was offering rewards which were entirely beyond my means. I close-reefed my ears—that is to say, I bent the flaps of them down and furled them into five or six folds, and pressed them against the hearing-orifice—but it did no good: the faculty was so sharpened by nervous excitement that it was become a microphone and could hear through the overlays without trouble.

My anger grew to a frenzy. I finally did what all persons before me have done, clear back to Adam,—resolved to throw something. I reached down and got my walking-shoes, then sat up in bed and listened, in order to exactly locate the noise. But I couldn't do it; it was as unlocatable as a cricket's noise; and where one thinks that that is, is always the very place where it isn't. So I presently hurled a shoe at random, and with a vicious vigor. It struck the wall over Harris's head and fell down on him; I had not imagined I could throw so far. It woke Harris, and I was glad of it until I found he was not angry; then I was sorry. He soon went to sleep again, which pleased me; but straightway the mouse began again, which roused my temper once more. I did not want to wake Harris a second time, but the gnawing continued until I was compelled to throw the other shoe. This time I broke a mirror—there were two in the room—I got the largest one, of course. Harris woke again, but did not complain, and I was sorrier than ever. I resolved that I would suffer all possible torture before I would disturb him a third time.

The mouse eventually retired, and by and by I was sinking to sleep, when a clock began to strike; I counted till it was done, and was about to drowse again when another clock began; I counted; then the two great *Rathhaus* clock angels began to send forth soft, rich, melodious blasts from their long trumpets. I had never heard anything that was so lovely, or weird, or mysterious—but when they got to blowing the quarter-hours, they seemed to me to be overdoing the thing. Every time I dropped off for a moment, a new noise woke me. Each time I woke I missed my coverlet, and had to reach down to the floor and get it again.

At last all sleepiness forsook me. I recognized the fact that I was hopelessly and permanently wide awake. Wide awake, and feverish and thirsty. When I had lain tossing there as long as I could endure it, it occurred to me that it would be a good idea to dress and go out in the great square and take a refreshing wash in the fountain, and smoke and reflect there until the remnant of the night was gone.

I believed I could dress in the dark without waking Harris. I had banished my shoes after the mouse, but my slippers would do for a summer night. So I rose softly, and gradually got on everything—down to one sock. I couldn't seem to get on the track of that sock, any way I could fix it. But I had to have it; so I went down on my hands and knees, with one slipper on and the other in my hand, and began to paw gently around and rake the floor, but with no success. I enlarged my circle, and went on pawing and raking. With every pres-

sure of my knee, how the floor creaked! and every time I chanced to
rake against any article, it seemed to give out thirty-five or thirty-six
times more noise than it would have done in the daytime. In those
cases I always stopped and held my breath till I was sure Harris had
not awakened—then I crept along again. I moved on and on, but I
could not find the sock; I could not seem to find anything but furniture.
I could not remember that there was much furniture in the room when
I went to bed, but the place was alive with it now—especially chairs—
chairs everywhere—had a couple of families moved in, in the mean
time? And I never could seem to *glance* on one of those chairs, but
always struck it full and square with my head. My temper rose, by
steady and sure degrees, and as I pawed on and on, I fell to making
vicious comments under my breath.

Finally, with a venomous access of irritation, I said I would leave
without the sock; so I rose up and made straight for the door—as I
supposed—and suddenly confronted my dim spectral image in the un-
broken mirror. It startled the breath out of me, for an instant; it also
showed me that I was lost, and had no sort of idea where I was. When
I realized this, I was so angry that I had to sit down on the floor and
take hold of something to keep from lifting the roof off with an explosion of opinion. If there had been only one mirror, it might possibly
have helped to locate me; but there were two, and two were as bad as
a thousand; besides, these were on opposite sides of the room. I could
see the dim blur of the windows, but in my turned-around condition
they were exactly where they ought not to be, and so they only confused me instead of helping me.

I started to get up, and knocked down an umbrella; it made a noise
like a pistol-shot when it struck that hard, slick, carpetless floor; I
grated my teeth and held my breath—Harris did not stir. I set the
umbrella slowly and carefully on end against the wall, but as soon as
I took my hand away, its heel slipped from under it, and down it came
again with another bang. I shrunk together and listened a moment in
silent fury—no harm done, everything quiet. With the most painstak-
ing care and nicety I stood the umbrella up once more, took my hand
away, and down it came again.

I have been strictly reared, but if it had not been so dark and solemn
and awful there in that lonely, vast room, I do believe I should have
said something then which could not be put into a Sunday-school book
without injuring the sale of it. If my reasoning powers had not been already sapped dry by my harassments, I would have known better than
to try to set an umbrella on end on one of those glassy German floors

in the dark; it can't be done in the daytime without four failures to one success. I had one comfort, though—Harris was yet still and silent —he had not stirred.

The umbrella could not locate me—there were four standing around the room, and all alike. I thought I would feel along the wall and find the door in that way. I rose up and began this operation, but raked down a picture. It was not a large one, but it made noise enough for a panorama. Harris gave out no sound, but I felt that if I experimented any further with the pictures I should be sure to wake him. Better give up trying to get out. Yes, I would find King Arthur's Round Table once more—I had already found it several times—and use it for a base of departure on an exploring tour for my bed; if I could find my bed I could then find my water pitcher; I would quench my raging thirst and turn in. So I started on my hands and knees, because I could go faster that way, and with more confidence, too, and not knock down things. By and by I found the table—with my head—rubbed the bruise a little, then rose up and started, with hands abroad and fingers spread, to balance myself. I found a chair; then the wall; then another chair; then a sofa; then an alpenstock, then another sofa; this confounded me, for I had thought there was only one sofa. I hunted up the table again and took a fresh start; found some more chairs.

It occurred to me, now, as it ought to have done before, that as the table was round, it was therefore of no value as a base to aim from; so I moved off once more, and at random among the wilderness of chairs and sofas—wandered off into unfamiliar regions, and presently knocked a candlestick off a mantelpiece; grabbed at the candlestick and knocked off a lamp, grabbed at the lamp and knocked off a water pitcher with a rattling crash, and thought to myself, "I've found you at last—I judged I was close upon you." Harris shouted "murder," and "thieves," and finished with "I'm absolutely drowned."

The crash had roused the house. Mr. X pranced in, in his long night-garment, with a candle, young Z after him with another candle; a procession swept in at another door, with candles and lanterns—land-lord and two German guests in their nightgowns, and a chambermaid in hers.

I looked around; I was at Harris's bed, a Sabbath-day's journey from my own. There was only one sofa; it was against the wall; there was only one chair where a body could get at it—I had been revolving around it like a planet, and colliding with it like a comet half the night.

I explained how I had been employing myself, and why. Then the landlord's party left, and the rest of us set about our preparations for

breakfast, for the dawn was ready to break. I glanced furtively at my
pedometer, and found I had made 47 miles. But I did not care, for I
had come out for a pedestrian tour anyway.

From A TRAMP ABROAD, 1880

Nicodemus Dodge

When I was a boy in a printing-office in Missouri, a loose-jointed,
long-legged, tow-headed, jeans-clad, countrified cub of about sixteen
lounged in one day, and without removing his hands from the depths
of his trousers pockets or taking off his faded ruin of a slouch hat,
whose broken rim hung limp and ragged about his eyes and ears like
a bug-eaten cabbage leaf, stared indifferently around, then leaned
his hip against the editor's table, crossed his mighty brogans, aimed at
a distant fly from a crevice in his upper teeth, laid him low, and said
with composure:

"Whar's the boss?"

"I am the boss," said the editor, following this curious bit of architecture wonderingly along up to its clock-face with his eye.

"Don't want anybody fur to learn the business, 'tain't likely?"

"Well, I don't know. Would you like to learn it?"

"Pap's so po' he cain't run me no mo', so I want to git a show somers
if I kin, 'tain't no diffunce what—I'm strong and hearty, and I don't
turn my back on no kind of work, hard nur soft."

"Do you think you would like to learn the printing business?"

"Well, I don't re'ly k'yer a durn what I *do* learn, so's I git a chance
fur to make my way. I'd jist as soon learn print'n's anything."

"Can you read?"

"Yes—middlin'."

"Write?"

"Well, I've seed people could lay over me thar."

"Cipher?"

"Not good enough to keep store, I don't reckon, but up as fur as
twelve-times-twelve I ain't no slouch. 'Tother side of that is what gits
me."

"Where is your home?"

"I'm f'm old Shelby."

"What's your father's religious denomination?"

"Him? Oh, he's a blacksmith."

"No, no—I don't mean his trade. What's his *religious* denomination?"

"*Oh*—I didn't understand you befo'. He's a Freemason."

"No, no, you don't get my meaning yet. What I mean is, does he belong to any *church?*"

"*Now* you're talkin'! Couldn't make out what you was a-tryin' to git through yo' head no way. B'long to a *church!* Why, boss, he's ben the pizenest kind of a Free-will Babtis' for forty year. They ain't no pizener ones 'n what *he* is. Mighty good man, pap is. Everybody says that. If they said any diffrunt they wouldn't say it whar *I* wuz—not *much* they wouldn't."

"What is your own religion?"

"Well, boss, you've kind o' got me, thar—and yit you hain't got me so mighty much, nuther. I think 't if a feller he'ps another feller when he's in trouble, and don't cuss, and don't do no mean things, nur noth'n' he ain' no business to do, and don't spell the Saviour's name with a little g, he ain't runnin' no resks—he's about as saift as if he b'longed to a church."

"But suppose he did spell it with a little g— what then?"

"Well, if he done it a-purpose, I reckon he wouldn't stand no chance —he *oughtn't* to have no chance, anyway, I'm most rotten certain 'bout that."

"What is your name?"

"Nicodemus Dodge."

"I think maybe you'll do, Nicodemus. We'll give you a trial, anyway."

"All right."

"When would you like to begin?"

"Now."

So, within ten minutes after we had first glimpsed this nondescript he was one of us, and with his coat off and hard at it.

Beyond that end of our establishment which was furthest from the street, was a deserted garden, pathless, and thickly grown with the bloomy and villainous "jimpson" weed and its common friend the stately sunflower. In the midst of this mournful spot was a decayed and aged little "frame" house with but one room, one window, and no ceiling—it had been a smoke-house a generation before. Nicodemus was given this lonely and ghostly den as a bedchamber.

The village smarties recognized a treasure in Nicodemus, right away

—a butt to play jokes on. It was easy to see that he was inconceivably green and confiding. George Jones had the glory of perpetrating the first joke on him; he gave him a cigar with a firecracker in it and winked to the crowd to come; the thing exploded presently and swept away the bulk of Nicodemus's eyebrows and eyelashes. He simply said: "I consider them kind of seeg'yars dangersome,"—and seemed to suspect nothing. The next evening Nicodemus waylaid George and poured a bucket of ice-water over him.

One day, while Nicodemus was in swimming, Tom McElroy "tied" his clothes. Nicodemus made a bonfire of Tom's by way of retaliation.

A third joke was played upon Nicodemus a day or two later—he walked up the middle aisle of the village church, Sunday night, with a staring handbill pinned between his shoulders. The joker spent the remainder of the night, after church, in the cellar of a deserted house, and Nicodemus sat on the cellar door till toward breakfast-time to make sure that the prisoner remembered that if any noise was made, some rough treatment would be the consequence. The cellar had two feet of stagnant water in it, and was bottomed with six inches of soft mud.

But I wander from the point. It was the subject of skeletons that brought this boy back to my recollection. Before a very long time had elapsed, the village smarties began to feel an uncomfortable consciousness of not having made a very shining success out of their attempts on the simpleton from "old Shelby." Experimenters grew scarce and chary. Now the young doctor came to the rescue. There was delight and applause when he proposed to scare Nicodemus to death, and explained how he was going to do it. He had a noble new skeleton—the skeleton of the late and only local celebrity, Jimmy Finn, the village drunkard—a grisly piece of property which he had bought of Jimmy Finn himself, at auction, for fifty dollars, under great competition, when Jimmy lay very sick in the tanyard a fortnight before his death. The fifty dollars had gone promptly for whisky and had considerably hurried up the change of ownership in the skeleton. The doctor would put Jimmy Finn's skeleton in Nicodemus's bed!

This was done—about half past ten in the evening. About Nicodemus's usual bedtime—midnight—the village jokers came creeping stealthily through the jimpson weeds and sunflowers toward the lonely frame den. They reached the window and peeped in. There sat the long-legged pauper, on his bed, in a very short shirt, and nothing more; he was dangling his legs contentedly back and forth, and wheezing the music of "Camptown Races" out of a paper-overlaid comb which he was pressing against his mouth; by him lay a new jewsharp, a new top, a solid india-rubber ball, a handful of painted marbles, five pounds of "store" candy, and a well-gnawed slab of gingerbread as big and as thick as a volume of sheet-music. He had sold the skeleton to a traveling quack for three dollars and was enjoying the result!

From A TRAMP ABROAD, 1880

Skeleton for Black Forest Novel

Rich old farmer, named Huss. Has inherited great wealth of manure, and by diligence has added to it. It is double-starred in Baedeker.[1] The Black Forest artist paints it—his masterpiece. The king comes to see it. Gretchen Huss, daughter and heiress. Paul Hoch, young neighbor, suitor for Gretchen's hand—ostensibly; he really wants the manure. Hoch has a good many cart-loads of the Black Forest currency himself, and therefore is a good catch; but he is sordid, mean, and without sentiment, whereas Gretchen is all sentiment and poetry. Hans Schmidt, young neighbor, full of sentiment, full of poetry, loves Gretchen, Gretchen loves him. But he has no manure. Old Huss forbids him the house. His heart breaks, he goes away to die in the woods, far from the cruel world—for he says, bitterly, "What is man, without manure?"

[Interval of six months.]

Paul Hoch comes to old Huss and says, "I am at last as rich as you required—come and view the pile." Old Huss views it and says, "It is sufficient—take her and be happy,"—meaning Gretchen.

[Interval of two weeks.]

Wedding party assembled in old Huss's drawing-room. Hoch placid and content, Gretchen weeping over her hard fate. Enter old Huss's head bookkeeper. Huss says fiercely, "I gave you three weeks to find out why your books don't balance, and to prove that you are not a defaulter; the time is up—find me the missing property or you go to prison as a thief." Bookkeeper: "I have found it." "Where?" Bookkeeper

[1] When Baedeker's guide-books mention a thing and put two stars (**) after it, it means well worth visiting.

M. T.

(sternly—tragically): "In the bridegroom's pile!—behold the thief—see him blench and tremble!" [Sensation.] Paul Hoch: "Lost, lost!"—falls over the cow in a swoon and is handcuffed. Gretchen: "Saved!" Falls over the calf in a swoon of joy, but is caught in the arms of Hans Schmidt, who springs in at that moment. Old Huss: "What, you here, varlet? Unhand the maid and quit the place." Hans (still supporting the insensible girl): "Never! Cruel old man, know that I come with claims which even you cannot despise."

HUSS: "What, *you?* name them."

HANS: "Then listen. The world had forsaken me, I forsook the world, I wandered in the solitude of the forest, longing for death but finding none. I fed upon roots, and in my bitterness I dug for the bitterest, loathing the sweeter kind. Digging, three days agone, I struck a manure mine!—a Golconda, a limitless Bonanza, of solid manure! I can buy you *all*, and have mountain ranges of manure left! Ha-ha, *now* thou smilest a smile!" [Immense sensation.] Exhibition of specimens from the mine. Old Huss (enthusiastically): "Wake her up, shake her up, noble young man, she is yours!" Wedding takes place on the spot; bookkeeper restored to his office and emoluments; Paul Hoch led off to jail. The Bonanza king of the Black Forest lives to a good old age, blessed with the love of his wife and of his twenty-seven children, and the still sweeter envy of everybody around.

From A TRAMP ABROAD, 1880

A Telephonic Conversation

Consider that a conversation by telephone—when you are simply sitting by and not taking any part in that conversation—is one of the solemnest curiosities of this modern life. Yesterday I was writing a deep article on a sublime philosophical subject while such a conversation was going on in the room. I notice that one can always write best when somebody is talking through a telephone close by. Well, the thing began in this way. A member of our household came in and asked me to have our house put into communication with Mr. Bagley's, down-town. I have observed, in many cities, that the sex always shrink from calling up the central office themselves. I don't know why, but they do. So I touched the bell, and this talk ensued:

CENTRAL OFFICE. (*Gruffly.*) Hello!

I. Is it the Central Office?

C. O. Of course it is. What do you want?

I. Will you switch me on to the Bagleys, please?

C. O. All right. Just keep your ear to the telephone.

Then I heard, *k-look, k-look k'look—klook-klook-klook-look-look!* then a horrible "gritting" of teeth, and finally a piping female voice: Y-e-s? (*Rising inflection.*) Did you wish to speak to me?

Without answering, I handed the telephone to the applicant, and sat down. Then followed that queerest of all the queer things in this world—a conversation with only one end to it. You hear questions asked; you don't hear the answer. You hear invitations given; you hear no thanks in return. You have listening pauses of dead silence, followed by apparently irrelevant and unjustifiable exclamations of glad surprise or sorrow or dismay. You can't make head or tail of the talk, because you never hear anything that the person at the other end of the wire says. Well, I heard the following remarkable series of observations, all from the one tongue, and all shouted—for you can't ever persuade the sex to speak gently into a telephone:

Yes? Why, how did *that* happen?

Pause.

What did you say?

Pause.

Oh no, I don't think it was.

Pause.

No! Oh no, I didn't mean *that.* I meant, put it in while it is still boiling—or just before it *comes* to a boil.

Pause.

WHAT?

Pause.

I turned it over with a backstitch on the selvage edge.

Pause.

Yes, I like that way, too; but I think it's better to baste it on with Valenciennes or bombazine, or something of that sort. It gives it such an air—and attracts so much notice.

Pause.

It's forty-ninth Deuteronomy, sixty-fourth to ninety-seventh inclusive. I think we ought all to read it often.

Pause.

Perhaps so; I generally use a hair-pin.

Pause.

What did you say? (*Aside.*) Children, do be quiet!

Pause.

Oh, B *flat!* Dear me, I thought you said it was the cat!

Pause.

Since *when?*

Pause.

Why, *I* never heard of it.

Pause.

You astound me! It seems utterly impossible!

Pause.

Who did?

Pause.

Good-ness gracious!

Pause.

Well, what *is* this world coming to? Was it right in *church?*

Pause.

And was her *mother* there?

Pause.

Why, Mrs. Bagley, I should have died of humiliation! What did
they *do?*

Long pause.

I can't be perfectly sure, because I haven't the notes by me; but I
think it goes something like this: te-rolly-loll-loll, loll lolly-loll-loll, O
tolly-loll-loll-*lee-ly-li-i*-do! And then *repeat,* you know.

Pause.

Yes, I think it *is* very sweet—and very solemn and impressive, if you
get the andantino and the pianissimo right.

Pause.

Oh, gum-drops, gum-drops! But I never allow them to eat striped
candy. And of course they *can't,* till they get their teeth, anyway.

Pause.

What?

Pause.

Oh, not in the least—go right on. He's here writing—it doesn't bother
him.

Pause.

Very well, I'll come if I can. (*Aside.*) Dear me, how it does tire a
person's arm to hold this thing up so long! I wish she'd—

Pause.

Oh no, not at all; I *like* to talk—but I'm afraid I'm keeping you from your affairs.

Pause.

Visitors?

Pause.

No, we never use butter on them.

Pause.

Yes, that is a very good way; but all the cookbooks say they are very unhealthy when they are out of season. And *he* doesn't like them, anyway—especially canned.

Pause.

Oh, I think that is too high for them; we have never paid over fifty cents a bunch.

Pause.

Must you go? Well, *good*-by.

Pause.

Yes, I think so. *Good*-by.

Pause.

Four o'clock, then—I'll be ready. *Good*-by.

Pause.

Thank you ever so much. *Good*-by.

Pause.

Oh, not at all!—just as fresh— *Which?* Oh, I'm glad to hear you say that. *Good*-by.

(Hangs up the telephone and says, "Oh, it *does* tire a person's arm so!")

A man delivers a single brutal "Good-by," and that is the end of it. Not so with the gentle sex—I say it in their praise; they cannot abide abruptness.

1880

Two Works of Art

I found more pleasure in contemplating the Old Masters this time than I did when I was in Europe in former years, but still it was a calm pleasure; there was nothing overheated about it. When I was in

Venice before, I think I found no picture which stirred me much, but this time there were two which enticed me to the Doge's palace day after day, and kept me there hours at a time. One of these was Tintoretto's three-acre picture in the Great Council Chamber. When I saw it twelve years ago I was not strongly attracted to it—the guide told me it was an insurrection in heaven—but this was an error.

The movement of this great work is very fine. There are ten thousand figures, and they are all doing something. There is a wonderful "go" to the whole composition. Some of the figures are diving headlong downward, with clasped hands, others are swimming through the cloud-shoals—some on their faces, some on their backs—great processions of bishops, martyrs, and angels are pouring swiftly centerward from various outlying directions—everywhere is enthusiastic joy, there is rushing movement everywhere. There are fifteen or twenty figures scattered here and there, with books, but they cannot keep their attention on their reading—they offer the books to others, but no one wishes to read, now. The Lion of St. Mark is there with his book; St. Mark is there with his pen uplifted; he and the Lion are looking each other earnestly in the face, disputing about the way to spell a word—the Lion looks up in rapt admiration while St. Mark spells. This is wonderfully interpreted by the artist. It is the master-stroke of this incomparable painting.

THE LION OF ST. MARK

I visited the place daily, and never grew tired of looking at that grand picture. As I have intimated, the movement is almost unimaginably vigorous; the figures are singing, hosannahing, and many are blowing trumpets. So vividly is noise suggested, that spectators who become absorbed in the picture almost always fall to shouting comments in each other's ears, making ear-trumpets of their curved hands, fearing they may not otherwise be heard. One often sees a tourist, with the eloquent tears pouring down his cheeks, funnel his hands at his wife's ear, and hears him roar through them, "OH, TO BE THERE AND AT REST!"

None but the supremely great in art can produce effects like these with the silent brush.

Twelve years ago I could not have appreciated this picture. One year ago I could not have appreciated it. My study of Art in Heidelberg has been a noble education to me. All that I am to-day in Art, I owe to that.

The other great work which fascinated me was Bassano's immortal Hair Trunk. This is in the Chamber of the Council of Ten. It is in one of the three forty-foot pictures which decorate the walls of the room. The composition of this picture is beyond praise. The Hair Trunk is not hurled at the stranger's head—so to speak—as the chief feature of an immortal work so often is; no, it is carefully guarded from prominence, it is subordinated, it is restrained, it is most deftly and cleverly held in reserve, it is most cautiously and ingeniously led up to, by the master, and consequently when the spectator reaches it at last, he is taken unawares, he is unprepared, and it bursts upon him with a stupefying surprise.

One is lost in wonder at all the thought and care which this elaborate planning must have cost. A general glance at the picture could never suggest that there was a hair trunk in it; the Hair Trunk is not mentioned in the title even—which is, "Pope Alexander III. and the Doge Ziani, the Conqueror of the Emperor Frederick Barbarossa"; you see, the title is actually utilized to help divert attention from the Trunk; thus, as I say, nothing suggests the presence of the Trunk, by any hint, yet everything studiedly leads up to it, step by step. Let us examine into this, and observe the exquisitely artful artlessness of the plan.

At the extreme left end of the picture are a couple of women, one of them with a child looking over her shoulder at a wounded man sitting with bandaged head on the ground. These people seem needless, but no, they are there for a purpose; one cannot look at them without seeing the gorgeous procession of grandees, bishops, halberdiers, and banner-bearers which is passing along behind them; one cannot see the procession without feeling a curiosity to follow it and learn whither it is going; it leads him to the Pope, in the center of the picture, who is talking with the bonnetless Doge—talking tranquilly, too, although within twelve feet of them a man is beating a drum, and not far from the drummer two persons are blowing horns, and many horsemen are plunging and rioting about—indeed, twenty-two feet of this great work is all a deep and happy holiday serenity and Sunday-school procession, and then we come suddenly upon eleven and one-half feet of turmoil and racket and insubordination. This latter state of things is not an accident, it has its purpose. But for it, one would linger upon the Pope and the Doge, thinking them to be the motive and supreme feature of the picture; whereas one is drawn along, almost unconsciously, to see what the trouble is about. Now at the very *end* of this riot, within four feet of the end of the picture, and full thirty-six feet from the beginning of it, the Hair Trunk bursts with an electrifying suddenness upon the spectator, in all its matchless perfection, and the great master's triumph is sweeping and complete. From that moment no other thing in those forty feet of canvas has any charm; one sees the Hair Trunk, and the Hair Trunk only—and to see it is to worship it. Bassano even placed objects in the immediate vicinity of the Supreme Feature whose pretended purpose was to divert attention from it yet a little longer and thus delay and augment the surprise; for instance, to the right of it he has placed a stooping man with a cap so red that it is sure to hold the eye for a moment—to the left of it, some six feet away, he has placed a red-coated man on an inflated horse, and that coat plucks your eye to that locality the next moment —then, between the Trunk and the red horseman he has intruded a man, naked to his waist, who is carrying a fancy flour-sack on the middle of his back instead of on his shoulder—this admirable feat interests you, of course—keeps you at bay a little longer, like a sock or a jacket thrown to the pursuing wolf—but at last, in spite of all distractions and detentions, the eye of even the most dull and heedless spectator is sure to fall upon the World's Masterpiece, and in that moment he totters to his chair or leans upon his guide for support.

Descriptions of such a work as this must necessarily be imperfect, yet they are of value. The top of the Trunk is arched; the arch is a perfect half-circle, in the Roman style of architecture, for in the then rapid decadence of Greek art, the rising influence of Rome was already beginning to be felt in the art of the Republic. The Trunk is bound or bordered with leather all around where the lid joins the main body. Many critics consider this leather too cold in tone; but I consider this its highest merit, since it was evidently made so to emphasize by contrast the impassioned fervor of the hasp. The high lights in this part of the work are cleverly managed, the *motif* is admirably subordinated to the ground tints, and the technique is very fine. The brass nail-heads are in the purest style of the early Renaissance. The strokes, here, are very firm and bold—every nailhead is a portrait. The handle on the end of the Trunk has evidently been retouched—I think, with a piece of chalk—but one can still see the inspiration of the Old Master in the tranquil, almost too tranquil, hang of it. The hair of this Trunk is *real* hair—so to speak—white in patches, brown in patches. The details are finely worked out; the repose proper to hair in a recumbent and inactive attitude is charmingly expressed. There is a feeling about this part of the work which lifts it to the highest altitudes of art; the sense of sordid realism vanishes away—one recognizes that there is *soul* here.

View this Trunk as you will, it is a gem, it is a marvel, it is a miracle. Some of the effects are very daring, approaching even to the boldest flights of the rococo, the sirocco, and the Byzantine schools—yet the master's hand never falters—it moves on, calm, majestic, confident—and, with that art which conceals art, it finally casts over the *tout ensemble*, by mysterious methods of its own, a subtle something which refines, subdues, etherealizes the arid components and endues them with the deep charm and gracious witchery of poesy.

Among the art-treasures of Europe there are pictures which approach the Hair Trunk—there are two which may be said to equal it, possibly—but there is none that surpasses it. So perfect is the Hair Trunk that it moves even persons who ordinarily have no feeling for art. When an Erie baggagemaster saw it two years ago, he could hardly keep from checking it; and once when a customs inspector was brought into its presence, he gazed upon it in silent rapture for some moments, then slowly and unconsciously placed one hand behind him with the palm uppermost, and got out his chalk with the other. These facts speak for themselves.

From A TRAMP ABROAD, 1880

Why Germans Wear Spectacles

A mile or two above Eberbach we saw a peculiar ruin projecting above the foliage which clothed the peak of a high and very steep hill. This ruin consisted of merely a couple of crumbling masses of masonry which bore a rude resemblance to human faces; they leaned forward and touched foreheads, and had the look of being absorbed in conversation. This ruin had nothing very imposing or picturesque about it, and there was no great deal of it, yet it was called the "Spectacular Ruin."

LEGEND OF THE "SPECTACULAR RUIN"

The captain of the raft, who was as full of history as he could stick, said that in the Middle Ages a most prodigious fire-breathing dragon used to live in that region, and made more trouble than a tax-collector. He was as long as a railway-train, and had the customary impenetrable green scales all over him. His breath bred pestilence and conflagration, and his appetite bred famine. He ate men and cattle impartially, and was exceedingly unpopular. The German emperor of that day made the usual offer: he would grant to the destroyer of the dragon, any one solitary thing he might ask for; for he had a surplusage of daughters, and it was customary for dragon-killers to take a daughter for pay.

So the most renowned knights came from the four corners of the earth and retired down the dragon's throat one after the other. A panic arose and spread. Heroes grew cautious. The procession ceased. The dragon became more destructive than ever. The people lost all hope of succor, and fled to the mountains for refuge.

At last Sir Wissenschaft, a poor and obscure knight, out of a far country, arrived to do battle with the monster. A pitiable object he was, with his armor hanging in rags about him, and his strange-shaped knapsack strapped upon his back. Everybody turned up their noses at him, and some openly jeered him. But he was calm. He simply inquired if the emperor's offer was still in force. The emperor said it was —but charitably advised him to go and hunt hares and not endanger so precious a life as his in an attempt which had brought death to so many of the world's most illustrious heroes.

But this tramp only asked—"Were any of these heroes men of science?" This raised a laugh, of course, for science was despised in those days. But the tramp was not in the least ruffled. He said he might be a little in advance of his age, but no matter—science would come to be honored, some time or other. He said he would march against the dragon in the morning. Out of compassion, then, a decent spear was offered him, but he declined, and said, "spears were useless to men of science." They allowed him to sup in the servants' hall, and gave him a bed in the stables.

When he started forth in the morning, thousands were gathered to see. The emperor said:

"Do not be rash, take a spear, and leave off your knapsack."

But the tramp said:

"It is not a knapsack," and moved straight on.

The dragon was waiting and ready. He was breathing forth vast volumes of sulphurous smoke and lurid blasts of flame. The ragged knight stole warily to a good position, then he unslung his cylindrical knapsack—which was simply the common fire-extinguisher known to modern times—and the first chance he got he turned on his hose and shot the dragon square in the center of his cavernous mouth. Out went the fires in an instant, and the dragon curled up and died.

This man had brought brains to his aid. He had reared dragons from the egg, in his laboratory, he had watched over them like a mother, and patiently studied them and experimented upon them while they grew. Thus he had found out that fire was the life principle of a dragon; put out the dragon's fires and it could make steam no longer, and must die. He could not put out a fire with a spear, therefore he invented the extinguisher. The dragon being dead, the emperor fell on the hero's neck and said:

"Deliverer, name your request," at the same time beckoning out behind with his heel for a detachment of his daughters to form and advance. But the tramp gave them no observance. He simply said:

"My request is, that upon me be conferred the monopoly of the manufacture and sale of spectacles in Germany."

The emperor sprang aside and exclaimed:

"This transcends all the impudence I ever heard! A modest demand, by my halidome! Why didn't you ask for the imperial revenues at once, and be done with it?"

But the monarch had given his word, and he kept it. To everybody's surprise, the unselfish monopolist immediately reduced the price of spectacles to such a degree that a great and crushing burden was removed from the nation. The emperor, to commemorate this generous act, and to testify his appreciation of it, issued a decree commanding everybody to buy this benefactor's spectacles and wear them, whether they needed them or not.

So originated the wide-spread custom of wearing spectacles in Germany; and as a custom once established in these old lands is imperishable, this one remains universal in the empire to this day. Such is the legend of the monopolist's once stately and sumptuous castle, now called the "Spectacular Ruin."

From A TRAMP ABROAD, 1880

Young Cholley Adams

One of the first persons we encountered, as we walked up the street, was the Rev. Mr. ——, an old friend from America—a lucky encounter, indeed, for his is a most gentle, refined, and sensitive nature, and his company and companionship are a genuine refreshment. We knew he had been in Europe some time, but were not at all expecting to run across him. Both parties burst forth into loving enthusiasms, and Rev. Mr. —— said:

"I have got a brimful reservoir of talk to pour out on you, and an empty one ready and thirsting to receive what you have got; we will sit up till midnight and have a good satisfying interchange, for I leave here early in the morning." We agreed to that, of course.

I had been vaguely conscious, for a while, of a person who was walking in the street abreast of us; I had glanced furtively at him once or twice, and noticed that he was a fine, large, vigorous young fellow, with an open, independent countenance, faintly shaded with a pale and even almost imperceptible crop of early down, and that he was clothed from head to heel in cool and enviable snow-white linen. I thought I had also noticed that his head had a sort of listening tilt to it. Now about this time the Rev. Mr. —— said:

"The sidewalk is hardly wide enough for three, so I will walk behind; but keep the talk going, keep the talk going, there's no time to lose, and you may be sure I will do my share." He ranged himself behind us, and straightway that stately snow-white young fellow closed up to the sidewalk alongside him, fetched him a cordial slap on the shoulder with his broad palm, and sung out with a hearty cheeriness:

"*Americans* for two-and-a-half and the money up! *Hey?*"

The Reverend winced, but said mildly:

"Yes—we are Americans."

"Lord love you, you can just bet that's what *I* am, every time! Put it there!"

He held out his Sahara of a palm, and the Reverend laid his diminutive hand in it, and got so cordial a shake that we heard his glove burst under it.

"Say, didn't I put you up right?"

"Oh, yes."

"Sho! I spotted you for *my* kind the minute I heard your clack. You been over here long?"

"About four months. Have you been over long?"

"*Long?* Well, I should say so! Going on two *years*, by geeminy! Say, are you homesick?"

"No, I can't say that I am. Are you?"

"Oh, *hell*, yes!" This with immense enthusiasm.

The Reverend shrunk a little, in his clothes, and we were aware, rather by instinct than otherwise, that he was throwing out signals of distress to us; but we did not interfere or try to succor him, for we were quite happy.

The young fellow hooked his arm into the Reverend's, now, with the confiding and grateful air of a waif who has been longing for a friend, and a sympathetic ear, and a chance to lisp once more the sweet accents of the mother-tongue—and then he limbered up the muscles of his mouth and turned himself loose—and with such a relish! Some of his words were not Sunday-school words, so I am obliged to put blanks where they occur.

"Yes indeedy! If *I* ain't an American there *ain't* any Americans, that's all. And when I heard you fellows gassing away in the good old American language, I'm —— if it wasn't all I could do to keep from hugging you! My tongue's all warped with trying to curl it around these ———— forsaken wind-galled nine-jointed German words here; now I *tell* you it's awful good to lay it over a Christian word once more and kind of let the old taste soak in. I'm from western New

York. My name is Cholley Adams. I'm a student, you know. Been here going on two years. I'm learning to be a horse-doctor! I *like* that part of it, you know, but —————— these people, they won't learn a fellow in his own language, they make him learn in German; so before I could tackle the horse-doctoring I had to tackle this miserable language.

"First off, I thought it would certainly give me the botts, but I don't mind it now. I've got it where the hair's short, I think; and dontchuknow, they made me learn Latin, too. Now between you and me, I wouldn't give a ——— for all the Latin that was ever jabbered; and the first thing *I* calculate to do when I get through, is to just sit down and forget it. 'Twon't take me long, and I don't mind the time, anyway. And I tell you what! the difference between school-teaching over yonder and school-teaching over here—sho! *We* don't know anything about it! Here you've got to peg and peg and peg and there just ain't any let-up—and what you learn here, you've got to *know,* dontchuknow—or else you'll have one of these ———— spavined, spectacled, ring-boned, knock-kneed old professors in your hair. I've been here long *enough,* and I'm getting blessed tired of it, mind I *tell* you. The old man wrote me that he was coming over in June, and said he'd take me home in August, whether I was done with my education or not, but durn him, he didn't come; never said why; just sent me a hamper of Sunday-school books, and told me to be good, and hold on a while. I don't take to Sunday-school books, dontchuknow— I don't hanker after them when I can get pie—but I *read* them, anyway, because whatever the old man tells me to do, that's the thing that I'm a-going to *do,* or tear something, you know. I buckled in and read all of those books, because he wanted me to; but that kind of thing don't excite *me,* I like something *hearty.* But I'm awful homesick. I'm homesick from ear-socket to crupper, and from crupper to hock-joint; but it ain't any use, I've got to stay here, till the old man drops the rag and gives the word—yes, *sir,* right here in this ————— country I've got to linger till the old man says *Come!*—and you bet your bottom dollar, Johnny, it *ain't* just as easy as it is for a cat to have twins!"

At the end of this profane and cordial explosion he fetched a prodigious *"Whoosh!"* to relieve his lungs and make recognition of the heat, and then he straightway dived into his narrative again for "Johnny's" benefit, beginning, "Well, ————— it ain't any use talking, some of those old American words *do* have a kind of a bully swing to them; a man can *express* himself with 'em—a man can get at what he wants to *say,* dontchuknow."

When we reached our hotel and it seemed that he was about to lose the Reverend, he showed so much sorrow, and begged so hard and so earnestly that the Reverend's heart was not hard enough to hold out against the pleadings—so he went away with the parent-honoring student, like a right Christian, and took supper with him in his lodgings, and sat in the surf-beat of his slang and profanity till near midnight, and then left him—left him pretty well talked out, but grateful "clear down to his frogs," as he expressed it. The Reverend said it had transpired during the interview that "Cholley" Adams's father was an extensive dealer in horses in western New York; this accounted for Cholley's choice of a profession. The Reverend brought away a pretty high opinion of Cholley as a manly young fellow, with stuff in him for a useful citizen; he considered him rather a rough gem, but a gem, nevertheless.

From A TRAMP ABROAD, 1880

Plymouth Rock and the Pilgrims

*Address at the First Annual Dinner, N. E. Society,
Philadelphia, December 22, 1881*

On calling upon Mr. Clemens to make response, President Rollins said:

"This sentiment has been assigned to one who was never *exactly* born in New England, nor, perhaps, were any of his ancestors. He is not *technically,* therefore, of New England descent. Under the painful circumstances in which he has found himself, however, he has done the best he could—he has had all his children born there,[1] and has made of *himself* a New England *ancestor.* He is a self-made man. More than this, and better even, in cheerful, hopeful, helpful literature he is of New England *ascent.* To *ascend* there in anything that's reasonable is difficult, for—confidentially, with the door shut—we all know that they are the brightest, ablest sons of that goodly land who never leave it, and it is among and above *them* that Mr. Twain has made his brilliant and permanent ascent—become a man of mark."

[1] A slight mistake: Mark Twain's children were born at Elmira, in the state of New York.

I rise to protest. I have kept still for years, but really I think there is no sufficient justification for this sort of thing. What do you want to celebrate those people for?—those ancestors of yours of 1620—the *May-flower* tribe, I mean. What do you want to celebrate *them* for? Your pardon: the gentleman at my left assures me that you are not celebrating the Pilgrims themselves, but the landing of the Pilgrims at Plymouth Rock on the 22d of December. So you are celebrating their landing. Why, the other pretext was thin enough, but this is thinner than ever; the other was tissue, tinfoil, fish-bladder, but this is gold-leaf. Celebrating their landing! What was there remarkable about it, I would like to know? What can you be thinking of? Why, those Pilgrims had been at sea three or four months. It was the very middle of winter: it was as cold as death off Cape Cod there. Why shouldn't they come ashore? If they *hadn't* landed there would be some reason for celebrating the fact. It would have been a case of monumental leatherheadedness which the world would not willingly let die. If it had been *you*, gentlemen, you probably wouldn't have landed, but you have no shadow of right to be celebrating, in your ancestors, gifts which they did not exercise, but only transmitted. Why, to be celebrating the mere landing of the Pilgrims—to be trying to make out that this most natural and simple and customary procedure was an extraordinary circumstance—a circumstance to be amazed at, and admired, aggrandized and glorified, at orgies like this for two hundred and sixty years—hang it, a horse would have known enough to land; a horse— Pardon again; the gentleman on my right assures me that it was not merely the landing of the Pilgrims that we are celebrating, but the Pilgrims themselves. So we have struck an inconsistency here—one says it was the landing, the other says it was the Pilgrims. It is an inconsistency characteristic of you intractable and disputatious tribe, for you never agree about anything but Boston. Well, then, what do you want to celebrate those Pilgrims for? They were a mighty hard lot—you know it. I grant you, without the slightest unwillingness, that they were a deal more gentle and merciful and just than were the people of Europe of that day; I grant you that they are better than their predecessors. But what of that?—that is nothing. People always progress. You are better than your fathers and grandfathers were (this is the first time I have ever aimed a measureless slander at the departed, for I consider such things improper). Yes, those among you who have not been in the penitentiary, if such there be, are better than your fathers and grandfathers were; but is that any sufficient reason for getting up annual dinners and celebrating you? No, by no means

—by no means. Well, I repeat, those Pilgrims were a hard lot. They took good care of themselves, but they abolished everybody else's ancestors. I am a border-ruffian from the State of Missouri. I am a Connecticut Yankee by adoption. In me, you have Missouri morals, Connecticut culture; this, gentlemen, is the combination which makes the perfect man. But where are my ancestors? Whom shall I celebrate? Where shall I find the raw material?

My first American ancestor, gentlemen, was an Indian—an early Indian. Your ancestors skinned him alive, and I am an orphan. Later ancestors of mine were the Quakers William Robinson, Marmaduke Stevenson, *et al.* Your tribe chased them out of the country for their religion's sake; promised them death if they came back; for your ancestors had forsaken the homes they loved, and braved the perils of the sea, the implacable climate, and the savage wilderness, to acquire that highest and most precious of boons, freedom for every man on this broad continent to worship according to the dictates of his own conscience—and they were not going to allow a lot of pestiferous Quakers to interfere with it. Your ancestors broke forever the chains of political slavery, and gave the vote to every man in this wide land, excluding none!—none except those who did not belong to the ortho- dox church. Your ancestors—yes, they were a hard lot; but, neverthe- less, they gave us religious liberty to worship as they required us to worship, and political liberty to vote as the church required; and so I the bereft one, I the forlorn one, am here to do my best to help you celebrate them right.

The Quaker woman Elizabeth Hooton was an ancestress of mine. Your people were pretty severe with her—you will confess that. But, poor thing! I believe they changed her opinions before she died, and took her into their fold; and so we have every reason to presume that when she died she went to the same place which your ancestors went to. It is a great pity, for she was a good woman. Roger Williams was an ancestor of mine. I don't really remember what your people did with him. But they banished him to Rhode Island, anyway. And then, I believe, recognizing that this was really carrying harshness to an un- justifiable extreme, they took pity on him and burned him. They were a hard lot! All those Salem witches were ancestors of mine! Your people made it tropical for them. Yes, they did; by pressure and the gallows they made such a clean deal with them that there hasn't been a witch and hardly a halter in our family from that day to this, and that is one hundred and eighty-nine years. The first slave brought into New England out of Africa by your progenitors was an ancestor of mine—for I am of a mixed breed, an infinitely shaded and exquisite Mongrel. I'm not one of your sham meerschaums that you can color in a week. No, my complexion is the patient art of eight generations. Well, in my own time, I had acquired a lot of my kin—by purchase, and swapping around, and one way and another—and was getting along very well. Then, with the inborn perversity of your lineage, you got up a war, and took them all away from me. And so, again am I bereft, again am I forlorn; no drop of my blood flows in the veins of any living being who is marketable.

O my friends, hear me and reform! I seek your good, not mine. You have heard the speeches. Disband these New England societies —nurseries of a system of steadily augmenting laudation and hosanna-ing, which, if persisted in uncurbed, may some day in the remote future beguile you into prevaricating and bragging. Oh, stop, stop, while you are still temperate in your appreciation of your ancestors! Hear me, I beseech you; get up an auction and sell Plymouth Rock! The Pilgrims were a simple and ignorant race. They never had seen any good rocks before, or at least any that were not watched, and so they were excusable for hopping ashore in frantic delight and clapping an iron fence around this one. But you, gentlemen, are educated; you are enlightened; you know that in the rich land of your nativity, opulent New England, overflowing with rocks, this one isn't worth, at the outside, more than thirty-five cents. Therefore, sell it, before it is injured by exposure, or at least throw it open to the patent-medicine advertisements, and let it earn its taxes.

Yes, hear your true friend—your only true friend—list to his voice. Disband these societies, hotbeds of vice, of moral decay—perpetuators of ancestral superstition. Here on this board I see water, I see milk, I see the wild and deadly lemonade. These are but steps upon the downward path. Next we shall see tea, then chocolate, then coffee—hotel coffee. A few more years—all too few, I fear—mark my words, we shall have cider! Gentlemen, pause ere it be too late. You are on the broad road which leads to dissipation, physical ruin, moral decay, gory crime, and the gallows! I beseech you, I implore you, in the name of your anxious friends, in the name of your impending widows and orphans, stop ere it be too late. Disband these New England societies, renounce these soul-blistering saturnalia, cease from varnishing the rusty reputations of your long-vanished ancestors—the super-high-moral old iron-clads of Cape Cod, the pious buccaneers of Plymouth Rock —go home, and try to learn to behave!

However, chaff and nonsense aside, I think I honor and appreciate your Pilgrim stock as much as you do yourselves, perhaps; and I indorse and adopt a sentiment uttered by a grandfather of mine once—a man of sturdy opinions, of sincere make of mind, and not given to flattery. He said: "People may talk as they like about that Pilgrim stock, but, after all's said and done, it would be pretty hard to improve on those people; and, as for me, I don't mind coming out flatfooted and saying there ain't any way to improve on them—except having them born in Missouri!"

1881

Concerning the American Language*

There was an Englishman in our compartment, and he complimented me on—on what? But you would never guess. He complimented me on my English. He said Americans in general did not speak the English language as correctly as I did. I said I was obliged to him for his compliment, since I knew he meant it for one, but that I was not fairly entitled to it, for I did not speak English at all—I only spoke American.

He laughed, and said it was a distinction without a difference. I said no, the difference was not prodigious, but still it was considerable. We fell into a friendly dispute over the matter. I put my case as well as I could, and said:

"The languages were identical several generations ago, but our changed conditions and the spread of our people far to the south and far to the west have made many alterations in our pronunciation, and have introduced new words among us and changed the meanings of many old ones. English people talk through their noses; we do not. We say *know*, English people say *näo;* we say *cow*, the Briton says *käow;* we—"

"Oh, come! that is pure Yankee; everybody knows that."

"Yes, it is pure Yankee; that is true. One cannot hear it in America outside of the little corner called New England, which is Yankee land. The English themselves planted it there, two hundred and fifty years

* Being part of a chapter which was crowded out of "A Tramp Abroad."—M. T.

ago, and there it remains; it has never spread. But England talks
through her nose yet; the Londoner and the backwoods New-
Englander pronounce 'know' and 'cow' alike, and then the Briton unconsciously satirizes himself by making fun of the Yankee's pronunciation."

We argued this point at some length; nobody won; but no matter,
the fact remains—Englishmen say *näo* and *käow* for "know" and "cow,"
and that is what the rustic inhabitant of a very small section of America
does.

"You conferred your *a* upon New England, too, and there it remains; it has not traveled out of the narrow limits of those six little
states in all these two hundred and fifty years. All England uses it,
New England's small population—say four millions—use it, but we have
forty-five millions who do not use it. You say 'glahs of wawtah,' so does
New England; at least, New England says *glahs*. America at large
flattens the *a*, and says 'glass of water.' These sounds are pleasanter
than yours; you may think they are not right—well, in English they
are *not* right, but in 'American' they are. You say *flahsk*, and *bahsket*,
and *jackahss*; we say 'flask,' 'basket,' 'jackass'—sounding the *a* as it is in
'tallow,' 'fallow,' and so on. Up to as late as 1847 Mr. Webster's Dictionary had the impudence to still pronounce 'basket' *bahsket*, when
he knew that outside of his little New England all America shortened
the *a* and paid no attention to his English broadening of it. However,
it called itself an English Dictionary, so it was proper enough that it
should stick to English forms, perhaps. It still calls itself an English
Dictionary today, but it has quietly ceased to pronounce 'basket' as
if it were spelt *bahsket*. In the American language the *h* is respected;
the *h* is not dropped or added improperly."

"The same is the case in England—I mean among the educated
classes, of course."

"Yes, that is true; but a nation's language is a very large matter.
It is not simply a manner of speech obtaining among the educated
handful; the manner obtaining among the vast uneducated multitude
must be considered also. Your uneducated masses speak English, you
will not deny that; our uneducated masses speak American—it won't be
fair for you to deny that, for you can see, yourself, that when your
stable-boy says, 'It isn't the 'unting that 'urts the 'orse, but the 'ammer,
'ammer, 'ammer on the 'ard 'ighway,' and our stable-boy makes the
same remark without suffocating a single *h*, these two people are
manifestly talking two different languages. But if the signs are to be
trusted, even your educated classes used to drop the *h*. They say
humble, now, and *heroic*, and *historic*, etc., but I judge that they used

to drop those *h*'s because your writers still keep up the fashion of putting *an* before those words, instead of *a*. This is what Mr. Darwin might call a 'rudimentary' sign that an *an* was justifiable once, and useful—when your educated classes used to say '*umble*, and '*eroic*, and '*istorical*. Correct writers of the American language do not put *an* before those words."

The English gentleman had something to say upon this matter, but never mind what he said—I'm not arguing his case. I have him at a disadvantage, now. I proceeded:

"In England you encourage an orator by exclaiming, 'H'yaah! h'yaah!' We pronounce it *heer* in some sections, 'h'*yer*' in others, and so on; but our whites do not say 'h'yaah,' pronouncing the *a*'s like the *a* in *ah*. I have heard English ladies say 'don't you'—making two separate and distinct words of it; your Mr. Burnand has satirized it. But we always say 'dontchu.' This is much better. Your ladies say, 'Oh, it's *o*ful nice!' Ours says, 'Oh, it's *aw*ful nice!' We say, '*Four* hundred,' you say '*For*' —as in the word *or*. Your clergymen speak of 'the Lawd,' ours of 'the Lord'; yours speak of 'the gawds of the heathen,' ours of 'the gods of the heathen.' When you are exhausted, you say you are 'knocked up.' We don't. When you say you will do a thing 'directly,' you mean 'immediately'; in the American language—generally speaking—the word signifies 'after a little.' When you say 'clever,' you mean 'capable'; with us the word used to mean 'accommodating,' but I don't know what it means now. Your word 'stout' means 'fleshy'; our word 'stout' usually means 'strong.' Your words 'gentleman' and 'lady' have a very restricted meaning; with us they include the barmaid, butcher, burglar, harlot, and horse-thief. You say, 'I haven't *got* any stockings on,' 'I haven't *got* any memory,' 'I haven't *got* any money in my purse'; we usually say, 'I haven't any stockings on,' 'I haven't any memory,' 'I haven't any money in my purse.' You say 'out of window'; we always put in a *the*. If one asks 'How old is that man?' the Briton answers, 'He will be about forty'; in the American language we should say, 'He *is* about forty.' However, I won't tire you, sir; but if I wanted to, I could pile up differences here until I not only convinced you that English and American are separate languages, but that when I speak my native tongue in its utmost purity an Englishman can't understand me at all."

"I don't wish to flatter you, but it is about all I can do to understand you *now*."

That was a very pretty compliment, and it put us on the pleasantest terms directly—I use the word in the English sense.

[*Later*—1882. Esthetes in many of our schools are now beginning to teach the pupils to broaden the *a*, and to say "don't you," in the elegant foreign way.]

1882

Legend of Sagenfeld, in Germany*

I

More than a thousand years ago this small district was a kingdom—a little bit of a kingdom, a sort of dainty little toy kingdom, as one might say. It was far removed from the jealousies, strifes, and turmoils of that old warlike day, and so its life was a simple life, its people a gentle and guileless race; it lay always in a deep dream of peace, a soft Sabbath tranquillity; there was no malice, there was no envy, there was no ambition, consequently there were no heart-burnings, there was no unhappiness in the land.

In the course of time the old king died and his little son Hubert came to the throne. The people's love for him grew daily; he was so good and so pure and so noble, that by and by his love became a passion, almost a worship. Now at his birth the soothsayers had diligently studied the stars and found something written in that shining book to this effect:

In Hubert's fourteenth year a pregnant event will happen; the animal whose singing shall sound sweetest in Hubert's ear shall save Hubert's life. So long as the king and the nation shall honor this animal's race for this good deed, the ancient dynasty shall not fail of an heir, nor the nation know war or pestilence or poverty. But beware an erring choice!

All through the king's thirteenth year but one thing was talked of by the soothsayers, the statesmen, the little parliament, and the general people. That one thing was this: How is the last sentence of the prophecy to be understood? What goes before seems to mean that the

* Left out of "A Tramp Abroad" because its authenticity seemed doubtful, and could not at that time be proved.—M. T.

saving animal will choose *itself* at the proper time; but the closing
sentence seems to mean that the *king* must choose beforehand, and
say what singer among the animals pleases him best, and that if he
choose wisely the chosen animal will save his life, his dynasty, his
people, but that if he should make "an erring choice"—beware!

By the end of the year there were as many opinions about this
matter as there had been in the beginning; but a majority of the wise
and the simple were agreed that the safest plan would be for the little
king to make choice beforehand, and the earlier the better. So an edict
was sent forth commanding all persons who owned singing creatures
to bring them to the great hall of the palace in the morning of the first
day of the new year. This command was obeyed. When everything
was in readiness for the trial, the king made his solemn entry with the
great officers of the crown, all clothed in their robes of state. The king
mounted his golden throne and prepared to give judgment. But he
presently said:

"These creatures all sing at once; the noise is unendurable; no one
can choose in such a turmoil. Take them all away, and bring back one
at a time."

This was done. One sweet warbler after another charmed the young
king's ear and was removed to make way for another candidate. The
precious minutes slipped by; among so many bewitching songsters he
found it hard to choose, and all the harder because the promised
penalty for an error was so terrible that it unsettled his judgment and
made him afraid to trust his own ears. He grew nervous and his face
showed distress. His ministers saw this, for they never took their eyes
from him a moment. Now they began to say in their hearts:

"He has lost courage—the cool head is gone—he will err—he and his
dynasty and his people are doomed!"

At the end of an hour the king sat silent awhile, and then said:
"Bring back the linnet."

The linnet trilled forth her jubilant music. In the midst of it the king
was about to uplift his scepter in sign of choice, but checked himself
and said:

"But let us be sure. Bring back the thrush; let them sing together."

The thrush was brought, and the two birds poured out their marvels
of song together. The king wavered, then his inclination began to
settle and strengthen—one could see it in his countenance. Hope
budded in the hearts of the old ministers, their pulses began to beat
quicker, the scepter began to rise slowly, when: There was a hideous
interruption! It was a sound like this—just at the door:

"Waw . . . *he!* waw . . . *he!*—waw-he!—waw-he!—waw-he!"

Everybody was sorely startled—and enraged at himself for showing it.

The next instant the dearest, sweetest, prettiest little peasant-maid of nine years came tripping in, her brown eyes glowing with childish eagerness; but when she saw that august company and those angry faces she stopped and hung her head and put her poor coarse apron to her eyes. Nobody gave her welcome, none pitied her. Presently she looked up timidly through her tears, and said:

"My lord the king, I pray you pardon me, for I meant no wrong. I have no father and no mother, but I have a goat and a donkey, and they are all in all to me. My goat gives me the sweetest milk, and when my dear good donkey brays it seems to me there is no music like to it. So when my lord the king's jester said the sweetest singer among all the animals should save the crown and nation, and moved me to bring him here—"

All the court burst into a rude laugh, and the child fled away crying, without trying to finish her speech. The chief minister gave a private order that she and her disastrous donkey be flogged beyond the precincts of the palace and commanded to come within them no more.

Then the trial of the birds was resumed. The two birds sang their best, but the scepter lay motionless in the king's hand. Hope died slowly out in the breasts of all. An hour went by; two hours, still no decision. The day waned to its close, and the waiting multitudes outside the palace grew crazed with anxiety and apprehension. The twilight came on, the shadows fell deeper and deeper. The king and his court could no longer see each other's faces. No one spoke—none called for lights. The great trial had been made; it had failed; each and all wished to hide their faces from the light and cover up their deep trouble in their own hearts.

Finally—hark! A rich, full strain of the divinest melody streamed forth from a remote part of the hall—the nightingale's voice!

"Up!" shouted the king, "let all the bells make proclamation to the people, for the choice is made and we have not erred. King, dynasty, and nation are saved. From henceforth let the nightingale be honored throughout the land forever. And publish it among all the people that whosoever shall insult a nightingale, or injure it, shall suffer death. The king hath spoken."

All that little world was drunk with joy. The castle and the city blazed with bonfires all night long, the people danced and drank and sang, and the triumphant clamor of the bells never ceased.

From that day the nightingale was a sacred bird. Its song was heard in every house; the poets wrote its praises; the painters painted it; its sculptured image adorned every arch and turret and fountain and public building. It was even taken into the king's councils; and no grave matter of state was decided until the soothsayers had laid the thing before the state nightingale and translated to the ministry what it was that the bird had sung about it.

II

The young king was very fond of the chase. When the summer was come he rode forth with hawk and hound, one day, in a brilliant company of his nobles. He got separated from them by and by, in a great forest, and took what he imagined a near cut, to find them again; but it was a mistake. He rode on and on, hopefully at first, but with sinking courage finally. Twilight came on, and still he was plunging through a lonely and unknown land. Then came a catastrophe. In the dim light he forced his horse through a tangled thicket overhanging a steep and rocky declivity. When horse and rider reached the bottom, the former had a broken neck and the latter a broken leg. The poor little king lay there suffering agonies of pain, and each hour seemed a long month to him. He kept his ear strained to hear any sound that might promise hope of rescue; but he heard no voice, no sound of horn or bay of hound. So at last he gave up all hope, and said, "Let death come, for come it must."

Just then the deep, sweet song of a nightingale swept across the still wastes of the night.

"Saved!" the king said. "Saved! It is the sacred bird, and the prophecy is come true. The gods themselves protected me from error in the choice."

He could hardly contain his joy; he could not word his gratitude. Every few moments now he thought he caught the sound of approaching succor. But each time it was a disappointment; no succor came. The dull hours drifted on. Still no help came—but still the sacred bird sang on. He began to have misgivings about his choice, but he stifled them. Toward dawn the bird ceased. The morning came, and with it thirst and hunger; but no succor. The day waxed and waned. At last the king cursed the nightingale.

Immediately the song of the thrush came from out the wood. The king said in his heart, "This was the true bird—my choice was false—succor will come now."

But it did not come. Then he lay many hours insensible. When he came to himself, a linnet was singing. He listened—with apathy. His faith was gone. "These birds," he said, "can bring no help; I and my house and my people are doomed." He turned him about to die; for he was grown very feeble from hunger and thirst and suffering, and felt that his end was near. In truth, he wanted to die, and be released from pain. For long hours he lay without thought or feeling or motion. Then his senses returned. The dawn of the third morning was breaking. Ah, the world seemed very beautiful to those worn eyes. Suddenly a great longing to live rose up in the lad's heart, and from his soul welled a deep and fervent prayer that Heaven would have mercy upon him and let him see his home and his friends once more. In that instant a soft, a faint, a far-off sound, but oh, how inexpressibly sweet to his waiting ear, came floating out of the distance:

"Waw . . . *he!* waw . . . *he!*—waw-he!—waw-he!—waw-he!"

"*That,* oh, *that* song is sweeter, a thousand times sweeter than the voice of the nightingale, thrush, or linnet, for it brings not mere hope, but *certainty* of succor; and now, indeed, am I saved! The sacred singer has chosen itself, as the oracle intended; the prophecy is fulfilled, and my life, my house, and my people are redeemed. The ass shall be sacred from this day!"

The divine music grew nearer and nearer, stronger and stronger—and ever sweeter and sweeter to the perishing sufferer's ear. Down the declivity the docile little donkey wandered, cropping herbage and singing as he went; and when at last he saw the dead horse and the wounded king, he came and snuffed at them with simple and marveling curiosity. The king petted him, and he knelt down as had been his wont when his little mistress desired to mount. With great labor and pain the lad drew himself upon the creature's back, and held himself there by aid of the generous ears. The ass went singing forth from the place and carried the king to the little peasant-maid's hut. She gave him her pallet for a bed, refreshed him with goat's milk, and then flew to tell the great news to the first scouting-party of searchers she might meet.

The king got well. His first act was to proclaim the sacredness and inviolability of the ass; his second was to add this particular ass to his cabinet and make him chief minister of the crown; his third was to have all the statues and effigies of nightingales throughout his kingdom destroyed, and replaced by statues and effigies of the sacred donkey; and his fourth was to announce that when the little peasant-maid should reach her fifteenth year he would make her his queen—and he kept his word.

Such is the legend. This explains why the moldering image of the ass adorns all these old crumbling walls and arches; and it explains why, during many centuries, an ass was always the chief minister in that royal cabinet, just as is still the case in most cabinets to this day; and it also explains why, in that little kingdom, during many centuries, all great poems, all great speeches, all great books, all public solemnities, and all royal proclamations, always began with these stirring words:

"Waw . . . *he!* waw . . . *he!*—waw-he!—waw-he!—waw-he!"

1882

On the Decay of the Art of Lying

Essay, for Discussion, Read at a Meeting of the Historical and Antiquarian Club of Hartford, and Offered for the Thirty-Dollar Prize. Now First Published.[1]

Observe, I do not mean to suggest that the *custom* of lying has suffered any decay or interruption—no, for the Lie, as a Virtue, a Principle, is eternal; the Lie, as a recreation, a solace, a refuge in time of need, the fourth Grace, the tenth Muse, man's best and surest friend, is immortal, and cannot perish from the earth while this Club remains. My complaint simply concerns the decay of the *art* of lying. No high-minded man, no man of right feeling, can contemplate the lumbering and slovenly lying of the present day without grieving to see a noble art so prostituted. In this veteran presence I naturally enter upon this scheme with diffidence; it is like an old maid trying to teach nursery matters to the mothers in Israel. It would not become me to criticize you, gentlemen, who are nearly all my elders—and my superiors, in this thing—and so, if I should here and there *seem* to do it, I trust it will in most cases be more in a spirit of admiration

---

[1] Did not take the prize.

than of fault-finding; indeed, if this finest of the fine arts had everywhere received the attention, encouragement, and conscientious practice and development which this Club has devoted to it, I should not
need to utter this lament or shed a single tear. I do not say this to
flatter: I say it in a spirit of just and appreciative recognition.

[It had been my intention, at this point, to mention names and
give illustrative specimens, but indications observable about me admonished me to beware of particulars and confine myself to generali-
ties.]

No fact is more firmly established than that lying is a necessity of
our circumstances—the deduction that it is then a Virtue goes without saying. No virtue can reach its highest usefulness without careful
and diligent cultivation—therefore, it goes without saying that this
one ought to be taught in the public schools—at the fireside—even in
the newspapers. What chance has the ignorant, uncultivated liar
against the educated expert? What chance have I against Mr. Per-
against a lawyer? *Judicious* lying is what the world needs. I sometimes
think it were even better and safer not to lie at all than to lie
injudiciously. An awkward, unscientific lie is often as ineffectual as
the truth.

Now let us see what the philosophers say. Note that venerable
proverb: Children and fools *always* speak the truth. The deduction
is plain—adults and wise persons never speak it. Parkman, the historian,
says, "The principle of truth may itself be carried into an absurdity."
In another place in the same chapter he says, "The saying is old that
truth should not be spoken at all times; and those whom a sick
conscience worries into habitual violation of the maxim are imbeciles
and nuisances." It is strong language, but true. None of us could *live*
with an habitual truth-teller; but, thank goodness, none of us has to.
An habitual truth-teller is simply an impossible creature; he does not
exist; he never has existed. Of course there are people who *think* they
never lie, but it is not so—and this ignorance is one of the very things
that shame our so-called civilization. Everybody lies—every day; every
hour; awake; asleep; in his dreams; in his joy; in his mourning; if he
keeps his tongue still, his hands, his feet, his eyes, his attitude, will
convey deception—and purposely. Even in sermons—but that is a
platitude.

In a far country where I once lived the ladies used to go around
paying calls, under the humane and kindly pretense of wanting to see
each other; and when they returned home, they would cry out with a
glad voice, saying, "We made sixteen calls and found fourteen of

them out"—not meaning that they found out anything against the fourteen—no, that was only a colloquial phrase to signify that they were not at home—and their manner of saying it expressed their lively satisfaction in that fact. Now their pretense of wanting to see the fourteen—and the other two whom they had been less lucky with—was that commonest and mildest form of lying which is sufficiently described as a deflation from the truth. Is it justifiable? Most certainly. It is beautiful, it is noble; for its object is, *not* to reap profit, but to convey a pleasure to the sixteen. The iron-souled truth-monger would plainly manifest, or even utter the fact, that he didn't want to see those people—and he would be an ass, and inflict a totally unnecessary pain. And next, those ladies in that far country—but never mind, they had a thousand pleasant ways of lying, that grew out of gentle impulses, and were a credit to their intelligence and an honor to their hearts. Let the particulars go.

The men in that far country were liars, every one. Their mere howdy-do was a lie, because *they* didn't care how you did, except they were undertakers. To the ordinary inquirer you lied in return; for you made no conscientious diagnosis of your case, but answered at random, and usually missed it considerably. You lied to the undertaker, and said your health was failing—a wholly commendable lie, since it cost you nothing and pleased the other man. If a stranger called and interrupted you, you said with your hearty tongue, "I'm glad to see you," and said with your heartier soul, "I wish you were with the cannibals and it was dinner-time." When he went, you said regretfully, "*Must* you go?" and followed it with a "Call again"; but you did no harm, for you did not deceive anybody nor inflict any hurt, whereas the truth would have made you both unhappy.

I think that all this courteous lying is a sweet and loving art, and should be cultivated. The highest perfection of politeness is only a beautiful edifice, built, from the base to the dome, of graceful and gilded forms of charitable and unselfish lying.

What I bemoan is the growing prevalence of the brutal truth. Let us do what we can to eradicate it. An injurious truth has no merit over an injurious lie. Neither should ever be uttered. The man who speaks an injurious truth, lest his soul be not saved if he do otherwise, should reflect that that sort of a soul is not strictly worth saving. The man who tells a lie to help a poor devil out of trouble is one of whom the angels doubtless say, "Lo, here is an heroic soul who casts his own welfare into jeopardy to succor his neighbor's; let us exalt this magnanimous liar."

An injurious lie is an uncommendable thing; and so, also, and in the same degree, is an injurious truth—a fact which is recognized by the law of libel.

Among other common lies, we have the *silent* lie—the deception which one conveys by simply keeping still and concealing the truth. Many obstinate truth-mongers indulge in this dissipation, imagining that if they *speak* no lie, they lie not at all. In that far country where I once lived, there was a lovely spirit, a lady whose impulses were always high and pure, and whose character answered to them. One day I was there at dinner, and remarked, in a general way, that we are all liars. She was amazed, and said, "Not *all?*" It was before "Pinafore's" time, so I did not make the response which would naturally follow in our day, but frankly said, "Yes, *all*—we are all liars; there are no exceptions." She looked almost offended, and said, "Why, do you include *me?*" "Certainly," I said, "I think you even rank as an expert." She said, "'Sh!—'sh! the children!" So the subject was changed in deference to the children's presence, and we went on talking about other things. But as soon as the young people were out of the way, the lady came warmly back to the matter and said, "I have made it the rule of my life to never tell a lie; and I have never departed from it in a single instance." I said, "I don't mean the least harm or disrespect, but really you have been lying like smoke ever since I've been sitting here. It has caused me a good deal of pain, because I am not used to it." She required of me an instance—just a single instance. So I said:

"Well, here is the unfilled duplicate of the blank which the Oakland hospital people sent to you by the hand of the sick-nurse when she came here to nurse your little nephew through his dangerous illness. This blank asks all manner of questions as to the conduct of that sick-nurse: 'Did she ever sleep on her watch? Did she ever forget to give the medicine?' and so forth and so on. You are warned to be very careful and explicit in your answers, for the welfare of the service requires that the nurses be promptly fined or otherwise punished for derelictions. You told me you were perfectly delighted with that nurse —that she had a thousand perfections and only one fault: you found you never could depend on her wrapping Johnny up half sufficiently while he waited in a chilly chair for her to rearrange the warm bed. You filled up the duplicate of this paper, and sent it back to the hospital by the hand of the nurse. How did you answer this question —'Was the nurse at any time guilty of a negligence which was likely to result in the patient's taking cold?' Come—everything is decided by a bet here in California: ten dollars to ten cents you lied when you answered that question." She said, "I didn't; *I left it blank!*" "Just so— you have told a *silent* lie; you have left it to be inferred that you had no fault to find in that matter." She said, "Oh, was that a lie? And how *could* I mention her one single fault, and she so good?—it would have been cruel." I said, "One ought always to lie when one can do good by it; your impulse was right, but your judgment was crude; this comes of unintelligent practice. Now observe the result of this inexpert deflection of yours. You know Mr. Jones's Willie is lying very low with scarlet fever; well, your recommendation was so enthusiastic that that girl is there nursing him, and the worn-out family have all been trustingly sound asleep for the last fourteen hours, leaving their darling with full confidence in those fatal hands, because you, like young George Washington, have a reputa— However, if you are not going to have anything to do, I will come around to-morrow and we'll attend the funeral together, for, of course, you'll naturally feel a peculiar interest in Willie's case—as personal a one, in fact, as the under-taker."

But that was all lost. Before I was half-way through she was in a carriage and making thirty miles an hour toward the Jones mansion to save what was left of Willie and tell all she knew about the deadly nurse. All of which was unnecessary, as Willie wasn't sick; I had been lying myself. But that same day, all the same, she sent a line to the hospital which filled up the neglected blank, and stated the *facts,* too, in the squarest possible manner.

Now, you see, this lady's fault was *not* in lying, but only in lying injudiciously. She should have told the truth, *there,* and made it up to the nurse with a fraudulent compliment further along in the paper. She could have said, "In one respect the sick-nurse is perfection— when she is on watch, she never snores." Almost any little pleasant lie would have taken the sting out of that troublesome but necessary expression of the truth.

Lying is universal—we *all* do it; we all *must* do it. Therefore, the wise thing is for us diligently to train ourselves to lie thoughtfully, judiciously; to lie with a good object, and not an evil one; to lie for others' advantage, and not our own; to lie healingly, charitably, humanely, not cruelly, hurtfully, maliciously; to lie gracefully and gra-ciously, not awkwardly and clumsily; to lie firmly, frankly, squarely, with head erect, not haltingly, tortuously, with pusillanimous mien, as being ashamed of our high calling. Then shall we be rid of the rank and pestilent truth that is rotting the land; then shall we be great and good and beautiful, and worthy dwellers in a world where even benign Nature habitually lies, except when she promises execrable weather. Then— But I am but a new and feeble student in this gracious art; I cannot instruct *this* Club.

Joking aside, I think there is much need of wise examination into what sorts of lies are best and wholesomest to be indulged, seeing we *must* all lie and *do* all lie, and what sorts it may be best to avoid— and this is a thing which I feel I can confidently put into the hands of this experienced Club—a ripe body, who may be termed, in this regard, and without undue flattery, Old Masters.

1882

Paris Notes*

The Parisian travels but little, he knows no language but his own, reads no literature but his own, and consequently he is pretty narrow and pretty self-sufficient. However, let us not be too sweeping; there are Frenchmen who know languages not their own: these are the waiters. Among the rest, they know English; that is, they know it on the European plan—which is to say, they can speak it, but can't understand it. They easily make themselves understood, but it is next to impossible to word an English sentence in such a way as to enable them to comprehend it. They think they comprehend it; they pretend they do; but they don't. Here is a conversation which I had with one of these beings; I wrote it down at the time, in order to have it exactly correct.

I: These are fine oranges. Where are they grown?

HE: More? Yes, I will bring them.

I: No, do not bring any more; I only want to know where they are from—where they are raised.

HE: Yes? (with imperturbable mien and rising inflection.)

I: Yes. Can you tell me what country they are from?

HE: Yes? (blandly, with rising inflection.)

I (disheartened): They are very nice.

HE: Good night. (Bows, and retires, quite satisfied with himself.)

* Crowded out of "A Tramp Abroad" to make room for more vital statistics.—M. T.

That young man could have become a good English scholar by
taking the right sort of pains, but he was French, and wouldn't do that.
How different is the case with our people; they utilize every means
that offers. There are some alleged French Protestants in Paris, and
they built a nice little church on one of the great avenues that lead
away from the Arch of Triumph, and proposed to listen to the correct
thing, preached in the correct way, there, in their precious French
tongue, and be happy. But their little game does not succeed. Our
people are always there ahead of them Sundays, and take up all the
room. When the minister gets up to preach, he finds his house full of
devout foreigners, each ready and waiting, with his little book in his
hand—a morocco-bound Testament, apparently. But only apparently;
it is Mr. Bellows's admirable and exhaustive little French-English
dictionary, which in look and binding and size is just like a Testament
—and those people are there to study French. The building has been
nicknamed "The Church of the Gratis French Lesson."

These students probably acquire more language than general information, for I am told that a French sermon is like a French speech
—it never names a historical event, but only the date of it; if you are
not up in dates, you get left. A French speech is something like this:

Comrades, citizens, brothers, noble parts of the only sublime and perfect
nation, let us not forget that the 21st January cast off our chains; that the
10th August relieved us of the shameful presence of foreign spies; that the
5th September was its own justification before heaven and humanity; that
the 18th Brumaire contained the seeds of its own punishment; that the
14th July was the mighty voice of liberty proclaiming the resurrection,
the new day, and inviting the oppressed peoples of the earth to look upon
the divine face of France and live; and let us here record our everlasting
curse against the man of the 2d December, and declare in thunder tones,
the native tones of France, that but for him there had been no 17th March
in history, no 12th October, no 19th January, no 22d April, no 16th November, no 30th September, no 2d July, no 14th February, no 29th June,
no 15th August, no 31st May—that but for him, France the pure, the grand,
the peerless, had had a serene and vacant almanac to-day!

I have heard of one French sermon which closed in this odd yet
eloquent way:

My hearers, we have sad cause to remember the man of the 13th
January. The results of the vast crime of the 13th January have been in
just proportion to the magnitude of the act itself. But for it there had been
no 30th November—sorrowful spectacle! The grisly deed of the 16th June
had not been done but for it, nor had the man of the 16th June known

existence; to it alone the 3d September was due, also the fatal 12th October. Shall we, then, be grateful for the 13th January, with its freight of death for you and me and all that breathe? Yes, my friends, for it gave us also that which had never come but for it, and it alone—the blessed 25th December.

It may be well enough to explain, though in the case of many of my readers this will hardly be necessary. The man of the 13th January is Adam; the crime of that date was the eating of the apple; the sorrow-ful spectacle of the 30th November was the expulsion from Eden; the grisly deed of the 16th June was the murder of Abel; the act of the 3d September was the beginning of the journey to the land of Nod; the 12th day of October, the last mountain-tops disappeared under the flood. When you go to church in France, you want to take your almanac with you—annotated.

1882

The Art of Inhumation

About the same time I encountered a man in the street whom I had not seen for six or seven years; and something like this talk followed. I said:

"But you used to look sad and oldish; you don't now. Where did you get all this youth and bubbling cheerfulness? Give me the address."

He chuckled blithely, took off his shining tile, pointed to a notched pink circlet of paper pasted into its crown, with something lettered on it, and went on chuckling while I read, "J. B., UNDERTAKER." Then he clapped his hat on, gave it an irreverent tilt to leeward, and cried out:

"That's what's the matter! It used to be rough times with me when you knew me—insurance-agency business, you know; mighty irregular. Big fire, all right—brisk trade for ten days while people scared; after that, dull policy business till next fire. Town like this don't have fires often enough—a fellow strikes so many dull weeks in a row that he gets discouraged. But you bet you, *this* is the business! People don't wait for examples to *die*. No, sir, they drop off right along—there ain't any dull spots in the undertaker line. I just started in with two or three little old coffins and a hired hearse, and *now* look at the thing! I've worked up a business here that would satisfy any man, don't care who he is. Five years ago, lodged in an attic; live in a swell house now, with a mansard roof, and all the modern inconveniences."

"Does a coffin pay so well? Is there much profit on a coffin?"

"*Go*-way! How you talk!" Then, with a confidential wink, a dropping of the voice, and an impressive laying of his hand on my arm: "Look here; there's one thing in this world which isn't ever cheap. That's a coffin. There's one thing in this world which a person don't ever try to jew you down on. That's a coffin. There's one thing in this world which a person don't say—'I'll look around a little, and if I find I can't do better I'll come back and take it.' That's a coffin. There's one thing in this world which a person won't take in pine if he can go walnut; and won't take in walnut if he can go mahogany; and won't take in mahogany if he can go an iron casket with silver door-plate and bronze handles. That's a coffin. And there's one thing in this world which you don't have to worry around after a person to get him to pay for. And *that's* a coffin. Undertaking?—why it's the dead-surest business in Christendom, and the nobbiest.

"Why, just look at it. A rich man won't have anything but your very best; and you can just pile it on, too—pile it on and sock it to him—he won't ever holler. And you take in a poor man, and if you work him right he'll bust himself on a single lay-out. Or especially a woman. F'r instance: Mrs. O'Flaherty comes in—widow—wiping her eyes and kind of moaning. Unhandkerchiefs one eye, bats it around tearfully over the stock; says:

"'And fhat might ye ask for that wan?'

"'Thirty-nine dollars, madam,' says I.

"'It's a foine big price, sure, but Pat shall be buried like a gintleman, as he was, if I have to work me fingers off for it. I'll have that wan, sor.'

"'Yes, madam,' says I, 'and it is a very good one, too; not costly, to be sure, but in this life we must cut our garments to our cloth, as the saying is.' And as she starts out, I heave in, kind of casually, 'This one with the white satin lining is a beauty, but I am afraid—well, sixty-five dollars *is* a rather—rather—but no matter, I felt obliged to say to Mrs. O'Shaughnessy—'

"'D'ye mane to soy that Bridget O'Shaughnessy bought the mate to that joo-ul box to ship that dhrunken divil to Purgatory in?'

"'Yes, madam.'

"'Then Pat shall go to heaven in the twin to it, if it takes the last rap the O'Flahertys can raise; and moind you, stick on some extras, too, and I'll give ye another dollar.'

"And as I lay in with the livery stables, of course I don't forget to mention that Mrs. O'Shaughnessy hired fifty-four dollars' worth of hacks and flung as much style into Dennis's funeral as if he had been a duke or an assassin. And of course she sails in and goes the O'Shaughnessy about four hacks and an omnibus better. That *used* to be, but that's all played now; that is, in this particular town. The Irish got to piling up hacks so, on their funerals, that a funeral left them ragged and hungry for two years afterward; so the priest pitched in and broke it all up. He don't allow them to have but two hacks now, and sometimes only one."

"Well," said I, "if you are so light-hearted and jolly in ordinary times, what *must* you be in an epidemic?"

He shook his head.

"No, you're off, there. We don't like to see an epidemic. An epidemic don't pay. Well, of course I don't mean that, exactly; but it don't pay in proportion to the regular thing. Don't it occur to you why?"

"No."

"Think."

"I can't imagine. What is it?"

"It's just two things."

"Well, what *are* they?"

"One's Embamming."

"And what's the other?"

"Ice."

"How is that?"

"Well, in ordinary times, a person dies, and we lay him up in ice; one day, two days, maybe three, to wait for friends to come. Takes a lot of it—melts fast. We charge jewelry rates for that ice, and war prices for attendance. Well, don't you know, when there's an epidemic, they rush 'em to the cemetery the minute the breath's out. No market for ice in an epidemic. Same with Embamming. You take a family that's able to embam, and you've got a soft thing. You can mention sixteen different ways to do it—though there *ain't* only one or two ways, when you come down to the bottom facts of it—and they'll take the highest-priced way, every time. It's human nature—human nature in grief. It don't reason, you see. Time being, it don't care a d——n. All it wants is physical immortality for deceased, and they're willing to pay for it. All you've got to do is to just be ca'm and stack it up—they'll stand the racket. Why, man, you can take a defunct that you couldn't *give* away; and get your embamming traps around you and go to work; and in a couple of hours he is worth a cool six hundred—that's what *he's* worth. There ain't anything equal to it but trading rats for diamonds in time of famine. Well, don't you see, when there's an epidemic, people don't wait to embam. No, indeed they don't; and it hurts the business like hellth, as we say—hurts it like hell-th, *health,* see?—our little joke in the trade. Well, I must be going. Give me a call whenever you need any—I mean, when you're going by, some time."

In his joyful high spirits, he did the exaggerating himself, if any had been done. I have not enlarged on him.

With the above brief references to inhumation, let us leave the subject. As for me, I hope to be cremated. I made that remark to my pastor once, who said, with what he seemed to think was an impressive manner:

"I wouldn't worry about that, if I had your chances."

Much he knew about it—the family all so opposed to it.

From LIFE ON THE MISSISSIPPI, 1883

Keelboat Talk and Manners

By way of illustrating keelboat talk and manners, and that now departed and hardly remembered raft life, I will throw in, in this place, a chapter from a book which I have been working at, by fits and starts, during the past five or six years, and may possibly finish in the course of five or six more. The book is a story which details some passages in the life of an ignorant village boy, Huck Finn, son of the town drunkard of my time out West, there. He has run away from his persecuting father, and from a persecuting good widow who wishes to make a nice, truth-telling, respectable boy of him; and with him a slave of the widow's has also escaped. They have found a fragment of a lumber-raft (it is high water and dead summer-time), and are floating down the river by night, and hiding in the willows by day—bound for Cairo, whence the negro will seek freedom in the heart of the free states. But, in a fog, they pass Cairo without knowing it. By

and by they begin to suspect the truth, and Huck Finn is persuaded
to end the dismal suspense by swimming down to a huge raft which
they have seen in the distance ahead of them, creeping aboard under
cover of the darkness, and gathering the needed information by eaves-
dropping:

But you know a young person can't wait very well when he is impatient to find a thing out. We talked it over, and by and by Jim said
it was such a black night, now, that it wouldn't be no risk to swim
down to the big raft and crawl aboard and listen—they would talk
about Cairo, because they would be calculating to go ashore there for
a spree, maybe; or anyway they would send boats ashore to buy
whisky or fresh meat or something. Jim had a wonderful level head,
for a nigger: he could most always start a good plan when you wanted
one.

I stood up and shook my rags off and jumped into the river, and
struck out for the raft's light. By and by, when I got down nearly to
her, I eased up and went slow and cautious. But everything was all
right—nobody at the sweeps. So I swum down along the raft till I was
most abreast the camp-fire in the middle, then I crawled aboard
and inched along and got in among some bundles of shingles on the
weather side of the fire. There was thirteen men there—they was the
watch on deck of course. And a mighty rough-looking lot, too. They
had a jug, and tin cups, and they kept the jug moving. One man was
singing—roaring, you may say; and it wasn't a nice song—for a parlor,
anyway. He roared through his nose, and strung out the last word of
every line very long. When he was done they all fetched a kind of
Injun war-whoop, and then another was sung. It begun:

> "There was a woman in our towdn,
>   In our towdn did dwed'l [dwell],
>   She loved her husband dear-i-lee,
>   But another man twyste as wed'l.
>
> "Singing too, riloo, riloo, riloo,
>   Ri-too, riloo, rilay - - - e,
>   She loved her husband dear-i-lee,
>   But another man twyste as wed'l."

And so on—fourteen verses. It was kind of poor, and when he was
going to start on the next verse one of them said it was the tune the
old cow died on; and another one said: "Oh, give us a rest!" And another one told him to take a walk. They made fun of him till he got

mad and jumped up and begun to cuss the crowd, and said he could lam any thief in the lot.

They was all about to make a break for him, but the biggest man there jumped up and says:

"Set whar you are, gentlemen. Leave him to me; he's my meat."

Then he jumped up in the air three times, and cracked his heels together every time. He flung off a buckskin coat that was all hung with fringes, and says, "You lay thar tell the chawin-up's done"; and flung his hat down, which was all over ribbons, and says, "You lay thar tell his sufferin's is over."

Then he jumped up in the air and cracked his heels together again, and shouted out:

"Whoo-oop! I'm the old original iron-jawed, brass-mounted, copper-bellied corpse-maker from the wilds of Arkansaw! Look at me! I'm the man they call Sudden Death and General Desolation! Sired by a hurricane, dam'd by an earthquake, half-brother to the cholera, nearly related to the smallpox on the mother's side! Look at me! I take nineteen alligators and a bar'l of whisky for breakfast when I'm in robust health, and a bushel of rattlesnakes and a dead body when I'm ailing. I split the everlasting rocks with my glance, and I squench the thunder when I speak! Whoo-oop! Stand back and give me room according to my strength! Blood's my natural drink, and the wails of the dying is music to my ear. Cast your eye on me, gentlemen! and lay low and hold your breath, for I'm 'bout to turn myself loose!"

All the time he was getting this off, he was shaking his head and looking fierce, and kind of swelling around in a little circle, tucking up his wristbands, and now and then straightening up and beating his breast with his fist, saying, "Look at me, gentlemen!" When he got through, he jumped up and cracked his heels together three times, and let off a roaring "Whoo-oop! I'm the bloodiest son of a wildcat that lives!"

Then the man that had started the row tilted his old slouch hat down over his right eye; then he bent stooping forward, with his back sagged and his south end sticking out far, and his fists a-shoving out and drawing in in front of him, and so went around in a little circle about three times, swelling himself up and breathing hard. Then he straightened, and jumped up and cracked his heels together three times before he lit again (that made them cheer), and he began to shout like this:

"Whoo-oop! bow your neck and spread, for the kingdom of sorrow's a-coming! Hold me down to the earth, for I feel my powers a-working!

whoo-oop! I'm a child of sin, *don't* let me get a start! Smoked glass, here, for all! Don't attempt to look at me with the naked eye, gentlemen! When I'm playful I use the meridians of longitude and parallels of latitude for a seine, and drag the Atlantic Ocean for whales! I scratch my head with the lightning and purr myself to sleep with the thunder! When I'm cold, I bile the Gulf of Mexico and bathe in it; when I'm hot I fan myself with an equinoctial storm; when I'm thirsty I reach up and suck a cloud dry like a sponge; when I range the earth hungry, famine follows in my tracks! Whoo-oop! Bow your neck and spread! I put my hand on the sun's face and make it night in the earth; I bite a piece out of the moon and hurry the seasons; I shake myself and crumble the mountains! Contemplate me through leather—*don't* use the naked eye! I'm the man with a petrified heart and biler-iron bowels! The massacre of isolated communities is the pastime of my idle moments, the destruction of nationalities the serious business of my life! The boundless vastness of the great American desert is my inclosed property, and I bury my dead on my own premises!" He jumped up and cracked his heels together three times before he lit (they cheered him again), and as he come down he shouted out: "Whoo-oop! bow your neck and spread, for the Pet Child of Calamity's a-coming!"

Then the other one went to swelling around and blowing again— the first one—the one they called Bob; next, the Child of Calamity chipped in again, bigger than ever; then they both got at it at the same time, swelling round and round each other and punching their fists most into each other's faces, and whooping and jawing like Injuns; then Bob called the Child names, and the Child called him names back again; next, Bob called him a heap rougher names, and the Child come back at him with the very worst kind of language; next, Bob knocked the Child's hat off, and the Child picked it up and kicked Bob's ribbony hat about six foot; Bob went and got it and said never mind, this warn't going to be the last of this thing, because he was a man that never forgot and never forgive, and so the Child better look out, for there was a time a-coming, just as sure as he was a living man, that he would have to answer to him with the best blood in his body. The Child said no man was willinger than he for that time to come, and he would give Bob fair warning, *now*, never to cross his path again, for he could never rest till he had waded in his blood, for such was his nature, though he was sparing him now on account of his family, if he had one.

Both of them was edging away in different directions, growling and shaking their heads and going on about what they was going to do; but a little black-whiskered chap skipped up and says:

"Come back here, you couple of chicken-livered cowards, and I'll thrash the two of ye!"

And he done it, too. He snatched them, he jerked them this way and that, he booted them around, he knocked them sprawling faster than they could get up. Why, it warn't two minutes till they begged like dogs—and how the other lot did yell and laugh and clap their hands all the way through, and shout, "Sail in, Corpse-Maker!" "Hi! at him again, Child of Calamity!" "Bully for you, little Davy!" Well, it was a perfect pow-wow for a while. Bob and the Child had red noses and black eyes when they got through. Little Davy made them own up that they was sneaks and cowards and not fit to eat with a dog or drink with a nigger; then Bob and the Child shook hands with each other, very solemn, and said they had always respected each other and was willing to let bygones be bygones. So then they washed their faces in the river; and just then there was a loud order to stand by for a crossing, and some of them went forward to man the sweeps there, and the rest went aft to handle the after sweeps.

I lay still and waited for fifteen minutes, and had a smoke out of a pipe that one of them left in reach; then the crossing was finished, and they stumped back and had a drink around and went to talking and singing again. Next they got out an old fiddle, and one played, and another patted juba, and the rest turned themselves loose on a regular old-fashioned keelboat breakdown. They couldn't keep that up very long without getting winded, so by and by they settled around the jug again.

They sung "Jolly, Jolly Raftsman's the Life for Me," with a rousing chorus, and then they got to talking about differences betwixt hogs, and their different kind of habits; and next about women and their different ways; and next about the best ways to put out houses that was afire; and next about what ought to be done with the Injuns; and next about what a king had to do, and how much he got; and next about how to make cats fight; and next about what to do when a man has fits; and next about differences betwixt clear-water rivers and muddy-water ones. The man they called Ed said the muddy Mississippi water was wholesomer to drink than the clear water of the Ohio; he said if you let a pint of this yaller Mississippi water settle, you would have about a half to three-quarters of an inch of mud in the bottom, according to the stage of the river, and then it warn't no better than Ohio water—what you wanted to do was to keep it stirred up—

and when the river was low, keep mud on hand to put in and thicken the water up the way it ought to be.

The Child of Calamity said that was so; he said there was nutritiousness in the mud, and a man that drunk Mississippi water could grow corn in his stomach if he wanted to. He says:

"You look at the graveyards; that tells the tale. Trees won't grow worth shucks in a Cincinnati graveyard, but in a Sent Louis graveyard they grow upwards of eight hundred foot high. It's all on account of the water the people drunk before they laid up. A Cincinnati corpse don't richen a soil any."

And they talked about how Ohio water didn't like to mix with Mississippi water. Ed said if you take the Mississippi on a rise when the Ohio is low, you'll find a wide band of clear water all the way down the east side of the Mississippi for a hundred mile or more, and the minute you get out a quarter of a mile from shore and pass the line, it is all thick and yaller the rest of the way across. Then they talked about how to keep tobacco from getting moldy, and from that they went into ghosts and told about a lot that other folks had seen; but Ed says:

"Why don't you tell something that you've seen yourselves? Now let me have a say. Five years ago I was on a raft as big as this, and right along here it was a bright moonshiny night, and I was on watch and boss of the stabboard oar forrard, and one of my pards was a man named Dick Allbright, and he come along to where I was sitting, forrard—gaping and stretching, he was—and stooped down on the edge of the raft and washed his face in the river, and come and set down by me and got out his pipe, and had just got it filled, when he looks up and says:

"'Why looky-here,' he says, 'ain't that Buck Miller's place, over yander in the bend?'

"'Yes,' says I, 'it is—why?' He laid his pipe down and leaned his head on his hand, and says:

"'I thought we'd be furder down.' I says:

"'I thought it, too, when I went off watch'—we was standing six hours on and six off—'but the boys told me,' I says, 'that the raft didn't seem to hardly move, for the last hour,' says I, 'though she's a-slipping along all right now,' says I. He give a kind of a groan, and says:

"'I've seed a raft act so before, along here,' he says, ''pears to me the current has most quit above the head of this bend durin' the last two years,' he says.

"Well, he raised up two or three times, and looked away off and around on the water. That started me at it, too. A body is always doing what he sees somebody else doing, though there mayn't be no sense in it. Pretty soon I see a black something floating on the water away off to stabboard and quartering behind us. I see he was looking at it, too. I says:

" 'What's that?' He says, sort of pettish:

" ' 'Tain't nothing but an old empty bar'l.'

" 'An empty bar'll" says I, 'why,' says I, 'a spy-glass is a fool to *your* eyes. How can you tell it's an empty bar'l?' He says:

" 'I don't know; I reckon it ain't a bar'l, but I thought it might be,' says he.

" 'Yes,' I says, 'so it might be, and it might be anything else, too; a body can't tell nothing about it, such a distance as that,' I says.

"We hadn't nothing else to do, so we kept on watching it. By and by I says:

" 'Why, looky-here, Dick Allbright, that thing's a-gaining on us, I believe.'

"He never said nothing. The thing gained and gained, and I judged it must be a dog that was about tired out. Well, we swung down into the crossing, and the thing floated across the bright streak of the moonshine, and by George, it *was* a bar'l. Says I:

" 'Dick Allbright, what made you think that thing was a bar'l, when it was half a mile off?' says I. Says he:

" 'I don't know.' Says I:

" 'You tell me, Dick Allbright.' Says he:

" 'Well, I knowed it was a bar'l; I've seen it before; lots has seen it; they says it's a ha'nted bar'l.'

"I called the rest of the watch, and they come and stood there, and I told them what Dick said. It floated right along abreast, now, and didn't gain any more. It was about twenty foot off. Some was for having it aboard, but the rest didn't want to. Dick Allbright said rafts that had fooled with it had got bad luck by it. The captain of the watch said he didn't believe in it. He said he reckoned the bar'l gained on us because it was in a little better current than what we was. He said it would leave by and by.

"So then we went to talking about other things, and we had a song, and then a breakdown; and after that the captain of the watch called for another song; but it was clouding up now, and the bar'l stuck right thar in the same place, and the song didn't seem to have much warm-up to it, somehow, and so they didn't finish it, and there warn't any cheers, but it sort of dropped flat, and nobody said anything for a minute. Then everybody tried to talk at once, and one chap got off a joke, but it warn't no use, they didn't laugh, and even the chap that made the joke didn't laugh at it, which ain't usual. We all just settled down glum, and watched the bar'l, and was oneasy and oncomfortable. Well, sir, it shut down black and still, and then the wind began to moan around, and next the lightning began to play and the thunder to grumble. And pretty soon there was a regular storm, and in the middle of it a man that was running aft stumbled and fell and sprained his ankle so that he had to lay up. This made the boys shake their heads. And every time the lightning come, there was that bar'l, with the blue lights winking around it. We was always on the lookout for it. But by and by, toward dawn, she was gone. When the day come we couldn't see her anywhere, and we warn't sorry, either.

"But next night about half past nine, when there was songs and high jinks going on, here she comes again, and took her old roost on the stabboard side. There warn't no more high jinks. Everybody got solemn; nobody talked; you couldn't get anybody to do anything but set around moody and look at the bar'l. It begun to cloud up again. When the watch changed, the off watch stayed up, 'stead of turning in. The storm ripped and roared around all night, and in the middle of it another man tripped and sprained his ankle, and had to knock off. The bar'l left toward day, and nobody see it go.

"Everybody was sober and down in the mouth all day. I don't mean the kind of sober that comes of leaving liquor alone—not that. They was quiet, but they all drunk more than usual—not together, but each man sidled off and took it private, by himself.

"After dark the off watch didn't turn in; nobody sung, nobody talked; the boys didn't scatter around, neither; they sort of huddled together, forrard; and for two hours they set there, perfectly still, looking steady in the one direction, and heaving a sigh once in a while. And then, here comes the bar'l again. She took up her old place. She stayed there all night; nobody turned in. The storm come on again, after midnight. It got awful dark; the rain poured down; hail, too; the thunder boomed and roared and bellowed; the wind blowed a hurricane; and the lightning spread over everything in big sheets of glare, and showed the whole raft as plain as day; and the river lashed up white as milk as far as you could see for miles, and there was that bar'l jiggering along, same as ever. The captain ordered the watch to man the after sweeps for a crossing, and nobody would go—no more sprained ankles for them, they said. They wouldn't even *walk* aft. Well, then, just then the sky split wide open, with a crash, and the lightning killed two men of the after watch, and crippled two more. Crippled them how, say you? Why, *sprained their ankles!*

"The bar'l left in the dark betwixt lightnings, toward dawn. Well, not a body eat a bite at breakfast that morning. After that the men loafed around, in twos and threes, and talked low together. But none of them herded with Dick Allbright. They all give him the cold shake. If he come around where any of the men was, they split up and sidled away. They wouldn't man the sweeps with him. The captain had all the skiffs hauled up on the raft, alongside of his wigwam, and wouldn't let the dead men be took ashore to be planted; he didn't believe a man that got ashore would come back; and he was right.

"After night come, you could see pretty plain that there was going to be trouble if that bar'l come again; there was such a muttering going on. A good many wanted to kill Dick Allbright, because he'd seen the bar'l on other trips, and that had an ugly look. Some wanted to put him ashore. Some said: 'Let's all go ashore in a pile, if the bar'l comes again.'

"This kind of whispers was still going on, the men being bunched together forrard watching for the bar'l, when lo and behold you! here she comes again. Down she comes, slow and steady, and settles into her old tracks. You could 'a' heard a pin drop. Then up comes the captain, and says:

" 'Boys, don't be a pack of children and fools; I don't want this bar'l to be dogging us all the way to Orleans, and *you* don't: Well, then, how's the best way to stop it? Burn it up—that's the way. I'm going to fetch it aboard,' he says. And before anybody could say a word, in he went.

"He swum to it, and as he come pushing it to the raft, the men spread to one side. But the old man got it aboard and busted in the head, and there was a baby in it! Yes, sir; a stark-naked baby. It was Dick Allbright's baby; he owned up and said so.

" 'Yes,' he says, a-leaning over it, 'yes, it is my own lamented darling, my poor lost Charles William Allbright deceased,' says he—for he could curl his tongue around the bulliest words in the language when he was a mind to, and lay them before you without a jint started anywheres. Yes, he said, he used to live up at the head of this bend, and one night he choked his child, which was crying, not intending to kill it—which was prob'ly a lie—and then he was scared, and buried it in a bar'l, before his wife got home, and off he went, and struck the northern trail and went to rafting; and this was the third year that the bar'l had chased him. He said the bad luck always begun light, and lasted till four men was killed, and then the bar'l didn't come any more after that. He said if the men would stand it one more night—and was a-going on like that—but the men had got enough. They started to get out a boat to take him ashore and lynch him, but he grabbed the little child all of a sudden and jumped overboard with it, hugged up to his breast and shedding tears, and we never see him again in this life, poor old suffering soul, nor Charles William neither."

"*Who* was shedding tears?" says Bob; "was it Allbright or the baby?"

"Why, Allbright, of course; didn't I tell you the baby was dead? Been dead three years—how could it cry?"

"Well, never mind how it could cry—how could it *keep* all that time?" says Davy. "You answer me that."

"I don't know how it done it," says Ed. "It done it, though—that's all I know about it."

"Say—what did they do with the bar'l?" says the Child of Calamity.

"Why, they hove it overboard, and it sunk like a chunk of lead."

"Edward, did the child look like it was choked?" says one.

"Did it have its hair parted?" says another.

"What was the brand on that bar'l, Eddy?" says a fellow they called Bill.

"Have you got the papers for them statistics, Edmund?" says Jimmy.

"Say, Edwin, was you one of the men that was killed by the lightning?" says Davy.

"Him? Oh, no! he was both of 'em," says Bob. Then they all haw-hawed.

"Say, Edward, don't you reckon you'd better take a pill? You look bad—don't you feel pale?" says the Child of Calamity.

"Oh, come, now, Eddy," says Jimmy, "show up; you must 'a' kept part of that bar'l to prove the thing by. Show us the bung-hole—*do*—and we'll all believe you."

"Say, boys," says Bill, "less divide it up Thar's thirteen of us. I can swaller a thirteenth of the yarn, if you can worry down the rest."

Ed got up mad and said they could all go to some place which he ripped out pretty savage, and then walked off aft, cussing to himself, and they yelling and jeering at him, and roaring and laughing so you could hear them a mile.

"Boys, we'll split a watermelon on that," says the Child of Calamity; and he came rummaging around in the dark amongst the shingle bundles where I was, and put his hand on me. I was warm and soft and naked; so he says "Ouch!" and jumped back.

"Fetch a lantern or a chunk of fire here, boys—there's a snake here as big as a cow!"

So they run there with a lantern, and crowded up and looked in on me.

"Come out of that, you beggar!" says one.

"Who are you?" says another.

"What are you after here? Speak up prompt, or overboard you go."

"Snake him out, boys. Snatch him out by the heels."

I began to beg, and crept out amongst them trembling. They looked me over, wondering, and the Child of Calamity says:

"A cussed thief! Lend a hand and less heave him overboard!"

"No," says Big Bob, "less get out the paint-pot and paint him a sky-blue all over from head to heel, and *then* heave him over."

"Good! that's it. Go for the paint, Jimmy."

When the paint come, and Bob took the brush and was just going to begin, the others laughing and rubbing their hands, I begun to cry, and that sort of worked on Davy, and he says:

"'Vast there. He's nothing but a cub. I'll paint the man that teches him!"

So I looked around on them, and some of them grumbled and growled, and Bob put down the paint, and the others didn't take it up.

"Come here to the fire, and less see what you're up to here," says Davy. "Now set down there and give an account of yourself. How long have you been aboard here?"

"Not over a quarter of a minute, sir," says I.

"How did you get dry so quick?"

"I don't know, sir. I'm always that way, mostly."

"Oh, you are, are you? What's your name?"

I warn't going to tell my name. I didn't know what to say, so I just says:

"Charles William Allbright, sir."

Then they roared—the whole crowd; and I was mighty glad I said that, because, maybe, laughing would get them in a better humor.

When they got done laughing, Davy says:

"It won't hardly do, Charles William. You couldn't have growed this much in five year, and you was a baby when you come out of the bar'l, you know, and dead at that. Come, now, tell a straight story, and nobody'll hurt you, if you ain't up to anything wrong. What *is* your name?"

"Aleck Hopkins, sir. Aleck James Hopkins."

"Well, Aleck, where did you come from, here?"

"From a trading-scow. She lays up the bend yonder. I was born on her. Pap has traded up and down here all his life; and he told me to swim off here, because when you went by he said he would like to get some of you to speak to a Mr. Jonas Turner, in Cairo, and tell him—"

"Oh, come!"

"Yes, sir, it's as true as the world. Pap he says—"

"Oh, your grandmother!"

They all laughed, and I tried again to talk, but they broke in on me and stopped me.

"Now, looky-here," says Davy; "you're scared, and so you talk wild. Honest, now, do you live in a scow, or is it a lie?"

"Yes, sir, in a trading-scow. She lays up at the head of the bend. But I warn't born in her. It's our first trip."

"Now you're talking! What did you come aboard here for? To steal?"

"No, sir, I didn't. It was only to get a ride on the raft. All boys does that."

"Well, I know that. But what did you hide for?"

"Sometimes they drive the boys off."

"So they do. They might steal. Looky-here; if we let you off this time, will you keep out of these kind of scrapes hereafter?"

" 'Deed I will, boss. You try me."

"All right, then. You ain't but little ways from shore. Overboard with you, and don't you make a fool of yourself another time this way. Blast it, boy, some raftsmen would rawhide you till you were black and blue!"

I didn't wait to kiss good-by, but went overboard and broke for shore. When Jim come along by and by, the big raft was away out of sight around the point. I swum out and got aboard, and was mighty glad to see home again.

The boy did not get the information he was after, but his adventure has furnished the glimpse of the departed raftsman and keelboatman which I desire to offer in this place.

I now come to a phase of the Mississippi River life of the flush times of steamboating, which seems to me to warrant full examination—the marvelous science of piloting, as displayed there. I believe there has been nothing like it elsewhere in the world.

From LIFE ON THE MISSISSIPPI, 1883

Introduction to "The New Guide of the Conversation in Portuguese and English"

by Pedro Carolino

In this world of uncertainties, there is, at any rate, one thing which may be pretty confidently set down as a certainty: and that is, that this celebrated little phrase-book will never die while the English language lasts. Its delicious unconscious ridiculousness, and its enchanting naïveté, are as supreme and unapproachable, in their way, as are Shakespeare's sublimities. Whatsoever is perfect in its kind, in literature, is imperishable: nobody can add to the absurdity of this book, nobody can imitate it successfully, nobody can hope to produce its fellow; it is perfect, it must and will stand alone: its immortality is secure.

It is one of the smallest books in the world, but few big books have received such wide attention, and been so much pondered by the grave and the learned, and so much discussed and written about by the thoughtful, the thoughtless, the wise, and the foolish. Long notices of it have appeared, from time to time, in the great English reviews, and in erudite and authoritative philological periodicals; and it has been laughed at, danced upon, and tossed in a blanket by nearly every newspaper and magazine in the English-speaking world. Every scribbler, almost, has had his little fling at it, at one time or another; I had mine fifteen years ago. The book gets out of print, every now and then, and one ceases to hear of it for a season; but presently the nations and near and far colonies of our tongue and lineage call for it once more, and once more it issues from some London or Continental or American press, and runs a new course around the globe, wafted on its way by the wind of a world's laughter.

Many persons have believed that this book's miraculous stupidities were studied and disingenuous; but no one can read the volume carefully through and keep that opinion. It was written in serious good faith and deep earnestness, by an honest and upright idiot who believed he knew something of the English language, and could impart his knowledge to others. The amplest proof of this crops out somewhere or other upon each and every page. There are sentences in the book which could have been manufactured by a man in his right mind, and with an intelligent and deliberate purpose to seem innocently ignorant; but there are other sentences, and paragraphs, which no mere pretended ignorance could ever achieve—nor yet even the most genuine and comprehensive ignorance, when unbacked by inspiration.

It is not a fraud who speaks in the following paragraph of the author's Preface, but a good man, an honest man, a man whose conscience is at rest, a man who believes he has done a high and worthy work for his nation and his generation, and is well pleased with his performance:

We expect then, who the little book (for the care what we wrote him, and for her typographical correction) that may be worth the acceptation of the studious persons, and especialy of the Youth, at which we dedicate him particularly.

One cannot open this book anywhere and not find richness. To prove that this is true, I will open it at random and copy the page I happen to stumble upon. Here is the result:

DIALOGUE 16

FOR TO SEE THE TOWN

Anothony, go to accompany they gentilsmen, do they see the town.

We won't to see all that is it remarquable here.

Come with me, if you please. I shall not folget nothing what can to merit your attention. Here we are near to cathedral; will you come in there?

We will first to see him in oudside, after we shall go in there for to look the interior.

Admire this master piece gothic architecture's.

The chasing of all they figures is astonishing' indeed.

The cupola and the nave are not less curious to see.

What is this palace how I see youder?

It is the town hall.

And this tower here at this side?

It is the Observatory.

The bridge is very fine, it have ten arches, and is constructed of free stone.

The streets are very layed out by line and too paved.
What is the circuit of this town?
Two leagues.
There is it also hospitals here?
It not fail them.
What are then the edifices the worthest to have seen?
It is the arsnehal, the spectacle's hall, the Cusiomhouse, and the Purse.
We are going too see the others monuments such that the public pawn-broker's office, the plants garden's, the money office's, the library.
That it shall be for another day; we are tired.

DIALOGUE 17

TO INFORM ONE'SELF OF A PERSON

How is that gentilman who you did speak by and by?
Is a German.
I did think him Englishman.
He is of the Saxony side.
He speak the french very well.
Tough he is German, he speak so much well italyan, french, spanish and english, that among the Italyans, they believe him Italyan, he speak the frenche as the Frenches himselves. The Spanishesmen believe him Spanish-ing, and the Englishes, Englisman. It is difficult to enjoy well so much several langages.

The last remark contains a general truth; but it ceased to be a truth when one contracts it and applies it to an individual—provided that that individual is the author of this book, Senhor Pedro Carolino. I am sure I should not find it difficult "to enjoy well so much several langages"—or even a thousand of them—if he did the translating for me from the originals into his ostensible English.

1883

A Petition to
the Queen of England

Hartford, Nov. 6, 1887

Madam: You will remember that last May Mr. Edward Bright, the clerk of the Inland Revenue Office, wrote me about a tax which he said was due from me to the government on books of mine published in London—that is to say, an income tax on the royalties. I do not know Mr. Bright, and it is embarrassing to me to correspond with strangers; for I was raised in the country and have always lived there, the early part in Marion County, Missouri, before the war, and this part in Hartford County, Connecticut, near Bloomfield and about eight miles this side of Farmington, though some call it nine, which it is impossible to be, for I have walked it many and many a time in considerably under three hours, and General Hawley says he has done it in two and a quarter, which is not likely; so it has seemed best that I write your Majesty. It is true that I do not know your Majesty personally, but I have met the Lord Mayor, and if the rest of the family are like him, it is but just that it should be named royal; and likewise plain that in a family matter like this, I cannot better forward my case than to frankly carry it to the head of the family itself. I have also met the Prince of Wales once in the fall of 1873, but it was not in any familiar way, but in a quite informal way, being casual, and was, of course, a surprise to us both. It was in Oxford Street, just where you come out of Oxford into Regent Circus, and just as he turned up one side of the circle at the head of a procession, I went down the other side on the top of an omnibus. He will remember me on account of a gray coat with flap pockets that I wore, as I was the only person on the omnibus that had on that kind of a coat; I remember him of course as easy as I would a comet. He looked quite proud and satisfied, but that is not to be wondered at, he has a good situation. And once I called on your Majesty, but you were out.

But this is no matter, it happens with everybody. However, I have wandered a little away from what I started about. It was this way. Young Bright wrote my London publishers, Chatto and Windus—their place is the one on the left as you come down Piccadilly, about a block and a half above where the minstrel show is—he wrote them that he wanted them to pay income tax on the royalties of some foreign authors, namely, "Miss De La Ramé (Ouida), Dr. Oliver Wendell Holmes, Mr. Francis Bret Harte, and Mr. Mark Twain." Well, Mr. Chatto diverted him from the others, and tried to divert him from me, but in this case he failed. So then young Bright wrote me. And not only that, but he sent me a printed document the size of a newspaper, for me to sign all over in different places. Well, it was that kind of a document that the more you study it the more it undermines you and makes everything seem uncertain to you; and so, while in that condition, and really not responsible for my acts, I wrote Mr. Chatto to pay the tax and charge to me. Of course my idea was that it was for only one year, and that the tax would be only about one per cent, or along there somewhere, but last night I met Professor Sloane of Princeton—you may not know him, but you have probably seen him every now and then, for he goes to England a good deal, a large man and very handsome and absorbed in thought, and if you have noticed such a man on platforms after the train is gone, that is the one, he generally gets left, like all those specialists and other scholars who know everything but how to apply it—and he said it was a back tax for *three* years, and not one per cent., but two and a half!

That gave what had seemed a little matter a new aspect. I then began to study the printed document again, to see if I could find anything in it that might modify my case, and I had what seems to be a quite promising success. For instance, it opens thus—polite and courteous, the way those English government documents always are—I do not say that to hear myself talk, it is just the fact, and it is a credit:

"To Mr. Mark Twain: IN PURSUANCE of the Acts of Parliament for granting to Her Majesty Duties and Profits," etc.

I had not noticed that before. My idea had been that it was for the government, and so I wrote *to* the government; but now I saw that it was a private matter, a family matter, and that the proceeds went to yourself, not the government. I would always rather treat with principals, and I am glad I noticed that clause. With a principal, one can always get at a fair and right understanding, whether it is about potatoes, or continents, or any of those things, or something entirely different; for the size or nature of the thing does not affect the fact; whereas, as a rule, a subordinate is more or less troublesome to satisfy. And yet this is not against them, but the other way. They have their duties to do, and must be harnessed to rules, and not allowed any

discretion. Why, if your Majesty should equip young Bright with
discretion—I mean his own discretion—it is an even guess that he would
discretion you out of house and home in two or three years. He would
not *mean* to get the family into straits, but that would be the upshot,
just the same. Now then, with Bright out of the way, this is not going
to be any Irish question; it is going to be settled pleasantly and
satisfactorily for all of us, and when it is finished your Majesty is going
to stand with the American people just as you have stood for fifty
years, and surely no monarch can require better than that of an alien
nation. They do not all pay a British income tax, but the most of
them will in time, for we have shoals of new authors coming along
every year; and of the population of your Canada, upward of four-
fifths are wealthy Americans, and more going there all the time.

Well, another thing which I noticed in the Document was an item
about "Deductions." I will come to that presently, your Majesty. And
another thing was this: that Authors are not mentioned in the Document at all. No, we have "Quarries, Mines, Iron-works, Salt-springs,
Alum-mines, Water-works, Canals, Docks, Drains, Levels, Fishings,
Fairs, Tolls, Bridges, Ferries," and so forth and so forth and so on—
well, as much as a yard or a yard and a half of them, I should think—
anyway a very large quantity or number. I read along—down, and
down, and down the list, further, and further, and further, and as I
approached the bottom my hopes began to rise higher and higher,
because I saw that everything in England *that* far was taxed by name
and in detail, except perhaps the family, and maybe Parliament, and
yet still no mention of Authors. Apparently they were going to be
overlooked. And sure enough, they were! My heart gave a great bound.
But I was too soon. There was a footnote, in Mr. Bright's hand, which
said: "You are taxed under Schedule D, section 14." I turned to that
place, and found these three things: "Trades, Offices, Gas-works."

Of course, after a moment's reflection, hope came up again, and
then certainty: Mr. Bright was in error, and clear off the track; for
Authorship is not a Trade, it is an inspiration; Authorship does not
keep an Office, its habitation is all out under the sky, and everywhere
where the winds are blowing and the sun is shining and the creatures
of God are free. Now then, since I have no Trade and keep no Office,
I am not taxable under Schedule D, section 14, Your Majesty sees
that; so I will go on to that other thing that I spoke of, the "deductions"
—deductions from my tax which I may get allowed, under conditions.
Mr. Bright says all deductions to be claimed by me must be restricted
to the provisions made in Paragraph No. 8, entitled "Wear and Tear

of Machinery, or Plant." This is curious, and shows how far he has gotten away on his wrong course after once he has got started wrong: for Offices and Trades do not have Plant, they do not have Machinery, such a thing was never heard of; and, moreover, they do not wear and tear. You see that, your Majesty, and that it is true. Here is the Paragraph No. 8:

Amount claimed as a deduction for diminished value by reason of Wear and Tear, where the Machinery or Plant belongs to the Person or Company carrying on the Concern, or is let to such Person or Company so that the Lessee is bound to maintain and deliver over the same in good condition:—

Amount £————————————

There it is—the very words.

I could answer Mr. Bright thus:

It is my pride to say that my Brain is my Plant; and I do not claim any deduction for diminished value by reason of Wear and Tear, for the reason that it does not wear and tear, but stays sound and whole all the time. Yes, I could say to him, my Brain is my Plant, my Skull is my Workshop, my Hand is my Machinery, and I am the Person carrying on the Concern; it is not leased to anybody, and so there is no Lessee bound to maintain and deliver over the same in good condition. There. I do not wish to any way overrate this argument and answer, dashed off just so, and not a word of it altered from the way I first wrote it, your Majesty, but indeed it does seem to pulverize that young fellow, you can see that yourself. But that is all I say; I stop there; I never pursue a person after I have got him down.

Having thus shown your Majesty that I am not taxable, but am the victim of the error of a clerk who mistakes the nature of my commerce, it only remains for me to beg that you will of your justice annul my letter that I spoke of, so that my publisher can keep back that tax-money which, in the confusion and aberration caused by the Document, I ordered him to pay. You will not miss the sum, but this is a hard year for authors; and as for lectures, I do not suppose your Majesty ever saw such a dull season.

With always great and ever-increasing respect, I beg to sign myself your Majesty's servant to command,

MARK TWAIN

HER MAJESTY THE QUEEN, LONDON

1887

A Majestic Literary Fossil

If I were required to guess offhand, and without collusion with higher minds, what is the bottom cause of the amazing material and intellectual advancement of the last fifty years, I should guess that it was the modern-born and previously non-existent disposition on the part of men to believe that a new idea can have value. With the long roll of the mighty names of history present in our minds, we are not privileged to doubt that for the past twenty or thirty centuries every conspicuous civilization in the world has produced intellects able to invent and create the things which make our day a wonder; perhaps we may be justified in inferring, then, that the reason they did not do it was that the public reverence for old ideas and hostility to new ones always stood in their way, and was a wall they could not break down or climb over. The prevailing tone of old books regarding new ideas is one of suspicion and uneasiness at times, and at other times contempt. By contrast, our day is indifferent to old ideas, and even considers that their age makes their value questionable, but jumps at a new idea with enthusiasm and high hope—a hope which is high because it has not been accustomed to being disappointed. I make no guess as to just when this disposition was born to us, but it certainly is ours, was not possessed by any century before us, is our peculiar mark and badge, and is doubtless the bottom reason why we are a race of lightning-shod Mercuries, and proud of it—instead of being, like our ancestors, a race of plodding crabs, and proud of that.

So recent is this change from a three or four thousand year twilight to the flash and glare of open day that I have walked in both, and yet am not old. Nothing is to-day as it was when I was an urchin; but when I was an urchin, nothing was much different from what it had always been in the world. Take a single detail, for example—medicine. Galen could have come into my sick-room at any time during my first seven years—I mean any day when it wasn't fishing weather, and there wasn't any choice but school or sickness—and he could have sat down there and stood my doctor's watch without asking a question. He would have smelt around among the wilderness of cups and bottles and vials on the table and the shelves, and missed not a stench that used to glad him two thousand years before, nor discovered one that was of a later date. He would have examined me, and run across only one disappointment—I was already salivated; I would have him there; for I was always salivated, calomel was so cheap. He would get out his lancet then; but I would have him again; our family doctor didn't allow blood to accumulate in the system. However, he could take dipper and ladle, and freight me up with old familiar doses that had come down from Adam to his time and mine; and he could go out with a wheelbarrow and gather weeds and offal, and build some more, while those others were getting in their work. And if our reverend doctor came and found him there, he would be dumb with awe, and would get down and worship him. Whereas if Galen should appear among us to-day, he could not stand anybody's watch; he would inspire no awe; he would be told he was a back number, and it would surprise him to see that that fact counted against him, instead of in his favor. He wouldn't know our medicines; he wouldn't know our practice; and the first time he tried to introduce his own we would hang him.

This introduction brings me to my literary relic. It is a *Dictionary of Medicine*, by Dr. James, of London, assisted by Mr. Boswell's Doctor Samuel Johnson, and is a hundred and fifty years old, it having been published at the time of the rebellion of '45. If it had been sent against the Pretender's troops there probably wouldn't have been a survivor. In 1861 this deadly book was still working the cemeteries —down in Virginia. For three generations and a half it had been going quietly along, enriching the earth with its slain. Up to its last free day it was trusted and believed in, and its devastating advice taken, as was shown by notes inserted between its leaves. But our troops captured it and brought it home, and it has been out of business since. These remarks from its preface are in the true spirit of the olden time, sodden with worship of the old, disdain of the new:

If we inquire into the Improvements which have been made by the Moderns, we shall be forced to confess that we have so little Reason to value ourselves beyond the Antients, or to be tempted to contemn them, that we cannot give stronger or more convincing Proofs of our own Ignorance, as well as our Pride.

Among all the systematical Writers, I think there are very few who refuse the Preference to *Hieron, Fabricius ab Aquapendente,* as a Person of unquestion'd Learning and Judgment; and yet is he not asham'd to let his Readers know that *Celsus* among the Latins, *Paulus Aegineta* among the Greeks, and *Albucasis* among the Arabians, whom I am unwilling to place among the Moderns, tho' he liv'd but six hundred Years since, are the Triumvirate to whom he principally stands indebted, for the Assistance he had receiv'd from them in composing his excellent Book.

[In a previous paragraph are puffs of Galen, Hippocrates, and other debris of the Old Silurian Period of Medicine.] How many Operations are there now in Use which were unknown to the Antients?

That is true. The surest way for a nation's scientific men to prove that they were proud and ignorant was to claim to have found out something fresh in the course of a thousand years or so. Evidently the peoples of this book's day regarded themselves as children, and their remote ancestors as the only grown-up people that had existed. Consider the contrast: without offense, without over-egotism, our own scientific men may and do regard themselves as grown people and their grandfathers as children. The change here presented is probably the most sweeping that has ever come over mankind in the history of the race. It is the utter reversal, in a couple of generations, of an attitude which had been maintained without challenge or interruption from the earliest antiquity. It amounts to creating man over again on a new plan; he was a canal-boat before, he is an ocean greyhound to-day. The change from reptile to bird was not more tremendous, and it took longer.

It is curious. If you read between the lines what this author says about Brer Albucasis, you detect that in venturing to compliment him he has to whistle a little to keep his courage up, because Albucasis "liv'd but six hundred Years since," and therefore came so uncomfortably near being a "modern" that one couldn't respect him without risk.

Phlebotomy, Venesection—terms to signify bleeding—are not often heard in our day, because we have ceased to believe that the best way to make a bank or a body healthy is to squander its capital; but in our author's time the physician went around with a hatful of lancets on his person all the time, and took a hack at every patient whom he found still alive. He robbed his man of pounds and pounds of blood at a single operation. The details of this sort in this book make terrific reading. Apparently even the healthy did not escape, but were bled twelve times a year, on a particular day of the month, and exhaustively purged besides. Here is a specimen of the vigorous old-time practice; it occurs in our author's adoring biography of a Doctor Aretaeus, a licensed assassin of Homer's time, or thereabouts:

In a Quinsey he used Venesection, and allow'd the Blood to flow till the Patient was ready to faint away.

There is no harm in trying to cure a headache—in our day. You can't do it, but you get more or less entertainment out of trying, and that is something; besides, you live to tell about it, and that is more. A century or so ago you could have had the first of these features in rich variety, but you might fail of the other once—and once would do. I quote:

As Dissections of Persons who have died of severe Head-achs, which have been related by Authors, are too numerous to be inserted in this Place, we shall here abridge some of the most curious and important Observations relating to this Subject, collected by the celebrated *Bonetus*.

The celebrated Bonetus's "Observation No. 1" seems to me a sufficient sample, all by itself, of what people used to have to stand any time between the creation of the world and the birth of your father and mine when they had the disastrous luck to get a "Head-ach":

A certain Merchant, about forty Years of Age, of and Melancholic Habit, and deeply involved in the Cares of the World, was, during the Dog-days, seiz'd with a violent pain of his Head, which some time after oblig'd him to keep his Bed.

I, being call'd, order'd Venesection in the Arms, the Application of Leeches to the Vessels of his Nostrils, Forehead, and Temples, as also to those behind his Ears; I likewise prescrib'd the Application of Cupping-glasses, with Scarification, to his Back: But notwithstanding these Precautions, he dy'd. If any Surgeon, skill'd in Arteriotomy, had been present, I should have also order'd that Operation.

I looked for "Arteriotomy" in this same Dictionary, and found this definition: "The opening of an Artery with a View of taking away Blood." Here was a person who was being bled in the arms, forehead, nostrils, back, temples, and behind the ears, yet the celebrated Bonetus was not satisfied, but wanted to open an artery "with a View" to insert a pump, probably. "Notwithstanding these Precautions"—he dy'd. No art of speech could more quaintly convey this butcher's innocent surprise. Now that we know what the celebrated Bonetus did when he wanted to relieve a Head-ach, it is no trouble to infer that if he wanted to comfort a man that had a Stomach-ach he disemboweled him.

I have given one "Observation"—a single Head-ach case; but the celebrated Bonetus follows it with eleven more. Without enlarging upon the matter, I merely note this coincidence—they all "dy'd." Not one of these people got well; yet this obtuse hyena sets down every little gory detail of the several assassinations as complacently as if he imagined he was doing a useful and meritorious work in perpetuating the methods of his crimes. "Observations," indeed! They are confessions.

According to this book, "the Ashes of an Ass's hoof mix'd with Woman's milk cures chilblains." Length of time required not stated. Another item: "The constant Use of Milk is bad for the Teeth, and causes them to rot, and loosens the Gums." Yet in our day babies use it constantly without hurtful results. This author thinks you ought to wash out your mouth with wine before venturing to drink milk. Presently, when we come to notice what fiendish decoctions those people introduced into their stomachs by way of medicine, we shall wonder that they could have been afraid of milk.

It appears that they had false teeth in those days. They were made of ivory sometimes, sometimes of bone, and were thrust into the natural sockets, and lashed to each other and to the neighboring teeth with wires or with silk threads. They were not to eat with, nor to laugh with, because they dropped out when not in repose. You could smile with them, but you had to practise first, or you would overdo it. They were not for business, but just decoration. They filled the bill according to their lights.

This author says "the Flesh of Swine nourishes above all other eatables." In another place he mentions a number of things, and says "these are very easy to be digested; so is Pork." This is probably a lie. But he is pretty handy in that line; and when he hasn't anything of the sort in stock himself he gives some other expert an opening. For instance, under the head of "Attractives" he introduces Paracelsus, who tells of a nameless "Specific"—quantity of it not set down—which is able to draw a hundred pounds of flesh to itself—distance not stated—and then proceeds, "It happen'd in our own Days that an Attractive of this Kind drew a certain Man's Lungs up into his Mouth, by which he had the Misfortune to be suffocated." This is more than doubtful. In the first place, his Mouth couldn't accommodate his Lungs—in fact, his Hat couldn't; secondly, his Heart being more eligibly Situated, it would have got the Start of his Lungs, and, being a lighter Body, it would have Sail'd in ahead and Occupied the Premises; thirdly, you will Take Notice a Man with his Heart in his Mouth hasn't any Room left for his Lungs—he has got all he can Attend to; and finally, the Man must have had the Attractive in his Hat, and when he saw what was going to Happen he would have Remov'd it and Sat Down on it. Indeed, he would; and then how could it Choke him to Death? I don't believe the thing ever happened at all.

Paracelsus adds this effort: "I myself saw a Plaister which attracted as much Water as was sufficient to fill a Cistern; and by these very Attractives Branches may be torn from Trees; and, which is still more surprising, a Cow may be carried up into the Air." Paracelsus is dead now; he was always straining himself that way.

They liked a touch of mystery along with their medicine in the olden time; and the medicine-man of that day, like the medicine-man of our Indian tribes, did what he could to meet the requirement:

Arcanum. A Kind of Remedy whose Manner of Preparation, or singular Efficacy, is industriously concealed, in order to enhance its Value. By the Chymists it is generally defined a thing secret, incorporeal, and immortal, which cannot be Known by Man, unless by Experience; for it is the Virtue of every thing, which operates a thousand times more than the thing itself.

To me the butt end of this explanation is not altogether clear. A little of what they knew about natural history in the early times is exposed here and there in the Dictionary.

The Spider. It is more common than welcome in Houses. Both the Spider and its Web are used in Medicine: The Spider is said to avert the Paroxysms of Fevers, if it be apply'd to the Pulse of the Wrist, or the Temples; but it is peculiarly recommended against a Quartan, being enclosed in the Shell of a Hazlenut.

Among approved Remedies, I find that the distill'd Water of Black Spiders is an excellent Cure for Wounds, and that this was one of the choice Secrets of Sir Walter Raleigh.

The Spider which some call the Catcher, or Wolf, being beaten into a Plaister, then sew'd up in Linen, and apply'd to the Forehead or Temples, prevents the Returns of a Tertian.

There is another Kind of Spider, which spins a white, fine, and thick Web. One of this Sort, wrapp'd in Leather, and hung about the Arm, will avert the Fit of a Quartan. Boil'd in Oil of Roses, and instilled into the Ears, it eases Pains in those Parts. *Dioscorides, Lib. 2, Cap. 68.*

Thus we find that Spiders have in all Ages been celebrated for their febrifuge Virtues; and it is worthy of Remark, that a Spider is usually given to Monkeys, and is esteem'd a sovereign Remedy for the Disorders those Animals are principally subject to.

Then follows a long account of how a dying woman, who had suffered nine hours a day with an ague during eight weeks, and who had been bled dry some dozens of times meantime without apparent benefit, was at last forced to swallow several wads of "Spiders-web," whereupon she straightway mended, and promptly got well. So the sage is full of enthusiasm over the spider-webs, and mentions only in the most casual way the discontinuance of the daily bleedings, plainly never suspecting that this had anything to do with the cure.

As concerning the venomous Nature of Spiders, *Scaliger* takes notice of a certain Species of them (which he had forgotten) whose Poison was of so great Force as to affect one *Vincentinus* thro' the Sole of his Shoe, by only treading on it.

The sage takes that in without a strain, but the following case was a trifle too bulky for him, as his comment reveals:

In Gascony, observes *Scaliger,* there is a very small Spider, which, running over a Looking-glass, will crack the same by the Force of her Poison. (*A mere Fable.*)

But he finds no fault with the following facts:

Remarkable is the Enmity recorded between this Creature and the Serpent, as also the Toad: Of the former it is reported, That, lying (as he thinks securely) under the Shadow of some Tree, the Spider lets herself down by her Thread, and, striking her Proboscis or Sting into the Head, with that Force and Efficacy, injecting likewise her venomous Juice, that, wringing himself about, he immediately grows giddy, and quickly after dies.

When the Toad is bit or stung in Fight with this Creature, the Lizard, Adder, or other that is poisonous, she finds relief from Plantain, to which she resorts. In her Combat with the Toad, the Spider useth the same Stratagem as with the Serpent, hanging by her own Thread from the Bough of some Tree, and striking her Sting into her enemy's Head, upon which the other, enraged, swells up, and sometimes bursts.

To this Effect is the Relation of *Erasmus,* which he saith he had from one of the Spectators, of a Person lying along upon the Floor of his Chamber, in the Summer-time, to sleep in a supine Posture, when a Toad, creeping out of some green Rushes, brought just before in, to adorn the Chimney, gets upon his Face, and with his Feet sits across his Lips. To force off the Toad, says the Historian, would have been accounted sudden Death to the Sleeper; and to leave her there, very cruel and dangerous; so that upon Consultation it was concluded to find out a Spider, which, together with her Web, and the Window she was fasten'd to, was brought carefully, and so contrived as to be held perpendicularly to the Man's Face; which was no sooner done, but the Spider, discovering his Enemy, let himself down, and struck in his Dart, afterwards betaking himself up again to his Web; the Toad swell'd, but as yet kept his station: The second Wound is given quickly after by the Spider, upon which he swells yet more, but remain'd alive still.—The Spider, coming down again by his Thread, gives the third Blow; and the Toad, taking off his Feet from over the Man's Mouth, fell off dead.

To which the sage appends this grave remark, "And so much for the historical Part." Then he passes on to a consideration of "the Effects and Cure of the Poison."

One of the most interesting things about this tragedy is the double sex of the Toad, and also of the Spider.

Now the sage quotes from one Turner:

I remember, when a very young Practitioner, being sent for to a certain Woman, whose Custom was usually, when she went to the Cellar by Candle-light, to go also a Spider-hunting, setting Fire to their Webs, and burning them with the Flame of the Candle still as she pursued them. It happen'd at length, after this Whimsy had been follow'd a long time, one of them sold his Life much dearer than those Hundreds she had destroy'd; for, lighting upon the melting Tallow of her Candle, near the Flame, and his legs being entangled therein, so that he could not extricate himself, the Flame or Heat coming on, he was made a Sacrifice to his cruel Persecutor, who delighting her Eyes with the Spectacle, still waiting for the Flame to take hold of him, he presently burst with a great Crack, and threw his Liquor, some into her Eyes, but mostly upon her Lips; by means of which, flinging away her Candle, she cry'd out for Help, as fansying herself kill'd already with the Poison. However in the Night her Lips swell'd up excessively, and one of her Eyes was much inflam'd; also her Tongue and Gums were somewhat affected; and, whether from the Nausea excited by the Thoughts of the Liquor getting into her Mouth, or from the poisonous Impressions communicated by the nervous *Fibrillae* of those Parts to those of the Ventricle, a continual Vomiting attended: To take off which, when I was call'd, I order'd a Glass of mull'd Sack, with a Scruple of Salt of Wormwood, and some hours after a Theriacal Bolus, which she flung up again. I embrocated the Lips with the Oil of Scorpions mix'd with the Oil of Roses; and, in Consideration of the Ophthalmy, tho' I was not certain but the Heat of the Liquor, rais'd by the Flame of the Candle before the Body of the Creature burst, might, as well as the Venom, excite the Disturbance, (altho' Mr. *Boyle's* Case of a Person blinded by this Liquor dropping from the living Spider, makes the latter sufficient;) yet observing the great Tumefaction of the Lips, together with the other Symptoms not likely to arise from simple Heat, I was inclin'd to believe a real Poison in the Case; and therefore not daring to let her Blood in the Arm [If a man's throat were cut in those old days, the doctor would come and bleed the other end of him], I did, however, with good Success, set Leeches to her Temples, which took off much of the Inflammation; and her Pain was likewise abated, by instilling into her Eyes a thin Mucilage of the Seeds of Quinces and white Poppies extracted with Rose-water; yet the Swelling on the Lips increased; upon which, in the Night, she wore a Cataplasm prepared by boiling the Leaves of Scordium, Rue, and Elder-flowers, and afterwards thicken'd with the Meal of Vetches. In the mean time, her Vomiting having left her,

she had given her, between whiles, a little Draught of Distill'd Water of
Carduus Benedictus and Scordium, with some of the Theriaca dissolved;
and upon going off of the Symptoms, an old Woman came luckily in, who,
with Assurance suitable to those People, (whose Ignorance and Poverty is
their Safety and Protection,) took off the Dressings, promising to cure her in
two Days' time, altho' she made it as many Weeks, yet had the Reputation
of the Cure; applying only Plantain Leaves bruis'd and mixed with Cobwebs,
dropping the Juice into her Eye, and giving some Spoonfuls of the same
inwardly, two or three times a day.

So ends the wonderful affair. Whereupon the sage gives Mr. Turner
the following shot—strengthening it with italics—and passes calmly on:

*I must remark upon this History, that the Plantain, as a Cooler, was much
more likely to cure this Disorder than warmer Applications and Medicines.*

How strange that narrative sounds to-day, and how grotesque,
when one reflects that it was a grave contribution to medical "science"
by an old and reputable physician! Here was all this to-do—two weeks
of it—over a woman who had scorched her eye and her lips with
candle grease. The poor wench is as elaborately dosed, bled, embrocated, and otherwise harried and bedeviled as if there had been
really something the matter with her; and when a sensible old woman
comes along at last, and treats the trivial case in a sensible way, the
educated ignoramus rails at her ignorance, serenely unconscious of
his own. It is pretty suggestive of the former snail-pace of medical
progress that the spider retained his terrors during three thousand
years, and only lost them within the last thirty or forty.

Observe what imagination can do. "This same young Woman" used
to be so affected by the strong (imaginary) smell which emanated
from the burning spiders that "the Objects about her seem'd to turn
round; she grew faint also with cold Sweats, and sometimes a light
Vomiting." There could have been Beer in that cellar as well as
Spiders.

Here are some more of the effects of imagination: "*Sennertus* takes
Notice of the Signs of the Bite or Sting of this Insect to be a Stupor or
Numbness upon the Part, with a sense of Cold, Horror, or Swelling
of the Abdomen, Paleness of the Face, involuntary Tears, Trembling,
Contractions, a (. . .), Convulsions, cold Sweats; but these latter
chiefly when the Poison has been received inwardly," whereas the
modern physician holds that a few spiders taken inwardly, by a bird or
a man, will do neither party any harm.

The above "Signs" are not restricted to spider bites—often they merely indicate fright. I have seen a person with a hornet in his pantaloons exhibit them all.

As to the Cure, not slighting the usual Alexipharmics taken internally, the Place bitten must be immediately washed with Salt Water, or a Sponge dipped in hot Vinegar, or fomented with a Decoction of Mallows, Origanum, and Mother of Thyme; after which a Cataplasm must be laid on of the Leaves of Bay, Rue, Leeks, and the Meal of Barley, boiled with Vinegar, or of Garlick and Onions, contused with Goat's Dung and fat Figs. Meantime the Patient should eat Garlick and drink Wine freely.

As for me, I should prefer the spider bite. Let us close this review with a sample or two of the earthquakes which the old-time doctor used to introduce into his patient when he could find room. Under this head we have "Alexander's Golden Antidote," which is good for— well, pretty much everything. It is probably the old original first patent-medicine. It is built as follows:

Take of Afarabocca, Henbane, Carpobalsamum, each two Drams and a half; of Cloves, Opium, Myrrh, Cyperus, each two Drams; of Opobalsamum, Indian Leaf, Cinnamon, Zedoary, Ginger, Coftus, Coral, Cassia, Euphorbium, Gum Tragacanth, Frankincense, Styrax Calamita, Celtic, Nard, Spignel, Hartwort, Mustard, Saxifrage, Dill, Anise, each one Dram; of Xylaloes, Rheum, Ponticum, Alipta Moschata, Castor, Spikenard, Galangals, Opoponax, Anacardium, Mastich, Brimstone, Peony, Eringo, Pulp of Dates, red and white Hermodactyls, Roses, Thyme, Acorns, Penyroyal, Gentian, the Bark of the Root of Mandrake, Germander, Valerian, Bishops Weed, Bay-berries, long and white Pepper, Xylobalsamum, Carnabadium, Macodonian, Parsley-seeds, Lovage, the Seeds of Rue, and Sinon, of each a Dram and a half; of pure Gold, pure Silver, Pearls not perforated, the Blatta Byzantina, the Bone of the Stag's Heart, of each the Quantity of fourteen Grains of Wheat; of Sapphire, Emerald, and Jasper Stones, each one Dram; of Haslenut, two Drams; of Pellitory of Spain, Shavings of Ivory, Calamus Odoratus, each the Quantity of twenty-nine Grains of Wheat; of Honey or Sugar a sufficient Quantity.

Serve with a shovel. No; one might expect such an injunction after such formidable preparation; but it is not so. The dose recommended is "the Quantity of an Haslenut." Only that; it is because there is so much jewelry in it, no doubt.

Aqua Limacum. Take a great Peck of Garden-snails, and wash them in a great deal of Beer, and make your Chimney very clean, and set a Bushel of Charcoal on Fire; and when they are thoroughly kindled, make a Hole in the Middle of the Fire, and put the Snails in, and scatter more Fire amongst them, and let them roast till they make a Noise; then take them out, and, with a Knife and coarse Cloth, pick and wipe away all the green froth: Then break them, Shells and all, in a Stone Mortar. Take also a Quart of Earthworms, and scour them with Salt, divers times over. Then take two Handfuls of Angelica and lay them in the Bottom of the Still; next lay two Handfuls of Celandine; next a Quart of Rosemary-flowers; then two Handfuls of Bearsfoot and Agrimony; then Fenugreek; then Turmerick; of each one Ounce: Red Dock-root, Bark of Barberry-trees, Wood-sorrel, Betony, of each two Handfuls.—Then lay the Snails and Worms on the top of the Herbs; and then two Handfuls of Goose Dung, and two Handfuls of Sheep Dung. Then put in three Gallons of Strong Ale, and place the pot where you mean to set Fire under it: Let it stand all Night, or longer; in the Morning put in three Ounces of Cloves well beaten, and a small Quantity of Saffron, dry'd to Powder; then six Ounces of Shavings of Hartshorn, which must be uppermost. Fix on the Head and Refrigeratory, and distil according to Art.

There. The book does not say whether this is all one dose, or whether you have a right to split it and take a second chance at it, in case you live. Also, the book does not seem to specify what ailment it was for; but it is of no consequence, for of course that would come out on the inquest.

Upon looking further, I find that this formidable nostrum is "good for raising Flatulencies in the Stomach"—meaning *from* the stomach, no doubt. So it would appear that when our progenitors chanced to swallow a sigh, they emptied a sewer down their throats to expel it. It is like dislodging skippers from cheese with artillery.

When you reflect that your own father had to take such medicines as the above, and that you would be taking them to-day yourself but for the introduction of homeopathy, which forced the old-school doctor to stir around and learn something of a rational nature about his business, you may honestly feel grateful that homeopathy survived the attempts of the allopathists to destroy it, even though you may never employ any physician but an allopathist while you live.

1890

About All Kinds of Ships

We are victims of one common superstition—the superstition that we realize the changes that are daily taking place in the world because we read about them and know what they are. I should not have supposed that the modern ship could be a surprise to me, but it is. It seems to be as much of a surprise to me as it could have been if I had never read anything about it. I walk about this great vessel, the *Havel*, as she plows her way through the Atlantic, and every detail that comes under my eye brings up the miniature counterpart of it as it existed in the little ships I crossed the ocean in fourteen, seventeen, eighteen, and twenty years ago.

In the *Havel* one can be in several respects more comfortable than he can be in the best hotels on the continent of Europe. For instance, she has several bathrooms, and they are as convenient and as nicely equipped as the bathrooms in a fine private house in America; whereas in the hotels of the Continent one bathroom is considered sufficient, and it is generally shabby and located in some out-of-the-way corner of the house; moreover, you need to give notice so long beforehand that you get over wanting a bath by the time you get it. In the hotels there are a good many different kinds of noises, and they spoil sleep; in my room in the ship I hear no sounds. In the hotels they usually shut off the electric light at midnight; in the ship one may burn it in one's room all night.

In the steamer *Batavia*, twenty years ago, one candle, set in the bulkhead between two staterooms, was there to light both rooms, but did not light either of them. It was extinguished at eleven at night, and so were all the saloon lamps except one or two, which were left burning to help the passenger see how to break his neck trying to get around in the dark. The passengers sat at table on long benches made of the hardest kind of wood; in the *Havel* one sits on a swivel chair with a cushioned back to it. In those old times the dinner bill of fare was always the same: a pint of some simple, homely soup or other, boiled codfish and potatoes, slab of boiled beef, stewed prunes for

dessert—on Sundays "dog in a blanket," on Thursdays "plum duff."
In the modern ship the menu is choice and elaborate, and is changed
daily. In the old times dinner was a sad occasion; in our day a concealed orchestra enlivens it with charming music. In the old days the
decks were always wet; in our day they are usually dry, for the
promenade-deck is roofed over, and a sea seldom comes aboard. In a
moderately disturbed sea, in the old days, a landsman could hardly
keep his legs, but in such a sea in our day the decks are as level as
a table. In the old days the inside of a ship was the plainest and
barrenest thing, and the most dismal and uncomfortable that ingenuity
could devise; the modern ship is a marvel of rich and costly decoration
and sumptuous appointment, and is equipped with every comfort and
convenience that money can buy. The old ships had no place of
assembly but the dining-room, the new ones have several spacious and
beautiful drawing-rooms. The old ships offered the passenger no
chance to smoke except in the place that was called the "fiddle." It
was a repulsive den made of rough boards (full of cracks) and its
office was to protect the main hatch. It was grimy and dirty; there
were no seats; the only light was a lamp of the rancid oil-and-rag kind;
the place was very cold, and never dry, for the seas broke in through
the cracks every little while and drenched the cavern thoroughly. In
the modern ship there are three or four large smoking-rooms, and
they have card-tables and cushioned sofas, and are heated by steam
and lighted by electricity. There are few European hotels with such
smoking-rooms.

The former ships were built of wood, and had two or three water-
tight compartments in the hold with doors in them which were often
left open, particularly when the ship was going to hit a rock. The
modern leviathan is built of steel, and the water-tight bulkheads
have no doors in them; they divide the ship into nine or ten water-
tight compartments and endow her with as many lives as a cat. Their
complete efficiency was established by the happy results following
the memorable accident to the *City of Paris* a year or two ago.

One curious thing which is at once noticeable in the great modern
ship is the absence of hubbub, clatter, rush of feet, roaring of orders.
That is all gone by. The elaborate manoeuvers necessary in working
the vessel into her dock are conducted without sounds; one sees
nothing of the processes, hears no commands. A Sabbath stillness
and solemnity reign, in place of the turmoil and racket of the earlier
days. The modern ship has a spacious bridge fenced chin-high with
sail-cloth and floored with wooden gratings; and this bridge, with its

fenced fore-and-aft annexes, could accommodate a seated audience of a hundred and fifty men. There are three steering equipments, each competent if the others should break. From the bridge the ship is steered, and also handled. The handling is not done by shout or whistle, but by signaling with patent automatic gongs. There are three telltales, with plainly lettered dials—for steering, handling the engines, and for communicating orders to the invisible mates who are conducting the landing of the ship or casting off. The officer who is astern is out of sight and too far away to hear trumpet-calls; but the gongs near him tell him to haul in, pay out, make fast, let go, and so on; he hears, but the passengers do not, and so the ship seems to land herself without human help.

This great bridge is thirty or forty feet above the water, but the sea climbs up there sometimes; so there is another bridge twelve or fifteen feet higher still, for use in these emergencies. The force of water is a strange thing. It slips between one's fingers like air, but upon occasion it acts like a solid body and will bend a thin iron rod. In the *Havel* it has splintered a heavy oaken rail into broomstraws instead of merely breaking it in two, as would have been the seemingly natural thing for it to do. At the time of the awful Johnstown disaster, according to the testimony of several witnesses, rocks were carried some distance on the surface of the stupendous torrent; and at St. Helena, many years ago, a vast sea-wave carried a battery of cannon forty feet up a steep slope and deposited the guns there in a row. But the water has done a still stranger thing, and it is one which is credibly vouched for. A marlin-spike is an implement about a foot long which tapers from its butt to the other extremity and ends in a sharp point. It is made of iron and is heavy. A wave came aboard a ship in a storm and raged aft, breast high, carrying a marlin-spike point first with it, and with such lightning-like swiftness and force as to drive it three or four inches into a sailor's body and kill him.

In all ways the ocean greyhound of to-day is imposing and impressive to one who carries in his head no ship pictures of a recent date. In bulk she comes near to rivaling the Ark; yet this monstrous mass of steel is driven five hundred miles through the waves in twenty-four hours. I remember the brag run of a steamer which I traveled in once on the Pacific—it was two hundred and nine miles in twenty-four hours; a year or so later I was a passenger in the excursion tub *Quaker City*, and on one occasion in a level and glassy sea it was claimed that she reeled off two hundred and eleven miles between noon and noon, but it was probably a campaign lie. That little steamer had seventy passengers, and a crew of forty men, and seemed a good deal of a beehive. But in this present ship we are living in a sort of solitude, these soft summer days, with sometimes a hundred passengers scattered about the spacious distances, and sometimes nobody in sight at all; yet, hidden somewhere in the vessel's bulk, there are (including crew) near eleven hundred people.

The stateliest lines in the literature of the sea are these:

> Britannia needs no bulwarks, no towers along the steep—
> Her march is o'er the mountain waves, her home is on
> the deep!

There it is. In those old times the little ships climbed over the waves and wallowed down into the trough on the other side; the giant ship of our day does not climb over the waves, but crushes her way through them. Her formidable weight and mass and impetus give her mastery over any but extraordinary storm waves.

The ingenuity of man! I mean in this passing generation. To-day I found in the chart-room a frame of removable wooden slats on the wall, and on the slats was painted uninforming information like this.

Trim-Tank	Empty
Double-Bottom No. 1	Full
Double-Bottom No. 2	Full
Double-Bottom No. 3	Full
Double-Bottom No. 4	Full

While I was trying to think out what kind of a game this might be and how a stranger might best go to work to beat it, a sailor came in and pulled out the "Empty" end of the first slat and put it back with its reverse side to the front, marked "Full." He made some other change, I did not notice what. The slat-frame was soon explained. Its function was to indicate how the ballast in the ship was distributed. The striking thing was that the ballast was water. I did not know that a ship had ever been ballasted with water. I had merely read, some time or other, that such an experiment was to be tried. But that is the modern way; between the experimental trial of a new thing and its adoption, there is no wasted time, if the trial proves its value.

On the wall, near the slat-frame, there was an outline drawing of the ship, and this betrayed the fact that this vessel has twenty-two considerable lakes of water in her. These lakes are in her bottom; they are imprisoned between her real bottom and a false bottom. They are separated from each other, thwartships, by water-tight bulkheads, and separated down the middle by a bulkhead running from the bow four-fifths of the way to the stern. It is a chain of lakes four hundred feet long and from five to seven feet deep. Fourteen of the lakes contain fresh-water brought from shore, and the aggregate weight of it is four hundred tons. The rest of the lakes contain salt-water—six hundred and eighteen tons. Upward of a thousand tons of water, altogether.

Think how handy this ballast is. The ship leaves port with the lakes all full. As she lightens forward through consumption of coal, she loses trim—her head rises, her stern sinks down. Then they spill one of the sternward lakes into the sea, and the trim is restored. This can be repeated right along as occasion may require. Also, a lake at one end of the ship can be moved to the other end by pipes and steam-pumps. When the sailor changed the slat-frame to-day, he was posting a transference of that kind. The seas had been increasing, and the vessel's head needed more weighting, to keep it from rising on the waves instead of plowing through them; therefore, twenty-five tons of water had been transferred to the bow from a lake situated well toward the stern.

A water compartment is kept either full or empty. The body of water must be compact, so that it cannot slosh around. A shifting ballast would not do, of course.

The modern ship is full of beautiful ingenuities, but it seems to me that this one is the king. I would rather be the originator of that idea than of any of the others. Perhaps the trim of a ship was never perfectly ordered and preserved until now. A vessel out of trim will not steer, her speed is maimed, she strains and labors in the seas. Poor creature, for six thousand years she had had no comfort until these latest days. For six hundred years she swam through the best and cheapest ballast in the world, the only perfect ballast, but she couldn't tell her master and he had not the wit to find it out for himself. It is odd to reflect that there is nearly as much water inside of this ship as there is outside, and yet there is no danger.

NOAH'S ARK

The progress made in the great art of shipbuilding since Noah's time is quite noticeable. Also, the looseness of the navigation laws in the time of Noah is in quite striking contrast with the strictness of the navigation laws of our time. It would not be possible for Noah to do in our day what he was permitted to do in his own. Experience has taught us the necessity of being more particular, more conservative,

more careful of human life. Noah would not be allowed to sail from
Bremen in our day. The inspectors would come and examine the Ark,
and make all sorts of objections. A person who knows Germany can
imagine the scene and the conversation without difficulty and without
missing a detail. The inspector would be in a beautiful military uniform; he would be respectful, dignified, kindly, the perfect gentleman,
but steady as the north star to the last requirement of his duty. He
would make Noah tell him where he was born, and how old he was,
and what religious sect he belonged to, and the amount of his income,
and the grade and position he claimed socially, and the name and
style of his occupation, and how many wives and children he had,
and how many servants, and the name, sex, and age of the whole of
them; and if he hadn't a passport he would be courteously required
to get one right away. Then he would take up the matter of the Ark:

"What is her length?"

"Six hundred feet."

"Depth?"

"Sixty-five."

"Beam?"

"Fifty or sixty."

"Built of—"

"Wood."

"What kind?"

"Shittim and gopher."

"Interior and exterior decorations?"

"Pitched within and without."

"Passengers?"

"Eight."

"Sex?"

"Half male, the others female."

"Ages?"

"From a hundred years up."

"Up to where?"

"Six hundred."

"Ah—going to Chicago; good idea, too. Surgeon's name?"

"We have no surgeon."

"Must provide a surgeon. Also an undertaker—particularly the undertaker. These people must not be left without the necessities of life
at their age. Crew?"

"The same eight."

"The same eight?"

"The same eight."

"And half of them women?"

"Yes, sir."

"Have they ever served as seamen?"

"No, sir."

"Have the men?"

"No, sir."

"Have any of you ever been to sea?"

"No, sir."

"Where were you reared?"

"On a farm—all of us."

"This vessel requires a crew of eight hundred men, she not being a steamer. You must provide them. She must have four mates and nine cooks. Who is captain?"

"I am, sir."

"You must get a captain. Also a chambermaid. Also sick-nurses for the old people. Who designed this vessel?"

"I did, sir."

"Is it your first attempt?"

"Yes, sir."

"I partly suspected it. Cargo?"

"Animals."

"Kind?"

"All kinds."

"Wild, or tame?"

"Mainly wild."

"Foreign or domestic?"

"Mainly foreign."

"Principal wild ones?"

"Megatherium, elephant, rhinoceros, lion, tiger, wolf, snakes—all the wild things of all climes—two of each."

"Securely caged?"

"No, not caged.

"They must have iron cages. Who feeds and waters the menagerie?"

"We do."

"The old people?"

"Yes, sir."

"It is dangerous—for both. The animals must be cared for by a competent force. How many animals are there?"

"Big ones, seven thousand; big and little together, ninety-eight thousand."

"You must provide twelve hundred keepers. How is the vessel lighted?"

"By two windows."

"Where are they?"

"Up under the eaves."

"Two windows for a tunnel six hundred feet long and sixty-five feet deep? You must put in the electric light—a few arc-lights and fifteen hundred incandescents. What do you do in case of leaks? How many pumps have you?"

"None, sir."

"You must provide pumps. How do you get water for the passengers and the animals?"

"We let down the buckets from the windows."

"It is inadequate. What is your motive power?"

"What is my which?"

"Motive power. What power do you use in driving the ship?"

"None."

"You must provide sails or steam. What is the nature of your steering apparatus?"

"We haven't any."

"Haven't you a rudder?"

"No, sir."

"How do you steer the vessel?"

"We don't."

"You must provide a rudder, and properly equip it. How many anchors have you?"

"None."

"You must provide six. One is not permitted to sail a vessel like this without that protection. How many life-boats have you?"

"None, sir."

"Provide twenty-five. How many life-preservers?"

"None."

"You will provide two thousand. How long are you expecting your voyage to last?"

"Eleven or twelve months."

"Eleven or twelve months. Pretty slow—but you will be in time for the Exposition. What is your ship sheathed with—copper?"

"Her hull is bare—not sheathed at all."

"Dear man, the wood-boring creatures of the sea would riddle her like a sieve and send her to the bottom in three months. She *cannot* be allowed to go away in this condition; she must be sheathed. Just a word more: Have you reflected that Chicago is an inland city and not reachable with a vessel like this?"

"Shecargo? What is Shecargo? I am not going to Shecargo."

"Indeed? Then may I ask what the animals are for?"

"Just to breed others from."

"Others? Is it possible that you haven't enough?"

"For the present needs of civilization, yes; but the rest are going to be drowned in a flood, and these are to renew the supply."

"A flood?"

"Yes, sir."

"Are you sure of that?"

"Perfectly sure. It is going to rain forty days and forty nights."

"Give yourself no concern about that, dear sir, it often does that here."

"Not this kind of rain. This is going to cover the mountain-tops, and the earth will pass from sight."

"Privately—but of course not officially—I am sorry you revealed this, for it compels me to withdraw the option I gave you as to sails or steam. I must require you to use steam. Your ship cannot carry the hundredth part of an eleven-months' water-supply for the animals. You will have to have condensed water."

"But I tell you I am going to dip water from outside with buckets."

"It will not answer. Before the flood reaches the mountain-tops the fresh waters will have joined the salt seas, and it will all be salt. You must put in steam and condense your water. I will now bid you good day, sir. Did I understand you to say that this was your very first attempt at ship-building?"

"My very first, sir, I give you the honest truth. I built this Ark without having ever had the slightest training or experience or instruction in marine architecture."

"It is a remarkable work, sir, a most remarkable work. I consider that it contains more features that are new—absolutely new and unhackneyed—than are to be found in any other vessel that swims the seas."

"This compliment does me infinite honor, dear sir, infinite; and I shall cherish the memory of it while life shall last. Sir, I offer my duty and most grateful thanks. Adieu."

No, the German inspector would be limitlessly courteous to Noah, and would make him feel that he was among friends, but he wouldn't let him go to sea with that Ark.

COLUMBUS'S CRAFT

Between Noah's time and the time of Columbus naval architecture underwent some changes, and from being unspeakably bad was improved to a point which may be described as less unspeakably bad. I have read somewhere, some time or other, that one of Columbus's ships was a ninety-ton vessel. By comparing that ship with the ocean greyhounds of our time one is able to get down to a comprehension of how small that Spanish bark was, and how little fitted she would be to run opposition in the Atlantic passenger trade to-day. It would take seventy-four of her to match the tonnage of the *Havel* and carry the *Havel's* trip. If I remember rightly, it took her ten weeks to make the passage. With our ideas this would now be considered an objectionable gait. She probably had a captain, a mate, and a crew consisting of four seamen and a boy. The crew of a modern greyhound numbers two hundred and fifty persons.

Columbus's ship being small and very old, we know that we may draw from these two facts several absolute certainties in the way of minor details which history has left unrecorded. For instance: being small, we know that she rolled and pitched and tumbled in any ordinary sea, and stood on her head or her tail, or lay down with her ear in the water, when storm seas ran high; also, that she was used to having billows plunge aboard and wash her decks from stem to stern; also, that the storm racks were on the table all the way over, and that nevertheless a man's soup was oftener landed in his lap than in his stomach; also, that the dining-saloon was about ten feet by seven, dark, airless, and suffocating with oil-stench; also, that there was only about one stateroom, the size of a grave, with a tier of two or three berths in it of the dimensions and comfortableness of coffins, and that when the light was out the darkness in there was so thick and real that you could bite into it and chew it like gum; also, that the only promenade was on the lofty poop-deck astern (for the ship was shaped like a high-quarter shoe)—a streak sixteen feet long by three feet wide, all the rest of the vessel being littered with ropes and flooded by the seas.

We know all these things to be true, from the mere fact that we know the vessel was small. As the vessel was old, certain other truths follow, as matters of course. For instance: she was full of rats; she was full of cockroaches; the heavy seas made her seams open and shut like your fingers, and she leaked like a basket; where leakage is, there also, of necessity, is bilge-water; and where bilge-water is, only the dead can enjoy life. This is on account of the smell. In the presence of bilge-water, Limburger cheese becomes odorless and ashamed.

From these abolsutely sure data we can competently picture the daily life of the great discoverer. In the early morning he paid his devotions at the shrine of the Virgin. At eight bells he appeared on the poop-deck promenade. If the weather was chilly he came up clad from plumed helmet to spurred heel in magnificent plate armor inlaid with arabesque of gold, having previously warmed it at the galley fire. If the weather was warm he came up in the ordinary sailor toggery of the time—great slouch hat of blue velvet with a flowing brush of snowy ostrich plumes, fastened on with a flashing cluster of diamonds and emeralds; gold-embroidered doublet of green velvet with slashed sleeves exposing under-sleeves of crimson satin; deep collar and cuff ruffles of rich limp lace; trunk hose of pink velvet, with big knee-knots of brocaded yellow ribbon; pearl-tinted silk stockings, clocked and daintily embroidered; lemon-colored buskins of unborn kid, funnel-topped, and drooping low to expose the pretty stockings; deep gauntlets of finest white heretic skin, from the factory of the Holy Inquisition, formerly part of the person of a lady of rank; rapier with sheath crusted with jewels, and hanging from a broad baldric upholstered with rubies and sapphires.

He walked the promenade thoughtfully, he noted the aspects of the sky and the course of the wind; he kept an eye out for drifting vegetation and other signs of land; he jawed the man at the wheel for pastime; he got out an imitation egg and kept himself in practice on his old trick of making it stand on end; now and then he hove a life-line below and fished up a sailor who was drowning on the quarter-deck; the rest of his watch he gaped and yawned and stretched, and said he wouldn't make the trip again to discover six Americas. For that was the kind of natural human person Columbus was when not posing for posterity.

At noon he took the sun and ascertained that the good ship had made three hundred yards in twenty-four hours, and this enabled him to win the pool. Anybody can win the pool when nobody but himself has the privilege of straightening out the ship's run and getting it right.

The Admiral has breakfasted alone, in state: bacon, beans, and gin; at noon he dines alone, in state: bacon, beans and gin; at six he sups alone, in state: bacon, beans, and gin; at eleven P.M. he takes a night relish alone, in state: bacon, beans, and gin. At none of these orgies

is there any music; the ship orchestra is modern. After his final meal
he returned thanks for his many blessings, a little overrating their
value, perhaps, and then he laid off his silken splendors or his gilded
hardware, and turned in, in his little coffin-bunk, and blew out his
flickering stencher and began to refresh his lungs with inverted sighs
freighted with the rich odors of rancid oil and bilge-water. The sighs
returned as snores, and then the rats and the cockroaches swarmed
out in brigades and divisions and army corps and had a circus all over
him. Such was the daily life of the great discoverer in his marine
basket during several historic weeks; and the difference between his
ship and his comforts and ours is visible almost at a glance.

When he returned, the King of Spain, marveling, said—as history
records:

"This ship seems to be leaky. Did she leak badly?"

"You shall judge for yourself, sire. I pumped the Atlantic Ocean
through her sixteen times on the passage."

This is General Horace Porter's account. Other authorities say fifteen.

It can be shown that the differences between that ship and the one
I am writing these historical contributions in are in several respects
remarkable. Take the matter of decoration, for instance. I have been
looking around again, yesterday and to-day, and have noted several
details which I conceive to have been absent from Columbus's ship,
or at least slurred over and not elaborated and perfected. I observe
stateroom doors three inches thick, of solid oak and polished. I note
companionway vestibules with walls, doors, and ceilings paneled in
polished hard woods, some light, some dark, all dainty and delicate
joiner-work, and yet every point compact and tight; with beautiful
pictures inserted, composed of blue tiles—some of the pictures containing as many as sixty tiles—and the joinings of those tiles perfect. These
are daring experiments. One would have said that the first time the
ship went straining and laboring through a storm-tumbled sea those
tiles would gape apart and drop out. That they have not done so is
evidence that the joiner's art has advanced a good deal since the days
when ships were so shackly that when a giant sea gave them a wrench
the doors came unbolted. I find the walls of the dining-saloon upholstered with mellow pictures wrought in tapestry and the ceiling
aglow with pictures done in oil. In other places of assembly I find
great panels filled with embossed Spanish leather, the figures rich
with gilding and bronze. Everywhere I find sumptuous masses of
color—color, color, color—color all about, color of every shade and tint

and variety; and, as a result, the ship is bright and cheery to the eye, and this cheeriness invades one's spirit and contents it. To fully appreciate the force and spiritual value of this radiant and opulent dream of color, one must stand outside at night in the pitch dark and the rain, and look in through a port, and observe it in the lavish splendor of the electric lights. The old-time ships were dull, plain, graceless, gloomy, and horribly depressing. They compelled the blues; one could not escape the blues in them. The modern idea is right: to surround the passenger with conveniences, luxuries, and abundance of inspiriting color. As a result, the ship is the pleasantest place one can be in, except, perhaps, one's home.

A VANISHED SENTIMENT

One thing is gone, to return no more forever—the romance of the sea. Soft sentimentality about the sea has retired from the activities of this life, and is but a memory of the past, already remote and much faded. But within the recollection of men still living, it was in the breast of every individual; and the farther any individual lived from salt-water the more of it he kept in stock. It was as pervasive, as universal, as the atmosphere itself. The mere mention of the sea, the romantic sea, would make any company of people sentimental and mawkish at once. The great majority of the songs that were sung by the young people of the back settlements had the melancholy wanderer for subject and his mouthings about the sea for refrain. Picnic parties paddling down a creek in a canoe when the twilight shadows were gathering always sang:

> Homeward bound, homeward bound,
> From a foreign shore;

and this was also a favorite in the West with the passengers on stern-wheel steamboats. There was another:

> My boat is by the shore
> And my bark is on the sea,
> But before I go, Tom Moore,
> Here's a double health to thee.

And this one, also:

> O pilot, 'tis a fearful night,
> There's danger on the deep.

And this:

> A life on the ocean wave
> And a home on the rolling deep,
> Where the scattered waters rave
> And the winds their revels keep!

And this:

> A wet sheet and a flowing sea,
> And a wind that follows fair.

And this:

> My foot is on my gallant deck,
> Once more the rover is free!

And the "Larboard Watch"—the person referred to below is at the masthead, or somewhere up there:

> Oh, who can tell what joy he feels,
> As o'er the foam his vessel reels,
> And his tired eyelids slumb'ring fall,
> He rouses at the welcome call
> Of "Larboard watch—ahoy!"

Yes, and there was forever and always some jackass-voiced person braying out:

> Rocked in the cradle of the deep,
> I lay me down in peace to sleep!

Other favorites had these suggestive titles: "The Storm at Sea"; "The Bird at Sea"; "The Sailor Boy's Dream"; "The Captive Pirate's Lament"; "We are far from Home on the Stormy Main"—and so on, and so on, the list is endless. Everybody on a farm lived chiefly amid the dangers of the deep in those days, in fancy.

But all that is gone now. Not a vestige of it is left. The iron-clad, with her unsentimental aspect and frigid attention to business, banished romance from the war marine, and the unsentimental steamer has banished it from the commercial marine. The dangers and uncertainties which made sea life romantic have disappeared and carried the poetic element along with them. In our day the passengers never sing sea-songs on board a ship, and the band never plays them. Pathetic songs about the wanderer in strange lands far from home, once so popular and contributing such fire and color to the imagination by reason of the rarity of that kind of wanderer, have lost their charm and fallen silent, because everybody is a wanderer in the far lands now, and the interest in that detail is dead. Nobody is worried about the wanderer; there are no perils of the sea for him, there are no uncertainties. He is safer in the ship than he would probably be at home, for there he is always liable to have to attend some friend's funeral and stand over the grave in the sleet, bareheaded—and that means pneumonia for him, if he gets his deserts; and the uncertainties of his voyage are reduced to whether he will arrive on the other side in the appointed afternoon, or have to wait till morning.

The first ship I was ever in was a sailing-vessel. She was twenty-eight days going from San Francisco to the Sandwich Islands. But the main reason for this particularly slow passage was that she got becalmed and lay in one spot fourteen days in the center of the Pacific two thousand miles from land. I hear no sea-songs in this present vessel, but I heard the entire lay-out in that one. There were a dozen young people—they are pretty old now, I reckon—and they used to group themselves on the stern, in the starlight or the moonlight, every evening, and sing sea-songs till after midnight, in that hot, silent, motionless calm. They had no sense of humor, and they always sang "Homeward Bound," without reflecting that that was practically ridiculous, since they were standing still and not proceeding in any direction at all; and they often followed that song with "'Are we almost there, are we almost there?' said the dying girl as she drew near home."

It was a very pleasant company of young people, and I wonder where they are now. Gone, oh, none knows whither; and the bloom and grace and beauty of their youth, where is that? Among them was a liar; all tried to reform him, but none could do it. And so, gradually, he was left to himself; none of us would associate with him. Many a time since I have seen in fancy that forsaken figure, leaning forlorn against the taffrail, and have reflected that perhaps if we had tried harder, and been more patient, we might have won him from his fault and persuaded him to relinquish it. But it is hard to tell; with him the vice was extreme, and was probably incurable. I like to think —and, indeed, I do think—that I did the best that in me lay to lead him to higher and better ways.

There was a singular circumstance. The ship lay becalmed that entire fortnight in exactly the same spot. Then a handsome breeze came fanning over the sea, and we spread our white wings for flight. But the vessel did not budge. The sails bellied out, the gale strained at the ropes, but the vessel moved not a hair's-breadth from her place.

The captain was surprised. It was some hours before we found out what the cause of the detention was. It was barnacles. They collect very fast in that part of the Pacific. They had fastened themselves to the ship's bottom; then others had fastened themselves to the first bunch, others to these, and so on, down and down and down, and the last bunch had glued the column hard and fast to the bottom of the sea, which is five miles deep at that point. So the ship was simply become the handle of a walking-cane five miles long—yes, no more moveable by wind and sail than a continent is. It was regarded by every one as remarkable.

Well, the next week—however, Sandy Hook is in sight.

1893

A Cure for the Blues

By courtesy of Mr. Cable I came into possession of a singular book eight or ten years ago. It is likely that mine is now the only copy in existence. Its title-page, unabbreviated, reads as follows:

"The Enemy Conquered; or, Love Triumphant. By G. Ragsdale McClintock,[1] author of 'An Address,' etc., delivered at Sunflower Hill, South Carolina, and member of the Yale Law School. New Haven: published by T. H. Pease, 83 Chapel Street, 1845."

No one can take up this book and lay it down again unread. Whoever reads one line of it is caught, is chained; he has become the contented slave of its fascinations; and he will read and read, devour and devour, and will not let it go out of his hand till it is finished to the last line, though the house be on fire over his head. And after a first reading he will not throw it aside, but will keep it by him, with his Shakespeare and his Homer, and will take it up many and many a time, when the world is dark and his spirits are low, and be straightway cheered and refreshed. Yet this work has been allowed to lie wholly neglected, unmentioned, and apparently unregretted, for nearly half a century.

The reader must not imagine that he is to find in it wisdom, bril-

[1] The name here given is a substitute for the one actually attached to the pamphlet.

liancy, fertility of invention, ingenuity of construction, excellence of form, purity of style, perfection of imagery, truth to nature, clearness of statement, humanly possible situations, humanly possible people, fluent narrative, connected sequence of events—or philosophy, or logic, or sense. No; the rich, deep, beguiling charm of the book lies in the total and miraculous *absence* from it of all these qualities—a charm which is completed and perfected by the evident fact that the author, whose naïve innocence easily and surely wins our regard, and almost our worship, does not know that they are absent, does not even suspect that they are absent. When read by the light of these helps to an understanding of the situation, the book is delicious—profoundly and satisfyingly delicious.

I call it a book because the author calls it a book, I call it a work because he calls it a work; but, in truth, it is merely a duodecimo pamphlet of thirty-one pages. It was written for fame and money, as the author very frankly—yes, and very hopefully, too, poor fellow—says in his preface. The money never came—no penny of it ever came; and how long, how pathetically long, the fame has been deferred—forty-seven years! He was young then, it would have been so much to him then; but will he care for it now?

As time is measured in America, McClintock's epoch is antiquity. In his long-vanished day the Southern author had a passion for "eloquence"; it was his pet, his darling. He would be eloquent, or perish. And he recognized only one kind of eloquence—the lurid, the tempestuous, the volcanic. He liked words—big words, fine words, grand words, rumbling, thundering, reverberating words; with sense attaching if it could be got in without marring the sound, but not otherwise. He loved to stand up before a dazed world, and pour forth flame and smoke and lava and pumice-stone into the skies, and work his sub-terranean thunders, and shake himself with earthquakes, and stench himself with sulphur fumes. If he consumed his own fields and vineyards, that was a pity, yes; but he would have his eruption at any cost. Mr. McClintock's eloquence—and he is always eloquent, his crater is always spouting—is of the pattern common to his day, but he departs from the custom of the time in one respect: his brethren allowed sense to intrude when it did not mar the sound, but he does not allow it to intrude at all. For example, consider this figure, which he uses in the village "Address" referred to with such candid complacency in the title-page above quoted—"like the topmost topaz of an ancient tower." Please read it again; contemplate it; measure it; walk around it; climb up it; try to get at an approximate realization of the size of it. Is the fellow to that to be found in literature, ancient or modern, foreign or domestic, living or dead, drunk or sober? One notices how fine and grand it sounds. We know that if it was loftily uttered, it got a noble burst of applause from the villagers; yet there isn't a ray of sense in it, or meaning to it.

McClintock finished his education at Yale in 1843, and came to Hartford on a visit that same year. I have talked with men who at that time talked with him, and felt of him, and knew he was real. One needs to remember that fact and to keep fast hold of it; it is the only way to keep McClintock's book from undermining one's faith in Mc-Clintock's actuality.

As to the book. The first four pages are devoted to an inflamed eulogy of Woman—simply Woman in general, or perhaps as an Institution—wherein, among other compliments to her details, he pays a unique one to her voice. He says it "fills the breast with fond alarms, echoed by every rill." It sounds well enough, but it is not true. After the eulogy he takes up his real work and the novel begins. It begins in the woods, near the village of Sunflower Hill.

> Brightening clouds seemed to rise from the mist of the fair Chattahoochee, to spread their beauty over the thick forest, to guide the hero whose bosom beats with aspirations to conquer the enemy that would tarnish his name, and to win back the admiration of his long-tried friend.

It seems a general remark, but it is not general; the hero mentioned is the to-be hero of the book; and in this abrupt fashion, and without name or description, he is shoveled into the tale. "With aspirations to conquer the enemy that would tarnish his name" is merely a phrase flung in for the sake of the sound—let it not mislead the reader. No one is trying to tarnish this person; no one has thought of it. The rest of the sentence is also merely a phrase; the man has no friend as yet, and of course has had no chance to try him, or win back his admiration, or disturb him in any other way.

The hero climbs up over "Sawney's Mountain," and down the other side, making for an old Indian "castle"—which becomes "the red man's hut" in the next sentence; and when he gets there at last, he "surveys with wonder and astonishment" the invisible structure, "which time had buried in the dust, and thought to himself his happiness was not yet complete." One doesn't know why it wasn't, nor how near it came to being complete, nor what was still wanting to round it up and make it so. Maybe it was the Indian; but the book does not say. At this point we have an episode:

Beside the shore of the brook sat a young man, about eighteen or twenty, who seemed to be reading some favorite book, and who had a remarkably noble countenance—eyes which betrayed more than a common mind. This of course made the youth a welcome guest, and gained him friends in whatever condition of life he might be placed. The traveler observed that he was a well-built figure which showed strength and grace in every movement. He accordingly addressed him in quite a gentlemanly manner, and inquired of him the way to the village. After he had received the desired information, and was about taking his leave, the youth said, "Are you not Major Elfonzo, the great musician[1]—the champion of a noble cause—the modern Achilles, who gained so many victories in the Florida War?" "I bear that name," said the Major, "and those titles, trusting at the same time that the ministers of grace will carry me triumphantly through all my laudable undertakings, and if," continued the Major, "you, sir, are the patronizer of noble deeds, I should like to make you my confidant and learn your address." The youth looked somewhat amazed, bowed low, mused for a moment, and began: "My name is Roswell. I have been recently admitted to the bar, and can only give a faint outline of my future success in that honorable profession; but I trust, sir, like the Eagle, I shall look down from lofty rocks upon the dwellings of man, and shall ever be ready to give you any assistance in my official capacity, and whatever this muscular arm of mine can do, whenever it shall be called from its buried *greatness*." The Major grasped him by the hand, and exclaimed: "O! thou exalted spirit of inspiration—thou flame of burning prosperity, may the Heaven-directed blaze be the glare of thy soul, and battle down every rampart that seems to impede your progress!"

There is a strange sort of originality about McClintock; he imitates other people's styles, but nobody can imitate his, not even an idiot. Other people can be windy, but McClintock blows a gale; other people can blubber sentiment, but McClintock spews it; other people can mishandle metaphors, but only McClintock knows how to make a business of it. McClintock is always McClintock, he is always consistent, his style is always his own style. He does not make the mistake of being relevant on one page and irrelevant on another; he is irrelevant on all of them. He does not make the mistake of being lucid in one place and obscure in another; he is obscure all the time. He does not make the mistake of slipping in a name here and there that is out of character with his work; he always uses names that exactly and fantastically fit his lunatics. In the matter of undeviating consistency he stands alone in authorship. It is this that makes his style unique, and entitles it to a name of its own—McClintockian. It is this that

[1] Further on it will be seen that he is a country expert on the fiddle, and has a three-township fame.

protects it from being mistaken for anybody else's. Uncredited quotations from other writers often leave a reader in doubt as to their authorship, but McClintock is safe from that accident; an uncredited quotation from him would always be recognizable. When a boy nineteen years old, who had just been admitted to the bar, says, "I trust, sir, like the Eagle, I shall look down from lofty rocks upon the dwellings of man," we know who is speaking through that boy; we should recognize that note anywhere. There be myriads of instruments in this world's literary orchestra, and a multitudinous confusion of sounds that they make, wherein fiddles are drowned, and guitars smothered, and one sort of drum mistaken for another sort; but whensoever the brazen note of the McClintockian trombone breaks through that fog of music, that note is recognizable, and about it there can be no blur of doubt.

The novel now arrives at the point where the Major goes home to see his father. When McClintock wrote this interview he probably believed it was pathetic.

The road which led to the town presented many attractions. Elfonzo had bid farewell to the youth of deep feeling, and was now wending his way to the dreaming spot of his fondness. The south winds whistled through the woods, as the waters dashed against the banks, as rapid fire in the pent furnace roars. This brought him to remember while alone, that he quietly left behind the hospitality of a father's house, and gladly entered the world, with higher hopes than are often realized. But as he journeyed onward, he was mindful of the advice of his father, who had often looked sadly on the ground, when tears of cruelly deceived hope moistened his eyes. Elfonzo had been somewhat of a dutiful son; yet fond of the amusements of life—had been in distant lands—had enjoyed the pleasure of the world, and had frequently returned to the scenes of his boyhood, almost destitute of many of the comforts of life. In this condition, he would frequently say to his father, "Have I offended you, that you look upon me as a stranger, and frown upon me with stinging looks? Will you not favor me with the sound of your voice? If I have trampled upon your veneration, or have spread a humid veil of darkness around your expectations, send me back into the world, where no heart beats for me—where the foot of man has never yet trod; but give me at least one kind word —allow me to come into the presence sometimes of thy winter-worn locks." "Forbid it, Heaven, that I should be angry with thee," answered the father, "my son, and yet I send thee back to the children of the world—to the cold charity of the combat, and to a land of victory. I read another destiny in thy countenance—I learn thy inclinations from the flame that has already kindled in my soul a strange sensation. It will seek thee, my dear *Elfonzo*, it will find thee—thou canst not escape that lighted torch, which shall blot out from the remembrance of men a long train of prophecies which they have foretold against thee. I once thought not so. Once, I was blind; but now the path of life is plain before me, and my sight is clear; yet, Elfonzo, return to thy worldly occupation—take again in thy hand that chord of sweet sounds—struggle with the civilized world and with your own heart; fly swiftly to the enchanted ground—let the night-*Owl* send forth its screams from the stubborn oak—let the sea sport upon the beach, and the stars sing together; but learn of these, Elfonzo, thy doom, and thy hiding-place. Our most innocent as well as our most lawful *desires* must often be denied us, that we may learn to sacrifice them to a Higher will."

Remembering such admonitions with gratitude, Elfonzo was immediately urged by the recollection of his father's family to keep moving.

McClintock has a fine gift in the matter of surprises; but as a rule they are not pleasant ones, they jar upon the feelings. His closing sentence in the last quotation is of that sort. It brings one down out of the tinted clouds in too sudden and collapsed a fashion. It incenses one against the author for a moment. It makes the reader want to take him by his winter-worn locks, and trample on his veneration, and deliver him over to the cold charity of combat, and blot him out with his own lighted torch. But the feeling does not last. The master takes again in his hand that concord of sweet sounds of his, and one is reconciled, pacified.

His steps became quicker and quicker—he hastened through the *piny* woods, dark as the forest was, and with joy he very soon reached the little village of repose, in whose bosom rested the boldest chivalry. His close attention to every important object—his modest questions about whatever was new to him—his reverence for wise old age, and his ardent desire to learn many of the fine arts, soon brought him into respectable notice.

One mild winter day, as he walked along the streets toward the Academy, which stood upon a small eminence, surrounded by native growth—some venerable in its appearance, others young and prosperous—all seemed inviting, and seemed to be the very place for learning as well as for genius to spend its research beneath its spreading shads. He entered its classic walls in the usual mode of southern manners.

The artfulness of this man! None knows so well as he how to pique the curiosity of the reader—and how to disappoint it. He raises the hope, here, that he is going to tell all about how one enters a classic wall in the usual mode of Southern manners; but does he? No; he smiles in his sleeve, and turns aside to other matters.

The principal of the Institution begged him to be seated and listen to the recitations that were going on. He accordingly obeyed the request, and seemed to be much pleased. After the school was dismissed, and the young hearts regained their freedom, with the songs of the evening, laughing at the anticipated pleasures of a happy home, while others tittered at the actions of the past day, he addressed the teacher in a tone that indicated a resolution—with an undaunted mind. He said he had determined to become a student, if he could meet with his approbation. "Sir," said he, "I have spent much time in the world. I have traveled among the uncivilized inhabitants of America. I have met with friends, and combated with foes; but none of these gratify my ambition, or decide what is to be my destiny. I see the learned world have an influence with the voice of the people themselves. The despoilers of the remotest kingdoms of the earth refer their differences to this class of persons. This the illiterate and inexperienced little dream of; and now if you will receive me as I am, with these deficiencies—with all my misguided opinions, I will give you my honor, sir, that I will never disgrace the Institution, or those who have placed you in this honorable station." The instructor, who had met with many disappointments, knew how to feel for a stranger who had been thus turned upon the charities of an unfeeling community. He looked at him earnestly, and said: "Be of good cheer—look forward, sir, to the high destination you may attain. Remember, the more elevated the mark at which you aim, the more sure, the more glorious, the more magnificent the prize." From wonder to wonder, his encouragement led the impatient listener. A strange nature bloomed before him—giant streams promised him success—gardens of hidden treasures opened to his view. All this, so vividly described, seemed to gain a new witchery from his glowing fancy.

It seems to me that this situation is new in romance. I feel sure it has not been attempted before. Military celebrities have been disguised and set at lowly occupations for dramatic effect, but I think McClintock is the first to send one of them to school. Thus, in this book, you pass from wonder to wonder, through gardens of hidden treasure, where giant streams bloom before you, and behind you, and all around, and you feel as happy, and groggy, and satisfied with your quart of mixed metaphor aboard as you would if it had been mixed in a sample-room and delivered from a jug.

Now we come upon some more McClintockian surprises—a sweetheart who is sprung upon us without any preparation, along with a name for her which is even a little more of a surprise than she herself is.

In 1842 he entered the class, and made rapid progress in the English and Latin departments. Indeed, he continued advancing with such rapidity that he was like to become the first in his class, and made such unexpected progress, and was so studious, that he had almost forgotten the pictured saint of his affections. The fresh wreaths of the pine and cypress had waited anxiously to drop once more the dews of Heaven upon the heads of those who had so often poured forth the tender emotions of their souls under its boughs. He was aware of the pleasure that he had seen there. So one evening, as he was returning from his reading, he concluded he would pay a visit to this enchanting spot. Little did he think of witnessing a shadow of his former happiness, though no doubt he wished it might be so. He continued sauntering by the roadside, meditating on the past. The nearer he approached the spot, the more anxious he became. At that moment a tall female figure flitted across his path, with a bunch of roses in her hand; her countenance showed uncommon vivacity, with a resolute spirit; her ivory teeth already appeared as she smiled beautifully, promenading—while her ringlets of hair dangled unconsciously around her snowy neck. Nothing was wanting to complete her beauty. The tinge of the rose was in full bloom upon her cheek; the charms of sensibility and tenderness were always her associates. In Ambulinia's bosom dwelt a noble soul—one that never faded—one that never was conquered.

Ambulinia! It can hardly be matched in fiction. The full name is Ambulinia Valeer. Marriage will presently round it out and perfect it. Then it will be Mrs. Ambulinia Valeer Elfonzo. It takes the chromo.

Her heart yielded to no feeling but the love of Elfonzo, on whom she gazed with intense delight, and to whom she felt herself more closely bound, because he sought the hand of no other. Elfonzo was roused from his apparent reverie. His books no longer were his inseparable companions—his thoughts arrayed themselves to encourage him to the field of victory. He endeavored to speak to his supposed Ambulinia, but his speech appeared not in words. No, his effort was a stream of fire, that kindled his soul into a flame of admiration, and carried his senses away captive. Ambulinia had disappeared, to make him more mindful of his duty. As she walked speedily away through the piny woods, she calmly echoed: "O! Elfonzo, thou wilt now look from thy sunbeams. Thou shalt now walk in a new path—perhaps thy way leads through darkness; but fear not, the stars foretell happiness."

To McClintock that jingling jumble of fine words meant something, no doubt, or seemed to mean something; but it is useless for us to try to divine what it was. Ambulinia comes—we don't know whence nor why; she mysteriously intimates—we don't know what; and then she goes echoing away—we don't know whither; and down comes the curtain. McClintock's art is subtle; McClintock's art is deep.

Not many days afterward, as surrounded by fragrant flowers she sat one evening at twilight, to enjoy the cool breeze that whispered notes of melody along the distant groves, the little birds perched on every side, as if to watch the movements of their new visitor. The bells were tolling, when Elfonzo silently stole along by the wild wood flowers, holding in his hand his favorite instrument of music—his eye continually searching for Ambulinia, who hardly

seemed to perceive him, as she played carelessly with the songsters that
hopped from branch to branch. Nothing could be more striking than the
difference between the two. Nature seemed to have given the more tender
soul to Elfonzo, and the stronger and more courageous to Ambulinia. A deep
feeling spoke from the eyes of Elfonzo—such a feeling as can only be expressed by those who are blessed as admirers, and by those who are able to
return the same with sincerity of heart. He was a few years older than Ambulinia: she had turned a little into her seventeenth. He had almost grown up
in the Cherokee country, with the same equal proportions as one of the
natives. But little intimacy had existed between them until the year forty-one—
because the youth felt that the character of such a lovely girl was too exalted
to inspire any other feeling than that of quiet reverence. But as lovers will not
always be insulted, at all times and under all circumstances, by the frowns
and cold looks of crabbed old age, which should continually reflect dignity
upon those around, and treat the unfortunate as well as the fortunate with a
graceful mien, he continued to use diligence and perseverance. All this lighted
a spark in his heart that changed his whole character, and like the unyielding
Diety that follows the storm to check its rage in the forest, he resolves for the
first time to shake off his embarrassment and return where he had before only
worshiped.

At last we begin to get the Major's measure. We are able to put
this and that casual fact together, and build the man up before our
eyes, and look at him. And after we have got him built, we find him
worth the trouble. By the above comparison between his age and
Ambulinia's, we guess the war-worn veteran to be twenty-two; and
the other facts stand thus: he had grown up in the Cherokee country
with the same equal proportions as one of the natives—how flowing
and graceful the language, and yet how tantalizing as to meaning!—he
had been turned adrift by his father, to whom he had been "somewhat
of a dutiful son"; he wandered in distant lands; came back frequently
"to the scenes of his boyhood, almost destitute of many of the comforts of life," in order to get into the presence of his father's winter-
worn locks, and spread a humid veil of darkness around his expectations; but he was always promptly sent back to the cold charity of the
combat again; he learned to play the fiddle, and made a name for
himself in that line; he had dwelt among the wild tribes; he had
philosophized about the despoilers of the kingdoms of the earth, and
found out—the cunning creature—that they refer their differences to
the learned for settlement; he had achieved a vast fame as a military
chieftain, the Achilles of the Florida campaigns, and then had got him
a spelling-book and started to school; he had fallen in love with
Ambulinia Valeer while she was teething, but had kept it to himself

awhile, out of the reverential awe which he felt for the child; but now at last, like the unyielding Deity who follows the storm to check its rage in the forest, he resolves to shake off his embarrassment, and to return where before he had only worshiped. The Major, indeed, has made up his mind to rise up and shake his faculties together, and to see if *he* can't do that thing himself. This is not clear. But no matter about that: there stands the hero, compact and visible; and he is no mean structure, considering that his creator had never created anything before, and hadn't anything but rags and wind to build with this time. It seems to me that no one can contemplate this odd creature, this quaint and curious blatherskite, without admiring McClintock, or, at any rate, loving him and feeling grateful to him; for McClintock made him, he gave him to us; without McClintock we could not have had him, and would now be poor.

But we must come to the feast again. Here is a courtship scene, down there in the romantic glades among the raccoons, alligators, and things, that has merit, peculiar literary merit. See how Achilles woos. Dwell upon the second sentence (particularly the close of it) and the beginning of the third. Never mind the new personage, Leos, who is intruded upon us unheralded and unexplained. That is McClintock's way; it is his habit; it is a part of his genius; he cannot help it; he never interrupts the rush of his narrative to make introductions.

It could not escape Ambulinia's penetrating eye that he sought an interview with her, which she as anxiously avoided, and assumed a more distant calmness than before, seemingly to destroy all hope. After many efforts and struggles with his own person, with timid steps the Major approached the damsel, with the same caution as he would have done in a field of battle. "Lady Ambulinia," said he, trembling, "I have long desired a moment like this. I dare not let it escape. I fear the consequences; yet I hope your indulgence will at least hear my petition. Can you not anticipate what I would say, and what I am about to express? Will not you, like Minerva, who sprung from the brain of Jupiter, release me from thy winding chains or cure me—" "Say no more, Elfonzo," answered Ambulinia, with a serious look, raising her hand as if she intended to swear eternal hatred against the whole world; "another lady in my place would have perhaps answered your question in bitter coldness. I know not the little arts of my sex. I care but little for the vanity of those who would chide me, and am unwilling as well as ashamed to be guilty of anything that would lead you to think 'all is not gold that glitters'; so be not rash in your resolution. It is better to repent now, than to do it in a more solemn hour. Yes, I know what you would say. I know you have a costly gift for me—the noblest that man can make—*your heart!* You should not offer it to one so unworthy. Heaven, you know, has allowed my father's

house to be made a house of solitude, a home of silent obedience, which my
parents say is more to be admired than big names and high-sounding titles.
Notwithstanding all this, let me speak the emotions of an honest heart—
allow me to say in the fullness of my hopes that I anticipate better days. The
bird may stretch its wings toward the sun, which it can never reach; and
flowers of the field appear to ascend in the same direction, because they
cannot do otherwise; but man confides his complaints to the saints in whom
he believes; for in their abodes of light they know no more sorrow. From
your confession and indicative looks, I must be that person; if so deceive not
yourself."

Elfonzo replied, "Pardon me, my dear madam, for my frankness. I have
loved you from my earliest days—everything grand and beautiful hath borne
the image of Ambulinia; while precipices on every hand surrounded me,
your *guardian angel* stood and beckoned me away from the deep abyss. In
every trial, in every misfortune, I have met with your helping hand; yet I
never dreamed or dared to cherish thy love, till a voice impaired with age
encouraged the cause, and declared they who acquired thy favor should win
a victory. I saw how Leos worshiped thee. I felt my own unworthiness. I
began to *know jealousy*, a strong guest—indeed, in my bosom,—yet I could see
if I gained your admiration Leos was to be my rival. I was aware that he had
the influence of your parents, and the wealth of a deceased relative, which is
too often mistaken for permanent and regular tranquillity; yet I have determined by your permission to beg an interest in your prayers—to ask you to
animate my drooping spirits by your smiles and your winning looks; for if
you but speak I shall be conqueror, my enemies shall stagger like Olympus
shakes. And though earth and sea may tremble, and the charioteer of the sun
may forget his dashing steed, yet I am assured that it is only to arm me with
divine weapons which will enable me to complete my long-tried intention."

"Return to yourself, Elfonzo," said Ambulinia, pleasantly: "a dream of
of vision has disturbed your intellect; you are above the atmosphere, dwelling in the celestial regions; nothing is there that urges or hinders, nothing
that brings discord into our present litigation. I entreat you to condescend a
little, and be a man, and forget it all. When Homer describes the battle of
the gods and noble men fighting with giants and dragons, they represent
under this image our struggles with the delusions of our passions. You have
exalted me, an unhappy girl, to the skies; you have called me a saint, and
portrayed in your imagination an angel in human form. Let her remain such
to you, let her continue to be as you have supposed, and be assured that she
will consider a share in your esteem as her highest treasure. Think not that
I would allure you from the path in which your conscience leads you; for you
know I respect the conscience of others, as I would die for my own. Elfonzo,
if I am worthy of thy love, let such conversation never again pass between us.
Go, seek a nobler theme! we will seek it in the stream of time, as the sun set
in the Tigris." As she spake these words she grasped the hand of Elfonzo,

saying at the same time—"Peace and prosperity attend you, my hero; be up and doing!" Closing her remarks with this expression, she walked slowly away, leaving Elfonzo astonished and amazed. He ventured not to follow or detain her. Here he stood alone, gazing at the stars; confounded as he was, here he stood.

Yes; there he stood. There seems to be no doubt about that. Nearly half of this delirious story has now been delivered to the reader. It seems a pity to reduce the other half to a cold synopsis. Pity! it is more than a pity, it is a crime; for to synopsize McClintock is to reduce a sky-flushing conflagration to dull embers, it is to reduce barbaric splendor to ragged poverty. McClintock never wrote a line that was not precious; he never wrote one that could be spared; he never framed one from which a word could be removed without damage. Every sentence that this master has produced may be likened to a perfect set of teeth, white, uniform, beautiful. If you pull one, the charm is gone.

Still, it is now necessary to begin to pull, and to keep it up; for lack of space requires us to synopsize.

We left Elfonzo standing there amazed. At what, we do not know. Not at the girl's speech. No; we ourselves should have been amazed at it, of course, for none of us has ever heard anything resembling it; but Elfonzo was used to speeches made up of noise and vacancy, and could listen to them with undaunted mind like the "topmost topaz of an ancient tower"; he was used to making them himself; he—but let it go, it cannot be guessed out; we shall never know what it was that astonished him. He stood there awhile; then he said, "Alas! am I now Grief's disappointed son at last?" He did not stop to examine his mind, and to try to find out what he probably meant by that, because, for one reason, "a mixture of ambition and greatness of soul moved upon his young heart," and started him for the village. He resumed his bench in school, "and reasonably progressed in his education." His heart was heavy, but he went into society, and sought surcease of sorrow in its light distractions. He made himself popular with his violin, "which seemed to have a thousand chords—more symphonious than the Muses of Apollo, and more enchanting than the ghost of the Hills." This is obscure, but let it go.

During this interval Leos did some unencouraged courting, but at last, "choked by his undertaking," he desisted.

Presently "Elfonzo again wends his way to the stately walls and new-built village." He goes to the house of his beloved; she opens the door herself. To my surprise—for Ambulinia's heart had still seemed free at the time of their last interview—love beamed from the girl's eyes. One sees that Elfonzo was surprised, too; for when he caught that light, "a halloo of smothered shouts ran through every vein." A neat figure—a very neat figure, indeed! Then he kissed her. "The scene was overwhelming." They went into the parlor. The girl said it was safe, for her parents were abed, and would never know. Then we have this fine picture—flung upon the canvas with hardly an effort, as you will notice.

Advancing toward him, she gave a bright display of her rosy neck, and from her head the ambrosial locks breathed divine fragrance; her robe hung waving to his view, while she stood like a goddess confessed before him.

There is nothing of interest in the couple's interview. Now at this point the girl invites Elfonzo to a village show, where jealousy is the motive of the play, for she wants to teach him a wholesome lesson, if he is a jealous person. But this is a sham, and pretty shallow. McClintock merely wants a pretext to drag in a plagiarism of his upon a scene or two in "Othello."

The lovers went to the play. Elfonzo was one of the fiddlers. He and Ambulinia must not be seen together, lest trouble follow with the girl's malignant father; we are made to understand that clearly. So the two sit together in the orchestra, in the midst of the musicians. This does not seem to be good art. In the first place, the girl would be in the way, for orchestras are always packed closely together, and there is no room to spare for people's girls; in the next place, one cannot conceal a girl in an orchestra without everybody taking notice of it. There can be no doubt, it seems to me, that this is bad art.

Leos is present. Of course, one of the first things that catches his eye is the maddening spectacle of Ambulinia "leaning upon Elfonzo's chair." This poor girl does not seem to understand even the rudiments of concealment. But she is "in her seventeenth," as the author phrases it, and that is her justification.

Leos meditates, constructs a plan—with personal violence as a basis, of course. It was their way down there. It is a good plain plan, without any imagination in it. He will go out and stand at the front door, and when these two come out he will "arrest Ambulinia from the hands of the insolent Elfonzo," and thus make for himself a "more prosperous field of immortality than ever was decreed by Omnipotence, or ever pencil drew or artist imagined." But, dear me, while he is waiting there the couple climb out at the back window and scurry home! This is romantic enough, but there is a lack of dignity in the situation.

At this point McClintock puts in the whole of his curious play—which we skip.

Some correspondence follows now. The bitter father and the distressed lovers write the letters. Elopements are attempted. They are idiotically planned, and they fail. Then we have several pages of romantic powwow and confusion signifying nothing. Another elopement is planned; it is to take place on Sunday, when everybody is at church. But the "hero" cannot keep the secret; he tells everybody. Another author would have found another instrument when he decided to defeat this elopement; but that is not McClintock's way. He uses the person that is nearest at hand.

The evasion failed, of course. Ambulinia, in her flight, takes refuge in a neighbor's house. Her father drags her home. The villagers gather, attracted by the racket.

Elfonzo was moved at this sight. The people followed on to see what was going to become of Ambulinia, while he, with downcast looks, kept at a distance, until he saw them enter the abode of the father, thrusting her, that was the sight of his soul, out of his presence into a solitary apartment, when she exclaimed, "Elfonzo! Elfonzo! oh, Elfonzo! where art thou, with all thy heroes? haste, oh! haste, come thou to my relief. Ride on the wings of the wind! Turn thy force loose like a tempest, and roll on thy army like a whirlwind, over this mountain of trouble and confusion. Oh, friends! if any pity me, let your last efforts throng upon the green hills, and come to the relief of Ambulinia, who is guilty of nothing but innocent love." Elfonzo called out with a loud voice, "My God, can I stand this! arouse up, I beseech you, and put an end to this tyranny. Come, my brave boys," said he, "are you ready to go forth to your duty?" They stood around him. "Who," said he, "will call us to arms? Where are my thunderbolts of war? Speak ye, the first who will meet the foe! Who will go forward with me in this ocean of grievous temptation? If there is one who desires to go, let him come and shake hands upon the altar of devotion, and swear that he will be a hero; yes, a Hector in a cause like this, which calls aloud for a speedy remedy." "Mine be the deed," said a young lawyer, "and mine alone; Venus alone shall quit her station before I will forsake one jot or tittle of my promise to you; what is death to me? what is all this warlike army, if it is not to win a victory? I love the sleep of the lover and the mighty; nor would I give it over till the blood of my enemies should wreak with that of my own. But God forbid that our fame should soar on the blood of the slumberer." Mr. Valeer stands at his door with the frown of a demon upon his brow, with his dangerous weapon[1] ready to strike the first man who should enter his door. "Who will arise and go forward through

[1] It is a crowbar.

blood and carnage to the rescue of my Ambulinia?" said Elfonzo. "All,"
exclaimed the multitude; and onward they went, with their implements of
battle. Others, of a more timid nature, stood among the distant hills to see
the result of the contest.

It will hardly be believed that after all this thunder and lightning
not a drop of rain fell; but such is the fact. Elfonzo and his gang
stood up and blackguarded Mr. Valeer with vigor all night, getting
their outlay back with interest; then in the early morning the army
and its general retired from the field, leaving the victory with their
solitary adversary and his crowbar. This is the first time this has happened in romantic literature. The invention is original. Everything in
this book is original; there is nothing hackneyed about it anywhere.
Always, in other romances, when you find the author leading up to a
climax, you know what is going to happen. But in this book it is
different; the thing which seems inevitable and unavoidable never
happens; it is circumvented by the art of the author every time.

Another elopement was attempted. It failed.

We have now arrived at the end. But it is not exciting. McClintock
thinks it is; but it isn't. One day Elfonzo sent Ambulinia another note
—a note proposing elopement No. 16. This time the plan is admirable;
admirable, sagacious, ingenious, imaginative, deep—oh, everything,
and perfectly easy. One wonders why it was never thought of before.
This is the scheme. Ambulinia is to leave the breakfast-table, ostensibly
to "attend to the placing of those flowers, which should have been
done a week ago"—artificial ones, of course; the others wouldn't keep
so long—and then, instead of fixing the flowers, she is to walk out to
the grove, and go off with Elfonzo. The invention of this plan over-
strained the author, that is plain, for he straightway shows failing
powers. The details of the plan are not many or elaborate. The author
shall state them himself—this good soul, whose intentions are always
better than his English:

"You walk carelessly toward the academy grove, where you will find me
with a lightning steed, elegantly equipped to bear you off where we shall
be joined in wedlock with the first connubial rights."

Last scene of all, which the author, now much enfeebled, tries to
smarten up and make acceptable to his spectacular heart by introducing some new properties—silver bow, golden harp, olive branch—
things that can all come good in an elopement, no doubt, yet are not
to be compared to an umbrella for real handiness and reliability in an
excursion of that kind.

And away she ran to the sacred grove, surrounded with glittering pearls, that indicated her coming. Elfonzo hails her with his silver bow and his golden harp. They meet—Ambulinia's countenance brightens—Elfonzo leads up the winged steed. "Mount," said he, "ye true-hearted, ye fearless soul—the day is ours." She sprang upon the back of the young thunderbolt, a brilliant star sparkles upon her head, with one hand she grasps the reins, and with the other she holds an olive branch. "Lend thy aid, ye strong winds," they exclaimed, "ye moon, ye sun, and all ye fair host of heaven, witness the enemy conquered." "Hold," said Elfonzo, "thy dashing steed." "Ride on," said Ambulinia, "the voice of thunder is behind us." And onward they went, with such rapidity that they very soon arrived at Rural Retreat, where they dismounted, and were united with all the solemnities that usually attend such divine operations.

There is but one Homer, there is but one Shakespeare, there is but one McClintock—and his immortal book is before you. Homer could not have written this book, Shakespeare could not have written it, I could not have done it myself. There is nothing just like it in the literature of any country or of any epoch. It stands alone; it is monumental. It adds G. Ragsdale McClintock's to the sum of the republic's imperishable names.

1893

The Enemy Conquered; or,
Love Triumphant

COMPLETE

[The foregoing review of the great work of G. Ragsdale McClintock is liberally illuminated with sample extracts, but these cannot appease the appetite. Only the complete book, unabridged, can do that. Therefore it is here printed.—M. T.]

> Sweet girl, thy smiles are full of charms,
>   Thy voice is sweeter still,
> It fills the breast with fond alarms,
>   Echoed by every rill.

I begin this little work with an eulogy upon woman, who has ever been distinguished for her perseverance, her constancy, and her devoted attention to those upon whom she has been pleased to place her *affections*. Many have been the themes upon which writers and public speakers have dwelt with intense and increasing interest. Among these delightful themes stands that of woman, the balm to all our sighs and disappointments, and the most pre-eminent of all other topics. Here the poet and orator have stood and gazed with wonder and with admiration; they have dwelt upon her innocence, the ornament of all her virtues. First viewing her external charms, such as are set forth in her form and her benevolent countenance, and then passing to the deep hidden springs of loveliness and disinterested devotion. In every clime, and in every age, she has been the pride of her *nation*. Her watchfulness is untiring; she who guarded the sepulcher was the first to approach it, and the last to depart from its awful yet sublime scene. Even here, in this highly favored land, we look to her for the security of our institutions, and for our future greatness as a nation. But, strange as it may appear, woman's charms and virtues are but slightly appreciated by thousands. Those who should raise the standard of female worth, and paint her value with her virtues, in living colors, upon the banners that are fanned by the zephyrs of heaven, and hand them down to posterity as emblematical of a rich inheritance, do not properly estimate them.

Man is not sensible, at all times, of the nature and the emotions which bear that name; he does not understand, he will not comprehend; his intelligence has not expanded to that degree of glory which drinks in the vast revolution of humanity, its end, its mighty destination, and the causes which operated, and are still operating, to produce a more elevated station, and the objects which energize and enliven its consummation. This he is a stranger to; he is not aware that woman is the recipient of celestial love, and that man is dependent upon her to perfect his character; that without her, philosophically and truly speaking, the brightest of his intelligence is but the coldness of a winter moon, whose beams can produce no fruit, whose solar light is not its own, but borrowed from the great dispenser of effulgent beauty. We have no disposition in the world to flatter the fair sex, we would raise them above those dastardly principles which only exist in little souls, contracted hearts, and a distracted brain. Often does she unfold herself in all her fascinating loveliness, presenting the most captivating charms; yet we find man frequently treats such purity of purpose with indifference. Why does he do it? Why does he baffle that which is inevitably the source of his better days? Is he so much of a stranger to those excellent qualities as not to appreciate woman, as not to have respect to her dignity? Since her art and beauty first captivated man, she has been his delight and his comfort; she has shared alike in his misfortunes and in his prosperity.

Whenever the billows of adversity and the tumultuous waves of trouble beat high, her smiles subdue their fury. Should the tear of sorrow and the mournful sigh of grief interrupt the peace of his mind, her voice removes them all, and she bends from her circle to encourage him onward. When darkness would obscure his mind, and a thick cloud of gloom would bewilder its operations, her intelligent eye darts a ray of streaming light into his heart. Mighty and charming is that disinterested devotion which she is ever ready to exercise toward man, not waiting till the last moment of his danger, but seeks to relieve him in his early afflictions. It gushes forth from the expansive fullness of a tender and devoted heart, where the noblest, the purest, and the most elevated and refined feelings are matured and developed in those many kind offices which invariably make her character.

In the room of sorrow and sickness, this unequaled characteristic may always be seen, in the performance of the most charitable acts; nothing that she can do to promote the happiness of him who she claims to be her protector will be omitted; all is invigorated by the animating sunbeams which awaken the heart to songs of gaiety. Leaving this point, to notice another prominent consideration, which is generally one of great moment and of vital importance. Invariably she is firm and steady in all her pursuits and aims. There is required a combination of forces and extreme opposition to drive her from her position; she takes her stand, not to be moved by the sound of Apollo's lyre or the curved bow of pleasure.

Firm and true to what she undertakes, and that which she requires by her own aggrandizement, and regards as being within the strict rules of propriety, she will remain stable and unflinching to the last. A more genuine principle is not to be found in the most determined, resolute heart of man. For this she deserves to be held in the highest commendation, for this she deserves the purest of all other blessings, and for this she deserves the most laudable reward of all others. It is a noble characteristic and is worthy the imitation of any age. And when we look at it in one particular aspect, it is still magnified, and grows brighter and brighter the more we reflect upon its eternal duration. What will she not do, when her word as well as her affections and *love* are pledged to her lover? Everything that is dear to her on

earth, all the hospitalities of kind and loving parents, all the sincerity
and loveliness of sisters, and the benevolent devotion of brothers,
who have surrounded her with every comfort; she will forsake them all,
quit the harmony and sweet sound of the lute and the harp, and throw
herself upon the affections of some devoted admirer, in whom she
fondly hopes to find more than she has left behind, which is not often
realized by many. Truth and virtue all combined! How deserving our
admiration and love! Ah! cruel would it be in man, after she has thus
manifested such an unshaken confidence in him, and said by her determination to abandon all the endearments and blandishments of home,
to act a villainous part, and prove a traitor in the revolution of his
mission, and then turn Hector over the innocent victim whom he swore
to protect, in the presence of Heaven, recorded by the pen of an angel.

Striking as this trait may unfold itself in her character, and as pre-
eminent as it may stand among the fair display of her other qualities,
yet there is another, which struggles into existence, and adds an additional luster to what she already possesses. I mean that disposition
in woman which enables her, in sorrow, in grief, and in distress, to bear
all with enduring patience. This she has done, and can and will do,
amid the din of war and clash of arms. Scenes and occurrences which,
to every appearance, are calculated to rend the heart with the pro-
foundest emotions of trouble, do not fetter that exalted principle im-
bued in her very nature. It is true, her tender and feeling heart may
often be moved (as she is thus constituted), but still she is not conquered, she has not given up to the harlequin of disappointments,
her energies have not become clouded in the last moment of misfortune, but she is continually invigorated by the archetype of her
affections. She may bury her face in her hands, and let the tear of
anguish roll, she may promenade the delightful walks of some garden,
decorated with all the flowers of nature, or she may steal out along
some gently rippling stream, and there, as the silver waters unin-
terruptedly move forward, shed her silent tears; they mingle with the
waves, and take a last farewell of their agitated home, to seek a
peaceful dwelling among the rolling floods; yet there is a voice rushing
from her breast, that proclaims *victory* along the whole line and battle-
ment of her affections. That voice is the voice of patience and resignation; that voice is one that bears everything calmly and dispassionately,
amid the most distressing scenes; when the fates are arrayed against
her peace, and apparently plotting for her destruction, still she is
resigned.

Woman's affections are deep, consequently her troubles may be made to sink deep. Although you may not be able to mark the traces of her grief and the furrowings of her anguish upon her winning countenance, yet be assured they are nevertheless preying upon her inward person, sapping the very foundation of that heart which alone was made for the weal and not the woe of man. The deep recesses of the soul are fields for their operation. But they are not destined simply to take the regions of the heart for their dominion, they are not satisfied merely with interrupting her better feelings; but after a while you may see the blooming cheek beginning to droop and fade, her intelligent eye no longer sparkles with the starry light of heaven, her vibrating pause long since changed its regular motion, and her palpitating bosom beats once more for the midday of her glory. Anxiety and care ultimately throw her into the arms of the haggard and grim monster death. But, oh, how patient, under every pining influence! Let us view the matter in bolder colors; see her when the dearest object of her affections recklessly seeks every bacchanalian pleasure, contents himself with the last rubbish of creation. With what solicitude she awaits his return! Sleep fails to perform its office—she weeps while the nocturnal shades of the night triumph in the stillness. Bending over some favorite book, whilst the author throws before her mind the most beautiful imagery, she startles at every sound. The midnight silence is broken by the solemn announcement of the return of another morning. He is still absent; she listens for that voice which has so often been greeted by the melodies of her own; but, alas! stern silence is all that she receives for her vigilance.

Mark her unwearied watchfulness, as the night passes away. At last, brutalized by the accursed thing, he staggers along with rage, and, shivering with cold, he makes his appearance. Not a murmur is heard from her lips. On the contrary, she meets him with a smile— she caresses him with her tender arms, with all the gentleness and softness of her sex. Here, then, is seen her disposition, beautifully arrayed. Woman, thou art more to be admired than the spicy gales of Arabia, and more sought for than the gold of Golconda. We believe that Woman should associate freely with man, and we believe that it is for the preservation of her rights. She should become acquainted with the metaphysical designs of those who condescend to sing the siren song of flattery. This, we think, should be according to the unwritten law of decorum, which is stamped upon every innocent heart. The precepts of prudery are often steeped in the guilt of contamination, which blasts the expectations of better moments. Truth, and beautiful dreams—loveliness, and delicacy of character, with cherished

affections of the ideal woman—gentle hopes and aspirations, are enough
to uphold her in the storms of darkness, without the transferred color-
ings of a stained sufferer. How often have we seen it in our public
prints, that woman occupies a false station in the world! and some
have gone so far as to say it was an unnatural one. So long has she
been regarded a weak creature, by the rabble and illiterate—they
have looked upon her as an insufficient actress on the great stage of
human life—a mere puppet, to fill up the drama of human existence—
a thoughtless, inactive being—that she has too often come to the same
conclusion herself, and has sometimes forgotten her high destination,
in the meridian of her glory. We have but little sympathy or patience
for those who treat her as a mere Rosy Melindi—who are always
fishing for pretty compliments—who are satisfied by the gossamer of
Romance, and who can be allured by the verbosity of high-flown
words, rich in language, but poor and barren in sentiment. Beset, as
she has been, by the intellectual vulgar, the selfish, the designing, the
cunning, the hidden, and the artful—no wonder she has sometimes
folded her wings in despair, and forgotten her *heavenly* mission in
the delirium of imagination; no wonder she searches out some wild
desert, to find a peaceful home. But this cannot always continue. A
new era is moving gently onward, old things are rapidly passing away;
old superstitions, old prejudices, and old notions are now bidding farewell to their old associates and companions, and giving way to one
whose wings are plumed with the light of heaven and tinged by the
dews of the morning. There is a remnant of blessedness that clings to
her in spite of all evil influence, there is enough of the Divine Master
left to accomplish the noblest work ever achieved under the canopy
of the vaulted skies; and that time is fast approaching, when the
picture of the true woman will shine from its frame of glory, to
captivate, to win back, to restore, and to call into being once more,
the object of her mission.

> Star of the brave! thy glory shed,
> O'er all the earth, thy army led—
> Bold meteor of immortal birth!
> Why come from Heaven to dwell on Earth?

Mighty and glorious are the days of youth; happy the moments of
the *lover*, mingled with smiles and tears of his devoted, and long to
be remembered are the achievements which he gains with a palpitating heart and a trembling hand. A bright and lovely dawn, the harbin-
ger of a fair and prosperous day, had arisen over the beautiful little

village of Cumming, which is surrounded by the most romantic scenery in the Cherokee country. Brightening clouds seemed to rise from the mist of the fair Chattahoochee, to spread their beauty over the thick forest, to guide the hero whose bosom beats with aspirations to conquer the enemy that would tarnish his name, and to win back the admiration of his long-tried friend. He endeavored to make his way through Sawney's Mountain where many meet to catch the gales that are continually blowing for the refreshment of the stranger and the traveler. Surrounded as he was by hills on every side, naked rocks dared the efforts of his energies. Soon the sky became overcast, the sun buried itself in the clouds, and the fair day gave place to gloomy twilight, which lay heavily on the Indian Plains. He remembered an old Indian Castle, that once stood at the foot of the mountain. He thought if he could make his way to this, he would rest contented for a short time. The mountain air breathed fragrance—a rosy tinge rested on the glassy waters that murmured at its base. His resolution soon brought him to the remains of the red man's hut: he surveyed with wonder and astonishment the decayed building, which time had buried in the dust, and thought to himself, his happiness was not yet complete. Beside the shore of the brook sat a young man, about eighteen or twenty, who seemed to be reading some favorite book, and who had a remarkably noble countenance—eyes which betrayed more and a common mind. This of course made the youth a welcome guest, and gained him friends in whatever condition of life he might be placed. The traveler observed that he was a well-built figure, which showed strength and grace in every movement. He accordingly addressed him in quite a gentlemanly manner, and inquired of him the way to the village. After he had received the desired information, and was about taking his leave, the youth said, "Are you not Major Elfonzo, the great musician—the champion of a noble cause—the modern Achilles, who gained so many victories in the Florida War?" "I bear that name," said the Major, "and those titles, trusting at the same time that the ministers of grace will carry me triumphantly through all my laudable undertakings, and if," continued the Major, "you, sir, are the patronizer of noble deeds, I should like to make you my confidant and learn your address." The youth looked somewhat amazed, bowed low, mused for a moment, and began: "My name is Roswell. I have been recently admitted to the bar, and can only give a faint outline of my future success in that honorable profession; but I trust, sir, like the Eagle, I shall look down from lofty rocks upon the dwellings of man, and shall ever be ready to give you any assistance in my official capacity,

and whatever this muscular arm of mine can do, whenever it shall be
called from its buried *greatness.*" The Major grasped him by the hand,
and exclaimed: "O! thou exalted spirit of inspiration—thou flame of
burning prosperity, may the Heaven-directed blaze be the glare of
thy soul, and battle down every rampart that seems to impede your
progress!"

The road which led to the town presented many attractions. Elfonzo
had bid farewell to the youth of deep feeling, and was now wending
his way to the dreaming spot of his fondness. The south winds whistled
through the woods, as the waters dashed against the banks, as rapid
fire in the pent furnace roars. This brought him to remember while
alone, that he quietly left behind the hospitality of a father's house,
and gladly entered the world, with higher hopes than are often realized. But as he journeyed onward, he was mindful of the advice of
his father, who had often looked sadly on the ground when tears of
cruelly deceived hope moistened his eye. Elfonzo had been somewhat
of a dutiful son; yet fond of the amusements of life—had been in
distant lands—had enjoyed the pleasure of the world and had frequently returned to the scenes of his boyhood, almost destitute of
many of the comforts of life. In this condition, he would frequently
say to his father, "Have I offended you, that you look upon me as a
stranger, and frown upon me with stinging looks? Will you not favor
me with the sound of your voice? If I have trampled upon your
veneration, or have spread a humid veil of darkness around your
expectations, send me back into the world where no heart beats for
me—where the foot of man has never yet trod; but give me at least
one kind word—allow me to come into the presence sometimes of thy
winter-worn locks." "Forbid it, Heaven, that I should be angry with
thee," answered the father, "my son, and yet I send thee back to the
children of the world—to the cold charity of the combat, and to a land
of victory. I read another destiny in thy countenance—I learn thy inclinations from the flame that has already kindled in my soul a strange
sensation. It will seek thee, my dear *Elfonzo,* it will find thee—thou
canst not escape that lighted torch, which shall blot out from the remembrance of men a long train of prophecies which they have foretold against thee. I once thought not so. Once, I was blind; but now
the path of life is plain before me, and my sight is clear; yet Elfonzo,
return to thy worldly occupation—take again in thy hand that chord of
sweet sounds—struggle with the civilized world, and with your own
heart; fly swiftly to the enchanted ground—let the night-*Owl* send
forth its screams from the stubborn oak—let the sea sport upon the

beach, and the stars sing together; but learn of these, Elfonzo, thy doom, and thy hiding-place. Our most innocent as well as our most lawful *desires* must often be denied us, that we may learn to sacrifice them to a Higher will."

Remembering such admonitions with gratitude, Elfonzo was immediately urged by the recollection of his father's family to keep moving. His steps became quicker and quicker—he hastened through the *piny* woods, dark as the forest was, and with joy he very soon reached the little village of repose, in whose bosom rested the boldest chivalry. His close attention to every important object—his modest questions about whatever was new to him—his reverence for wise old age, and his ardent desire to learn many of the fine arts, soon brought him into respectable notice.

One mild winter day as he walked along the streets toward the Academy, which stood upon a small eminence, surrounded by native growth—some venerable in its appearance, others young and prosperous—all seemed inviting, and seemed to be the very place for learning as well as for genius to spend its research beneath its spreading shades. He entered its classic walls in the usual mode of southern manners. The principal of the Institution begged him to be seated and listen to the recitations that were going on. He accordingly obeyed the request, and seemed to be much pleased. After the school was dismissed, and the young hearts regained their freedom, with the songs of the evening, laughing at the anticipated pleasures of a happy home, while others tittered at the actions of the past day, he addressed the teacher in a tone that indicated a resolution—with an undaunted mind. He said he had determined to become a student, if he could meet with his approbation. "Sir," said he, "I have spent much time in the world. I have traveled among the uncivilized inhabitants of America. I have met with friends, and combated with foes; but none of these gratify my ambition, or decide what is to be my destiny. I see the learned world have an influence with the voice of the people themselves. The despoilers of the remotest kingdoms of the earth refer their differences to this class of persons. This the illiterate and inexperienced little dream of; and now if you will receive me as I am, with these deficiencies—with all my misguided opinions, I will give you my honor, sir, that I will never disgrace the Institution, or those who have placed you in this honorable station." The instructor, who had met with many disappointments, knew how to feel for a stranger who had been thus turned upon the charities of an unfeeling community. He looked at him earnestly, and said: "Be of good cheer—look forward,

sir, to the high destination you may attain. Remember, the more elevated the mark at which you aim, the more sure, the more glorious,
the more magnificent the prize." From wonder to wonder, his encouragement led the impatient listener. A strange nature bloomed before him—giant streams promised him success—gardens of hidden treasures opened to his view. All this, so vividly described, seemed to gain
a new witchery from his glowing fancy.

In 1842 he entered the class, and made rapid progress in the English and Latin departments. Indeed, he continued advancing with
such rapidity that he was like to become the first in his class, and
made such unexpected progress, and was so studious, that he had
almost forgotten the pictured saint of his affections. The fresh wreaths
of the pine and cypress had waited anxiously to drop once more the
dews of Heaven upon the heads of those who had so often poured
forth the tender emotions of their souls under its boughs. He was aware
of the pleasure that he had seen there. So one evening, as he was returning from his reading, he concluded he would pay a visit to this
enchanting spot. Little did he think of witnessing a shadow of his
former happiness, though no doubt he wished it might be so. He
continued sauntering by the roadside, meditating on the past. The
nearer he approached the spot, the more anxious he became. At that
moment a tall female figure flitted across his path, with a bunch of
roses in her hand; her countenance showed uncommon vivacity, with
a resolute spirit; her ivory teeth already appeared as she smiled beautifully, promenading—while her ringlets of hair dangled unconsciously
around her snowy neck. Nothing was wanting to complete her beauty.
The tinge of the rose was in full bloom upon her cheek; the charms
of sensibility and tenderness were always her associates. In Ambulinia's
bosom dwelt a noble soul—one that never faded—one that never was
conquered. Her heart yielded to no feeling but the love of Elfonzo,
on whom she gazed with intense delight, and to whom she felt herself
more closely bound, because he sought the hand of no other. Elfonzo
was roused from his apparent reverie. His books no longer were his
inseparable companions—his thoughts arrayed themselves to encourage
him to the field of victory. He endeavored to speak to his supposed
Ambulinia, but his speech appeared not in words. No, his effort was
a stream of fire, that kindled his soul into a flame of admiration, and
carried his senses away captive. Ambulinia had disappeared, to make
him more mindful of his duty. As she walked speedily away through
the piny woods she calmly echoed: "O! Elfonzo, thou wilt now look
from thy sunbeams. Thou shalt now walk in a new path—perhaps thy

way leads through darkness; but fear not, the stars foretell happiness."

Not many days afterward, as surrounded by fragrant flowers she sat one evening at twilight, to enjoy the cool breeze that whispered notes of melody along the distant groves, the little birds perched on every side, as if to watch the movements of their new visitor. The bells were tolling when Elfonzo silently stole along by the wild wood flowers, holding in his hand his favorite instrument of music—his eye continually searching for Ambulinia, who hardly seemed to perceive him, as she played carelessly with the songsters that hopped from branch to branch. Nothing could be more striking than the difference between the two. Nature seemed to have given the more tender soul to Elfonzo, and the stronger and more courageous to Ambulinia. A deep feeling spoke from the eyes of Elfonzo—such a feeling as can only be expressed by those who are blessed as admirers, and by those who are able to return the same with sincerity of heart. He was a few years older than Ambulinia: she had turned a little into her seventeenth. He had almost grown up in the Cherokee country, with the same equal proportions as one of the natives. But little intimacy had existed between them until the year forty-one—because the youth felt that the character of such a lovely girl was too exalted to inspire any other feeling than that of quiet reverence. But as lovers will not always be insulted, at all times and under all circumstances, by the frowns and cold looks of crabbed old age, which should continually reflect dignity upon those around, and treat the unfortunate as well as the fortunate with a graceful mien, he continued to use diligence and perseverance. All this lighted a spark in his heart that changed his whole character, and like the unyielding Deity that follows the storm to check its rage in the forest, he resolves for the first time to shake off his embarrassment and return where he had before only worshiped.

It could not escape Ambulinia's penetrating eye that he sought an interview with her, which she as anxiously avoided, and assumed a more distant calmness than before, seemingly to destroy all hope. After many efforts and struggles with his own person, with timid steps the Major approached the damsel, with the same caution as he would have done in a field of battle. "Lady Ambulinia," said he, trembling, "I have long desired a moment like this. I dare not let it escape. I fear the consequences; yet I hope your indulgence will at least hear my petition. Can you not anticipate what I would say, and what I am about to express? Will not you, like Minerva, who sprung from the brain of Jupiter, release me from thy winding chains or cure me—" "Say no more, Elfonzo," answered Ambulinia, with a serious look, raising her hand as if she intended to swear eternal hatred against the whole world; "another lady in my place would have perhaps answered your question in bitter coldness. I know not the little arts of my sex. I care but little for the vanity of those who would chide me, and am un- willing as well as ashamed to be guilty of anything that would lead you to think 'all is not gold that glitters'; so be not rash in your resolu- tion. It is better to repent now than to do it in a more solemn hour. Yes, I know what you would say. I know you have a costly gift for me— the noblest that man can make—*your heart!* you should not offer it to one so unworthy. Heaven, you know, has allowed my father's house to be made a house of solitude, a home of silent obedience, which my parents say is more to be admired than big names and high-sounding titles. Notwithstanding all this, let me speak the emotions of an honest heart; allow me to say in the fullness of my hopes that I anticipate better days. The bird may stretch its wings toward the sun, which it can never reach; and flowers of the field appear to ascend in the same direction, because they cannot do otherwise; but man confides his complaints to the saints in whom he believes; for in their abodes of light they know no more sorrow. From your confession and indicative looks, I must be that person; if so, deceive not yourself."

Elfonzo replied, "Pardon me, my dear madam, for my frankness. I have loved you from my earliest days; everything grand and beautiful hath borne the image of Ambulinia; while precipices on every hand surrounded me, your *guardian angel* stood and beckoned me away from the deep abyss. In every trial, in every misfortune, I have met with your helping hand; yet I never dreamed or dared to cherish thy love till a voice impaired with age encouraged the cause, and declared they who acquired thy favor should win a victory. I saw how Leos worshiped thee. I felt my own unworthiness. I began to *know jealousy* —a strong guest, indeed, in my bosom—yet I could see if I gained your admiration Leos was to be my rival. I was aware that he had the influence of your parents, and the wealth of a deceased relative, which is too often mistaken for permanent and regular tranquillity; yet I have determined by your permission to beg an interest in your prayers —to ask you to animate my drooping spirits by your smiles and your winning looks; for if you but speak I shall be conqueror, my enemies shall stagger like Olympus shakes. And though earth and sea may tremble, and the charioteer of the sun may forget his dashing steed, yet I am assured that it is only to arm me with divine weapons which will enable me to complete my long-tried intention."

"Return to your self, Elfonzo," said Ambulinia, pleasantly; "a dream of vision has disturbed your intellect; you are above the atmosphere, dwelling in the celestial regions; nothing is there that urges or hinders, nothing that brings discord into our present litigation. I entreat you to condescend a little, and be a man, and forget it all. When Homer describes the battle of the gods and noble men fighting with giants and dragons, they represent under this image our struggles with the delusions of our passions. You have exalted me, an unhappy girl, to the skies; you have called me a saint, and portrayed in your imagination an angel in human form. Let her remain such to you, let her continue to be as you have supposed, and be assured that she will consider a share in your esteem as her highest treasure. Think not that I would allure you from the path in which your conscience leads you; for you know I respect the conscience of others, as I would die for my own. Elfonzo, if I am worthy of thy love, let such conversation never again pass between us. Go, seek a nobler theme! we will seek it in the stream of time, as the sun set in the Tigris." As she spake these words she grasped the hand of Elfonzo, saying at the same time, "Peace and prosperity attend you, my hero: be up and doing!" Closing her remarks with this expression, she walked slowly away, leaving Elfonzo astonished and amazed. He ventured not to follow or detain her. Here he stood alone, gazing at the stars; confounded as he was, here he stood. The rippling stream rolled on at his feet. Twilight had already begun to draw her sable mantle over the earth, and now and then the fiery smoke would ascend from the little town which lay spread out before him. The citizens seemed to be full of life and good-humor; but poor Elfonzo saw not a brilliant scene. No; his future life stood before him, stripped of the hopes that once adorned all his sanguine desires. "Alas!" said he, "am I now Grief's disappointed son at last." Ambulinia's image rose before his fancy. A mixture of ambition and greatness of soul moved upon his young heart, and encouraged him to bear all his crosses with the patience of a Job, notwithstanding he had to encounter with so many obstacles. He still endeavored to prosecute his studies, and reasonably progressed in his education. Still, he was not content; there was something yet to be done before his happiness was complete. He would visit his friends and acquaintances. They would invite him to social parties, insisting that he should partake of the amusements that were going on. This he enjoyed tolerably well. The ladies and gentlemen were generally well pleased with the Major; as he delighted all with his violin, which seemed to have a thousand chords—more symphonious than the Muses of Apollo and more enchanting than the ghosts of the Hills. He passed some days in the country. During that time Leos had made many calls upon Ambulinia, who was generally received with a great deal of courtesy by the family. They thought him to be a young man worthy of attention, though he had but little in his soul to attract the attention or even win the affections of her whose graceful manners had almost made him a slave to every bewitching look that fell from her eyes. Leos made several attempts to tell her of his fair prospects—how much he loved her, and how much it would add to his bliss if he could but think she would be willing to share these blessings with him; but, choked by his undertaking, he made himself more like an inactive drone than he did like one who bowed at beauty's shrine.

Elfonzo again wends his way to the stately walls and new-built village. He now determines to see the end of the prophecy which had been foretold to him. The clouds burst from his sight; he believes if he can but see his Ambulinia, he can open to her view the bloody altars that have been misrepresented to stigmatize his name. He knows that her breast is transfixed with the sword of reason, and ready at all times to detect the hidden villainy of her enemies. He resolves to see her in her own home, with the consoling theme: "'I can but perish if I go.' Let the consequences be what they may," said he, "if I die, it shall be contending and struggling for my own rights."

Night had almost overtaken him when he arrived in town. Colonel Elder, a noble-hearted, high-minded, and independent man, met him at his door as usual, and seized him by the hand. "Well, Elfonzo," said the Colonel, "how does the world use you in your efforts?" "I have no objection to the world," said Elfonzo, "but the people are rather singular in some of their opinions." "Aye, well," said the Colonel, "you must remember that creation is made up of many mysteries; just take things by the right handle; be always sure you know which is the smooth side before you attempt your polish; be reconciled to your fate, be it what it may; and never find fault with your condition, unless your complaining will benefit it. Perseverance is a principle that should be commendable in those who have judgment to govern it. I should never have been so successful in my hunting excursions had I waited till the deer, by some magic dream, had been drawn to the muzzle of the gun before I made an attempt to fire at the game that dared my boldness in the wild forest. The great mystery in hunting seems to be—a good marksman, a resolute mind, a fixed determination, and my word for it, you will never return home without sounding your horn with the breath of a new victory. And so with every other undertaking. Be confident that your ammunition is of the right kind—always pull your trigger with a steady hand, and so soon as you perceive a calm, touch her off, and the spoils are yours."

This filled him with redoubled vigor, and he set out with a stronger anxiety than ever to the home of Ambulinia. A few short steps soon brought him to the door, half out of breath. He rapped gently. Ambulinia, who sat in the parlor alone, suspecting Elfonzo was near, ventured to the door, opened it, and beheld the hero, who stood in an humble attitude, bowed gracefully, and as they caught each other's looks the light of peace beamed from the eyes of Ambulinia. Elfonzo caught the expression; a halloo of smothered shouts ran through every vein, and for the first time he dared to impress a kiss upon her cheek. The scene was overwhelming; had the temptation been less animating, he would not have ventured to have acted so contrary to the desired wish of his Ambulinia; but who could have withstood the irresistible temptation! What society condemns the practice but a cold, heartless, uncivilized people that know nothing of the warm attachments of refined society? Here the dead was raised to his long-cherished hopes, and the lost was found. Here all doubt and danger were buried in the vortex of oblivion; sectional differences no longer disunited their opinions; like the freed bird from the cage, sportive claps its rustling wings, wheels about to heaven in a joyful strain, and raises its notes to the upper sky. Ambulinia insisted upon Elfonzo to be seated, and give her a history of his unnecessary absence; assuring him the family had retired, consequently they would ever remain ignorant of his visit. Advancing toward him, she gave a bright display of her rosy neck, and from her head the ambrosial locks breathed divine fragrance; her robe hung waving to his view, while she stood like a goddess confessed before him.

"It does seem to me, my dear sir," said Ambulinia, "that you have been gone an age. Oh, the restless hours I have spent since I last saw you, in yon beautiful grove. There is where I trifled with your feelings for the express purpose of trying your attachment for me. I now find you are devoted; but ah! I trust you live not unguarded by the powers of Heaven. Though oft did I refuse to join my hand with thine, and as oft did I cruelly mock thy entreaties with borrowed shapes: yes, I feared to answer thee by terms, in words sincere and undissembled. O! could I pursue, and you had leisure to hear the annals of my woes, the evening star would shut Heaven's gates upon the impending day before my tale would be finished, and this night would find me soliciting your forgiveness."

"Dismiss thy fears and thy doubts," replied Elfonzo.

"Look, O! look: that angelic look of thine—bathe not thy visage in tears; banish those floods that are gathering; let my confession and my presence bring thee some relief." "Then, indeed, I will be cheerful," said Ambulinia, "and I think if we will go to the exhibition this evening, we certainly will see something worthy of our attention. One of the most tragical scenes is to be acted that has ever been witnessed, and one that every jealous-hearted person should learn a lesson from. It cannot fail to have a good effect, as it will be performed by those who are young and vigorous, and learned as well as enticing. You are aware, Major Elfonzo, who are to appear on the stage, and what the characters are to represent." "I am acquainted with the circumstances," replied Elfonzo, "and as I am to be one of the musicians upon that interesting occasion, I should be much gratified if you would favor me with your company during the hours of the exercises."

"What strange notions are in your mind?" inquired Ambulinia. "Now I know you have something in view, and I desire you to tell me why it is that you are so anxious that I should continue with you while the exercises are going on; though if you think I can add to your happiness and predilections, I have no particular objection to acquiesce in your request. Oh, I think I foresee, now, what you anticipate." "And will you have the goodness to tell me what you think it to be?" inquired Elfonzo. "By all means," answered Ambulinia; "a rival, sir, you would fancy in your own mind; but let me say to you, fear not! fear not! I will be one of the last persons to disgrace my sex by thus encouraging every one who may feel disposed to visit me, who may honor me with their graceful bows and their choicest compliments. It is true that young men too often mistake civil politeness for the finer emotions of the heart, which is tantamount to courtship; but, ah! how often are they deceived, when they come to test the weight of sunbeams with those on whose strength hangs the future happiness of an untried life."

The people were now rushing to the Academy with impatient anxiety; the band of music was closely followed by the students; then the parents and guardians; nothing interrupted the glow of spirits which ran through every bosom, tinged with the songs of a Virgil and the tide of a Homer. Elfonzo and Ambulinia soon repaired to the scene, and fortunately for them both the house was so crowded that they took their seats together in the music department, which was not in view of the auditory. This fortuitous circumstance added more to the bliss of the Major than a thousand such exhibitions would have done. He forgot that he was man; music had lost its charms for him; whenever he attempted to carry his part, the string of the instrument would

break, the bow became stubborn, and refused to obey the loud calls
of the audience. Here, he said, was the paradise of his home, the long-
sought-for opportunity; he felt as though he could send a million supplications to the throne of Heaven for such an exalted privilege. Poor
Leos, who was somewhere in the crowd, looking as attentively as if he
was searching for a needle in a haystack; here he stood, wondering to
himself why Ambulinia was not there. "Where can she be? Oh! if she
was only here, how I could relish the scene! Elfonzo is certainly not
in town; but what if he is? I have got the wealth, if I have not the
dignity, and I am sure that the squire and his lady have always been
particular friends of mine, and I think with this assurance I shall be
able to get upon the blind side of the rest of the family and make
the heaven-born Ambulinia the mistress of all I possess." Then, again,
he would drop his head, as if attempting to solve the most difficult
problem in Euclid. While he was thus conjecturing in his own mind,
a very interesting part of the exhibition was going on, which called
the attention of all present. The curtains of the stage waved continually by the repelled forces that were given to them, which caused
Leos to behold Ambulinia leaning upon the chair of Elfonzo. Her lofty
beauty, seen by the glimmering of the chandelier, filled his heart with
rapture, he knew not how to contain himself; to go where they were
would expose him to ridicule; to continue where he was, with such an
object before him, without being allowed an explanation in that trying
hour, would be to the great injury of his mental as well as of his physical powers; and, in the name of high heaven, what must he do? Finally, he resolved to contain himself as well as he conveniently could,
until the scene was over, and then he would plant himself at the door,
to arrest Ambulinia from the hands of the insolent Elfonzo, and thus
make for himself a more prosperous field of immortality than ever was
decreed by Omnipotence, or ever pencil drew or artist imagined. Accordingly he made himself sentinel, immediately after the performance of the evening—retained his position apparently in defiance of
all the world; he waited, he gazed at every lady, his whole frame
trembled; here he stood, until everything like human shape had disappeared from the institution, and he had done nothing; he had failed
to accomplish that which he so eagerly sought for. Poor, unfortunate
creature! he had not the eyes of an Argus, or he might have seen his
Juno and Elfonzo, assisted by his friend Sigma, make their escape
from the window, and, with the rapidity of a race-horse, hurry through
the blast of the storm to the residence of her father, without being
recognized. He did not tarry long, but assured Ambulinia the end-

less chain of their existence was more closely connected than ever,
since he had seen the virtuous, innocent, imploring, and the constant
Amelia murdered by the jealous-hearted Farcillo, the accursed of the
land.

The following is the tragical scene, which is only introduced to
show the subject-matter that enabled Elfonzo to come to such a
determinate resolution that nothing of the kind should ever dispossess
him of his true character, should he be so fortunate as to succeed
in his present undertaking.

Amelia was the wife of Farcillo, and a virtuous woman; Gracia, a
young lady, was her particular friend and confidant. Farcillo grew
jealous of Amelia, murders her, finds out that he was deceived, *and
stabs himself*. Amelia appears alone, talking to herself.

A. Hail, ye solitary ruins of antiquity, ye sacred tombs and silent
walks! it is your aid I invoke; it is to you, my soul, wrapt in deep
meditation, pours forth its prayer. Here I wander upon the stage of
mortality, since the world hath turned against me. Those whom I
believed to be my friends, alas! are now my enemies, planting thorns
in all my paths, poisoning all my pleasures, and turning the past to
pain. What a lingering catalogue of sighs and tears lies just before me,
crowding my aching bosom with the fleeting dream of humanity, which
must shortly terminate. And to what purpose will all this bustle of
life, these agitations and emotions of the heart have conduced, if it
leave behind it nothing of utility, if it leave no traces of improvement?
Can it be that I am deceived in my conclusions? No, I see that I
have nothing to hope for, but everything to fear, which tends to drive
me from the walks of time.

> Oh! in this dead night, if loud winds arise,
> To lash the surge and bluster in the skies,
> May the west its furious rage display,
> Toss me with storms in the watery way.

(Enter Gracia.)

G. Oh, Amelia, is it you, the object of grief, the daughter of opulence,
of wisdom and philosophy, that thus complaineth? It cannot be you are
the child of misfortune, speaking of the monuments of former ages,
which were allotted not for the reflection of the distressed, but for the
fearless and bold.

A. Not the child of poverty, Gracia, or the heir of glory and peace,
but of fate. Remember, I have wealth more than wit can number; I
have had power more than kings could encompass; yet the world

seems a desert; all nature appears an afflictive spectacle of warring passions. This blind fatality, that capriciously sports with the rules and lives of mortals, tells me that the mountains will never again send forth the water of their springs to my thirst. Oh, that I might be freed and set at liberty from wretchedness! But I fear, I fear this will never be.

G. Why, Amelia, this untimely grief? What has caused the sorrows that bespeak better and happier days, to thus lavish out such heaps of misery? You are aware that your instructive lessons embellish the mind with holy truths, by wedding its attention to none but great and noble affections.

A. This, of course, is some consolation. I will ever love my own species with feelings of a fond recollection, and while I am studying to advance the universal philanthropy, and the spotless name of my own sex, I will try to build my own upon the pleasing belief that I have accelerated the advancement of one who whispers of departed confidence.

> And I, like some poor peasant fated to reside
> Remote from friends, in a forest wide.
> Oh, see what woman's woes and human wants require,
> Since that great day hath spread the seed of sinful fire.

G. Look up, thou poor disconsolate; you speak of quitting earthly enjoyments. Unfold they bosom to a friend, who would be willing to sacrifice every enjoyment for the restoration of that dignity and gentleness of mind which used to grace your walks, and which is so natural to yourself; not only that, but your paths were strewed with flowers of every hue and of every order.

> With verdant green the mountains glow,
> For thee, for thee, the lilies grow;
> Far stretched beneath the tented hills,
> A fairer flower the valley fills.

A. Oh, would to Heaven I could give you a short narrative of my former prospects for happiness, since you have acknowledged to be an unchangeable confidant—the richest of all other blessings. Oh, ye names forever glorious, ye celebrated scenes, ye renowned spot of my hymeneal moments; how replete is your chart with sublime reflections! How many profound vows, decorated with immaculate deeds, are written upon the surface of that precious spot of earth where I yielded up my life of celibacy, bade youth with all its beauties a final adieu, took a last farewell of the laurels that had accompanied me up the hill of my juvenile career. It was then I began to descend toward the valley of disappointment and sorrow; it was then I cast my little bark upon a mysterious ocean of wedlock, with him who then smiled and caressed me, but, alas! now frowns with bitterness, and has grown jealous and cold toward me, because the ring he gave me is misplaced or lost. Oh, bear me, ye flowers of memory, softly through the eventful history of past times; and ye places that have witnessed the progression of man in the circle of so many societies, and, oh, aid my recollection, while I endeavor to trace the vicissitudes of a life devoted in endeavoring to comfort him that I claim as the object of my wishes.

> Ah! ye mysterious men, of all the world, how few
> Act just to Heaven and to your promise true!
> But He who guides the stars with a watchful eye,
> The deeds of men lay open without disguise;
> Oh, this alone will avenge the wrongs I bear,
> For all the oppressed are His peculiar care.

(F. makes a slight noise.)

A. Who is there—Farcillo?

G. Then I must be gone. Heaven protect you. Oh, Amelia, farewell, be of good cheer.

> May you stand, like Olympus' towers,
> Against earth and all jealous powers!
> May you, with loud shouts ascend on high
> Swift as an eagle in the upper sky.

A. Why so cold and distant to-night, Farcillo? Come, let us each other greet, and forget all the past, and give security for the future.

F. Security! talk to me about giving security for the future—what an insulting requisition! Have you said your prayers to-night, Madam Amelia?

A. Farcillo, we sometimes forget our duty, particularly when we expect to be caressed by others.

F. If you bethink yourself of any crime, or of any fault, that is yet concealed from the courts of Heaven and the thrones of grace, I bid you ask and solicit forgiveness for it now.

A. Oh, be kind, Farcillo, don't treat me so. What do you mean by all this?

F. Be kind, you say; you, madam, have forgot that kindness you owe to me, and bestowed it upon another; you shall suffer for your conduct when you make your peace with your God. I would not slay thy unprotected spirit. I call to Heaven to be my guard and my watch—I would not kill thy soul, in which all once seemed just, right, and perfect; but I must be brief, woman.

A. What, talk you of killing? Oh, Farcillo, Farcillo, what is the matter?

F. Aye, I do, without doubt; mark what I say, Amelia.

A. Then, O God, O Heaven, and Angels, be propitious, and have mercy upon me.

F. Amen to that, madam, with all my heart, and with all my soul.

A. Farcillo, listen to me one moment; I hope you will not kill me.

F. Kill you, aye, that I will; attest it, ye fair host of light, record it ye dark imps of hell!

A. Oh, I fear you—you are fatal when darkness covers your brow; yet I know not why I should fear, since I never wronged you in all my life. I stand, sir, guiltless before you.

F. You pretend to say you are guiltless! Think of thy sins, Amelia; think, oh, think, hidden woman.

A. Wherein have I not been true to you? That death is unkind, cruel, and unnatural, that kills for loving.

F. Peace, and be still while I unfold to thee.

A. I will, Farcillo, and while I am thus silent, tell me the cause of such cruel coldness in an hour like this.

F. That *ring*, oh that ring I so loved, and gave thee as the ring of my heart; the allegiance you took to be faithful, when it was presented; the kisses and smiles with which you honored it. You became tired of the donor, despised it as a plague, and finally gave it to Malos, the hidden, the vile traitor.

A. No, upon my word and honor, I never did; I appeal to the Most High to bear me out in this matter. Send for Malos, and ask him.

F. Send for Malos, aye! Malos you wish to see; I thought so. I knew you could not keep his name concealed. Amelia, sweet Amelia, take heed, take heed of perjury; you are on the stage of death, to suffer for *your sins.*

A. What, not to die I hope, my Farcillo, my ever beloved.

F. Yes, madam, to die a traitor's death. Shortly your spirit shall take its exit; therefore confess freely thy sins, for to deny tends only to make me groan under the bitter cup thou hast made for me. Thou art to die with the name of traitor on thy brow!

A. Then, O Lord, have mercy upon me; give me courage, give me grace and fortitude to stand this hour of trial.

F. Amen, I say, with all my heart.

A. And, oh, Farcillo, will you have mercy, too? I never intentionally offended you in all my life; never *loved* Malos, never gave him cause to think so, as the high court of Justice will acquit me before its tribunal.

F. Oh, false, perjured woman, thou dost chill my blood, and makest me a demon like thyself. I saw the ring.

A. He found it, then, or got it clandestinely; send for him, and let him confess the truth; let his confession be sifted.

F. And you still wish to see him! I tell you, madam, he hath already confessed, and thou knowest the darkness of thy heart.

A. What, my deceived Farcillo, that I gave him the ring, in which all my affections were concentrated? Oh, surely not.

F. Aye, he did. Ask thy conscience, and it will speak with a voice of thunder to thy soul.

A. He will not say so, he dare not, he cannot.

F. No, he will not say so now, because his mouth, I trust, is hushed in death, and his body stretched to the four winds of heaven, to be torn to pieces by carnivorous birds.

A. What, is he dead, and gone to the world of spirits with that declaration in his mouth? Oh, unhappy man! Oh, insupportable hour!

F. Yes, and had all his sighs and looks and tears been lives, my great revenge could have slain them all, without the least condemnation.

A. Alas! he is ushered into eternity without testing the matter for which I am abused and sentenced and condemned to die.

F. Cursed, infernal woman! Weepest thou for him to my face? He that hath robbed me of my peace, my energy, the whole love of my life? Could I call the fabled Hydra, I would have him live and perish, survive and die, until the sun itself would grow dim with age. I would make him have the thirst of a Tantalus, and roll the wheel of an Ixion, until the stars of heaven should quit their brilliant stations.

A. Oh, invincible God, save me! Oh, unsupportable moment! Oh, heavy hour! Banish me, Farcillo—send me where no eye can ever see me, where no sound shall ever greet my ear; but, oh, slay me not, Farcillo; vent thy rage and thy spite upon this emaciated frame of mine, only spare my life.

F. Your petitions avail nothing, cruel Amelia.

A. Oh, Farcillo, perpetrate the dark deed to-morrow; let me live till then, for my past kindness to you, and it may be some kind angel will show to you that I am not only the object of innocence, but one who never loved another but your noble self.

F. Amelia, the decree has gone forth, it is to be done, and that quickly; thou art to die, madam.

A. But half an hour allow me, to see my father and my only child, to tell her the treachery and vanity of this world.

F. There is no alternative, there is no pause: my daughter shall not see its deceptive mother die; your father shall not know that his daughter fell disgraced, despised by all but her enchanting Malos.

A. Oh, Farcillo, put up thy threatening dagger into its scabbard; let it rest and be still, just while I say one prayer for thee and for my child.

F. It is too late, thy doom is fixed, thou hast not confessed to Heaven or to me, my child's protector—thou art to die. Ye powers of earth and heaven, protect and defend me in this alone. (*Stabs her while imploring for mercy.*)

A. Oh, Farcillo, Farcillo, a guiltless death I die.

F. Die! die! die!

(Gracia enters running, falls on her knees weeping, and kisses Amelia.)

G. Oh, Farcillo, Farcillo! oh, Farcillo!

F. I am here, the genius of the age, and the avenger of my wrongs.

G. Oh, lady, speak once more; sweet Amelia, oh, speak again. Gone, gone—yes, forever gone! Farcillo, oh, cold-hearted Farcillo, some evil fiend hath urged you to do this, Farcillo.

F. Say not so again, or you shall receive the same fate. I did the glorious deed, madam—beware, then, how you talk.

G. I fear not your implements of war; I will let you know you have not the power to do me harm. If you have a heart of triple brass, it shall be reached and melted, and thy blood shall chill thy veins and grow stiff in thy arteries. Here is the ring of the virtuous and innocent murdered Amelia; I obtained it from Malos, who yet lives, in hopes that he will survive the wound given him, and says he got it clandestinely—declares Amelia to be the princess of truth and virtue, invulnerable to anything like forgetting her first devotion to thee. The world has heard of your conduct and your jealousy, and with one universal voice declares her to be the best of all in piety; that she is the star of this great universe, and a more virtuous woman never lived since the wheels of time began. Oh, had you waited till to-morrow, or until I had returned, some kind window would have been opened to her relief. But, alas! she is gone—yes, forever gone, to try the realities of an unknown world!

(Farcillo leaning over the body of Amelia.)

F. Malos not dead, and here is my ring! Oh, Amelia! falsely, falsely
murdered! Oh, bloody deed! Oh, wretch that I am! Oh, angels forgive
me! Oh, God, withhold thy vengeance! Oh, Amelia! if Heaven would
make a thousand worlds like this, set with diamonds, and all of one
perfect chrysolite, I would not have done this for them all, I would not
have frowned and cursed as I did. Oh, she was heavenly true, nursed
in the very lap of bright angels! Cursed slave that I am! Jealousy, oh!
thou infernal demon! Lost, lost to every sense of honor! Oh! Amelia—
heaven-born Amelia—dead, dead! Oh! oh! oh!—then let me die with
thee. Farewell! farewell! ye world that deceived me! (*Stabs himself.*)

Soon after the excitement of this tragical scene was over, and the
enlisted feeling for Amelia had grown more buoyant with Elfonzo
and Ambulinia, he determined to visit his retired home, and make the
necessary improvements to enjoy a better day; consequently he conveyed the following lines to Ambulinia:

> Go tell the world that hope is glowing,
>   Go bid the rocks their silence break,
> Go tell the stars that love is glowing,
>   Then bid the hero his lover take.

In the region where scarcely the foot of man hath ever trod, where
the woodman hath not found his way, lies a blooming grove, seen
only by the sun when he mounts his lofty throne, visited only by the
light of the stars, to whom are intrusted the guardianship of earth,
before the sun sinks to rest in his rosy bed. High cliffs of rocks surround
the romantic place, and in the small cavity of the rocky wall grows the
daffodil clear and pure; and as the wind blows along the enchanting
little mountain which surrounds the lonely spot, it nourishes the flowers
with the dewdrops of heaven. Here is the seat of Elfonzo; darkness
claims but little victory over this dominion, and in vain does she spread
out her gloomy wings. Here the waters flow perpetually, and the trees
lash their tops together to bid the welcome visitor a happy muse.
Elfonzo, during his short stay in the country, had fully persuaded
himself that it was his duty to bring this solemn matter to an issue. A
duty that he individually owed, as a gentleman, to the parents of
Ambulinia, a duty in itself involving not only his own happiness and
his own standing in society, but one that called aloud the act of the
parties to make it perfect and complete. How he should communicate
his intentions to get a favorable reply, he was at a loss to know; he
knew not whether to address Esq. Valeer in prose or in poetry, in a
jocular or an argumentative manner, or whether he should use moral

suasion, legal injunction, or seize and take by reprisal; if it was to do the latter, he would have no difficulty in deciding in his own mind, but his gentlemanly honor was at stake; so he concluded to address the following letter to the father and mother of Ambulinia, as his address in person he knew would only aggravate the old gentleman, and perhaps his lady.

Cumming, Ga., January 22, 1844

MR. AND MRS. VALEER—

Again I resume the pleasing task of addressing you, and once more beg an immediate answer to my many salutations. From every circumstance that has taken place, I feel in duty bound to comply with my obligations; to forfeit my word would be more than I dare do; to break my pledge, and my vows that have been witnessed, sealed, and delivered in the presence of an unseen Deity, would be disgraceful on my part, as well as ruinous to Ambulinia. I wish no longer to be kept in suspense about this matter. I wish to act gentlemanly in every particular. It is true, the promises I have made are unknown to any but Ambulinia, and I think it unnecessary to here enumerate them, as they who promise the most generally perform the least. Can you for a moment doubt my sincerity or my character? My only wish is, sir, that you may calmly and dispassionately look at the situation of the case, and if your better judgment should dictate otherwise, my obligations may induce me to pluck the flower that you so diametrically opposed. We have sworn by the saints—by the gods of battle, and by that faith whereby just men are made perfect—to be united. I hope, my dear sir, you will find it convenient as well as aggreeable to give me a favorable answer, with the signature of Mrs. Valeer, as well as yourself.

With very great esteem,
your humble servant,
J. I. ELFONZO

The moon and stars had grown pale when Ambulinia had retired to rest. A crowd of unpleasant thoughts passed through her bosom. Solitude dwelt in her chamber—no sound from the neighboring world penetrated its stillness; it appeared a temple of silence, of repose, and of mystery. At that moment she heard a still voice calling her father. In an instant, like the flash of lightning, a thought ran through her mind that it must be the bearer of Elfonzo's communication. "It is not a dream!" she said, "no, I cannot read dreams. Oh! I would to Heaven I was near that glowing eloquence—that poetical language—it charms the mind in an inexpressible manner, and warms the coldest heart." While consoling herself with this strain, her father rushed into her room almost frantic with rage, exclaiming: "Oh, Ambulinia! Ambulinia!! undutiful, ungrateful daughter! What does this mean? Why does this letter bear such heart-rending intelligence? Will you quit a father's house with this debased wretch, without a place to lay his distracted head; going up and down the country; with every novel object that may chance to wander through this region. He is a pretty man to make love known to his superiors, and you, Ambulinia, have done but little credit to yourself by honoring his visits. Oh, wretchedness! can it be that my hopes of happiness are forever blasted! Will you not listen to a father's entreaties, and pay some regard to a mother's tears. I know, and I do pray that God will give me fortitude to bear with this sea of troubles, and rescue my daughter, my Ambulinia, as a brand from the eternal burning." "Forgive me, father, oh! forgive thy child," replied Ambulinia. "My heart is ready to break, when I see you in this grieved state of agitation. Oh! think not so meanly of me, as that I mourn for my own danger. Father, I am only woman. Mother, I am only the templement of thy youthful years, but will suffer courageously whatever punishment you think proper to inflict upon me, if you will but allow me to comply with my most sacred promises—if you will but give me my personal right and my personal liberty. Oh, father! if your generosity will but give me these, I ask nothing more. When Elfonzo offered me his heart, I gave him my hand, never to forsake him, and now may the mighty God banish me before I leave him in adversity. What a heart must I have to rejoice in prosperity with him whose offers I have accepted, and then, when poverty comes, haggard as it may be, for me to trifle with the oracles of Heaven, and change with every fluctuation that may interrupt our happiness—like the politician who runs the political gantlet for office one day, and the next day, because the horizon is darkened a little, he is seen running for his life, for fear he might perish in its ruins. Where is the philosophy, where is the consistency, where is the charity, in conduct like this? Be happy then, my beloved father, and forget me; let the sorrow of parting break down the wall of separation and make us equal in our feeling; let me now say how ardently I love you; let me kiss that age-worn cheek, and should my tears bedew thy face, I will wipe them away. Oh, I never can forget you; no, never, never!"

"Weep not," said the father, "Ambulinia. I will forbid Elfonzo my house, and desire that you may keep retired a few days. I will let him know that my friendship for my family is not linked together by cankered chains; and if he ever enters upon my premises again, I will send him to his long home." "Oh, father! let me entreat you to be calm upon this occasion, and though Elfonzo may be the sport of the clouds and winds, yet I feel assured that no fate will send him to the silent tomb until the God of the Universe calls him hence with a triumphant voice."

Here the father turned away, exclaiming: "I will answer his letter in a very few words, and you, madam, will have the goodness to stay at home with your mother; and remember, I am determined to protect you from the consuming fire that looks so fair to your view."

Cumming, January 22, 1844

Sir—In regard to your request, I am as I ever have been, utterly opposed to your marrying into my family; and if you have any regard for yourself, or any gentlemanly feeling, I hope you will mention it to me no more; but seek some other one who is not so far superior to you in standing.

W. W. Valeer

When Elfonzo read the above letter, he became so much depressed in spirits that many of his friends thought it advisable to use other means to bring about the happy union. "Strange," said he, "that the contents of this diminutive letter should cause me to have such depressed feelings; but there is a nobler theme than this. I know not why my *military title* is not as great as that of *Squire Valeer*. For my life I cannot see that my ancestors are inferior to those who are so bitterly opposed to my marriage with Ambulinia. I know I have seen huge mountains before me, yet, when I think that I know gentlemen will insult me upon this delicate matter, should I become angry at fools and babblers, who pride themselves in their impudence and ignorance? No. My equals! I know not where to find them. My inferiors! I think it beneath me; and my superiors! I think it presumption; therefore, if this youthful heart is protected by any of the divine rights, I never will betray my trust."

He was aware that Ambulinia had a confidence that was, indeed, as firm and as resolute as she was beautiful and interesting. He hastened to the cottage of Louisa, who received him in her usual mode of pleasantness, and informed him that Ambulinia had just that moment left. "Is it possible?" said Elfonzo. "Oh, murdered hours! Why did she not remain and be the guardian of my secrets? But hasten and tell me how she has stood this trying scene, and what are her future determinations." "You know," said Louisa, "Major Elfonzo, that you have Ambulinia's first love, which is of no small consequence. She came here about twilight, and shed many precious tears in consequence of her own fate with yours. We walked silently in yon little valley you see, where we spent a momentary repose. She seemed to be quite as determined as ever, and before we left that beautiful spot she offered up a prayer to Heaven for thee." "I will see her then," replied Elfonzo, "though legions of enemies may oppose. She is mine by fore-ordination—she is mine by prophecy—she is mine by her own free will, and I will rescue her from the hands of her oppressors. Will you not, Miss Louisa, assist me in my capture?"

"I will certainly, by the aid of Divine Providence," answered Louisa, "endeavor to break those slavish chains that bind the richest of prizes; though allow me, Major, to entreat you to use no harsh means on this important occasion; take a decided stand, and write freely to Ambulinia upon this subject, and I will see that no intervening cause hinders its passage to her. God alone will save a mourning people. Now is the day and now is the hour to obey a command of such valuable worth." The Major felt himself grow stronger after this short interview with Louisa. He felt as if he could whip his weight in wild-cats—he knew he was master of his own feelings, and could now write a letter that would bring this litigation to *an issue*.

Cumming, January 24, 1844

DEAR AMBULINIA—

We have now reached the most trying moment of our lives; we are pledged not to forsake our trust; we have waited for a favorable hour to come, think-ing your friends would settle the matter agreeably among themselves, and finally be reconciled to our marriage; but as I have waited in vain, and looked in vain, I have determined in my own mind to make a proposition to you, though you may think it not in accord with your station, or compatible with your rank; yet, "sub hoc signo vinces." You know I cannot resume my visits, in consequence of the utter hostilty that your father has to me; therefore the consummation of our union will have to be sought for in a more sublime sphere, at the residence of a respectable friend of this village. You cannot have any scruples upon this mode of proceeding, if you will but remember it emanates from one who loves you better than his own life—who is more than anxious to bid you welcome to a new and happy home. Your warmest as-sociates say come; the talented, the learned, the wise, and the experienced say come;—all these with their friends say, come. Viewing these, with many other inducements, I flatter myself that you will come to the embraces of your Elfonzo; for now is the time of your acceptance and the day of your liberation. You cannot be ignorant, Ambulinia, that thou art the desire of my heart; its thoughts are too noble, and too pure, to conceal themselves from you. I shall wait for your answer to this impatiently, expecting that you will set the time to make your departure, and to be in readiness at a moment's warning to share the joys of a more preferable life. This will be handed to you by Louisa, who will take a pleasure in communicating anything to you that may relieve your

dejected spirits, and will assure you that I now stand ready, willing, and
waiting to make good my vows.

> I am, dear Ambulinia, yours
> truly, and forever,
> J. I. ELFONZO

Louisa made it convenient to visit Mr. Valeer's, though they did not
suspect her in the least the bearer of love epistles; consequently, she
was invited in the room to console Ambulinia, where they were left
alone. Ambulinia was seated by a small table—her head resting on
her hand—her brilliant eyes were bathed in tears. Louisa handed her
the letter of Elfonzo, when another spirit animated her features—the
spirit of renewed confidence that never fails to strengthen the female
character in an hour of grief and sorrow like this, and as she pronounced the last accent of his name, she exclaimed, "And does he love
me yet! I never will forget your generosity, Louisa. Oh, unhappy and
yet blessed Louisa! may you never feel what I have felt—may you
never know the pangs of love. Had I never loved, I never would have
been unhappy; but I turn to Him who can save, and if His wisdom
does not will my expected union, I know He will give me strength to
bear my lot. Amuse yourself with this little book, and take it as an
apology for my silence," said Ambulinia, "while I attempt to answer
this volume of consolation." "Thank you," said Louisa, "you are excusable upon this occasion; but I pray you, Ambulinia, to be expert upon
this momentous subject, that there may be nothing mistrustful upon
my part." "I will," said Ambulinia, and immediately resumed her seat
and addressed the following to Elfonzo:

> *Cumming, Ga., January 28, 1844*

DEVOTED ELFONZO—

I hail your letter as a welcome messenger of faith, and can now say truly
and firmly that my feelings correspond with yours. Nothing shall be wanting
on my part to make my obedience your fidelity. Courage and perseverance
will accomplish success. Receive this as my oath, that while I grasp your
hand in my own imagination, we stand united before a higher tribunal than
any on earth. All the powers of my life, soul, and body, I devote to thee.
Whatever dangers may threaten me, I fear not to encounter them. Perhaps
I have determined upon my own destruction, by leaving the house of the
best of parents; be it so; I flee to you; I share your destiny, faithful to the
end. The day that I have concluded upon for this task is *Sabbath* next, when
the family with the citizens are generally at church. For Heaven's sake let
not that day pass unimproved: trust not till to-morrow, it is the cheat of
life—the future that never comes—the grave of many noble births—the cavern
of ruined enterprise: which like the lightning's flash is born, and dies, and

perishes, ere the voice of him who sees can cry, *behold! behold!!* You may trust to what I say, no power shall tempt me to betray confidence. Suffer me to add one word more.

> I will soothe thee, in all thy grief,
> Beside the gloomy river;
> And though thy love may yet be brief;
> Mine is fixed forever.

Receive the deepest emotions of my heart for thy constant love, and may the power of inspiration be thy guide, thy portion, and thy all. In great haste,
Yours faithfully,
AMBULINIA

"I now take my leave of you, sweet girl," said Louisa, "sincerely wishing you success on Sabbath next." When Ambulinia's letter was handed to Elfonzo, he perused it without doubting its contents. Louisa charged him to make but few confidants; but like most young men who happened to win the heart of a beautiful girl, he was so elated with the idea that he felt as a commanding general on parade, who had confidence in all, consequently gave orders to all. The appointed Sabbath, with a delicious breeze and cloudless sky, made its appearance. The people gathered in crowds to the church—the streets were filled with the neighboring citizens, all marching to the house of worship. It is entirely useless for me to attempt to describe the feelings of Elfonzo and Ambulinia, who were silently watching the movements of the multitude, apparently counting them as they entered the house of God, looking for the last one to darken the door. The impatience and anxiety with which they waited, and the bliss they anticipated on the eventful day, is altogether indescribable. Those that have been so fortunate as to embark in such a noble enterprise know all its realities; and those who have not had this inestimable privilege will have to taste its sweets before they can tell to others its joys, its comforts, and its Heaven-born worth. Immediately after Ambulinia had assisted the family off to church, she took the advantage of that opportunity to make good her promises. She left a home of enjoyment to be wedded to one whose love had been justifiable. A few short steps brought her to the presence of Louisa, who urged her to make good use of her time, and not to delay a moment, but to go with her to her brother's house, where Elfonzo would forever make her happy. With lively speed, and yet a graceful air, she entered the door and found herself protected by the champion of her confidence. The necessary arrangements were fast making to have the two lovers united—

everything was in readiness except the parson; and as they are generally very sanctimonious on such occasions, the news got to the parents of Ambulinia before the everlasting knot was tied, and they both came running, with uplifted hands and injured feelings, to arrest their daughter from an unguarded and hasty resolution. Elfonzo desired to maintain his ground, but Ambulinia thought it best for him to leave, to prepare for a greater contest. He accordingly obeyed, as it would have been a vain endeavor for him to have battled against a man who was armed with deadly weapons; and besides, he could not resist the request of such a pure heart. Ambulinia concealed herself in the upper story of the house, fearing the rebuke of her father; the door was locked, and no chastisement was now expected. Esquire Valeer, whose pride was already touched, resolved to preserve the dignity of his family. He entered the house almost exhausted, looking wildly for Ambulinia. "Amazed and astonished indeed I am," said he, "at a people who call themselves civilized, to allow such behavior as this. Ambulinia, Ambulinia!" he cried, "come to the calls of your first, your best, and your only friend. I appeal to you, sir," turning to the gentle-man of the house, "to know where Ambulinia has gone, or where is she?" "Do you mean to insult me, sir, in my own house?" inquired the confounded gentleman. "I will burst," said Mr. V., "asunder every door in your dwelling, in search of my daughter, if you do not speak quickly, and tell me where she is. I care nothing about that outcast rubbish of creation, that mean, low-lived Elfonzo, if I can but obtain Ambulinia. Are you not going to open this door?" said he. "By the Eternal that made Heaven and earth! I will go about the work in-stantly, if it is not done." The confused citizens gathered from all parts of the village, to know the cause of this commotion. Some rushed into the house; the door what was locked flew open, and there stood Ambulinia, weeping. "Father, be still," said she, "and I will follow thee home." But the agitated man seized her, and bore her off through the gazing multitude. "Father!" she exclaimed, "I humbly beg your pardon —I will be dutiful—I will obey thy commands. Let the sixteen years I have lived in obedience to thee be my future security." "I don't like to be always giving credit, when the old score is not paid up, madam," said the father. The mother followed almost in a state of derangement, crying and imploring her to think beforehand, and ask advice from experienced persons, and they would tell her it was a rash undertaking. "Oh!" said she, "Ambulinia, my daughter, did you know what I have suffered—did you know how many nights I have

whiled away in agony, in pain, and in fear, you would pity the
sorrows of a heartbroken mother."

"Well, mother," replied Ambulinia, "I know I have been disobedient;
I am aware that what I have done might have been done much better;
but oh! what shall I do with my honor? it is so dear to me; I am
pledged to Elfonzo. His high moral worth is certainly worth some
attention; moreover, my vows, I have no doubt, are recorded in the
book of life, and must I give these all up? must my fair hopes be forever blasted? Forbid it, father; oh! forbid it, mother; forbid it, Heaven."

"I have seen so many beautiful skies overclouded," replied the mother,
"so many blossoms nipped by the frost, that I am afraid to trust you
to the care of those fair days, which may be interrupted by thundering and tempestuous nights. You no doubt think as I did—life's devious
ways were strewed with sweet-scented flowers, but ah! how long
they have lingered around me and took their flight in the vivid hope
that laughs at the drooping victims it has murdered." Elfonzo was
moved at this sight. The people followed on to see what was going
to become of Ambulinia, while he, with downcast looks, kept at a
distance, until he saw them enter the abode of the father, thrusting
her, that was the sigh of his soul, out of his presence into a solitary
apartment, when she exclaimed, "Elfonzo! Elfonzo! oh, Elfonzo! where
art thou, with all thy heroes? haste, oh! haste, come thou to my
relief. Ride on the wings of the wind! Turn thy force loose like a
tempest, and roll on thy army like a whirlwind, over this mountain of
trouble and confusion. Oh, friends! if any pity me, let your last efforts
throng upon the green hills, and come to the relief of Ambulinia, who
is guilty of nothing but innocent love." Elfonzo called out with a loud
voice, "My God, can I stand this! arouse up, I beseech you, and put
an end to this tyranny. Come, my brave boys," said he, "are you ready
to go forth to your duty?" They stood around him. "Who," said he,
"will call us to arms? Where are my thunderbolts of war? Speak ye,
the first who will meet the foe! Who will go forward with me in this
ocean of grievous temptation? If there is one who desires to go, let
him come and shake hands upon the altar of devotion, and swear
that he will be a hero; yes, a Hector in a cause like this, which calls
aloud for a speedy remedy." "Mine be the deed," said a young lawyer,
"and mine alone; Venus alone shall quit her station before I will
forsake one jot or tittle of my promise to you; what is death to me?
what is all this warlike army, if it is not to win a victory? I love the
sleep of the lover and the mighty; nor would I give it over till the
blood of my enemies should wreak with that of my own. But God

forbid that our fame should soar on the blood of the slumberer." Mr. Valeer stands at his door with the frown of a demon upon his brow, with his dangerous weapon ready to strike the first man who should enter his door. "Who will arise and go forward through blood and carnage to the rescue of my Ambulinia?" said Elfonzo. "All," exclaimed the multitude; and onward they went, with their implements of battle. Others, of a more timid nature, stood among the distant hills to see the result of the contest.

Elfonzo took the lead of his band. Night arose in clouds; darkness concealed the heavens; but the blazing hopes that stimulated them gleamed in every bosom. All approached the anxious spot; they rushed to the front of the house and, with one exclamation, demanded Ambulinia. "Away, begone, and disturb my peace no more," said Mr. Valeer. "You are a set of base, insolent, and infernal rascals. Go, the northern star points your path through the dim twilight of the night; go, and vent your spite upon the lonely hills; pour forth your love, you poor, weak-minded wretch, upon your idleness and upon your guitar, and your fiddle; they are fit subjects for your admiration, for let me assure you, though this sword and iron lever are cankered, yet they frown in sleep, and let one of you dare to enter my house this night and you shall have the contents and the weight of these instruments." "Never yet did base dishonor blur my name," said Elfonzo; "mine is a cause of renown; here are my warriors; fear and tremble, for this night, though hell itself should oppose, I will endeavor to avenge her whom thou hast banished in solitude. The voice of Ambulinia shall be heard from that dark dungeon." At that moment Ambulinia appeared at the window above, and with a tremulous voice said, "Live, Elfonzo! oh! live to raise my stone of moss! why should such language enter your heart? why should thy voice rend the air with such agitation? I bid thee live, once more remembering these tears of mine are shed alone for thee, in this dark and gloomy vault, and should I perish under this load of trouble, join the song of thrilling accents with the raven above my grave, and lay this tattered frame beside the banks of the Chattahoochee or the stream of Sawney's brook; sweet will be the song of death to your Ambulinia. My ghost shall visit you in the smiles of Paradise, and tell your high fame to the minds of that region, which is far more preferable than this lonely cell. My heart shall speak for thee till the latest hour; I know faint and broken are the sounds of sorrow, yet our souls, Elfonzo, shall hear the peaceful songs together. One bright name shall be ours on high, if we are not permitted to be united here; bear in mind that

I still cherish my old sentiments, and the poet will mingle the names of Elfonzo and Ambulinia in the tide of other days." "Fly, Elfonzo," said the voices of his united band, "to the wounded heart of your beloved. All enemies shall fall beneath thy sword. Fly through the clefts, and the dim spark shall sleep in death." Elfonzo rushes forward and strikes his shield against the door, which was barricaded, to prevent any intercourse. His brave sons throng around him. The people pour along the streets, both male and female, to prevent or witness the melancholy scene.

"To arms, to arms!" cried Elfonzo; "here is a victory to be won, a prize to be gained that is more to me than the whole world beside." "It cannot be done to-night," said Mr. Valeer. "I bear the clang of death; my strength and armor shall prevail. My Ambulinia shall rest in this hall until the break of another day, and if we fall, we fall together. If we die, we die clinging to our tattered rights, and our blood alone shall tell the mournful tale of a murdered daughter and a ruined father." Sure enough, he kept watch all night, and was successful in defending his house and family. The bright morning gleamed upon the hills, night vanished away, the Major and his associates felt somewhat ashamed that they had not been as fortunate as they expected to have been; however, they still leaned upon their arms in dispersed groups; some were walking the streets, others were talking in the Major's behalf. Many of the citizens suspended business, as the town presented nothing but consternation. A novelty that might end in the destruction of some worthy and respectable citizens. Mr. Valeer ventured in the streets, though not without being well armed. Some of his friends congratulated him on the decided stand he had taken, and hoped he would settle the matter amicably with Elfonzo, without any serious injury. "Me," he replied, "what, me, condescend to fellowship with a coward, and a low-lived, lazy, undermining villain? no, gentlemen, this cannot be; I had rather be borne off, like the bubble upon the dark blue ocean, with Ambulinia by my side, than to have him in the ascending or descending line of relationship. Gentlemen," continued he, "if Elfonzo is so much of a distinguished character, and is so learned in the fine arts, why do you not patronize such men? why not introduce him into your families, as a gentleman of taste and of unequaled magnanimity? why are you so very anxious that he should become a relative of mine? Oh, gentlemen, I fear you yet are tainted with the curiosity of our first parents, who were beguiled by the poisonous kiss of an old ugly serpent, and who, for one *apple, damned* all mankind. I wish to divest myself, as far as possible, of that untutored custom. I have long since learned that the perfection of wisdom, and the end of true philosophy, is to proportion our wants to our possessions, our ambition to our capacities; we will then be a happy and a virtuous people." Ambulinia was sent off to prepare for a long and tedious journey. Her new acquaintances had been instructed by her father how to treat her, and in what manner, and to keep the anticipated visit entirely secret. Elfonzo was watching the movements of everybody; some friends had told him of the plot that was laid to carry off Ambulinia. At night, he rallied some two or three of his forces, and went silently along to the stately mansion; a faint and glimmering light showed through the windows; lightly he steps to the door; there were many voices rallying fresh in fancy's eye; he tapped the shutter; it was opened instantly, and he beheld once more, seated beside several ladies, the hope of all his toils; he rushed toward her, she rose from her seat, rejoicing; he made one mighty grasp, when Ambulinia exclaimed, "Huzza for Major Elfonzo! I will defend myself and you, too, with this conquering instrument I hold in my hand; huzza, I say, I now invoke time's broad wing to shed around us some dewdrops of verdant spring."

But the hour had not come for this joyous reunion; her friends struggled with Elfonzo for some time, and finally succeeded in arresting her from his hands. He dared not injure them, because they were matrons whose courage needed no spur; she was snatched from the arms of Elfonzo, with so much eagerness, and yet with such expressive signification, that he calmly withdrew from this lovely enterprise, with an ardent hope that he should be lulled to repose by the zephyrs which whispered peace to his soul. Several long days and nights passed unmolested, all seemed to have grounded their arms of rebellion, and no callidity appeared to be going on with any of the parties. Other arrangements were made by Ambulinia; she feigned herself to be entirely the votary of a mother's care, and said, by her graceful smiles, that manhood might claim his stern dominion in some other region, where such boisterous love was not so prevalent. This gave the parents a confidence that yielded some hours of sober joy; they believed that Ambulinia would now cease to love Elfonzo, and that her stolen affections would now expire with her misguided opinions. They therefore declined the idea of sending her to a distant land. But oh! they dreamed not of the rapture that dazzled the fancy of Ambulinia, who would say, when alone, youth should not fly away on his rosy pinions, and leave her to grapple in the conflict with unknown admirers.

> No frowning age shall control
> The constant current of my soul,
> Nor a tear from pity's eye
> Shall check my sympathetic sigh.

With this resolution fixed in her mind, one dark and dreary night, when the winds whistled and the tempest roared, she received intelligence that Elfonzo was then waiting, and every preparation was then ready, at the residence of Dr. Tully, and for her to make a quick escape while the family were reposing. Accordingly she gathered her books, went to the wardrobe supplied with a variety of ornamental dressing, and ventured alone in the streets to make her way to Elfonzo, who was near at hand, impatiently looking and watching her arrival. "What forms," said she, "are those rising before me? What is that dark spot on the clouds? I do wonder what frightful ghost that is, gleaming on the red tempest? Oh, be merciful and tell me what region you are from. Oh, tell me, ye strong spirits, or ye dark and fleeting clouds, that I yet have a friend." "A friend," said a low, whispering voice. "I am thy unchanging, thy aged, and thy disappointed mother. Oh, Ambulinia why hast thou deceived me? Why brandish in that hand of thine a javelin of pointed steel? Why suffer that lip I have kissed a thousand times to equivocate? My daughter, let these tears sink deep into thy soul, and no longer persist in that which may be your destruction and ruin. Come, my dear child, retract your steps, and bear me company to your welcome home." Without one retorting word, or frown from her brow, she yielded to the entreaties of her mother, and with all the mildness of her former character she went along with the silver lamp of age, to the home of candor and benevolence. Her father received her cold and formal politeness—"Where has Ambulinia been, this blustering evening, Mrs. Valeer?" inquired he. "Oh, she and I have been taking a solitary walk," said the mother; "all things, I presume, are now working for the best."

Elfonzo heard this news shortly after it happened. "What," said he, "has heaven and earth turned against me? I have been disappointed times without number. Shall I despair?—must I give it over? Heaven's decrees will not fade; I will write again—I will try again; and if it traverses a gory field, I pray forgiveness at the altar of justice."

Desolate Hill, Cumming, Geo., 1844

UNCONQUERED AND BELOVED AMBULINIA—

I have only time to say to you, not to despair; thy fame shall not perish; my visions are brightening before me. The whirlwind's rage is past, and we now shall subdue our enemies without doubt. On Monday morning, when your friends are at breakfast, they will not suspect your departure, or even mistrust me being in town, as it has been reported advantageously that I have left for the west. You walk carelessly toward the academy grove, where you will find me with a lightning steed, elegantly equipped to bear you off where we shall be joined in wedlock with the first connubial rights. Fail not to do this—think not of the tedious relations of our wrongs—be invincible. You alone occupy all my ambition, and I alone will make you my happy spouse, with the same unimpeached veracity. I remain, forever, your devoted friend and admirer,   J. I. ELFONZO.

The appointed day ushered in undisturbed by any clouds; nothing disturbed Ambulinia's soft beauty. With serenity and loveliness she obeys the request of Elfonzo. The moment the family seated themselves at the table—"Excuse my absence for a short time," said she, "while I attend to the placing of those flowers, which should have been done a week ago." And away she ran to the sacred grove, surrounded with glittering pearls, that indicated her coming. Elfonzo hails her with his silver bow and his golden harp. They meet—Ambulinia's countenance brightens—Elfonzo leads up his winged steed. "Mount," said he, "ye true-hearted, ye fearless soul—the day is ours." She sprang upon the back of the young thunderbolt, a brilliant star sparkles upon her head, with one hand she grasps the reins, and with the other she holds an olive branch. "Lend thy aid, ye strong winds," they exclaimed, "ye moon, ye sun, and all ye fair host of heaven, witness the enemy conquered." "Hold," said Elfonzo, "thy dashing steed." "Ride on," said Ambulinia, "the voice of thunder is behind us." And onward they went, with such rapidity that they very soon arrived at Rural Retreat, where they dismounted, and were united with all the solemnities that usually attend such divine operations. They passed the day in thanksgiving and great rejoicing, and on that evening they visited their uncle, where many of their friends and acquaintances had gathered to congratulate them in the field of untainted bliss. The kind old gentleman met them in the yard: "Well," said he, "I wish I may die, Elfonzo, if you and Ambulinia haven't tied a knot with your tongue that you can't untie with your teeth. But come in, come in, never mind, all is right—the world still moves on, and no one has fallen in this great battle."

Happy now is their lot! Unmoved by misfortune, they live among the fair beauties of the South. Heaven spreads their peace and fame upon the arch of the rainbow, and smiles propitiously at their triumph, *through the tears of the storm.*

                                                                    1893

Traveling with a Reformer

Last spring I went out to Chicago to see the Fair, and although I did not see it my trip was not wholly lost—there were compensations. In New York I was introduced to a major in the regular army who said he was going to the Fair, and we agreed to go together. I had to go to Boston first, but that did not interfere; he said he would go along, and put in the time. He was a handsome man, and built like a gladiator. But his ways were gentle, and his speech was soft and persuasive. He was companionable, but exceedingly reposeful. Yes, and wholly destitute of the sense of humor. He was full of interest in everything that went on around him, but his serenity was indestructible; nothing disturbed him, nothing excited him.

But before the day was done I found that deep down in him somewhere he had a passion, quiet as he was—a passion for reforming petty public abuses. He stood for citizenship—it was his hobby. His idea was that every citizen of the republic ought to consider himself an unofficial policeman, and keep unsalaried watch and ward over the laws and their execution. He thought that the only effective way of preserving and protecting public rights was for each citizen to do his share in preventing or punishing such infringements of them as came under his personal notice.

It was a good scheme, but I thought it would keep a body in trouble all the time; it seemed to me that one would be always trying to get offending little officials discharged, and perhaps getting laughed at for all reward. But he said no, I had the wrong idea; that there was no occasion to get anybody discharged; that in fact you *mustn't* get anybody discharged; that that would itself be a failure; no, one must reform the man—reform him and make him useful where he was.

"Must one report the offender and then beg his superior not to discharge him, but reprimand him and keep him?"

"No, that is not the idea; you don't report him at all, for then you risk his bread and butter. You can act as if you are *going* to report him —when nothing else will answer. But that's an extreme case. That is a sort of *force,* and force is bad. Diplomacy is the effective thing. Now if a man has tact—if a man will exercise diplomacy—"

For two minutes we had been standing at a telegraph wicket, and during all this time the Major had been trying to get the attention of one of the young operators, but they were all busy skylarking. The Major spoke now, and asked one of them to take his telegram. He got for reply:

"I reckon you can wait a minute, can't you?" and the skylarking went on.

The Major said yes, he was not in a hurry. Then he wrote another telegram:

President Western Union Tel. Co.:
Come and dine with me this evening. I can tell you how business is conducted in one of your branches.

Presently the young fellow who had spoken so pertly a little before reached out and took the telegram, and when he read it he lost color and began to apologize and explain. He said he would lose his place if this deadly telegram was sent, and he might never get another. If he could be let off this time he would give no cause of complaint again. The compromise was accepted.

As we walked away, the Major said:

"Now, you see, that was diplomacy—and you see how it worked. It wouldn't do any good to bluster, the way people are always doing—that boy can always give you as good as you send, and you'll come out defeated and ashamed of yourself pretty nearly always. But you see he stands no chance against diplomacy. Gentle words and diplomacy—those are the tools to work with."

"Yes, I see; but everybody wouldn't have had your opportunity. It isn't everybody that is on those familiar terms with the president of the Western Union."

"Oh, you misunderstand. I don't know the president—I only used him diplomatically. It is for his good and for the public good. There's no harm in it."

I said, with hesitation and diffidence:

"But is it ever right or noble to tell a lie?"

He took no note of the delicate self-righteousness of the question, but answered, with undisturbed gravity and simplicity:

"Yes, sometimes. Lies told to injure a person, and lies told to profit yourself are not justifiable, but lies told to help another person, and lies told in the public interest—oh, well, that is quite another matter. Anybody knows that. But never mind about the methods: you see the result. That youth is going to be useful now, and well behaved.

He had a good face. He was worth saving. Why, he was worth saving on his mother's account if not his own. Of course, he has a mother—sisters, too. Damn those people who are always forgetting that! Do you know, I've never fought a duel in my life—never once—and yet have been challenged, like other people. I could always see the other man's unoffending women folks or his little children standing between him and me. *They* hadn't done anything—I couldn't break *their* hearts, you know."

He corrected a good many little abuses in the course of the day, and always without friction—always with a fine and dainty "diplomacy" which left no sting behind; and he got such happiness and such contentment out of these performances that I was obliged to envy him his trade—and perhaps would have adopted it if I could have managed the necessary deflections from fact as confidently with my mouth as I believe I could with a pen, behind the shelter of print, after a little practice.

Away late that night we were coming up-town in a horse-car when three boisterous roughs got aboard, and began to fling hilarious obscenities and profanities right and left among the timid passengers, some of whom were women and children. Nobody resisted or retorted; the conductor tried soothing words and moral suasion, but the roughs only called him names and laughed at him. Very soon I saw that the Major realized that this was a matter which was in his line; evidently he was turning over his stock of diplomacy in his mind and getting ready. I felt that the first diplomatic remark he made in this place would bring down a landslide of ridicule upon him and maybe something worse; but before I could whisper to him and check him he had begun, and it was too late. He said, in a level and dispassionate tone: "Conductor, you must put these swine out. I will help you."

I was not looking for that. In a flash the three roughs plunged at him. But none of them arrived. He delivered three such blows as one could not expect to encounter outside the prize-ring, and neither of the men had life enough left in him to get up from where he fell. The Major dragged them out and threw them off the car, and we got under way again.

I was astonished; astonished to see a lamb act so; astonished at the strength displayed, and the clean and comprehensive result; astonished at the brisk and business-like style of the whole thing. The situation had a humorous side to it, considering how much I had been hearing about mild persuasion and gentle diplomacy all day from this pile-driver, and I would have liked to call his attention to that feature and do some sarcasms about it; but when I looked at him I saw that it would be of no use—his placid and contented face had no ray of humor in it; he would not have understood. When we left the car, I said:

"That was a good stroke of diplomacy—three good strokes of diplomacy, in fact."

"*That?* That wasn't diplomacy. You are quite in the wrong. Diplomacy is a wholly different thing. One cannot apply it to that sort; they would not understand it. No, that was not diplomacy; it was force."

"Now that you mention it, I—yes, I think perhaps you are right."

"Right? Of course I am right. It was just force."

"I think, myself, it had the outside aspect of it. Do you often have to reform people in that way?"

"Far from it. It hardly ever happens. Not oftener than once in half a year, at the outside."

"Those men will get well?"

"Get well? Why, certainly they will. They are not in any danger. I know how to hit and where to hit. You noticed that I did not hit them under the jaw. That would have killed them."

I believed that. I remarked—rather wittily, as I thought—that he had been a lamb all day, but now had all of a sudden developed into a ram—battering-ram; but with dulcet frankness and simplicity he said no, a battering-ram was quite a different thing and not in use now. This was maddening, and I came near bursting out and saying he had no more appreciation of wit than a jackass—in fact, I had it right on my tongue, but did not say it, knowing there was no hurry and I could say it just as well some other time over the telephone.

We started to Boston the next afternoon. The smoking-compartment in the parlor-car was full, and we went into the regular smoker. Across the aisle in the front seat sat a meek, farmer-looking old man with a sickly pallor in his face, and he was holding the door open with his foot to get the air. Presently a big brakeman came rushing through, and when he got to the door he stopped, gave the farmer an ugly scowl, then wrenched the door to with such energy as to almost snatch the old man's boot off. Then on he plunged about his business. Several passengers laughed, and the old gentleman looked pathetically shamed and grieved.

After a little the conductor passed along, and the Major stopped him and asked him a question in his habitually courteous way:

"Conductor, where does one report the misconduct of a brakeman? Does one report to you?"

"You can report him at New Haven if you want to. What has he been doing?"

The Major told the story. The conductor seemed amused. He said, with just a touch of sarcasm in his bland tones:

"As I understand you, the brakeman didn't *say* anything."

"No, he didn't say anything."

"But he scowled, you say."

"Yes."

"And snatched the door loose in a rough way."

"Yes."

"That's the whole business, is it?"

"Yes, that is the whole of it."

The conductor smiled pleasantly, and said:

"Well, if you want to report him, all right, but I don't quite make out what it's going to amount to. You'll say—as I understand you—that the brakeman insulted this old gentleman. They'll ask you what he *said*. You'll say he didn't say anything at all. I reckon they'll say, how are you going to make out an insult when you acknowledge yourself that he didn't say a word."

There was a murmur of applause at the conductor's compact reasoning, and it gave him pleasure—you could see it in his face. But the Major was not disturbed. He said:

"There—now you have touched upon a crying defect in the complaint system. The railway officials—as the public think and as you also seem to think—are not aware that there are any kind of insults except *spoken* ones. So nobody goes to headquarters and reports insults of manner, insults of gesture, look, and so forth; and yet these are sometimes harder to bear than any words. They are bitter hard to bear because there is nothing tangible to take hold of; and the insulter can always say, if called before the railway officials, that he never dreamed of intending any offense. It seems to me that the officials ought to specially and urgently request the public to report *unworded* affronts and incivilities."

The conductor laughed, and said:

"Well, that *would* be trimming it pretty fine, sure!"

"But not too fine, I think. I will report this matter at New Haven, and I have an idea that I'll be thanked for it."

The conductor's face lost something of its complacency; in fact, it settled to a quite sober cast as the owner of it moved away. I said:

"You are not really going to bother with that trifle, are you?"

"It isn't a trifle. Such things ought always to be reported. It is a public duty, and no citizen has a right to shirk it. But I sha'n't have to report this case."

"Why?"

"It won't be necessary. Diplomacy will do the business. You'll see."

Presently the conductor came on his rounds again, and when he reached the Major he leaned over and said:

"That's all right. You needn't report him. He's responsible to me, and if he does it again I'll give him a talking to."

The Major's response was cordial:

"Now that is what I like! You mustn't think that I was moved by any vengeful spirit, for that wasn't the case. It was duty—just a sense of duty, that was all. My brother-in-law is one of the directors of the road, and when he learns that you are going to reason with your brakeman the very next time he brutally insults an unoffending old man it will please him, you may be sure of that."

The conductor did not look as joyous as one might have thought he would, but on the contrary looked sickly and uncomfortable. He stood around a little; then said:

"I think something ought to be done to him *now*. I'll discharge him."

"Discharge him? What good would that do? Don't you think it would be better wisdom to teach him better ways and keep him?"

"Well, there's something in that. What would you suggest?"

"He insulted the old gentleman in presence of all these people. How would it do to have him come and apologize in their presence?"

"I'll have him here right off. And I want to say this: If people would do as you've done, and report such things to me instead of keeping mum and going off and blackguarding the road, you'd see a different state of things pretty soon. I'm much obliged to you."

The brakeman came and apologized. After he was gone the Major said:

"Now, you see how simple and easy that was. The ordinary citizen would have accomplished nothing—the brother-in-law of a director can accomplish anything he wants to."

"But are you really the brother-in-law of a director?"

"Always. Always when the public interests require it. I have a brother-in-law on all the boards—everywhere. It saves me a world of trouble."

"It is a good wide relationship."

"Yes. I have over three hundred of them."

"Is the relationship never doubted by a conductor?"

"I have never met with a case. It is the honest truth—I never have."

"Why didn't you let him go ahead and discharge the brakeman, in spite of your favorite policy? You know he deserved it."

The Major answered with something which really had a sort of distant resemblance to impatience:

"If you would stop and think a moment you wouldn't ask such a question as that. Is a brakeman a dog, that nothing but dog's methods will do for him? He is a man, and has a man's fight for life. And he always has a sister, or a mother, or wife and children to support. Always—there are no exceptions. When you take his living away from him you take theirs away too—and what have they done to you? Nothing. And where is the profit in discharging an uncourteous brakeman and hiring another just like him? It's unwisdom. Don't you see that the rational thing to do is to *reform* the brakeman and keep him? Of course it is."

Then he quoted with admiration the conduct of a certain division superintendent of the Consolidated road, in a case where a switchman of two years' experience was negligent once and threw a train off the track and killed several people. Citizens came in a passion to urge the man's dismissal, but the superintendent said:

"No, you are wrong. He has learned his lesson, he will throw no more trains for the track. He is twice as valuable as he was before. I shall keep him."

We had only one more adventure on the trip. Between Hartford and Springfield the train-boy came shouting in with an armful of literature and dropped a sample into a slumbering gentleman's lap, and the man woke up with a start. He was very angry, and he and a couple of friends discussed the outrage with much heat. They sent for the parlor-car conductor and described the matter, and were determined to have the boy expelled from his situation. The three complainants were wealthy Holyoke merchants, and it was evident that the conductor stood in some awe of them. He tried to pacify them, and explained that the boy was not under his authority, but under that of one of the news companies; but he accomplished nothing.

Then the Major volunteered some testimony for the defense. He said:

"I saw it all. You gentlemen have not meant to exaggerate the circumstances, but still that is what you have done. The boy has done nothing more than all train-boys do. If you want to get his ways softened down and his manners reformed, I am with you and ready to help, but it isn't fair to get him discharged without giving him a chance."

But they were angry, and would hear of no compromise. They were well acquainted with the president of the Boston & Albany, they said, and would put everything aside next day and go up to Boston and fix that boy.

The Major said he would be on hand too, and would do what he could to save the boy. One of the gentlemen looked him over, and said:

"Apparently it is going to be a matter of who can wield the most influence with the president. Do you know Mr. Bliss personally?"

The Major said, with composure:

"Yes; he is my uncle."

The effect was satisfactory. There was an awkward silence for a minute or more; than the hedging and the half-confessions of over-haste and exaggerated resentment began, and soon everything was smooth and friendly and sociable, and it was resolved to drop the matter and leave the boy's bread-and-butter unmolested.

It turned out as I had expected: the president of the road was not the Major's uncle at all—except by adoption, and for this day and train only.

We got into no episodes on the return journey. Probably it was because we took a night train and slept all the way.

We left New York Saturday night by the Pennsylvania road. After breakfast the next morning we went into the parlor-car, but found it a dull place and dreary. There were but few people in it and nothing going on. Then we went into the little smoking-compartment of the same car and found three gentlemen in there. Two of them were grumpling over one of the rules of the road—a rule which forbade card-playing on the trains on Sunday. They had started an innocent game of high-low-jack and been stopped. The Major was interested. He said to the third gentleman:

"Did you object to the game?"

"Not at all. I am a Yale professor and a religious man, but my prejudices are not extensive."

Then the Major said to the others:

"You are at perfect liberty to resume your game, gentlemen; no one here objects."

One of them declined the risk, but the other one said he would like to begin again if the Major would join him. So they spread an overcoat

over their knees and the game proceeded. Pretty soon the parlor-car
conductor arrived, and said brusquely:

"There, there, gentlemen, that won't do. Put up the cards—it's not
allowed."

The Major was shuffling. He continued to shuffle, and said:

"By whose order is it forbidden?"

"It's my order. I forbid it."

The dealing began. The Major asked:

"Did you invent the idea?"

"What idea?"

"The idea of forbidding card-playing on Sunday."

"No—of course not."

"Who did?"

"The company."

"Then it isn't your order, after all, but the company's. Is that it?"

"Yes. But you don't stop playing; I have to require you to stop
playing immediately."

"Nothing is gained by hurry, and often much is lost. Who authorized
the company to issue such an order?"

"My dear sir, that is a matter of no consequence to me, and—"

"But you forget that you are not the only person concerned. It may
be a matter of consequence to me. It is indeed a matter of very great
importance to me. I cannot violate a legal requirement of my country
without dishonoring myself; I cannot allow any man or corporation
to hamper my liberties with illegal rules—a thing which railway companies are always trying to do—without dishonoring my citizenship.
So I come back to that question: By whose authority has the company
issued this order?"

"I don't *know*. That's *their* affair."

"Mine, too. I doubt if the company has any right to issue such a rule.
This road runs through several states. Do you know what state we
are in now, and what its laws are in matters of this kind?"

"Its laws do not concern me, but the company's orders do. It is my
duty to stop this game, gentlemen, and it *must* be stopped."

"Possibly; but still there is no hurry. In hotels they post certain
rules in the rooms, but they always quote passages from the state laws
as authority for these requirements. I see nothing posted here of this
sort. Please produce your authority and let us arrive at a decision,
for you see yourself that you are marring the game."

"I have nothing of the kind, but I have my orders, and that
is sufficient. They must be obeyed."

"Let us not jump to conclusions. It will be better all around to examine into the matter without heat or haste, and see just where we stand before either of us makes a mistake—for the curtailing of the liberties of a citizen of the United States is a much more serious matter than you and the railroads seem to think, and it cannot be done in my person until the curtailer proves his right to do so. Now—"

"My dear sir, *will* you put down those cards?"

"All in good time, perhaps. It depends. You say this order must be obeyed. *Must.* It is a strong word. You see yourself how strong it is. A wise company would not arm you with so drastic an order as this, of *course*, without appointing a penalty for its infringement. Otherwise it runs the risk of being a dead letter and a thing to laugh at. What is the appointed penalty for an infringement of this law?"

"Penalty? I never heard of any."

"Unquestionably you must be mistaken. Your company orders you to come here and rudely break up an innocent amusement, and furnishes you no way to enforce the order? Don't you see that that is nonsense? What do you *do* when people refuse to obey this order? Do you take the cards away from them?"

"No."

"Do you put the offender off at the next station?"

"Well, no—of course we couldn't if he had a ticket."

"Do you have him up before a court?"

The conductor was silent and apparently troubled. The Major started a new deal, and said:

"You see that you are helpless, and that the company has placed you in a foolish position. You are furnished with an arrogant order, and you deliver it in a blustering way, and when you come to look into the matter you find you haven't any way of enforcing obedience."

The conductor said, with chill dignity:

"Gentlemen, you have heard the order, and my duty is ended. As to obeying it or not, you will do as you think fit." And he turned to leave.

"But wait. The matter is not yet finished. I think you are mistaken about your duty being ended; but if it really is, I myself have a duty to perform yet."

"How do you mean?"

"Are you going to report my disobedience at headquarters in Pittsburg?"

"No. What good would that do?"

"You must report me, or I will report you."

"Report me for what?"

"For disobeying the company's orders in not stopping this game. As a citizen it is my duty to help the railway companies keep their servants to their work."

"Are you in earnest?"

"Yes, I am in earnest. I have nothing against you as a man, but I have this against you as an officer—that you have not carried out that order, and if you do not report me I must report you. And I will."

The conductor looked puzzled, and was thoughtful a moment; then he burst out with:

"I seem to be getting *myself* into a scrape! It's all a muddle; I can't make head or tail of it; it's never happened before; they always knocked under and never said a word, and so *I* never saw how ridiculous that stupid order with no penalty is. *I* don't want to report anybody, and I don't want to *be* reported—why, it might do me no end of harm! Now *do* go on with the game—play the whole day if you want to—and don't let's have any more trouble about it!"

"No, I only sat down here to establish this gentleman's rights—he can have his place now. But before you go won't you tell me what you think the company made this rule for? Can you imagine an excuse for it? I mean a rational one—an excuse that is not on its face silly, and the invention of an idiot?"

"Why, surely I can. The reason it was made is plain enough. It is to save the feelings of the other passengers—the religious ones among them, I mean. They would not like it, to have the Sabbath desecrated by card-playing on the train."

"I just thought as much. They are willing to desecrate it themselves by traveling on Sunday, but they are not willing that other people—"

"By gracious, you've hit it! I never thought of that before. The fact is, it *is* a silly rule when you come to look into it."

At this point the train-conductor arrived, and was going to shut down the game in a very high-handed fashion, but the parlor-car conductor stopped him and took him aside to explain. Nothing more was heard of the matter.

I was ill in bed eleven days in Chicago and got no glimpse of the Fair, for I was obliged to return east as soon as I was able to travel. The Major secured and paid for a stateroom in a sleeper the day before we left, so that I could have plenty of room and be comfortable; but when we arrived at the station a mistake had been made and our car had not been put on. The conductor had reserved a section for us —it was the best he could do, he said. But the Major said we were not in a hurry, and would wait for the car to be put on. The conductor responded, with pleasant irony:

"It may be that *you* are not in a hurry, just as you say, but we *are*. Come, get aboard, gentlemen, get aboard—don't keep us waiting."

But the Major would not get aboard himself nor allow me to do it. He wanted his car, and said he must have it. This made the hurried and perspiring conductor impatient, and he said:

"It's the best we can *do*—we can't do impossibilities. You will take the section or go without. A mistake has been made and can't be rectified at this late hour. It's a thing that happens now and then, and there is nothing for it but to put up with it and make the best of it. Other people do."

"Ah, that is just it, you see. If they had stuck to their rights and enforced them you wouldn't be trying to trample mine under foot in this bland way now. I haven't any disposition to give you unnecessary trouble, but it is my duty to protect the next man from this kind of imposition. So I must have my car. Otherwise I will wait in Chicago and sue the company for violating its contract."

"Sue the company?—for a thing like that!"

"Certainly."

"Do you really mean that?"

"Indeed, I do."

The conductor looked the Major over wonderingly, and then said:

"It beats me—it's bran-new—I've never struck the mate to it before. But I swear I think you'd do it. Look here, I'll send for the station-master."

When the station-master came he was a good deal annoyed—at the Major, not at the person who had made the mistake. He was rather brusque, and took the same position which the conductor had taken in the beginning; but he failed to move the soft-spoken artilleryman, who still insisted that he must have his car. However, it was plain that there was only one strong side in this case, and that that side was the Major's. The station-master banished his annoyed manner, and became pleasant and even half apologetic. This made a good opening for a compromise, and the Major made a concession. He said he would give up the engaged stateroom, but he must have *a* stateroom. After a deal of ransacking, one was found whose owner was persuadable; he exchanged it for our section, and we got away at last. The conductor called on us in the evening, and was kind and courteous and obliging, and we had a long talk and got to be good friends. He said he wished the public would make trouble oftener—it would have a good effect.

He said that the railroads could not be expected to do their whole duty by the traveler unless the traveler would take some interest in the matter himself.

I hoped that we were done reforming for the trip now, but it was not so. In the hotel-car, in the morning, the Major called for broiled chicken. The waiter said:

"It's not in the bill of fare, sir; we do not serve anything but what is in the bill."

"That gentleman yonder is eating a broiled chicken."

"Yes, but that is different. He is one of the superintendents of the road."

"Then all the more must I have broiled chicken. I do not like these discriminations. Please hurry—bring me a broiled chicken."

The waiter brought the steward, who explained in a low and polite voice that the thing was impossible—it was against the rule, and the rule was rigid.

"Very well, then, you must either apply it impartially or break it impartially. You must take that gentleman's chicken away from him or bring me one."

The steward was puzzled, and did not quite know what to do. He began an incoherent argument, but the conductor came along just then, and asked what the difficulty was. The steward explained that here was a gentleman who was insisting on having a chicken when it was dead against the rule and not in the bill. The conductor said:

"Stick by your rules—you haven't any option. Wait a moment—is this the gentleman?" Then he laughed and said: "Never mind your rules—it's my advice, and sound; give him anything he wants—don't get him started on his rights. Give him whatever he asks for; and if you haven't got it, stop the train and get it."

The Major ate the chicken, but said he did it from a sense of duty and to establish a principle, for he did not like chicken.

I missed the Fair, it is true, but I picked up some diplomatic tricks which I and the reader may find handy and useful as we go along.

1893

Private History of the
"Jumping Frog" Story

Five or six years ago a lady from Finland asked me to tell her a story in our negro dialect, so that she could get an idea of what that variety of speech was like. I told her one of Hopkinson Smith's negro stories, and gave her a copy of *Harper's Monthly* containing it. She translated it for a Swedish newspaper, but by an oversight named me as the author of it instead of Smith. I was very sorry for that, because I got a good lashing in the Swedish press, which would have fallen to his share but for that mistake; for it was shown that Boccaccio had told that very story, in his curt and meager fashion, five hundred years before Smith took hold of it and made a good and tellable thing out of it.

I have always been sorry for Smith. But my own turn has come now. A few weeks ago Professor Van Dyke, of Princeton, asked this question:

"Do you know how old your Jumping Frog story is?"

And I answered:

"Yes—forty-five years. The thing happened in Calaveras County in the spring of 1849."

"No; it happened earlier—a couple of thousand years earlier; it is a Greek story."

I was astonished—and hurt. I said:

"I am willing to be a literary thief if it has been so ordained; I am even willing to be caught robbing the ancient dead alongside of Hopkinson Smith, for he is my friend and a good fellow, and I think would be as honest as any one if he could do it without occasioning remark; but I am not willing to antedate his crimes by fifteen hundred years. I must ask you to knock off part of that."

But the professor was not chaffing; he was in earnest, and could not abate a century. He named the Greek author, and offered to get the book and send it to me and the college text-book containing the English translation also. I thought I would like the translation best, because Greek makes me tired. January 30th he sent me the English version, and I will presently insert it in this article. It is my Jumping Frog tale in every essential. It is not strung out as I have strung it out, but it is all there.

To me this is very curious and interesting. Curious for several reasons. For instance:

I heard the story told by a man who was not telling it to his hearers as a thing new to them, but as a thing which *they had witnessed and would remember*. He was a dull person, and ignorant; he had no gift as a story-teller, and no invention; in his mouth this episode was merely history—history and statistics; and the gravest sort of history, too; he was entirely serious, for he was dealing with what to him were austere facts, and they interested him solely because they *were* facts; he was drawing on his memory, not his mind; he saw no humor in his tale, neither did his listeners; neither he nor they never smiled or laughed; in my time I have not attended a more solemn conference. To him and to his fellow gold-miners there were just two things in the story that were worth considering. One was the smartness of the stranger in taking in its hero, Jim Smiley, with a loaded frog; and the other was the stranger's deep knowledge of a frog's nature—for he knew (as the narrator asserted and the listeners conceded) that a frog *likes shot* and is always ready to eat it. Those men discussed those two points, and those only. They were hearty in their admiration of them, and none of the party was aware that a first-rate story had been told in a first-rate way, and that it was brimful of a quality whose presence they never suspected—humor.

Now, then, the interesting question is, *did* the frog episode happen in Angel's Camp in the spring of '49, as told in my hearing that day in the fall of 1865? I am perfectly sure that it did. I am also sure that its duplicate happened in Boeotia a couple of thousand years ago. I think it must be a case of history actually repeating itself, and not a case of a good story floating down the ages and surviving because too good to be allowed to perish.

I would now like to have the reader examine the Greek story and the story told by the dull and solemn Californian, and observe how exactly alike they are in essentials.

[*Translation*]

THE ATHENIAN AND THE FROG[1]

An Athenian once fell in with a Boeotian who was sitting by the roadside looking at a frog. Seeing the other approach, the Boeotian said his was a remarkable frog, and asked if he would agree to start a contest of frogs, on condition that he whose frog jumped farthest should receive a large sum of money. The Athenian replied that he would if the other would fetch him a frog, for the lake was near. To this he agreed, and when he was gone the Athenian took the frog, and, opening its mouth, poured some stones into its stomach, so that it did not indeed seem larger than before, but could not jump. The Boeotian soon returned with the other frog, and the contest began. The second frog first was pinched, and jumped moderately; then they pinched the Boeotian frog. And he gathered himself for a leap, and used the utmost effort, but he could not move his body the least. So the Athenian departed with the money. When he was gone the Boeotian, wondering what was the matter with the frog, lifted him up and examined him. And being turned upside down, he opened his mouth and vomited out the stones.

And here is the way it happened in California:

FROM "THE CELEBRATED JUMPING FROG OF CALAVERAS COUNTY"

Well, thish-yer Smiley had rat-tarriers, and chicken cocks, and tom-cats, and all them kind of things, till you couldn't rest, and you couldn't fetch nothing for him to bet on but he'd match you. He ketched a frog one day, and took him home, and said he cal'lated to educate him; and so he never done nothing for three months but set in his back yard and learn that frog to jump. And you bet you he *did* learn him, too. He'd give him a little punch behind, and the next minute you'd see that frog whirling in the air like a doughnut—see him turn one summerset, or maybe a couple if he got a good start, and come down flat-footed and all right, like a cat. He got him up so in the matter of ketching flies, and kep' him in practice so constant, that he'd nail a fly every time as fur as he could see him. Smiley said all a frog wanted was education, and he could do 'most anything —and I believe him. Why, I've seen him set Dan'l Webster down here on this floor—Dan'l Webster was the name of the frog—and sing out

---

[1] Sidgwick, *Greek Prose Composition*, page 116.

"Flies, Dan'l, flies!" and quicker'n you could wink he'd spring straight up and snake a fly off'n the counter there, and flop down on the floor ag'in as solid as a gob of mud, and fall to scratching the side of his head with his hind foot as indifferent as if he hadn't no idea he'd been doin' any more'n any frog might do. You never see a frog so modest and straightfor'ard as he was, for all he was so gifted. And when it come to fair and square jumping on a dead level, he could get over more ground at one straddle than any animal of his breed you ever see. Jumping on a dead level was his strong suit, you understand; and when it came to that, Smiley would ante up money on him as long as he had a red. Smiley was monstrous proud of his frog, and well he might be, for fellers that had traveled and been everywheres all said he laid over any frog that ever *they* see.

Well, Smiley kep' the beast in a little lattice box, and he used to fetch him down-town sometimes and lay for a bet. One day a feller— a stranger in the camp, he was—come acrost him with his box, and says:

"What might it be that you've got in the box?"

And Smiley says, sorter indifferent-like, "It might be a parrot, or it might be a canary, maybe, but it ain't—it's only just a frog."

And the feller took it, and looked at it careful, and turned it round this way and that, and says, "H'm—so 'tis. Well, what's *he* good for?"

"Well," Smiley says, easy and careless, "he's good enough for *one* thing, I should judge—he can outjump any frog in Calaveras County."

The feller took the box again and took another long, particular look, and gave it back to Smiley, and says, very deliberate, "Well," he says, "I don't see no p'ints about that frog that's any better'n any other frog."

"Maybe you don't," Smiley says. "Maybe you understand frogs and maybe you don't understand 'em; maybe you've had experience, and maybe you ain't only a amature, as it were. Anyways, I've got *my* opinion, and I'll resk forty dollars that he can outjump any frog in Calaveras County."

And the feller studies a minute, and then says, kinder sad-like, "Well, I'm only a stranger here, and I ain't got no frog, but if I had a frog I'd bet you."

And then Smiley sais: "That's all right—that's all right—if you'll hold my box a minute, I'll go and get you a frog." And so the feller took the box and put up his forty dollars along with Smiley's and set down to wait.

So he set there a good while thinking and thinking to hisself, and then he got the frog out and prized his mouth open and took a teaspoon and filled him full of quail-shot—filled him pretty near up to his chin—and set him on the floor. Smiley he went to the swamp and slopped around in the mud for a long time, and finally he ketched a frog and fetched him in and give him to this feller, and says:

"Now, if you're ready, set him alongside of Dan'l, with his fore paws just even with Dan'l's, and I'll give the word." Then he says, "One—two—three—git!" and him and the feller touched up the frogs from behind, and the new frog hopped off lively; but Dan'l give a heave, and hysted up his shoulders—so—like a Frenchman, but it warn't no use—he couldn't budge; he was planted as solid as a church, and he couldn't no more stir than if he was anchored out. Smiley was a good deal surprised, and he was disgusted, too, but he didn't have no idea what the matter was, of course.

The feller took the money and started away; and when he was going out at the door he sorter jerked his thumb over his shoulder—so—at Dan'l, and says again, very deliberate: "Well," he says, "*I* don't see no p'ints about that frog that's any better'n any other frog."

Smiley he stood scratching his head and looking down at Dan'l a long time, and at last he says, "I do wonder what in the nation that frog throw'd off for—I wonder if there ain't something the matter with him—he 'pears to look mighty baggy, somehow." And he ketched Dan'l by the nap of the neck, and hefted him, and says, "Why, blame my cats if he don't weigh five pound!" and turned him upside down, and he belched out a double handful of shot. And then he see how it was, and he was the maddest man—he set the frog down and took out after that feller, but he never ketched him.

The resemblances are deliciously exact. There you have the wily Boeotian and the wily Jim Smiley waiting—two thousand years apart —and waiting, each equipped with his frog and "laying" for the stranger. A contest is proposed—for money. The Athenian would take a chance "if the other would fetch him a frog"; the Yankee says: "I'm only a stranger here, and I ain't got no frog; but if I had a frog I'd bet you." The wily Boeotian and the wily Californian, with that vast gulf of two thousand years between, retire eagerly and go frogging in the marsh; the Athenian and the Yankee remain behind and work a base advantage, the one with pebbles, the other with shot. Presently the contest began. In the one case "they pinched the Boeotian frog"; in the other, "him and the feller touched up the frogs from behind." The Boeotian frog "gathered himself for a leap" (you can just *see* him!), "but could not move his body in the least"; the Californian frog "give a heave, but it warn't no use—he couldn't budge." In both the ancient and the modern cases the strangers departed with the money. The Boeotian and the Californian wonder what is the matter with their frogs; they lift them and examine; they turn them upside down and out spills the informing ballast.

Yes, the resemblances are curiously exact. I used to tell the story of the Jumping Frog in San Francisco, and presently Artemus Ward came along and wanted it to help fill out a little book which he was about to publish; so I wrote it out and sent it to his publisher, Carleton; but Carleton thought the book had enough matter in it, so he gave the story to Henry Clapp as a present, and Clapp put it in his *Saturday Press,* and it killed that paper with a suddenness that was beyond praise. At least the paper died with that issue, and none but envious people have ever tried to rob me of the honor and credit of killing it. The "Jumping Frog" was the first piece of writing of mine that spread itself through the newspapers and brought me into public notice. Consequently, the *Saturday Press* was a cocoon and I the worm in it; also, I was the gay-colored literary moth which its death set free. This simile has been used before.

Early in '66 the "Jumping Frog" was issued in book form, with other sketches of mine. A year or two later Madame Blanc translated it into French and published it in the *Revue des Deux Mondes,* but the result was not what should have been expected, for the *Revue* struggled along and pulled through, and is alive yet. I think the fault must have been in the translation. I ought to have translated it myself. I think so because I examined into the matter and finally retranslated the sketch from the French back into English, to see what the trouble was; that is, to see just what sort of a focus the French people got upon it. Then the mystery was explained. In French the story is too confused, and chaotic, and unreposeful, and ungrammatical, and insane; consequently it could only cause grief and sickness—it could not kill. A glance at my retranslation will show the reader that this must be true.

[My Retranslation]

THE FROG JUMPING OF THE COUNTY OF CALAVERAS

Eh bien! this Smiley nourished some terriers à rats, and some cocks of combat, and some cats, and all sort of things; and with his rage of betting one no had more of repose. He trapped one day a frog and him imported with him (*et l'emporta chez lui*) saying that he pretended to make his education. You me believe if you will, but during three months he not has nothing done but to him apprehend to jump (*apprendre à sauter*) in a court retired of her mansion (*de sa maison*). And I you respond that he have succeeded. He him gives a small blow by behind, and the instant after you shall see the frog turn in the air like a grease-biscuit, make one summersault, sometimes two, when she was well started, and re-fall upon his feet like a cat. He him had accomplished in the art of to gobble the flies (*gober des mouches*), and him there exercised continually—so well that a fly at the most far that she appeared was a fly lost. Smiley had custom to say that all which lacked to a frog it was the education, but with the education she could do nearly all—and I him believe. *Tenez*, I him have seen pose Daniel Webster there upon this plank—Daniel Webster was the name of the frog—and to him sing, "Some flies, Daniel, some flies!" —in a flash of the eye Daniel had bounded and seized a fly here upon the counter, then jumped anew at the earth, where he rested truly to himself scratch the head with his behind-foot, as if he no had not the least idea of his superiority. Never you not have seen frog as modest, as natural, sweet as she was. And when he himself agitated to jump purely and simply upon plain earth, she does more ground in one jump than any beast of his species than you can know.

To jump plain—this was his strong. When he himself agitated for that Smiley multiplied the bets upon her as long as there to him remained a red. It must to know, Smiley was monstrously proud of his frog, and he of it was right, for some men who were traveled, who had all seen, said that they to him would be injurious to him compare to another frog. Smiley guarded Daniel in a little box latticed which he carried by times to the village for some bet.

One day an individual stranger at the camp him arrested with his box and him said:

"What is this that you have then shut up there within?"

Smiley said, with an air indifferent:

"That could be a paroquet, or a syringe (*ou un serin*), but this no is nothing of such, it not is but a frog."

The individual it took, it regarded with care, it turned from one side and from the other, then he said:

"*Tiens!* in effect!—At what is she good?"

"My God!" respond Smiley, always with an air disengaged, "she is good for one thing, to my notice (*à mon avis*), she can batter in jumping (*elle peut batter en sautant*) all frogs of the county of Calaveras."

The individual re-took the box, it examined of new longly, and it rendered to Smiley in saying with an air deliberate:

"*Eh bien!* I no saw not that that frog had nothing of better than each frog." (*Je ne vois pas que cette grenouille ait rien de mieux qu'aucune grenouille.*) [If that isn't grammar gone to seed, then I count myself no judge.—M. T.]

"Possible that you not it saw not," said Smiley, "possible that you—you comprehend frogs; possible that you not you there comprehend nothing; possible that you had of the experience, and possible that you not be but an amateur. Of all manner (*De toute manière*) I bet forty dollars that she batter in jumping no matter which frog of the county of Calaveras."

The individual reflected a second, and said like sad:

"I not am but a stranger here, I no have not a frog; but if I of it had one, I would embrace the bet."

"Strong, well!" respond Smiley; "nothing of more facility. If you will hold my box a minute, I go you to search a frog (*j'irai vous chercher*)."

Behold, then, the individual, who guards the box, who puts his forty dollars upon those of Smiley, and who attends (*et qui attend*). He attended enough longtimes, reflecting all solely. And figure you that he takes Daniel, him opens the mouth by force and with a teaspoon him fills with shot of the hunt, even him fills just to the chin, then he him puts by the earth. Smiley during these times was at slopping in a swamp. Finally he trapped (*attrape*) a frog, him carried to that individual, and said:

"Now if you be ready, put him all against Daniel, with their before-feet upon the same line, and I give the signal"—then he added: "One, two, three—advance!"

Him and the individual touched their frogs by behind, and the frog new put to jump smartly, but Daniel himself lifted ponderously, exalted the shoulders thus, like a Frenchman—to what good? he could not budge, he is planted solid like a church, he not advance no more than if one him had put at the anchor.

Smiley was surprised and disgusted, but he not himself doubted not of the turn being intended (*mais il ne se doutait pas du tour bien entendu*). The individual empocketed the silver, himself with it went, and of it himself in going is that he no gives not a jerk of thumb over the shoulder—like that—at the poor Daniel, in saying with his air deliberate—(*L'individu empoche l'argent s'en va et en s'en allant est ce qu'il ne donne pas un coup de pouce par-dessus l'épaule, comme ça, au pauvre Daniel, en disant de son air délibéré.*)

"Eh bein! I no see not that that frog has nothing of better than an-other."

Smiley himself scratched longtimes the head, the eyes fixed upon Daniel, until that which at last he said:

"I me demand how the devil it makes itself that this beast has re-fused. Is it that she had something? One would believe that she is stuffed."

He grasped Daniel by the skin of the neck, him lifted and said: "The wolf me bite if he no weigh not five pounds."

He him reversed and the unhappy belched two handfuls of shot (*et le malheureux,* etc.).—When Smiley recognized how it was, he was like mad. He deposited his frog by the earth and ran after the individual, but he not him caught never.

It may be that there are people who can translate better than I can, but I am not acquainted with them.

So ends the private and public history of the Jumping Frog of Cala-veras County, an incident which has this unique feature about it—that it is both old and new, a "chestnut" and not a "chestnut"; for it was original when it happened two thousand years ago, and was again original when it happened in California in our own time.

1894

Fenimore Cooper's Literary
Offenses

The Pathfinder and *The Deerslayer* stand at the head of Cooper's novels as artistic creations. There are others of his works which contain parts as perfect as are to be found in these, and scenes even more thrilling. Not one can be compared with either of them as a finished whole.

The defects in both of these tales are comparatively slight. They were pure works of art.—*Prof. Lounsbury.*

The five tales reveal an extraordinary fullness of invention.

. . . One of the very greatest characters in fiction, Natty Bumppo. . . .

The craft of the woodsman, the tricks of the trapper, all the delicate art of the forest, were familiar to Cooper from his youth up.–*Prof. Brander Matthews.*

Cooper is the greatest artist in the domain of romantic fiction yet produced by America.–*Wilkie Collins.*

It seems to me that it was far from right for the Professor of English Literature in Yale, the Professor of English Literature in Columbia, and Wilkie Collins to deliver opinions on Cooper's literature without having read some of it. It would have been much more decorous to keep silent and let persons talk who have read Cooper.

Cooper's art has some defects. In one place in *Deerslayer,* and in the restricted space of two-thirds of a page, Cooper has scored 114 offenses against literary art out of a possible 115. It breaks the record.

There are nineteen rules governing literary art in the domain of romantic fiction—some say twenty-two. In *Deerslayer* Cooper violated eighteen of them. These eighteen require:

1. That a tale shall accomplish something and arrive somewhere. But the *Deerslayer* tale accomplishes nothing and arrives in the air.

2. They require that the episodes of a tale shall be necessary parts of the tale, and shall help to develop it. But as the *Deerslayer* tale is not a tale, and accomplishes nothing and arrives nowhere, the episodes have no rightful place in the work, since there was nothing for them to develop.

3. They require that the personages in a tale shall be alive, except in the case of corpses, and that always the reader shall be able to tell the corpses from the others. But this detail has often been overlooked in the *Deerslayer* tale.

4. They require that the personages in a tale, both dead and alive, shall exhibit a sufficient excuse for being there. But this detail also has been overlooked in the *Deerslayer* tale.

5. They require that when the personages of a tale deal in conversation, the talk shall sound like human talk, and be talk such as human beings would be likely to talk in the given circumstances, and have a discoverable meaning, also a discoverable purpose, and a show of relevancy, and remain in the neighborhood of the subject in hand, and be interesting to the reader, and help out the tale, and stop when the people cannot think of anything more to say. But this requirement has been ignored from the beginning of the *Deerslayer* tale to the end of it.

6. They require that when the author describes the character of a personage in his tale, the conduct and conversation of that personage

shall justify said description. But this law gets little or no attention in the *Deerslayer* tale, as Natty Bumppo's case will amply prove.

7. They require that when a personage talks like an illustrated, gilt-edged, tree-calf, hand-tooled, seven-dollar Friendship's Offering in the beginning of a paragraph, he shall not talk like a negro minstrel in the end of it. But this rule is flung down and danced upon in the *Deerslayer* tale.

8. They require that crass stupidities shall not be played upon the reader as "the craft of the woodsman, the delicate art of the forest," by either the author or the people in the tale. But this rule is persistently violated in the *Deerslayer* tale.

9. They require that the personages of a tale shall confine themselves to possibilities and let miracles alone; or, if they venture a miracle, the author must so plausibly set it forth as to make it look possible and reasonable. But these rules are not respected in the *Deerslayer* tale.

10. They require that the author shall make the reader feel a deep interest in the personages of his tale and in their fate; and that he shall make the reader love the good people in the tale and hate the bad ones. But the reader of the *Deerslayer* tale dislikes the good people in it, is indifferent to the others, and wishes they would all get drowned together.

11. They require that the characters in a tale shall be so clearly defined that the reader can tell beforehand what each will do in a given emergency. But in the *Deerslayer* tale this rule is vacated.

In addition to these large rules there are some little ones. These require that the author shall

12. *Say* what he is proposing to say, not merely come near it.

13. Use the right word, not its second cousin.

14. Eschew surplusage.

15. Not omit necessary details.

16. Avoid slovenliness of form.

17. Use good grammar.

18. Employ a simple and straightforward style.

Even these seven are coldly and persistently violated in the *Deerslayer* tale.

Cooper's gift in the way of invention was not a rich endowment; but such as it was he liked to work it, he was pleased with the effects, and indeed he did some quite sweet things with it. In his little box of stage-properties he kept six or eight cunning devices, tricks, artifices for his savages and woodsmen to deceive and circumvent each other

with, and he was never so happy as when he was working these innocent things and seeing them go. A favorite one was to make a
moccasined person tread in the tracks of the moccasined enemy, and
thus hide his own trail. Cooper wore out barrels and barrels of moc-
casins in working that trick. Another stage-property that he pulled
out of his box pretty frequently was his broken twig. He prized his
broken twig above all the rest of his effects, and worked it the hardest.
It is a restful chapter in any book of his when somebody doesn't step
on a dry twig and alarm all the reds and whites for two hundred yards
around. Every time a Cooper person is in peril, and absolute silence is
worth four dollars a minute, he is sure to step on a dry twig. There
may be a hundred handier things to step on, but that wouldn't satisfy
Cooper. Cooper requires him to turn out and find a dry twig; and if
he can't do it, go and borrow one. In fact, the Leatherstocking Series
ought to have been called the Broken Twig Series.

I am sorry there is not room to put in a few dozen instances of the
delicate art of the forest, as practised by Natty Bumppo and some of
the other Cooperian experts. Perhaps we may venture two or three
samples. Cooper was a sailor—a naval officer; yet he gravely tells us
how a vessel, driving toward a lee shore in a gale, is steered for a particular spot by her skipper because he knows of an *undertow* there
which will hold her back against the gale and save her. For just pure
woodcraft, or sailorcraft, or whatever it is, isn't that neat? For several
years Cooper was daily in the society of artillery, and he ought to have
noticed that when a cannon-ball strikes the ground it either buries
itself or skips a hundred feet or so; skips again a hundred feet or so—
and so on, till finally it gets tired and rolls. Now in one place he loses
some "females"—as he always calls women—in the edge of a wood near
a plain at night in a fog, on purpose to give Bumppo a chance to show
off the delicate art of the forest before the reader. These mislaid people
are hunting for a fort. They hear a cannon-blast, and a cannon-ball
presently comes rolling into the wood and stops at their feet. To the
females this suggests nothing. The case is very different with the admirable Bumppo. I wish I may never know peace again if he doesn't
strike out promptly and *follow the track* of that cannon-ball across the
plain through the dense fog and find the fort. Isn't it a daisy? If
Cooper had any real knowledge of Nature's ways of doing things,
he had a most delicate art in concealing the fact. For instance: one
of his acute Indian experts, Chingachgook (pronounced Chicago, I
think), has lost the trail of a person he is tracking through the forest.
Apparently that trail is hopelessly lost. Neither you nor I could ever

have guessed out the way to find it. It was very different with Chicago. Chicago was not stumped for long. He turned a running stream out of its course, and there, in the slush in its old bed, were that person's moccasin tracks. The current did not wash them away, as it would have done in all other like cases—no, even the eternal laws of Nature have to vacate when Cooper wants to put up a delicate job of wood-craft on the reader.

We must be a little wary when Brander Matthews tell us that Cooper's books "reveal an extraordinary fullness of invention." As a rule, I am quite willing to accept Brander Matthews's literary judg-ments and applaud his lucid and graceful phrasing of them; but that particular statement needs to be taken with a few tons of salt. Bless your heart, Cooper hadn't any more invention than a horse; and I don't mean a high-class horse, either; I mean a clothes-horse. It would be very difficult to find a really clever "situation" in Cooper's books, and still more difficult to find one of any kind which he has failed to render absurd by his handling of it. Look at the episodes of "the caves"; and at the celebrated scuffle between Maqua and those others on the table-land a few days later; and at Hurry Harry's queer water-transit from the castle to the ark; and at Deerslayer's half-hour with his first corpse; and at the quarrel between Hurry Harry and Deerslayer later; and at—but choose for yourself; you can't go amiss.

If Cooper had been an observer his inventive faculty would have worked better; not more interestingly, but more rationally, more plau-sibly. Cooper's proudest creations in the way of "situations" suffer noticeably from the absence of the observer's protecting gift. Cooper's eye was splendidly inaccurate. Cooper seldom saw anything correctly. He saw nearly all things as through a glass eye, darkly. Of course a man who cannot see the commonest little every-day matters accurately is working at a disadvantage when he is constructing a "situation." In the *Deerslayer* tale Cooper has a stream which is fifty feet wide where it flows out of a lake; it presently narrows to twenty as it meanders along for no given reason, and yet when a stream acts like that it ought to be required to explain itself. Fourteen pages later the width of the brook's outlet from the lake has suddenly shrunk thirty feet, and become "the narrowest part of the stream." This shrinkage is not accounted for. The stream has bends in it, a sure indication that it has alluvial banks and cuts them; yet these bends are only thirty and fifty feet long. If Cooper had been a nice and punctilious observer he would have noticed that the bends were oftener nine hundred feet long than short of it.

Cooper made the exit of that stream fifty feet wide, in the first place, for no particular reason; in the second place, he narrowed it to less than twenty to accommodate some Indians. He bends a "sapling" to the form of an arch over this narrow passage, and conceals six Indians in its foliage. They are "laying" for a settler's scow or ark which is coming up the stream on its way to the lake; it is being hauled against the stiff current by a rope whose stationary end is anchored in the lake; its rate of progress cannot be more than a mile an hour. Cooper describes the ark, but pretty obscurely. In the matter of dimensions "it was little more than a modern canal-boat." Let us guess, then, that it was about one hundred and forty feet long. It was of "greater breadth than common." Let us guess, then, that it was about sixteen feet wide. This leviathan had been prowling down bends which were but a third as long as itself, and scraping between banks where it had only two feet of space to spare on each side. We cannot too much admire this miracle. A low-roofed log dwelling occupies "two-thirds of the ark's length"—a dwelling ninety feet long and sixteen feet wide, let us say—a kind of vestibule train. The dwelling has two rooms—each forty-five feet long and sixteen feet wide, let us guess. One of them is the bedroom of the Hutter girls, Judith and Hetty; the other is the parlor in the daytime, at night it is papa's bedchamber. The ark is arriving at the stream's exit now, whose width has been reduced to less than twenty feet to accommodate the Indians—say to eighteen. There is a foot to spare on each side of the boat. Did the Indians notice that there was going to be a tight squeeze there? Did they notice that they could make money by climbing down out of that arched sapling and just stepping aboard when the ark scraped by? No, other Indians would have noticed these things, but Cooper's Indians never notice anything. Cooper thinks they are marvelous creatures for noticing, but he was almost always in error about his Indians. There was seldom a sane one among them.

The ark is one hundred and forty-feet long; the dwelling is ninety feet long. The idea of the Indians is to drop softly and secretly from the arched sapling to the dwelling as the ark creeps along under it at the rate of a mile an hour, and butcher the family. It will take the ark a minute and a half to pass under. It will take the ninety-foot dwelling a minute to pass under. Now, then, what did the six Indians do? It would take you thirty years to guess, and even then you would have to give it up, I believe. Therefore, I will tell you what the Indians did. Their chief, a person of quite extraordinary intellect for a Cooper Indian, warily watched the canal-boat as it squeezed along under him, and when he had got his calculations fined down to exactly the right shade, as he judged, he let go and dropped. And *missed the house!* That is actually what he did. He missed the house, and landed in the stern of the scow. It was not much of a fall, yet it knocked him silly. He lay there unconscious. If the house had been ninety-seven feet long he would have made the trip. The fault was Cooper's, not his. The error lay in the construction of the house. Cooper was no architect.

There still remained in the roost five Indians. The boat has passed under and is now out of their reach. Let me explain what the five did —you would not be able to reason it out for yourself. No. 1 jumped for the boat, but fell in the water astern of it. Then No. 2 jumped for the boat, but fell in the water still farther astern of it. Then No. 3 jumped for the boat, and fell a good way astern of it. Then No. 4 jumped for the boat, and fell in the water *away* astern. Then even No. 5 made a jump for the boat—for he was a Cooper Indian. In the matter of intellect, the difference between a Cooper Indian and the Indian that stands in front of the cigar-shop is not spacious. The scow episode is really a sublime burst of invention; but it does not thrill, because the inaccuracy of the details throws a sort of air of fictitiousness and general improbability over it. This comes of Cooper's inadequacy as an observer.

The reader will find some examples of Cooper's high talent for in-accurate observation in the account of the shooting-match in *The Pathfinder*.

A common wrought nail was driven lightly into the target, its head having been first touched with paint.

The color of the paint is not stated—an important omission, but Cooper deals freely in important omissions. No, after all, it was not an important omission; for this nail-head is *a hundred yards from* the marksmen, and could not be seen by them at that distance, no matter what its color might be. How far can the best eyes see a common house-fly? A hundred yards? It is quite impossible. Very well; eyes that cannot see a house-fly that is a hundred yards away cannot see an ordinary nail-head at that distance, for the size of the two objects is the same. It takes a keen eye to see a fly or a nail-head at fifty yards—one hundred and fifty feet. Can the reader do it?

The nail was lightly driven, its head painted, and game called. Then the Cooper miracles began. The bullet of the first marksman chipped an edge of the nail-head; the next man's bullet drove the nail a little way into the target—and removed all the paint. Haven't the miracles gone far enough now? Not to suit Cooper; for the purpose of this whole scheme is to show off his prodigy, Deerslayer-Hawkeye-Long-Rifle-Leatherstocking-Pathfinder-Bumppo before the ladies.

"Be all ready to clench it, boys!" cried out Pathfinder, stepping into his friend's tracks the instant they were vacant. "Never mind a new nail; I can see that, though the paint is gone, and what I can see I can hit at a hundred yards, though it were only a mosquito's eye. Be ready to clench!"

The rifle cracked, the bullet sped its way, and the head of the nail was buried in the wood, covered by the piece of flattened lead.

There, you see, is a man who could hunt flies with a rifle, and command a ducal salary in a Wild West show to-day if we had him back with us.

The recorded feat is certainly surprising just as it stands; but it is not surprising enough for Cooper. Cooper adds a touch. He has made Pathfinder do this miracle with another man's rifle; and not only that, but Pathfinder did not have even the advantage of loading it himself. He had everything against him, and yet he made that impossible shot; and not only made it, but did it with absolute confidence, saying, "Be ready to clench." Now a person like that would have undertaken that same feat with a brickbat, and with Cooper to help he would have achieved it, too.

Pathfinder showed off handsomely that day before the ladies. His very first feat a thing which no Wild West show can touch. He was standing with the group of marksmen, observing—a hundred yards from the target, mind; one Jasper raised his rifle and drove the center of the bull's-eye. Then the Quartermaster fired. The target exhibited no result this time. There was a laugh. "It's a dead miss," said Major Lundie. Pathfinder waited an impressive moment or two; then said, in that calm, indifferent, know-it-all way of his, "No, Major, he has covered Jasper's bullet, as will be seen if any one will take the trouble to examine the target."

Wasn't it remarkable! How *could* he see that little pellet fly through the air and enter that distant bullet-hole? Yet that is what he did; for nothing is impossible to a Cooper person. Did any of those people have any deep-seated doubts about this thing? No; for that would imply sanity, and these were all Cooper people.

The respect for Pathfinder's skill and for his *quickness and accuracy of sight* [the italics are mine] was so profound and general, that the instant he made this declaration the spectators began to distrust their own opinions, and a dozen rushed to the target in order to ascertain the fact. There, sure enough, it was found that the Quartermaster's bullet had gone through the hole made by Jasper's, and that, too, so accurately as to require a minute examination to be certain of the circumstance, which, however, was soon clearly established by discovering one bullet over the other in the stump against which the target was placed.

They made a "minute" examination; but never mind, how could they know that there were two bullets in that hole without digging the latest one out? for neither probe nor eyesight could prove the presence of any more than one bullet. Did they dig? No; as we shall see. It is the Pathfinder's turn now; he steps out before the ladies, takes aim, and fires.

But, alas! here is a disappointment; an incredible, an unimaginable disappointment—for the target's aspect is unchanged; there is nothing there but that same old bullet-hole!

"If one dared to hint at such a thing," cried Major Duncan, "I should say that the Pathfinder has also missed the target!"

As nobody had missed it yet, the "also" was not necessary; but never mind about that, for the Pathfinder is going to speak.

"No, no, Major," said he, confidently, "that *would* be a risky declaration. I didn't load the piece, and can't say what was in it; but if it was lead, you will find the bullet driving down those of the Quartermaster and Jasper, else is not my name Pathfinder."

A shout from the target announced the truth of this assertion.

Is the miracle sufficient as it stands? Not for Cooper. The Pathfinder speaks again, as he "now slowly advances toward the stage occupied by the females":

"That's not all, boys, that's not all; if you find the target touched at all, I'll own to a miss. The Quartermaster cut the wood, but you'll find no wood cut by that last messenger."

The miracle is at last complete. He knew—doubtless *saw*—at the distance of a hundred yards—that his bullet had passed into the hole *without fraying the edges*. There were now three bullets in that one hole—three bullets embedded processionally in the body of the stump back of the target. Everybody knew this—somehow or other—and yet nobody had dug any of them out to make sure. Cooper is not a close observer, but he is interesting. He is certainly always that, no matter what happens. And he is more interesting when he is not noticing what he is about than when he is. This is a considerable merit.

The conversations in the Cooper books have a curious sound in our modern ears. To believe that such talk really ever came out of people's mouths would be to believe that there was a time when time was of no value to a person who thought he had something to say; when it was the custom to spread a two-minute remark out to ten; when a man's mouth was a rolling-mill, and busied itself all day long in turning four-foot pigs of thought into thirty-foot bars of conversational railroad iron by attenuation; when subjects were seldom faithfully stuck to, but the talk wandered all around and arrived nowhere; when conversations consisted mainly of irrelevancies, with here and there a relevancy, a relevancy with an embarrassed look, as not being able to explain how it got there.

Cooper was certainly not a master in the construction of dialogue. Inaccurate observation defeated him here as it defeated him in so many other enterprises of his. He even failed to notice that the man who talks corrupt English six days in the week must and will talk it on the seventh, and can't help himself. In the *Deerslayer* story he lets Deerslayer talk the showiest kind of book-talk sometimes, and at other times the basest of base dialects. For instance, when some one asks him if he has a sweetheart, and if so, where she abides, this is his majestic answer:

"She's in the forest—hanging from the boughs of the trees, in a soft rain—in the dew on the open grass—the clouds that float about in the blue heavens—the birds that sing in the woods—the sweet springs where I slake my thirst—and in all the other glorious gifts that come from God's Providence!"

And he preceeded that, a little before, with this:

"It consarns me as all things that touches a fri'nd consarns a fri'nd."

And this is another of his remarks:

"If I was Injin born, now, I might tell of this, or carry in the scalp and boast of the expl'ite afore the whole tribe; or if my inimy had only been a bear"—[and so on].

We cannot imagine such a thing as a veteran Scotch Commander-in-Chief comporting himself in the field like a windy melodramatic actor, but Cooper could. On one occasion Alice and Cora were being chased by the French through a fog in the neighborhood of their father's fort:

"*Point de quartier aux coquins!*" cried an eager pursuer, who seemed to direct the operations of the enemy.

"Stand firm and be ready, my gallant 60ths!" suddenly exclaimed a voice above them; "wait to see the enemy; fire low, and sweep the glacis."

"Father! father" exclaimed a piercing cry from out the mist. "it is I! Alice! thy own Elsie! spare, O! save your daughters!"

"Hold!" shouted the former speaker, in the awful tones of parental agony, the sound reaching even to the woods, and rolling back in solemn echo. " 'Tis she! God has restored me my children! Throw open the sally-port; to the field, 6oths, to the field! pull not a trigger, l st ye kill my lambs! Drive off these dogs of France with your steel!"

Cooper's word-sense was singularly dull. When a person has a poor ear for music he will flat and sharp right along without knowing it. He keeps near the tune, but it is *not* the tune. When a person has a poor ear for words, the result is a literary flatting and sharping; you perceive what he is intending to say, but you also perceive that he doesn't *say* it. This is Cooper. He was not a word-musician. His ear was satisfied with the *approximate* word. I will furnish some circumstantial evidence in support of this charge. My instances are gathered from half a dozen pages of the tale called *Deerslayer*. He uses "Verbal" for "oral"; "precision" for "facility"; "phenomena" for "marvels"; "necessary" for "predetermined"; "unsophisticated" for "primitive"; "preparation" for "expectancy"; "rebuked" for "subdued"; "dependent on" for "resulting from"; "fact" for "condition"; "fact" for "conjecture"; "precaution" for "caution"; "explain" for "determine"; "mortified" for "disappointed"; "meretricious" for "factitious"; "materially" for "considerably"; "decreasing" for "deepening"; "increasing" for "disappearing"; "embedded" for "inclosed"; "treacherous" for "hostile"; "stood" for "stooped"; "softened" for "replaced"; "rejoined" for "remarked"; "situation" for "condition"; "different" for "differing"; "insensible" for "unsentient"; "brevity" for "celerity"; "distrusted" for "suspicious"; "mental imbecility" for "imbecility"; "eyes" for "sight"; "counteracting" for "opposing"; "funeral obsequies" for "obsequies."

There have been daring people in the world who claimed that Cooper could write English, but they are all dead now—all dead but Lounsbury. I don't remember that Lounsbury makes the claim in so many words, still he makes it, for he says that *Deerslayer* is a "pure work of art." Pure, in that connection, means faultless—faultless in all details—and language is a detail. If Mr. Lounsbury had only compared Cooper's English with the English which he writes himself—but it is plain that he didn't; and so it is likely that he imagines until this day that Cooper's is as clean and compact as his own. Now I feel sure, deep down in my heart, that Cooper wrote about the poorest English that exists in our language, and that the English of *Deerslayer* is the very worst that even Cooper ever wrote.

I may be mistaken, but it does seem to me that *Deerslayer* is not a work of art in any sense; it does seem to me that it is destitute of every detail that goes to the making of a work of art; in truth, it seems to me that *Deerslayer* is just simply a literary *delirium tremens*.

A work of art? It has no invention; it has no order, system, sequence, or result; it has no lifelikeness, no thrill, no stir, no seeming of reality; its characters are confusedly drawn, and by their acts and words they prove that they are not the sort of people the author claims that they are; its humor is pathetic; its pathos is funny; its conversations are—oh! indescribable; its love-scenes odious; its English a crime against the language.

Counting these out, what is left is Art. I think we must all admit that.

1895

A Hell of a Hotel at Maryborough

November 11. On the road. This train—express—goes twenty and one-half miles an hour, schedule time; but it is fast enough, the outlook upon sea and land is so interesting, and the cars so comfortable. They are not English, and not American; they are the Swiss combination of the two. A narrow and railed porch along the side, where a person can walk up and down. A lavatory in each car. This is progress; this is nineteenth-century spirit. In New Zealand, these fast expresses run twice a week. It is well to know this if you want to be a bird and fly through the country at a twenty-mile gait; otherwise you may start on one of the five wrong days, and then you will get a train that can't overtake its own shadow.

By contrast, these pleasant cars call to mind the branch-road cars at Maryborough, Australia, and a passenger's talk about the branch-road and the hotel.

Somewhere on the road to Maryborough I changed for a while to a smoking-carriage. There were two gentlemen there; both riding backward, one at each end of the compartment. They were acquaintances of each other. I sat down facing the one that sat at the starboard window. He had a good face, and a friendly look, and I judged from his dress that he was a dissenting minister. He was along toward fifty. Of his own motion he struck a match, and shaded it with his hand for me to light my cigar. I take the rest from my diary:

In order to start conversation I asked him something about Maryborough. He said, in a most pleasant—even musical—voice, but with quiet and cultured decision:

"It's a charming town, with a hell of a hotel."

I was astonished. It seemed so odd to hear a minister swear out loud. He went placidly on:

"It's the worst hotel in Australia. Well, one may go further, and say in Australasia."

"Bad beds?"

"No—none at all. Just sand-bags."

"The pillows, too?"

"Yes, the pillows, too. Just sand. And not a good quality of sand. It packs too hard, and has never been screened. There is too much gravel in it. It is like sleeping on nuts."

"Isn't there any good sand?"

"Plenty of it. There is as good bed-sand in this region as the world can furnish. Aerated sand—and loose; but they won't buy it. They want something that will pack solid, and petrify."

"How are the rooms?"

"Eight feet square; and a sheet of iced oil-cloth to step on in the morning when you get out of the sand-quarry."

"As to lights?"

"Coal-oil lamp."

"A good one?"

"No. It's the kind that sheds a gloom."

"I like a lamp that burns all night."

"This one won't. You must blow it out early."

"That is bad. One might want it again in the night. Can't find it in the dark."

"There's no trouble; you can find it by the stench."

"Wardrobe?"

"Two nails on the door to hang seven suits of clothes on—if you've got them."

"Bells?"

"There aren't any."

"What do you do when you want service?"

"Shout. But it won't fetch anybody."

"Suppose you want the chambermaid to empty the slop-jar?"

"There isn't any slop-jar. The hotels don't keep them. That is, outside of Sydney and Melbourne."

"Yes, I knew that. I was only talking. It's the oddest thing in Australia. Another thing: I've got to get up in the dark, in the morning, to take the five-o'clock train. Now if the boots—"

"There isn't any."

"Well, the porter."

"There isn't any."

"But who will call me?"

"Nobody. You'll call yourself. And you'll light yourself, too. There'll not be a light burning in the halls or anywhere. And if you don't carry a light, you'll break your neck."

"But who will help me down with my baggage?"

"Nobody. However, I will tell you what to do. In Maryborough there's an American who has lived there half a lifetime; a fine man, and prosperous and popular. He will be on the lookout for you; you won't have any trouble. Sleep in peace; he will rout you out, and you will make your train. Where is your manager?"

"I left him at Ballarat, studying the language. And besides, he had to go to Melbourne and get us ready for New Zealand. I've not tried to pilot myself before, and it doesn't look easy."

"Easy! You've selected the very most difficult piece of railroad in Australia for your experiment. There are twelve miles of this road which no man without good executive ability can ever hope—tell me, have you good executive ability?—first-rate executive ability?"

"I—well, I think so, but—"

"That settles it. The tone of—oh, *you* wouldn't ever make it in the world. However, that American will point you right, and you'll go. You've got tickets?"

"Yes—round trip; all the way to Sydney."

"Ah, there it is, you see! You are going in the five o'clock by Castlemaine—twelve miles—instead of the seven-fifteen by Ballarat—in order to save two hours of fooling along the road. Now then, don't interrupt —let me have the floor. You're going to save the government a deal of hauling, but that's nothing; your ticket is by Ballarat, and it isn't good over that twelve miles, and so—"

"But why should the government care which way I go?"

"Goodness knows! Ask of the winds that far away with fragments strewed the sea, as the boy that stood on the burning deck used to say. The government chooses to do its railway business in its own way, and it doesn't know as much about it as the French. In the beginning they tried idiots; then they imported the French—which was going backward, you see; now it runs the roads itself—which is going backward again, you see. Why, do you know, in order to curry favor with the voters, the government puts down a road wherever anybody wants it—anybody that owns two sheep and a dog; and by consequence we've got, in the colony of Victoria, eight hundred railway-stations, and the business done at eighty of them doesn't foot up twenty shillings a week."

"Five dollars? Oh, come!"

"It's true. It's the absolute truth."

"Why, there are three or four men on wages at every station."

"I know it. And the station business doesn't pay for the sheep-dip to sanctify their coffee with. It's just as I say. And accommodating? Why, if you shake a rag the train will stop in the midst of the wilderness to pick you up. All that kind of politics costs, you see. And then, besides, any town that has a good many votes and wants a fine station, gets it. Don't you overlook that Maryborough station, if you take an interest in governmental curiosities. Why, you can put the whole population of Maryborough into it, and give them a sofa apiece, and have room for more. You haven't fifteen stations in America that are as big, and you probably haven't five that are half as fine. Why, it's perfectly elegant. And the clock! Everybody will show you the clock. There isn't a station in Europe that's got such a clock. It doesn't strike—and that's one mercy. It hasn't any bell; and as you'll have cause to remember, if you keep your reason, all Australia is simply bedamned with bells. On every quarter-hour, night and day, they jingle a tiresome chime of half a dozen notes—all the clocks in town at once, all the clocks in Australasia at once, and all the *very same* notes; first, downward scale: *mi, re, do, sol*—then upward scale: *sol, si, re, do*—down again: *mi, re, do, sol*—up again: *sol, si, re, do*—then the clock—say at midnight: *clang—clang—clang—clang—clang—clang—clang—clang—clang—clang—clang—clang!—and*, by that time you're—hello, what's all this excitement about? Oh, I see—a runaway—scared by the train; why, you wouldn't think *this* train could scare anything. Well, of course, when they build and run eighty stations at a loss, and a lot of palace-stations and clocks like Maryborough's at another loss, the government has got to economize somewhere, hasn't it? Very well—look at the rolling stock! That's where they save the money. Why, that train from Maryborough will consist of eighteen freight-cars and two passenger-kennels; cheap, poor, shabby, slovenly; no drinking-water, no sanitary arrangements, every imaginable inconvenience; and slow?

—oh, the gait of cold molasses; no air-brake, no springs, and they'll jolt your head off every time they start or stop. That's where they make their little economies, you see. They spend tons of money to house you palatially while you wait fifteen minutes for a train, then degrade you to six hours' convict-transportation to get the foolish outlay back. What a rational man really needs is discomfort while he's waiting, then his journey in a nice train would be a grateful change. But no, that would be common sense—and out of place in a government. And then, besides, they save in that other little detail, you know—repudiate their own tickets, and collect a poor little illegitimate extra shilling out of you for that twelve miles, and—"

"Well, in any case—"

"Wait—there's more. Leave that American out of the account and see what would happen. There's nobody on hand to examine your ticket when you arrive. But the conductor will come and examine it when the train is ready to start. It is too late to buy your extra ticket now; the train can't wait, and won't. You must climb out."

"But can't I pay the conductor?"

"No, he is not authorized to receive the money, and he won't. You must climb out. There's no other way. I tell you, the railway management is about the only thoroughly European thing here—continentally European I mean, not English. It's the continental business in perfection; down *fine*. Oh, yes, even to the peanut-commerce of weighing baggage."

The train slowed up at his place. As he stepped out he said:

"Yes, you'll like Maryborough. Plenty of intelligence there. It's a charming place—with a hell of a hotel."

Then he was gone. I turned to the other gentleman:

"Is your friend in the ministry?"

"No—studying for it."

From FOLLOWING THE EQUATOR, 1897

The Indian Crow

Some natives—I don't remember how many—went into my bedroom, now, and put things to rights and arranged the mosquito-bar,
and I went to bed to nurse my cough. It was about nine in the evening.
What a state of things! For three hours the yelling and shouting of
natives in the hall continued, along with the velvety patter of their
swift bare feet—what a racket it was! They were yelling orders and
messages down three flights. Why, in the matter of noise it amounted
to a riot, an insurrection, a revolution. And then there were other
noises mixed up with these and at intervals tremendously accent-
ing them—roofs falling in, I judged, windows smashing, persons being murdered, crows squawking, and deriding, and cursing, canaries
screeching, monkeys jabbering, macaws blaspheming, and every now
and then fiendish bursts of laughter and explosions of dynamite. By
midnight I had suffered all the different kinds of shocks there are,
and knew that I could never more be disturbed by them, either isolated or in combination. Then came peace—stillness deep and solemn
—and lasted till five.

Then it all broke loose again. And who restarted it? The Bird of
Birds—the Indian crow. I came to know him well, by and by, and be
infatuated with him. I suppose he is the hardest lot that wears feathers.
Yes, and the cheerfulest, and the best satisfied with himself. He never
arrived at what he is by any careless process, or any sudden one; he is
a work of art, and "art is long"; he is the product of immemorial ages,
and of deep calculation; one can't make a bird like that in a day. He
has been reincarnated more times than Shiva; and he has kept a
sample of each incarnation, and fused it into his constitution. In the
course of his evolutionary promotions, his sublime march toward ultimate perfection, he has been a gambler, a low comedian, a dissolute
priest, a fussy woman, a blackguard, a scoffer, a liar, a thief, a spy, an
informer, a trading politician, a swindler, a professional hypocrite, a
patriot for cash, a reformer, a lecturer, a lawyer, a conspirator, a rebel,
a royalist, a democrat, a practicer and propagator of irreverence, a
meddler, an intruder, a busybody, an infidel, and a wallower in sin for
the mere love of it. The strange result, the incredible result, of this

648   MARK TWAIN

patient accumulation of all damnable traits is, that he does not know
what care is, he does not know what sorrow is, he does not know what
remorse is; his life is one long thundering ecstasy of happiness, and
he will go to his death untroubled, knowing that he will soon turn
up again as an author or something, and be even more intolerably
capable and comfortable than ever he was before.

In his straddling wide forward-step, and his springy sidewise series
of hops, and his impudent air, and his cunning way of canting his
head to one side upon occasion, he reminds one of the American
blackbird. But the sharp resemblances stop there. He is much bigger
than the blackbird; and he lacks the blackbird's trim and slender and
beautiful build and shapely beak; and of course his sober garb of
gray and rusty black is a poor and humble thing compared with the
splendid luster of the blackbird's metallic sables and shifting and
flashing bronze glories. The blackbird is a perfect gentleman, in de-
portment and attire, and is not noisy, I believe, except when holding
religious services and political conventions in a tree; but this Indian
sham Quaker is just a rowdy, and is always noisy when awake—always
chaffing, scolding, scoffing, laughing, ripping, and cursing, and carrying
on about something or other. I never saw such a bird for delivering
opinions. Nothing escapes him; he notices everything that happens,
and brings out his opinion about it, particularly if it is a matter that is
none of his business. And it is never a mild opinion, but always violent
—violent and profane—the presence of ladies does not affect him. His
opinions are not the outcome of reflection, for he never thinks about
anything, but heaves out the opinion that is on top in his mind, and
which is often an opinion about some quite different thing and does
not fit the case. But that is his way; his main idea is to get out an
opinion, and if he stopped to think he would lose chances.

I suppose he has no enemies among men. The whites and Mohammedans never seemed to molest him; and the Hindus, because of their
religion, never take the life of any creature, but spare even the snakes
and tigers and fleas and rats. If I sat on one end of the balcony, the
crows would gather on the railing at the other end and talk about me;
and edge closer, little by little, till I could almost reach them; and
they would sit there, in the most unabashed way, and talk about my
clothes, and my hair, and my complexion, and probable character and
vocation and politics, and how I came to be in India, and what I had
been doing, and how many days I had got for it, and how I had happened to go unhanged so long, and when would it probably come off,
and might there be more of my sort where I came from, and when

would *they* be hanged—and so on, and so on, until I could not longer endure the embarrassment of it; then I would shoo them away, and they would circle around in the air a little while, laughing and deriding and mocking, and presently settle on the rail and do it all over again.

They were very sociable when there was anything to eat—oppressively so. With a little encouragement they would come in and light on the table and help me eat my breakfast; and once when I was in the other room and they found themselves alone, they carried off everything they could lift; and they were particular to choose things which they could make no use of after they got them. In India their number is beyond estimate, and their noise is in proportion. I suppose they cost the country more than the government does; yet that is not a light matter. Still, they pay; their company pays; it would sadden the land to take their cheerful voice out of it.

From FOLLOWING THE EQUATOR, 1897

At the Appetite Cure

This establishment's name is Hochberghaus. It is in Bohemia, a short day's journey from Vienna, and being in the Austrian Empire is, of course, a health resort. The empire is made up of health resorts; it distributes health to the whole world. Its waters are all medicinal. They are bottled and sent throughout the earth; the natives themselves drink beer. This is self-sacrifice, apparently—but outlanders who have drunk Vienna beer have another idea about it. Particularly the Pilsener which one gets in a small cellar up an obscure back lane in the First Bezirk— the name has escaped me, but the place is easily found: You inquire for the Greek church; and when you get to it, go right along by—the next house is that little beer-mill. It is remote from all traffic and all noise; it is always Sunday there. There are two small rooms, with low ceilings supported by massive arches; the arches and ceilings are whitewashed, otherwise the rooms would pass for cells in the dungeons of a bastile. The furniture is plain and cheap, there is no ornamentation anywhere; yet it is a heaven for the self-sacrificers, for the beer there is incomparable; there is nothing like it elsewhere in the world. In the first room you will find twelve or fifteen ladies and gentlemen of civilian quality; in the other one a dozen generals and ambassadors. One may live in Vienna many months and not hear of this place; but having once heard of it and sampled it the sampler will afterward infest it.

However, this is all incidental—a mere passing note of gratitude for blessings received—it has nothing to do with my subject. My subject is health resorts. All unhealthy people ought to domicile themselves in Vienna, and use that as a base, making flights from time to time to the outlying resorts, according to need. A flight to Marienbad to get rid of fat; a flight to Carlsbad to get rid of rheumatism; a flight to Kaltenleutgeben to take the water cure and get rid of the rest of the diseases. It is all so handy. You can stand in Vienna and toss a biscuit into Kaltenleutgeben, with a twelve-inch gun. You can run out thither at any time of the day; you go by the phenomenally slow trains, and yet inside of an hour you have exchanged the glare and swelter of the city for wooded hills, and shady forest paths, and soft, cool airs, and the music of birds, and the repose and peace of paradise.

And there are plenty of other health resorts at your service and convenient to get at from Vienna; charming places, all of them; Vienna sits in the center of a beautiful world of mountains with now and then a lake and forests; in fact, no other city is so fortunately situated.

There are abundance of health resorts, as I have said. Among them this place—Hochberghaus. It stands solitary on the top of a densely wooded mountain, and is a building of great size. It is called the Appetite Anstalt, and people who have lost their appetites come here to get them restored. When I arrived I was taken by Professor Haimberger to his consulting-room and questioned:

"It is six o'clock. When did you eat last?"

"At noon."

"What did you eat?"

"Next to nothing."

"What was on the table?"

"The usual things."

"Chops, chickens, vegetables, and so on?"

"Yes; but don't mention them—I can't bear it."

"Are you tired of them?"

"Oh, utterly. I wish I might never hear of them again."

"The mere sight of food offends you, does it?"

"More, it revolts me."

The doctor considered awhile, then got out a long menu and ran his eye slowly down it.

"I think," said he, "that what you need to eat is—but here, choose for yourself."

I glanced at the list, and my stomach threw a handspring. Of all the barbarous layouts that were ever contrived, this was the most atrocious. At the top stood "tough, underdone, overdue tripe, garnished with garlic"; half-way down the bill stood "young cat; old cat; scrambled cat"; at the bottom stood "sailor-boots, softened with tallow —served raw." The wide intervals of the bill were packed with dishes calculated to insult a cannibal. I said:

"Doctor, it is not fair to joke over so serious a case as mine. I came here to get an appetite, not to throw away the remnant that's left."

He said, gravely, "I am not joking; why should I joke?"

"But I can't eat these horrors."

"Why not?"

He said it with a naïveté that was admirable, whether it was real or assumed.

"Why not? Because—why, doctor, for months I have seldom been able to endure anything more substantial than omelettes and custards. These unspeakable dishes of yours—"

"Oh, you will come to like them. They are very good. And you *must* eat them. It is the rule of the place, and is strict. I cannot permit any departure from it."

I said, smiling: "Well, then, doctor, you will have to permit the departure of the patient. I am going."

He looked hurt, and said in a way which changed the aspect of things:

"I am sure you would not do me that injustice. I accepted you in good faith—you will not shame that confidence. This appetite cure is my whole living. If you should go forth from it with the sort of appetite which you now have, it could become known, and you can see, yourself, that people would say my cure failed in your case and hence can fail in other cases. You will not go; you will not do me this hurt."

I apologized and said I would stay.

"That is right. I was sure you would not go; it would take the food from my family's mouths."

"Would they mind that? Do they eat these fiendish things?"

"They? My family?" His eyes were full of gentle wonder. "Of course not."

"Oh, they don't! Do you?"

"Certainly not."

"I see. It's another case of a physician who doesn't take his own medicine."

"I don't need it. It is six hours since you lunched. Will you have supper now—or later?"

"I am not hungry, but now is as good a time as any, and I would like to be done with it and have it off my mind. It is about my usual time, and regularity is commanded by all the authorities. Yes, I will try to nibble a little now—I wish a light horse-whipping would answer instead."

The professor handed me that odious menu.

"Choose—or will you have it later?"

"Oh, dear me, show me to my room; I forgot your hard rule."

"Wait just a moment before you finally decide. There is another rule. If you choose now, the order will be filled at once; but if you wait, you will have to await my pleasure. You cannot get a dish from that entire bill until I consent."

"All right. Show me to my room, and send the cook to bed; there is not going to be any hurry."

The professor took me up one flight of stairs and showed me into a most inviting and comfortable apartment consisting of parlor, bed-chamber, and bath-room.

The front windows looked out over a far-reaching spread of green glades and valleys, and tumbled hills clothed with forests—a noble solitude unvexed by the fussy world. In the parlor were many shelves filled with books. The professor said he would now leave me to myself; and added:

"Smoke and read as much as you please, drink all the water you like. When you get hungry, ring and give your order, and I will decide whether it shall be filled or not. Yours is a stubborn, bad case, and I think the first fourteen dishes in the bill are each and all too delicate for its needs. I ask you as a favor to restrain yourself and not call for them."

"Restrain myself, is it? Give yourself no uneasiness. You are going to save money by me. The idea of coaxing a sick man's appetite back with this buzzard fare is clear insanity."

I said it with bitterness, for I felt outraged by this calm, cold talk over these heartless new engines of assassination. The doctor looked grieved, but not offended. He laid the bill of fare on the commode at my bed's head, "so that it would be handy," and said:

"Yours is not the worst case I have encountered, by any means; still it is a bad one and requires robust treatment; therefore I shall be gratified if you will restrain yourself and skip down to No. 15 and begin with that."

Then he left me and I began to undress, for I was dog-tired and very sleepy. I slept fifteen hours and woke up finely refreshed at ten the next morning. Vienna coffee! It was the first think I thought of—that unapproachable luxury—that sumptuous coffee-house coffee, compared with which all other European coffee and all American hotel coffee is mere fluid poverty. I rang, and ordered it; also Vienna bread, that delicious invention. The servant spoke through the wicket in the door and said—but you know what he said. He referred me to the bill of fare. I allowed him to go—I had no further use for him.

After the bath I dressed and started for a walk, and got as far as the door. It was locked on the outside. I rang and the servant came and explained that it was another rule. The seclusion of the patient was required until after the first meal. I had not been particularly anxious to get out before; but it was different now. Being locked in makes a person wishful to get out. I soon began to find it difficult to put in the time. At two o'clock I had been twenty-six hours without food. I had been growing hungry for some time; I recognized that I was not only hungry now, but hungry with a strong adjective in front of it. Yet I was not hungry enough to face the bill of fare.

I must put in the time somehow. I would read and smoke. I did it; hour by hour. The books were all of one breed—shipwrecks; people lost in deserts; people shut up in caved-in mines; people starving in besieged cities. I read about all the revolting dishes that ever famishing men had stayed their hunger with. During the first hours these things nauseated me; hours followed in which they did not so affect me; still other hours followed in which I found myself smacking my lips over some tolerably infernal messes. When I had been without food forty-five hours I ran eagerly to the bell and ordered the second dish in the bill, which was a sort of dumplings containing a compost made of caviar and tar.

It was refused me. During the next fifteen hours I visited the bell every now and then and ordered a dish that was further down the list. Always a refusal. But I was conquering prejudice after prejudice, right along; I was making sure progress; I was creeping up on No. 15 with deadly certainty, and my heart beat faster and faster, my hopes rose higher and higher.

At last when food had not passed my lips for sixty hours, victory was mine, and I ordered No. 15:

"Soft-boiled spring chicken—in the egg; six dozen, hot and fragrant!"

In fifteen minutes it was there; and the doctor along with it, rubbing his hands with joy. He said with great excitement:

"It's a cure, it's a cure! I knew I could do it. Dear sir, my grand system never fails—never. You've got your appetite back—you know you have; say it and make me happy."

"Bring on your carrion—I can eat anything in the bill!"

"Oh, this is noble, this is splendid—but I knew I could do it, the system never fails. How are the birds?"

"Never was anything so delicious in the world; and yet as a rule I don't care for game. But don't interrupt me, don't— I can't spare my mouth, I really can't."

Then the doctor said:

"The cure is perfect. There is no more doubt nor danger. Let the poultry alone; I can trust you with a beefsteak now."

The beefsteak came—as much as a basketful of it—with potatoes, and Vienna bread and coffee; and I ate a meal then that was worth all the costly preparation I had made for it. And dripped tears of gratitude into the gravy all the time—gratitude to the doctor for putting a little plain common sense into me when I had been empty of it so many, many years.

II

Thirty years ago Haimberger went off on a long voyage in a sailing-ship. There were fifteen passengers on board. The table-fare was of the regulation pattern of the day: At seven in the morning, a cup of bad coffee in bed; at nine, breakfast: bad coffee, with condensed milk; soggy rolls, crackers, salt fish; at 1 P.M., luncheon: cold tongue, cold ham, cold corned beef, soggy cold rolls, crackers; 5 P.M., dinner: thick pea-soup, salt fish, hot corned beef and sauerkraut, boiled pork and beans, pudding; 9 till 11 P.M., supper: tea, with condensed milk, cold tongue, cold ham, pickles, sea-biscuit, pickled oysters, pickled pig's feet, grilled bones, golden buck.

At the end of the first week eating had ceased, nibbling had taken its place. The passengers came to the table, but it was partly to put in the time, and partly because the wisdom of the ages commanded them to be regular in their meals. They were tired of the coarse and monotonous fare, and took no interest in it, had no appetite for it. All day and every day they roamed the ship half hungry, plagued by their gnawing stomachs, moody, untalkative, miserable. Among them were three confirmed dyspeptics. These became shadows in the course of three weeks. There was also a bedridden invalid; he lived on boiled rice; he could not look at the regular dishes.

Now came shipwreck and life in open boats, with the usual paucity of food. Provisions ran lower and lower. The appetites improved, then. When nothing was left but raw ham and the ration of that was down to two ounces a day per person, the appetites were perfect. At the end of fifteen days the dyspeptics, the invalid and the most delicate ladies in the party were chewing sailor-boots in ecstasy, and only complaining because the supply of them was limited. Yet these were the same people who couldn't endure the ship's tedious corned beef and sauerkraut and other crudities. They were rescued by an English vessel. Within ten days the whole fifteen were in as good condition as they had been when the shipwreck occurred.

"They had suffered no damage by their adventure," said the professor. "Do you note that?"

"Yes."

"Do you note it well?"

"Yes—I think I do."

"But you don't. You hesitate. You don't rise to the importance of it. I will say it again—with emphasis—*not one of them suffered any damage.*"

"Now I begin to see. Yes, it was indeed remarkable."

"Nothing of the kind. It was perfectly natural. There was no reason why they should suffer damage. They were undergoing Nature's Appetite Cure, the best and wisest in the world."

"Is that where you got your idea?"

"That is where I got it."

"It taught those people a valuable lesson."

"What makes you think that?"

"Why shouldn't I? You seem to think it taught you one."

"That is nothing to the point. I am not a fool."

"I see. Were they fools?"

"They were human beings."

"Is it the same thing?"

"Why do you ask? You know it yourself. As regards his health—and the rest of the things—the average man is what his environment and his superstitions have made him; and their function is to make him an ass. He can't add up three or four new circumstances together and perceive what they mean; it is beyond him. He is not capable of observing for himself. He has to get everything at second hand. If what

are miscalled the lower animals were as silly as man is, they would all
perish from the earth in a year."

"Those passengers learned no lesson, then?"

"Not a sign of it. They went to their regular meals in the English
ship, and pretty soon they were nibbling again—nibbling, appetiteless,
disgusted with the food, moody, miserable, half hungry, their outraged stomachs cursing and swearing and whining and supplicating
all day long. And in vain, for they were the stomachs of fools."

"Then, as I understand it, your scheme is—"

"Quite simple. Don't eat till you are hungry. If the food fails to taste
good, fails to satisfy you, rejoice you, comfort you, don't eat again until
you are *very* hungry. Then it will rejoice you—and do you good, too."

"And I observe no regularity, as to hours?"

"When you are conquering a bad appetite—no. After it is conquered,
regularity is no harm, so long as the appetite remains good. As soon as
the appetite wavers, apply the corrective again—which is starvation,
long or short according to the needs of the case."

"The best diet, I suppose—I mean the wholesomest—"

"All diets are wholesome. Some are wholesomer than others, but all
the ordinary diets are wholesome enough for the people who use them.
Whether the food be fine or coarse, it will taste good and it will
nourish if a watch be kept upon the appetite and a little starvation introduced every time it weakens. Nansen was used to fine fare, but
when his meals were restricted to bear-meat months at a time he suffered no damage and no discomfort, because his appetite was kept at
par through the difficulty of getting his bear-meat regularly."

"But doctors arrange carefully considered and delicate diets for invalids."

"They can't help it. The invalid is full of inherited superstitions and
won't starve himself. He believes it would certainly kill him."

"It would weaken him, wouldn't it?"

"Nothing to hurt. Look at the invalids in our shipwreck. They lived
fifteen days on pinches of raw ham, a suck at sailor-boots, and general
starvation. It weakened them, but it didn't hurt them. It put them in
fine shape to eat heartily of hearty food and build themselves up to a
condition of robust health. But they did not perceive that; they lost
their opportunity; they remained invalids; it served them right. Do
you know the tricks that the health-resort doctors play?"

"What is it?"

"My system disguised—covert starvation. Grape-cure, bath-cure,
mud-cure—it is all the same. The grape and the bath and the mud

AT THE APPETITE CURE   657

make a show and do a trifle of the work—the real work is done by the
surreptitious starvation. The patient accustomed to four meals and
late hours—at both ends of the day—now consider what he has to do
at a health resort. He gets up at six in the morning. Eats one egg.
Tramps up and down a promenade two hours with the other fools.
Eats a butterfly. Slowly drinks a glass of filtered sewage that smells
like a buzzard's breath. Promenades another two hours, but alone; if
you speak to him he says anxiously, 'My water!—I am walking off my
water!—please don't interrupt,' and goes stumping along again. Eats
a candied rose-leaf. Lies at rest in the silence and solitude of his room
for hours; mustn't speak, mustn't read, mustn't smoke. The doctor
comes and feels of his heart, now, and his pulse, and thumps his
breast and his back and his stomach, and listens for results through a
penny flageolet; then orders the man's bath—half a degree, Réaumur,
cooler than yesterday. After the bath, another egg. A glass of sewage
at three or four in the afternoon, and promenade solemnly with the
other freaks. Dinner at six—half a doughnut and a cup of tea. Walk
again. Half past eight, supper—more butterfly; at nine, to bed. Six
weeks of this régime—think of it. It starves a man out and puts him in
splendid condition. It would have the same effect in London, New
York, Jericho—anywhere."

"How long does it take to put a person in condition here?"

"It ought to take but a day or two; but in fact it takes from one to six
weeks, according to the character and mentality of the patient."

"How is that?"

"Do you see that crowd of women playing football, and boxing, and
jumping fences yonder? They have been here six or seven weeks.
They were spectral poor weaklings when they came. They were accustomed to nibbling at dainties and delicacies at set hours four times
a day, and they had no appetite for anything. I questioned them, and
then locked them into their rooms, the frailest ones to starve nine or
ten hours, the others twelve or fifteen. Before long they began to beg;
and indeed they suffered a good deal. They complained of nausea,
headache, and so on. It was good to see them eat when the time was
up. They could not remember when the devouring of a meal had
afforded them such rapture—that was their word. Now, then, that
ought to have ended their cure, but it didn't. They were free to go to
any meals in the house, and they chose their accustomed four. Within
a day or two I had to interfere. Their appetites were weakening. I
made them knock out a meal. That set them up again. Then they
resumed the four. I begged them to learn to knock out a meal them-

selves, without waiting for me. Up to a fortnight ago they couldn't;
they really hadn't manhood enough; but they were gaining it, and
now I think they are safe. They drop out a meal every now and then
of their own accord. They are in fine condition now, and they might
safely go home, I think, but their confidence is not quite perfect yet,
so they are waiting awhile."

"Other cases are different?"

"Oh, yes. Sometimes a man learns the whole trick in a week. Learns
to regulate his appetite and keep it in perfect order. Learns to drop
out a meal with frequency and not mind it."

"But why drop the entire meal out? Why not a part of it?"

"It's a poor device, and inadequate. If the stomach doesn't call
vigorously—with a shout, as you may say—it is better not to pester it,
but just give it a real rest. Some people can eat more meals than
others, and still thrive. There are all sorts of people, and all sorts of
appetites. I will show you a man presently who was accustomed to
nibble at eight meals a day. It was beyond the proper gait of his
appetite by two. I have got him down to six a day, now, and he is all
right, and enjoys life. How many meals do you effect per day?"

"Formerly—for twenty-two years—a meal and a half; during the
past two years, two and a half: coffee and a roll at nine, luncheon at
one, dinner at seven-thirty or eight."

"Formerly a meal and a half—that is, coffee and a roll at nine,
dinner in the evening, nothing between—is that it?"

"Yes."

"Why did you add a meal?"

"It was the family's idea. They were uneasy. They thought I was
killing myself."

"You found a meal and a half per day enough, all through the
twenty-two years?"

"Plenty."

"Your present poor condition is due to the extra meal. Drop it out.
You are trying to eat oftener than your stomach demands. You don't
gain, you lose. You eat less food now, in a day, on two and a half
meals, than you formerly ate on one and a half."

"True—a good deal less; for in those old days my dinner was a very
sizable thing."

"Put yourself on a single meal a day, now—dinner—for a few days,
till you secure a good, sound, regular, trustworthy appetite, then take
to your one and a half permanently, and don't listen to the family any
more. When you have any ordinary ailment, particularly of a feverish

sort, eat nothing at all during twenty-four hours. That will cure it. It will cure the stubbornest cold in the head, too. No cold in the head can survive twenty-four hours on modified starvation."

"I know it. I have proved it many a time."

1898

The Austrian Edison Keeping School Again

By a paragraph in the *Freie Presse* it appears that Jan Szczepanik, the youthful inventor of the "telelectroscope" (for seeing at great distances; and some other scientific marvels, has been having an odd adventure, by help of the state.

Vienna is hospitably ready to smile whenever there is an opportunity, and this seems to be a fair one. Three or four years ago, when Szczepanik was nineteen or twenty years old, he was a schoolmaster in a Moravian village, on a salary of—I forget the amount, but no matter; there was not enough of it to remember. His head was full of inventions, and in his odd hours he began to plan them out. He soon perfected an ingenious invention for applying photography to pattern-designing as used in the textile industries, whereby he proposed to reduce the customary outlay of time, labor, and money expended on that department of loom-work to next to nothing. He wanted to carry his project to Vienna and market it; and as he could not get leave of absence, he made his trip without leave. This lost him his place, but did not gain him his market. When his money ran out he went back home, and was presently reinstated. By and by he deserted once more, and went to Vienna, and this time he made some friends who assisted him, and his invention was sold to England and Germany for a great sum. During the past three years he has been experimenting and investigating in velvety comfort. His most picturesque achievement in his telelectroscope, a device which a number of able men—including Mr. Edison, I think—had already tried their hands at, with prospects of eventual success. A Frenchman came near to solving the difficult

and intricate problem fifteen years ago, but an essential detail was
lacking which he could not master, and he suffered defeat. Szczepanik's
experiments with his pattern-designing project revealed to him the
secret of the lacking detail. He perfected his invention, and a French
syndicate has bought it, and saved it for exhibition and fortune-
making at the Paris world's fair.

As a schoolmaster Szczepanik was exempt from military duty. When
he ceased from teaching, being an educated man he could have had
himself enrolled as a one-year volunteer; but he forgot to do it, and
this exposed him to the privilege, and also the necessity, of serving
three years in the army. In the course of duty, the other day, an official
discovered the inventor's indebtedness to the state, and took the
proper measures to collect. At first there seemed to be no way for the
inventor (and the state) out of the difficulty. The authorities were
loath to take the young man out of his great laboratory, where he was
helping to shove the whole human race along on its road to new
prosperities and scientific conquests, and suspend operations in his
mental Klondike three years, while he punched the empty air with a
bayonet in a time of peace; but there was the law, and how was it to
be helped? It was a difficult puzzle, but the authorities labored at it
until they found a forgotten law somewhere which furnished a loophole—a large one, and a long one, too, as it looks to me. By this piece
of good luck Szczepanik is saved from soldiering, but he becomes a
schoolmaster again; and it is a sufficiently picturesque billet, when
you examine it. He must go back to his village every two months, and
teach his school half a day—from early in the morning until noon; and,
to the best of my understanding of the published terms, he must keep
this up the rest of his life! I hope so, just for the romantic poeticalness
of it. He is twenty-four, strongly and compactly built, and comes of an
ancestry accustomed to waiting to see its great-grandchildren married.
It is almost certain that he will live to be ninety. I hope so. This
promises him sixty-six years of useful school service. Dissected, it gives
him a chance to teach school 396 half-days, make 396 railway trips
going and 396 back, pay bed and board 396 times in the village, and
lose possibly 1,200 days from his laboratory work—that is to say, three
years and three months or so. And he already owes three years to this
same account. This has been overlooked; I shall call the attention of
the authorities to it. It may be possible for him to get a compromise on
this compromise by doing his three years in the army, and saving one;
but I think it can't happen. This government "holds the age" on him;
it has what is technically called a "good thing" in financial circles, and

knows a good thing when it sees it. I know the inventor very well, and he has my sympathy. This is friendship. But I am throwing my influence with the government. This is politics.

Szczepanik left for his village in Moravia day before yesterday to "do time" for the first time under his sentence. Early yesterday morning he started for the school in a fine carriage, which was stocked with fruits, cakes, toys, and all sorts of knick-knacks, rarities, and surprises for the children, and was met on the road by the school and a body of schoolmasters from the neighboring districts, marching in column, with the village authorities at the head, and was received with the enthusiastic welcome proper to the man who had made their village's name celebrated, and conducted in state to the humble doors which had been shut against him as a deserter three years before. It is out of materials like these that romances are woven; and when the romancer has done his best, he has not improved upon the unpainted facts. Szczepanik put the sapless school-books aside, and led the children a holiday dance through the enchanted lands of science and invention, explaining to them some of the curious things which he had contrived, and the laws which governed their construction and performance, and illustrating these matters with pictures and models and other helps to a clear understanding of their fascinating mysteries. After this there was play and a distribution of the fruits and toys and things; and after this, again, some more science, including the story of the invention of the telephone, and an explanation of its character and laws, for the convict had brought a telephone along. The children saw that wonder for the first time, and they also personally tested its powers and verified them. Then school "let out"; the teacher got his certificate, all signed, stamped, taxed, and so on, said good-by, and drove off in his carriage under a storm of *"Do widzenia!"* (*"Au revoir!"*) from the children, who will resume their customary sobrieties until he comes in August and uncorks his flask of scientific fire-water again.

1898

From the "London Times" of 1904

I

Correspondence of the "London Times"

Chicago, April 1, 1904

I resume by cable-telephone where I left off yesterday. For many hours, now, this vast city—along with the rest of the globe, of course—has talked of nothing but the extraordinary episode mentioned in my last report. In accordance with your instructions, I will now trace the romance from its beginnings down to the culmination of yesterday—or to-day; call it which you like. By an odd chance, I was a personal actor in a part of this drama myself. The opening scene plays in Vienna. Date, one o'clock in the morning, March 31, 1898. I had spent the evening at a social entertainment. About midnight I went away, in company with the military attachés of the British, Italian, and American embassies, to finish with a late smoke. This function had been appointed to take place in the house of Lieutenant Hillyer, the third attaché mentioned in the above list. When we arrived there we found several visitors in the room: young Szczepanik;[1] Mr. K., his financial backer; Mr. W., the latter's secretary; and Lieutenant Clayton of the United States army. War was at that time threatening between Spain and our country, and Lieutenant Clayton had been sent to Europe on military business. I was well acquainted with young Szczepanik and his two friends, and I knew Mr. Clayton slightly. I had met him at West Point years before, when he was a cadet. It was when General Merritt was superintendent. He had the reputation of being an able officer, and also of being quick-tempered and plain-spoken.

This smoking-party had been gathered together partly for business. This business was to consider the availability of the telelectroscope for military service. It sounds oddly enough now, but it is nevertheless true that at that time the invention was not taken seriously by any one except its inventor. Even his financial supporter regarded it merely as a curious and interesting toy. Indeed, he was so convinced of this that he had actually postponed its use by the general world to the end of

---

[1] Pronounced (approximately) Ze*pann*ik.

the dying century by granting a two years' exclusive lease of it to a syndicate, whose intent was to exploit it at the Paris World's Fair.

When we entered the smoking-room we found Lieutenant Clayton and Szczepanik engaged in a warm talk over the telelectroscope in the German tongue. Clayton was saying:

"Well, you know *my* opinion of it, anyway!" and he brought his fist down with emphasis upon the table.

"And I do not value it," retorted the young inventor, with provoking calmness of tone and manner.

Clayton turned to Mr. K., and said:

"*I* cannot see why you are wasting money on this toy. In my opinion, the day will never come when it will do a farthing's worth of real service for any human being."

"That may be; yes, that may be; still, I have put the money in it, and am content. I think, myself, that it is only a toy; but Szczepanik claims more for it, and I know him well enough to believe that he can see farther than I can—either with his telelectroscope or without it."

The soft answer did not cool Clayton down; it seemed only to irritate him the more; and he repeated and emphasized his conviction that the invention would never do any man a farthing's worth of real service. He even made it a "brass" farthing, this time. Then he laid an English farthing on the table, and added:

"Take that, Mr. K., and put it away; and if ever the telelectroscope does any man an actual service,—mind, a *real* service—please mail it to me as a reminder, and I will take back what I have been saying. Will you?"

"I will"; and Mr. K. put the coin in his pocket.

Mr. Clayton now turned toward Szczepanik, and began with a taunt—a taunt which did not reach a finish; Szczepanik interrupted it with a hardy retort, and followed this with a blow. There was a brisk fight for a moment or two; then the attachés separated the men.

The scene now changes to Chicago. Time, the autumn of 1901. As soon as the Paris contract released the telelectroscope, it was delivered to public use, and was soon connected with the telephonic systems of the whole world. The improved "limitless-distance" telephone was presently introduced, and the daily doings of the globe made visible to everybody, and audibly discussable, too, by witnesses separated by any number of leagues.

By and by Szczepanik arrived in Chicago. Clayton (now captain) was serving in that military department at the time. The two men resumed the Viennese quarrel of 1898. On three different occasions

they quarreled, and were separated by witnesses. Then came an
interval of two months, during which time Szczepanik was not seen by
any of his friends, and it was at first supposed that he had gone off on a
sight-seeing tour and would soon be heard from. But no; no word
came from him. Then it was supposed that he had returned to Europe.
Still, time drifted on, and he was not heard from. Nobody was troubled, for he was like most inventors and other kinds of poets, and went
and came in a capricious way, and often without notice.

Now comes the tragedy. On the 29th of December, in a dark and
unused compartment of the cellar under Captain Clayton's house, a
corpse was discovered by one of Clayton's maid-servants. It was easily
identified as Szczepanik's. The man had died by violence. Clayton
was arrested, indicted, and brought to trial, charged with this murder.
The evidence against him was perfect in every detail, and absolutely
unassailable. Clayton admitted this himself. He said that a reasonable
man could not examine this testimony with a dispassionate mind and
not be convinced by it; yet the man would be in error, nevertheless.
Clayton swore that he did not commit the murder, and that he had
had nothing to do with it.

As your readers will remember, he was condemned to death. He
had numerous and powerful friends, and they worked hard to save
him, for none of them doubted the truth of his assertion. I did what
little I could to help, for I had long since become a close friend of his,
and thought I knew that it was not in his character to inveigle an
enemy into a corner and assassinate him. During 1902 and 1903 he
was several times reprieved by the governor; he was reprieved once
more in the beginning of the present year, and the execution-day
postponed to March 31st.

The governor's situation had been embarrassing, from the day of
the condemnation, because of the fact that Clayton's wife is the governor's niece. The marriage took place in 1899, when Clayton was thirty-
four and the girl twenty-three, and has been a happy one. There is
one child, a little girl three years old. Pity for the poor mother and
child kept the mouths of grumblers closed at first; but this could not
last forever—for in America politics has a hand in everything—and by
and by the governor's political opponents began to call attention to
his delay in allowing the law to take its course. These hints have grown
more and more frequent of late, and more and more pronounced. As
a natural result, his own party grew nervous. Its leaders began to visit
Springfield and hold long private conferences with him. He was now
between two fires. On the one hand, his niece was imploring him to

pardon her husband; on the other were the leaders, insisting that he stand to his plain duty as chief magistrate of the State, and place no further bar to Clayton's execution. Duty won in the struggle, and the governor gave his word that he would not again respite the condemned man. This was two weeks ago. Mrs. Clayton now said:

"Now that you have given your word, my last hope is gone, for I know you will never go back from it. But you have done the best you could for John, and I have no reproaches for you. You love him, and you love me, and we both know that if you could honorably save him, you would do it. I will go to him now, and be what help I can to him, and get what comfort I may out of the few days that are left to us before the night comes which will have no end for me in life. You will be with me that day? You will not let me bear it alone?"

"I will take you to him myself, poor child, and I will be near you to the last."

By the governor's command, Clayton was now allowed every indulgence he might ask for which could interest his mind and soften the hardships of his imprisonment. His wife and child spent the days with him; I was his compainon by night. He was removed from the narrow cell which he had occupied during such a dreary stretch of time, and given the chief warden's room and comfortable quarters. His mind was always busy with the catastrophe of his life, and with the slaughtered inventor, and he now took the fancy that he would like to have the telelectroscope and divert his mind with it. He had his wish. The connection was made with the international telephone-station, and day by day, and night by night, he called up one corner of the globe after another, and looked upon its life, and studied its strange sights, and spoke with its people, and realized that by grace of this marvelous instrument he was almost as free as the birds of the air, although a prisoner under locks and bars. He seldom spoke, and I never interrupted him when he was absorbed in this amusement. I sat in his parlor and read and smoked, and the nights were very quiet and reposefully sociable, and I found them pleasant. Now and then I would hear him say, "Give me Yedo"; next, "Give me Hong-Kong"; next, "Give me Melbourne." And I smoked on, and read in comfort, while he wandered about the remote under-world, where the sun was shining in the sky, and the people were at their daily work. Sometimes the talk that came from those far regions through the microphone attachment interested me, and I listened.

Yesterday—I keep calling it yesterday, which is quite natural, for certain reasons—the instrument remained unused, and that, also, was natural, for it was the eve of the execution-day. It was spent in tears and lamentations and farewells. The governor and the wife and child remained until a quarter past eleven at night, and the scenes I witnessed were pitiful to see. The execution was to take place at four in the morning. A little after eleven a sound of hammering broke out upon the still night, and there was a glare of light, and the child cried out "What is that, papa?" and ran to the window before she could be stopped, and clapped her small hands, and said: "Oh, come and see, mamma—such a pretty thing they are making!" The mother knew—and fainted. It was the gallows!

She was carried away to her lodging, poor woman, and Clayton and I were alone—alone, and thinking, brooding, dreaming. We might have been statues, we sat so motionless and still. It was a wild night, for winter was come again for a moment, after the habit of this region in the early spring. The sky was starless and black, and a strong wind was blowing from the lake. The silence in the room was so deep that all outside sounds seemed exaggerated by contrast with it. These sounds were fitting ones; they harmonized with the situation and the conditions: the boom and thunder of sudden storm-gusts among the roofs and chimneys, then the dying down into moanings and wailings about the eaves and angles; now and then a gnashing and lashing rush of sleet along the window-panes; and always the muffled and uncanny hammering of the gallows-builders in the courtyard. After an age of this, another sound—far off, and coming smothered and faint through the riot of the tempest—a bell tolling twelve! Another age, and it tolled again. By and by, again. A dreary, long interval after this, then the spectral sound floated to us once more—one, two, three; and this time we caught our breath: sixty minutes of life left!

Clayton rose, and stood by the window, and looked up into the black sky, and listened to the thrashing sleet and the piping wind; then he said: "That a dying man's last of earth should be—this!" After a little he said: "I must see the sun again—the sun!" and the next moment he was feverishly calling: "China! Give me China—Peking!"

I was strangely stirred, and said to myself: "To think that it is a mere human being who does this unimaginable miracle—turns winter into summer, night into day, storm into calm, gives the freedom of the great globe to a prisoner in his cell, and the sun in his naked splendor to a man dying in Egyptian darkness!"

I was listening.

"What light! what brilliancy! what radiance! . . . This is Peking?"

"Yes."

"The time?"

"Mid-afternoon."

"What is the great crowd for, and in such gorgeous costumes? What masses and masses of rich color and barbaric magnificence! And how they flash and glow and burn in the flooding sunlight! What *is* the occasion of it all?"

"The coronation of our new emperor—the Czar."

"But I thought that that was to take place yesterday."

"This *is* yesterday—to you."

"Certainly it is. But my mind is confused, these days; there are reasons for it . . . Is this the beginning of the procession?"

"Oh, no, it began to move an hour ago."

"Is there much more of it still to come?"

"Two hours of it. Why do you sigh?"

"Because I should like to see it all."

"And why can't you?"

"I have to go—presently."

"You have an engagement?"

After a pause, softly: "Yes." After another pause: "Who are these in the splendid pavilion?"

"The imperial family, and visiting royalties from here and there and yonder in the earth."

"And who are those in the adjoining pavilions to the right and left?"

"Ambassadors and their families and suites to the right; unofficial foreigners to the left."

"If you will be so good, I—"

Boom! That distant bell again, tolling the half-hour faintly through the tempest of wind and sleet. The door opened, and the governor and the mother and child entered—the woman in widow's weeds! She fell upon her husband's breast in a passion of sobs, and I—I could not stay; I could not bear it. I went into the bedchamber, and closed the door. I sat there waiting—waiting—waiting, and listening to the rattling sashes and the blustering of the storm. After what seemed a long, long time, I heard a rustle and movement in the parlor, and knew that the clergyman and the sheriff and the guard were come. There was some low-voiced talking; then a hush; then a prayer, with a sound of sobbing; presently, footfalls—the departure for the gallows; then the child's happy voice: "Don't cry *now*, mamma, when we've got papa again, and taking him home."

The door closed; they were gone. I was ashamed: I was the only friend of the dying man that had no spirit, no courage. I stepped into the room, and said I would be a man and would follow. But we are made as we are made, and we cannot help it. I did not go.

I fidgeted about the room nervously, and presently went to the window, and softly raised it—drawn by that dread fascination which the terrible and the awful exert—and looked down upon the courtyard. By the garish light of the electric lamps I saw the little group of privileged witnesses, the wife crying on her uncle's breast, the condemned man standing on the scaffold with the halter around his neck, his arms strapped to his body, the black cap on his head, the sheriff at his side with his hand on the drop, the clergyman in front of him with bare head and his book in his hand.

"*I am the resurrection and the life—*"

I turned away. I could not listen; I could not look. I did not know whither to go or what to do. Mechanically, and without knowing it, I put my eye to that strange instrument, and there was Peking and the Czar's procession! The next moment I was leaning out of the window, gasping, suffocating, trying to speak, but dumb from the very imminence of the necessity of speaking. The preacher could speak, but I, who had such need of words—

"*And may God have mercy upon your soul. Amen.*"

The sheriff drew down the black cap, and laid his hand upon the lever. I got my voice.

"Stop, for God's sake! The man is innocent. Come here and see Szczepanik face to face!"

Hardly three minutes later the governor had my place at the window, and was saying:

"Strike off his bonds and set him free!"

Three minutes later all were in the parlor again. The reader will imagine the scene; I have no need to describe it. It was a sort of mad orgy of joy.

A messenger carried word to Szczepanik in the pavilion, and one could see the distressed amazement dawn in his face as he listened to the tale. Then he came to his end of the line, and talked with Clayton and the governor and the others; and the wife poured out her gratitude upon him for saving her husband's life, and in her deep thankfulness she kissed him at twelve thousand miles' range.

The telelectrophonoscopes of the globe were put to service now, and for many hours the kings and queens of many realms (with here and there a reporter) talked with Szczepanik, and praised him; and the few scientific societies which had not already made him an honorary member conferred that grace upon him.

How had he come to disappear from among us? It was easily explained. He had not grown used to being a world-famous person, and had been forced to break away from the lionizing that was robbing him of all privacy and repose. So he grew a beard, put on colored glasses, disguised himself a little in other ways, then took a fictitious name, and went off to wander about the earth in peace.

Such is the tale of the drama which began with an inconsequential quarrel in Vienna in the spring of 1898, and came near ending as a tragedy in the spring of 1904.

MARK TWAIN

II

Correspondence of the "London Times"

Chicago, April 5, 1904

To-day, by a clipper of the Electric Line, and the latter's Electric Railway connections, arrived an envelope from Vienna, for Captain Clayton, containing an English farthing. The receiver of it was a good deal moved. He called up Vienna, and stood face to face with Mr. K., and said:

"I do not need to say anything; you can see it all in my face. My wife has the farthing. Do not be afraid—she will not throw it away."   M.T.

III

Correspondence of the "London Times"

Chicago, April 23, 1904

Now that the after developments of the Clayton case have run their course and reached a finish, I will sum them up. Clayton's romantic escape from a shameful death steeped all this region in an enchantment of wonder and joy—during the proverbial nine days. Then the sobering process followed, and men began to take thought, and to say: "But *a man was killed*, and Clayton killed him." Others replied: "That is true: we have been overlooking that important detail: we have been led away by excitement."

The feeling soon became general that Clayton ought to be tried again. Measures were taken accordingly, and the proper representations conveyed to Washington; for in America, under the new paragraph added to the Constitution in 1899, second trials are not state affairs, but national, and must be tried by the most august body in the land—the Supreme Court of the United States. The justices were, therefore, summoned to sit in Chicago. The session was held day before yesterday, and was opened with the usual impressive formalities, the nine judges appearing in their black robes, and the new chief justice (Lemaître) presiding. In opening the case, the chief justice said:

"It is my opinion that this matter is quite simple. The prisoner at the bar was charged with murdering the man Szczepanik; he was tried for murdering the man Szczepanik; he was fairly tried, and justly condemned and sentenced to death for murdering the man Szcze-panik. It turns out that the man Szczepanik was not murdered at all. By the decision of the French courts in the Dreyfus matter, it is established beyond cavil or question that the decisions of courts are permanent and cannot be revised. We are obliged to respect and adopt this precedent. It is upon precedents that the enduring edifice of jurisprudence is reared. The prisoner at the bar has been fairly and righteously condemned to death for the murder of the man Szczepanik, and, in my opinion, there is but one course to pursue in the matter: he must be hanged."

Mr. Justice Crawford said:

"But, your Excellency, he was pardoned on the scaffold for that."

"The pardon is not valid, and cannot stand, because he was par-doned for killing a man whom he had not killed. A man cannot be pardoned for a crime which he has not committed; it would be an absurdity."

"But, your Excellency, he did kill a man."

"That is an extraneous detail; we have nothing to do with it. The court cannot take up this crime until the prisoner has expiated the other one."

Mr. Justice Halleck said:

"If we order his execution, your Excellency, we shall bring about a miscarriage of justice; for the governor will pardon him again."

"He will not have the pardon. He cannot pardon a man for a crime which he has not committed. As I observed before it, it would be an absurdity."

After a consultation, Mr. Justice Wadsworth said:

"Several of us have arrived at the conclusion, your Excellency, that it would be an error to hang the prisoner for killing Szczepanik, but only for killing the other man, since it is proven that he did not kill Szczepanik."

"On the contrary, it is proven that he *did* kill Szczepanik. By the French precedent, it is plain that we must abide by the finding of the court."

"But Szczepanik is still alive."

"So is Dreyfus."

In the end it was found impossible to ignore or get around the French precedent. There could be but one result: Clayton was delivered over to the executioner. It made an immense excitement; the state rose as one man and clamored for Clayton's pardon and re-trial. The governor issued the pardon, but the Supreme Court was in duty bound to annul it, and did so, and poor Clayton was hanged yesterday. The city is draped in black, and, indeed, the like may be said of the state. All America is vocal with scorn of "French justice," and of the malignant little soldiers who invented it and inflicted it upon the other Christian lands.

1898

My First Lie, and How I
Got Out of It

As I understand it, what you desire is information about "my first lie, and how I got out of it." I was born in 1835; I am well along, and my memory is not as good as it was. If you had asked about my first truth it would have been easier for me and kinder of you, for I remember that fairly well; I remember it as if it were last week. The family think it was week before, but that is flattery and probably has a selfish project back of it. When a person has become seasoned by experience and has reached the age of sixty-four, which is the age of discretion, he likes a family compliment as well as ever, but he does not lose his head over it as in the old innocent days.

I do not remember my first lie, it is too far back; but I remember my second one very well. I was nine days old at the time, and had noticed that if a pin was sticking in me and I advertised it in the usual fashion, I was lovingly petted and coddled and pitied in a most agreeable way and got a ration between meals besides. It was human nature to want to get these riches, and I fell. I lied about the pin—advertising one when there wasn't any. You would have done it; George Washington did it; anybody would have done it. During the first half of my life I never knew a child that was able to rise above that temptation and keep from telling that lie. Up to 1867 all the civilized children that were ever born into the world were liars— including George. Then the safety-pin came in and blocked the game. But is that reform worth anything? No; for it is reform by force and has no virtue in it; it merely stops that form of lying; it doesn't impair the disposition to lie, by a shade. It is the cradle application of con- version by fire and sword, or of the temperance principle through prohibition.

To return to that early lie. They found no pin, and they realized that another liar had been added to the world's supply. For by grace of a rare inspiration, a quite commonplace but seldom noticed fact was borne in upon their understandings—that almost all lies are acts, and speech has no part in them. Then, if they examined a little further they recognized that all people are liars from the cradle onward, without exception, and that they begin to lie as soon as they wake in the morning, and keep it up, without rest or refreshment, until they go to sleep at night. If they arrived at that truth it probably grieved them— did, if they had been heedlessly and ignorantly educated by their books and teachers; for why should a person grieve over a thing which by the eternal law of his make he cannot help? He didn't invent the law; it is merely his business to obey it and keep still; join the universal conspiracy and keep so still that he shall deceive his fellow-conspirators into imagining that he doesn't know that the law exists. It is what we all do—we that know. I am speaking of the lie of silent assertion; we can tell it without saying a word, and we all do it —we that know. In the magnitude of its territorial spread it is one of the most majestic lies that the civilizations make it their sacred and anxious care to guard and watch and propagate.

For instance: It would not be possible for a humane and intelligent person to invent a rational excuse for slavery; yet you will remember that in the early days of the emancipation agitation in the North, the agitators got but small help or countenance from any one. Argue and plead and pray as they might, they could not break the universal stillness that reigned, from pulpit and press all the way down to the bottom of society—the clammy stillness created and maintained by the lie of silent assertion—the silent assertion that there wasn't anything going on in which humane and intelligent people were interested.

From the beginning of the Dreyfus case to the end of it, all France, except a couple of dozen moral paladins, lay under the smother of the silent-assertion lie that no wrong was being done to a persecuted and unoffending man. The like smother was over England lately, a good half of the population silently letting on that they were not aware that Mr. Chamberlain was trying to manufacture a war in South Africa and was willing to pay fancy prices for the materials.

Now there we have instances of three prominent ostensible civilizations working the silent-assertion lie. Could one find other instances in the three countries? I think so. Not so very many, perhaps, but say a billion—just so as to keep within bounds. Are those countries working that kind of lie, day in and day out, in thousands and thousands of varieties, without ever resting? Yes, we know that to be true. The universal conspiracy of the silent-assertion lie is hard at work always and everywhere, and always in the interest of a stupidity or a sham, never in the interest of a thing fine or respectable. Is it the most timid and shabby of all lies? It seems to have the look of it. For ages and ages it has mutely labored in the interest of despotisms and aristocracies and chattel slaveries, and military slaveries, and religious slaveries, and has kept them alive; keeps them alive yet, here and there and yonder, all about the globe; and will go on keeping them alive until the silent-assertion lie retires from business—the silent assertion that nothing is going on which fair and intelligent men are aware of and are engaged by their duty to try to stop.

What I am arriving at is this: When whole races and peoples conspire to propagate gigantic mute lies in the interest of tyrannies and shams, why should we care anything about the trifling lies told by individuals? Why should we try to make it appear that abstention from lying is a virtue? Why should we want to beguile ourselves in that way? Why should we without shame help the nation lie, and then be ashamed to do a little lying on our own account? Why shouldn't we be honest and honorable, and lie every time we get a chance? That is to say, why shouldn't we be consistent, and either lie all the time or not at all? Why should we help the nation lie the whole day long and then object to telling one little individual private lie in our own interest to go to bed on? Just for the refreshment of it, I mean, and to take the rancid taste out of our mouth.

Here in England they have the oddest ways. They won't tell a spoken lie—nothing can persuade them. Except in a large moral interest, like politics or religion, I mean. To tell a spoken lie to get even the poorest little personal advantage out of it is a thing which is impossible to them. They make me ashamed of myself sometimes, they are so bigoted. They will not even tell a lie for the fun of it; they will not tell it when it hasn't even a suggestion of damage or advantage in it for any one. This has a restraining influence upon me in spite of reason, and I am always getting out of practice.

Of course, they tell all sorts of little unspoken lies, just like anybody; but they don't notice it until their attention is called to it. They have got me so that sometimes I never tell a verbal lie now except in a modified form; and even in the modified form they don't approve of it. Still, that is as far as I can go in the interest of the growing friendly relations between the two countries; I must keep some of my self-respect—and my health. I can live on a low diet, but I can't get along on no sustenance at all.

Of course, there are times when these people have to come out with a spoken lie, for that is a thing which happens to everybody once in a while, and would happen to the angels if they came down here much. Particularly to the angels, in fact, for the lies I speak of are self-sacrificing ones told for a generous object, not a mean one; but even when these people tell a lie of that sort it seems to scare them and unsettle their minds. It is a wonderful thing to see, and shows that they are all insane. In fact, it is a country full of the most interesting superstitions.

I have an English friend of twenty-five years' standing, and yesterday when we were coming downtown on top of the bus I happened to tell him a lie—a modified one, of course; a half-breed, a mulatto: I can't seem to tell any other kind now, the market is so flat. I was explaining to him how I got out of an embarrassment in Austria last year. I do not know what might have become of me if I hadn't happened to remember to tell the police that I belonged to the same family as the Prince of Wales. That made everything pleasant, and they let me go; and apologized, too, and were ever so kind and obliging and polite, and couldn't do too much for me, and explained how the mistake came to be made, and promised to hang the officer that did it, and hoped I would let bygones be bygones and not say anything about it; and I said they could depend on me. My friend said, austerely:

"You call it a modified lie? Where is the modification?"

I explained that it lay in the form of my statement to the police.

"I didn't say I belonged to the royal family: I only said I belonged to the same family as the Prince—meaning the human family, of course;

and if those people had had any penetration they would have known it. I can't go around furnishing brains to the police; it is not to be expected."

"How did you feel after that performance?"

"Well, of course I was distressed to find that the police had misunderstood me, but as long as I had not told any lie I knew there was no occasion to sit up nights and worry about it."

My friend struggled with the case several minutes, turning it over and examining it in his mind; then he said that so far as he could see the modification was itself a lie, being a misleading reservation of an explanatory fact; so I had told two lies instead of one.

"I wouldn't have done it," said he: "I have never told a lie, and I should be very sorry to do such a thing."

Just then he lifted his hat and smiled a basketful of surprised and delighted smiles down at a gentleman who was passing in a hansom.

"Who was that, G——?"

"I don't know."

"Then why did you do that?"

"Because I saw he thought he knew me and was expecting it of me. If I hadn't done it he would have been hurt. I didn't want to embarrass him before the whole street."

"Well, your heart was right, G——, and your act was right. What you did was kindly and courteous and beautiful; I would have done it myself: but it was a lie."

"A lie? I didn't say a word. How do you make it out?"

"I know you didn't speak, still you said to him very plainly and enthusiastically in dumb show, 'Hello! you in town? Awful glad to see you, old fellow; when did you get back?' Concealed in your actions was what you have called 'a misleading reservation of an explanatory fact'—the fact that you had never seen him before. You expressed joy in encountering him—a lie; and you made that reservation—another lie. It was my pair over again. But don't be troubled—we all do it."

Two hours later, at dinner, when quite other matters were being discussed, he told how he happened along once just in the nick of time to do a great service for a family who were old friends of his. The head of it had suddenly died in circumstances and surroundings of a ruinously disgraceful character. If known, the facts would break the hearts of the innocent family and put upon them a load of unendurable shame. There was no help but in a giant lie, and he girded up his loins and told it.

"The family never found out, G——?"

"Never. In all these years they have never suspected. They were proud of him, and always had reason to be; they are proud of him yet, and to them his memory is sacred and stainless and beautiful."

"They had a narrow escape, G——."

"Indeed they had."

"For the very next man that came along might have been one of these heartless and shameless truth-mongers. You have told the truth a million times in your life, G——, but that one golden lie atones for it all. Persevere."

Some may think me not strict enough in my morals, but that position is hardly tenable. There are many kinds of lying which I do not approve. I do not like an injurious lie, except when it injures somebody else; and I do not like the lie of bravado, nor the lie of virtuous ecstasy: the latter was affected by Bryant, the former by Carlyle.

Mr. Bryant said, "Truth crushed to earth will rise again."

I have taken medals at thirteen world's fairs, and may claim to be not without capacity, but I never told as big a one as that which Mr. Bryant was playing to the gallery; we all do it. Carlyle said, in substance, this—I do not remember the exact words: "This gospel is eternal—that a lie shall not live."

I have a reverent affection for Carlyle's books, and have read his *Revolution* eight times; and so I prefer to think he was not entirely at himself when he told that one. To me it is plain that he said it in a moment of excitement, when chasing Americans out of his back yard with brickbats. They used to go there and worship. At bottom he was probably fond of them, but he was always able to conceal it. He kept bricks for them, but he was not a good shot, and it is matter of history that when he fired they dodged, and carried off the brick; for as a nation we like relics, and so long as we get them we do not much care what the reliquary thinks about it. I am quite sure that when he told that large one about a lie not being able to live, he had just missed an American and was over-excited. He told it above thirty years ago, but it is alive yet; alive, and very healthy and hearty, and likely to outlive any fact in history. Carlyle was truthful when calm, but give him Americans enough and bricks enough and he could have taken medals himself.

As regards that time that George Washington told the truth, a word must be said, of course. It is the principal jewel in the crown of America, and it is but natural that we should work for all it is worth, as Milton says in his "Lay of the Last Minstrel." It was a timely and judicious truth, and I should have told it myself in the circumstances. But I should have stopped there. It was a stately truth, a lofty truth—a Tower; and I think it was a mistake to go on and distract attention from its sublimity by building another Tower alongside of it fourteen times as high. I refer to his remark that he "could not lie." I should have fed that to the marines: or left it to Carlyle; it is just in his style. It would have taken a medal at any European fair, and would have got an Honorable Mention even at Chicago if it had been saved up. But let it pass: the Father of his Country was excited. I have been in those circumstances, and I recollect.

With the truth he told I have no objection to offer, as already indicated. I think it was not premeditated, but an inspiration. With his fine military mind, he had probably arranged to let his brother Edward in for the cherry-tree results, but by an inspiration he saw his opportunity in time and took advantage of it. By telling the truth he could astonish his father; his father would tell the neighbors; the neighbors would spread it; it would travel to all firesides; in the end it would make him President, and not only that, but First President. He was a far-seeing boy and would be likely to think of these things. Therefore, to my mind, he stands justified for what he did. But not for the other Tower: it was a mistake. Still, I don't know about that; upon reflection I think perhaps it wasn't. For indeed it is that Tower that makes the other one live. If he hadn't said "I cannot tell a lie," there would have been no convulsion. That was the earthquake that rocked the planet. That is the kind of statement that lives forever, and a fact barnacled to it has a good chance to share its immortality.

To sum up, on the whole I am satisfied with things the way they are. There is a prejudice against the spoken lie, but none against any other, and by examination and mathematical computation I find that the proportion of the spoken lie to the other varieties is as 1 to 22,894. Therefore the spoken lie is of no consequence, and it is not worth while to go around fussing about it and trying to make believe that it is an important matter. The silent colossal National Lie that is the support and confederate of all the tyrannies and shams and inequalities and unfairnesses that afflict the peoples—that is the one to throw bricks and sermons at. But let us be judicious and let somebody else begin.

And then— But I have wandered from my text. How did I get out of my second lie? I think I got out with honor, but I cannot be sure, for it was a long time ago and some of the details have faded out of my memory. I recollect that I was reversed and stretched across some one's knee, and that something happened, but I cannot now remember what it was. I think there was music; but it is all dim now and blurred by the lapse of time, and this may be only a senile fancy.

1899

My Boyhood Dreams

The dreams of my boyhood? No, they have not been realized. For all who are old, there is something infinitely pathetic about the subject which you have chosen, for in no gray-head's case can it suggest any but one thing—disappointment. Disappointment is its own reason for its pain: the quality or dignity of the hope that failed is a matter aside. The dreamer's valuation of a thing lost—not another man's—is the only standard to measure it by, and his grief for it makes it large and great and fine, and is worthy of our reverence in all cases. We should carefully remember that. There are sixteen hundred million people in the world. Of these there is but a trifling number—in fact, only thirty-eight million—who can understand why a person should have an ambition to belong to the French army; and why, belonging to it, he should be proud of that; and why, having got down that far, he should want to go on down, down, down till he struck bottom and got on the General Staff; and why, being stripped of his livery, or set free and reinvested with his self-respect by any other quick and thorough process, let it be what it might, he should wish to return to his strange serfage. But no matter: the estimate put upon these things by the fifteen hundred and sixty millions is no proper measure of their value: the proper measure, the just measure, is that which is put upon them by Dreyfus, and is cipherable merely upon the littleness or the vastness of the *disappointment* which their loss cost him.

There you have it: the measure of the magnitude of a dream-failure is the measure of the disappointment the failure cost the dreamer; the value, in others' eyes, of the thing lost, has nothing to do with the matter. With this straightening-out and classification of the dreamer's position to help us, perhaps we can put ourselves in his place and respect his dream—Dreyfus's, and the dreams our friends have cherished and reveal to us. Some that I call to mind, some that have been revealed to me, are curious enough; but we may not smile at them, for they were precious to the dreamers, and their failure has left scars which give them dignity and pathos. With this theme in my mind, dear heads that were brown when they and mine were young together rise old and white before me now, beseeching me to speak for them, and most lovingly will I do it.

Howells, Hay, Aldrich, Matthews, Stockton, Cable, Remus—how their young hopes and ambitions come flooding back to my memory now, out of the vague far past, the beautiful past, the lamented past! I remember it so well—that night we met together—it was in Boston, and Mr. Fields was there, and Mr. Osgood, and Ralph Keeler, and Boyle O'Reilly, lost to us now these many years—and under the seal of confidence revealed to each other what our boyhood dreams had been: dreams which had not as yet been blighted, but over which was stealing the gray of the night that was to come—a night which we prophetically *felt*, and this feeling oppressed us and made us sad. I remember that Howells's voice broke twice, and it was only with great difficulty that he was able to go on; in the end he wept. For he had hoped to be an auctioneer. He told of his early struggles to climb to his goal, and how at last he attained to within a single step of the coveted summit. But there misfortune after misfortune assailed him, and he went down, and down, and down, until now at last, weary and disheartened, he had for the present given up the struggle and become editor of the *Atlantic Monthly*. This was in 1830. Seventy years are gone since, and where now is his dream? It will never be fulfilled. And it is best so; he is no longer fitted for the position; no one would take him now; even if he got it, he would not be able to do himself credit in it, on account of his deliberateness of speech and lack of trained professional vivacity; he would be put on real estate, and would have the pain of seeing younger and abler men intrusted with the furniture and other such goods—goods which draw a mixed and intellectually low order of customers, who must be beguiled of their bids by a vulgar and specialized humor and sparkle, accompanied with antics.

But it is not the thing lost that counts, but only the *disappointment* the loss brings to the dreamer that had coveted that thing and had set his heart of hearts upon it; and when we remember this, a great wave of sorrow for Howells rises in our breasts, and we wish for his sake that his fate could have been different.

At that time Hay's boyhood dream was not yet past hope of reali-

zation, but it was fading, dimming, wasting away, and the wind of a
growing apprehension was blowing cold over the perishing summer
of his life. In the pride of his young ambition he had aspired to be a
steamboat mate; and in fancy saw himself dominating a forecastle
some day on the Mississippi and dictating terms to roustabouts in
high and wounding tones. I look back now, from this far distance of
seventy years, and note with sorrow the stages of that dream's destruction. Hay's history is but Howells's, with differences of detail.
Hay climbed high toward his ideal; when success seemed almost sure,
his foot upon the very gangplank, his eye upon the capstan, misfortune came and his fall began. Down—down—down—ever down:
Private Secretary to the President; Colonel in the field; Chargé
d'Affaires in Paris; Chargé d'Affaires in Vienna; Poet; Editor of the
Tribune; Biographer of Lincoln; Ambassador to England; and now
at last there he lies—Secretary of State, Head of Foreign Affairs. And
he has fallen like Lucifer, never to rise again. And his dream—where
now is his dream? Gone down in blood and tears with the dream of
the auctioneer.

And the young dream of Aldrich—where is that? I remember yet
how he sat there that night fondling it, petting it; seeing it recede
and ever recede; trying to be reconciled and give it up, but not able
yet to bear the thought; for it had been his hope to be a horse-doctor.
He also climbed high, but, like the others, fell; then fell again, and
yet again, and again and again. And now at last he can fall no further.
He is old now, he has ceased to struggle, and is only a poet. No one
would risk a horse with him now. His dream is over.

Has *any* boyhood dream ever been fulfilled? I must doubt it. Look
at Brander Matthews. He wanted to be a cowboy. What is he to-day?
Nothing but a professor in a university. Will he ever be a cowboy? It
is hardly conceivable.

Look at Stockton. What was Stockton's young dream? He hoped to
be a barkeeper. See where *he* has landed.

Is it better with Cable? What was Cable's young dream? To be
ring-master in the circus, and swell around and crack the whip. What
is he to-day? Nothing but a theologian and novelist.

And Uncle Remus—what was his young dream? To be a buccaneer.
Look at him now.

Ah, the dreams of our youth, how beautiful they are, and how
perishable! The ruins of these might-have-beens, how pathetic! The
heart-secrets that were revealed that night now so long vanished, how

they touch me as I give them voice! Those sweet privacies, how they endeared us to each other! We were under oath never to tell any of these things, and I have always kept that oath inviolate when speaking with persons whom I thought not worthy to hear them.

Oh, our lost Youth—God keep its memory green in our hearts! for Age is upon us, with the indignity of its infirmities, and Death beckons!

TO THE ABOVE OLD PEOPLE

Sleep! for the Sun that scores another Day
Against the Tale allotted You to stay,
    Reminding You, is Risen, and now
Serves Notice—ah, ignore it while You may!

The chill Wind blew, and those who stood before
The Tavern murmured, "Having drunk his Score,
    Why tarries He with empty Cup? Behold,
The Wine of Youth once poured, is poured no more.

"Come leave the Cup, and on the Winter's Snow
Your Summer Garment of Enjoyment throw:
    Your Tide of Life is ebbing fast, and it,
Exhausted once, for You no more shall flow."

While yet the Phantom of false Youth was mine,
I heard a Voice from out the Darkness whine,
    "O Youth, O whither gone? Return,
And bathe my Age in thy reviving Wine."

In this subduing Draught of tender green
And kindly Absinthe, with its wimpling Sheen
    Of dusky half-lights, let me drown
The haunting Pathos of the Might-Have-Been.

For every nickeled Joy, marred and brief,
We pay some day its Weight in golden Grief
    Mined from our Hearts. Ah, murmur not—
From this one-sided Bargain dream of no Relief!

The Joy of Life, that streaming through their Veins
Tumultuous swept, falls slack—and wanes
    The Glory in the Eye—and one by one
Life's Pleasures perish and make place for Pains.

Whether one hide in some secluded Nook—
Whether at Liverpool or Sandy Hook—
    'Tis one. Old Age will search him out—and He—
He—He—when ready will know where to look.

From Cradle unto Grave I keep a House
Of Entertainment where may drowse
    Bacilli and kindred Germs—or feed—or breed
Their festering Species in a deep Carouse.

Think—in this battered Caravanserai,
Whose Portals open stand all Night and Day,
    How Microbe after Microbe with his Pomp
Arrives unasked, and comes to stay.

Our ivory Teeth, confessing to the Lust
Of masticating, once, now own Disgust
    Of Clay-plug'd Cavities—full soon our Snags
Are emptied, and our Mouths are filled with Dust.

Our Gums forsake the Teeth and tender grow,
And fat, like over-ripened Figs—we know
    The Sign—the Riggs Disease is ours, and we
Must list this Sorrow, add another Woe.

Our Lungs begin to fail and soon we Cough,
And chilly Streaks play up our Backs, and off
    Our fever'd Foreheads drips an icy Sweat—
We scoffed before, but now we may not scoff.

Some for the Bunions that afflict us prate
Of Plasters unsurpassable, and hate
    To cut a Corn—ah cut, and let the Plaster go,
Nor murmur if the Solace come too late.

Some for the Honors of Old Age, and some
Long for its Respite from the Hum
    And Clash of sordid Strife—O Fools,
The Past should teach them what's to Come:

Lo, for the Honors, cold Neglect instead!
For Respite, disputatious Heirs a Bed
    Of Thorns for them will furnish. Go,
Seek not Here for Peace—but Yonder—with the Dead.

For whether Zal and Rustam heed this Sign,
And even smitten thus, will not repine,
    Let Zal and Rustam shuffle as they may,
The Fine once levied they must Cash the Fine.

O Voices of the Long Ago that were so dear!
Fall'n Silent, now, for many a Mold'ring Year,
    O whither are ye flown? Come back,
And break my Heart, but bless my grieving ear.

Some happy Day my Voice will Silent fall,
And answer not when some that love it call:
    Be glad for Me when this you note—and think
I've found the Voices lost, beyond the pall.

So let me grateful drain the Magic Bowl
That medicines hurt Minds and on the Soul
    The Healing of its Peace doth lay—if then
Death claim me—Welcome be his Dole!

SANNA, SWEDEN, *September 15th*

Private.—If you don't know what Rigg's Disease of the Teeth is, the dentist will tell you. I've had it—and it is more than interesting.

                                                                S.L.C.

EDITORIAL NOTE

Fearing that there might be some mistake, we submitted a proof of this article to the (American) gentlemen named in it, and asked them to correct any errors of detail that might have crept in among the facts. They reply with some asperity that errors cannot creep in among facts where there are no facts for them to creep in among; and that none are discoverable in this article, but only baseless aberrations of a disordered mind. They have no recollection of any such night in Boston, nor elsewhere; and in their opinion there was never any such night. They have *met* Mr. Twain, but have had the prudence not to intrust any privacies to him—particularly under oath; and they think they now see that this prudence was justified, since he has been untrustworthy enough to even betray privacies which had no existence. Further, they think it a strange thing that Mr. Twain, who was never invited to meddle with anybody's boyhood dreams but his own, has been so gratuitously anxious to see that other people's are placed before the world that he has quite lost his head in his zeal and forgotten to make any mention of his own at all. Provided we insert this explanation, they are willing to let his article pass; otherwise they must require its suppression in the interest of truth.

P.S.—These replies having left us in some perplexity, and also in some fear lest they might distress Mr. Twain if published without his privity, we judged it but fair to submit them to him and give him an opportunity to defend himself. But he does not seem to be troubled, or even aware that he is in a delicate situation. He merely says:

"Do not worry about those former young people. They can write good literature, but when it comes to speaking the truth, they have not had my training.—MARK TWAIN."

The last sentence seems obscure, and liable to an unfortunate construction. It plainly needs refashioning, but we cannot take the responsibility of doing it.—EDITOR.

1900

Amended Obituaries

To the Editor:

SIR,—I am approaching seventy; it is in sight; it is only three years away. Necessarily, I must go soon. It is but matter-of-course wisdom, then, that I should begin to set my worldly house in order now, so that it may be done calmly and with thoroughness, in place of waiting until the last day, when, as we have often seen, the attempt to set both houses in order at the same time has been marred by the necessity for haste and by the confusion and waste of time arising from the inability of the notary and the ecclesiastic to work together harmoniously, taking turn about and giving each other friendly assistance—not perhaps in fielding, which could hardly be expected, but at least in the minor offices of keeping game and umpiring; by consequence of which conflict of interests and absence of harmonious action a draw has frequently resulted where this ill-fortune could not have happened if the houses had been set in order one at a time and hurry avoided by beginning in season, and giving to each the amount of time fairly and justly proper to it.

In setting my earthly house in order I find it of moment that I should attend in person to one or two matters which men in my position have long had the habit of leaving wholly to others, with consequences often most regrettable. I wish to speak of only one of these matters at this time: Obituaries. Of necessity, an Obituary is a thing which cannot be so judiciously edited by any hand as by that of the subject

of it. In such a work it is not the Facts that are of chief importance, but the light which the obituarist shall throw upon them, the meanings which he shall dress them in, the conclusions which he shall draw from them, and the judgments which he shall deliver upon them. The Verdicts, you understand: that is the danger-line.

In considering this matter, in view of my approaching change, it has seemed to me wise to take such measures as may be feasible, to acquire, by courtesy of the press, access to my standing obituaries, with the privilege—if this is not asking too much—of editing, not their Facts, but their Verdicts. This, not for present profit, further than as concerns my family, but as a favorable influence usable on the Other Side, where there are some who are not friendly to me.

With this explanation of my motives, I will now ask you of your courtesy to make an appeal for me to the public press. It is my desire that such journals and periodicals as have obituaries of me lying in their pigeonholes, with a view to sudden use some day, will not wait longer, but will publish them now, and kindly send me a marked copy. My address is simply New York City—I have no other that is permanent and not transient.

I will correct them—not the Facts, but the Verdicts—striking out such clauses as could have a deleterious influence on the Other Side, and replacing them with clauses of a more judicious character. I should, of course, expect to pay double rates for both the omissions and the substitutions; and I should also expect to pay quadruple rates for all obituaries which proved to be rightly and wisely worded in the originals, thus requiring no emendations at all.

It is my desire to leave these Amended Obituaries neatly bound behind me as a perennial consolation and entertainment to my family, and as an heirloom which shall have a mournful but definite commercial value for my remote posterity.

I beg, sir, that you will insert this Advertisement (1t-eow, agate, inside), and send the bill to

Yours very respectfully.

Mark Twain

P.S.—For the best Obituary—one suitable for me to read in public, and calculated to inspire regret—I desire to offer a Prize, consisting of a Portrait of me* done entirely by myself in pen and ink without previous instructions. The ink warranted to be the kind used by the very best artists.

1902

Does the Race of Man Love a Lord?

Often a quite assified remark becomes sanctified by use and petrified by custom; it is then a permanency, its term of activity a geologic period.

The day after the arrival of Prince Henry I met an English friend, and he rubbed his hands and broke out with a remark that was charged to the brim with joy—joy that was evidently a pleasant salve to an old sore place:

"Many a time I've had to listen without retort to an old saying that

* See p. 685 for portrait.—c.n.

is irritatingly true, and until now seemed to offer no chance for a return jibe: 'An Englishman does dearly love a lord'; but after this I shall talk back, and say 'How about the Americans?'"

It is a curious thing, the currency that an idiotic saying can get. The man that first says it thinks he has made a discovery. The man he says it to, thinks the same. It departs on its travels, is received everywhere with admiring acceptance, and not only as a piece of rare and acute observation, but as being exhaustively true and profoundly wise; and so it presently takes its place in the world's list of recognized and established wisdoms, and after that no one thinks of examining it to see whether it is really entitled to its high honors or not. I call to mind instances of this in two well-established proverbs, whose dullness is not surpassed by the one about the Englishman and his love for a lord: one of them records the American's Adoration of the Almighty Dollar, the other the American millionaire-girl's ambition to trade cash for a title, with a husband thrown in.

It isn't merely the American that adores the Almighty Dollar, it is the human race. The human race has always adored the hatful of shells, or the bale of calico, or the half-bushel of brass rings, or the handful of steel fish-hooks, or the houseful of black wives, or the zareba full of cattle, or the two-score camels and asses, or the factory, or the farm, or the block of buildings, or the railroad bonds, or the bank stock, or the hoarded cash, or—anything that stands for wealth and consideration and independence, and can secure to the possessor that most precious of all things, another man's envy. It was a dull person that invented the idea that the American's devotion to the dollar is more strenuous than another's.

Rich American girls do buy titles, but they did not invent that idea; it had been worn threadbare several hundred centuries before America was discovered. European girls still exploit it as briskly as ever; and, when a title is not to be had for the money in hand, they buy the husband without it. They must put up the "dot," or there is no trade. The commercialization of brides is substantially universal, except in America. It exists with us, to some little extent, but in no degree approaching a custom.

"The Englishman dearly loves a lord."

What is the soul and source of his love? I think the thing could be more correctly worded:

"The human race dearly envies a lord."

That is to say, it envies the lord's place. Why? On two accounts, I think: its Power and its Conspicuousness.

Where Conspicuousness carries with it a Power which, by the light of our own observation and experience, we are able to measure and comprehend, I think our envy of the possessor is as deep and as passionate as is that of any other nation. No one can care less for a lord than the backwoodsman, who has had no personal contact with lords and has seldom heard them spoken of; but I will not allow that any Englishman has a profounder envy of a lord than has the average American who has lived long years in a European capital and fully learned how immense is the position the lord occupies.

Of any ten thousand Americans who eagerly gather, at vast inconvenience, to get a glimpse of Prince Henry, all but a couple of hundred will be there out of an immense curiosity; they are burning up with desire to see a personage who is so much talked about. They envy him; but it is Conspicuousness they envy mainly, not the Power that is lodged in his royal quality and position, for they have but a vague and spectral knowledge and appreciation of that; through their environment and associations they have been accustomed to regard such things lightly, and as not being very real; consequently, they are not able to value them enough to consumingly envy them.

But, whenever an American (or other human being) is in the presence, for the first time, of a combination of great Power and Conspicuousness which he thoroughly understands and appreciates, his eager curiosity and pleasure will be well-sodden with that other passion—envy—whether he suspect it or not. At any time, on any day, in any part of America, you can confer a happiness upon any passing stranger by calling his attention to any other passing stranger and saying:

"Do you see that gentleman going along there? It is Mr. Rockfeller."

Watch his eye. It is a combination of power and conspicuousness which the man understands.

When we understand rank, we always like to rub against it. When a man is conspicuous, we always want to see him. Also, if he will pay us an attention we will manage to remember it. Also, we will mention it now and then, casually; sometimes to a friend, or if a friend is not handy, we will make out with a stranger.

Well, then, what is rank, and what is conspicuousness? At once we think of kings and aristocracies, and of world-wide celebrities in soldierships, the arts, letters, etc., and we stop there. But that is a mistake. Rank holds its court and receives its homage on every round of the ladder, from the emperor down to the rat-catcher; and distinction, also, exists on every round of the ladder, and commands its due of deference and envy.

To worship rank and distinction is the dear and valued privilege of all the human race, and it is freely and joyfully exercised in democracies as well as well as in monarchies—and even, to some extent, among those creatures whom we impertinently call the Lower Animals. For even they have some poor little vanities and foibles, though in this matter they are paupers as compared to us.

A Chinese Emperor has the worship of his four hundred million of subjects, but the rest of the world is indifferent to him. A Christian Emperor has the worship of his subjects and of a large part of the Christian world outside of his dominions; but he is a matter of indifference to all China. A king, class A, has an extensive worship; a king, class B, has a less extensive worship; class C, class D, class E get a steadily diminishing share of worship; class L (Sultan of Zanzibar), class P (Sultan of Sulu), and class W (half-king of Samoa), get no worship at all outside their own little patch of sovereignty.

Take the distinguished people along down. Each has his group of homage-payers. In the navy, there are many groups; they start with the Secretary and the Admiral, and go down to the quartermaster— and below; for there will be groups among the sailors, and each of these groups will have a tar who is distinguished for his battles, or his strength, or his daring, or his profanity, and is admired and envied by his group. The same with the army; the same with the literary and journalistic craft, the publishing craft; the cod-fishery craft; Standard Oil; U. S. Steel; the class A hotel—and the rest of the alphabet in that line; the class A prize-fighter—and the rest of the alphabet in his line —clear down to the lowest and obscurest six-boy gang of little gamins, with its one boy that can thrash the rest, and to whom he is king of Samoa, bottom of the royal race, but looked up to with a most ardent admiration and envy.

There is something pathetic, and funny, and pretty, about this human race's fondness for contact with power and distinction, and for the reflected glory it gets out of it. The king, class A, is happy in the state banquet and the military show which the emperor provides for him, and he goes home and gathers the queen and the princelings around him in the privacy of the spare room, and tells them all about it, and says:

"His Imperial Majesty put his hand on my shoulder in the most friendly way—just as friendly and familiar, oh, you can't imagine it!— and everybody *seeing* him do it; charming, perfectly charming!"

The king, class G, is happy in the cold collation and the police parade provided for him by the king, class B, and goes home and tells the family all about it, and says:

"And His Majesty took me into his own private cabinet for a smoke and a chat, and there we sat just as sociable, and talking away and laughing and chatting, just the same as if we had been born in the same bunk; and all the servants in the anteroom could see us doing it! Oh, it was too lovely for anything!"

The king, class Q, is happy in the modest entertainment furnished him by the king, class M, and goes home and tells the household about it, and is as grateful and joyful over it as were his predecessors in the gaudier attentions that had fallen to their larger lot.

Emperors, kings, artisans, peasants, big people, little people—at bottom we are all alike and all the same; all just alike on the inside, and when our clothes are off, nobody can tell which of us is which. We are unanimous in the pride we take in good and genuine compliments paid us, in distinctions conferred upon us, in attentions shown us. There is not one of us, from the emperor down, but is made like that. Do I mean attentions shown us by the great? No, I mean simply flattering attentions, let them come whence they may. We despise no source that can pay us a pleasing attention—there is no source that is humble enough for that. You have heard a dear little girl say to a frowzy and disreputable dog: "He came right to me and let me pat him on the head, and he wouldn't let the others touch him!" and you have seen her eyes dance with pride in that high distinction. You have often seen that. If the child were a princess, would that random dog be able to confer the like glory upon her with his pretty compliment? Yes; and even in her mature life and seated upon a throne, she would still remember it, still recall it, still speak of it with frank satisfaction. That charming and lovable German princess and poet, Carmen Sylva, Queen of Roumania, remembers yet that the flowers of the woods and fields "talked to her" when she was a girl, and she sets it down in her latest book; and that the squirrels conferred upon her and her father the valued compliment of not being afraid of them; and "once one of them, holding a nut between its sharp little teeth, ran right up against my father"—it has the very note of "He came right to me and let me pat him on the head"—"and when it saw itself reflected in his boot it was very much surprised, and stopped for a long time to contemplate itself in the polished leather"—then it went its way. And the birds! she still remembers with pride that "they came boldly into my room," when she had neglected her "duty" and put no food on the window-sill for them; she knew all the wild birds, and forgets the royal crown on her head to remember with pride that they knew her; also that the wasp and the bee were personal friends of hers, and never forgot that gracious relationship to her injury: "never have I been stung by a wasp or a bee." And here is that proud note again that sings in that little child's elation in being singled out, among all the company of children, for the random dog's honor-conferring attentions. "Even in the very worst summer for wasps, when, in lunching out of doors, our table was covered with them and every one else was stung, they never hurt me."

When a queen whose qualities of mind and heart and character are able to add distinction to so distinguished a place as a throne, remembers with grateful exultation, after thirty years, honors and distinctions conferred upon her by the humble, wild creatures of the forest, we are helped to realize that complimentary attentions, homage, distinctions, are of no caste, but are above all caste—that they are a nobility-conferring power apart.

We all like these things. When the gate-guard at the railway-station passes me through unchallenged and examines other people's tickets, I feel as the king, class A, felt when the emperor put the imperial hand on his shoulder, "everybody seeing him do it"; and as the child felt when the random dog allowed her to pat his head and ostracized the others; and as the princess felt when the wasps spared her and stung the rest; and I felt just so, four years ago in Vienna (and remember it yet), when the helmeted police shut me off, with fifty others, from a street which the Emperor was to pass through, and the captain of the squad turned and saw the situation and said indignantly to that guard:

"Can't you see it is the Herr Mark Twain? Let him through!"

It was four years ago; but it will be four hundred before I forget the wind of self-complacency that rose in me, and strained my buttons when I marked the deference for me evoked in the faces of my fellow-rabble, and noted, mingled with it, a puzzled and resentful expression which said, as plainly as speech could have worded it: "And who in the nation is the Herr Mark Twain *um Gotteswillen?*"

How many times in your life have you heard this boastful remark:

"I stood as close to him as I am to you; I could have put out my hand and touched him."

We have all heard it many and many a time. It was a proud distinction to be able to say those words. It brought envy to the speaker, a kind of glory; and he basked in it and was happy through all his veins. And who was it he stood so close to? The answer would cover all the grades. Sometimes it was a king; sometimes it was a renowned highwayman; sometimes it was an unknown man killed in an extraordinary way and made suddenly famous by it; always it was a person who was for the moment the subject of public interest—the public interest of a nation, maybe only the public interest of a village.

"I was there, and I saw it myself." That is a common and envy-compelling remark. It can refer to a battle; to a hanging; to a coronation, to the killing of Jumbo by the railway-train; to the arrival of Jenny Lind at the Battery; to the meeting of the President and Prince Henry; to the chase of a murderous maniac; to the disaster in the tunnel; to the explosion in the subway; to a remarkable dog-fight; to a village church struck by lightning. It will be said, more or less casually, by everybody in America who has seen Prince Henry do anything, or try to. The man who was absent and didn't see him do anything, will scoff. It is his privilege; and he can make capital out of it, too; he will seem, even to himself, to be different from other Americans, and better. As his opinion of his superior Americanism grows, and swells, and concentrates and coagulates, he will go further and try to belittle the distinction of those that saw the Prince do things, and will spoil their pleasure in it if he can. My life has been embittered by that kind of persons. If you are able to tell of a special distinction that has fallen to your lot, it gravels them; they cannot bear it; and they try to make believe that the thing you took for a special distinction was nothing of the kind and was meant in quite another way. Once I was received in private audience by an emperor. Last week I was telling a jealous person about it, and I could see him wince under it, see it bite, see him suffer. I revealed the whole episode to him with considerable elaboration and nice attention to detail. When I was through, he asked me what had impressed me most. I said:

"His Majesty's delicacy. They told me to be sure and back out from the presence, and find the door-knob as best I could; it was not allowable to face around. Now the Emperor knew it would be a difficult ordeal for me, because of lack of practice; and so, when it was time to part, he turned, with exceeding delicacy, and pretended to fumble with things on his desk, so that I could get out in my own way, without his seeing me."

It went home! It was vitriol! I saw the envy and disgruntlement rise in the man's face; he couldn't keep it down. I saw him trying to fix up something in his mind to take the bloom off that distinction. I enjoyed that, for I judged that he had his work cut out for him. He struggled along inwardly for quite a while; then he said, with the manner of a person who has to say something and hasn't anything relevant to say:

"You said he had a handful of special-brand cigars lying on the table?"

"Yes; I never saw anything to match them."

I had him again. He had to fumble around in his mind as much as another minute before he could play; then he said in as mean a way as I ever heard a person say anything:

"He could have been counting the cigars, you know."

I cannot endure a man like that. It is nothing to him how unkind he is, so long as he takes the bloom off. It is all he cares for.

"An Englishman (or other human being) does dearly love a lord," (or other conspicuous person). It includes us all. We love to be noticed by the conspicuous person; we love to be associated with such, or with a conspicuous event, even in a seventh-rate fashion, even in a forty-seventh, if we cannot do better. This accounts for some of our curious tastes in mementos. It accounts for the large private trade in the Prince of Wales's hair, which chambermaids were able to drive in that article of commerce when the Prince made the tour of the world in the long ago—hair which probably did not always come from his brush, since enough of it was marketed to refurnish a bald comet; it accounts for the fact that the rope which lynches a negro in the presence of ten thousand Christian spectators is salable five minutes later at two dollars an inch; it accounts for the mournful fact that royal personage does not venture to wear buttons on his coat in public.

We do love a lord—and by that term I mean any person whose situation is higher than our own. The lord of a group, for instance: a group of peers, a group of millionaires, a group of hoodlums, a group of sailors, a group of newsboys, a group of saloon politicians, a group of college girls. No royal person has ever been the object of a more delirious loyalty and slavish adoration than is paid by the vast Tammany herd to its squalid idol of Wantage. There is not a bifurcated animal in that menagerie that would not be proud to appear in a newspaper picture in his company. At the same time, there are some in that organization who would scoff at the people who have been daily pictured in company with Prince Henry, and would say vigorously that *they* would not consent to be photographed with him—a statement which would not be true in any instance. There are hundreds of people in America who would frankly say to you that they would not be proud to be photographed in a group with the Prince, if invited; and some of these unthinking people would believe it when they said it; yet in no instance would it be true. We have a large population, but we have not a large enough one, by several millions, to furnish that man. He has not yet been begotten, and in fact he is not begettable.

You may take any of the printed groups, and there isn't a person in it who isn't visibly glad to be there; there isn't a person in the dim background who isn't visibly trying to be vivid; if it is a crowd of ten thousand—ten thousand proud, untamed democrats, horny-handed sons of toil and of politics, and fliers of the eagle—there isn't one who isn't conscious of the camera, there isn't one who is trying to keep out of range, there isn't one who isn't plainly meditating a purchase of the paper in the morning, with the intention of hunting himself out in the picture and of framing and keeping it if he shall find so much of his person in it as his starboard ear.

We all love to get some of the drippings of Conspicuousness, and we will put up with a single, humble drip, if we can't get any more. We may pretend otherwise, in conversation; but we can't pretend it to ourselves privately—and we don't. We do confess in public that we are the noblest work of God, being moved to it by long habit, and teaching, and superstition; but deep down in the secret places of our souls we recognize that, if we *are* the noblest work, the less said about it the better.

We of the North poke fun at the South for its fondness for titles—a fondness for titles pure and simple, regardless of whether they are genune or pinchbeck. We forget that whatever a Southerner likes the rest of the human race likes, and that there is no law of predilection lodged in one people that is absent from another people. There is no variety in the human race. We are all children, all children of the one Adam, and we love toys. We can soon acquire that Southern disease if some one will give it a start. It already has a start, in fact. I have been personally acquainted with over eighty-four thousand persons who, at one time or another in their lives, have served for a year or two on the staffs of our multitudinous governors, and through that fatality have been generals temporarily, and colonels temporarily, and judge-advocates temporarily; but I have known only nine among them who could be hired to let the title go when it ceased to be legitimate. I know thousands and thousands of governors who ceased to be governors away back in the last century; but I am acquainted with only three who would answer your letter if you failed to call them "Governor" in it. I know acres and acres of men who have done time in a legislature in prehistoric days, but among them is not half an acre whose resentment you would not raise if you addressed them as "Mr." instead of "Hon." The first thing a legislature does is to convene in an impressive legislative attitude, and get itself photographed. Each member frames his copy and takes it to the woods and hangs it up in the most aggressively conspicuous place in his house; and if you visit the house and fail to inquire what that accumulation is, the conversation will be brought around to it by that aforetime legislator, and he will show you a figure in it which in the course of years he has almost obliterated with the smut of his finger-marks, and say with a solemn joy, "It's me!"

Have you ever seen a country Congressman enter the hotel breakfast-room in Washington with his letters?—and sit at his table and let on to read them?—and wrinkle his brows and frown statesman-like? —keeping a furtive watch-out over his glasses all the while to see if he is being observed and admired?—those same old letters which he fetches in every morning? Have you seen it? Have you seen him show off? It is *the* sight of the national capital. Except one; a pathetic one. That is the ex-Congressman: the poor fellow whose life has been ruined by a two-year taste of glory and of fictitious consequence; who has been superseded, and ought to take his heartbreak home and hide it, but cannot tear himself away from the scene of his lost little grandeur; and so he lingers, and still lingers, year after year, unconsidered, sometimes snubbed, ashamed of his fallen estate, and valiantly trying to look otherwise; dreary and depressed, but counterfeiting breeziness and gaiety, hailing with chummy familiarity, which is not always welcomed, the more-fortunates who are still in place and were once his mates. Have you seen him? He clings piteously to the one little shred that is left of his departed distinction—the "privilege of the floor"; and works it hard and gets what he can out of it. That is the saddest figure I know of.

Yes, we do so love our little distinctions! And then we loftily scoff at a Prince for enjoying his larger ones; forgetting that if we only had his chance—ah! "Senator" is not a legitimate title. A Senator has no more right to be addressed by it than have you or I; but, in the several state capitals and in Washington, there are five thousand Senators who take very kindly to that fiction, and who purr gratefully when you call them by it—which you may do quite unrebuked. Then those same

Senators smile at the self-constructed majors and generals and judges of the South!

Indeed, we do love our distinctions, get them how we may. And we work them for all they are worth. In prayer we call ourselves "worms of the dust," but it is only on a sort of tacit understanding that the remark shall not be taken at par. *We*—worms of the dust! Oh, no, we are not that. Except in fact; and we do not deal much in fact when we are contemplating ourselves.

As a race, we do certainly love a lord—let him be Croker, or a duke, or a prize-fighter, or whatever other personage shall chance to be the head of our group. Many years ago, I saw a greasy youth in overalls standing by the *Herald* office, with an expectant look in his face. Soon a large man passed out, and gave him a pat on the shoulder. That was what the boy was waiting for—the large man's notice. The pat made him proud and happy, and the exultation inside of him shone out through his eyes; and his mates were there to see the pat and envy it and wish they could have that glory. The boy belonged down cellar in the press-room, the large man was king of the upper floors, foreman of the composing-room. The light in the boy's face was worship, the foreman was his lord, head of his group. The pat was an accolade. It was as precious to the boy as it would have been if he had been an aristocrat's son and the accolade had been delivered by his sovereign with a sword. The quintessence of the honor was all there; there was no difference in values; in truth there was no difference present except an artificial one—clothes.

All the human race loves a lord—that is, it loves to look upon or be noticed by the possessor of Power or Conspicuousness; and sometimes animals, born to better things and higher ideals, descend to man's level in this matter. In the Jardin des Plantes I have seen a cat that was so vain of being the personal friend of an elephant that I was ashamed of her.

1902

Instructions in Art

(With Illustrations by the Author)

The great trouble about painting a whole gallery of portraits at the same time is, that the housemaid comes and dusts, and does not put them back the way they were before, and so when the public flock to the studio and wish to know which is Howells and which is Depew and so on, you have to dissemble, and it is very embarrassing at first. Still, you know they are there, and this knowledge presently gives you more or less confidence, and you say sternly, *"This* is Howells," and watch the visitor's eye. If you see doubt there, you correct yourself and try another. In time you find one that will satisfy, and then you feel relief and joy, but you have suffered much in the meantime; and you know that this joy is only temporary, for the next inquirer will settle on another Howells of a quite different aspect, and one which you suspect is Edward VII or Cromwell, though you keep that to yourself, of course. It is much better to label a portrait when you first paint it, then there is no uncertainty in your mind and you can get bets out of the visitor and win them.

I believe I have had the most trouble with a portrait which I painted in installments—the head on one canvas and the bust on another.

The housemaid stood the bust up sideways, and now I don't know which way it goes. Some authorities think it belongs with the breastpin at the top, under the man's chin; others think it belongs the reverse way, on account of the collar, one of these saying, "A person can wear a breastpin on his stomach if he wants to, but he can't wear his collar anywhere he dern pleases." There is a certain amount of sense in that view of it. Still, there is no way to determine the matter for certain; when you join the installments, with the pin under the chin, that seems to be right; then when you reverse it and bring the collar under the chin it seems as right as ever; whichever way you fix it the lines come together snug and convincing, and either way you do it the portrait's face looks equally surprised and rejoiced, and as if it wouldn't be satisfied to have it any way but just that one; in fact, even if you take the bust away altogether the face seems surprised and happy

THE HEAD ON ONE CANVAS

just the same—I have never seen an expression before, which no vicis-situdes could alter. I wish I could remember who it is. It looks a little like Washington, but I do not think it can be Washington, because he had as many ears on one side as the other. You can always tell Washington by that; he was very particular about his ears, and about having them arranged the same old way all the time.

By and by I shall get out of these confusions, and then it will be plain sailing; but first-off the confusions were natural and not to be avoided. My reputation came very suddenly and tumultuously when I published my own portrait, and it turned my head a little, for indeed there was never anything like it. In a single day I got orders from

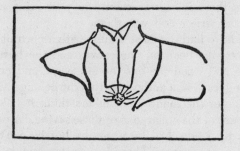

AND THE BUST ON ANOTHER

sixty-two people not to paint their portraits, some of them the most distinguished persons in the country—the President, the Cabinet, authors, governors, admirals, candidates for office on the weak side—almost everybody that was anybody, and it would really have turned the head of nearly any beginner to get so much notice and have it come with such a frenzy of cordiality. But I am growing calm and settling down to business, now; and pretty soon I shall cease to be flurried, and then when I do a portrait I shall be quite at myself and able on the instant to tell it from the others and pick it out when wanted.

I am living a new and exalted life of late. It steeps me in a sacred rapture to see a portrait develop and take soul under my hand. First, I

FIRST YOU THINK IT'S DANTE; NEXT YOU THINK
IT'S EMERSON; THEN YOU THINK IT'S WAYNE
MAC VEAGH. YET IT ISN'T ANY OF THEM; IT'S
THE BEGINNINGS OF DEPEW

throw off a study—just a mere study, a few apparently random lines— and to look at it you would hardly ever suspect who it was going to be; even I cannot tell, myself. Take this picture, for instance:

First you think it's Dante; next you think it's Emerson; then you think it's Wayne Mac Veagh. Yet it isn't any of them; it's the beginnings of Depew. Now you wouldn't believe Depew could be devolved out of that; yet the minute it is finished here you have him to the life, and you say, yourself, "If that isn't Depew it isn't anybody."

Some would have painted him speaking, but he isn't always speaking, he has to stop and think sometimes.

That is a *genre* picture, as we say in the trade, and differs from the encaustic and other schools in various ways, mainly technical, which you wouldn't understand if I should explain them to you. But you will get the idea as I go along, and little by little you will learn all that is valuable about Art without knowing how it happened, and without any sense of strain or effort, and then you will know what school a picture belongs to, just at a glance, and whether it is an animal picture or a landscape. It is then that the joy of life will begin for you.

When you come to examine my portraits of Mr. Joe Jefferson and the rest, your eye will have become measurably educated by that time, and you will recognize at once that no two of them are alike. I will close the present chapter with an example of the nude, for your instruction.

This creation is different from any of the other works. The others are from real life, but this is an example of still-life; so called because it is a portrayal of a fancy only, a thing which has no actual and active existence. The purpose of a still-life picture is to concrete to the eye the spiritual, the intangible, a something which we feel, but cannot see with the fleshy vision—such as joy, sorrow, resentment, and so on. This is best achieved by the employment of that treatment which we call the impressionist, in the trade. The present example is an impressionist picture, done in distemper, with a chiaroscuro motif modified by monochromatc technique, so as to secure tenderness of feeling and spirituality of expression. At a first glance it would seem to be a Botticelli, but it is not that; it is only a humble imitation of that great master of longness and slimness and limbfulness.

The work is imagined from Greek story, and represents Proserpine or Persepolis, or one of those other Bacchantes doing the solemnities of welcome before the altar of Isis upon the arrival of the annual shipload of Athenian youths in the island of Minos to be sacrificed in appeasement of the Dordonian Cyclops.

The figure symbolizes solemn joy. It is severely Greek, therefore does not call details of drapery or other factitious helps to its aid, but depends wholly upon grace of action and symmetry of contour for its effects. It is intended to be viewed from the south or southeast, and I think that that is best; for while it expresses more and larger joy when viewed from the east or the north, the features of the face are too much foreshortened and wormy when viewed from that point. That thing in the right hand is not a skillet; it is a tambourine.

This creation will be exhibited at the Paris Salon in June, and will compete for the *Prix de Rome*.

THAT THING IN THE RIGHT HAND IS NOT A SKILLET;
IT IS A TAMBOURINE

THE PORTRAIT REPRODUCES MR. JOSEPH JEFFER-
SON, THE COMMON FRIEND OF THE HUMAN RACE

The above is a marine picture, and is intended to educate the eye in the important matters of perspective and foreshortening. The mountainous and bounding waves in the foreground, contrasted with the tranquil ship fading away as in a dream the other side of the fishing-pole, convey to us the idea of space and distance as no words could do. Such is the miracle wrought by that wondrous device, perspective.

The portrait reproduces Mr. Joseph Jefferson, the common friend of the human race. He is fishing, and is not catching anything. This is finely expressed by the moisture in the eye and the anguish of the mouth. The mouth is holding back words. The pole is bamboo, the line is foreshortened. This foreshortening, together with the smoothness of the water away out there where the cork is, gives a powerful impression of distance, and is another way of achieving a perspective effect.

We now come to the next portrait, which is either Mr. Howells or Mr. Laffan. I cannot tell which, because the label is lost. But it will do for both, because the features are Mr. Howells's, while the expression is Mr. Laffan's. This work will bear critical examination.

EITHER MR. HOWELLS OR MR.
LAFFAN. I CANNOT TELL WHICH
BECAUSE THE LABEL IS LOST

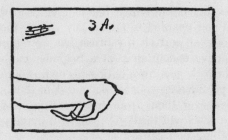

THE FRONT END OF IT WENT AROUND
A CORNER BEFORE I COULD GET TO IT

The next picture is part of an animal, but I do not know the name of it. It is not finished. The front end of it went around a corner before I could get to it.

We will conclude with the portrait of a lady in the style of Raphael. Originally I started it out for Queen Elizabeth, but was not able to do the lace hopper her head projects out of, therefore I tried to turn it into Pocahontas, but was again baffled, and was compelled to make further modifications, this time achieving success. By spiritualizing it and turning it into the noble mother of our race and throwing into the

THE BEST AND MOST WINNING AND
ELOQUENT   PORTRAIT   MY   BRUSH
HAS   EVER   PRODUCED

countenance the sacred joy which her first tailor-made outfit infuses into her spirit, I was enabled to add to my gallery the best and most winning and eloquent portrait my brush has ever produced.

The most effective encouragement a beginner can have is the encouragement which he gets from noting his own progress with an alert and persistent eye. Save up your works and date them; as the years go by, run your eye over them from time to time, and measure your advancing stride. This will thrill you, this will nerve you, this will inspire you as nothing else can.

It has been my own course, and to it I owe the most that I am to-day in Art. When I look back and examine my first effort and then compare it with my latest, it seems unbelievable that I have climbed so high in thirty-one years. Yet so it is. Practice—that is the secret. From three to seven hours a day. It is all that is required. The results are sure; whereas indolence achieves nothing great.

IT SEEMS UNBELIEV-
ABLE THAT I HAVE
CLIMBED SO HIGH IN
THIRTY-ONE YEARS

1903

Italian with Grammar

I found that a person of large intelligence could read this beautiful language with considerable facility without a dictionary, but I presently found that to such a person a grammar could be of use at times. It is because, if he does not know the *Were's* and the *Was's* and the

May-be's and the *Has-been's* apart, confusions and uncertainties can arise. He can get the idea that a thing is going to happen next week when the truth is that it has already happened week before last. Even more previously, sometimes. Examination and inquiry showed me that the adjectives and such things were frank and fair-minded and straightforward, and did not shuffle; it was the Verb that mixed the hands, it was the Verb that lacked stability, it was the Verb that had no permanent opinion about anything, it was the Verb that was always dodging the issue and putting out the light and making all the trouble.

Further examination, further inquiry, further reflection, confirmed this judgment, and established beyond peradventure the fact that the Verb was the storm-center. This discovery made plain the right and wise course to pursue in order to acquire certainty and exactness in understanding the statements which the newspaper was daily endeavoring to convey to me: I must catch a Verb and tame it. I must find out its ways, I must spot its eccentricities, I must penetrate its disguises, I must intelligently foresee and forecast at least the commoner of the dodges it was likely to try upon a stranger in given circumstances, I must get in on its main shifts and head them off, I must learn its game and play the limit.

I had noticed, in other foreign languages, that verbs are bred in families, and that the members of each family have certain features or resemblances that are common to that family and distinguish it from the other families—the other kin, the cousins and what not. I had noticed that this family-mark is not usually the nose or the hair, so to speak, but the tail—the Termination—and that these tails are quite definitely differentiated; insomuch that an expert can tell a Pluperfect from a Subjunctive by its tail as easily and as certainly as a cowboy can tell a cow from a horse by the like process, the result of observation and culture. I should explain that I am speaking of legitimate verbs, those verbs which in the slang of the grammar are called Regular. There are others—I am not meaning to conceal this; others called Irregulars, born out of wedlock, of unknown and uninteresting parentage, and naturally destitute of family resemblances, as regards all features, tails included. But of these pathetic outcasts I have nothing to say. I do not approve of them, I do not encourage them; I am prudishly delicate and sensitive, and I do not allow them to be used in my presence.

But, as I have said, I decided to catch one of the others and break it to harness. One is enough. Once familiar with its assortment of tails, you are immune; after that, no regular verb can conceal its specialty from you and make you think it is working the past or the future or the conditional or the unconditional when it is engaged in some other line of business—its tail will give it away. I found out all these things by myself, without a teacher.

I selected the verb *Amare, to love.* Not for any personal reason, for I am indifferent about verbs; I care no more for one verb than for another, and have little or no respect for any of them; but in foreign languages you always begin with that one. Why, I do not know. It is merely habit, I suppose; the first teacher chose it, Adam was satisfied, and there hasn't been a successor since with originality enough to start a fresh one. For they *are* a pretty limited lot, you will admit that? Originality is not in their line; they can't think up anything new, anything to freshen up the old moss-grown dullness of the language lesson and put life and "go" into it, and charm and grace and picturesqueness.

I knew I must look after those details myself; therefore I thought them out and wrote them down, and sent for the *facchino* and explained them to him, and said he must arrange a proper plant, and get together a good stock company among the *contadini,* and design the costumes, and distribute the parts; and drill the troupe, and be ready in three days to begin on this Verb in a shipshape and workman-like manner. I told him to put each grand division of it under a fore-man, and each subdivision under a subordinate of the rank of sergeant or corporal or something like that, and to have a different uniform for each squad, so that I could tell a Pluperfect from a Compound Future without looking at the book; the whole battery to be under his own special and particular command, with the rank of Brigadier, and I to pay the freight.

I then inquired into the character and possibilities of the selected verb, and was much disturbed to find that it was over my size, it being chambered for fifty-seven rounds—fifty-seven ways of saying *I love* without reloading; and yet none of them likely to convince a girl that was laying for a title, or a title that was laying for rocks.

It seemed to me that with my inexperience it would be foolish to go into action with this mitrailleuse, so I ordered it to the rear and told the facchino to provide something a little more primitive to start with, something less elaborate, some gentle old-fashioned flint-lock, smooth-bore, double-barreled thing, calculated to cripple at two hundred yards and kill at forty—an arrangement suitable for a beginner who could be satisfied with moderate results on the offstart and did not wish to take the whole territory in the first campaign.

But in vain. He was not able to mend the matter, all the verbs being
of the same build, all Gatlings, all of the same caliber and delivery,
fifty-seven to the volley, and fatal at a mile and a half. But he said the
auxiliary verb AVERE, *to have,* was a tidy thing, and easy to handle in
a seaway, and less likely to miss stays in going about than some of the
others; so, upon his recommendation I chose that one, and told him to
take it along and scrape its bottom and break out its spinnaker and
get it ready for business.

I will explain that a facchino is a general-utility domestic. Mine
was a horse-doctor in his better days, and a very good one.

At the end of three days the facchino-doctor-brigadier was ready.
I was also ready, with a stenographer. We were in the room called the
Rope-Walk. This is a formidably long room, as is indicated by its
facetious name, and is a good place for reviews. At 9.30 the F.-D.-B.
took his place near me and gave the word of command; the drums
began to rumble and thunder, the head of the forces appeared at an
upper door, and the "march-past" was on. Down they filed, a blaze of
variegated color, each squad gaudy in a uniform of its own and bearing a banner inscribed with its verbal rank and quality: first the Present Tense in Mediterranean blue and old gold, then the Past Definite
in scarlet and black, then the Imperfect in green and yellow, then the
Indicative Future in the stars and stripes, then the Old Red Sandstone
Subjunctive in purple and silver—and so on and so on, fifty-seven
privates and twenty commissioned and non-commissioned officers; certainly one of the most fiery and dazzling and eloquent sights I have
ever beheld. I could not keep back the tears. Presently:

"Halt!" commanded the Brigadier.

"Front—face!"

"Right dress!"

"Stand at ease!"

"One—two—three. In unison—*recite!*"

It was fine. In one noble volume of sound all the fifty-seven Haves
in the Italian language burst forth in an exalting and splendid confusion. Then came commands:

"About—face! Eyes—front! Helm alee—hard aport! Forward—march!"
and the drums let go again.

When the last Termination had disappeared, the commander said
the instruction drill would now begin, and asked for suggestions. I
said:

"They say *I have, thou hast, he has,* and so on, but they don't say *what*. It will be better, and more definite, if they have something to have; just an object, you know, a something—anything will do; anything that will give the listener a sort of personal as well as grammatical interest in their joys and complaints, you see."

He said:

"It is a good point. Would a dog do?"

I said I did not know, but we could try a dog and see. So he sent out an aide-de-camp to give the order to add the dog.

The six privates of the Present Tense now filed in, in charge of Sergeant AVERE (*to have*), and displaying their banner. They formed in line of battle, and recited, one at a time, thus:

"*Io ho un cane*, I have a dog."

"*Tu hai un cane*, thou hast a dog."

"*Egli ha un cane*, he has a dog."

"*Noi abbiamo un cane*, we have a dog."

"*Voi avete un cane*, you have a dog."

"*Eglino hanno un cane*, they have a dog."

No comment followed. They returned to camp, and I reflected a while. The commander said:

"I fear you are disappointed."

"Yes," I said; "they are too monotonous, too singsong, too dead-and-alive; they have no expression, no elocution. It isn't natural; it could never happen in real life. A person who had just acquired a dog is either blame' glad or blame' sorry. He is not on the fence. I never saw a case. What the nation do you suppose is the matter with these people?"

He thought maybe the trouble was with the dog. He said:

"These are *contadini*, you know, and they have a prejudice against dogs—that is, against marimane. Marimana dogs stand guard over people's vines and olives, you know, and are very savage, and thereby a grief and an inconvenience to persons who want other people's things at night. In my judgment they have taken this dog for a marimana, and have soured on him."

I saw that the dog was a mistake, and not functionable: we must try something else; something, if possible, that could evoke sentiment, interest, feeling.

"What is cat, in Italian?" I asked.

"Gatto."

"Is it a gentleman cat, or a lady?"

"Gentleman cat."

"How are these people as regards that animal?"

"We-ll, they—they—"

"You hesitate: that is enough. How are they about chickens?"

He tilted his eyes toward heaven in mute ecstasy. I understood.

"What is chicken, in Italian?" I asked.

"Pollo, *podere*." (Podere is Italian for master. It is a title of courtesy, and conveys reverence and admiration.) "Pollo is one chicken by itself; when there are enough present to constitute a plural, it is *polli*."

"Very well, polli will do. Which squad is detailed for duty next?"

"The Past Definite."

"Send out and order it to the front—with chickens. And let them understand that we don't want any more of this cold indifference."

He gave the order to an aide, adding, with a haunting tenderness in his tone and a watering mouth in his aspect:

"Convey to them the conception that these are unprotected chickens." He turned to me, saluting with his hand to his temple, and explained, "It will inflame their interest in the poultry, sire."

A few minutes elapsed. Then the squad marched in and formed up, their faces glowing with enthusiasm, and the file-leader shouted:

"*Ebbi polli*, I had chickens!"

"Good!" I said. "Go on, the next."

"*Avesti polli*, thou hadst chickens!"

"Fine! Next!"

"*Ebbe polli*, he had chickens!"

"Moltimoltissimo! Go on, the next!"

"*Avemmo polli*, we had chickens!"

"Basta-basta aspettatto avanti—last man—*charge!*"

"*Ebbero polli*, they had chickens!"

Then they formed in echelon, by columns of fours, refusing the left, and retired in great style on the double-quick. I was enchanted, and said:

"Now, doctor, that is something *like!* Chickens are the ticket, there is no doubt about it. What is the next squad?"

"The Imperfect."

"How does it go?"

"*Io aveva*, I had, *tu avevi*, thou hadst, *egli aveva*, he had, *noi av—*"

"Wait—we've just *had* the hads. What are you giving me?"

"But this is another breed."

"What do we want of another breed? Isn't one breed enough? *Had* is HAD, and your tricking it out in a fresh way of spelling isn't going to make it any hadder than it was before; now you know that yourself."

"But there is a distinction—they are not just the same Hads."

"How do you make it out?"

"Well, you use that first Had when you are referring to something that happened at a named and sharp and perfectly definite moment; you use the other when the thing happened at a vaguely defined time and in a more prolonged and indefinitely continuous way."

"Why, doctor, it is pure nonsense; you know it yourself. Look here: If I have had a had, or have wanted to have had a had, or was in a position right then and there to have had a had that hadn't had any chance to go out hadding on account of this foolish discrimination which lets one Had go hadding in any kind of indefinite grammatical weather but restricts the other one to definite and datable meteoric convulsions, and keeps it pining around and watching the barometer all the time, and liable to get sick through confinement and lack of exercise, and all that sort of thing, why—why, the inhumanity of it is enough, let alone the wanton superfluity and uselessness of any such a loafing consumptive hospital-bird of a Had taking up room and cumbering the place for nothing. These finical refinements revolt me; it is not right, it is not honorable; it is constructive nepotism to keep in office a Had that is so delicate it can't come out when the wind's in the nor'west—I won't have this dude on the pay-roll. Cancel his exequatur; and look here—"

"But you miss the point. It is like this. You see—"

"Never mind explaining, I don't care anything about it. Six Hads is enough for me; anybody that needs twelve, let him subscribe; I don't want any stock in a Had Trust. Knock out the Prolonged and Indefinitely Continuous; four-fifths of it is water, anyway."

"But I beg you, podere! It is often quite indispensable in cases where—"

"Pipe the next squad to the assault!"

But it was not to be; for at that moment the dull boom of the noon gun floated up out of far-off Florence, followed by the usual softened jangle of church-bells, Florentine and suburban, that bursts out in murmurous response; by labor-union law the *colazione*[1] must stop; stop promptly, stop instantly, stop definitely, like the chosen and best of the breed of Hads.

1904

[1] Colazione is Italian for a collection, a meeting, a séance, a sitting.—M. T.

Italian without a Master

It is almost a fortnight now that I am domiciled in a medieval villa in the country, a mile or two from Florence. I cannot speak the language; I am too old not to learn how, also too busy when I am busy, and too indolent when I am not; wherefore some will imagine that I am having a dull time of it. But it is not so. The "help" are all natives; they talk Italian to me, I answer in English; I do not understand them, they do not understand me, consequently no harm is done, and everybody is satisfied. In order to be just and fair, I throw in an Italian word when I have one, and this has a good influence. I get the word out of the morning paper. I have to use it while it is fresh, for I find that Italian words do not keep in this climate. They fade toward night, and next morning they are gone. But it is no matter; I get a new one out of the paper before breakfast, and thrill the domestics with it while it lasts. I have no dictionary, and I do not want one; I can select my words by the sound, or by orthographic aspect. Many of them have a French or German or English look, and these are the ones I enslave for the day's service. That is, as a rule. Not always. If I find a learnable phrase that has an imposing look and warbles musically along I do not care to know the meaning of it; I pay it out to the first applicant, knowing that if I pronounce it carefully *he* will understand it, and that's enough.

Yesterday's word was *avanti*. It sounds Shakespearian, and probably means Avaunt and quit my sight. To-day I have a whole phrase: *sono dispiacentissimo*. I do not know what it means, but it seems to fit in everywhere and give satisfaction. Although as a rule my words and phrases are good for one day and train only, I have several that stay by me all the time, for some unknown reason, and these come very handy when I get into a long conversation and need things to fire up with in monotonous stretches. One of the best ones is *Dov' è il gatto*. It nearly always produces a pleasant surprise, therefore I save it up for places where I want to express applause or admiration. The fourth word has a French sound, and I think the phrase means "that takes the cake."

During my first week in the deep and dreamy stillness of this woodsy and flowery place I was without news of the outside world,

and was well content without it. It had been four weeks since I had
seen a newspaper, and this lack seemed to give life a new charm and
grace, and to saturate it with a feeling verging upon actual delight.
Then came a change that was to be expected: the appetite for news
began to rise again, after this invigorating rest. I had to feed it, but I
was not willing to let it make me its helpless slave again; I determined
to put it on a diet, and a strict and limited one. So I examined an
Italian paper, with the idea of feeding it on that, and on that exclusively. On that exclusively, and without help of a dictionary. In
this way I should surely be well protected against overloading and
indigestion.

A glance at the telegraphic page filled me with encouragement.
There were no scare-heads. That was good—supremely good. But
there were headings—one-liners and two-liners—and that was good
too; for without these, one must do as one does with a German paper
—pay our precious time in finding out what an article is about, only
to discover, in many cases, that there is nothing in it of interest to you.
The head-line is a valuable thing.

Necessarily we are all fond of murders, scandals, swindles, robberies,
explosions, collisions, and all such things, when we know the people,
and when they are neighbors and friends, but when they are strangers
we do not get any great pleasure out of them, as a rule. Now the
trouble with an American paper is that it has no discrimination; it
rakes the whole earth for blood and garbage, and the result is that you
are daily overfed and suffer a surfeit. By habit you stow this muck
every day, but you come by and by to take no vital interest in it—
indeed, you almost get tired of it. As a rule, forty-nine-fiftieths of it
concerns strangers only—people away off yonder, a thousand miles,
two thousand miles, ten thousand miles from where you are. Why,
when you come to think of it, who cares what becomes of those people? I would not give the assassination of one personal friend for a
whole massacre of those others. And, to my mind, one relative or
neighbor mixed up in a scandal is more interesting than a whole
Sodom and Gomorrah of outlanders gone rotten. Give me the home
product every time.

Very well. I saw at a glance that the Florentine paper would suit
me: five out of six of its scandals and tragedies were local; they were
adventures of one's very neighbors, one might almost say one's friends.
In the matter of world news there was not too much, but just about
enough. I subscribed. I have had no occasion to regret it. Every morning I get all the news I need for the day; sometimes from the head-

lines, sometimes from the text. I have never had to call for a dictionary yet. I read the paper with ease. Often I do not quite understand, often some of the details escape me, but no matter, I get the idea. I will cut out a passage or two, then you will see how limpid the language is:

ILL RITORNO, DEI REALI D'ITALIA
ELARGIZIONE DEL RE ALL' OSPEDALE ITALIANO

The first line means that the Italian sovereigns are coming back—they have been to England. The second line seems to mean that they enlarged the King at the Italian hospital. With a banquet, I suppose. An English banquet has that effect. Further:

IL RITORNO DEI SOVRANI
A ROMA

ROMA, 24, ore 22,50. - I Sovrani e le
Principessine Reali si attendono a Roma do-
mani alle ore 15,51.

Return of the sovereigns to Rome, you see. Date of the telegram, Rome, November 24, ten minutes before twenty-three o'clock. The telegram seems to say, "The Sovereigns and the Royal Children expect themselves at Rome to-morrow at fifty-one minutes after fifteen o'clock."

I do not know about Italian time, but I judge it begins at midnight and runs through the twenty-four hours without breaking bulk. In the following ad. the theaters open at half-past twenty. If these are not matinées, 20.30 must mean 8.30 P.M., by my reckoning.

SPETTACOLL DEL DI 25

TEATRO DELLA PERGOLA — (Ore 20,30) — Opera: *Bohème*.

TEATRO ALFIERI. — Compagnia drammatica Drago —(Ore 20,30)— *La Legge*.

ALHAMBRA — (Ore 20,30) — Spettacolo variato.

SALA EDISON — Grandioso spettacolo Cinematografico: *Quo-Vadis?* - Inaugurazione della Chiesa Russa — In coda al Direttissimo — Vedute di Firenze con gran movimento — America: Trasporto tronchi giganteschi — I ladri in casa del Diavolo – Scene comiche.

CINEMATOGRAFO – Via Brunelleschi n. 4. — Programma straordinario, *Don Chisciotte* — Prezzi popolari.

The whole of that is intelligible to me—and sane and rational, too—
except the remark about the Inauguration of a Russian Cheese. That
one oversizes my hand. Gimme five cards.

This is a four-page paper; and as it is set in long primer leaded
and has a page of advertisements, there is no room for the crimes,
disasters, and general sweepings of the outside world—thanks bel To-
day I find only a single importation of the off-color sort:

UNA PRINCIPESSA
CHE FUGGE CON UN COCCHIERE

PARIGI, 24. - Il *Matin* ha da Berlino che la
principessa Schovenbsre-Waldenbura scomparve il 9
novembre. Sarebbe partita col suo cocchiere.
La Principessa ha 27 anni.

Twenty-seven years old, and scomparve—scampered—on the 9th November. You see by the added detail that she departed with her coachman. I hope Sarebbe has not made a mistake, but I am afraid the
chances are that she has. *Sono dispiacentissimo.*

There are several fires: also a couple of accidents. This is one of
them:

GRAVE DISGRAZIA SUL PONTE VECCHIO

Stamattina, circa le 7,30, mentre Giuseppe Sciatti,
di anni 55, di Casellina e Torri, passava dal-Ponte
Vecchio, stando seduto sopra un barroccio carico di
verdura, perse l' equilibrio e cadde al suolo,
rimanendo con la gamba destra sotto una ruota del
veicolo.
Lo Sciatti fu subito raccolto da alcuni cittadini, che,
per mezzo della pubblica vettura n. 365, lo
trasportarono a San Giovanni di Dio.
Ivi il medico di guardia gli riscontrò la frattura della
gamba destra e alcune lievi escoriazioni giudicandolo
guaribile in 50 giorni salvo complicazioni.

What it seems to say is this: "Serious Disgrace on the Old Old
Bridge. This morning about 7.30, Mr. Joseph Sciatti, aged 55, of
Casellina and Torri, while standing up in a sitting posture on top of a
carico barrow of verdure (foliage? hay? vegetables?), lost his equi-
librium and fell on himself, arriving with his left leg under one of the
wheels of the vehicle.

"Said Sciatti was suddenly harvested (gathered in?) by several citizens, who by means of public cab No. 365 transported him to St. John of God."

Paragraph No. 3 is a little obscure, but I think it says that the medico set the broken left leg—right enough, since there was nothing the matter with the other one—and that several are encouraged to hope that fifty days will fetch him around in quite giudicandolo-guaribile way, if no complications intervene.

I am sure I hope so myself.

There is a great and peculiar charm about reading news-scraps in a language which you are not acquainted with—the charm that always goes with the mysterious and the uncertain. You can never be absolutely sure of the meaning of anything you read in such circumstances; you are chasing an alert and gamy riddle all the time, and the baffling turns and dodges of the prey make the life of the hunt. A dictionary would spoil it. Sometimes a single word of doubtful purport will cast a veil of dreamy and golden uncertainty over a whole paragraph of cold and practical certainties, and leave steeped in a haunting and adorable mystery an incident which had been vulgar and commonplace but for that benefaction. Would you be wise to draw a dictionary on that gracious word? would you be properly grateful?

After a couple of days' rest I now come back to my subject and seek a case in point. I find it without trouble, in the morning paper; a cablegram from Chicago and Indiana by way of Paris. All the words save one are guessable by a person ignorant of Italian:

REVOLVERATE IN TEATRO

> PARIGI, 27. - La *Patrie* ha da Chicago:
> Il guardiano del teatro dell'opera di Wallace (Indiana), avendo voluto espellere uno spettatore che continuava a fumare malgrado il divieto, questo spalleggiato dai suoi amici tirò diversi colpi di rivoltella. Il guardiano rispose. Nacque una scarica generale. Grande panico tra-gli spettatori. Nessun ferito.

Translation.—"REVOLVERATION IN THEATER. *Paris, 27th. La Patrie* has from Chicago: The cop of the theater of the opera of Wallace, Indiana, had willed to expel a spectator which continued to smoke in spite of the prohibition, who, spalleggiato by his friends, tirò (Fr. *tiré*, Anglice *pulled*) manifold revolver-shots. The cop responded. Result, a general scare; great panic among the spectators. Nobody hurt."

It is bettable that that harmless cataclysm in the theater of the opera of Wallace, Indiana, excited not a person in Europe but me, and so came near to not being worth cabling to Florence by way of France. But it does excite me. It excites me because I cannot make out, for sure, what it was that moved that spectator to resist the officer. I was gliding along smoothly and without obstruction or accident, until I came to that word "spalleggiato," then the bottom fell out. You notice what a rich gloom, what a somber and pervading mystery, that word sheds all over the whole Wallachian tragedy. That is the charm of the thing, that is the delight of it. This is where you begin, this is where you revel. You can guess and guess, and have all the fun you like; you need not be afraid there will be an end to it; none is possible, for no amount of guessing will ever furnish you a meaning for that word that you can be sure is the right one. All the other words give you hints, by their form, their sound, or their spelling—this one doesn't, this one throws out no hints, this one keeps its secret. If there is even the slight-est slight shadow of a hint anywhere, it lies in the very meagerly sug-gestive fact that "spalleggiato" carries our word "egg" in its stomach. Well, make the most out of it, and then where are you at? You con-jecture that the spectator which was smoking in spite of the pro-hibition and become reprohibited by the guardians, was "egged on" by his friends, and that it was owing to that evil influence that he initiated the revolveration in theater that has galloped under the sea and come crashing through the European press without exciting any-body but me. But are you sure, are you dead sure, that that was the way of it? No. Then the uncertainty remains, the mystery abides, and with it the charm. Guess again.

If I had a phrase-book of a really satisfactory sort I would study it, and not give all my free time to undictionarial readings, but there is no such work on the market. The existing phrase-books are inadequate. They are well enough as far as they go, but when you fall down and skin your leg they don't tell you what to say.

1904

APPENDIX

The Petrified Man

A WASHOE JOKE

[From *San Francisco Bulletin*, October 15, 1862.]

The *Territorial Enterprise* has a joke of a "petrified man" having been found on the plains, which the interior journals seem to be copying in good faith. Our authority gravely says:

A petrified man was found some time ago in the mountains south of Gravelly Ford. Every limb and feature of the stony mummy was perfect, not even excepting the left leg, which has evidently been a wooden one during the lifetime of the owner—which lifetime, by the way, came to a close about a century ago, in the opinion of a *savan* who has examined the defunct. The body was in a sitting posture and leaning against a huge mass of croppings; the attitude was pensive, the right thumb resting against the side of the nose; the left thumb partially supported the chin, the forefinger pressing the inner corner of the left eye and drawing it partly open; the right eye was closed, and the fingers of the right hand spread apart. [!] This strange freak of nature created a profound sensation in the vicinity, and our informant states that, by request, Justice Sewell or Sowell of Humboldt City at once proceeded to the spot and held an inquest on the body. The verdict of the jury was that "deceased came to his death from protracted exposure," etc. The people of the neighborhood volunteered to bury the poor unfortunate, and were even anxious to do so; but it was discovered, when they attempted to remove him, that the water which had dripped upon him for ages from the crag above, had coursed down his back and deposited a limestone sediment under him which had glued him to the bed rock upon which he sat, as with a cement of adamant, and Judge S. refused to allow the charitable citizens to blast him from his position. The opinion expressed by his Honor that such a course would be little less than sacrilege, was eminently just and proper. Everybody goes to see the stone man, as many as 300 persons having visited the hardened creature during the past five or six weeks.

1862

The Dutch Nick Massacre

THE LATEST SENSATION

A Victim to Jeremy Diddling Trustees—He Cuts his Throat from Ear to Ear, Scalps his Wife, and Dashes Out the Brains of Six Helpless Children!

From Abram Curry, who arrived here yesterday afternoon from Carson, we learn the following particulars concerning a bloody massacre which was committed in Ormsby County night before last. It seems that during the past six months a man named P. Hopkins, or Philip Hopkins, has been residing with his family in the old log-house just at the edge of the great pine forest which lies between Empire City and Dutch Nick's. The family consisted of nine children—five girls and four boys—the oldest of the group, Mary, being nineteen years old, and the youngest, Tommy, about a year and a half. Twice in the past two months Mrs. Hopkins, while visiting Carson, expressed fears concerning the sanity of her husband, remarking that of late he had been subject to fits of violence, and that during the prevalence of one of these he had threatened to take her life. It was Mrs. Hopkins's misfortune to be given to exaggeration, however, and but little attention was given to what she said.

About 10 o'clock on Monday evening Hopkins dashed into Carson on horseback, with his throat cut from ear to ear, and bearing in his hand a reeking scalp, from which the warm, smoking blood was still dripping, and fell in a dying condition in front of the Magnolia saloon. Hopkins expired, in the course of five minutes, without speaking. The long, red hair of the scalp he bore marked it as that of Mrs. Hopkins. A number of citizens, headed by Sheriff Gasherie, mounted at once and rode down to Hopkins's house, where a ghastly scene met their eyes. The scalpless corpse of Mrs. Hopkins lay across the threshold, with her head split open and her right hand almost severed from the wrist. Near her lay the ax with which the murderous deed had been committed. In one of the bedrooms six of the children were found, one in bed and the others scattered about the floor. They were all dead. Their brains had evidently been dashed out with a club, and every mark about them seemed to have been made with a blunt instrument. The children must have struggled hard for their lives, as articles of clothing and broken furniture were strewn about the room in the utmost confusion. Julia and Emma, aged respectively fourteen and seventeen, were found in the kitchen, bruised and insensible, but it is thought their recovery is possible. The eldest girl, Mary, must have sought refuge, in her terror, in the garret, as her body was found there frightfully mutilated, and the knife with which her wounds had been inflicted still sticking in her side. The two girls Julia and Emma, who had recovered sufficiently to be able to talk yesterday morning, declare that their father knocked them down with a billet of wood and stamped on them. They think they were the first attacked. They further state that Hopkins had shown evidence of derangement all day, but had exhibited no violence. He flew into a passion and attempted to murder them because they advised him to go to bed and compose his mind.

Curry says Hopkins was about forty-two years of age, and a native of western Pennsylvania; he was always affable and polite, and until very recently no one had ever heard of his ill-treating his family. He had been a heavy owner in the best mines of Virginia and Gold Hill, but when the San Francisco papers exposed our game of cooking dividends in order to bolster up our stocks he grew afraid and sold out, and invested an immense amount in the Spring Valley Water Company, of San Francisco. He was advised to do this by a relative of his, one of the editors of the San Francisco *Bulletin,* who had suffered pecuniarily by the dividend-cooking system as applied to the Daney Mining Company recently. Hopkins had not long ceased to own in the various claims on the Comstock lead, however, when several dividends were cooked on his newly acquired property, their water totally dried up, and Spring Valley stock went down to nothing. It is presumed that this misfortune drove him mad, and resulted in his killing himself and the greater portion of his family. The newspapers of San Francisco permitted this water company to go on borrowing money and cooking dividends, under cover of which the cunning financiers crept out of the tottering concern, leaving the crash to come upon poor and un-suspecting stockholders, without offering to expose the villainy at work. We hope the fearful massacre detailed above may prove the saddest result of their silence.

1863

INDEX OF TITLES